H

D0390713

NICARAGUA

RANDALL WOOD & JOSHUA BERMAN

Contents

Discover Nicaragua

A land of clay-tiled villages and soaring cathedrals, of volcanic heat and Caribbean cool, Nicaragua is as charming as it is diverse, enticing as it is unfathomable. Its seven million proud, outspoken inhabitants continue to reinvent themselves amid unending political, geological, and economic drama.

Nicaragua's volcanoes, lagoons, highlands, rivers, and valleys provide opportunities for hiking, paddling, and exploring. An endless network of dusty roads and mule trails carry curious travelers to country villages throughout the interior. The Atlantic coast is a remote labyrinth of mangrove swamps and classic Caribbean colors while the Pacific side is a bold stretch of hills, plains, and pueblos, its bays and beaches washed by superb surf. Ride a horse among mountain villas, duck through cloud forest canopy, summit an active volcano – or just soak up a series of languid afternoons over homecooked meals and the company of your Nica hosts.

What was once a nascent travel industry in a little-known, misunderstood nation is finally coming into its own. A decade of economic growth has catalyzed the slowly-maturing Nicaraguan tourism industry, from resurfaced roads and new hotels to a panoply of chic clubs and restaurants – with service to match (sometimes). Granada has blossomed into a destination the international press can't keep quiet about, and outside of San Juan del Sur, traditional fields of sugarcane and corn now abut gated gringo retirement communities and a smattering of luxury resorts.

Still, travel in most of Nicaragua involves compromises you wouldn't be asked to make in more prosperous countries. Patience is key, and Nicaragua's greatest adventures require daring and imagination, not to mention some conversational Spanish (if your Spanish is rusty, enroll in one of the many excellent language schools, where you can brush up in beachfront classrooms and colonial cities).

Nicaragua is a place where independent spirits can easily fall off the map, to live simply and witness life at a slower pace. Red beans and toasted corn tortillas cooked over a wood fire, a crisp night sky behind a volcano's silhouette, a simple, friendly exchange with a *campesino* in the town plaza. . . . There's something to see and learn around every corner.

Planning Your Trip

In general, destinations south of Managua are more developed for travelers, especially Granada and San Juan del Sur, whose exploding number of colonial hotels, upscale surf camps, and convenient shuttle services have drastically altered the tourism landscape. The rest of the country—north and east of Managua, and the Río San Juan in the southeast—is a different story. In these places, with some basic Spanish, patience, and persistence, you can pueblo-hop on public buses till the Chontales cattle come home. Basic room and board are found in even small pueblos, as are community homestay and rural tourism programs. Fancier hotels and restaurants are found in most department capitals, usually on or near the central plaza.

Most travelers begin in Granada and with good reason. It is smaller and more manageable than Managua and you can get a shuttle directly to Granada from the airport (under one hour). Granada is a beautiful, tranquil place to get acclimated to the heat and pace of things, and provides access to numerous day trips.

Las Isletas de Granada

IF YOU HAVE . . .

seaside restaurant, San Juan del Sur

- **ONE WEEK:** Visit Granada and San Juan del Sur.

- **TWO WEEKS:** Add La Isla de Ometepe and/or a side trip to León and the northwest beaches.

- **THREE WEEKS:** Add the Solentiname Islands and a trip down the Río San Juan. Take the time to hike a volcano or explore the Estero Reál. Or work your way up the Pacific coast, one beach at a time.

- **FOUR WEEKS:** Go deep. After visiting the above, get off the beaten track using Matagalpa, Jinotega, or Estelí as a base, or spend a couple days camping in the more remote wildlife reserves of Matagalpa and the Río San Juan.

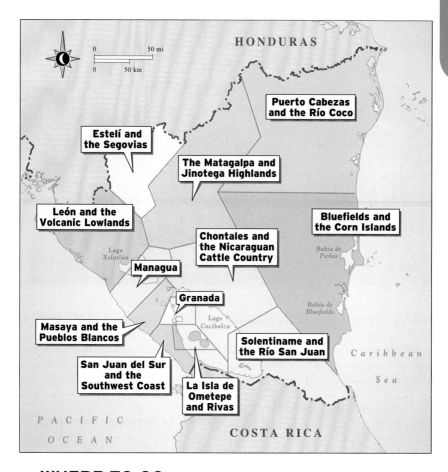

HONDURAS

Puerto Cabezas
and the Río Coco

Estelí and
the Segovias

The Matagalpa and
Jinotega Highlands

León and the
Volcanic Lowlands

Bluefields and
the Corn Islands

Lago Xolotlán

Chontales and
the Nicaraguan
Cattle Country

Bahía de Perlas

Managua

Granada

Bahía de Bluefields

Masaya and the
Pueblos Blancos

Lago Cocibolca

Solentiname and
the Río San Juan

Caribbean

Sea

San Juan del Sur
and the
Southwest Coast

La Isla de
Ometepe
and Rivas

PACIFIC

OCEAN

COSTA RICA

▶ WHERE TO GO

Managua

The most chaotic of Central American capitals, Managua used to be a modern, cosmopolitan center until it was flattened by an earthquake in 1972, the first of a series of recent major disasters to strike the city. Today, amid an ongoing building boom and expansion of Managua's middle class, *la capital* can be a fun stopover if traveling through on business or pleasure. Though you could conceivably pass through Nicaragua without visiting

Managua at all, its central location makes it an important transport hub and the place to go for services not available elsewhere. You can see Managua's small cadre of attractions in half a day, but if you're here on a weekend, consider staying to sample the vibrant nightlife.

Granada

The most colorful and comfortable of Nicaragua's cities, Granada has been charming

cathedral in Granada

travelers with its red-tiled roofs, grand cathedrals, breezy lakeshore, and drowsy lifestyle since the days of the Spanish, who used the city as their first Atlantic port (via Lake Cocibolca and the Río San Juan). Today, Granada is the undisputed hub of tourism in the country, and it's got the international cuisine and café culture to prove it. Many visitors opt to stay in Granada throughout their trip, as a tranquil base from which to explore the 365 *isletas* and the cloud forests of Volcán Mombacho, as well as Masaya, the Pueblos Blancos, and the Laguna de Apoyo.

Masaya and the Pueblos Blancos

Less than an hour south of the capital, Masaya and the dozens of villages that comprise the Pueblos Blancos are known for their residents' artistry. Start with a trip to Volcán Masaya, where you can peer into Nicaragua's fiery entrails, then visit the shaded stalls of Masaya's craft markets. Spend a lazy afternoon driving through the Pueblos Blancos and take a dip in the Laguna de Apoyo, the country's nicest swimming hole. You could easily devote two full days to this region, either by staying in Masaya or the Laguna, or by traveling here each day from Granada. The Pueblos make a nice diversion for those spending a longer time in Managua, as the hills are markedly cooler.

La Isla de Ometepe and Rivas

An old administrative city with a vibrant colonial history, Rivas may be worth a stop on your way to the beaches of San Juan del Sur or to Nicaragua's crown jewel: La Isla de Ometepe, a few kilometers across Lake Cocibolca. Visible from the entire southern highway, Ometepe's twin volcanic peaks—Concepción is hot and active, Maderas is dormant and forested—offer challenging, unique treks. Or stick to the lakeshore, enjoying island-grown coffee, lagoons, waterfalls, and the call of howler monkeys. The slopes of Maderas are home to an array of rustic, farm-based hostels, surrounded by old-growth hardwoods, petroglyphs, barnyard animals, and memorable views.

San Juan del Sur and the Southwest Coast

Nicaragua's favorite beach town is also the most popular with foreign tourists. In addition to a crescent bay lined with barefoot restaurants and sandy bars, San Juan del Sur offers a slow-paced, tranquil setting, fresh seafood, and charming guesthouses. Go fishing and sailing, try the canopy tour, or learn surfing and Spanish. From San Juan's bay, the Pacific coastline extends in both directions in a series of hidden beaches, hills, and wave-strewn coves. The southwest coast is an important habitat for the Paslama turtle—witnessing the hatching is breathtaking.

León and the Volcanic Lowlands

Lying at the feet of the imposing Maribio volcanoes, León and Chinandega are colonial cities in the arid lowlands of Nicaragua's Pacific northwest. León's importance as a political and economic center over the past four centuries has bequeathed it a rich history. Stop in at the baroque cathedral, the

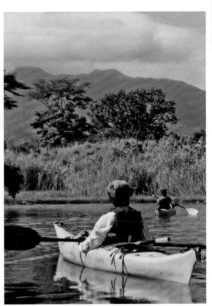

kayaking Las Isletas de Granada

largest in Central America, or wander the indigenous Subtiava neighborhood, with a magnificent church of its own. Most travelers stroll León's streets, walk up (and ride down) Cerro Negro, and then head back south or east. With a week or more, you can work your way farther northwest. In addition to beaches near León, there are a number of remote protected areas throughout the Cosigüina Peninsula.

Estelí and the Segovias

Nicaragua's mountainous north is accessible by comfortable public transportation, its main city, Estelí, only a few hours from Managua. Farther north, the peaks are some of the oldest in Central America, and they boast an unforgettable landscape with hardwood and pine forests, stony river valleys, and fields of tobacco, coffee, and corn. Spend a day at the Estanzuelas waterfall and the Tisey wildlife reserve, or head into the hills for

riding through the wetlands on the Cosigüina Peninsula

There are countless bays and coves along Nicaragua's southwest coast.

a weekend in Miraflor, a precious habitat for some of Nicaragua's rarest species of birds and orchids. Press farther northward to the small towns of the Segovias—Somoto and Ocotal—dry as dust but alive with history, legends, and lore.

The Matagalpa and Jinotega Highlands

Nicaragua's rugged interior is coffee country, where the unrushed traveler will find rough, undeveloped adventure. Green valleys and steep peaks define the landscape, and the hard-working, sometimes aloof residents define its character. Everyone's got a war story in these mountains, and hearing them adds texture to your travels. Matagalpa has steep streets, famous steaks, and long vistas; Jinotega is the gateway to the untrodden, as most of Nicaragua's landmass lies farther afield to the east. A guide in Matagalpa can take you trekking to summits, waterfalls, and forgotten gold mines. Spend a weekend in a rural lodge, tour coffee plantations, or participate in a village guest program for a closer look at *campesino* life.

Chontales and the Nicaraguan Cattle Country

The golden hillsides beyond the east shore of Lake Cocibolca fold upward into the rocky precipices of the Amerrisque mountains, stomping grounds of the Chontal people during pre-Columbian times. Today, the area runs thick with cattle ranches that produce most of Nicaragua's cheese and milk. To the north and east, the roads dwindle to rutted tracks and old, rural encampments. It was here that the Chontal people carved their totemlike statues, a few of which are on display in the museum in Juigalpa. Most travelers speed through on buses bound for El Rama and the Atlantic coast, but spending a night in Juigalpa or Boaco, where the wild west vibe hasn't lost its edge, may lead you on to the area's hot springs, petroglyphs, horseback treks, and burly hikes.

Solentiname and the Río San Juan

Life moves slowly along the broad river that drains Lake Cocibolca to the Caribbean. This gorgeous, verdant lowland is Nicaragua's wettest, and its remoteness means you'll spend more time and more money getting around. The Spanish fort at El Castillo has watched over river traffic since the 17th century. Along the southern shore of Cocibolca, you'll find wildlife reserves and cultural curiosities. The Solentiname archipelago isn't easy to get to, but you'll be rewarded with an up-close look at the birthplace of liberation theology and a thriving colony of artists. Explore the wilds of Los Guatuzos, habitat for monkeys, birds, and amphibians, then set sail downstream for San Juan de Nicaragua, home to the bones of English pirates and more ghosts than residents.

Bluefields and the Corn Islands

The isolated Atlantic coast may as well be a country unto itself. Nicaragua's Caribbean is tough, muddy, and quite unlike any Cancún-tainted visions you may harbor. Most tourists fly straight from Managua to Big Corn, but a few hardy souls still visit Bluefields to experience Creole culture and crab soup. When you tire of Bluefields's grittiness, board a boat for Pearl Lagoon, the coastal fishing communities, Pearl Cays, or Greenfields

reserve. Both Corn Island and Little Corn Island are Caribbean gems as gorgeous below the waterline as above. There are kilometers of coral reef, a handful of hotels, and only one dive shop on each island. Little Corn has no roads so the only sound you hear should be the wind in the trees.

Puerto Cabezas and the Río Coco

The northeast Miskito communities of Puerto Cabezas (Bilwi), Waspám, and the Río Coco are a far removed, embattled corner of the country, where resources go more toward fighting the drug trade and recovering from natural disasters than developing tourism. Still, there are basic services in Puerto Cabezas, including decent oceanfront accommodations and low-budget tour guides to take you to nearby rivers, beaches, and Miskito communities. Even farther north, Waspám is the commercial center for villages up the Río Coco, mostly indigenous communities where Miskito is still the first language and where foreign visitors may arouse more suspicion than hospitality.

The rustic end of Little Corn Island has varied lodging.

▶ WHEN TO GO

Generally speaking, the best months—when the land is still green from the rains and the days are sunny and dry—are December, January, and February. June, July, and August are nice as well, with cooler temperatures, fewer North Americans, and more European travelers. March, April, and May are the hottest, driest months, prone to pervasive dust and smoke caused by agricultural burning; September–November are the wettest months, and also hurricane season, when you can expect periodic tropical depressions to raise the rivers.

Nicaragua's *invierno* (winter, or rainy season) lasts approximately May–October, and *verano* (summer, or dry season) lasts November–April. Rain during these months may mean just a quick shower each afternoon, or it may go on for days. As you travel east toward the Atlantic coast or down the Río San Juan, the rainy season grows longer and wetter; in these areas, the dry season sometimes lasts only a month or two (around April).

Several fiestas are worth planning your trip around: the fiestas in Diriamba around January 19, the Palo de Mayo on the Atlantic

rain and coconuts: a familiar combo on the Atlantic coast

coast (throughout May), the Crab Soup Festival on Corn Island (August 27–28), and the Fiesta del Toro Venado in Masaya (last Sunday of October). The first weeks of December, when Nicaraguans celebrate the Immaculate Conception with various *purísima* and *gritería* parades, are particularly lively in Granada and León.

▶ BEFORE YOU GO

Passport and Visa Requirements

Every traveler to Nicaragua must have a passport valid for at least six months following the date of entry. A visa is required only for citizens of the following countries: Afghanistan, Albania, Bosnia and Herzegovina, Colombia, Cuba, Haiti, India, Iran, Iraq, Jordan, Lebanon, Libya, Nepal, Pakistan, People's Republic of China, People's Republic of Korea, Somalia, Sri Lanka, Vietnam, and Yugoslavia. Everyone else is automatically given a tourist pass good for three months.

Vaccinations

Required: A certificate of vaccination against yellow fever is required for all travelers over one year of age and arriving from affected areas.

Recommended: Before traveling to Nicaragua, be sure your tetanus, diphtheria, measles, mumps, rubella, and polio vaccines are up-to-date. Protection against hepatitis A and typhoid fever is also recommended for all travelers.

Explore Nicaragua

► THE 21-DAY BEST OF NICARAGUA

Like other countries in the region, Nicaragua has a popular, carved-out tourist route based on its principal, most-developed attractions. Nicaragua's beaten path is made up of the Granada–Ometepe–San Juan del Sur circuit, which can be done in about one week; save another week for tackling the northwestern lowlands and a third week for the Atlantic coast or Río San Juan. Wherever you head, Granada is a good place to ease into things, with colorful surroundings, wonderful cuisine, and more creature comforts than elsewhere in the country.

Day 1

Arrive in the afternoon at Managua's International Airport. Transfer to a hotel in town, catch a performance, enjoy some of the local restaurants, and above all, get accustomed to the heat and relax after your flight.

Days 2-3

Hop a bus to Granada and spend at least two or three days there. Tour the city the first day, visit museums and enjoy the languid waterfront. Your second day, paddle to the nearby *isletas* or go hiking on Volcán Mombacho, whose heights above the city make for a cool day.

Iglesia de Guadalupe, Granada

SURFING

Swells from South Pacific storms pound Central America during the North American summer months, especially in June and July. The shape of Nicaragua's long, isolated beaches and direction of the shoreline help form these pushes of water into perfect overhead barrels. On the southwest coast around San Juan del Sur, lake-generated offshore breezes often blow year-round.

Waves are still being "discovered" and named, and more than once, we have been asked not to print details about certain legendary breaks and knowledgable boat drivers. One old-school surfer we encountered compared Nicaragua to Hawaii's unspoiled North Shore in the 1970s.

Nicaragua, once a blank spot on the world's surfing map, now hosts international competitions and draws an increasingly well-informed crew of sponsored and non-sponsored shredders from across the planet. Meanwhile, a few young Nicaraguans have picked up the sport and caught the attention of surf journalists and documentary filmmakers, while small eco-surf camps spring up along the entire Pacific coast. In short, the secret is out.

Most surfers head straight to **San Juan del Sur** (a.k.a Sin City) where they can get oriented, rent or buy a board, socialize, and arrange transport to breaks north and south of town. You'll find plenty of accommodations, guides, surf shops, and beach shuttles — none of which existed only a few years ago.

Start your research with the **Nicaragua Surf Report** (www.nicaraguasurfreport.com), the longest-running online daily wave report in the country, plus a full complement of services for visiting surfers (rentals, equipment, transport, etc.). Another option, especially if you'd prefer to explore the north coast, **Rise Up Surf Tours Nicaragua** (www.riseupsurftoursnicaragua. com) offers fully-guided surf tour packages to Nicaragua's Central and Northwest Pacific coast; the owners are surfers based in León.

Women surfers can check out the **ChicaBrava Surf Camp** (U.S. tel. 832/519-0253, www.chicabrava.com), the first all-girls surf operation in the country. The second, **Suave Dulce Women's Surf Retreat** (SuaveDulce@gmail.com, www.suavedulce. com), was opened in 2010 by pro-surfer Holley Beck, on the Nicaraguan north coast.

Nicaragua's surf spots are no longer a secret.

Most visitors come to San Juan del Sur for the nearby beaches.

Day 4

Using Granada as your base, make a day trip to the city of Masaya and its the active volcano of the same name. Start early at Volcán Masaya National Park, then browse the handicrafts in the Old Market. Return to Granada that evening.

Days 5-7

Pack up and head south. Catch the boat at San Jorge to Ometepe. Spend 2–3 days exploring the island's unique getaways, or arrange a guide to take you to the top of one of the volcanoes for more adventurous travel.

Days 8-9

Catch the boat back to San Jorge and bus it south through Rivas to the beach at San Juan del Sur. Spend at least one night there, but tag on a few more if the surf's up or the turtles are laying.

Days 10-11

Catch the early express bus to Managua. Transfer directly to León. It's been a long trip, so relax, walk around the hot town, check out a few museums, and save time for ice cream in the park.

Days 12-13

Catch a ride to Matagalpa, then continue east to the village of San Ramón. It will take you the better part of a day to get here, so enjoy the afternoon and that plate of *gallo pinto* waiting for you in the mountains. Spend the next two days hiking to the mines and touring a coffee farm or two.

Days 14-19

Return to Managua and take the afternoon flight to Corn Island. Spend two days on Corn Island and two days on Little Corn, soaking up sun, fresh lobster, island vibes, and perhaps a dive on the reef.

Day 20

Take the morning flight back to Managua to see a few more of the city's sights before last-minute shopping at the Mercado Roberto Huembes.

Day 21

¡Adios, jodido! ¡Feliz viaje!

HANDICRAFTS AND *ARTESANÍAS*

Nicaragua is a nation with a rich diversity of handicrafts as beautiful as they are practical. If you're interested in shopping, the city of Masaya and its surrounding pueblos present the nation's best opportunity to admire – and acquire – elaborate pottery, intricately woven hammocks, wood carvings, ceramic miniatures, leatherwork, and embroidered *guayaberas*. Shop at the source, or browse the market stalls in Masaya and Managua before your flight home. Here's a brief guide to some of the items you'll find in Nicaragua.

HAMMOCKS

Nicaraguan hammocks are well made and reasonably priced: around $30-60, depending on size and quantity. Though you can also find good-quality hammocks at the **Roberto Huembes market** in Managua, the heart of Nicaragua's home-crafted hammock industry is **Masaya,** and visiting the many family "factories" is as easy as walking up to the porch and saying *"Buenos días."* Check the weave and the quality of the cord – stiffer cord tends to last longer and tighter weaves tend to be more comfortable.

SOAPSTONE

The soapstone (*marmolina*) sculptors of **San Juan de Limay** (a small village north of

Masaya handicraft market

Estelí) produce polished figurines inspired by animals, Rubenesque (and pregnant) women, and pre-Columbian designs. Smaller pieces are simple to transport, but in **Masaya,** you can have larger pieces packed and shipped home. You'll see iguanas, parrots, frogs, oxen, wagons, and more, plus ornately carved nativity scenes and chess sets, all carefully rendered in

► HIKING THE RING OF FIRE

Volcano hopping, anyone? Pack some sturdy boots and hike one or all of the more than a dozen ascents detailed in this book. Nicaragua's Maribio and Dirián mountain ranges contain both dormant and active cones, each one completely unique in scenery, difficulty, vegetation, and length. A few of these hikes have established, well-blazed trails (Mombacho and Masaya), most don't. In undeveloped-for-tourism areas, "hiking" means turning off the pavement, taking a poor dirt road to an even poorer one, and then entering the country's vast network of mule- and footpaths that have connected rural communities for centuries. You'll share the road with horses, cattle, and families walking to and from their fields. You'll discover small adobe chapels, hidden shrines to the Virgin Mary, and cool watering holes, all on your way to or from another crater. Always hire a local guide, both as a way to both support the community and to not get lost, both the salmon and ivory hues natural to the Limay soapstone.

POTTERY

Nicaraguan pottery designs have continued uninterrupted from pre-Columbian times to the present. Today's potters produce all manner of vases, bowls, urns, pots, and other forms in rich earthy hues, some delicately etched, some left crude. You'll find fantastic mobiles and wind chimes of clay birds, bells, or ornamental shapes, like stars and planets. Get gorgeous, export-quality pieces in **Masaya** or **San Juan del Oriente** (Catarina and increasingly the other pueblos are getting into the act now, too). Or find earthy, rustic pieces not too different from what the Nahuatls must have used up north: Jinotega's black pottery or red clay pieces in Estelí and Matagalpa.

WOODEN FURNITURE

The carpenters and craftspeople of the small towns around **Masaya** turn out gorgeous wooden furniture which you'll see lining the roadside during your drive-by browsing. Rocking chairs called *abuelitas* ("little grandmothers") or *mecedoras* are sturdy and comfortable, and if you ask, they'll gladly disassemble them and condense their products into well-wrapped airline-suitable packages.

BASKETWORK

The basketwork you'll find around the country is an extension of the bamboo baskets you see stacked up with produce in countryside markets. **Nueva Segovia** and the northeast Miskito regions of Nicaragua, in contrast, produce curious baskets and urns from bundles of wrapped pine needles that have been bound into long coils, then wound in concentric coils. Look for them in **Ocotal** and the markets in **Managua.**

PRIMITIVIST PAINTINGS

The first primitivist paintings from the Solentiname archipelago came into the world spotlight in the 1960s as an offshoot of Padre Ernesto Cardenal's liberation theology movement on the islands. Instantly recognized the world over as an art form unique to Nicaragua, the vibrant paintings typically portray romanticized scenes of tropical Latin America: markets, oxen, trees laden with fruit, and skies full of toucans and parrots. You'll have a better story to tell if you buy them from the source on the **Solentiname islands,** but if your schedule doesn't permit, you can do just as well at the **Galería Solentiname** in **Managua.** Lower-priced pieces are available in Huembes market, but you'll have to look harder to find the better works.

---

respectable goals: León has an excellent selection of guides and tour services specializing in volcano treks.

Following is a quickie weeklong jaunt up a couple of favorites, but after seeing the long chain of gas-streaming peaks stretching off into the horizon, you'll realize that this is only the beginning.

Day 1

Arrive at Managua International Airport and transfer to Granada.

Day 2

After enjoying the specter of Volcán Mombacho looming over the colonial streets, get a ride to its summit and walk the various ridge trails around its jungled craters; the wonderful loops make a good warm-up for what's to come.

Day 3

Spend the morning at Volcán Masaya's gaping crater, only an hour from Granada and guaranteed to impress. On the way back, enjoy a swim in the Laguna de Apoyo, an unspoiled crater lake, easily accessed by bus from Masaya.

Day 4

Transfer to León and find someone to take you to Cerro Negro, a relatively short but stout and rewarding hike.

Day 5

Rest up on the beach at Las Peñitas and paddle out to Isla Juan Venado.

Day 6

Today's the big day. Hook back up with your guides in León and set out early to tackle Momotombo, a 1,300-meter, eight-hour round-trip on horseback and foot. Celebrate with a fancy dinner in León that night.

the Maribio volcano chain, seen from Cerro Negro

Day 7

Back to Managua, back to work, or back to the beach.

enjoying live music overlooking Laguna de Apoyo

▶ THE GREAT GREEN NORTH

Nicaragua north of Managua is offbeat and little-traveled, and gives the creative traveler lots of opportunities. Pueblo-hopping through the Segovia mountains and participating in the Ruta de Café will immerse you in an authentic and sublime world you won't soon forget. Each town has a swimming hole, local hike, or archaeological site that will beckon you farther. Alternate legs include passing through San Juan de Limay and the back roads to León; or from Jinotega, looping through Yalí to Condega. This sample itinerary will give you a taste of what to expect.

Day 1

From Managua, head north to Estelí and spend the day walking the streets of this bustling commercial center, viewing the murals and markets, and enjoying cool weather.

Days 2-3

Take an early-morning bus to the Estanzuela waterfall; stay in a cabin on the Tisey Reserve, where you can arrange hikes, horseback expeditions, and farm tours. Return to Estelí at the end of day three.

Days 4-5

From Estelí, go east and up, into the Miraflor Reserve, where you can experience a rural homestay, photograph orchids, and try to spot elusive wildlife. Even if you don't find any quetzals or ocelots, the locals will regale you with legends and ghost stories. Spend the night, return in the morning, and grab a bus north.

Day 6

Stop in for lunch at one of the quiet northern agricultural towns, like Condega, or Palacagüina; press on to Ocotal, and

SPORTFISHING

WHERE TO GO

Most sportfishing trips are available out of San Juan del Sur, an increasing number of Pacific beach towns, and along the Río San Juan. There are also opportunities on the Atlantic coast, especially off the Corn Islands. Bonefishing in the flats around Little Corn Island is exciting, but you'll have to have some idea of what you are doing, as experienced guides are limited. There are freshwater fish to be caught in Lake Apanás and El Dorado in Jinotega, and of course, in Lake Cocibolca and down the Río San Juan.

WHAT YOU'LL CATCH

Saltwater sportfishing on the Pacific coast is focused primarily on *hurel* (jacks), *pargo* (snapper), *pez gallo* (roosterfish), bonito, *pez vela* (sailfish), and *dorado* (mahimahi). All commonly reach sizes in excess of 50 pounds.

Off the Corn Islands, you'll find kingfish, amberjack, red snapper, and barracuda. In the lakes, the giant freshwater bull sharks and sawfish are all but gone, but mammoth catch-and-release *sábalos* (tarpon), bigger than your mother and carrying up to 50 pounds of meat, are still abundant, as are *robalos*, *guapote*, and the basin's newest invasive resident, tilapia.

spend the evening roaming the park and city center.

Day 7

Day trips galore await from Ocotal—seek out the ruins, or head northeast to Jalapa if you have the time. Otherwise, check out the humble church and exhibits in the Ocotal *casa de cultura* and hop an express bus back to Estelí.

There are scores of tranquil mountain pueblos dotting the northern countryside.

Day 8

Leave Estelí in the morning and make your way through Sébaco to Matagalpa. Enjoy the city for the day, maybe even take a quick hike up Cerro Apante.

Day 9

Here's your chance to visit a coffee plantation and witness the process that brings us that magical beverage. You can stay in San Ramón, Finca Esperanza Verde, or in the cozy stone cottages at Selva Negra.

Day 10

Enjoy a beautiful, fun-filled day of monkeys in the trees, hearty country dining, and a guided tour through the farm.

Day 11

Return to Managua, hopefully with a few pounds of freshly roasted coffee in your pack.

▶ DOWN THE RÍO SAN JUAN

The watery "Golden Route" through southern Lake Cocibolca and down the Río San Juan is tougher to access than it was when boat service was more frequent, so you'll need a minimum of 7–10 days to get there, get around, and get back. Once you reach San Carlos (by boat, bus, or small plane), public boat transportation is regular and cheap, but limited to a handful of boats per week. As a result, unless you drop a lot of cash to hire your own personal boat and driver, you may find yourself stranded on one of 36 Solentiname islands for three days, with nothing to do but go fishing or bird- and crocodile-watching in a dugout canoe—we can think of worse. The Río San Juan is unquestionably worth a visit, especially the photogenic fort and river town at El Castillo.

CELEBRATIONS AND FIESTAS

When planning your trip, consider timing your visit to coincide with one of Nicaragua's many celebrations and festivals. Conversely, you might want to *avoid* festivals and all the fireworks, drunken masses, altered transportation schedules, and spiked hotel prices that they bring. Additionally, airlines are well aware of when expatriate Nicas living in the United States like to return home for family time and celebration, and at these times you can expect airfares to nearly double. Here are a few times of the year when services are affected by celebrations.

CHRISTMAS SEASON

La Navidad is one of the times you can expect airfare to increase. Christmas celebrations begin a full week before December 25 and nothing truly returns to normal until after January 7. That's not to say you won't be able to get around, but expect a higher demand for hotel rooms. Banks are open (except on actual holidays), but government agencies operate on a limited schedule if at all.

SEMANA SANTA

Semana Santa (Holy Week) is an even bigger event than Christmas. The week that precedes Easter Sunday is an important and much-loved holiday, when every Nica that can finds his or her way to the beach (or lake, river, waterfall, etc.) for some fun in the sun. At the very least, Wednesday, Thursday, and Friday before Easter are completely lost days, but many Nicas take off Monday and Tuesday as well and make a long vacation out of it. During this period bus service slackens, banks reduce hours, and government officials, if you can find them, will deal with you between clenched teeth. You are keeping them from the beach and will be made to suffer for it.

REGIONAL CELEBRATIONS

Additional city-specific festivals happen throughout the year with great amounts of local pride and traditional revelry. Participating in these events is a memorable and enjoyable experience. Every city has its own patron saint, and that saint is celebrated annually in an event as lavish as the locals can afford; the most elaborate festivals often involve bands and parades and food throughout the night.

Masaya's is the most jubilant, with well over a dozen festivals throughout the year. One of the most unique festivals, the festival of San Sebastián, takes place in **Diriamba,** Carazo, during the third week of January. **Granada** puts on an international poetry festival in mid-February, a gastronomy, folklore, and handicraft festival in late March, and celebrates the Assumption of Mary on August 15. **Managua** puts on its patron saint festival twice: on August 1, when the patron saint is paraded down from a hillside chapel to a small church on the eastern side of the capital, then again on August 10 when it is paraded back up. **Estelí** puts on a lively festival of "Mariachis and Mazurkas" (the mazurka is a traditional dance) the third week in August. On **Ometepe** there's an Equestrian Rally November 3-5, and between November 12-18 **Altagracia** celebrates its patron saint, San Diego de Alcalá.

The festival of San Sebastián takes place in January in Diriamba.

the main attraction and namesake of the riverside village of El Castillo

Day 1

Fly from Managua to San Carlos in the early morning. If you really want the full-blown adventure, take the slow boat from Granada on Monday: You'll arrive Tuesday morning. Poke around San Carlos until the afternoon, when the boat leaves for Solentiname.

Days 2-3

Enjoy the island artist colony of Solentiname, set in a unique area of profound natural splendor. You can hire boats to take you among the islands, enjoy scarlet sunsets, and absorb the intense tranquility of the archipelago. Return to San Carlos Thursday morning to catch the boat to Los Guatuzos. If you'd rather go directly and bypass San Carlos, strike a deal with a local Solentiname boat owner.

Days 4-6

Hike and explore the fascinating tropical landscape of the Los Guatuzos Reserve. A two-day stay will give you a taste for the reserve, but real outdoors enthusiasts will probably prefer to stay until the next boat (Tuesday, unless you make other arrangements). Arrival in San Carlos on Saturday means you are just in time to catch a boat downstream. Cast away and start your adventure down the mighty Río San Juan, bound for El Castillo.

Day 7

Start your day off in El Castillo early, so you can hear the sky fill with birds. Visit the old Spanish fort or rent a horse for a bush trip.

Day 8 and Beyond

Most travelers return to San Carlos for a flight to Managua at this point, but if the downstream horizon is beckoning, then keep on floating.

MANAGUA

If Nicaragua's capital were a vehicle, it would be a battered 1960s school bus, dented and dinged on all sides, paint chipping through multiple layers of color, four bald tires rolling slightly akilter, but sporting a brand new, $2,000 sound system blaring a merengue classic for its smiling passengers, both rich and poor. Managua rarely impresses; its labrynthine, unnamed streets are complicated to navigate, it is loud and architecturally uninspiring, and there's no city center to speak of. Though it's relatively safe, it doesn't *feel* that way, and its understated charms don't exactly jump out at you.

Home to nearly a quarter of Nicaragua's population, Managua sets the tone for the political and economic dialogue that shapes the nation's destiny. The story of Managua and Nicaragua are largely parallel, from earthquake to revolution to economic revival and onward, so the better you understand Managua, the better you will understand the history of Nicaragua itself.

Managua is also the best place in the country to get your gear repaired, see a doctor or dentist, see a movie or show, and party like a salsa star. It also has the nation's most varied selection of restaurants and night spots. You likely won't plan your trip around a visit to Managua, but neither should you necessarily avoid it, as Managua does have a charm of its own that will become apparent once you've spent a little time here. You may even discover you like the place.

PLANNING YOUR TIME

Managua's main historical attractions are clustered in a four-block-square area along

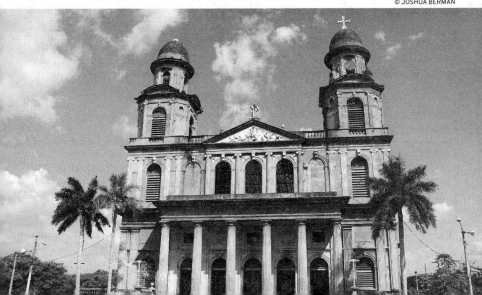

HIGHLIGHTS

◖ **La Laguna de Tiscapa:** Just one of the area's many volcanic lakes, this is the only one you can zip over while tethered to a steel cable; or just enjoy the view (page 34).

◖ **Catedral Santiago de los Caballeros:** This cathedral is standing testimony to the earthquake of 1972 (page 34).

◖ **Plaza de la Revolución:** Most of Managua's historical sights are clustered in this four-block area, still the cultural heart of Nicaragua's capital (page 34).

◖ **Malecón (Waterfront):** Managua's Malecón is the gateway to lakeside adventure (page 37).

◖ **Las Huellas de Acahualinca:** This glimpse of Managua's mysterious past is haunting for the questions it raises, not the ones it answers (page 38).

◖ **Chocoyero-El Brujo Nature Reserve:** Located just south of Managua, in a gorgeous patch of protected hillsides and ravines, this community-based tourism venture offers some wonderful day hikes (page 53).

Lago Xolotlán

La Laguna de Tiscapa

Catedral Santiago de los Caballeros

Plaza de la Revolución

Managua ◖ — Malecón (Waterfront)

Las Huellas de Acahualinca

Chocoyero-El Brujo ◖ Nature Reserve

○ La Concepción

○ Granada

Jinotepe ○

○ Nandaime

PACIFIC OCEAN

0   20 mi
0   20 km

LOOK FOR ◖ TO FIND RECOMMENDED SIGHTS, ACTIVITIES, DINING, AND LODGING.

the lakeshore, and you can easily visit all of them in about an hour by taxi, or reserve another two hours if you'd like to take one of the lake cruises. It pays however to stick around for an evening, as Managua's biggest attraction is its nightlife, and its beauty is enhanced by dim (or absent) urban lighting. For the intrepid or for those with more than just an evening to spend in the capital, Managua offers a number of other attractions, including theaters and museums. Just outside the city you'll find a few excellent, usually overlooked, outdoor activities. You can also visit the Pacific beaches and the Chocoyero–El Brujo Nature Reserve without entering the chaos of the capital. If you're just passing

through, consider a stop at the Tiscapa crater for an amazing view that reveals just how many trees there are in the city.

HISTORY

Managua's modern layout is the very embodiment of its history, in a tale that leads inexorably from the water's edge in the direction of Masaya. Mana-huac ("the big water vessel") has been inhabited since 4000 B.C.; you can see the footsteps of some of the earliest inhabitants in the Museum of the Footprints of Acahualinca at the city's western edge. The Nahuatls met the Spanish so fiercely there the Spanish retaliated by razing the city in the 15th century; the land remained abandoned another 300

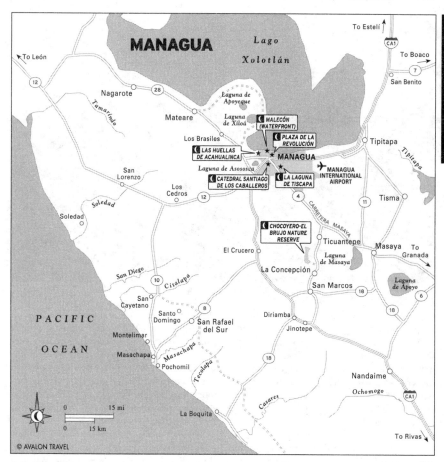

MANAGUA

Lago
Xolotlán

To León

To Estelí

To Boaco

San Benito

Nagarote

Laguna de
Apoyeque

Mateare

Laguna
de Xiloá

Los Brasiles

Tipitapa

▮ MALECÓN
(WATERFRONT)

▮ PLAZA DE LA
REVOLUCIÓN

▮ LAS HUELLAS
DE ACAHUALINCA

MANAGUA

San
Lorenzo

Laguna de Asososca

MANAGUA
INTERNATIONAL
AIRPORT

Los
Cedros

▮ CATEDRAL SANTIAGO
DE LOS CABALLEROS

▮ LA LAGUNA
DE TISCAPA

Tisma

Soledad

▮ CHOCOYERO-EL
BRUJO NATURE
RESERVE

Ticuantepe

Masaya

To
Granada

El Crucero

Laguna
de Masaya

Laguna
de Apoyo

La Concepción

San Diego

San Marcos

San
Cayetano

Santo
Domingo

San Rafael
del Sur

Diriamba

Montelimar

Jinotepe

PACIFIC

OCEAN

Masachapa

Pochomil

Nandaime

Ochomogo

To Rivas

La Boquita

0   15 mi

0   15 km

© AVALON TRAVEL

years. By the mid-1800s, when both León and Granada rivaled for political control of the nation, Managua was again a prosperous fishing village. The Conservatives and Liberals compromised by making Managua the capital, and the fishing village began to grow. But in 1931, by which time Managua was a small municipality of 10 square city blocks, an earthquake of 5.6 on the Richter scale leveled Managua and killed more than 1,000 people. For five years, Managuans rebuilt their city, only to see it consumed by flames in the Fire of 1936. Again, they rebuilt.

By the late 1960s, Managua was the most modern capital in Central America, home to nearly half a million inhabitants, with a modern center and two skyscrapers. But at 27 minutes past midnight on December 23, 1972, an earthquake of 6.3 on the Richter scale laid waste to the five square miles of the city. The quake killed 10,000 people, destroyed 50,000 homes, and reduced the city's entire infrastructure to rubble. Managua was left without water, sewers, or electricity, hospitals lay in ruins, and the roads were choked with debris.

This was a disaster from which Managua

Managua's skyline is dominated more by volcanoes than office buildings.

has never quite recovered, as little of the initial material aid arrived at its intended destination. President Anastasio Somoza Debayle saw to it that humanitarian assistance channeled through the "emergency committee" under his control ended up in his personal bank accounts. For Nicaraguans who'd lost everything, being forced to purchase donated relief items from the National Guard was the last straw: The revolution would fully erupt only seven years later. Today, the ruins of old Managua have been largely left to rot at the south shore of Lake Xolotlán, a depressing reminder of the city's glory years. The old cathedral and several other buildings still remain standing, though squatters occupy the derelict buildings that were not cleared away.

But the Sandinista Revolution brought destruction, not healing, to the capital. Managua bore the brunt of the Revolution's final battles. As the Sandinistas advanced, Somoza began bombing his own capital, concentrating his ire on the barrios of Riguera and El Dorado. Managua remained wrecked throughout Somoza's war against the Sandinistas. And once the Sandinistas took power, fighting the Contras left no money to rebuild Managua according to any sort of plan. It was during this time Managuans shoveled themselves out, and the city began to grow organically, forming the twisting, homogenous neighborhoods of small houses and shanties that make Managua so difficult for foreigners to decipher today.

The end of the Sandinista era brought new investment capital and new opportunities and since 1990 Managua has grown quickly and impressively. But rather than risk rebuilding in the seismic zone, new, up-scale establishments stretch down the city's outskirts in the direction of Masaya, where they now form the city's Zona Rosa.

ORIENTATION

Managua city has no obvious city center and its unnamed streets do not follow a grid pattern, so staying oriented is a challenge. Focus on the following specific zones of interest and avoid the rest: From **Plaza de la Revolución** and the **Malecón** (waterfront) south to the

© JOSHUA BERMAN

FOLLOWING DIRECTIONS IN MANAGUA

Locating addresses in Managua is unlike any system you've ever seen, but with a few tips, some basic vocabulary, and a couple of examples, you'll master Managua in no time. Street names and house numbers are few and far between, and where they do exist, they are universally ignored. Addresses in Managua begin with a landmark (either existing or historical), which is followed by the number of *cuadras* (blocks) and a direction. Remember this: **North** is *al lago* (toward the lake); **east** is *arriba* (up, referring to the sunrise); **south** is *al sur* (to the south); and **west** is *abajo* (down, where the sun sets).

Some other key phrases to know are *contiguo a* (next door to), *frente a* (across from), *casa esquinera* (corner house), and *a mano derecha/izquierda* (on the right-/left-hand side). Also note that *varas* are often used to measure distances of less than one block; this is an old colonial measurement just shy of a meter.

Directions throughout this chapter are given in English for consistency's sake, but always beginning with the landmark exactly as it is referred to in Spanish. By studying the following examples, you should be able to find your way around with few hassles.

De la Plaza España, tres cuadras abajo, tres c. al lago, casa esquinera.
From Plaza España, three blocks west, three north, corner house.

De donde fue el Sandy's, 200 varas arriba, frente al gran hotel.
From where Sandy's used to be, 200 meters to the east, across from the big hotel.

De los Semáforos El Dorado, dos cuadras al sur, una c. arriba, casa lila.
From the El Dorado traffic light, two blocks south, one east, purple house.

Reparto San Juan, de la UNIVAL, 50 varitas al lago, edificio de cinco pisos.
In the San Juan neighborhood, just 50 meters north of the UNIVAL, five-story building.

Laguna de Tiscapa you'll find the city's historical attractions, but little to eat or drink and no lodging. The various neighborhoods that flank **Carretera Masaya** south of the Plaza Metrocentro are where you'll find the bars, clubs, and restaurants that make Managua fun, and an increasing number of charming guesthouses. Lastly, **Barrio Martha Quezada** has historically been a backpacker and budget traveler center, and still houses most international bus companies for those making overland connections.

GETTING AROUND

Managua was not made for walking. Organize your day into trips to different regions of interest, and resign yourself to getting around by taxi, as the buses are slow and rather dangerous, and walkers are at risk not only to petty crime but general harrassment (not to mention heat stroke). Negotiate a rate with a taxi driver to take you around the sights (one hour is enough and should cost you about $10). Finish the driving tour at the Malecón, where you can enjoy a boat trip on Lake Xolotlán (Tuesday–Sunday), then move on. Any middle or upper range hotel can organize a guide and/or taxi to help you tour Managua. A taxi will cost around $20 per half day and a guide a similar amount.

SAFETY IN THE CITY

Managua is still statistically less dangerous than other Central American capitals, but you should keep your wits about you, as minor crime from pickpocketing and purse snatching to carjacking seems to be on the rise. The best way to stay out of trouble is to avoid areas where you'll find it. The safest and cleanest neighborhoods are Los Robles, Altamira along

MANAGUA

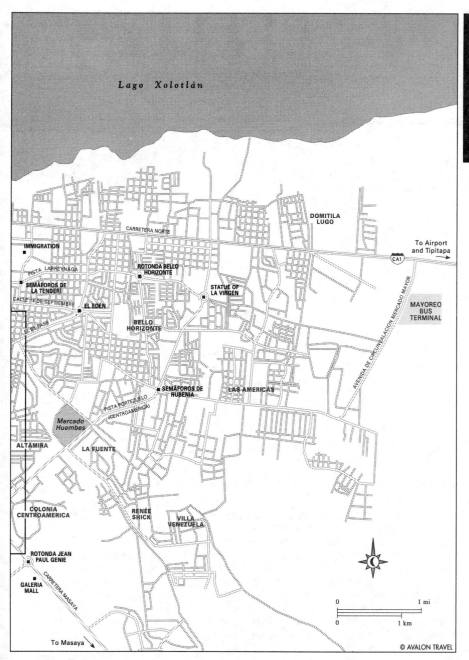

Lago Xolotlán

CARRETERA NORTE

DOMITILA LUGO

To Airport and Tipitapa

CA1

IMMIGRATION

PISTA LARREYNAGA

ROTONDA BELLO HORIZONTE

STATUE OF LA VIRGEN

SEMÁFOROS DE LA TENDERÍ

CALLE 14 DE SEPTIEMBRE

EL EDÉN

MAYOREO BUS TERMINAL

EL BY-PASS

BELLO HORIZONTE

AVENIDA DE CIRCUNVALACIÓN MERCADO MAYOR

SEMÁFOROS DE RUBENIA

LAS AMERICAS

PISTA PORTEZUELO (CENTROAMERICA)

Mercado Huembes

ALTAMIRA

LA FUENTE

COLONIA CENTROAMERICA

RENÉE SHICK

VILLA VENEZUELA

ROTONDA JEAN PAUL GENIE

CARRETERA MASAYA

GALERIA MALL

| 0 | | | | 1 mi |
| 0 | | | | 1 km |

To Masaya

© AVALON TRAVEL

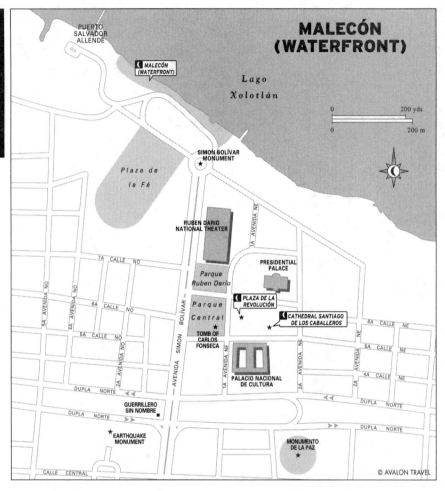

PUERTO
SALVADOR
ALLENDE

MALECÓN (WATERFRONT)

MALECÓN
(WATERFRONT)

*Lago
Xolotlán*

0   200 yds

0   200 m

SIMÓN BOLÍVAR
MONUMENT

*Plaza de
la Fé*

RUBEN DARÍO
NATIONAL THEATER

7A CALLE NO

PRESIDENTIAL
PALACE

*Parque
Ruben Darío*

5A AVENIDA NO
2A AVENIDA NO

6A CALLE NO

PLAZA DE LA
REVOLUCIÓN

*Parque
Central*

CATHEDRAL SANTIAGO
DE LOS CABALLEROS

6A CALLE NE

5A CALLE NO

TOMB OF
CARLOS
FONSECA

AVENIDA SIMÓN BOLÍVAR

5A CALLE NE

2A AVENIDA NO

1A AVENIDA NE

2A AVENIDA NE

4A CALLE NE

PALACIO NACIONAL
DE CULTURA

DUPLA   NORTE

DUPLA   NORTE

GUERRILLERO
SIN NOMBRE

DUPLA   NORTE

DUPLA   NORTE

EARTHQUAKE
MONUMENT

MONUMENTO
DE LA PAZ

CALLE   CENTRAL

© AVALON TRAVEL

Carretera Masaya, plus Reparto San Juan (near the University of Central America), and Bolonia (south of Plaza España), all of which offer more upscale accommodation and bed-and-breakfasts.

Dangerous neighborhoods include Renée Schick, Jorgé Dimitrov, La Fuente, San Judas, Villa Venezuela, Batahola, Las Americas, Bello Amanecer, Vida Nueva, Los Pescadores, Domitila Lugo, Santana, and Hialeah. You should be safe enough in and around the major shopping centers and the restaurants and clubs along Carretera Masaya, but in general you're better off staying in groups when possible—especially when traveling by taxi. And pay close attention to your surroundings. Don't get into taxis where the driver is keeping his face obscured by a baseball cap or where the driver is traveling with a "friend" in the passenger seat.

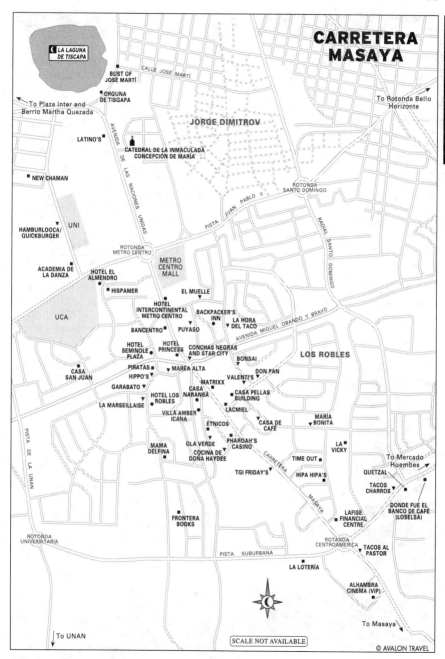

LA LAGUNA
DE TISCAPA

CARRETERA
MASAYA

BUST OF
JOSÉ MARTÍ

CALLE JOSÉ MARTÍ

CHGUNA
DE TISGAPA

To Plaza Inter and
Barrio Martha Quezada

To Rotonda Bello
Horizonte

JORGE DIMITROV

LATINO'S

CATEDRAL DE LA INMACULADA
CONCEPCIÓN DE MARÍA

NEW CHAMAN

ROTONDA
SANTO DOMINGO

PISTA JUAN PABLO II

HAMBURLOOCA/
QUICKBURGER

UNI

ACADEMIA DE
LA DANZA

HOTEL EL
ALMENDRO

ROTONDA
METRO CENTRO

METRO
CENTRO
MALL

HISPAMER

EL MUELLE

UCA

HOTEL
INTERCONTINENTAL
METRO CENTRO

BACKPACKER'S
INN

LA HORA
DEL TACO

RADIAL SANTO DOMINGO

BANCENTRO

PUYASO

AVENIDA MIGUEL OBANDO Y BRAVO

HOTEL
SEMINOLE
PLAZA

HOTEL
PRINCESS

CONCHAS NEGRAS
AND STAR CITY

LOS ROBLES

BONSAI

CASA
SAN JUAN

PIRATAS
HIPPO'S

MAREA ALTA

VALENTI'S

DON PAN

GARABATO

MATRIXX

CASA
NARANSA

CASA PELLAS
BUILDING

LA MARSEILLAISE

HOTEL LOS
ROBLES

LACMIEL

VILLA AMBER
ICANA

ÉTNICOS

CASA DE
CAFÉ

MARÍA
BONITA

MAMA
DELFINA

OLA VERDE

PHAROAH'S
CASINO

COCINA DE
DOÑA HAYDEE

LA
VICKY

To Mercado
Huembes

TIME OUT

TGI FRIDAY'S

HIPA HIPA'S

QUETZAL

TACOS
CHARROS

CARRETERA

DONDE FUE EL
BANCO DE CAFÉ
(LOSELSA)

PISTA DE LA UNAN

ROTONDA
UNIVERSITARIA

FRONTERA
BOOKS

MASAYA

LAFISE
FINANCIAL
CENTRE

ROTONDA
CENTROAMERICA

TACOS AL
PASTOR

PISTA SUBURBANA

LA LOTERÍA

ALHAMBRA
CINEMA (VIP)

To UNAN

To Masaya

SCALE NOT AVAILABLE

© AVALON TRAVEL

Sights

(LA LAGUNA DE TISCAPA

If you only have time to make one tourist stop in Managua, this is it. The **Parque Historica** occupies Managua's breeziest and highest point; follow the road just south of the Plaza Inter and Crowne Plaza Hotel upwards to get to it. The twin-towered monument halfway up the road is the **Monumento Roosevelt,** which delineated the southern terminus of the city pre-earthquake. Twenty meters farther up the hill is the statue of justice, sardonically decapitated ages ago. The **statue of Sandino** atop the crater lip is one of Managua's most recognizable symbols and is now a public park with impressive views of the old city and lake. The Sandinistas erected it atop the wreckage of Somoza's presidential mansion. A permanent exhibition of old photos of Sandino has been set up in the basement of the ruins. Just up the hill but closed to the public rests Las Masmorras, a prison

a zip line at Tiscapa Crater

in which Somoza tortured many political prisoners, including Daniel Ortega.

Older Managuans remember the Laguna de Tiscapa as a turquoise swimming hole and popular afternoon getaway. Under the Sandinista government of the 1980s it was turned into a sewer. A major cleanup began in 2005, including the diversion of sewer lines and a reoxygenation plant to treat the waters. See for yourself as you zoom across the lagoon on a **zip line** (tel. 505/8888-2566, 9 A.M.–5:30 P.M. Tues.–Sun., $15 for foreigners, $10 for Nicas).

(CATEDRAL SANTIAGO DE LOS CABALLEROS

Managua's most iconic and evocative landmark, the Catedral Santiago de los Caballeros in the Plaza de la Rvolución, had barely been completed when the earthquake of 1931 struck. It survived relatively unscathed that time, but was all but destroyed by the 1972 earthquake that leveled Managua. Still standing but structurally unsound, the **Ruinas de la Catedral Vieja** (as it is now known) are a poignant testimonial to the destruction caused by the quake. Until the late 1990s, the ruins of the cathedral were open to visitors, but due to continued structural degradation, it is no longer safe. You can still peer in, however, to appreciate its ravaged, sunlit interior—do so before the next quake finishes what the quake of '72 started. Across the street, heading toward the lake, the lavishly decorated and brightly painted **Casa Presidencial** was built in 1999 by former president Arnoldo Alemán despite popular outrage over the unjustifiable expense in Hurricane Mitch's aftermath. President Ortega turned it into "the people's house."

(PLAZA DE LA REVOLUCIÓN
South Side of the Plaza

The Plaza de la Revolución, ostensibly just an open area, has become a living monument to

© JOSHUA BERMAN

General Sandino's silhouette still graces the Tiscapa Crater in downtown Managua.

also housed the Ministry of Housing, the treasury, the comptroller-general, and the National Congress. Sandinista commandos raided the building in 1978 and held the entire Congress hostage, winning international recognition and the liberation of several political prisoners. In addition to the national library, several murals and the Institute of Culture can be found here.

The first two floors of the old Gran Hotel (severely damaged by the quake in 1972) are now Managua's official **cultural museum**— look for the murals around the outside. The building hosts art exhibits, concerts, puppet shows, and dances. The second floor holds studios of prominent Nicaraguan artists. The hallways are lined with striking black-and-white photographs of old Managua, pre- and post-earthquake and host handicraft fairs the first Saturday of each month. Sneak up to the roof to see how the upper floors of the old hotel were never replaced, yet another monument to the earthquake. There is a halfway decent café here as well, serving lunch only.

the incessant bickering of Nicaragua's political elite. Under Somoza, it was known as Plaza de la República. The rebel Sandinista movement assembled huge crowds there to manifest their outrage against the dictator, and upon overthrowing him, the Sandinista government renamed it Plaza de la Revolución. Renowned Sandinista-hater President Alemán, upon taking power, was thus thrilled to punch a hole in the symbolic Sandinista chakra by building an audiovisual fountain in its center. So naturally when President Ortega returned to power in 2006 he wasted no time in demolishing Alemán's fountain and holding political rallies and celebrations here. Visit in the morning, when the breeze off the lake is cool, the trees are full of birds, and the traffic is momentarily silent.

On the south side of the Plaza, the **Palacio Nacional de Cultura** houses Nicaragua's National Museum but at various times has

North Side of the Plaza

The **Plaza de la Cultura República de Guatemala** celebrates Guatemalan author Miguel Angel Asturias Rosales, winner of the Nobel Prize in literature in 1967 for his colorful writings about national individuality and Native American traditions. He wrote frequently of the tyranny of dictators, the beauty and hostility of nature, and the struggle against domination by U.S. interests, themes with which the Sandinista government is sympathetic.

Parque Rubén Darío, dominated by a stark, white marble statue, is adjacent to the Parque Central and honors Nicaragua's most-beloved poet. Built in 1933, it was restored in 1998 with the help of the Texaco Corporation. At the bottom of the hill, the marble and brass **Teatro Rubén Darío** was designed by the same architects that created New York's Metropolitan Opera House. It was one of few surviving buildings in the 1972 earthquake and remains to this day a classy place

REVOLUTIONARY DRIVING TOUR

Historical trivia buffs, take note! A lot of Managua's most historically salient points are close to invisible, in stark contrast to the role they played in the lead-up to the 1979 revolution. None of these destinations has gotten the granite monument they deserve, but their importance is no less diminished, even as life goes on around them. If you have a rainy afternoon in Managua some day, hop in a taxi, and revisit history on this driving tour (about 30 minutes). Start at your hotel and go first to **Plaza de la Revolución.**

One block south of the Guerrillero sin Nombre, the southwest corner with a lone wooden telephone pole marks the site of journalist **Pedro Joaquín Chamorro's assassination** as he drove to his office on January 10, 1978. Whether the drive-by was paid for by Tachito or his business partner in the infamous blood-bank business was never determined, but Chamorro's death helped spark the revolution. Look for a concrete monument directly behind the telephone pole.

Turn south onto Avenida Bolívar. You'll pass some government buildings and basketball courts before coming to the **National Arboretum** (8 A.M.–5 P.M. Mon.-Sat., $0.50) on your left, home to more than 180 species of trees found in Nicaragua. It is practically unvisited except by local school groups but is especially attractive in March, when the fragrant *sacuanjoche* (Nicaragua's national flower) blooms brightly; the scarlet flowers of the *malinche* tree blossom from May through August. The trees are planted atop the remnants of Somoza's Hormiguero (Anthill), a military base belonging to the National Guard and destroyed in 1972 by the earthquake. Popular legend has it that this was the site where, on February 21, 1934, General Sandino was ambushed and assassinated after meeting with President Sacasa at his home on the Tiscapa Crater.

Turn left at Plaza Inter and head in the direction of the El Dorado neighborhood. The **monument to Bill Stewart** is one block west and two blocks south of the Semáforo El Dorado. Bill Stewart was a U.S. journalist for ABC in the 1970s. While reporting on the early days of the Sandinista insurrection, he was brutally attacked and killed by members of Somoza's National Guard. Stewart's cameraman filmed and published the whole thing, forcing the U.S. government to stop turning a blind eye to the excesses of Nicaragua's dictator.

A few blocks south in the same neighborhood, the **Iglesia de los Angeles** is a living monument to the revolution, painted on all sides in bright murals that tell the story of Nicaragua. Beautiful on its own, it can be better appreciated with a guide: Contact Solentiname Tours (tel. 505/2270-9981, zerger@ibw.com.ni) for an expert who will lead you through the story.

Finally, and in the opposite direction, just west of the petroleum refinery on the road leading west out of town is **La Cuesta del Plomo** (accessible from *ruta* bus 183), the ravine where Somoza was allegedly fond of making folks "disappear." Families whose loved ones didn't come home after a few days would go to this hillside to search for their bodies.

Plaza de la Revolución

© JOSHUA BERMAN

© RANDALL WOOD

The port offers breezy cruises on Lake Xolotlán.

to enjoy dance, theater, or musical presentations. Check the newspaper for performances, its website www.tnrubendario.gob.ni, or call 505/2266-3630 or 505/2228-4021 for upcoming events.

West Side of the Plaza

Set in the small green space of the Parque Central are several monuments of historical significance. An eternal flame guards the **Tomb of Comandante Carlos Fonseca,** father of the Sandinista revolution. Buried across from him is Santos Lopez, a member of General Sandino's "crazy little army" in the 1930s, who helped train latter-day Sandinistas in the general's ideology and the art of guerrilla warfare. The historical frieze that circles the **Templo de la Música,** a brightly painted gazebo, highlights the arrival of Columbus, Rafael Herrera fighting pirates, independence from Spain, Andrés Castro fighting William Walker, and more, but it's just as interesting for the antics of the sparrows in its arches.

◖ MALECÓN (WATERFRONT)

The backsides of Simón Bolívar, hero of the Latin American liberation movement, and his horse greet you upon arrival (he's peering northward for impending Yanqui invasions, probably). It's an inauspicious welcome to one of Managua's more interesting quarters, though its full potential remains unmet for now.

Puerto Salvador Allende

It was a loudly decried pity that rather than capitalizing on Lake Xolotlán's windswept lakefront, Managuan mayors had instead chosen for decades to defile it. That has finally changed and the Malecón is becoming a halfway-decent place to spend some time. The Malecón benefitted from a facelift in 2007 and the Puerto Salvador Allende opened for business not long after.

The port offers **tourist cruises** (45 minutes round-trip) into the lake and around the Isla de Amor, an islet at Managua's western side once used by the dictator for trysts, as well as longer tours across to the mostly underwhelming

San Francisco Libre (famous for being the first village where illiteracy was eradicated in the 1980s). The lake is still polluted, mind you, but a Japanese-funded treatment plant that began operation in 2005, and an aggressive initiative to reroute city sewers have improved the lake's condition over all, and the cruise is pleasant and enjoyable, certainly one of the better ways to spend a late afternoon in the capital.

Cruises around Isla de Amor leave Tuesday–Sunday at 11 A.M., and 1, 3, 5, and 7 P.M., and cost $2.50 for adults, $1 for children ($2.50, $1.50 for upstairs seating with a better view—which is worth it). Cruises across the lake to San Francisco Libre leave Friday–Sunday at 10 A.M. and 1 P.M. (5-hour trip: 1 hour in each direction, plus 3 hours in San Francisco Libre). There is not much to see or do in San Francisco Libre, however.

OTHER SIGHTS
Plaza de la Fé
The Plaza de la Fé (Plaza of Faith) was built in 1996 in tribute to Pope John Paul II's second visit to Nicaragua; former Managua mayor Herty Lewites built the adjacent **La Concha Acustica** here for live concerts. Both are used mostly for Ortega political rallies these days.

Monumento de la Paz
Hugely representative of the peacemaking initiatives of former president Violeta Chamorro, the Monumento de la Paz celebrated a new era of peace. Beneath the concrete are buried the destroyed remains of thousands and thousands of weapons from the Contra war, many of which—including a tank—can be seen protruding through the cement. Almost directly across the street (just a bit west) is the unmistakable statue of the Guerrillero sin Nombre. This area was and may still be a favorite target for thieves. Despite continuous police presence now, play it safe: Visit it only during daylight hours.

El Guerrillero sin Nombre
You can't miss this guy. The Nameless Guerrilla Soldier grasps a pick-ax in one hand and an AK-47 in the disproportionately muscular other. This hulkish symbol of the revolution's aspirations is inscribed with one of Sandino's most treasured quotations: "Only the laborers and farmers will go to the end." Arnoldo Alemán's administration countered with a different statue just across the road, honoring the working class with two cowed and undernourished looking figures, one representing a construction worker and the other a domestic servant, both representative of Nicaragua's growing laborer community in neighboring Costa Rica.

Earthquake Monument
Across from the new *cancillería* (foreign affairs) building, where the old Iglesia de San Antonio used to stand, is the **monument to victims of the earthquake of 1972.** This touching statue, constructed in 1994, was the initiative of journalist Aldo Palacios and portrays a man standing amidst the wreckage of his home. It is inscribed with the poem, "Requiem a una Ciudad Muerta," by Pedro Rafael Gutierrez.

Catedral de la Inmaculada Concepción de María
At the center of an immense field of young coconut trees along the Carretera Masaya is the new cathedral, Catedral de la Inmaculada Concepción de María, constructed just two years after the conclusion of the civil war. Commissioned by American Thomas Monahan and designed by Mexican architect Ricardo Legorretta, this dynamic and open cathedral houses the Dutch bells of the old cathedral. Playing on the soaring forms of Spanish colonial architecture and using colors and materials of the Latin culture, the new cathedral is the pulpit of Nicaragua's famous and controversial Cardinal Miguel Obando y Bravo. Mass is celebrated Tuesday–Saturday at noon and 6 P.M. and Sunday at 11 A.M. and 6 P.M.

◖ Las Huellas de Acahualinca
If you visit only one historical site outside of the city center, this is the one. Modest but

intriguing, the site is a simple interpretation center built over the fossilized footprints of Managua's earliest known inhabitants who fished Lake Managua 4,000 years before Christ. The prehistoric footprints were found in the last century, four meters below the ground surface. Once thought to be the prints of people fleeing a volcanic eruption, forensic analysis now shows the walkers were unhurried. The women's prints are deeper, as they were carrying a heavier load, perhaps the children. The museum's exhibits on Nahuatl life and the volcanoes of Central America make clear that living in the shadow of imminent volcanic destruction is nothing new in town. The museum (tel. 505/2266-5774, open 8 A.M.–5 P.M. Mon.–Sat., $2) is a bit out of the way at the northwest end of the city, so call before going, and find a taxi to take you there and back (about $5 an hour; one hour should be enough). The taxi will inevitably drive you through some of Managua's poorer lakefront neighborhoods, another statement about the continuity of experience in Managua.

Museums and Art Galleries

Nicaragua's museum selection is pretty poor overall, but you can spend a rainy afternoon in **El Museo Nacional de Nicaragua** located in the Palacio de Cultura (tel. 505/2222-2905, open 7:30 A.M.–4:30 P.M. Mon.–Fri., 9 A.M.–5 P.M. Sun., $1). It highlights natural history, as well as pre-Columbian ceramics and statues from all over Nicaragua's territories. Managua's other art galleries individually showcase Nicaragua's creative artists. The best is probably **Galería Solentiname** (Barrio Edgard Munguía Transfer, 600 meters south of the UNAN, tel. 505/2277-0939, open 9 A.M.–5 P.M. Mon.–Sat.), set in the home of Doña Elena Pineda, a native Solentinameña who has done a great job of promoting the works of painters from the famous archipelago. Related, the **Galería de Los Tres Mundos** (Los Robles, two blocks north of the French restaurant La Marseillaise, open 8 A.M.–5 P.M. Mon.–Fri.) is Ernesto Cardenal's home base and showcases a variety of Solentiname artwork, from paintings to balsa work. More a cultural center than a museum, **Códice** (Colonial Los Robles *segunda etapa,* house #15, tel. 505/2267-2635, open 9 A.M.–7 P.M., sometimes later, Mon.–Sat.) displays changing exhibitions of sculpture, paintings, and ceramics, all set around a lovely courtyard. There are frequent evening musical performances here set in a lovely outdoor patio.

Entertainment and Events

Dancing is a central part of the Managua experience. The disco scene trends more towards the hip-hop-influenced *reggetón* these days, but there's plenty of salsa, merengue, bacchata, and cumbia as well. Managua also has several places to learn salsa and merengue if you are in town for a longer period of time.

If you prefer something more low-key, there are lots of bars and clubs with atmospheres that range from sultry to suspect, but they change on an annual basis, as Managuans flock inexorably to the newest scene. Otherwise, for classical, dance, and theater, there is usually something happening at the Rubén Darío Theater. For a full party and event listing, check www.hechomagazine.com.

DISCOS

Moods on the outskirts of town in Galería Santo Domingo is rather exclusive but the most upscale disco in town and gets consistently good reviews for its swanky atmosphere and great music, and skilled bartenders. You'll need to dress well to get in (no jeans, baseball caps, T-shirts, etc.) and maybe even catch the eye of the bouncer (Wed.–Sun., cover charge typically $5). The city's burgeoisie are upstairs in the VIP lounge, photographing themselves. Thursday is ladies' night, with varying specials.

The liveliest—and youngest—party in town is at the new **❰ Chamán,** a Mayan pyramid structure just south of the Laguna de Tiscapa and north of the UCA. Expect long lines, as Managua's youth have made this the place to be, but the wild, party atmosphere makes it worth it (Wed.–Sun., cover charge is typically $3).

Matrixx Disco is also impressive, with a lot of black lights and a slightly less university-crowd that knows how to dance. It's open Thursday–Sunday, though Friday is the best (cover charge typically $4).

Two other discos are largely spurned by the trendy, Facebook crowd. That makes them unpretentious, inexpensive, and still great places to dance. **El Quetzal** and **La Laguna de Tiscapa** are old Managua favorites, with a somewhat older crowd. The former is air-conditioned and glassy, the latter is open air on a balcony overlooking the crater. Both are recommended and open Friday–Sunday starting around 8 P.M., no cover charge.

Managua's Costeño crowd still loves **Island Taste** (Km 6 Carretera Norte, Thurs.–Sun., cover charge $4), somewhat far away from the rest of town and a bit run down these days, but still well-loved (and packed!). Palo de Mayo, *soca,* and reggae are what's playing. Go on a Thursday, when there's more elbow room.

BARS AND CLUBS

Low lighting, good service, and attention to ambience make **Etnicos,** next to the Ola Verde restaurant, almost romantic.

The block surrounding **Hipa Hipa's** bar hosts a rotating bar scene: The bars change from year to year, but the scene—and the crowd—remains the same. Start with the trendy Hipa Hipa itself, now less exclusive than it used to be (they got vilified for refusing entry to the dark-skinned daughter of a diplomat), this is still one of the best places to be seen, with an atmosphere straight out of Miami's South Beach (Wed.–Sun. after 7 P.M., but Hipa Hipa offers happy hour starting at

Carretera Masaya is Managua's main drag.

© JOSHUA BERMAN

4 P.M.). Below and adjacent to Hipa Hipa are three similar, but less popular bar-discos that take up the slack, including **Broder,** a college favorite (baseball cap at a 45 degree angle is all but mandatory here). Just down the street, **Time-Out** (from the Lafise financial center, half a block east, 3.5 blocks north) has 20 pool tables for $2.50 per hour, and serves cocktails, beer, and snacks.

A similar zone of tightly clustered fun spots where the bars serve food and the restaurants have a good bar scene, is Zona Hippos, west of Carretera Masaya. **Piratas** on the corner is a favorite and a good place to see-and-be-seen.

A surprise favorite, **Bar Rollos,** isn't near much of anything else, but its gauzy ambience, candlelit simplicity and cheap, cold beer has brought it success from international travelers and young Managuans. In the Colonia Centroamerica, open evenings after 6 P.M.

LIVE MUSIC

Managua's music scene, both intimate and refined, shows a lot of local talent and energy.

Without a doubt, the single best show in town is (C) **Casa de los Mejía Godoy** (in front of the Hotel Crowne Plaza, tel. 505/2270-4928 or 505/2278-4913, fmejiago@cablenet.com.ni). Both brothers perform here regularly, Carlos on Thursday and Saturday, with or without his band Los de Palacagüina. Luis Enrique does Latin rhythm nights on Friday, and Sunday features other Nicaraguan or international performers. Both brothers are born showmen and present a theatrical mix of stories, bawdy jokes, and famous songs. The club is expensive by Nica standards, but well worth it by any measure. Buy tickets the afternoon of the performance for $8–15; shows are Wednesday–Sunday only and start at 9 P.M.

Just up the block, (C) **El Caramanchel** (two blocks south and 15 meters west of the Crowne Plaza Hotel, open from 7 P.M. Wed.–Sat.) is a favorite Bohemian haunt, with an inviting, casual atmosphere, and a soundtrack that includes reggae, rhumba, and bossa nova. The cozy, open-air dance floor doubles as a stage and has hosted some fantastic bands from as far away as Brazil. This is a relaxed and comfortable atmosphere in which to enjoy live music.

The breezy, outdoor terrace of **La Ruta Maya** (150 meters east of the Estatua de Montoya, tel. 505/2268-0698, open Thurs.–Sat., $4–6) is a pleasant place to appreciate a wide variety of performers from singer-songwriters to reggae, jazz, and everything in between. Local talent includes names such as Macolla, Llama Viva, Dimensión Costeña, Elsa Basil, and Clara Grun, to name but a few. **Latino's** (600 meters north of the Metrocentro roundabout) gets a similar entourage of troubadours and has an attractive, modern decor and dance floor. This is the place if you want to dance rather than just listen. They have live music Thursday–Saturday, entrance $4.

MOVIES

Managua's five commercial centers each has a modern multiplex theater showing the same half-dozen films: mostly Hollywood fare, with some Spanish and Mexican films as well. **Cinemark** (tel. 505/2271-9037 or 505/2271-9000) is in the Plaza Metrocentro, **Cinema Plaza Inter** (tel. 505/2222-5090 or 505/2222-5122) is on the third floor of the Plaza Inter mall (remember to take a cab at night; the neighborhoods west of the theater are no longer walkable at night), and the **Galería Santo Domingo** shopping complex (tel. 505/2276-5065) is located on the Carretera Masaya just southeast of the Rotunda Jean Paul Genie.

Simply drop in, or check the *Revista Cinematógrafica* (a weekly bulletin distributed at most gas stations and some hotels and restaurants), or *Patadeperro* a free monthly arts magazine at the Casa de Café. Shows change every Thursday and cost about $3–5. Tuesdays and Wednesdays are often cut-price. Bring a jacket: Managua's theaters are glacially air-conditioned. In addition, Cinemark and Galería complexes host occasional film festivals with the support of the local embassies' cultural attachés. The **Alianza Francesa** (tel. 505/2267-8283 or 505/2267-8285) presents a variety of European DVDs on Tuesday nights. Also try the **Cinemateca** (tel. 505/2222-3845), located next to the **El Centro Cultural de Managua**, where cinema connoisseurs enjoy film classics.

Miercoles de Cine shows an artsy foreign flick each Wednesday at 7 P.M. at the Sala de Teatro Justo Rufino Garay (from Montoya, 3 blocks west, 20 meters north, tel. 505/2266-3714, www.rufinos.org, $2).

THEATER AND DANCE

Managua's finest theater, **El Teatro Nacional Rubén Darío** (at the Malecón, tel. 505/2266-3630 or 505/2228-4021) hosts top-name international acts. Check the newspaper for performances or call. **La Escuela Nacional de Teatro** (Palacio Nacional de Cultura, tel. 505/2222-4449) is primarily a teaching facility that presents performances on weekends by students and small professional troupes from all over Latin America; call for a list of events, as they're not always published. The **Sala de Teatro Justo Rufino Garay** (from Montoya, 3 blocks west, 20 meters north, next to Parque Las Palmas, tel. 505/2266-3714, www.rufinos.org)

NICARAGUAN FOLK MUSIC AND THE HOUSE OF MEJÍA GODOY

In the wide, vast — and incredibly loud — sea of music flowing through Nicaragua's living rooms, bars, vehicles, and airwaves, music of true Nicaraguan roots is not the easiest to hear. However, once you get to know the distinctive 6/8 rhythms, the sound of the *marimba*, and the melodies that every single Nicaraguan knows by heart, you'll realize just how much Nicaraguan music is woven into its society.

Only a few musical remnants of Nicaragua's indigenous societies survived the conquistadores; these precious acts of dance, costume, and distinctive melodies are best observed today during the *fiestas patronales* of Masaya, Diriamba, and the various pueblos dotting the hills between them. These pre-Columbian fragments were further enriched by the different cultures they encountered along the way. Much of this influence was Spanish, and at some point, the African marimba traveled up the Río San Juan, landed in Granada, and found its home among the *folkloricos* of Carazo and Masaya.

Things are different in the northern hills of Nicaragua, where **Carlos Mejía Godoy** was born in 1943. The music there, he explains, is composed of *campesino* versions of the waltz, polka, and mazurka. Born and taught to play the accordion and guitar in Somoto, Carlos Mejía Godoy is neither the "father" nor "inventor" of Nicaraguan folk music, as some would have it. In fact, he is only one in a line of multiple generations of songwriting Nicaraguans. However, his love and passion for Nicaraguan culture, combined with his sheer talent as a musician, songwriter, and performer, have made Carlos Mejía and his long catalog of songs central in any discussion (or jam session) involving Nicaraguan music.

Don Carlos says he wishes he had two lives: one to learn all there is to be learned about Nicaraguan culture and a second to perform and use that knowledge. To most observers (and fans), it would appear he has done an adequate job at squeezing both into the one life he was given. Not only did he join the Sandinista Revolution in 1973 and proceed to compose its soundtrack, but throughout his life, Carlos Mejía has delved deeply into the *campo*, always in search of the regionally distinct riches of his country's cultural fabric. His songs are vibrant, colorful celebrations of everything Nicaraguan — from its geography, food, and wildlife, to praise for the town gossip and shoe-shine boy.

When asked about the Nicaraguita flower that inspired him to write the most famous song in the country's history ("Nicaragua, Nicaraguita"), Carlos Mejía quoted a passage entitled "La Flor Escogida" (The Chosen Flower) by Profesor Carlos A. Bravo. In that passage, the rare variety of *sacuanjoche* (Nicaragua's national flower) is described as *"roja incendida, un clarinazo, listada de oro"* (burning red, a trumpet blast, with golden rays). Carlos Mejía called this "such a beautiful thing," and one is not sure if he was speaking of the flower or the lyrical words describing it — perhaps for him, there is no distinction between the two.

Pick up some of Carlos Mejía's music and learn his lyrics before you leave, but don't stop your discovery there. Carlos's brother Luis Enrique is a world-renowned salsa king, and they can both be found performing at their club in Managua, **La Casa de los Mejía Godoy.**

is better frequented and offers similar fare on weekends only; a calendar of events is often available at supermarkets and Texaco stations as well as in the arts magazine *Patadeperro* if you're lucky enough to find a copy.

Located across from the UCA, **La Academia de Danza** (tel. 505/2277-5557) has frequent performances and concerts. The students deliver professional and talented renditions of traditional, folk, modern jazz, Brazilian, and ballet; call or drop by for a schedule of events, or if you're in town for the long haul, consider taking one of their dance classes to prepare you for the club scene.

SPECIAL EVENTS

Las Fiestas Patronales each August are when Managua celebrates its patron saint Santo Domingo and are the highlight of the calendar year. On the first of the month, the saint (a diminutive little figure under a glass dome) is brought down from a small church in the hilly neighborhood of Santo Domingo and on the 10th he is returned. On both those dates, and for much of the time in between, Managua celebrates. Expect parades, horse shows, unlimited quantities of beer and rum, and a lot of fun and colors. INTUR sponsors a series of events during this time, like Las Noches Agostinas, featuring cultural presentations and live music throughout the capital.

Every **July 19th** since 1979, Nicaraguans have celebrated the final victory against Somoza during the Sandinista revolution. July 19th celebrations bring out the Sandinista party faithful, with a rally and presentations in Plaza de la Fé and a show choreographed by President Ortega's wife Rosario Murillo. The truly devout even stay through Ortega's predictable and lengthy speech at the end.

If you are in Managua during the first few weeks of December, be sure to catch the massive **IMPYME** crafts fair on Avenida Bolívar—arts, crafts, and food from all over the country, plus a two-week carnival. **Expica** is a permanent farming-related exhibition site in Barrio Acahualinca (Casa Pellas, two blocks west and one block north, tel. 505/2266-9634) and where in August ranchers descend upon the capital to exhibit and sell breeding stock, and generally show off their latest SUVs, ill-concealed revolvers, and beer-swilling prowess on the bar stool. The Nicaraguan cowboy elite show hundreds of some of the most magnificent and beautifully tended specimens of Brahman cattle in this part of the world, as well as impressive displays of horsemanship in the saddles of pure-bred Arabian and Peruvian equines.

Shopping

MERCADO ROBERTO HUEMBES

Mercado Huembes is a fun market: It's full of the exuberance, color, and life that so typifies Nicaragua, and is tourist friendly and easily-accessible. That's what makes it such a pleasant way to spend an afternoon in Managua, and you will be perfectly safe there while you shop. Although Managuans rely on Huembes for lots of day-to-day stuff (chicken cutlets, toothpaste, socks) the market also has a splendid selection of pottery, paintings, leatherwork, and other Nicaraguan artisan specialties. Only Masaya is a better place to shop. Open every day from around 7:30 A.M. to around 5 P.M.

ARTS, CRAFTS, AND SOUVENIRS

For a gorgeous selection of arts and crafts in a pleasant atmosphere, visit **Mama Delfina** (Enitel Villa Fontana, one block north, tel. 505/2267-8288), a boutique that collects the work of artisans from all over the country. At the little café on a breezy second-floor balcony, you can mull over your purchases with a tall glass of icy cacao.

BOOKSTORES

The best bilingual selection of local and international books is **Frontera Books** (200 meters north of the Enitel Villa Fontana intersection, tel. 550/2270-2345); great children's section, plus the latest maps and magazines.

Hispamer (Reparto Tiscapa, just east of the UCA, tel. 505/2278-1210) is the largest and oldest bookstore in the city. In the Centro Comercial, several small, but interesting bookstores compete for your attention, including **Librería El Güegüense** (tel. 505/2278-7399 or 505/2278-5285), one of the better choices for books about Nicaragua and foreign-language dictionaries; and **Librería**

Rigoberto López Pérez (tel. 505/2277-2240), named for the poet who, for love of his country, assassinated Anastasio Somoza García. The latter features a wide selection and friendly atmosphere.

GENERAL TRAVELER NEEDS

Managua has seen four U.S.-style malls built since 1998: **Plaza Inter, Plaza Metrocentro** on Carretera Masaya, **Galería Santo Domingo** farther south on the same road, and **Plaza Las Américas** in Bello Horizonte. At the upper end of the market, Galería Santo Domingo sells luxury goods over Cartier, LaCoste, and Chanel counters, and a selection of European fashions; at the lower end Plaza Inter has made a go at cheaper-quality imported goods from Asia (the Plaza is wholly owned by Taiwanese investors). Plaza Las Américas falls somewhere in the middle. Metrocentro and Plaza Las Américas are the most recommended for satisfying travelers' needs, but at any of them you should be able to pick up a cell phone or cell phone chip, a clean shirt, new shoes, a Swiss Army watch, sunglasses, a digital camera, a sun hat, and similar (these malls offer free wireless Internet as well).

The Centro Comercial de Managua is a pleasant open-air strip mall built in the Somoza era, offering a good selection of books, clothing, fabric, and sporting goods, plus two banks, an Internet café, and a post office—not a bad place to get some errands out of the way if malls aren't your cup of tea.

Accommodations

Where you should spend the night in Managua depends a lot on your reason for spending the night here. If all you need is the cheapest possible bed before boarding an international bus to a neighboring country, the *hospedaje* scene in Barrio Martha Quezada is probably your best bet. But if you're overnighting in order to make an early morning flight there are safer options elsewhere, especially if you're willing to spend a few extra dollars. You can catch an early-morning taxi to the airport from anywhere in the city, or you can roll out of bed at the Best Western La Mercedes and walk across the street to check in.

UNDER $10

Located in the shadow of the grand Hotel Intercontinental in central Managua, **Managua Backpacker's Inn** (Chaman Viejo, 75 meters south, house #55, tel. 505/2267-0006, www.managuahostel.com, contact@managuahostel.com, $8 shared dorm, $15 private room) blew away the competition as soon as it arrived a couple of years ago. It offers clean rooms, a friendly atmosphere, and a good value in a safe neighborhood, all within walking distance to Metrocentro and the Zona Rosa. It is very popular, so reserve (and even prepay) online.

Managua's former backpacker stronghold neighborhood, **Barrio Martha Quezada** is getting tougher to recommend to anyone but overnighters bound for an international bus line. The neighborhood that has hosted international budget travelers since the *sandalistas* poured south to support the Revolution is run-down and worse for the wear these days, and increasingly unsafe. Travel in groups and always take a taxi, especially to the nearby Plaza Inter shopping center.

If you do stay here, the new and family-run **Hostal Dulce Sueño** (75 meters east of TicaBus, 505/2228-4125 or 505/8424-0272, www.hostaldulcesueno.com, hospedaje_dulcesueno@yahoo.es, $8/s) is clean and safe, with private bathrooms and laundry service. Traditional Nica meals are available for $2 per person (recommended). **Guesthouse Santos** (from TicaBus, one block north and 1.5 blocks west, tel. 505/2222-3713, $6) remains quirky, gaudy, and well-liked by an ever-revolving international crowd. **Hospedaje El Dorado** (tel.

505/2222-6012, $15/d) is plain but secure under the watchful eye of a very demanding proprietress. The remaining guesthouses in this neighborhood will not be around for much longer as travelers increasingly pay more and go elsewhere.

$10-25

[Hotel Los Felipe (1.5 blocks west of TicaBus, tel. 505/2222-6501, www.hotellosfelipe.com.ni, $15/s with fan, $25 with a/c) is the best of the hotels in Barrio Martha Quezada. Rooms are clean and safe and have cable TV and phone; the hotel offers Internet, parking, pool, a shady patio area under a thatched roof, laundry service, and private baths. **Hotel Cisneros,** just opposite Guesthouse Santos, offers similar comforts but is slightly more expensive ($25 with fan, $40 with a/c) and not quite as pretty.

Hospedaje Mauricio Babilonia (six blocks south, half block west of El Zumen, Managua's Civic Center, house #238, tel. 505/2260-1258, babilonia@turbonett.com.ni, $20) is located in a quiet and safe neighborhood towards the southeast side of town, rather far from everything of interest. Run by a well-known local artist, Mauricio Mejía, the guesthouse's five comfortable and clean private rooms are also an art gallery. All rooms have cable TV, hot water, and private bathroom, and Internet is available.

$25-50

Posadita de Bolonia (three blocks west of Canal 2, then 75 meters south, tel. 505/2268-6692, www.posaditadebolonia.com, $40) is a comfortable and quiet place offering cable TV, Internet, hot water, and private showers. Breakfast is included. Other meals can be provided by arrangement. The hotel also offers a full range of tour and guide services. At about the same level of amenities, **Casa San Juan** (Reparto San Juan Calle Esperanza 560, tel. 505/2278-3220, sanjuan@cablenet.com.ni, $46) is quiet and close to the universities and offers wireless Internet throughout the hotel, cable TV, and hot-water showers.

Posada de Maria La Gorda (Reparto El Carmen, tel. 505/2268-2455 or 505/2268-2456, $35–60) is accustomed to the international set and provides Internet, laundry, and cable TV; check about special group rates.

$50-100

Increasingly, this is the kind of money you need to spend in Managua to get comfort, safety, and peace of mind, and travelers are increasingly willing to do so. This price category has more options than we can print. For this kind of money, expect hot water, cable TV, telephone, minibar, Internet, and probably airport pickup. Many of these hotels have a small pool, which you will appreciate in Managuan heat.

[Hotel Pyramide (Reparto San Juan, del Gimnasio Hercules one block south, one east, 2.5 south, tel. 505/2278-0687, pyramide@ibw.com.ni, www.lapyramidehotel.com, $75) gets consistently favorable reviews for the attentiveness of the owner, who will make sure you are comfortable as soon as you get to the airport. Good value for the money, but just a bit hard to get to the restaurants from here: The owner will help you get taxis. In the same neighborhood, **Hotel Brandt** (Reparto San Juan, from the north side of Hercules gym one block east, tel. 505/2270-2114, www.brandtshotel.com.ni, $75) is clean, safe, and pretty, and has been in business a long time.

[Hotel El Ritzo (from the Lacmiel, three blocks east, 25 meters south, tel. 505/2277-5616, hotelritzo@alianza.com.ni, www.hotelritzo.net, $65) is tastefully decorated, quiet, and gorgeous. (They've got a second hotel in Villa Fontana now, which is slightly less convenient.) Another great option for good access to Carretera Masaya is **Hotel El Almendro** (from the Metrocentro rotunda, two blocks west, half block south, tel. 505 /2270-1260, www.hotelelalmendro.com, almendro@cablenet.com.ni, $64). You can walk relatively easily about two blocks to the Plaza Metrocentro shopping center and the rooms are great, though somewhat geared towards business travelers and long-stay guests (suites, kitchenettes, etc.). Guarded parking is available for your rental car and a little pool for dipping, with breakfast included.

In the quiet Bolonia neighborhood, **Hotel Europeo** (75 meters west of Canal 2, tel. 505/2268-4930 or 505/2268-4933, www.hoteleuropeo.com.ni, reserv@hoteleuropeo.com.ni, europeo@ibw.com.ni, $60) is a good choice with a well-liked pool in an attractive garden patio. In the same neighborhood, **Hotel Real Bolonia** (from Plaza España 1.5 blocks north, across from the German Embassy, tel. 505/2266-8133, hotelreal@hotelreal.com.ni, $75) is on a more major street with easier access to restaurants but at the price of a bit more noise.

Hotel Mozonte (from the entrance to PriceSmart, 1.5 blocks north, across from the old French Embassy, tel. 505/2266-0686 or 505/8965-0855, www.hotelmozonte.com, info@hotelmozonte.com, $60) has attractive, clean rooms, pleasant common and sitting areas, and a gorgeous pool. Have them pick you up at the airport. Adjacent, the **Hotel Villa Americana B&B** (tel. 505/2278-6446 or 505/2267-5005, villamer@cablenet.com.ni, $68) is much less charming but safer-looking due to better lighting and a guard at the front door. Breakfast is included.

A convenient place to stay if you have an early flight is the **Best Western Las Mercedes** (tel. 505/2263-1011, $85), directly across from the airport. Decompress on the last night before your flight in a decent restaurant or with the mixed bag of travelers and diplomats lounging by the pool.

OVER $100

In the Los Robles area just west of Carretera Masaya, **Hotel Los Robles** (in front of Restaurante La Marseillaise, tel. 505/2267-3008, www.hotellosrobles.com, $102) blends colonial charm with business-minded amenities; their breakfast buffet is splendid. **Casa Naranja** (from Tip-top Chicken on Carretera Masaya, 1 block west, tel. 505/2277-3403, www.hotelcasanaranja.com, $110) gets consistently favorable reviews from travelers for its understated colonial style and green backyard patio—a welcome respite from Managua.

Managua's premium chain hotels cater to business travelers with expense accounts (and travelers who want to splurge at the end of their trip). Your safest bet in this category is **[C] Intercontinental Metrocentro** (tel. 505/2271-9483, mga-metro@interconti.com, www.ichotelsgroup.com, from $150), with its convenient location next to the Plaza Metrocentro and Zona Rosa, and its good service. **El Inter** is one of the tallest buildings in the city, has standard smallish rooms (club level are the nicest), pool, event center, and overpriced bar and restaurant. The old pyramidal Hotel Inter at the base of the Tiscapa Crater is now the **Hotel Crowne Plaza** (located in Plaza Inter, tel. 505/2228-3530, managua@interconti.com), a landmark since the Somoza days; its rooms afford supreme views of the lake.

Other nearby options include **Hotel Hilton Princess** (Carretera Masaya, tel. 505/2270-5045, $169–219). One block west and one block north of the Princess, and a short stroll from a dozen excellent restaurants, the **Hotel Seminole Plaza** (tel. 505/270-6496, www.seminoleplaza.com, $119) is owned by the Seminole Indian tribe of Florida; the hotel is typically a bit less expensive than the competition.

The **Holiday Inn** (Pista Juan Paul II, tel. 505/2270-4515, holidayinn@tmx.com.ni, from $100) is the least conveniently situated of the premium hotels, but its interior is lovely and the service excellent.

The **Camino Real** (U.S. tel. 800/948-3770, caminoreal@centralamerica.com, $120) is very close to the airport, just minutes away on Carretera Norte, and is adjacent to a casino.

LONG-TERM ACCOMMODATIONS

Visiting students tend to gravitate to **Arcoiris** (Barrio Los Robles, two blocks south and one block east of Plaza del Sol, house #97, tel. 505/2278-0905, $12/night), a clean, comfortable, family-run guesthouse in a safe neighborhood. The price includes breakfast, and minimum one-month stay applies. Internet is available, and laundry and other meals can be arranged. **Hostal Dulce Sueño** (75 meters east of TicaBus, tel. 505/2228-4125 or 505/8424-0272, hospedaje_dulcesueno@ yahoo.es, www.hostaldulcesueno.com) offers similar services plus free laundry for $180per month single or $300per month for a couple. **Belinda's House** (Canal 2, two blocks north and 75 meters west, tel. 505/2266-3856, $15) is a similar, cozy family-run long-term guesthouse. Next to Las Cazuelas restaurant and across from Guesthouse Santos, **Hotel/ Apartamentos Los Cisneros** (tel. 505/2222-3535) rents small, fully furnished apartments that include refrigerator, private phone, and parking facilities.

At the higher end, several boutique hotels can accomodate long-stay visitors in luxury with full cable TV, Internet, laundry service, and similar. **Hotel El Almendro** (from the Metrocentro rotunda, two blocks west, half block south, tel. 505/2270-1260, www.hotelelalmendro.com, almendro@cablenet.com.ni,

$54/s, $64/d) specializes in long-term accomodations, offering studio suites with kitchenettes and parking; pricing depends on the length of your stay but runs around $40 per day. Being able to cook your own meals once in awhile is a huge advantage. **Los Robles** (one block west, two blocks south of the Hotel Intercontinental Metrocentro, tel. 505/2278-6334), in the same class, has 12 rooms at $1,300 per month but you'll eat in the hotel restaurant (and love it). **Los Cedros** (Km 13, Carretera Sur, across from the Iglesia Monte Tabor, tel. 505/2265-8340) has 30 furnished rooms with bath, terrace, kitchen, pool, and plenty of green space.

If you're content living outside the city limits, several excellent long-term options line the far reaches of Carretera Masaya. **Hotel Campo Real** (Km 12.5, tel. 505/2279-7067, camporeal@ideay.net.ni, www.hotelcamporeal.com) has six fully furnished apartments with all the amenities to make you feel at home, from $60 a night, depending on how long you stay.

Food

Keeping up with restaurants is a challenge in a city where most restaurants thrive for a year and then vanish. Dining out is the mainstay of Managua's elite and they tend to abandon a place as soon as something newer and trendier comes along. But a few classics help hold the whole scene together. *¡Buen provecho!*

CARRETERA MASAYA AREA

Pizza Valenti is the heart of a tight little cluster of restaurants. Take a taxi here and you can find something to eat within one or two blocks. **Pizza Valenti** (Colonial Los Robles, two blocks east of Lacmiel, tel. 505/2277-5744) is now essentially a landmark—a family restaurant serving a variety of classic pizzas and cold beer. Their pizza is excellent, though not gourmet, and they've got pasta as well: Try their fresh pesto and their cannelloni. **Don Pan**

(across from Pizza Valenti) serves sandwiches and baked goods.

For simple, belly-warming "Californiastyle food," try **Moon River Burritos** (in the Los Robles neighborhood adjacent to the San Jeronimo book store,, two blocks from Backpacker's Inn, tel. 505/2277-5017, open Mon.–Sat. 11 A.M.–11 P.M.); they've also got nachos, tacos, and beer.

Managua's premier coffee shop is ◖ **La Casa de Café** with a selection of pastries, juice drinks, and Nicaraguan coffee all served on a gorgeous, second-story open terrace overlooking the street. The coffee is excellent, but the ambience is better (they now have branches in the commercial centers as well). Solid breakfasts are served in addition to other meals.

María Bonita (1.5 blocks west of Distribuidora Vicky, tel. 505/2270-4326) is another favorite, serving Mexican classics in an open, romantic atmosphere for about $6, and a traditional and European breakfast bar Monday–Saturday 6:45–10 A.M. for $3. **Tacos al Pastor** is unassuming but delicious and not expensive. Mexican and Central American specialties run about $3–7.

For tasty Peruvian-Asian fusion, **La Terraza Peruana** (De Pasteleria Sampson, 1 block north, Casa No. 14, Planes de Altamira, tel. 505/2278-0031) has exquisite ceviches and other seafood, and also a huge array of appetizers, chicken, and beef entrées ($5–10). **Bonsai** (1.5 blocks south of the Monte Olivos funeral parlor, tel. 505/2278-8585) is a newish but well-recommended sushi place, with executive lunches for $5–6 and a veritable sushi feast for $45 that would feed a marauding band of seven samurai.

VICINITY OF CARRETERA MASAYA

On your way to Granada, **Sushi Itto** (tel. 505/2278-4886), a Central American chain of good-quality sushi restaurants, has two branches in Managua, one in the Galería Santo Domingo and the other at the Rotunda El Periodista, about two kilometers west of the UCA, with meals starting at $10. **Hary's Grill** (next to the Texaco gas station, Las Colinas, Carretera Masaya, tel. 505/2276-1067) serves pricey imported Argentinian steak.

El Muelle (one block east of the Hotel Intercontinental Metrocentro, $6–8) also offers excellent seafood cocktails and main courses.

ZONA HIPPOS AND LOS ROBLES

Zona Hippos lies just off the Carretera Masaya and is thickly clustered with competing restaurants and lively sports bars with open-air seating. We recommend ◖ **El Garabato** (two blocks south of the Hotel Seminole Plaza, tel. 505/2278-2944) for their variety of Nicaraguan classic foods and internationally-inspired chicken and beef dishes in a pleasant indoor/outdoor environment that gets a bit noisy later at night.

One of the best seafood places in town, with

a choice of outdoor seating and air-conditioning indoors, is **Marea Alta** (from Hotel Seminole Plaza, two blocks south). The restaurant is the former residence of Chema Castillo, where in 1977 the Sandinistas took hostage of diplomats and government officials (Chema himself was killed). The Los Robles branch has become a core around which a dozen other restaurants have sprung up. Next door is **Rock and Grill,** which offers a brash and definitely un-Asiatic mixture of sushi and steak dishes for $8–15, and one set of street-front tables. Nearby **Sharky's** offers an excellent seafood paella for two for $15 and other seafood dishes for $7–15.

Driving south from Zona Hippos puts you in Los Robles, a relatively secure and well-serviced middle-class neighborhood only a few blocks west of Carretera Masaya. For home-cooked Nicaraguan cuisine in an upscale atmosphere, **La Cocina de Doña Haydee** (one block west of Casino Pharaoh, $3–7) has been around for ages and always gets good reviews. Her menu of Nica specialties, including her famous Indio Viejo (an assortment of small, classic dishes) taste better in this quiet and intimate place off the main road. ◖ **Ola Verde** (behind Pharoah's Casino, follow the road to the end and turn right, tel. 505/2270-3048, open from 9 A.M. daily, breakfast starts around $4, lunch around $6, more for dinner) features fresh juices, salads, soups, hummus, and babaghanoush on a pleasant and fresh menu of changing vegetarian and chicken dishes. Ola Verde also has a small shop of natural products and is a popular meeting spot for foreigners; ask about upcoming cooking classes.

El Puyaso (from old El Chamán, 75 meters south, Los Robles, tel. 505/2277-2485) is the Managua branch of a Matagalpan favorite, and their steak is top-notch and inexpensive. Otherwise, **La Plancha** (from the Semáforos Plaza del Café, 150 meters to the east) is home to some of the best meat in town. Ask for the *parrillada* rack or just go for the grill, *a la plancha,* about $10–12 a plate.

One of Managua's fanciest and oldest dining options, **La Marseillaise** (Calle Principal Los Robles, tel. 505/2277-0224) is a city classic since before the war, serving traditional French cuisine and stunning desserts, all in a classy building adorned with works of art. It's also one of the city's most expensive, so be prepared.

CARRETERA SUR

On the road out of town are several places that make for excellent and memorable lunches given their view of the capital. **Mi Pueblo** (Km 9, $6–12) is worth the trip for lunch or dinner to check out one of the best views in town, bar none. The menu is unsurprising—Nicaraguan classics like nacatamales and churrasco steak with red beans—but a lot of attention goes into the food.

Just a half kilometer farther south out of town is **Asados Milcas** ($3–6), with large helpings, quick service, reasonable prices, and good charcoal-grilled meats. Even farther south and newer, **Casa Hacienda** (Km 15, tel. 505/2265-8437) offers a similar menu, but serves meals on a gorgeous site once a former coffee plantation (ask to see the 850-year-old ceiba tree) where you can get an idea of how the outskirts of Managua looked before all the construction began.

ESTATUA MONTOYA

There are two reasons to eat in this part of town: One is that you plan on catching a show at the Ruta Maya, one of Managua's better musical venues; the second is the quality of the restaurants here. **Eskimo** (next door to the Fábrica Eskimo, tel. 505/2266-9701) serves a varied menu of meats, fish, and shellfish, all in the $6–9 range; the *pollo en vino* is a popular choice. **Los Ranchos** (Carretera Sur Km 3, tel. 505/2266-0526, open noon–3 P.M. and 6–11 P.M. daily) isn't cheap (about $15 per entrée), but they've served a fantastic steak au poivre since the days of Somoza. **El Churrasco** has similarly easy-to-recommend beef dishes for about $10–12 per person, located right on the Rotonda El Güegüense.

Managua's second most popular vegetarian place is **Licuados Ananda** (half a block east of the Estatua Montoya, tel. 505/2228-4140, open 7 A.M.–9 P.M. daily), with whole foods and a menu of several dozen fresh fruit juices and smoothies, well recommended on a hot day.

BARRIO MARTHA QUEZADA AND BOLONIA

The budget backpacker stronghold specializes in low-cost eating as well: nothing fancy, but the price is right. For breakfast, you can't go wrong at **Café Myrna** (one block west of TicaBus, open 6 A.M.–lunch daily, $3.50 for a full meal) for eggs any way you like them, fresh juices, and the best pancakes in the country. But if you prefer just a pastry, try **Cafetín Tonalli** (2.5 blocks south of Cine Cabrera), a unique women's cooperative that produces extraordinarily good breads and cakes, and sells juices, cheese, coffee, and more (Swiss training!). Take out or eat in their enclosed outdoor patio. Finally, **Frutilandia** (a block and a half east of the Calle 27 traffic light, look for the colorful storefront, open 7 A.M.–5 P.M. Mon.–Sat.), where you'll find a fresh, delicious menu of fruit smoothies, shakes, and simple meals.

Our favorite *fritanga* (Nicaraguan barbecue) in Managua has satisfied decades of backpack travelers and remains a great option for low cost dining. **Fritanga Doña Pilar** (one block west and half a block north of TicaBus, open nights about 6–9 P.M.) only serves dinner: chicken, *gallo pinto, tostones,* fresh avocado, an icy glass of fruit juice, and some fried cheese will fill you up for a price that can't be beat, if you're comfortable eating at a plastic table, roadside.

For more robust budgets, these two places provide a substantial, elegant meal in a classy atmosphere, with prices that correspond. **El Mesón Español y Barra La Tasca** (Bolonia Mansión Teodolinda 350 meters south, tel. 505/2266-8561) serves fantastic paella and shellfish for about $20. And right at the Rotonda El Güegüense (essentially across the circle from McDonalds, a nice irony, $12–18) is **El Churrasco,** probably the best bet in the neighborhood, with an impressive menu of steaks, chops, and grilled beef.

Information and Services

EMERGENCY

Dial 118 for police, 115 or 120 for the fire department, and 128 for the Red Cross ambulance. There are several hospitals in Managua; the most modern is the private **Hospital Vivian Pellas** (outside of Managua on the highway to Masaya), built in 2004. For less serious ailments and stomach disorders, **Hospital Bautista** (Barrio Largaespada, near the main fire station, tel. 505/2249-7070) is accustomed to dealing with foreigners.

LIBRARIES

Managua's public library, **Biblioteca Dr. Roberto Incer Barquero** (behind the bank at Carretera Sur Km 7, tel. 505/2265-0500 ext. 465, open 8:30 A.M.–4:30 P.M. Mon.–Fri.) was built in 1999 and houses a notable collection of newspapers from the war years. The old National Library is located in the Palacio de Cultura down by the waterfront. INHCA is a remarkable collection of historical and cultural resources housed within the UCA; accessing them requires a library card obtainable from the director by paying a $10 fee.

BANKS

Banking hours in Managua are 8 A.M.–4 P.M. Monday–Friday, and 8 A.M.–noon on Saturday. Along Carretera Masaya, you'll find the **Banco de América Central** (BAC), **Bancentro** (in the LAFISE financial center), **Banco de Finanzas (BDF), Banpro, Banco Uno** and the first truly international bank, **HSBC.** For travelers staying in Barrio Martha Quezada, the nearest bank is the BDF near the Hotel Crowne Plaza. Several other nearby banks are clustered around Plaza España, including BAC and Banco Uno, and branches of most can be found in all the main malls. You'll find shorter lines at Multicambios, on the south side of Plaza España.

Bancentro will change euros directly to local currency without first changing them to U.S.

dollars (and taking another commission). Avoid the *coyotes* (money changers) on the streets.

MAIL, FAX, AND PHONE

The Palacio de Comunicaciones, located across the plaza near the ruins of the old cathedral, contains the central office of both **Correos de Nicaragua** and **ENITEL,** with full mail, fax, telex, express courier, and phone services. In the *palacio,* the *oficina de filatelía* sells stamps from previous editions beginning in 1991 (Nicaragua is well known among philatelists for having the most beautiful postage stamps in Central America), plus postcards and greeting cards (open 8 A.M.–5 P.M. Mon.–Fri., 8 A.M.–1 P.M. Sat.). More compact, easier post offices to deal with are found in the Centro Comercial, Altamira, and the airport.

For packages, **DHL** (tel. 505/2255-8700) is located in front of the Hotel Intercontinental, and on Carretera Masaya near the Hotel Princess. **Federal Express** (tel. 505/2278-4500) has been operating in Nicaragua since 2000. Find it on Carretera Masaya near Subway, and in Ofiplaza El Retiro, Suite 515 (150 meters south of Rotonda Los Periodistas, tel. 505/2278-4500). **UPS** (tel. 505/2254-4892) is close to Barrio Martha Quezada and can be found two blocks north of Plaza España.

INTERNET

The cybercafés typically also offer VOIP (voice over Internet protocol) calling booths as well, but they are quickly losing ground to the free Wi-Fi spots in the commercial centers like Metrocentro. If you're sleeping in Barrio Martha Quezada, **Cyber Center Banisa,** located two blocks south of the stadium, is your best bet. Otherwise, head toward the university area, across from the main UCA gates, where there are a half dozen Internet joints, all with the cheapest rates in the city, usually open till 9 P.M. during the week. Macintosh addicts can

NOT YOUR TYPICAL COLLEGE TOWN

Nicaragua's next generation of leaders attends more than 30 Managuan universities, the three biggest of which are **La Universidad de Centroamerica** (La UCA, rhymes with "hookah"), **La Universidad Nacional Autónoma de Nicaragua** (La UNAN), and **La Universidad Nicaragüense de Ingeniería** (La UNI). Visiting the courtyards, soda shops, cafés, and bars on campus provides a great opportunity to mingle with up-and-coming revolutionaries and neoliberal capitalists alike. Find out about the latest student strike or tire-burning session in the fight for 6 percent of the national budget, cheaper tuition, and of course, a class-less society without corruption, war, or unfair wages. Actually, with the Sandinistas once again in power, and one of their principal student firebrands, Jasser Martínez, now a deputy in the National Assembly, it's probably safe to assume that the students will stay obediently off the streets unless Daniel Ortega's government needs some agitation to intimidate the opposition.

The intersection in front of the UCA and UNI is a hotspot during student strife, and a huge social scene at all other times. The parking lot across from the main gate, called La UCA, is also a transportation hub, with minivans departing the city daily for nearby destinations.

get their fix (or get their own Macs fixed) at the **Mac Center** (tel. 505/2270-5918, open 8 A.M.–5 P.M. daily), tucked behind the UCA, a few doors down from Hispamer bookstore.

SUPERMARKETS

The many branches of La Colonial and La Union not only stock their modern aisles with national and imported foodstuffs, they also sell clothing, sandals, books, CDs, cosmetics, and more. The easiest to reach from Barrio Martha Quezada is just up the road at Plaza España (8 A.M.–7 P.M. Mon.–Fri., 8 A.M.–5 P.M. Sat., 9 A.M.–3 P.M. Sun.). If you're in the Carretera Masaya area, you're better off at the La Colonial on the Rotonda Centroamerica. Visit Costco Familiar (located across the street from Valenti's Pizza, open 9 A.M.–10 P.M. Mon.–Sat., 9 A.M.–3 P.M. Sun.) for gourmet goodies, alcohol, and imported bulk items, including dark European beers (and crappy U.S. ones), shiitake mushrooms, chewing tobacco, and specialty olive oils and cheeses. There are several other supermarkets around the city, but most travelers will find what they need at one of the many smaller "mini-supers" and *pulperías* that populate the neighborhoods.

LAUNDRY AND DRY CLEANING

If you're roughing it, you'll have noticed most *hospedajes* have a *lavandero* (cement-ridged washboard). Buy a slug of bar soap ($0.30) at the local *pulpería*, roll up your sleeves, and scrub away like everybody else. Most *hospedajes* have someone who will wash and iron for a reasonable fee as well. Otherwise, try one of the **Dryclean USA** locations, such as behind the Tip Top Chicken on Carretera Masaya. The most convenient branch is located at the Plaza Bolonia right behind Santa Fé Steakhouse, but their prices will make you wish you'd bought the bar soap.

TRAVEL AGENTS

Many travel agents operate just southeast of the Plaza España and are a short cab ride from Barrio Martha Quezada. **Viajes Atlantida** (one block east and half block north of Plaza España, tel. 505/2266-4050 or 505 /266-8720) is a renowned agency and the official representative for American Express in Nicaragua. **Turismo Joven** (tel. 505/2222-2619, 8:30 A.M.–5:30 P.M. Mon.–Fri., 8:30 A.M.–noon Sat.) is the local representative for STA, the student travel association, and offers students discounted airfare. Close to

MANAGUA

Barrio Martha Quezada, **Viajes MTOM** (adjacent to Optica Nicaragüense, tel. 505/2266-8717) is quite professional.

CLASSES/STUDYING OPPORTUNITIES

You can join classes in Latin dancing any time at **La Academia Nicaragüense de la Danza** (50 meters north of the UCA gates, tel. 505/2277-5557). If you think you'll be in Managua long-term, you or your children can learn horseback riding on the beautiful facilities of **Escuela de Equitación Haras de Albanta** (Carretera Vieja a León Km 13, 500 meters north of the Entrada Chiquilistagua, tel. 505/8883-8899 or 505/8882-0369).

Getting There and Around

GETTING THERE

Four main bus terminals link Managua to the towns and cities of Nicaragua's farthest corners. In general, buses depart approximately every hour, 5 A.M.–5 P.M.

To Points North and East

Buses to Estelí, Matagalpa, Ocotal, Jinotega, Boaco, Juigalpa, El Rama, and San Carlos operate out of the **Mercado Mayoreo** bus terminal on the eastern edge of town. From the other end of Managua (i.e., Barrio Martha Quezada), you can take the 102 *ruta* bus to get there, but plan up to an additional hour's travel through Managua's heart; a taxi is much quicker and should cost no more than $3 for a solo traveler.

Expresos del Norte services the entire north of Nicaragua with express buses. Their fleet includes a few Scania luxury buses (a rare treat), and they have a posted schedule, ticket window, and office where you can call to check on times (tel. 505/2233-4729).

To Points West and Northwest

Buses to León, Chinandega, and Carazo depart from the **Israel Lewites** terminal (named for a Jewish-Nicaraguan martyr of the revolution but sometimes referred to by its post-Sandinista name, El Boer). The terminal is surrounded on all sides by a chaotic fruit market by the same name; watch your belongings and expect a slightly more aggressive crowd of *buseros.*

To Points South

Buses to Carazo, Masaya, Granada, Rivas, Ometepe, the border at Peñas Blancas, and San Juan del Sur depart from **Mercado Roberto Huembes** in south-central Managua. The taxi ride from Barrio Martha Quezada should cost no more than $2 a person. Before you get to Huembes, be sure to specify *parada de los buses* (bus stop) to your driver, as opposed to *el mercado de artesanía* (crafts market), located on the opposite side of the same market. This is a very busy terminal, serving thousands of commuters from points south, and its porters and bus assistants will swarm you as you get out of your taxi.

Fast, express minibuses known as *interlocales* are the best option for Jinotepe, Diriamba, Masaya, and Granada, and depart from a lot across the street from **La UCA**. Service starts around 6 A.M. and runs as late as 9 P.M. You can also get Carazo expresses at **Mercado Israel Lewites,** from *el portón rojo* (the big red door).

Finally, **Adelante Express** (tel. 505/8850-6070 or 505/8850-6064, www.adelanteexpress.com) offers fast, direct service between the Managua airport and San Juan del Sur for people looking to bypass Managua entirely.

GETTING AROUND

Managua is easiest to deal with by taxi, given the lack of landmarks and the lousy public transportation, and the addresses given in this book are written with that in mind. If you find yourself walking in Managua, watch your step. Thousands of uncovered, ankle-breaking manholes abound, sometimes up to three meters deep and known as "gringo traps."

Taxis

Not to fear, if you even approach the edge of the street, Managua's 14,000 taxis will circle you like vultures, beeping for your attention. Taxis will take you most places for $1–7, though the ride to and from the airport might cost you as much as $15 if you don't bargain well. Managua taxis have no meters, so settle on a price before getting in the vehicle! Hotel and guesthouse owners can usually arrange a reliable taxi driver if you feel insecure about taking a cab on the street.

Near Managua

◖ CHOCOYERO-EL BRUJO NATURE RESERVE

Less than 28 kilometers away from downtown Managua is a little pocket of wilderness so vibrant with wildlife you'll forget the capital is literally just over the horizon. The Chocoyero–El Brujo nature reserve (tel. 505/2278-3772 or 505/2279-9774, cnd@cablenet.com.ni) is a 41-square-kilometer protected hardwood forest that provides nearly 20 percent of Managua's water supply (20 million gallons of water per day). In the midst of moist hardwood forest and pineapple farms are two 25-meter waterfalls separated by a rocky knife-edge. El Brujo was named The Warlock because to the locals the fact that no river flows out from the waterfall meant it must be enchanted. The other fall, Chocoyero, was named for the incredible number of *chocoyos* (parakeets) that inhabit the adjacent cliff walls.

In fact, this protected area is a naturalist's paradise, with five kinds of *chocoyo* and 113 other bird species (including several owls), plus 49 species of mammals, and 21 species of reptiles and amphibians. Sharp-eyed travelers may even spot small cat species, like *tigrillos* and *gatos de monte,* and you'll likely hear both howler and capuchin monkeys in the treetops. In addition to having well-kept hiking trails, Chocoyero–El Brujo is also one of the few places in Nicaragua that encourages tent camping, making it a great place to spend an evening in the wild. Conditions are simple: a rustic, wooden base camp where guides will meet you and walk you the remaining way to the falls. The two best times to see the *chocoyos* are at around 5:30 A.M. when they leave their nests, and at around 4 P.M. , when the flocks return. To catch the morning commute, you'll obviously have to spend the previous night there.

The entrance fee for foreigners is $3.50; guides, available on weekends, charge a nominal fee ($2–5 for a group of 12, usually). You can rent two-person tents on the premises for $11 each, or set up your own. This is a safe, pretty, and easily accessible area in which to camp for a night. If you call ahead and make a reservation, they'll even cook simple, traditional Nica fare for you for about $2.50–$3 per meal. The reserve is actively promoting low-ropes courses, enviro-camps, and more to local schools and church groups.

Unless you have rented a vehicle, you'll need to charter a sturdy taxi from Managua with a group to take you all the way there. Otherwise, take any bus leaving Managua's Huembes terminal bound for La Concepción (called La Concha for short); buses leave Managua every 15 minutes. Get off at Km 21.5, where you'll see a wooden sign for the park entrance, then stretch out for a good, long walk. The dirt road that travels seven kilometers southwest to the reserve will lead you down a series of volcanic ridges and across a broad valley to the falls. It's an easy two-hour walk, passing through fields of pineapples, bananas, and coffee. Halfway down the road, you'll find a small community where you can rent bikes or horses to take you the rest of the way in (horse $1 per hour, guide $1 per hour, bicycle $0.50 per hour). There also may be some buses from Ticuantepe that take you all the way in—ask around.

MONTIBELLI WILDLIFE RESERVE

This 162-hectare private reserve and award-winning sustainable tourism project is set within the biological corridor between Chocoyero–El Brujo and Volcán Masaya National Park. In this setting, you'll find comfortable accommodations with private bathrooms and an ample deck perched on the edge of a valley—great for armchair birding. There are three trails to hike, with views of the Masaya Volcano and surrounding forest. The restaurant features family recipes and Sunday barbecues.

Over 155 bird species have been spotted here, including manakins, motmots, oropendolas, trogons, tanagers, toucans, and hummingbirds. This is one of the most accessible wildlife reserves in the country, making it really easy to escape from the city. To get there, drive south on Carretera Masaya, taking the turnoff through the town of Ticuantepe, then just after leaving town on Km 18.5 of the Ticuantepe–La Concha Highway, it's a 2.8-km road to the main lodge, known locally as La Casa Blanca. By bus, find a microbus heading south to La Concha and get off at Km 18.5 where you can take a mototaxi. Better yet, arrange for transport by contacting Claudia Belli in Managua (tel. 505/2270-4287, info@montibelli.com, www. montibelli.com).

THE LAGUNAS OF XILOÁ AND APOYEQUE

Less than a half hour from the capital on the highway to León, the Peninsula de Chiltepe protrudes into the southwestern shore of Lake Xolotlán, cradling two ancient volcanic cones drowned in clean rainwater. Part of the Maribios chain, the twin crater lagoons of Xiloá and Apoyeque are a fun day trip if you find yourself in Managua for more than a weekend and anxious for some greenery.

Legend says the **Xiloá** lagoon was formed when an indigenous princess of the same name, spurned by her Spanish lover, went down to the lake's edge to cry. She cried so much that the valley began to fill with tears, and the lagoon formed around her.

Broader and more easily accessed, Xiloá was a popular swimming hole for decades, but former Minister of Tourism director Herty Lewites took the initiative to develop the site more completely, with thatched-roof *ranchónes,* concrete pads, parking areas, and lunch stands. In 1998, Hurricane Mitch submerged the facilities under a meter of water. Rather forgotten, the lagoon will probably be deserted except for yourself and the occasional marine biologist, scuba diving to study the lake's endemic species.

Apoyeque still bears much of its original cone shape—the lagoon is enclosed in steep crater walls that form the highest part of the Chiltepe Peninsula. The Nicaraguan military occasionally uses it for training special forces in the art of rappelling, and a radio tower perches on the southwest lip of the crater. In 2001, Apoyeque was the epicenter of a series of seismic tremors.

Buses leave Managua's Mercado Israel Lewites infrequently and go directly to the water at Xiloá. It's easier to take any León-bound bus from the same market, get off at the top of the road to Xiloá, and walk (30 minutes). Pay $0.25 per person ($1 per vehicle) to enter the park facilities at the water's edge. Getting to Apoyeque is a more challenging hike, requiring good boots and some autonomy (compass, water bottles, etc.). Take the road from Mateare, which you can walk or hitch down until you reach the access road for the radio antenna. That road will lead you to the ridge, from where you'll have to painstakingly and carefully make your way into the crater.

From Xiloá, a well-marked but little-used dirt road circles the entire peninsula (28 km), coming out in Mateare. The rest of the peninsula and the lower slopes of the two volcanic peaks are lush cattle farms, many owned by the Seminole tribe of Florida, which has invested heavily in the area. The view from the northeastern side of the peninsula is particularly beautiful in the late afternoon when the sky fills with colors.

PACIFIC BEACHES

Roughly 65 kilometers due west of the capital are a handful of easy-to-reach beaches, with facilities ranging from low-key, grungy *hospedajes* to all-out, all-inclusive resorts. In fact, the diversity along the coastline couldn't be greater. Pochomíl attracts the casual day-tripper and increasingly, surfers, while Montelimar is a pricey but pleasurable all-inclusive resort. Los Cardones is an ecofriendly offbeat lodge also popular with surfers and families that's a bit harder to get to but worth the effort. But when you hear about all the foreign real estate investment in Nicaragua, much of it is happening right here, so watch for big changes over the next decade unless Ortega scares away the foreigners again.

Pochomíl

Pochomíl was named in the early 20th century by a farmer by the name of Felipe Gutierrez, in reference to all the *"pocho"* (money) he hoped to earn from his ambitious duck and goat farm. These days it's a once-popular beach town left to stagnate and now in the midst of an economic revival, as wealthy investors are building beachfront estates and hotel complexes.

Hotel and restaurant rates fluctuate wildly according to the calendar. Semana Santa and Christmas are the most expensive time of year to visit. In the wet season, prices become significantly more flexible, but at any month of the year, traveling with a group gives you significant leverage to bargain for a good deal. Travelers driving their own vehicles will pay a $1 entrance fee at the entrance to town.

One of the longest-established places on the beach, **Hotel Altamar** (tel. 505/2269-9204, $11 per room with private bath, $9 per room with shared bath) has 15 basic rooms and a pleasant restaurant overlooking the water. Otherwise, competition among hotel and restaurant owners is particularly fierce—as you get off the bus expect to be assaulted by employees of a dozen restaurants all trying to drag you into their establishments to eat and drink. No one place is any better than another; you can expect beachfront palm thatch huts, fried fish, and cold beer no matter where you go.

All the way down the road at the north end of the beach is the luxury **Hotel Villa del Mar** (tel. 505/2269-0426, $35 with private bath and a/c). Owned by the Universidad Americana (UAM) and run as part of the university's tourism/business administration curriculum, it has a nice stretch of beach, swimming pool, wading pool, wood-paneled conference room, palm-thatch huts set on a grassy lawn, and a fancy open-air restaurant serving three meals a day. The $7 entrance fee can be applied to meals and beverages served on the premises if you just come for the day. Otherwise try the more humble **Hotel Cabañas del Mar** (tel. 505/2269-0433, $18 d or $25 t with private bath and a/c) next door, offering a simple menu and some vegetarian dishes.

Buses leave Managua's Israel Lewites bus station for Pochomíl every 30 minutes all day until about 5 P.M. The last bus from Pochomíl back to Managua departs at 5:30 P.M. from the cul-de-sac.

Barceló Montelimar Beach

Somoza's former personal summer palace was converted into a resort in the 1980s and since being purchased by Barceló Resorts is now **Montelimar Beach** (tel. 505/2269-6769 or 505/2269-6752, U.S. and Canada tel. 800/227-2356, www.barcelomontelimarbeach.com, $72–135 per person), an all-inclusive five-star resort. It offers 88 double guest rooms with queen-size beds and 205 bungalows with king-size beds, private bath, air-conditioning, TV, strongbox, and mini-bar. The price includes 24 hours of unlimited feasting, drinking, swimming, and playing. Often crowded during weekends with visitors from Managua, it is more peaceful on week-days when you can swim in the largest pool in Central America by yourself. The Montelimar compound is enormous, with multiple beach-side bars, sports, and a spunky coed crew of "animators" to help you have a good time. It also has facilities for groups and conventions, plus airport shuttles, shopping, casino, travel agency, etc. Any bus to Pochomíl will also get you to Montelimar, and there are various tour operators that arrange for transfers from Managua airport or hotels. Ask about deep off-season discounts.

Los Cardones Surf Lodge

This is a unique, peaceful, highly recom-mended beach escape with direct access to con-sistent surf breaks nearly year-round. Set on five acres of organically managed land, **C Los Cardones** (tel. 505/8618-7314, info@loscar-dones.com, www.loscardones.com) rents half

a dozen simple but elegant bungalows made from wood and thatch; all have solar hot water, soft beds, no electricity, and composting toi-lets; all are also waterfront. Their inspired and creative menu involves lots of fresh fish, and their commitment to both the local commu-nity and the ecosystem is admirable. Rent surf or boogie boards for the waves, collect shells on the beach, or hike to nearby pre-Columbian petroglyphs. Ask about yoga and surf retreats. Rates ($69 plus tax per person) are all-inclusive, for lodging, meals, drinks, and transportation; great deals for a week's stay or other packages. The managers started **Arte Acción,** which promotes social change through art classes, in a neighboring village. Many guests often join in and help the class.

They'll send a car to Managua for you; or to get there by bus, take the bus to San Cayetano from Mercado Israel Lewites in Managua (leaves every 45 minutes 4 A.M.–9 P.M.) and get off at "California." Then walk or hitch 15 kilo-meters toward the ocean and follow the signs. To drive, take the Carretera Masachapa to Km 49, then drive 15 kilometers on the Playa San Diego Road until you hit the beach.

GRANADA

Arguably Nicaragua's most picturesque town, Granada is an easy place to love. Much of its colonial architecture is remarkably intact and is being painstakingly restored by a new generation of homeowners. The colorful facades lining old narrow streets practically glow in the late afternoon sun. It's sultry and tropical here but a fresh breeze blows off the waters of Lake Cocibolca. The views from along the lakeshore's broad, undeveloped shoreline—and the ever-looming silhouette of Volcán Mombacho—make for easy photos and good memories.

Granada has always been important politically for Nicaragua, and it is the home of many of the country's economic and political elite. Most travelers eschew Managua and flock to Granada because of its charm and lethargic pace, making it their base for further exploration. Some decide to stay, as evidenced by the many real estate offices that have sprung up over the last decade.

Granada is pleasant to explore by foot or old-fashioned horse carriage. Nights, the sky fills with stars and the neighbors come out to chit-chat on their front stoops; inside even the most nondescript colonial facade is an open, private courtyard designed to capture the evening breeze. Granada's restaurants are varied and high quality, offering something for just about everybody. Granada lacks the five-star luxury or business hotels of the capital and coast but instead offers a wide selection of small, charming guesthouses, bed-and-breakfasts, and colonial lodges.

HIGHLIGHTS

◖ **Antiguo Convento San Francisco:** The towering stone statues displayed in one of the Convento's many courtyards are a stunning glimpse into the nation's pre-Columbian past (page 61).

◖ **The Waterfront:** Lake Nicaragua is spectacular in different ways throughout the day, and nowhere is it more beautiful than Granada's landscaped lakefront (page 61).

◖ **Iglesia La Merced:** Climb the bell tower for the best view in all of Granada (page 64).

◖ **Las Isletas:** Spend a lazy day swimming, picnicking, and relaxing among the hundreds of gorgeous islands that comprise Las Isletas (page 78).

◖ **Parque Nacional Archipiélago Zapatera:** The stunning alter-ego statues in the museums came from these islands; an exciting lacustrine day trip leads you into Nicaragua's prehistory (page 79).

◖ **Volcán Mombacho:** More than a gorgeous background for your Granada photographs, Volcán Mombacho has a first-class set of hiking trails, an ecolodge, a canopy tour, and a lot more (page 80).

LOOK FOR ◖ TO FIND RECOMMENDED SIGHTS, ACTIVITIES, DINING, AND LODGING.

PLANNING YOUR TIME

A full day and night in Granada is the minimum and allows you to explore the streets, sleep somewhere interesting, and enjoy a good meal or two. But a lot of Granada's charm lies in the interesting excursions reachable if you use Granada as a base camp. Leave half a day for a boat ride in Las Isletas and another day for Volcán Mombacho. Most people devote another day for visiting the pueblos and markets in Masaya. While you could conceivably day-trip to the Laguna de Apoyo as well, the hotel options make it a fun place to stay (when was the last time you woke up inside a volcano crater?).

HISTORY

Granada has a history as long as colonial Nicaragua's, as it is in fact the oldest city in North America. Founded 1524 by Francisco Hernández de Córdoba on the edge of Lake Cocibolca, the Spanish built Granada strategically adjacent to the indigenous community of Xalteva, whose residents suddenly found themselves working for their new foreign "visitors." Granada grew quickly as a sort of trade hub; sailing vessels would navigate their way up the Río San Juan and across the lake to Granada. As a result, an affluent Spanish merchant class developed, largely of Veracruz, Cartagena, and La Habana origin. From its beginnings,

Granada was a symbol of Spanish opulence, an unsubtle show of mercantile success in the New World. The competing nations accepted the challenge, sacking and burning the city at every available opportunity (the English buccaneers were particularly effective).

After independence from Spain, Granada was the capital of Nicaragua each time the Conservatives took power (León was the capital when the Liberals won). As the Liberal-Conservative feud escalated, it was the Liberals who first called upon the American filibuster William Walker for support. He executed Granada's most ruthless sacking, even

by pirate standards. Before he was eventually driven from Granada, he finally burned the whole place to the ground, and buried a symbolic coffin in the central plaza under a wooden sign that read, Aquí Fue Granada (Here Was Granada).

Despite the sackings and reconstruction, Granada remains little changed from its earliest colonial incarnation; if Córdoba were to rise from the grave today and walk the streets of La Gran Sultana as it is sometimes called, he would find it eerily familiar. But these days, Granada is changing fast. Less influential than the old families these days is the influx of foreign capital, new ideas, and fast business. A decade ago, Granada was a "sleepy colonial jewel." The hum of the Internet cafés, chic eateries, tour services, and trendy hotels indicate it has woken up.

ORIENTATION

From Granada's central tree-lined plaza, a.k.a. **Parque Central** and **Parque Colón** look south to the giant Volcán Mombacho. Just behind the **cathedral** on the park's east side, **Calle La Calzada** runs due east about one kilometer to the municipal dock on the lake. A lot of the lodging and restaurants lie along this street or within a block or two of it.

At the lake, a paved road runs south along the water's edge to the Malecón (waterfront), a would-be tourist complex that's emptier than it should be, but remains a peaceful, wooded, lakeshore walking park. An easy taxi ride farther south are the marinas that provide boat access to the *isletas* and Zapatera.

West of the plaza is the **Xalteva** (pronounced more or less, with a hard "h") neighborhood and eventually the cemetery and road to Nandaime. In this neighborhood, one block west of the Plaza, is **Calle Atravesada,** running north-south between the old 1886 train station (now a museum, which has closed for lack of funds) to the bustling chaos of the municipal market. This is one of Granada's main thoroughfares and a modern commercial center, of sorts, for banks, movie theaters, and the like.

Sights

PARQUE COLÓN (CENTRAL PLAZA) AND CATHEDRAL

If Granada is the center of tourism in Nicaragua, then Granada's central plaza is the heart of it all. You'll pass through here dozens of times during your stay in Granada, and each time, sweat-drenched, you'll pause for something cold to drink. People-watchers will find it hard to leave, as the park is a steady stream of students gossiping, elderly men playing chess, and vendors hawking carved wooden toys, ceramics, jewelry, ice cream, and more. Order a glass of icy *fresco de cacao* at one of the corner kiosks, and enjoy the raucous bird-chatter in the treetops, and the hustle and bustle of life in North America's first city.

Cross the park to the magnificent cathedral on the plaza's east side. It's sometimes open to the public (even the bell towers). When the doors open for mass, it's worth a peek inside. The stone and wooden interior is dim and cool, and the bells echo overhead. Just outside the church's front step is the **Cruz del Siglo** (Century Cross), inaugurated January 1, 1900. Entombed in its cement are coins, pieces of art, and a gilded bottle from the 19th century.

LA PLAZUELA DE LOS LEONES

The pedestrian space guarded by the cannon off the northeast corner of the main plaza is where Henry Morgan once set 18 cannons during his sacking of the city, and where, a century later, William Walker was sworn in as President of Nicaragua. On the Plazuela's eastern side is the **Casa de los Leones,** a colonial era home whose lush interior has been transformed into an international cultural center. Don Diego de Montiel, governor of Costa Rica, built the Casa de los Leones in 1720. William Walker did not miss the opportunity to burn this place down, leaving nothing standing but the portal bearing the Montiel family crest (still visible). The unique, neoclassical colonnade facade was a product of the subsequent reconstruction. In 1987, the historical monument became the headquarters of the **Casa de los Tres Mundos Foundation** (tel. 505/2552-4176, www.c3mundos.org, open 8 A.M.–6 P.M. daily), bearing an art and music school, museum, historical archive, library, concert hall, literary café, bookstore, and exhibition space which hosts resident artists from around the world.

© RANDALL WOOD

La Plazuela de los Leones

🄲 ANTIGUO CONVENTO SAN FRANCISCO

The Antiguo Convento San Francisco and its trio of bells (one block north and two east of the main cathedral, tel. 505/2552-5535, open 8 A.M.–5 P.M. Mon.–Fri., 9 A.M.–4 P.M. weekends, $2) were once famously blue. Inside, set around open courtyards festooned with palm trees are centuries' worth of priceless artwork, and 30 alter-ego statues collected a century ago from Zapatera Island. The carved basalt shows human forms with the heads of jaguars, birds, and crocodiles whose spirits were thought to flow through humans' souls—a rare look into the cosmology of Nicaragua's pre-Columbian peoples. There is also a large to-scale replica of the city, and exhibits that represent the lifestyle of the Chorotega and Nahautl peoples. The convent was first built by Franciscan monks in 1529 and lasted 150 years before pirate Henry Morgan burned it to the ground. Since then it has housed William Walker's troops, U.S. Marines, a contingent of engineers surveying a possible canal route in the 1920s, and the National University.

CALLE LA CALZADA

Walk east from the park toward the lake along Granada's hippest strip, recently reworked with a modern pedestrian-friendly design, but with an old feel featuring cobblestone, street lamps, and wide sidewalks. Halfway to the lake, stop at the 17th-century **Iglesia de Guadalupe,** first built in 1626 and most recently refurbished in 1945. Continuing along the palm-lined boulevard, you'll reach the *muelle* and *malecón* (dock and quay) on the water's edge.

🄲 THE WATERFRONT

As you reach the lakeshore, turn right and pass through "the rooks" (a pair of statues)

GRANADA

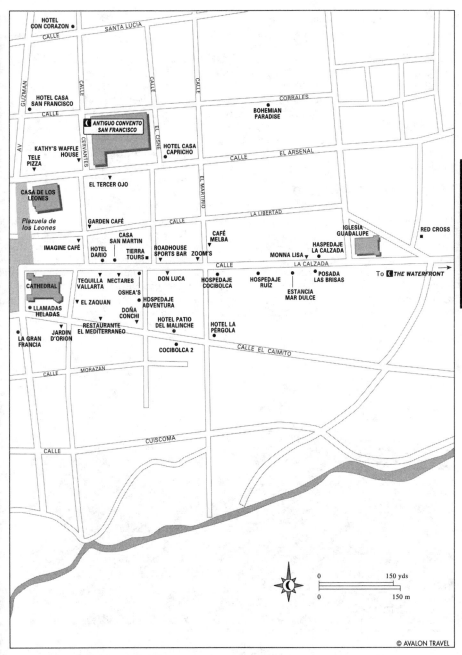

GRANADA

Map locations:

HOTEL CON CORAZON •
SANTA LUCIA
CALLE

HOTEL CASA SAN FRANCISCO •
CALLE
AV GUZMAN

(ANTIGUO CONVENTO SAN FRANCISCO

KATHY'S WAFFLE HOUSE ▼
TELE PIZZA ▼

CORRALES

BOHEMIAN PARADISE •

HOTEL CASA CAPRICHO •
EL CISNE
CALLE
EL ARSENAL

EL TERCER OJO ▼

CASA DE LOS LEONES

Plazuela de los Leones

GARDEN CAFÉ ▼
CALLE
LA LIBERTAD

EL MARTIRIO

CAFÉ MELBA •

IGLESIA GUADALUPE
RED CROSS ■

IMAGINE CAFÉ •
HOTEL DARIO ▼
CASA SAN MARTIN •
TIERRA TOURS ■
ROADHOUSE SPORTS BAR •
ZOOM'S •
MONNA LISA ▼
HASPEDAJE LA CALZADA •
LA CALZADA
CALLE

To (THE WATERFRONT

CATHEDRAL

TEQUILLA VALLARTA ▼
NECTARES •
OSHEA'S •
DON LUCA ▼
HOSPEDAJE COCIBOLCA •
HOSPEDAJE RUÍZ •
POSADA LAS BRISAS •
ESTANCIA MAR DULCE •

LLAMADAS HELADAS •
▼ EL ZAQUAN
HOSPEDAJE ADVENTURA •
DOÑA CONCHI •
HOTEL PATIO DEL MALINCHE •
HOTEL LA PÉRGOLA •

LA GRAN FRANCIA •
JARDIN D'ORION ▼
RESTAURANTE EL MEDITERRANEO •
COCIBOLCA 2 •
CALLE EL CAIMITO

CALLE
MORAZÁN

CUISCOMA

CALLE

0   150 yds
0   150 m

© AVALON TRAVEL

to enter the **Complejo Turístico,** a short row of restaurants and discos lining the lakeshore. None of the restaurants has a menu worth recommending, but the shady ambience and fresh lake breeze set the tone for languid afternoons (as long as the annoying no-see-ums called *chayules* aren't too numerous). Somehow this places fails to live up to its potential, and even the swimming is not good, but there remains no better place to appreciate Granada's gorgeous lacustrine panorama.

IGLESIA LA MERCED

Built in 1534, sacked and burned by Henry Morgan in 1670, then rebuilt, the church itself is pretty, but ascend the tight spiral stairs of the bell tower (open 10 A.M.–6 P.M. daily, $1 entrance fee) for the single most spectacular view in the city. Look over an ocean of tiled roofs to the lake and *isletas,* with Volcán Mombacho over your shoulder. The scene changes over the course of the day; late afternoons are best when the shadows are long.

FORTALEZA DE LA PÓLVORA AND CEMETERY

The old fort and powder storage facility is another seven blocks west of La Merced. Built in 1748 to secure Granada's gunpowder supply from marauding pirates, its medieval architecture speaks of simplicity and strength: five squat towers and one heavily guarded gate with two oak doors. In the 20th century, both the city government and later Somoza's National Guard used La Pólvora as a military garrison, and later, a jail. These days it's a museum of arms or art whose exhibitions rotate regularly. Climb the towers for a breath of wind and a good perspective of the skyline. No entrance fee; watch your head and watch your step. Adjacent, the 10-meter-high arched stone walls known as **Los Muros de Xalteva** were erected by the Spaniards in the mid-1700s to separate Spanish settlements from those of the

a sea of tiled roofs, from the bell tower of Iglesia La Merced

© JOSHUA BERMAN

WILLIAM WALKER: GREY-EYED MAN OF DESTINY

The year was 1853, and Nicaragua's Liberals and Conservatives were once again at each other's throats in a fierce competition for political power. The León-based Liberals saw a chance to beat the Conservatives of Granada once and for all by hiring foreign mercenaries; so they invited a self-styled North American adventurer, white supremacist, and filibuster from Tennessee named William Walker to join them in battle in Nicaragua. He accepted, and within the year, they realized they'd created a monster.

Walker, the self-proclaimed Grey-Eyed Man of Destiny, arrived from Nashville with a band of 300 thugs and ruffians he'd rounded up in the tough neighborhoods of San Francisco. Walker and his men promptly led the Liberals to a rousing victory, but he had no intentions of going home. Two years later, he usurped power, arranged for elections that he rigged to his advantage, and declared himself President of Nicaragua. His goal was to make Nicaragua a slave state loyal to the American South's nascent confederacy.

The United States, at the brink of civil war, officially recognized Walker as President of Nicaragua. Walker reinstituted slavery and declared English the official language of the country. But Walker did what no Nicaraguan leader has been able to accomplish since: He united the people. In a rare moment of fear-inspired solidarity, the Nicaraguans temporarily forgot their differences, banded together, and with the help of the other Central American nations and some financing from Cornelius Vanderbilt (who'd lost his steamship company to Walker) defeated Walker at the Battle of San Jacinto on September 14, 1856, now a national holiday. Not long afterward, he was captured and executed by a rifle squad in Honduras. The Liberals fell into disgrace, and the Conservatives effectively ruled the nation for the next 30 years.

The scars Walker wrought on the nation run deep. As he and his men fled Granada, they paused long enough to burn the city to the ground. On the highway leading north from Managua to Estelí, a statue commemorates the victory over Walker's troops by a mobilized populace at San Jacinto. And deep inside every Nicaraguan, you'll find a distaste for loud, impudent North Americans with ambitious plans and a confident gait. William Walker's own account, *La Guerra de Nicaragua*, tells his story in no uncertain terms. Just be careful who sees you reading it. Or read *Tycoon's War* by Stephen Dando-Collins (Da Capo Press, 2008), a fascinating play-by-play, street-by-street account of William Walker's battles (and Cornelius Vanderbilt's ambitions).

locals. There is a relaxing park across the street with interesting stone shapes.

Located at Granada's southwest corner, Granada's **cemetery** of enormous marble tombs—bigger than the homes of many Nicaraguans—shelters the bones of several centuries of elite from Granada's heyday, including a half-dozen presidents. Note the column-lined Capilla de Animas and the replica of the Magdalena de Paris, both built between 1876 and 1922.

BUTTERFLY RESERVE

Continuing two kilometers down the dirt road to the right of the cemetery (by foot or bicycle, the track is too rough for cars at least half the year) will take you to the **Nicaragua Butterfly Reserva** (tel. 505/8895-3012, www.backyard-nature.net/nbr, $6); take a bus to Km 50 near the police station, and it's less than a kilometer—an easy walk—from there. Tour the flight house and enjoy the ones flying around free outside on the lush grounds of an old fruit orchard.

TOUR OPERATORS IN GRANADA

Most of the national tour operators we list in the *Essentials* chapter have offices in Granada that provide all local trips and transfers. In addition, here are a few Granada specialists.

Leo Tours (tel. 505/8829-4372 or 505/8842-7905, leotoursgranada@gmail.com, leonica1971@yahoo.com, leotours.blogspot.com), run by Leopoldo Castillo, a Granada native, tries to work in a more community-minded spirit that will connect you to Nicaragua rather than just show you the sights. They can take you around Granada, Ometepe, Laguna de Apoyo, and Mombacho, or show by bike tour how the "rest" of Granada lives.

Mombotour (next to BDF in the Centro Comercial Granada, tel. 505/2552-4545 or 505/2552-3297, www.mombotour.com) offers several different canopy tours starting at $30 per person, including their popular Tarzan Swing. You can be on belay in 30 minutes from your hotel, and they pick you up. Also look for bike tours/rentals and canopy trips at the Cutirre Farm on Mombacho.

Tierra Tours (Calle La Calzada, two blocks east of park, tel. 505/8862-9580, www.tierratours.com) offers trips to Mombacho, Masaya, and Las Isletas, where they can coordinate kayak tours as well. They are also gaining traction as the go-to place for travelers – Spanish language students, usually – looking for longer term homestays. In addition to local tours of Granada, Masaya, and Catarina, Tierra offers night tours of Volcán Masaya and overnight cabins and tent platforms at a nearby Butterfly Reserve and coffee farm ($55 pp for full-service camping trip). Ask about shuttle service to other parts of Nicaragua, including León, where they have a sister office.

Servitur (tel. 505/8838-7820 or 505/2552-2955, orvind@hotmail.com) is connected to the Hotel Alhambra, offering travel agent services and a variety of local trips in the Granada area, including a horse-drawn-carriage city tour and fishing trips.

Amigo Tours (tel. 505/2552-4080, bernal@amigotours.net, www.amigotours.net), connected to the lobby of the Hotel Colonial, provides a higher-end option for tours, plus travel agency services like national airline bookings, car rentals, and transfers to and from Costa Rica.

Sports and Recreation

SPAS AND MASSAGE

The three blind masseuses at **Seeing Hands Massage** (in the back of Euro Cafe, 9 A.M.–5:30 P.M. Mon.–Sat.) will give you a chair or full body massage (15-minute chair massage under $5). **Hotel Spa Granada** (Calle Atravesada, across from Bancentro, tel. 505/2552-4678) is the city's first full-service luxury spa. **Swenja Janine** (tel. 505/8451-0891, SJSchlegel@gmx.de) offers Hawaiian massage, relaxation, and reflexology for about $25 per hour. **Maximus Spa** (401 Calle El Arsenal, tel. 505/2552-8422) offers full body massages.

SAILING, BOATING, AND SWIMMING

Getting out on the water is the right way to enjoy this beautiful corner of Nicaragua; watch weather conditions carefully as Lake Cocibolca gets choppy fast as the wind picks up. Taking a boat trip through Las Isletas is the best way to do that. The closest option for the active is renting a kayak from **Inuit Kayaks** (tel. 505/8691-0616, $12 per hour) in the Centro Turístico. They assemble groups that caravan out through the closer *isletas,* a safe and fun way to explore. There are a *lot* more options though.

GRANADA

© JOSHUA BERMAN

Rent a horse carriage on the west side of the main plaza.

Velago Nicaragua Sailing School (located at the Cabana Amarilla, tel. 505/2459-4699, velagoGranada@gmx.at, www.velagogranada.com) offers sailing day trips on the lake (but not through Las Isletas) at $30 pp, and will teach you to sail over the course of a few days, if you'd like. Their fleet consists mostly of Hobie Cat catamarans that will get your adrenaline pumping.

To beat the heat, it's well worth the $5 per person to use the swimming pool at the **Mombacho Beach Club**, located inside Hotel Spa Granada (Calle Atravesada, across from Bancentro, tel. 505/2552-4678, daily 10 A.M.–6 P.M.). You can make spa and beauty appointments there as well. Whether for swimming laps, cooling off, enjoying cocktails and light snacks, or checking e-mails, this place is right for you!

HORSEDRAWN CARRIAGE TOUR

Though Granada is easy to walk, the humidity will wear you down on the haul out to the lakeshore and back. Rather, explore Granada's narrow streets by enjoying a ride in horse and carriage. Find the carriages along the western, shady side of the plaza (prices vary, about $10–15 per hour). Please patronize only those drivers who seem to be taking good care of their animals (the situation is improving, but the occasional bag-o-bones with open saddle sores are still around). Not only is the tour pleasant, but it will help orient you for the rest of your stay in town.

BICYCLING

If you start early before the temperature rises, a bike ride down the Peninsula de Asese can be excellent, and the birdlife present there will astound you. Start at **NicarAgua Dulce** (Marina Cocibolca, tel. 505/8802-0285, www.nicaraguadulce.com) where you can rent a beater bike. Follow the signs for Balneario El Rayo, a small harbor out at the end of the Asese peninsula with a wonderful view of Ometepe. The road goes from bumpy to appalling over the course of the ride, but you should be pedalling slowly anyway so you can spot the animals (and so you don't get heatstroke). Bring lots of water and a bathing suit so you can cool off in the lake at the end.

VOLUNTEERING IN GRANADA

Nicaragua has lots of potential and there are lots of ways to help. If you can commit more than a couple of weeks and have decent Spanish already, you can turn your vacation into something more than just travel by volunteering with one of the several Granada-based organizations that helps travelers make a difference. Yes, you'll miss out on some hammock time, but look at what you'll gain:

Building New Hope (BNH) (U.S. tel. 412/421-1625, in Granada, call Donna Tabor at tel. 505/8852-0210, www.buildingnewhope. org), based in both Granada and Pittsburgh, Pennsylvania, is a nonprofit organization offering a number of ongoing programs and volunteer opportunities. Start by purchasing a pound (or six) of Fair Trade-certified organic, shade-grown coffee from their website, then mull over these options while sipping some hot Nica joe: BNH manages two neighborhood schools that welcome volunteer teachers' assistants. They often need mentors for young adult males attempting to enter the mainstream after life on the streets. BNH assists the community library and reading-in-schools program, and operates a veterinary clinic to help control the stray animal population in Granada, which is *always* looking for visiting veterinarians, vet techs, dog walkers, and vet students. BNH is also on the lookout for music teachers for their **Rhythm in the Barrios** project, physical education instructors, and other teachers (intermediate Spanish and one month minimum commitment). BNH assists the **Hogar Madre Albertina** (from Colegio Padre Misieri, two blocks north, tel. 505/2552-7661), an underfunded home for girls where volunteers are sometimes welcome to read to the girls or play games with them. They're also looking for Microsoft geeks and English instructors, for both the girls and the sisters in charge.

Empowerment International (tel. 505/2552-1653 or 8678-3341, U.S. tel. 303/823-6495, www.empowermentinternational.org) runs a community-based educational program for impoverished and at-risk youth. Direct work with the families and community is an integral part of their methodology, as are art and photography projects. There are many ways to volunteer for EI both in Nicaragua and from afar. See their website for a list of needs and ways to help. Currently they serve Villa Esperanza and Santa Ana de Malacos, two outlying communities of Granada. Intermediate Spanish is a must. There is a strong need for computer skills, pyschology, and teaching experience.

Sisters of Madre Teresa de Calcuta in Barrio Sabonetta have a very organized school and residence for girls up to the age of 18. Most have been rescued from precarious conditions in their homes or were at-risk for drug use, prostitution, and other crimes. The school grounds are beautifully manicured and immaculate; the sisters welcome volunteers to teach music (guitar and voice), English, and art; conversational Spanish is a must.

La Harmonía (Carraterra Masaya, two blocks west of La Colonia supermarket, eeap_aman@yahoo.com) is an organization for mentally and physically challenged children and young adults. They accept volunteers with basic Spanish who can teach handicrafts, weaving, haircutting, sign language, or have experience in special education.

La Esperanza Granada (Calle Libertad #307, tel. 505/8432-5420, la_esperanza_granada@yahoo.com, www.la-esperanza-granada.org) focuses on education, especially with very young children. Volunteers work in public schools on the outskirts of Granada; they tutor and teach arts and crafts, sports, English, etc. Volunteer housing in the center of Granada is $20 per week; preferred time frame is eight weeks with intermediate Spanish. No program fees or registration fee. They have experience with groups of international volunteers for short-term projects.

SHOPPING

Granada is not really the best place to shop for Nicaraguan handicrafts since most people save that activity for Masaya. But the steady volume of tourist traffic through Granada is slowly changing the picture. There are several gift shops around the plaza, as well as frequent street vendors. The municipal market is located one block south of the plaza, but spills up Calle Atravesada as well. It's geared more for the locals than for tourists, but is lots of fun to visit.

Maverick Reading & Smoothie Lounge (tel. 505/2552-4120, mavericks_granada@yahoo.ca, open 9 A.M.–6 P.M. Tues.–Sat., 10 A.M.–noon Sun.) has crafts, gifts, books, and magazines.

Granada is *guayabera* country, and there are several places to buy the elegant Latin shirts, the best (and most expensive) being **Guayabera Nora,** right around the corner from the Bearded Monkey. At **Sultan Cigars** (tel. 505/8803-9569, eddyreyes78@yahoo.es), Eddy Reyes and family can make you a custom labeled (your name on a cigar label) case in a couple of hours; otherwise visit **Doña Elba Cigar Factory** (located one block west of the Iglesia Xalteva, tel. 505/8860-6715, open 7 A.M.–7 P.M. daily). Antique lovers will adore **Casa de Antiguedades** (tel. 505/8874-2034, haroldsandino@hotmail.com) a block north of the park on Calle Arsenal.

Entertainment and Events

A concerted effort to raise Granada's profile, the annual February **Poetry Festival** is a knock-out, drawing not only Nicaragua's most acclaimed literati and musicians (Gioconda Belli, Ernesto Cardenal, Norma Elena Gadea), but an astonishing array of poets and artists from around the world as well. The event capitalizes on the open spaces of several Granada landmarks, including cathedrals, the San Francisco convent, and Granada's best plazas. If your trip coincides with this event, book your room early.

Throughout the rest of the year, the Casa de los Leones sponsors frequent events, including concerts by local musicians and visiting international artists. One block west of the plaza, Granada's humble movie theater, **El Teatro Karawala,** offers popular (often trashy) American movies; good for rainy evenings. **Cafe Melba** ups the bar with a better selection of international films.

BARS

Granada's two most popular gringo watering holes occupy opposite corners of the same block on La Calzada: **Roadhouse Sports Bar** (open noon–midnight daily) and **Zoom Bar**

(open from noon daily). There are half a dozen other bars within a stone's throw of this corner. The beer's cold at every one.

Café Nuit (Calle La Libertad, half block east of Piedra Bocona) is one of the city's prettiest bars, attracting mostly locals and often with live music. On the next corner, **El Club** offers frequent promotional bashes, bikini-clad beer babes, and theme parties.

A loungier, more romantic scene is found at **El Tercer Ojo** (Calle El Arsenal across from Convento San Francisco, open 11 A.M.–11 P.M. Tues.–Sun.); swank tapas, wine, cocktails, and more, especially popular during happy hour (4–7 P.M.).

Charly's Bar and Restaurante (from Petronic, 5 blocks west and 25 meters south, tel. 505/2552-2942, open 11 A.M.–11 P.M. daily except Tuesday) is an old-time, schnitzel-flinging favorite on the western fringes of town, specializing in German cuisine, barbecue, and draft beer in a huge crystal cowboy boots. It's a bit far from the city center but worth the trip.

El Balcón (southeast corner of the central plaza, tel. 505/2552-6002, daily noon–10 P.M.), on the second floor of the grand, yellow-painted Gran Francia, offers the best aerial streetside

© JOSHUA BERMAN

Granada's sidewalks at night are a destination unto themselves.

balcony from which to watch the foot and horse traffic below as you sip your Centenario and enjoy the delicious bar menu. The **Enoteca Wine Bar** (in the Hotel Plaza Colón, open 10 A.M.–11 P.M. daily) has a wide selection of international wines and monthly tastings, often with rum and cigars on hand as well.

CLUBS

Managua is better for dancing but a tiny club scene exists in Granada. **El Club** (3 blocks west of the park) hosts the upscale scene, with a calendar of DJs and events. More casual and a bit rowdier, **Inuit Bar** (Fridays and Saturdays only) is inside the Centro Turístico, serving cold beer and Reggaeton music. Similar but less popular (and closer to the entrance of the Centro Turístico) is the old classic **Cesar's.** For either of the two clubs inside the Centro Turístico, take a cab there and back—this area is not safe at night.

Accommodations

Granada lodging runs from youthful backpacker hostels to refurbished colonial homes; much of the accommodation is located conveniently near Plaza Central. Interestingly, the past five years have seen huge turnover in expat-owned places that appeared at the start of the real estate boom but then disappeared without a whisper. Locally-owned places on the other hand, have mostly weathered the storm. Expect higher rates during the high season (Dec.–Apr.).

UNDER $25

Hospedaje Aventura (tel. 505/2252-2270 or 505/8871-5554, laposadasanjose@gmail.com, www.laposadasanjose.com, $5/d with fan, some have a/c) has simple but really spartan rooms with ample sunlight on the second floor of a converted, family home.

The Bearded Monkey (across from the fire station, tel. 505/2552-4028, www.the-beardedmonkey.com, $6 dorm, $14 for a private room) is without a doubt, the backpacker set's favorite, with dorm-style rooms and a laid-back, communal atmosphere. Expect cool music, an eclectic crowd, movie nights, and free Internet access. A few other places in town have successfully copied the monkey vibe. **Hospedaje Samarcanda** (Calle la Libertad, five blocks west of the central plaza, tel. 505/2552-8069, www.hospedajesamarcanda.com, $6 dorm, $16–39 rooms) is farther away, but clean and decent, with breakfast.

Hospedaje El Chelero (two blocks west of the park, tel. 505/8379-2657 or 505/8955-2602, elchelerohostal@hotmail.com, $5 dorm beds, from $8–15 private rooms with a/c) is locally owned and basic, in an unrenovated colonial home sporting brand new beds. They rent bikes, too.

Hostel Oasis (one block north, one block east of the market, tel. 505/2552-8005, www.nicaraguahostel.com, $6 dorm bed, $19–28 rooms) is one of the quietest in this range, with the bonus of a swimming pool, which matters. Travelers have reported surly staff and bedbugs here, so have a close look at the mattress before sealing the deal. **Hospedaje La Calzada** (tel. 505/8475-9229, mariinez_1970@yahoo.com, $12.50 with private bath, $10 shared bath) has been around for over a decade at least; what it lacks in decor it makes up in location.

Hospedaje Cocibolca (Calle la Calzada, three blocks east of park, tel. 505/2552-7223, hospedaje_cocibolca@yahoo.com, www.hospedajecocibolca.com, $18) has wireless Internet, friendly and professional service, and over ten years of experience. **Hostal Dorado** (1.5 blocks west of the park on Calle Xalteva, tel. 505/2252-6932, info@hostaldorado.com, www.hostaldorado.com, $25) comes well recommended, but not all the rooms have private bathrooms. A supermarket is across the street, which is convenient.

Hospedaje Ruiz (Calle la Calzada, tel. 505/2552-2346, $20 with private bath) has been around longer than some of the competition; rooms are simple but well ventilated and quite clean. Similar but less experienced is **Posada las Brisas** (Calle la Calzada, tel. 505/2552-3984 or 8885-3989, tcristac@hotmail.es,

$20–25 with fans) is family-run, safe, and clean. Features include wireless Internet, refrigerator, and kitchen access but no air-conditioning. **Hospedaje La Libertad** (three blocks west of park on Calle la Libertad, tel. 505/2552-4017, hospedaje_lalibertad@hotmail.com, $8 dorm beds, $15/s with shared bath) offers dorm beds, but the dormitories are broad and well ventilated, and the bright colors are nice.

$25-50

Estancia Mar Dulce (Calle la Calzada, 3.5 blocks east of park, tel. 505/2552-3732, granadamardulce@hotmail.com, www.hotelmardulcenicaragua.com, $30 with fan, $40 with a/c, cable TV, breakfast) is locally owned, clean, and professional, and has large, pleasant rooms and a spacious interior courtyard with a landscaped swimming pool.

Casa Silas Bed and Breakfast (206 Calle La Concepción, 1.5 blocks west of El Mercado, tel. 505/8358-5852, casasilas@gmail.com, www.casasilas.com, $45) is an unassuming but comfortable option near the market, with a couple of nicely equipped queen-size bed rooms, small pool, Wi-Fi, air-conditioning, skylights, and great coffee. Very knowledgeable hosts can help you make the best of your time in Granada.

Hotel Kekoldi (3.5 blocks west of the park on Calle El Consulado, tel. 506/2248-0804, U.S. tel. 786/221-9011, reservations@kekoldi.com, www.kekoldi.com, $39) is spacious and colorful with well-planned architecture and plenty of open areas.

Hotel La Pérgola (three blocks east of the park on Calle El Caimito, tel. 505/2552-4221, lapergolanic@yahoo.com, www.lapergola.com.ni, $44) has 11 rooms with private bath, TV, air-conditioning, and access to a gorgeous open balcony (for which the hotel is named), plus tour service, Wi-Fi, and parking.

El Club (three blocks west of the northwest corner of the park, tel. 505/2552-4245, www.elclub-nicaragua.com, $45–65 high season, $20–50 low season) has a modern look with cozy, small windowless rooms and the city's longest bar. **Hotel Casa San Martín** (Calle

GRANADA

La Calzada, one block east of the plaza, tel. 505/2552-6185, reservaciones@hcasasanmartin.com, www.hcasasanmartin.com, $45–60) has eight rooms, all with gorgeous hardwood floors.

$50-100

Granada's midrange and upscale hotels offer remarkable value, each striving to offer an authentic but unique colonial experience with all the amenities. In this price range and above expect hot water, air-conditioning, private bathrooms, cable TV, artsy decor, and the ubiquitous open-air central patio with small swimming pool.

Casa San Francisco (kitty-corner to the Convento San Francisco, tel. 505/2552-8235, csfgranada@yahoo.com, www.casasanfrancisco.com, $45–55) is a charming colonial cluster of 13 decorated rooms with breakfast included. Run by a couple of dynamic and well-traveled ex–Peace Corps volunteer sisters, Casa San Francisco features a small pool and is located in a quiet and central neighborhood. You'll also find a great on-site restaurant and bar.

A few blocks up Calle Corrales from Casa San Francisco, look for **Bohemian Paradise** (tel. 505/2552-0286, www.seecentralamerica.com, $60), a small, high-quality retreat in a surprisingly quiet neighborhood, whose handful of über-comfortable rooms around a small garden are excellent (guests rave about the quality of the mattresses and sheets). Most basic services are available (including parking and laundry) except a bar and restaurant, since the owners encourage guests to explore the city; great for small groups, gay friendly.

Hotel Patio del Malinche (Calle El Caimito, 2.5 blocks east of the central plaza, tel. 505/2552-2235, www.patiodelmalinche.com, $75) is Catalan-owned and very comfortable. Fifteen rooms surround a huge patio, bar, and pool.

Better for families in this price range is **Hotel Casa Capricho** (Calle El Arsenal, a block east of Convento San Francisco, tel. 505/2552-8422, www.casacapricho.com, $55), with 11 rooms, a kitchen, a dining room, and common areas; it's colorful and pleasant.

Hotel con Corazón (Calle Santa Lucia 141, tel. 505/2552-8852, www.hotelconcorazon.com, $60–67) has Scandinavian styling and a noble mission: In addition to a hotel this is a foundation that invests heavily in the community, particularly in education. They have a cute little pool, 16 comfortable rooms with air-conditioning, ceiling fans, and TV, plus an on-site restaurant, making it hard not to recommend.

Finally in this class are two legitimate hotels, not restored colonial houses: **Hotel Alhambra** (northwest corner of the central plaza, tel. 505/2552-4486, www.hotelalhambra.com.ni, $60–90) was Granada's first luxury hotel and has the best spot in town, right on the park. Built around a gorgeous, landscaped patio, its 56 newly remodeled rooms (some with pleasing balcony views) have air-conditioning, TV, private bath, hot water, kitchenette, exposed wood beams, and tasteful decorations. The whole place has a classy, mahogany ambience.

Hotel Colonial (20 meters west of the park's northwest corner, tel. 505/2552-7299, www.nicaragua-vacations.com, $60–75) is newer, with 37 clean, well-appointed rooms surrounding an outdoor patio, pool, and bar.

OVER $100

Casa La Merced (Calle Real Xalteva, tel. 505/2552-2744, www.casalamerced.com, $90–125) is a stately bed-and-breakfast with eight ample, street-level rooms around an open patio garden. It's right across the street from the church of the same name. Its stately blue facade gracing Calle La Calzada, **Hotel Dario** (tel. 505/2552-3400, www.hoteldario.com, $100) has open walkways, gardens, and 22 rooms which make artful use of the available space; request one of the rooms with small balconies facing Mombacho.

One of Granada's first buildings (and one of

GRANADA

© RANDALL WOOD

Hotel Colonial

few that withstood the fire that consumed the rest of the city in the days of William Walker) has been painstakingly restored as ◖ **La Gran Francia Hotel y Restaurante** (southeast corner of the park, tel. 505/2552-6000, www. lagranfrancia.com, $110–150 includes tax and breakfast). A careful blend of neoclassical and colonial elements in hardwoods, wrought iron, and porcelain characterize La Gran Francia's every detail—down to the hand-painted sinks. Twenty-one rooms, some with balconies, are set around a courtyard and pool. The Duke's Suite, named after an 18th-century mystery man, is one of the few accommodations in Granada with a whirlpool tub.

Another class act is ◖ **Hotel Plaza Colón** (tel. 505/552-8489, www.hotelplazacolon.com, $100–130), whose 26 large, elegant rooms feature air-conditioning, hot water, cable TV, and ceiling fan; six rooms have vast wooden porches looking straight across the central plaza to the main cathedral, a beautiful—but sometimes noisy—vista. The other rooms face a quiet street or the sculpted inner courtyards and pool. A restaurant, bar, and wine cellar are on the premises, and parking is available.

Food

The Granada dining scene is in constant rotation, with old favorites disappearing, new contenders, and creative experimentation. We've pointed out some of our favorite picks here, but you won't go hungry if you simply stroll lakeward down Calle La Calzada, where the city's dining scene is at its most intense.

BREAKFAST

Garden Cafe (Calle la Libertad, one block east of central plaza, tel. 505/2552-8582, open 7 A.M.–3 P.M. Mon.–Sat., under $5) is great for breakfasts, or try the orange-infused French toast at **Hotel Casa San Francisco** (kitty-corner to the Convento San Francisco, from 7 A.M. daily); ask for a table on the sidewalk. **Kathy's Waffle House** (across from Convento San Francisco, open 7 A.M.–2 P.M. daily, $4) is a favorite for breakfast with its American-style pancakes, biscuits and gravy, eggs and bacon, omelets, and a lot more—Kathy, a young Granada native, passed away in 2010; we hope this town favorite remains open. Another greasy spoon–style breakfast joint is **Nica Buffet,** just south of the park, where you'll find both gringo breakfasts and heaping plates of *platano maduro* and *gallo pinto* (turn off your cell phone and behave if you don't want to end up on the owner's black list). Finally, in a pinch, you can always fall back on the infamous monster breakfast burritos at the **Bearded Monkey** hostel (across from the fire station).

CAFÉS

Euro Cafe (northwest corner of central plaza, open 7:30 A.M.–9 P.M. daily) serves homemade gelato, pastries, panini, fresh hummus, fruit juices, and strong coffee drinks; there's free Wi-Fi. And a block south of the park, **Jardin d'Orion** (open afternoons and evenings) serves quality salads, seafood specialities, and fruit juice blends.

❰ **Garden Cafe** (Calle la Libertad, one block east of central plaza, tel. 505/2552-8582, thegardencafe.granada@gmail.com,

open 7 A.M.–3 P.M. Mon.–Sat., under $4) is a wonderful respite from the heat, with a cool space to enjoy gourmet sandwiches, salads, smoothies, and coffee drinks; the artsy patio is a great place to crank the Wi-Fi.

Café Don Simon on the west side of the park serves up burgers, sandwiches, roast chicken, and more; but you can sample expertly prepared Nicaraguan classics at **Comida Típica,** just behind the cathedral.

PIZZA AND ITALIAN

Locals and backpackers rave about the prices at **Telepizza** (Calle El Arsenal, 1.5 blocks east of Bancentro, tel. 505/2552-4219, open 10 A.M.–10 P.M. daily), with large pies from $6 and delivery available; the gigantic $3 stuffed calzones may be one of the best deals in town. You'll find more authentic pizza at **Monna Lisa** (Calle La Calzada, tel. 505/2552-8187). Get real, thin-crust Italian pizza baked in a wood-fired oven at **Don Luca's** (Calle La Calzada, tel. 505/2552-7822).

UPSCALE

Find lamb chops with fresh mint, flaming breast of duck, and top-notch filet mignon, among other inspired dinners at **❰ Imagine Café** (tel. 505/2552-4672 or 505/8842-2587, www.imaginerestaurantandbar.com) which also has a decent bit of live music some evenings. All meals are carefully handcrafted from local, and usually organic, ingredients.

❰ El Tercer Ojo (Calle El Arsenal across from Convento San Francisco, tel. 505/2552-6451, open 11 A.M.–11 P.M. Tues.–Sun.) offers everything from Spanish tapas and sushi to gorgonzola pasta, kebabs, and fine wine in a gauzy lounge of candles and soothing music.

Nectars (a block east of the park, open 10:30 A.M.–11 P.M. daily has found the right spot between casual and classy, with a stylish appetizer menu featuring goat cheese and babaganoush, salads, and crepes, plus a long fruit juice menu.

Doña Conchi (Calle Caimito, two blocks east of the cathedral, tel. 505/2552-7376, closed Tues.) has one of the more intimate atmospheres in Granada, and serves fresh dinner salads, seafood, and pitchers of sangria in a lush garden setting. One door west, **El Mediterraneo** (tel. 505/2552-6764, closed Mon.) is another elegant Spanish restaurant set in an airy garden patio adorned with colorful artwork; readers love this place.

El Arcángel Restaurant at La Gran Francia (tel. 505/2552-6000, open at 7 A.M.

for breakfast, then noon–10 P.M. daily) features an exquisite fusion of Latin American ingredients with international cuisine; fancy entrées like whiskey-glazed steak, pastas, and banana and brown-sugar coated snapper fillet run $12–20.

For lip-smacking, upscale Nicaraguan dishes and steaks, don't miss ◖ **El Zaquan** (open noon–3 P.M. and 6 P.M.–closing daily), located behind the main cathedral—your nose should lead you to the meat-draped open-flame grill and dishes like *churrasco jalapeño* (around $9).

Services

Emergency

The **police** presence is pretty serious in Granada. You'll note an officer stationed full time in the park, and a lot of others patrolling to keep tourists safe. In case you are a victim of crime you can now file a report by email to webdenunciagr@policia.gob.ni, or visit the police station on the highway to Nandaime (tel. 505/2552-4712) and 75 meters west of the cinema (tel. 505/2552-2977 or 505/2552-2929). The biggest **hospital,** Bernardino Díaz Ochoa, is a few kilometers out of town, on the road toward Managua. On the same highway, a bit closer to town is the Hospital Privado Cocibolca (tel. 505/2552-2907 or 505/2552-4092). For minor treatments, the section of Calle Atravesada just south of the bridge is occupied by more than a dozen clinics, blood labs, and pharmacies.

Groceries

The two major supermarkets are the Palí (on Calle Atravesada just south of the market) and La Colonial, both open till 8 P.M. or so. As many of the lower priced *hospedajes* offer you the kitchen and fridge, you can stretch your travel dollars immensely by using these markets.

Internet

Internet cafés throughout the city usually offer

service for $1–1.25/hour and Internet phone service for around $0.10/minute. Start at **Alhambra Internet** (across the street from Hotel Colonial, open 8 A.M.–10 P.M. daily); they offer a variety of services and the shop is always air-conditioned. Also pleasant is the **Cafémail** (in the Casa de los Leones, open 7 A.M.–10 P.M. daily, $1/hr), offering a coffee-bar experience with both a row of PCs and Wi-Fi. In fact, most restaurants and hotels have free Wi-Fi in Granada, so you'll have no problem with your laptop.

Banks

Banco de America Central is on the southwest corner of the plaza, and Banpro and Bancentro are on Calle Atravesada, just a few blocks away. The sanctioned money changers are out in full force along this same section of Atravesada (they're on the street, waving wads of cash), and you'll find ATMs in most banks and at the Esso gas station on the edge of town.

Laundry

Mapache Laundry Service (Calle La Calzada, tel. 505/5611-3501, open 7 A.M.–5 P.M. Mon.–Sat.) will wash your duds in modern machines, delivery and pickup service for about $10 per load. Another laundry service with no name (from the middle of the central park, 1.5 blocks west, tel. 505/2552-6532) also offers pickup and delivery service for about $5/load.

GRANADA

COMMUNITY TOURISM NEAR GRANADA

For those seeking a full-immersion cultural experience, the most obvious option is to sign up for a homestay with one of the many Spanish schools in Granada. This is a good option if you want to stay with a Nicaraguan family and still have access to Granada's many restaurants, Internet cafés, and other distractions. If you'd really like to get out there, then consider arranging a few days (or weeks) with the **Unión de Cooperativas Agropecuarias Tierra y Agua,** also known as the **Earth and Water UCA** (tel. 505/8896-9361 or 505/2552-0238, turismo@ucatierrayagua.org, www.ucatierrayagua.org). The office in Granada is located 75 yards to the west of the Shell Palmira and is open Monday, Wednesday, and Friday 8:30 A.M.–2 P.M. The UCA is an association of rural farmers

on the slopes of Volcán Mombacho and Isla de Zapatera National Park who will be glad to be your hosts. You'll stay in primitive Nicaraguan lodging and eat typical food while getting to know your new neighborhood. Expect to pay about $5 per person per night for lodging in La Granadilla or Zonzapote, and about $3 per meal. Local guides will take you horseback riding, hiking, fishing, and more; cheap transport to and from Granada can be arranged.

Income generated by your visit goes directly to a cooperative collective fund to pay for meals, guides, maintenance, etc., and to distribute to families involved. The UCA also maintains a general fund for tourism, used for training and to make small loans for new tourist-related projects.

Getting There and Around

GETTING THERE AND AWAY

In addition to the options below, most tour operators listed in this chapter offer exclusive shuttles to San Juan del Sur, León, the dock for Ometepe, and the airport.

By Bus to Other Points in Nicaragua

There are four places to catch a bus out of town. The easiest and most popular way to get to Managua (or Masaya, which is on the way) is to grab a **COGRAN** *expreso* (1.5 blocks south of the central plaza's southwest corner, tel. 505/2552-2954); these medium-sized buses leave every 15–20 minutes 4:30 A.M.–7 or 8 P.M. Monday–Friday (they stop service a few hours earlier on Sunday). Another fleet of minivans leaves from the Parque Sandino on the north side of Granada near the old railroad station, with regular departures 5 A.M.–7:30 P.M. Both services travel to La UCA in Managua. From

there, the same vehicles leave for Granada every 15 minutes, 5:50 A.M.–8 P.M.

Regular bus service to Rivas, Nandaime, and Jinotepe works out of the **Shell Palmira,** on Granada's south side, just past the Palí supermarket. The first bus to Rivas leaves at 5:45 A.M. and takes 1.5 hours; service continues sporadically until the last one at 3:10 P.M. Nandaime buses leave every 20 minutes. Jinotepe *expresos* take a mere 45 minutes compared to the nearly two-hour *ordinario* trip through the pueblos. Around the corner, behind the Palí, is the bus terminal with service to Masaya (although any Managua-bound *expreso* will let you off in Masaya as well).

By Bus to Costa Rica and Panamá

Avenida Arrellano, on the west end of Granada, is part of the San José– and Panama City–bound routes for Central American bus lines.

The three offices are all located on the east side of the street, and reservations should be made at least two days in advance. The **TicaBus** terminal (tel. 505/2552-4301) is half a block south of the Old Hospital; be there at 6:15 A.M. for the 7 A.M. bus. **TransNica** (tel. 505/2552-6619) is three long blocks south of the Old Hospital, on the corner of Calle Xalteva; three daily south-bounders leave at 6:30 A.M., 8 A.M., and 11 A.M.; be there a half-hour before departure.

By Boat to Ometepe and San Carlos

Granada's crusty old ferry departs Granada's municipal dock (tel. 505/552-2966) Monday and Thursday at 2 P.M., arriving in San Carlos around 6 A.M. When weather permits, the boat stops at Altagracia before cutting across to the eastern lakeshore and port calls in Morrito and San Miguelito. The adventure costs $4 for air-conditioning and padded benches upstairs or $10 for no air-conditioning and hard wooden benches downstairs. The VIP suite/sleeper cabin is $110, and returns from San Carlos at 2 P.M. on Tuesdays and Fridays. The boat can get crowded and uncomfortable, especially around Semana Santa when the lake turns *bravo* (rough) and the weather is hot. Get to the port early and be aggressive to stake your territory. During the rest of the year, the ride is usually languid and uneventful, and you may even be able to get some sleep on the deck.

A new option, the **Barco Turistico** leaves Granada Fridays at 7 P.M., stopping only in Altagracia (on La Isla de Ometepe), then arriving in San Carlos the following morning at 6 A.M. It departs San Carlos Sunday evening at 6 P.M.; cost is $20 for first class (includes coffee and drink service), $13 for economy. For more info, contact Empersario Portuario (tel. 505/2583-0256).

GETTING AROUND

Most of what you'll want to visit or see lies in the kilometer between the lake and the plaza, and it's all walkable. That's really the best way to enjoy the city, but you'll be better off if you do your walking in the early morning when the sunlight is golden and the air temperature is still pleasant. Taxis are numerous and cheap if the heat really has you down. Better yet, hire a horse-drawn carriage from the west side of the plaza for an open-air local's view of town.

Car Rental

The **Budget** office is located in the Shell Guapinol gas station on the road to Managua (tel. 505/2552-2323, reserve@budget.com.ni, open 8 A.M.–6:30 P.M. daily). Cars rent from about $30–110 a day, and they rent cell phones. There is huge demand for their 28-vehicle fleet, so reservations are necessary, especially in the high season. Hotels also often maintain a list of trusted cars and drivers and many tour operators have extra vehicles. For car rentals, drivers, transfers, and 4WD, call Peter van der Meijs at **Armadillo Nicaragua** (tel. 505/8833-8663, info@armadillo-nicaragua.com, http://armadillo-nicaragua.com); from the Shell Guapinol gas station, their office is four blocks north and 1.5 blocks west.

GRANADA

Near Granada

◖ LAS ISLETAS

This 365-island archipelago formed when Volcán Mombacho erupted some 20,000 years ago, hurling its top half into the nearby lake in giant masses of rock, ash, and lava. Today, the islands are inhabited by a few hundred *campesinos* and an ever-increasing number of wealthy Nicaraguans and foreigners who continue to buy up the *isletas* and build garish vacation homes on them. The natural beauty of the *isletas* is spectacular, and history buffs will enjoy the **Fortín de San Pablo,** a Spanish fort that was largely unsuccessful in preventing pirate attacks on Granada. The islanders themselves are interesting and friendly, maintaining a rural lifestyle unique in Nicaragua: Children paddle dugout canoes or rowboats to school from an early age, and their parents get along by fishing and farming—or by taking camera-toting tourists for a ride in their boats.

To visit Las Isletas, begin at either Cabañas Amarillo or Puerto Asese, both a seven-minute drive south of Granada at the end of the waterfront road (about $1 via taxi). Puerto Asese is more popular, while Cabañas Amarillo (fork left at the Asese sign) provides more shade and wider views—as well as kayak tours. At both docks, you'll find a restaurant, snack bars, and a plethora of boats vying for your business. Choose a *lanchero* (boatman) and don't expect to haggle over prices, as gasoline is expensive. You'll pay about $10 a person for a half-hour tour, more for longer or farther trips. Beef up your visit by asking to visit an island where a family can serve you lunch—or pull up and "refuel" at one of the mellow island bars before continuing your tour. You can also take a dip in the lake water or have your *lanchero* bring you to the cemetery, old fort, or monkey island.

There are 365 *isletas* off the coast near Granada.

By Kayak

Touring the islands in a *lancha* is not recommended for those seeking a quiet wilderness experience—the loud motors spew smoke and scare the birds away and keep you far up out of the water. Much more enjoyable is the sound of birdsong over your kayak as you cut silently through the glassy water. **NicarAgua Dulce** (Marina Cocibolca, tel. 505/8802-0285 or 505/2552-6351, www.nicaraguadulce.com) rents rowboats, kayaks, and silent electric boats—all three can carry up to five persons—by the half or full day.

Find tours in the Mombotour office in Granada. The introductory class, which includes all equipment, sea kayaks, transportation, and tour of the Fortín San Pablo, costs $34 a person and lasts three hours. Special bird-watching kayak excursions run $20–30; Nica guides are available and for the full petroleum-free experience, try the bike-kayak combo tour.

Accommodations

The exclusive **Jicaro Lodge** (tel. 505/2552-6353, info@jicarolodge.com, www.jicarolodge.com, $380 for a three-day package for two people) is a spa, yoga and wellness retreat that opened in 2010. They've built nine cabins, will pick you up at the airport, and feed you a classy, custom menu prepared on-site. Watch your step on the steep, unrailed stairs at night; travelers report the islet is tinier than you think, but appreciate the courteous staff.

◖ PARQUE NACIONAL ARCHIPIÉLAGO ZAPATERA

About 34 kilometers south of Granada, Zapatera is an extinct volcano surrounded by Isla el Muerto and a dozen or so other islets, all of which comprise 45 square kilometers of land; the whole complex is home for some 500 residents. Zapatera is a natural wonder, rising 629 meters above sea level. Its virgin forest is rife with myriad wildlife such as parrots, toucans, herons, and other waterfowl, plus white-tailed deer, and an alleged population of jaguars no one ever seems to see.

© RANDALL WOOD

GRANADA

petroglyph on Zapatera

These islands were enormously important to the Nahuatl, who used them primarily as a vast burial ground and sacrifice spot. The sites of La Punta de las Figuras and Zonzapote are particularly rich in artifacts and have a network of caves that have never been researched. Also seek out the petroglyphs carved into the bedrock beaches of Isla el Muerto. An impressive selection of Zapatera's formidable stone idols is on display in the Convento San Francisco, but the islands' remaining archaeological treasures remain relatively unstudied and unprotected and (naturally) continue to disappear.

Officially declared a national park by the Sandinistas in 1983, the Zapatera Archipelago has never been adequately protected or funded. MARENA's thousand-page management plan document is just that—a document—while in reality, only one park ranger visits the islands a couple of times per month. It's no surprise then that inhabitants and visitors litter, loot the archaeological patrimony, hunt, and cut down trees for timber.

Visiting Zapatera

Access the islands from Granada's Puerto Asese, where you can strike a deal with returning Zapatera islanders or hire a tourist boat. The most reliable way is to arrange a trip with **Zapatera Tours** (tel. 505/8842-2587, www. zapateratours.com), a small company that specializes in creative lake tours, including overnight camping trips, fishing, waterskiing, you name it. You can also inquire about Zapatera trips with any of the other Granada tour companies above. With a fast, powerful motor, it's a 20-minute trip from Granada, partly over a stretch of open water that can get choppy.

There are a scattering of places to stay around the island, including a cheap dormitory and homestay options in Zonzapote. Or book a room at **Casa Hacienda Hotel Santa María** (tel. 505/8884-0606, zapateratour@gmail. com), where the Cordova family's 120-year-old tile-roofed ranch house has been outfitted with comfortably primitive double rooms with mosquito net, fan, and private bathrooms. The cost is $50 per person to use the place for the day, or $120 a night for two people plus meals, transport, and fishing trips. The hotel is on a relaxing sandy beach, looking north toward Isla el Muerto and Mombacho.

◖ VOLCÁN MOMBACHO

Mombacho is unavoidable; it towers over the southern horizon, lurks around every corner, creeps into your panoramic photos. In Granada, you are living in the shadow of a giant. Fortunately, this giant is gentle. Every bit of cool, misty, cloud forest higher than 850 meters above sea level is officially protected as a nature reserve. This equals about 700 hectares of park, rising to a peak elevation of 1,345 meters, and comprising a rich, concentrated island of flora and fauna. Thanks to the Fundación Cocibolca, the reserve is accessible and makes available the best-designed and maintained hiking trails in the nation.

Overgrown with hundreds of orchid and bromeliad species, tree ferns, and old-growth cloud and dwarf forests, Mombacho also boasts three species of monkeys, 168 observed birds (49 of which are migratory), 30 species of reptiles, 60 mammals (including at least one very secretive big cat), and 10 amphibians. The flanks of the volcano, 21 percent of which remains forested, are composed of privately owned coffee plantations and cattle ranches. Maintaining the forest canopy is a crucial objective of Fundación Cocibolca, since this is where more than 90 percent of Mombacho's 1,000 howler monkeys reside (the monkeys travel in 100 different troops, and venture into the actual reserve only to forage).

Although the majority of Mombacho's visitors arrive as part of a tour package, it is entirely possible to visit the reserve on your own, and it makes a perfect day trip from Managua, Granada, or Masaya. You'll start by taking a bus (or express minivan) headed for Nandaime or Rivas (or, from Granada, to Carazo as well); tell the driver to let you off at the Empalme el Guanacaste. This is a large intersection, and the road up to the parking lot and official reserve entrance is located 1.5 kilometers toward the mountain—look for the signs. The walk to the parking lot is a solid half-hour trek, mostly uphill and in the sun. Water and snacks are available at the parking lot—be sure to drink lots before and during this first leg of your journey. Once you arrive at the parking lot, you'll pay the entrance fee and then board one of the foundation's vehicles to make the half-hour, six-kilometer climb up to the Biological Station. The lumbering troop transports depart at 8:30 A.M., 10 A.M., 1 P.M., and 3 P.M. Thursday–Sunday, and return shortly after each climb up the hill (last bus down is 6 P.M.). In your own four-wheel drive vehicle, you'll be asked to pay $13 in addition to your entrance fee. The park is closed Monday and open on Tuesday by reservation only.

Trails

There is a short (half-hour) trail through the coffee farm at the bottom of the volcano, where you wait for your ride up. Once on top, there are two main trails to choose from: **Sendero el Cráter,** which encircles the forest-lined crater, and features a moss-lined tunnel, several

the view from Volcán Mombacho

lookouts, and a spur trail to the **fumaroles** (holes in the ground venting hot sulfurous air). The fumaroles area is an open, grassy part of the volcano with blazing wildflowers and an incredible view of Granada and the *isletas*. The whole loop, including the spur, is 1.5 kilometers, with a few ups and downs, and takes a casual hour to walk. The **Sendero la Puma** is considerably more challenging—a four-kilometer loop with several difficult climbs that lead to breathtaking viewpoints. It begins at a turnoff from the fumaroles trail, and you should allow a minimum of three hours to complete it (and lots of water). Well-trained, knowledgeable local guides (some with English) are available for $5 (per group, plus tip) for the Sendero el Cráter and $10 for the Sendero la Puma. Note, because of the altitude and the clouds, the visibility from these trails may be much diminished on bad-weather days.

The reserve is closed on Mondays for maintenance, and usually restricts Tuesdays and Wednesdays to organized groups. From Thursday to Sunday, all are welcome. The entrance fee ($7.50 for foreigners, $5 for Nicas and residents, $4 for students and children)

includes admission to the reserve, transport to and from the top of the volcano, and insurance. If you've got the time and the strong legs, feel free to hike all the way up the steep road yourself. Allow a couple of hours (and lots of water) to reach the top.

Volcán Mombacho Biological Center

Located at the base of one of Mombacho's 14 communications antennas, on a small plateau called Plan de las Flores at 1,150 meters, the research station is also an interpretive center, *hospedaje, cafetín,* ranger station, and conference center, technically completed in 2000 but still expanding. Find drinks and snacks here, including a simple meal for $3.50. As of press time, there are 10 dormitory beds in a loft above the interpretive center. It costs $25 to rent out the whole *albergue* (hostel), which sleeps up to 10 people. The package deal includes dinner, a guided night hike (on which you can search for the famous red-eyed frog and Mombacho salamander), and breakfast; or pitch a tent for $15 and buy meals on the side. To make a reservation, contact the Biological

Station (tel. 505/2248-8234/35 or 505/2552-5858); or contact Fundación Cocibolca in Managua (tel. 505/2278-3224 or 505/2277-1681, www.mombacho.org). Most tour companies will get you there; start with Mombotours or Tierra Tours.

Canopy Tours

Put yourself on belay at the **Mombacho Canopy Tour** (tel. 505/8888-2566 or 505/8852-9483, gloriamaria@cablenet.com.ni, $30 pp), located up the road from the parking lot, just before the road passes through the El Progreso coffee mill. Their 1,500-meter course involves 15 platforms and a 25-meter-long hanging bridge. Many tour operators offer a full-day Mombacho package that involves a visit to the reserve followed by a canopy tour on the way down, or you can arrange it yourself by calling Fundación Cocibolca.

On the opposite (east) face of Volcán Mombacho, cloud-forest coffee farm meets canopy tour at the Cutirre Farm. **Mombotour** (next to BDF, tel. 505/2552-4548, www.mombotour.com) offers a range of half-day trips, involving some combination of canopy tour,

horseback ride, bird-watching hike, and coffee-farm tour. Trips include transportation to and from Granada and lunch, about $55 per adult (add a kayak tour to make a full day out of it).

The 15-kilometer ride to the Cutirre Farm takes longer than you'd expect. The road turns into a river during the wet season, but the trip is worth it; once you arrive, the views from the lodge are spectacular, looking straight out at Isla de Zapatera, and behind it, the cone of Volcán Concepción. There is also a small but attractive insect museum, with a full butterfly farm in the works. Bird-watchers can take a walk through the plantation with guides experienced in spotting any of the 43 species observed here.

The canopy tour, suspended from 14 of the giant shade trees on the coffee farm, is a professional, safe system of 17 platforms, a hanging bridge, and 13 horizontal zip lines, ending with a 23-meter rappel from a massive ceiba tree. Show up at Mombotour's Granada office to arrange your trip, leaving at either 10 A.M. or 2 P.M. (arrive one hour prior), returning you to Granada about three hours later.

MASAYA AND THE PUEBLOS BLANCOS

Masaya is a city of artisans, metalworkers, leatherworkers, carpenters, painters, and musicians. In fact, no other region of Nicaragua is as blessed with a sense of artistry and creativity as Masaya and the surrounding villages, called the Pueblos Blancos. Many of the handicrafts found in markets throughout the country are Masayan: handwoven hammocks, terra cotta pottery, musical instruments, and more. "The City of Flowers," as Rubén Darío christened the town a century ago (he was talking about the girls, not the flora), rarely garners more than a brief afternoon market visit for most travelers. It is a city relatively devoid of monuments, historical buildings, and traditional sights. As a marketplace however, it is unsurpassed, and wandering through the cool alleys of the crafts markets is a cultural

tour through Nicaragua, a vivid expression of this people's vitality, passion, and creativity. If you are eager to come home from your trip with something special, this is the place to find it.

Adjacent, and an inextricable part not only of the landscape but of the culture is Volcán Masaya. One of the world's most accessible volcanoes, one of only two on earth where you can drive up to the crater lip and look inside, and Nicaragua's most thoughtfully planned national park, Volcán Masaya is extremely active. You'll smell the sulphur when the wind is right. As such it's a rewarding and memorable experience well worth your time, and possibly one of the top three things to do in Nicaragua.

To the south and west of Masaya the charming Pueblos Blancos are artisan villages whose

MASAYA

HIGHLIGHTS

◖ **El Mercado Viejo Craft Market:** The best handmade pottery, leatherwork, paintings, and more are all handsomely displayed in a professionally run market designed to showcase Nicaragua's finest (page 86).

◖ **El Malecón:** Take a stroll along the crater's lip, which marks Masaya's western edge, and enjoy the view of the lagoon below (page 87).

◖ **Volcán Masaya National Park:** Peer into the gates of hell, wherein dwell demon parakeets – then visit the museum of this popular national park (page 92).

◖ **Laguna de Apoyo:** Get away from it all in what might be the coolest swimming hole in the country, an enticing volcanic crater lake, ringed with forest (page 94).

◖ **Catarina Mirador:** This crater's lip patio terrace, with one of the best panoramas in Nicaragua, often offers live marimba music to accompany your beverage (page 98).

LOOK FOR ◖ TO FIND RECOMMENDED SIGHTS, ACTIVITIES, DINING, AND LODGING.

craftspeople produce what you find in the markets. It's easy to spend a day visiting their workshops or just enjoying the casual, friendly atmosphere of each town. In particular, the village of Catarina, perched on the crater lip above Laguna de Apoyo enjoys one of the most spectacular vistas in all of Nicaragua. The Pueblos run into Carazo, another group of small towns, closer to the Pacific, with a pleasant climate and somewhat middle-class feel in a country of economic extremes. Its cooler temperatures favor coffee production, often under the shade of beautiful hardwood trees. The towns of Diriamba and Jinotepe make delightful lunch stopovers on your way through from Managua to Masaya, but both have nice places to stay and Jinotepe's open-air market is more manageable than most.

A regional turquoise jewel, the Laguna de Apoyo is probably the most pleasant freshwater swimming hole in the country, imbued with both a sense of tranquility and isolation that make more than just the cool lake water refreshing. It's an easy day trip from Granada, but many choose to stay the night as well, and a growing number of hotels and restaurants make that possible. Unless you are truly water-averse, this delightful place should not be missed.

PLANNING YOUR TIME

Most people visit the craft markets, city, and volcano in one day, but if you are relying on public transportation, it may take longer. Naturalists more interested in the volcano can just as easily spend a long day on hiking trails, in the visitors center, and on guided tours. It's

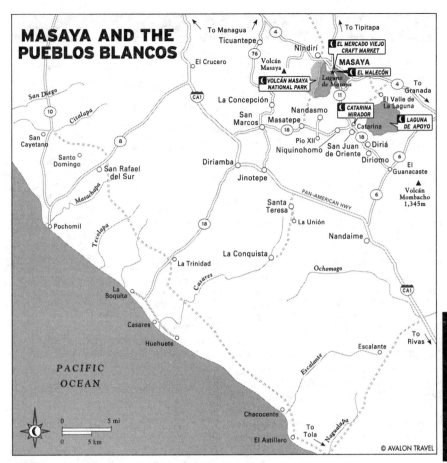

MASAYA AND THE PUEBLOS BLANCOS

To Managua
Ticuantepe
To Tipitapa
El Mercado Viejo Craft Market
Nindirí
MASAYA
El Crucero
Volcán Masaya
El Malecón
San Diego
Citalapa
Volcán Masaya National Park
Laguna de Masaya
To Granada
La Concepción
El Valle de La Laguna
Catarina Mirador
San Marcos
Nandasmo
Masatepe
Catarina
Laguna de Apoyo
San Cayetano
Santo Domingo
San Rafael del Sur
Pío XII
Niquinohomo
San Juan de Oriente
Diriá
Diriomo
El Guanacaste
Diriamba
Masachapa
Jinotepe
Pan-American Hwy
Volcán Mombacho 1,345m
Pochomil
Tecolapa
Santa Teresa
La Unión
Nandaime
La Conquista
Ochomogo
La Trinidad
Casares
To Rivas
La Boquita
Casares
Huehuete
Escalante
PACIFIC OCEAN
Escalante
Chacocente
To Tola
Nagualapa
El Astillero
© AVALON TRAVEL

0   5 mi
0   5 km

MASAYA

possible to make Masaya your base for excursions, but most travelers opt instead to stay in Granada, which has a better selection of hotels and restaurants. On any trip to the Masaya craft market, be sure to allow for time to walk to the cliff-top lookout near the baseball stadium *(el malecón),* where you'll also find the hammock factories. You can also kill an hour or two at the Coyotepe fortress, where the views are pleasant and the wind takes the edge off the heat.

A trip through the Pueblos Blancos can occupy a full day, even if driving. It's fun to start at one end, work your way up to Catarina, have lunch, and then continue. You can visit the Pueblos Blancos by public transportation, as the buses run this route frequently throughout the day, but having the freedom of a vehicle will greatly facilitate your ability to pick and choose as you work your way through the villages. Lastly, though very few travelers stay the night in Masaya, consider doing so during one of the city's colorful festivals, when the town really comes alive.

Masaya City

Masaya (population 90,000) sprawls over a tropical plain nestled against the slopes of the volcano by the same name; at its western edge, paths carved by the Chorotegas trace the steep hillside down to the Laguna de Masaya. Twenty indigenous villages of Darianes used to cluster at the water's edge. Masaya was officially founded as a city in 1819 and has grown ever since. Several centuries of rebellion and uprising—first against the Spaniards in 1529 and later against William Walker's forces in 1856, the U.S. Marines in 1912, and in a number of ferocious battles against the National Guard during the revolution, earned the Masayans a reputation as fierce fighters.

Travelers find Masaya less picturesque than Granada and it's true the streets and building facades in Masaya are less cared for. But the Masayans are a creative people with many traditions found nowhere else in Nicaragua, such as their solemn, mysterious funeral processions. Perhaps Masayan creative energy goes into its delightful arts and crafts instead of the architecture. Your best introduction to these delights is Masaya's Mercado Viejo (Old Market), which is so pleasant and compelling that many visitors choose not to stray beyond its stately stone walls. But it's well worth the money to charter a horse-drawn carriage to carry you to the breezy *malecón,* to see the crater lake 100 meters below.

ORIENTATION AND GETTING AROUND

Masaya sits due south of the Managua–Granada Carretera along the east side of the Laguna de Masaya. The street that runs north along the plaza's east side is the Calle Central, and as you travel it toward the Carretera, it becomes increasingly commercial. One block east of the southeast corner of the park, you'll find the stone walls of the Mercado Viejo (Old Market). Walking six blocks west of the central park takes you to the hammock factories, baseball stadium, and *malecón;* traveling due

LA LAGUNA DE MASAYA

The peaceful waters of the Laguna de Masaya belie the violent origin of the lake. Long before the first Chorotegas settled in 20 small villages around its perimeter, the lake was one of Volcán Masaya's gaping craters, choked off long ago by shifting channels of magma beneath the surface of the earth and abandoned to slowly fill up with rainwater. These days, the most impressive views of Laguna de Masaya are from the 100-meter-high vantage points of the *malecón* in the city of Masaya, or from the restaurants that line Carretera Masaya, just west of the city. It's one of Nicaragua's bigger crater lakes: 8.5 square kilometers set at the foot Volcán Masaya and 73 meters deep in the center. It's also one of the country's most polluted with sewage and trash. While several trails, some of which were made by the Chorotegas themselves, lead the intrepid hiker down to the water's edge, this is no swimming hole. Dip your heels in nearby Laguna de Apoyo instead.

south leads you to Barrio Monimbó; going five blocks north puts you in the heart of the Barrio San Jerónimo around the church of the same name, situated at the famous *siete esquinas* (seven corners) intersection. The heart of Masaya is easily walkable, but several hundred taxis, buses, horse-drawn carriages, and more exotic forms of transport will help you get out to the *malecón* or the highway.

SIGHTS AND ATTRACTIONS
◖ El Mercado Viejo Craft Market

All roads lead to El Mercado Viejo, built in 1891, destroyed by fires in 1966 and 1978, and refurbished in 1997 as a showcase for local handicrafts. Also known as El Mercado Nacionál de Artesanías, or simply the "tourist

© JOSHUA BERMAN

Most hammock "factories" are actually people's homes in Masaya.

market," El Mercado Viejo is safe, comfortable, and geared toward foreigners. Here you'll find all manner of delightful leather, brass, iron, carved wood, and textile handicrafts, plus paintings, clothing, hammocks, and the best of what Nicaragua's talented craftspeople have to offer. It's the best reason to come to Masaya and even if you don't buy anything, an enjoyable and colorful experience—of course you pay for the convenience in slightly higher prices. Right around the corner, **Chincheli** is a shop owned and run by talented local artists and former street kids. Not only do these artists sell high quality paintings, hammocks, and bracelets, they also teach other children, under the tutelage of NGO Los Quinchos.

◖ El Malecón

Cool off after an intense morning in the market on the windswept *malecón,* a beautiful cliffside promenade with long views over the Volcán Masaya crater lake to the north and west. It's easily reached from the city center. Skip the taxi; charter a horse carriage instead, which makes for a nice ride through some quiet neighborhoods.

Artisan Workshops

Nicaragua's most treasured souvenirs, woven hammocks are handmade by scores of Masaya families, and take 2–3 days each to make. The most obvious place to purchase one is in either of the markets described above. More fun than just buying is to visit one of the many *fábricas de hamacas,* most of which are in people's homes, clustered on the same block near the southwest edge of town, across from the old hospital on the road to the *malecón* and baseball stadium. There you'll find at least a half-dozen family porch-front businesses; all of these craftspeople will gladly show you how hammocks are woven.

Sergio Zepeda is a third-generation luthier (guitar builder) at **Guitarras Zepeda** (200 meters west of the Unión Fenosa, tel. 505/8883-0260, guitarraszepeda@yahoo. com). His shop is only a block off the Carretera Masaya, behind Hotel Rosalyn. Cheap children's and beater guitars start at

$60 or so; professional hardwood instruments with cocobolo rosewood back and sides and imported red cedar, mahogany, or spruce tops can go for up to $800. Allow at least two weeks to order, or show up in his shop and see what's available.

Historic Sights

Masaya's central plaza is officially called **Parque 17 de Octubre,** named for a battle against Somoza's Guardia in 1977. Plenty of remaining bullet holes are testimony, plus two imposing command towers immediately to the west. The church in the northeast corner is La Parroquia La Asunción. The unremarkable, triangular **Plaza de Monimbó** park on the southern side of Masaya comes to life every afternoon at around 3 P.M. as the throbbing social and commercial heart of the mostly indigenous Monimbó neighborhood. The **Museo y Galería Héroes y Mártires** (inside the Alcaldía, 1.5 blocks north of the park, open 8 A.M.–5 P.M. Mon.–Fri., donation requested) pays tribute to those Masayans who fought Somoza's National Guard during the revolution with a collection of guns and photos of the fallen but the highlight is the unexploded napalm bomb Somoza dropped on the city in '77.

ENTERTAINMENT AND EVENTS

Every Thursday 5–11 P.M., **Jueves de Verbena** consists of dance, theater, art expos, music, and more, all presented in the Old Market on one of several stages. Or rub elbows with the locals at the most popular local bar in town, **La Rhonda,** on the south side of the park, with beer, lots of space, and good appetizers.

If you're here on a weekend during baseball season (Nov.–May), be sure to catch the local team, San Fernando, who plays in **Estadio Roberto Clemente,** named for the Puerto Rico–born Pittsburgh Pirate who died in a plane crash in 1973 delivering aid to Nicaraguan earthquake victims. The tailgating scene atop the *malecón* may be one of the most scenic in the world. Tickets start at $0.50.

MASAYA

MASAYA CITY

FRITANGA CHEPA RATÓN
OLD TRAIN STATION
ENITEL
★ LIBRARY
MADERA'S INN HOTEL
IGLESIA SAN JERÓNIMO
🖂 SHELL
HOSTAL MI CASA
HOTEL REGIS
POLLO LOCO ▾
▾ PARAJE CENTRAL
ROAST CHICKEN ▾
CALLE EL CALVARIO
HOTEL IVANIA'S
CALLE CENTRAL
MUSEO Y GALERÍA HÉROES Y MÁRTIRES ★
BANK
LA JAROCHITA
CYBER-1
POST OFFICE
PASTELERÍA NORMA ▾
POLICE
Parque San Juan
CENTRO DE CULTURA ★
ENITEL
LA PARROQUIA LA ASUNCIÓN
EL MERCADO VIEJO CRAFT MARKET
CHE GRIS
IGLESIA SAN JUAN
BANCENTRO
Central Park
To New Market and Bus Terminal →
HOSPEDAJE MASAYITA
PALÍ
Parque San Miguel
BANPRO
INTERNET
← To Cocojambo
LA RHONDA ▾
BDF
LA EMILINA ÑATA
To Plaza Monimbó ▾
CALLE MONIMBÓ

0   100 yds
0   100 m

© AVALON TRAVEL

MASAYA

YEAR-ROUND FIESTA TOWN: A GUIDE TO MASAYA'S PARTIES

Masayans celebrate all year long, observing various religious, historical, and indigenous rites with a wild collage of marimba music, traditional costume, poetry, painting, food, drink, and age-old customs. Many of the dances are family traditions, in which certain roles – and their accompanying masks and costumes – are passed from generation to generation. Costumes are a key element of the festivals and are often elaborate and gorgeous.

A few weeks before Easter, the celebration of **San Lázaro** features believers promenading with their ornately costumed dogs, to thank their patron saint for keeping their household animals in good health.

The fiestas only get more interesting. In the **Festival of the Cross,** celebrated in May, people exchange thousands of palm-thatch crosses in honor of La Señora de la Asunción. The virgin icon is carried to Monimbó in remembrance of the miracle that occurred there during the last eruption of Volcán Masaya's Santiago Crater, in which the virgin saved the city from hot ashes.

September–December are peak fiesta months in Masaya. Things get started with the official **fiestas patronales** on September 20, in honor of Patron Saint Jerónimo. Toward the end of the three-month celebration, look for the extravagant **Fiesta del Toro Venado,** on the last Sunday of October. It's similar to the North American Halloween, but instead of ghosts and goblins, Masayans don disguises that poke fun at their favorite politicians, clergy, and other public figures.

Held on the penultimate Friday of October, the **Fiesta de los Agüisotes** (Fiesta of the Bad Omens) is a nod to Nicaragua's darker side: Folks dress up as scary figures from local legends, such as the chancha bruja, the mocuana, and the arre chavalo (a headless priest from León).

Patron-saint celebrations end the first Sunday of December with the **Procesión de San Jerónimo.** This is perhaps the most stunning of Masaya's fiestas, as the statue of the city's patron saint is paraded through the streets amidst a sea of flowers. Look for the **Baile de las Inditas** (Dance of the Little Indian Girls), **Baile de Negras** (Dance of the Black Women), and the **Baile de Fantasía** (Dance of Fantasy). Every Sunday from September through December features a folk dance of some sort, a competition between rival troops, or even dancers that go from house to house performing short dances to marimba music.

In mid-January, the **Festival of San Sebastian** explodes with life and energy in the indigenous Monimbó barrio. The celebration's highlight is the **Baile de Chinegro de Mozote y Verga,** in which participants engage in a mock battle, hitting each other with big sticks and finally coming together in a peace ritual. The tunkún drum (a Maya instrument) beats out the rhythm of the dance, along with a whistle called a pífano. At the end of the ritual, everybody screams together:

"¡Viva San Sebastian!" ("Long live San Sebastian!")

"¡Viva el Mayordomo!" ("Long live the Master of the Parade!")

"¡Viva Santa Marta Vencedera!" ("Long live Saint Martha the Conqueror!")

La Novena del Niño Dios is an interesting December ritual in which small children are given pots, pans, whistles, and firecrackers and sent into the streets at 5 A.M. to noisily call all the other children together for the 6 A.M. mass in celebration of the Christ child's birth.

Pieces and parcels of Masaya's festivals are found in the various fiestas patronales of the many surrounding pueblos, each of which present their own peculiar twist on the events. In mid-June, for example, San Juan de Oriente's party involves "warriors" dancing through the streets and whipping each other with stiffened bull penises.

ACCOMMODATIONS

Along the highway and outside of town, Masaya's hotels tend to be pay-by-the-hour *auto-hotels;* nifty car park curtains hide your license plate to spying eyes. In town, lodging is reasonable but not nearly as varied or exciting as in Granada.

Under $25

🄲 Hotel Regis (on Calle Central, 3.5 blocks north of the church on the main plaza, tel. 505/2522-2300, $5 pp) has a dozen neat, clean rooms (including some for groups and families), with shared bath and fan, and a respectable breakfast for $2. The couple that runs the place is friendly, knowledgeable about things to do in the area, and speaks some English—however, they are strict about running a clean shop, look down on partying, and close their doors at 10 P.M. There are several other options on the same block, including **Hostal Mi Casa** (tel. 505/2522-2500, $5 pp or $20 for a simple room with a/c) in a big, open, colorful space which includes the Fruti-Fruti smoothie bar and cafetín.

If you'd rather be closer to the *discotecas* and baseball stadium, get a bare-bones room in a family's home at **Hospedaje Masayita** (two blocks west of the central park, tel. 505/8667-7055, $4 and up).

At **🄲 Madera's Inn Hotel** (two blocks south of the fire station, tel. 505/2522-5825, maderasinn@yahoo.com, $15–45), some rooms have fan and shared bath, and more expensive ones have private bath and air-conditioning. The 12 rooms occupy two floors set around a beautifully furnished common room; you'll also find friendly service, Internet access, parking, tours, and laundry.

$25-50

Just a few kilometers outside Masaya, near the entrance to the national park with the same name, **Hotel Volcán Masaya** (tel. 505/2522-7114, $37) has 10 rooms with air-conditioning, private bath, warm water, and TV. There is a lovely garden and serene, remote feeling here,

but you're a bit isolated from everything except the volcano; a decent option if you have your own vehicle.

Over $50

A well-run, modern option in central Masaya, **Hotel Ivania's** (from Calvario church, 3.5 blocks west, tel. 505/2522-7632, hotelivanias@hotmail.com, www.hotelivanias.com, $65 includes tax and breakfast) has 17 clean, plain rooms with air-conditioning, television, hot water, refrigerators, and tiled floors, all surrounding an attractive courtyard; budget doubles without air-conditioning are $25. Ask about the family suite and local tours.

FOOD
Local Fare and *Fritanga*

Masaya is more famous for its street food than its restaurants and nowhere will you find more authentic cuisine *de la calle* than at **El Tiangue,** an open-air, multivendor food market in barrio Monimbó. Vendors set up in the small triangular plaza across from the Don Bosco school. It gets going every evening around 5 P.M. when you'll find everything from standard finger-licking *fritanga* served on a banana leaf to hard-core snout-to-tail pig dishes and organ meat, such as that featured on the Travel Channel's *Bizarre Foods with Andrew Zimmern,* "Nicaragua" episode.

Countless small *comedores* line both sides of the main street from the central park all the way up to the old train station, all fine places to find out why Masayans refer to themselves as *"come-yucas"* (yucca eaters). You'll find all sorts of juicy, greasy, fried, and roasted treasures at one of several locally famous street grills: **Fritanga Alvarez** is across from the entrance to Santa Rosa; **Fritanga San Jerónimo** is a few blocks west of the church with the same name; **La Emilina Ñata en el Barrio Loco,** or Flat-nose Emilina's in the Crazy Neighborhood is open every day from 5 P.M. till its world-famous grilled beef runs out. Still another savory sidewalk barbecue option is **La Chepa Ratona,** next to the old train station.

Cafés and Restaurants

Eateries close to El Mercado Viejo include **Pastelería Norma** (20 meters north of the Old Market), for baked goods, juices, and snacks, and **Che Gris** (on the east side of the Old Market), which offers traditional cooking in an air-conditioned setting. A livelier, more popular option is ◖ **Jarochito's** (tel. 505/2522-4831, open 11 A.M.–10 P.M. daily), just north of the central park, for Mexican with a Nicaraguan twist, with plates from $3–8. A bit farther up the main street is **Comedor La Criolla** (7 A.M.–5 P.M. daily), serving excellent local breakfast and lunch for $2.50–$4. It's a great place to sit and enjoy a fresh juice drink.

INFORMATION

The INTUR office is located within the Old Market, open business hours (closed for lunch, tel. 505/2522-7615) but of little use other than for upcoming events in the city.

SERVICES

Hospital Hilario Sanchez Vásquez (on the highway toward Granada, tel. 505/2522-2778) is the biggest facility in town, though you are much better off driving to Hospital Vivan Pellas, on the highway before you reach Managua.

The large, blue police station (tel. 505/2522-

4222 or 505/2522-2521) is half a block north of the Old Market across from Norma's bakery.

Besides the multiple ATMs within the Old Market, numerous banks are close by: Bancentro on the west side of the central park and a BDF one block north of the Old Market. Several cheap and crowded Internet places line the south side of the central park. Both Correos de Nicaragua and a DHL Worldwide Express are available inside the Old Market compound to facilitate sending gifts and packages, and the ENITEL phone office is a block south of the old train station.

GETTING THERE AND AWAY

Nearly every southbound bus leaving Managua from Roberto Huembes passes Masaya, which is right on the highway, only 27 kilometers from Managua. Faster still are the Masaya- or Granada-bound *expresos* from the UCA leaving regularly 7 A.M.–9:30 P.M., arriving in Masaya's Parque San Miguel; from there, they depart for Managua 6 A.M.–8 P.M. The ride costs under $1. Less recommended is the *expreso* service between Masaya's Plaza de Monimbó and Mercado Oriental in Managua, first leaving Masaya at 3 A.M. and running through 7 P.M. Ordinary bus service leaves and arrives at the main terminal in the parking lot of the Mercado Nuevo.

Near Masaya

◖ VOLCÁN MASAYA NATIONAL PARK

An extraordinary and easy day trip from Managua, Masaya, or Granada, Volcán Masaya National Park (tel. 505/2522-5415, open 9 A.M.–4:45 P.M. daily, $4) is Nicaragua's most impressive outdoor attraction and premier tourist site. There are very few volcanoes in the world where you can simply drive up to the crater edge and look into what the Spaniards declared to be the very "mouth of hell": That's exactly what Masaya offers, but there's a lot

more. One of the most visibly active volcanoes in the country, Volcán Masaya emits a nearly constant plume of sulfurous gas, smoke, and sometimes ash, visible from as far away as the airport in Managua. From one of its craters, you can sometimes glimpse incandescent rock and magma. A visitors center (where they'll ask you to park your car facing out "just in case") will help you interpret the geology and ecology of the site, as will the park's impressive nature museum. For the more actively inclined, hiking trails cover a portion of the volcano's slopes.

© JOSHUA BERMAN

the cross at Volcán Masaya

Volcán Masaya was called Popogatepe (mountain that burns) by the Chorotegas, who feared it and interpreted eruptions as displays of anger to be appeased with sacrifices, often human. In the early 1500s, Father Francisco Bobadilla placed a cross at the crater lip in order to exorcise the devil within and protect the villages below. Not long afterward, though, thinking the volcano might contain gold instead of the devil both Friar Blas del Castillo and Gonzalo Fernandez de Oviedo lowered themselves into the crater on ropes to search. They found neither the devil nor gold but probably singed their eyebrows.

The park is actually composed of several geologically linked volcanic craters: Volcán Nindirí, which last erupted in 1670, and Volcán Masaya, which blew its top in 1772. The relatively new Santiago Crater was formed between the other two in 1852, and is inhabited by a remarkable species of parakeet that nests contentedly in the rocky side of the crater walls, oblivious to the toxic gases and the scientists who had thought such a sulphurous

environment would be uninhabitable. You might see these *chocoyos del cráter* (crater parakeets) from the parking area along the crater's edge.

As for the sensation of "just in case," the danger is quite real. In April 2000, the Santiago crater burped up a single volcanic boulder that plummeted to earth, crushing an unfortunate Italian tourist's car in the parking lot.

Visiting Volcán Masaya

The exhibits at the **Visitors Interpretation Center** and museum include three-dimensional dioramas of Nicaragua and Central America, models of active volcanoes, and remnants of indigenous sacrifice urns and musical instruments found deep in the volcano's caves; there is also a display of old lithographs and paintings of the volcano as the Spaniards saw it. Consider one of the several guided tours ($10 pp, sign up at the visitors center), including an exciting night tour beginning at sunset. Of special interest is the walk to the Tzinancanostoc Bat Cave, a lava tube passageway melted out of solid rock.

Though most visitors only snap a few photos from the crater's edge before continuing, the park also contains several hiking trails through a veritable moonscape of lava formations and scrubby vegetation, making it easy to spend at least half a day here; carry lots of water and sunscreen (there is little to no shade); the trails are well worth your time and offer good opportunities to cross paths with some of the park's wildlife, including coyotes, deer, iguanas, and monkeys. The Coyote Trail will lead you east to the shore of the Laguna de Masaya.

Coyotepe

Just south of the volcano on a hill overlooking the highway, the battlements of this fort (open 8:30 A.M.–5 P.M., 365 days a year, $1) overlook the city of Masaya. Take a cab or hike up the road—the view of Masaya, its lagoon and volcano, both great lakes, and the far-reaching surrounding countryside is worth it; that's before you even descend into the dungeons. Built at the turn of the 20th

MASAYA

MASAYA

© RANDALL WOOD

Coyotepe fortress, near Masaya

century, this site witnessed a fierce battle between national troops and U.S. Marines in 1912. Somoza rehabilitated it as a particularly cruel prison. Today, Coyotepe is in the hands of the Nicaraguan Boy Scouts, who will accompany you through the pitch-black underground prison facilities in exchange for a small fee (for special attention, or at least a smile, greet your guide with the three-finger Scout salute and their motto in Spanish: *Siempre Listo*—Always Prepared).

Nindirí

Just north of the highway between the entrance to the national park and the city of Masaya, Nindirí was the most important and densely populated of the indigenous settlements in the area—up to 1,500 years before the arrival of the Spanish. Its name in Chorotega means Hill of the Small Pig, and its principal attraction is the 1,000-artifact collection in the **Museo Tenderí** (named after a local cacique) that celebrates pre-Columbian culture. Also, ask around about the Cailagua site, with petroglyphs overlooking the Laguna de Masaya. During the last week of July, the festival for patron saint Santa Ana employs many of the ancient dance, costume,

and music rituals popular to the whole Masaya and Carazo region.

◖ LAGUNA DE APOYO

Nicaragua's cleanest and most enticing swimming hole is Laguna de Apoyo, just outside of Masaya. Actually a lake that formed in the drowned volcanic crater of the long extinct Apoyo Volcano, the lagoon floor reaches 200 meters in depth—the lowest point in all of Central America. Considering how easy it is to reach the lagoon, it is surprisingly untouristed. Despite its continued seismicity—a minor earthquake in 2000 under the crater-rim town of Catarina caused Apoyo's water to slosh back and forth like a teapot and wrecked a few homes—for the most part the volcano is considered dormant, and a thick green forest has grown up the slopes over the years. These slopes harbor a few hiking trails and are protected from further development by law. The crater hosts a few fish species found nowhere else on earth; scientists at the Proyecto Ecologico are studying them. If you hike through the forests, expect to observe species of toucan, hummingbirds, blue jays, howler and white-face monkeys (which are prone to fling their feces at you if you approach), and rare butterflies. You will find very few places on earth quite like this charming, isolated community.

Accommodations and Food

The number of places to eat or lodge along the western shore of the crater lake is slowly increasing and diversifying, despite local grumbling about illegal development of the waterfront. At any establishment below, pay $6–10 to stay for the day and enjoy the docks, pool, inner tubes, hammocks, and other facilities. The area has no stores or shops, and few services, so either pack your essentials before coming, or count on one of the local hotels or restaurants. Most hotels offer cheap shuttles from Granada, or you can hire a taxi or take a bus.

The **Monkey Hut** (tel. 505/2552-4028 or 505/8887-3546, thebeardedmonkey@yahoo. com, www.thebeardedmonkey.com, $10 dorm, $25 d with shared bath and fan, $45–80 for nicer cabañas) is a well-liked retreat on a beautiful terraced piece of land at the water's edge, with a fully equipped kitchen and a small

selection of rooms. Soft drinks, water, wine, and beer can be purchased at the hut—all other supplies need to be packed in. Make reservations at the Bearded Monkey in Granada. **Crater's Edge** (tel. 505/8895-3202, www. craters-edge.com, $12 pp dorm, $24–44 private room) is also geared toward budget travelers, offering terraced patios, waterside bar, and floating dock. Cheap transport from Granada is provided and leaves Hostel Oasis in Granada at 10 A.M. and returns at 4:30 P.M. Rooms in the dormitory have a fabulous sunrise view. Also offered are three meals a day served at the restaurant, Wi-Fi, and local crafts for sale.

The **Proyecto Ecologico Spanish School and Hostel** (tel. 505/8882-3992, www.gaiani-caragua.org) is one of the oldest operations in the crater, a not-for-profit research station and Spanish school. Stay for $10 pp shared dorm, $19 d with fan and shared bath, breakfast included. They organize bird-watching, hikes, scuba diving expeditions ($60 for two tanks), and the chance to participate in a volunteer reforestation brigade (all-inclusive Spanish

© JOSHUA BERMAN

Laguna de Apoyo is a very swimmable crater lake.

school packages start at $190 per week). There is nowhere better to speak with knowledgeable ecologists who can help interpret this unique region, and the home-cooked meals ($4) are well recommended.

At "Grandma's" **Posada Ecologica La Abuela** (tel. 505/8880-0368, info@posadaecologicalaabuela.com, www.posadaecologicalaabuela.com, $70 includes breakfast) you'll find a series of wooden docks, rocker swings for splashing around in the water, and great views. The wooden *cabañas* are very comfortable and well appointed, with air-conditioning, private bath, nice mattresses; also great facilities for groups.

Neither hostel nor hotel, **Guest House La Orquidea** (tel. 505/8872-1866, www.laorquideanicaragua.com) is a stylish two-bedroom house, fully equipped for a relaxing stay; features include a gorgeous balcony, boats, and water toys. Rates run $120 a night for 4–7 guests, healthy breakfast provided; there is also a separate room for $40.

On the opposite end of the road, ⬛ San **Simian Eco-Resort** (tel. 505/8813-6866, info@sansimian.com, www.sansimian.com, $50 includes large breakfast), the sister hotel of Hotel Casa San Francisco in Granada, is a lovely waterside group of five private bungalows, each of which has a slightly different theme built from natural materials like thatch and bamboo. The tasteful, rustic rooms have bamboo beds with comfy mattresses, mosquito nets, fans, and fun outdoor showers and gardens; more features include great on-site meals, bar, and relaxing dock with water toys. Nearby trailheads lead up into the jungle and along the shore.

After several years of on-and-off neglect, a new management team has taken over **Norome Resort and Villas** (tel. 505/2552-8200, U.S. or Canada tel. 760/494-7331, www.noromevillas.

com, $75–166) and is bringing the property's 66 Caribbean-style villas back to glory. Apartments and suites (1–3 bedrooms) have hot water, bathtubs, air-conditioning, TV/ DVD, and kitchenettes. The restaurant and bar perched over the water are stunning (meals $6–12, Wi-Fi available). Relax by the lakeshore and swimming pools, book a massage, or go boating, biking, and hiking; day-trippers are welcome with a $5 minimum purchase at the restaurant.

Getting There and Away

Laguna de Apoyo is about a 20-minute ride from either Masaya or Granada, and about an hour from the airport in Managua. There are two paved roads that go up and over the crater lip and down to the water's edge; one originates on Carretera Masaya, at a spot called *el puentecito;* the other branches off the Masaya–Catarina road. They join just before passing through the village of Valle de Laguna, where you'll turn right at the T then make a quick left to begin your descent (pay a $1 entrance fee if driving). The road winds downward until the paved section ends exactly at the gate to former president Alemén's vacation home.

Regular backpacker buses leave Hostel Oasis and the Bearded Monkey in Granada, charging only a couple of bucks each. Or share a taxi from Granada or Masaya for about $15. Public buses headed for *bajo al plan* (i.e., lakefront) cost under $1 and leave the main Masaya market terminal at 10:30 A.M. and 3:10 P.M.; or you can hop one of the hourly buses for Valle de Laguna, then walk (30 minutes downhill) or wait for a stray taxi. Mototaxis run between the *puentecito* and Valle de Laguna. Three public buses can get you back up the hill, leaving at 6 A.M., 11:10 A.M., and 4:40 P.M. (3 P.M. on Sunday is the last bus).

The Pueblos Blancos and Carazo

Escaping the heat of Managua or Granada is as easy as a 40-minute bus ride to the Pueblos Blancos and Carazo, two regions that occupy a breezy 500-meter-high *meseta* south of Managua and are thus far cooler and more relaxing. The Pueblos Blancos, or White Villages, are named for the purity of color of their churches (some of which, naturally, are now other colors). They are separated to the north by the Sierras de Managua, to the east by the slopes of Volcán Masaya, to the south by the Laguna de Apoyo and Volcán Mombacho, and to the west by the dry, desolate decline toward the Pacific Ocean. Each town is well known for something particular—bamboo craftwork, wicker chairs, black magic, folk dances, Sandino's birthplace, crater lakes, beaches, or interesting festivals. Visiting the pueblos is an easy day trip best appreciated if you have a car, which permits you to tour furniture workshops, coffee plantations, or outdoor plant nurseries.

In nearby Carazo, the January celebration of San Sebastián is a dramatic and colorful festival not to be missed. Diriamba is home to Nicaragua's national soccer team but baseball is given equal attention; games are exciting and fun. This is also the gateway to several Pacific beaches quieter than their more developed neighbors.

ORIENTATION AND GETTING AROUND

Renting a car or taxi is the best way to visit the Pueblos, but you can get around almost as easily with the *expreso* minivan system. No more than 10 or 12 kilometers separate any two townst, all of which are easily accessible from Masaya, Granada, and Managua. Buses to the Pueblos Blancos leave from Huembes, continue south on the Carretera Masaya, and then turn west into the hills at various points, depending on the route. The Carazo buses—to

MASAYA

© JOSHUA BERMAN

Los Pueblos Blancos are named for their white churches.

Jinotepe and Diriamba—travel via Carretera Sur and leave from the Mercado Israel Lewites and from a lot across from the UCA.

◖ CATARINA MIRADOR

This hillside pueblo clings to the verdant lip of the spectacular Laguna de Apoyo crater lake. The Mirador is a blustery cliffside walkway and restaurant complex at the edge of the crater with one of the best panoramic views in Nicaragua—look for the distant red-tiled roofs and cathedral spires of Granada, broad Lake Cocibolca behind, and on a clear day, the twin volcanic peaks of Ometepe. Roaming marimba and guitar players will serenade you for a small fee (negotiate before they begin playing). Locals visit Catarina for its ornamental plant nurseries and the wares of local artisans and basket makers whose shops begin at roadside. Vehicles pay $1 each to enter the Mirador.

◖ **Hotel Casa Catarina** (tel. 505/2558-0034 or 505/2558-0227, reservaciones@hotelcasacatarina.com, www.casacatarina.com, $75) is a new, modern, and well-liked three-star hotel. It's the only choice other than the basic but clean **Hotel Jaaris** or **Hospedaje Euro,** both about $10 and one block west (i.e. downhill) from the Catarina church.

SAN JUAN DE ORIENTE

San Juan potters craft attractive ceramic vases, pots, plates, and more, in both a proud celebration of pre-Columbian styles and modern inspirations. Shop at one of the small cooperatives along the entrance to town, or in the many tiny displays in people's homes as you walk through the narrow streets. Many artisans are glad to invite you back into their workshops for a tour.

DIRIÁ AND DIRIOMO

Named for the indigenous Dirian people and their leader, Diriangén (the famed rebel cacique and martyr whose spilled blood at the hands of the conquistadores is immortalized in Carlos Mejía Godoy's anthem, "Nicaragua Nicaragüita"), Diriá and Diriomo face each other on both sides of the highway. Both

towns are well loved for their unique celebrations throughout the year, mixing elements of pre-Columbian, Catholic, and bizarre regional traditions (like the "dicking" festival in which participants smack each other with dried-out bull penises, sometimes practiced in San Juan de Oriente as well). Diriá, on the east, has a *mirador* smaller and less frequented than the more famous one at Catarina, as well as additional trails down to the Laguna de Apoyo. Across the highway, Diriomo is renowned for its sorcery: The intrepid traveler looking for a love potion or revenge should seek out one of the pueblo's *brujos* (or at least read the book *Sofía de los Presagios*)

Less famous than Catarina, Diriomo has a crater overlook of its own: **Diriomito Mirador,** which occasionally offers paragliding, or *parapente* (tel. 505/2522-2009).

NIQUINOHOMO

"The valley of the warriors," in Nahuatl, produced a famous warrior indeed: Augusto César Sandino, born there at the turn of the 20th century. Sandino's childhood home off the northwest corner of the park has been restored as a library and museum. A 4,000-pound, solid bronze statue of the man, with the famous hat and bandolier of bullets around his waist, stands at attention at the east side of town. Niquinohomo's 320-year-old church is also worth a look.

MASATEPE

Masatepe (Nahuatl for "place of the deer") is a quiet pueblo of about 12,000 that explodes in revelry the first Sunday of every June during its famous **Hípica** (horse parade). Stick around after the festivities for a steaming bowl of Masatepe's culinary claim to fame—*sopa de mondongo* (cow tripe soup), served hot in front of the town's gorgeous, architecturally unique church. The Hípica is just one part of the *fiestas patronales* in honor of La Santísima Trinidad, the black Christ icon a Chorotegan found in the trunk of a tree during the years of the Spanish colony. Find other meals in the Bar Sarapao or Eskimo shop on the north side of the park.

© JOSHUA BERMAN

Children's rocking chairs, crafted by Masatepe carpenters, are inexpensive and easy to pack down.

Outside of the city, both sides of the highway are lined with the workshops of the extraordinarily talented Masatepe carpenters, whose gorgeous, handcrafted hardwood and rattan furniture is prized throughout the country. You'll wish you could fit more of it in your luggage (a set of chairs and a coffee table go for about $100), but console yourself instead with a comfortable, old-fashioned hardwood rocking chair. They'll disassemble and pack it down to airline-acceptable size for you for a small fee.

If driving to Masatepe from the south, save time for a meal at **Mi Teruño Masatepino** (on the east side of the road, just north of the turnoff for Pio XII and Nandasmo), a delicious open-air restaurant featuring Nicaragua's traditional country cuisine.

SAN MARCOS

San Marcos is sort of the hub of the Pueblos Blancos and hosts Nicaragua's best (and most expensive) university, the **Ave Maria College of the Americas** (three blocks south of the park, www.avemaria.edu.ni), a Catholic, bilingual, four-year liberal arts university with about 400 students and a sister campus in Ann Arbor, Michigan. Before 1998, its modern facilities belonged to the University of Mobile (Alabama). Ave Maria is one of the beneficiaries of Catholic conservative and Domino Pizza founder, Thomas Monaghan. Not much to see here other than the church and town square, both of which are lovely. There's one very nice hotel: **Hotel Casablanca** (two blocks east of the church's southeast corner, tel. 505/2535-2717, $46–55), with Wi-Fi, hot water, breakfast included. There are several small restaurants; **La Casona** (near the park) is particularly recommended for its food and pleasant owner.

MARIPOSA ECO-HOTEL AND SPANISH SCHOOL

Tucked into the forest off the road to the village of San Juan de la Concepción (a.k.a. La Concha, 12 kilometers west of Ticuantepe, under an hour from Managua), this unique hideaway has spurred a stream of rave reviews from our readers. Mariposa Ecohotel and Spanish School (tel. 505/2418-4638, www.spanishschoolnica.com) uses part of its revenue to fund a range of grassroots environmental

MASAYA

THE FESTIVAL OF SAINT SEBASTIÁN

Every pueblo's *fiestas patronales* have something that make them unique, but Diriamba's celebration of the Holy Martyr San Sebastián stands above the rest as Nicaragua's most authentic connection to its indigenous roots. Many of the dances, songs, and costumes are true to traditions that predate the arrival of the Spanish by hundreds of years. But this is no nostalgia act – indeed, the integration of pre-Columbian ritual with Catholicism and the telling of modern history is as fascinating as the colors, costumes, and music.

This celebration is actually three fiestas for the price of one, since icons of San Santiago of Jinotepe, San Marcos of San Marcos, and San Sebastián of Diriamba have been observed together since the three of them first traveled from Spain, landing at nearby Casares beach. The icons are still believed to have the special bond they formed during their journey, and they get together to celebrate this three times a year during the fiesta of each of their towns. Santiago and Marcos meet up at the *tope* (end of the road) in Dolores on (or around) January 19, where they are danced around the village to a bombardment of cheers and homemade fireworks. The next day, they reunite with their pal, Sebastián, in Diriamba, where the town has been partying for four days in preparation.

The following day is the peak of activities, the actual **Día del Santo,** marked by special masses and, sometimes, groups of tourists that come to view the long, raucous procession, famous for its theatrical dances and costumes. The following are the most important acts:

The Dance of Toro Huaco is of indigenous ancestry and features peacock feather hats and a multigeneration snake dance, with the youngest children bringing up the rear and an old man with a special tambourine and whistle up front. **El Güegüense,** also called the **Macho Ratón,** is recognizable for its masks and costumes depicting burdened-down donkeys and the faces of Spanish conquistadores. The Güegüense (from the old word *güegüe,* which means something like grumpy old man) is a hard-handed social satire with cleverly vulgar undertones that depicts the indigenous peoples' first impression of the Spanish – it has been called the oldest comedy act on the continent. **El Gigante** is a dance that depicts the biblical story of David and Goliath, and **La Danza de las Inditas** is a group act, recognizable by the white cotton costumes and the sound of the marimba. Most of the dancers are carrying out a family tradition that has been kept for dozens of generations, and each usually has a grandma-led support team on the sidelines to make sure their costumes and performances are kept in order.

A true believer will tell you that Diriamba's fiesta begins not on January 19, but on February 2 of the previous year, when the official *fiesteros* apply for roles in the upcoming celebration; they then begin more than 11 months of preparation, all of which is seen as a display of faith and thanks to their beloved San Sebastián. Those that don't show their devotion by dancing or playing music do so by carrying the icons or fulfilling promises to walk a certain number of blocks on their knees, sometimes until bloody.

Bring plenty of film, and be sure to try the official beverage of the festival: *chicha con genibre,* a ginger-tinted, slightly fermented cornmeal drink. Most of the masks and costumes in the productions are also for sale, as are homemade action figures depicting the various dance characters.

and community projects. Guests are invited to help with the projects, from reforestation and chicken raising to literacy, education, and animal rescue. The hotel and rooms have excellent views of Volcán Masaya, use solar and wind power, and there is an organic farm with coffee, bananas, free-range eggs, and lots of fruit. Meals are typical Nicaraguan breakfast, buffet-style lunch (salads, meat, and vegetarian), and family-style dinner. The rooms are decorated with local handicrafts, each with their own bathroom and fan. There is a fully stocked library, quality one-on-one Spanish school, and the manager, Paulette Goudge, PhD, offers a three-month course in the "Politics of Development." This is a great place for families. There are volunteer and homestay opportunities as well. Rooms are $25 per night including breakfast, or look into their all-inclusive Spanish school packages ($300 a week).

JINOTEPE AND DIRIAMBA (CARAZO)
Jinotepe

Jinotepe (Xilotepetl, or "field of baby corn") is a sometimes-sleepy, sometimes-bustling villa of 27,000 set around **La Iglesia Parroquial de Santiago** (built in 1860) and a lively park shaded by the canopy of several immense hardwood trees. Thanks to a branch of UNAN, Jinotepe's student population keeps things youthful and lively, and its outdoor market is fun. Don't miss the beautiful two-block-long mural on the nursing school (three blocks west of the park's northwest corner) and the towering statue of Pope John Paul II in front of the church. While you're there, enjoy an icy, chocolatey *cacao con leche* in the kiosk under the shade trees of one of Nicaragua's shadiest parks.

The **Hotel Casa Mateo** (one block north of the park and two west, tel. 505/2532-3284, U.S. tel. 410/878-2252, $45–65) has 40 rooms with TV, private bath, hot water, and fan; also laundry service, a guard for your car, a restaurant (called Jardín de los Olivos), conference room, and Wi-Fi. This is a nonprofit hotel run by Glenn and Lynne Schweitzer, pastors and missionaries from

Maryland, to help fund Quinta Esperanza, a home for abused and orphaned children, preschool, and vocational center. They offer special group rates ($15–20 pp).

There are dozens of small, decent eateries, but Managua expats actually drive here to enjoy ◖ **Pizzería Coliseo** (one block north of Bancentro, tel. 505/2532-2150 or 505/2532-2646, open 12:30–9 P.M., closed Monday, $6 and up), a legitimate Italian restaurant run by Rome *originario* Fausto, who's been preparing delicious pizzas and pasta in Jinotepe for more than 20 years. Ask anyone and they'll guide you there. Not quite as authentic, **Pizza To Go** (half block east of the BDF, tel. 505/2532-0754, closed Tuesday) is half the price and twice as popular among locals; the place is packed every night and they deliver.

Diriamba

Diriamba's **Festival of San Sebastian** in the third week of January is an annual religious, theatrical, folklore celebration uninterrupted since colonial days. Featuring both pagan and Catholic elements, it is without rival in western Nicaragua, comparable perhaps only to Bluefield's Palo de Mayo.

Visit the **Museo Ecológico de Tropico Seco** (tel. 505/2422-2129, open Mon.–Fri.), for background on much of the region's unique dry tropical ecosystem. The MARENA office here ministers some of the local turtle-nesting refuges.

Hospedaje Diriangén (one block east, half block south of the Shell Station, tel. 505/2422-2428, $7 pp with private bath and fan) is clean enough and safe. The **Casa Hotel Diriamba** (one block east of the clock tower, tel. 505/2523-2523, $11) is more central.

Outside of town on the road to Managua, the ◖ **Eco Lodge El Jardín Tortuga Verde** (tel. 505/2534-2948 or 505/8905-5313, rorappal@turbonett.com.ni, www.ecolodgecarazo.com, $25–45) is truly a pleasant and peaceful guesthouse whose six clean, comfortable rooms are built around a beautiful garden filled with statues. They can show you around their converted coffee plantation now rife with lush flowers and vegetation; ask about their beach house in Casares and horseback riding trips.

Getting There and Away

Sleek, comfortable *interlocal* minibuses leave for both Jinotepe and Carazo from the UCA in Managua until 10 P.M. and much slower *rutas* leave from Terminal Israel Lewites.

From Jinotepe, buses leave from the COOTRAUS terminal—a dirt lot along the Pan-American Highway directly north of the park—at all hours for Managua, Masaya, Nandaime, and Rivas. Microbuses to Managua leave from the unofficial Sapasmapa terminal on the south side of the Instituto Alejandro, 4:45 A.M.–7:30 P.M. ($1). Your most comfortable choice is one of the *interlocales* to Diriamba and San Marcos queued up on the street in front of the Super Santiago—only the front one will load passengers, departing when the van is full.

From Diriamba, a fleet of *interlocales* run to and from Jinotepe for about $0.25, 6 A.M.–9 P.M. daily from a spot right next to the clock tower.

Walk east and take your first left to find *microbus expresos* to Managua's Mercado Israel Lewites and the UCA for $1, 5 A.M.–7 P.M. A little farther east at the first *caseta* (booth) on the left, you can ask about all the buses that pass from Jinotepe (Managua: 4:30 A.M.–6 P.M.; Masaya: 5 A.M.–6 P.M.).

CENTRO ECOTURÍSTICO LA MÁQUINA

This is one of the "private wild reserves" protected by MARENA and managed by the landowners; La Máquina remains almost completely unvisited by tourists. The views from the waterfall are gorgeous and the area is great for hiking and camping. There is a cheap food stand and a shallow bathing area; short hiking trails lead through the forest. La Máquina is located halfway (15 minutes) between Diriamba and the ocean, around Km 58. Buses pass the entrance all day long in both directions. The reserve is open daylight hours, entrance is $1.50, and it's closed Mondays.

CARAZO BEACHES

La Boquita and Casares are 35 kilometers due west of Diriamba. The road ends at the coast where you'll turn right to reach humble, run-down **La Boquita** tourist center (you'll pay a small admission fee to enter). Left takes you to **Casares**, a fishing village to the south. These beaches attract mostly Nicaraguan families on picnics and outings and the odd foreigner in search of fresh fish dishes. On a big swell, the surf can be up at both places, and you'll likely be the only gringo in the lineup (rental boards sometimes available). Note that this area—particularly La Boquita—is probably best avoided during Semana Santa and New Year's Day when they are overrun by drunken mobs.

Rent some shade under one of the *ranchos,* where you can order drinks, food, and wandering musicians. There are two decent hotels at La Boquita, **Hotel Palmas del Mar** (tel. 505/2552-8715, pglo@tmx.com.ni, $40) and **Suleyka Hotel** (tel. 505/8698-3355, swlagos@yahoo.com, from $10 per person and up), whose few excellent rooms have air conditioning and private bathrooms, and are right on the beach; the large room can sleep a family of 10, with bunkbeds, for $80. Otherwise at La Boquita, there are a handful of interchangeable *hospedajes* with basic (occasionally filthy) rooms for under $15.

Just down the coast, the beach at Casares is uncomfortably short on shade—but it's also short on crowds, has a decent hotel if you choose to stay, and features a long, wide beach great for watching the fishing boats coming in and out. On the drive between La Boquita and Casares, seek out **El Pozo del Padre,** a self-contained rocky bathtub that's loads of fun at high tide.

Public transportation leaves from the main market on the highway east of the clock tower. Express microbuses leave every 20 minutes for the 40-minute, $0.75 ride to La Boquita 6:20 A.M.–6 P.M. Regular buses take 90 minutes and leave between 6:40 A.M. and 6:30 P.M. From the beach at La Boquita the first bus leaves at 5 A.M., the last one at 6 P.M.

LA ISLA DE OMETEPE AND RIVAS

South of Managua, the land crumples into high cloudy ridges and the windblown peak of Las Nubes (934 meters), then falls off slowly until it spills into southwestern Nicaragua's plains. Here Lake Cocibolca presses the land into a narrow belt that barely separates the lake from the Pacific Ocean. In fact, geological evidence suggests at one point, it didn't separate them at all, and Lake Cocibolca once flowed across this slim margin of land to the west, draining into the Pacific near the fishing community of Brito rather than down the Río San Juan into the Atlantic Ocean, as it does today.

The isthmus of Rivas is replete with history. Although known as the land of Nicarao, the area was first inhabited by the Kiribisis tribe, whom the more powerful Chorotegas

pushed aside. The Nicaraos came afterward, and by the time the Spanish "discovered" the region, had been residents here for at least seven generations. Rivas, a languorous colonial town of traders and farmers, watched hundreds of thousands of passengers traveling between New York and California pass through its streets in horse-drawn carts between San Jorge and San Juan del Sur; this was the only dry-land crossing of the entire gold rush journey. At about the same time, one of filibuster William Walker's first military defeats took place here.

These days, Rivas draws less attention than the coastal communities of San Juan del Sur and La Isla de Ometepe, but retains a colonial charm appreciated by many. But it's hard to compete with La Isla de Ometepe for attention.

© RANDALL WOOD

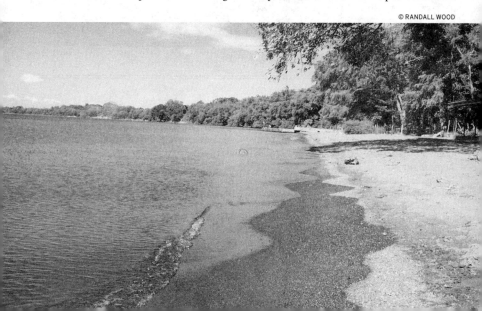

HIGHLIGHTS

🌙 Reserva Charco Verde: Verdant and cool, the reserve is a lovely little ecosystem with a sandy lakeshore beach in the shadows of tall trees; in a word, gorgeous (page 111).

🌙 El Ojo de Agua: The only place you can swim other than in the lake, the waters of El Ojo de Agua are crystal clear from the mountains, and bracing. Enjoy a languid afternoon in a garden setting (page 114).

🌙 Playa Santo Domingo: A sweeping crescent of black sand nestled on the "bridge" between the two volcanoes (page 114).

🌙 Río Istián: Paddling a kayak through these still waters early in the morning or during sunset is breathtaking (page 115).

🌙 Volcán Maderas: Santa Cruz to Balgüe The lower slopes are covered with petroglyphs dating from before Columbus (page 116).

🌙 Iglesia Parroquial de San Pedro: Rivas's historic church witnessed the entire gold rush of the 19th century, and emerged unscathed. A charming and photogenic piece of history (page 123).

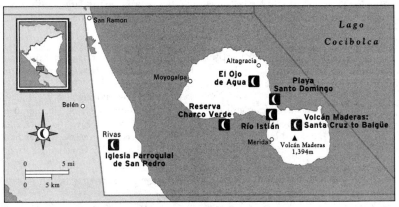

LOOK FOR 🌙 TO FIND RECOMMENDED SIGHTS, ACTIVITIES, DINING, AND LODGING.

The magnificent twin-peaked Ometepe rises like a crown from the center of Lake Cocibolca. An intensely volcanic island steeped in tradition and mystery, Ometepe was the ancestral home of the Nahuatl people and today is an alluring destination for travelers, with its sandy beaches, swimming holes, hiking trails, and of course, two breathtaking volcanoes: one hot, one cold (the former remains quite active).

Southwestern Nicaragua does not suffer the same intense, grinding poverty prevalent in the drier lands of the north and west. It rains more in the south, and the rivers flow nearly year-round. The volcanic soils on Lake Cocibolca's western shore are rich and productive. Cattle graze lazily in immense, lucrative ranches and sugarcane fields drape the valleys south of the foot of Mombacho, one of Nicaragua's most picturesque peaks.

PLANNING YOUR TIME

You will probably visit Rivas on the way to and from San Juan del Sur; half a day is acceptable to walk around the historical sites, appreciate the cathedral, and perhaps take in a museum. Travelers with a more leisurely schedule can easily spend another half day enjoying the lakeshore in San Jorge before continuing to Ometepe.

La Isla de Ometepe should not be missed on any but the shortest trips to Nicaragua, offering in a nutshell, a little of everything Nicaragua has to offer, from history to waterfalls and from volcanic trekking to horseback riding, all in an environment travelers routinely rave about as relaxing and delightful. You could feasibly

travel to and from the island in a single day, but such a short trip would be folly. Rather, allow at least two days and two nights (and an extra day and night if you'd like to hike a volcano, which is a full day activity in itself).

Note that travel in this region requires careful coordination of transport, as you can easily lose up to a half day waiting for boats and buses. Traveling around Ometepe is never easy; local transport is slow and erratic (especially on Sundays) and renting vehicles can be expensive.

La Isla de Ometepe

The twin-peaked island of Ometepe (Nahuatl for "two hills") is remarkably insulated from the rest of the country by the choppy waters of Lake Cocibolca. Ometepe's 38,000 proud residents live a mostly agrarian lifestyle, harvesting plantains, rice, tobacco, sorghum, sugarcane, corn, honey, and coffee on the slopes of the twin Cenozoic volcanoes. The two principal towns, Moyogalpa and Altagracia, are formerly sleepy commercial centers, port towns, and transportation hubs enjoying an upswing in ecotourism and accommodation.

Nicaragua's pre-Columbian history may have begun on and around Ometepe. According to legend, the Nahuatl people in modern-day Mexico fled the stronger Aztecs, guided southward by a vision of two volcanoes in the middle of a broad lake. Long before the Spanish arrived, the islanders considered Ometepe sacred ground, inhabited by gods of great power; even today the island remains awash in myths and legends, some of which date back to the days of the Nahuatl. Today's islanders prefer their home to what they call "over there." In 1957, as Volcán Concepción rumbled and threatened to erupt, the government ordered the islanders to evacuate Ometepe; they flatly refused, preferring to die on their island than live anywhere else.

At night, the slopes of the volcanoes echo with the deep roar of howler monkeys, and by day the air is filled with the sharp cry of the thousands of parakeets and *hurracas* (bright blue jays that scold you from the treetops). Ecologically, the island of Ometepe has been called the edge of the tropics, as a dividing line between tropical and dry falls right between the two volcanoes: Volcán Maderas is

A LOVE STORY – THE LEGEND OF OMETEPE AND ZAPATERA

It is said that long ago, neither Lake Cocibolca nor the islands existed. In their place was a broad green valley called Caopol, inhabited by animals that lived in thick forest. Not a single human lived in the forested valley, but the Chorotega, Chontales, Nagrandan, and Niquirano tribes all inhabited the edges of the valley, where they fought battles between tribes.

In the Niquirano tribe there was a lovely Indian maiden by the name of Ometepetl, who caught the eye of the young Nagrandan warrior named Nagrando. He fell deeply in love with her, and she with him. Their love remained a secret because the Niquiranos and Nagrandans were sworn enemies. The day Ometepetl's father learned of the illicit romance he grew furious and swore he would chase Nagrando to his death, rather than see his daughter marry a Nagrandan.

Ometepetl and Nagrando fled to the valley where they hid in the forest to escape the fury of Ometepetl's father. There they decided the only way they'd ever be able to have peace would be to die together. Ometepetl and Nagrando slit their wrists with a sharp blade and died in each others' arms.

Ometeptl, as death overcame her, leaned backwards, and her breasts swelled. The sadness that overwhelmed the valley caused the sky to darken and an intense rain to fall. The valley began to flood, and her breasts became the twin peaks of Concepción and Maderas. Nagrando grew into an island as well, the volcanic island of Zapatera, located halfway between the lands of the Nagrandan people and his love Ometepetl. Ometepetl's father and the men who accompanied him in the search to kill Nagrando all perished in the flood. They became the Isletas de Granada and the Solentiname archipelago.

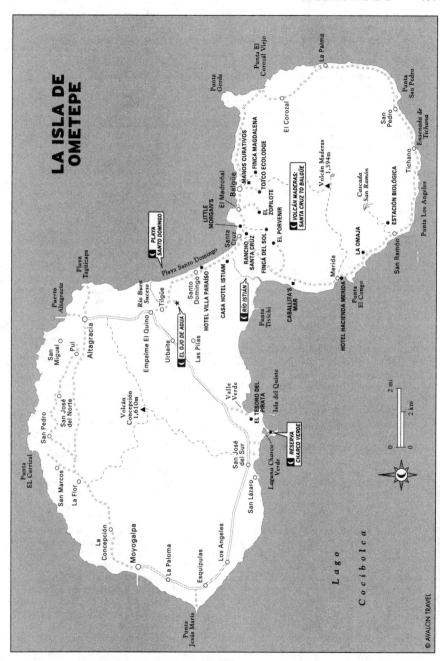

LA ISLA DE OMETEPE

Punta El Carrial

San Pedro

San Marcos

La Flor

San Miguel

Pul

San José del Norte

Altagracia

Puerto Altagracia

Playa Tagüizapa

Playa Santo Domingo

La Concepción

Moyogalpa

La Paloma

Esquipulas

Los Angeles

San Lázaro

San José del Sur

Punta Jesús María

Laguna Charco Verde

Isla del Quiste

EL TESORO DEL PIRATA

★ **RESERVA CHARCO VERDE**

Valle Verde

Volcán Concepción 1,610m ▲

Empalme El Quino

Urbaite

Las Pilas

★ **EL OJO DE AGUA**

Río Buen Suceso

Tilgüe

Santo Domingo

HOTEL VILLA PARAÍSO

CASA HOTEL ISTIAM

★ **PLAYA SANTO DOMINGO**

Playa Santo Domingo

◀ RÍO ISTIAN

Punta Tivichi

CABALLITA'S MAR ■

Punta El Congo

HOTEL HACIENDA MERIDA

Merida

San Ramón

LA OMAJA

ESTACIÓN BIOLÓGICA

Cascada San Ramón

Punta Los Angeles

Tichano

Ensenada de Tichana

Punta San Pedro

San Pedro

El Corozal

Volcán Maderas 1,394m ▲

FINCA MAGDALENA

TOTOCO ECOLODGE

EL ZOPILOTE

EL PORVENIR

FINCA DEL SOL

RANCHO SANTA CRUZ

✦ VOLCÁN MADERAS: SANTA CRUZ TO BALGÜE

Balgüe

MANOS CURATIVOS

Santa Cruz

LITTLE MORGAN'S

El Madroñal

Punta Gorda

Punta El Corozal Viejo

La Palma

LA ISLA DE OMETEPE

Lago Cocibolca

0   2 mi
0   2 km

© AVALON TRAVEL

LA ISLA DE OMETEPE

ALTERNATIVE TOURISM ON LA ISLA DE OMETEPE

There are numerous opportunities on the Oasis of Peace to get involved in community projects, learn about sustainable agriculture, and support everyday Nicaraguans with your tourism dollars. From long-standing solidarity partnerships to sustainable agriculture work and research projects, Ometepe awaits those looking for something a little different.

HOMESTAYS AND COMMUNITY TOURISM

There are a handful of community-based tourism projects, mostly in or around Moyogalpa, in which local residents provide accommodations and services to visitors.

At **Comunidad Indígina Urbaite-Las Pilas** (tel. 505/2569-4180, ask for Ulises Hernández) tourists can enjoy the flora and fauna of the island, live with local farmers and fishermen, and go on guided walking or fishing tours. More private lodging arrangements are available for $4 per person. To get to this community, take the bus from Moyogalpa to Urbaite and walk 15 minutes to Las Pilas.

In Moyogalpa **Escuela Hotel Teosintal** (tel. 505/2569-4105, tecuilturismo@intelnett. com, contact Migdalia Tórrez, $10 pp) aims to provide an additional source of income for the local producers and improve customer service and tourism services on the island. The theory is reinforced by the students' interaction with hotel guests. The hotel can arrange tours around the island or up to the volcanoes. The project, operating since 2005, can connect you with a network of agricultural cooperatives, many of which specialize in the production of sesame seeds for export. Escuela Hotel is located just north of the ENITEL office in Moyogalpa.

Moyogalpa is also home to **Pueblo Hotel** (tel. 505/2617-1405, contact Danelia López Ponce), a network of 25 women from various communities on Ometepe who produce organic fertilizer, conduct workshops on domestic violence, and host tourists in their homes. The goals of the program are to increase intercultural exchange (or *intercambio*), promote local culture, and share ecological knowledge and experience. The cost of a stay in one of the houses is $12 per person, which includes three meals per day and a complete immersion experience. Aside from traditional tourism activities offered elsewhere on the island, the Pueblo Hotel members can teach you traditional fishing techniques, take you to one of the local botanical gardens, and explain the incredible medicinal value of the Ometepe flora.

Experience authentic Nicaraguan living and invest in community tourism by spending a night with one of the **Puesta del Sol** (tel. 505/8619-0219, www.puestadelsol.org) families in the village of La Paloma, a few kilometers south of Moyogalpa. For $15 a night, you get three home-cooked meals, filtered water, and stories of *campesino* living to tell the folks back home. All bedrooms have a fan and access to toilets – don't worry, you won't be forced to use the latrine – but you'll share common spaces with dogs, chickens, and curious children. Basic Spanish would make your stay more enjoyable as the families involved don't speak much English.

VOLUNTEER OPPORTUNITIES

As you research your options, start helping by buying a bag of organic, shade-grown, fair trade certified **Café Oro de Ometepe** – coffee sold by the **Bainbridge-Ometepe Sisters Island Association** (www.bosia.org); the beans are grown at Finca Magdalena and profits are sent back to Nicaragua in the form of development projects around the town of Balgüe.

There are several projects on the island that lend a hand to youth at risk from around Nicaragua; a high level of Spanish is recommended, as this can be frustrating, difficult work (and equally rewarding, of course). In Altagracia is the residential center of **¡Sí a la Vida!** (Yes to Life, www.asalv.org), an organization that welcomes international volunteers who can expect to work with ex-street kids in sports, arts, handicrafts and tutoring, as well as specialized services like health care, construction, and agriculture. Volunteers accompany Nicaraguan staff on field trips to the streets and markets of Managua. A commitment of six months or more is usually required, and visitors are usually welcome. To volunteer, contact Tom Mueller (U.S. tel. 619/593-9567, vccmueller@hotmail.com). There's also the **Quincho Barrilete** chapter in the town of San José del Sur, which sometimes accepts volunteers.

In the community of San Lázaro, just to the east of Punta Jesús María, is the **Nuestros Pequeños Hermanos** (NPH, www.nphamigos.org) orphanage, run by Our Little Brothers and Sisters, who provide "a Christian family environment based on unconditional acceptance and love, sharing, working and responsibility." Adopt a godchild, come for a visit, or visit their website to apply to their volunteer program.

In the community of Santa Cruz, you'll find the **Fundación Entre Volcánes** (tel. 505/2569-4118), which runs projects all over Volcán Maderas. Contact Raúl Mayorga or Martín Juarez for details – Raúl works in Moyogalpa (two blocks south and one block east of the Shell station, tel. 505/8882-5562) and Martín is based out of the town of Los Angeles (Ometepe, not California).

In 2007, the folks at Hacienda Mérida founded the **Ometepe Bilingual School** (tel. 505/8868-8973, contact Alvaro Molina, alvaronica@gmail.com, www.hmerida.com), a free English-language school in the rural community of Mérida, on the southwestern side of the island. It is a before- and after-school program which children attend on their own initiative, in addition to their five-hour days at the public school. The school also provides oatmeal and granola porridge for all of the kids after classes. Methods of teaching include bilingual card games, movies, text and grammar book activities, singing, and field trips. The school hosts international volunteers and student groups and individuals come from around the world. You can teach English to local elementary and high school students. There is a two-week minimum commitment, a $150 fee, and accommodations with a local family, or in the dormitories at Hacienda Mérida.

The **Maderas Rainforest Conservancy** (formerly the Ometepe Biological Field Station, Miami tel. 305-666-9932, info@maderasrfc.org, www.maderasrfc.org) is located near Merida, on the slopes of Volcán Maderas. They manage numerous forward-thinking conservation projects in surrounding communities, including a botanical garden on the lake shore to serve as a refuge for endangered Blue Morpho butterflies and they operate a field school for birding groups and research students. Tourists are welcome to sample the restaurant or stay at the station for a small fee.

AGRI-TOURISM AND EARNING YOUR KEEP

To learn everything there is to know about organic agriculture, permaculture, and horticulture, spend a week (or four) at **Finca Bona Fide** (about 300 meters past Finca Magdalena, tel. 505/8616-4566, www.projectbonafide.com). Chris and Michael run a beautiful farm, have 18-day organic agriculture workshops (free for locals), have a nutritional kitchen in Balgüe, where they feed 70 kids breakfast every morning, and offer farm work internships and volunteer opportunities. Enjoy rustic lodging and three meals a day for $5-8 depending on how long you stay. The view from the communal tree shower hidden in the bushes is alone worth the work.

Similar agricultural work arrangements can be made at **La Finca Ecologica El Zopilote** (tel. 505/8419-0246, www.ometepezopilote.com), where volunteers are expected to stay for at least a week and receive a 20 percent discount on lodging, but have to cook for themselves. Be sure to check out the **Fincas Verdes** network (www.fincasverdes.com) to get a lowdown on the various agricultural and conservation ventures being offered on the island.

an extinct volcano whose crater is filled with a shallow lagoon and whose slopes are carpeted with more tropical and humid species, including actual cloud forest at the top. Concepción is an active volcano whose slopes are covered with tropical dry forest species like *guacimo* and *guanacaste*. Underneath the greenery, however, is fire. Beginning December 8, 1880, Volcán Concepción erupted with such force that lava and smoke flowed out of the crater for nearly a year. It was this eruption that created some of its more distinctive features visible today, like the Lava de Urbaite, Peña Bruja (a broad cliff visible from Altagracia), and Peña de San Marcos. Concepción erupted again in 1883, launching large rocks from the crater, and again in 1889 and 1902, ruining crops in Rivas. In 2005, Volcán Concepción has rumbled, fumed, and ejected tons of volcanic ash, smoke, and debris, in spectacular, frightening eruptions. There were also mini-eruptions in 2007 and 2009.

Plan carefully before you leave. Ometepe has one ATM machine that accepts VISA cards only and is closed on Sundays; bring cash and in particular, small bills. Transport can also be problematic and sporadic.

MOYOGALPA

Moyogalpa (Nahuatl for "place of the mosquitoes") is Ometepe's largest commercial center, and it's not that buggy, though it's a bit bland. There is plenty of fine accomodation here, but we recommend basing yourself outside of the town to experience the more isolated sides of the island.

Sights and Entertainment

At the top of the hill, Moyogalpa's **Catholic church** is charming, with a bell tower just high enough over the tree line to afford you a great view of the town, coastline, lake, and the statue of a boy urinating.

La Sala Arqueológica (or El Museo), located toward the top of main street, has a small but interesting collection of pre-Columbian artifacts found on the island over the years. Owner and amateur historian Herman García and his wife Ligia are very knowledgeable about island history and lore, and can point you to local artisan communities. The store in front of the museum sells contemporary works. Get oriented at the office of **Fundación Entre Volcanes** (across the street from the Moyogalpa ENITEL office), a small NGO involved in several community projects across the island; staff may be able to help you find ways to volunteer your time while on the island. They also have some representative handicrafts of the region on display.

On the main street, the **Ranchón El Chele** is a popular place to drink and relax. **Disco Johnny Bar,** just north of the dock, and **Disco Cocibolca,** near El Indio Viejo a few blocks east of the dock, also vie for the dancing crowd on the weekends.

The town of Moyogalpa celebrates its patron saint, Santa Ana, June 23–26. The **Baile de las Inditas** is performed in much the same way as the indigenous dance it replaced, with traditional costumes and the resonant sound of the marimba.

Accommodations

Be sure to consider a homestay in Moyogalpa and surrounding villages. In town, the best budget-traveler option is ◖ **El Indio Viejo** (three blocks east of the dock, one south, tel. 505/2569-4262), offering 17 dorm beds for $3 each, $10–14 for a private room for up to four people with clean beds, private bath, and fan. This is where backpackers turn for the familiar funkiness extended from Granada's popular Hospedaje Central; take a hammock or camp outside for less than $2. The bar/*comedor* has a hip world music soundtrack, satellite TV, movie lounge, washing machine and book exchange. Volcano hiking arrangements ($10–15 per group) can be made with Will. Artists are welcome to add to the organic murals and may even receive free lodging. The rooms at **Hotel Casa Familiar** (half a block south of main street, tel. 505/2459-4240) are similar and the establishment is clean and comfortable.

Hotel Restaurant La Bahía (located across from the Shell Station, tel. 505/823-5743, $4 pp) offers second-story rooms with tons of light and air, and a view of Concepción from the back porch. **Hotelito Aly** (a few blocks up from the dock on the left, tel. 505/2569-4196) has 11 rooms set around a garden patio and a decent restaurant that serves three meals. Rates are $6 per person with shared bath, $7 private bath, and up to $40 for nicer rooms with air-conditioning.

Easily recommendable is **(€ Hotel Ometepetl** (a few blocks up from the dock on the right, tel. 505/2569-4276, $12–25 private bath, a/c) whose staff is friendly and can help you with the logistics of preparing your trip (guides, cars, etc.). They have a gift shop on-site and accept credit cards. And the newer **American Café & Hotel** (100 meters up the hill on the right, tel. 505/8645-7193, $30 d) has five spotless and spacious rooms with high ceilings, hot water, and gringo-style breakfasts.

Food

All the aforementioned accommodations serve food, the nicest of which is found at the restaurant at Ometepetl, with meals for about $5. **La Casa Familiar** serves traditional Nicaraguan meals. **El Indio Viejo** offers spaghetti, burritos, and other favorites, but more importantly serves a large breakfast—important if you're off to hike a volcano. Doña Esperanza Jimenez, a half-block east of the park, serves huge, inexpensive meals as well, but not breakfast.

(€ Los Ranchitos (four blocks up the hill from the dock, then half a block south, tel. 505/2569-4112, open 7 A.M.–9 P.M. daily) is a favorite among locals and Peace Corps volunteers; its huge menu features surprisingly good pizza (large pie for only $6). Not far behind is **Yogi's Cafe and Sports Bar** (half a block south of El Indio Viejo, tel. 505/2403-6951), dishing out burgers, reggae music, and movies on a big projector screen.

Services

The sole ATM on the island is inside Banco ProCredito (up the hill on the right). But be forewarned, the machine only accepts Visa and is closed on Sunday. To be safe, bring plenty of cash to the island and make sure you have small bills; both dollars and córdobas are accepted. One of the few places that takes travelers checks is Hotel Ometepetl (minus 10 percent). The ENITEL office is located 1.5 blocks east of the main street and is closed on Sundays. The Moyogalpa hospital (tel. 505/2569-4247) is three blocks east of the park along the highway out of town. For Internet, go to the **Arcia Cyber Café,** which is air-conditioned and open 8 A.M.–8 P.M. daily, or continue up the main street and use one of the computers at the museum.

NEAR MOYOGALPA
San Marcos

Just northeast of Moyogalpa along the "back way around the island" is the small community of San Marcos, home to a women's group that makes and sells ceramic pieces, including authentic replicas of pre-Columbian art. Ask around in town for the *taller de artesanía.*

Punta Jesús María

The long, sandy peninsula of Punta Jesús María is lovely for swimming and relaxing in the dry season, and submerges in the rainy season. The restaurant will give you a beer to take with you on your walk up the kilometer-long sandbar with waves lapping at both sides. This is a good place to watch the sun set or enjoy a meal after a swim in the lake. Owner Joaquín Salazar may let you set up your tent on the beach and spend the night with the crickets. The entrance is a long driveway just north of the town of Esquipulas that takes 15 minutes to walk. Take the bus and ask to get off at the picturesquely named **Punta de la Paloma** (Dove's Point).

(€ Reserva Charco Verde

At Charco Verde you can swim in the lake accompanied only by the call of the monkeys in the treetops and the whir of colorful birds. This is still a relatively wild area, with enough tall trees remaining to harbor some very exciting wildlife. The entire area has been cordoned off to prevent development, leaving this cove an oasis of peace to be shared by you and the monkeys (who, incidentally, do their own part by throwing excrement from the trees at intruders). Pay $0.50 to walk along the Charco Verde nature reserve, a short trail where you may see (or at least hear) howler monkeys, birds, and other wildlife. Bring bug spray.

The three local hotels are each owned by a different Riveras sibling. Each rents horses and offers boat and kayak trips along the shoreline, fishing trips, and outings to Isla de Quiste. The family owns a cattle farm just up the beach you can also visit. **Hotel y Restaurante Charco Verde** (tel. 505/8887-9302, www.charcoverde. com.ni) is next to the reserve with easy trail access; a cute cabana with tile floors, oodles of windows, and front porch costs $35–45 for a private bath and air-conditioning. If you've been in-country a while, you'll appreciate the bedside reading lamps. Reservations are recommended during the high season.

Up the beach toward Moyogalpa, Rubén Riveras runs a family-style guesthouse on the beach called **Hotel Finca Venecia** (tel. 505/8872-7668, $27–35 for cabins, $7.50 pp for rooms with private bath). The hammock pavilion is quiet and, during the high season, not a bad place to spend the night (for $2) when all the beds are taken. The restaurant serves well-prepared pasta, chicken, fish, and beef dishes. From his place, it's an easy walk along the shore into the reserve of Charco Verde and to Playa Balcón.

Right next door is **La Posada de Chico Largo** (tel. 505/8886-4069, chicolargo@ yahoo.com, $4 dorm beds, $5 pp for room with private bath), the most economic of the three. Despite their nickname, "Los Diablos" are accommodating hosts and their restaurant is good. Ask about La Mirador del Diablo trail.

Isla de Quiste

Really just an islet, Quiste is overgrown and vacant, and a scant 100 meters long—a perfect place to pitch a tent and camp. Many Moyogalpa hotels will help you make arrangements with someone with a small boat.

The beach at Charco Verde is one of Nicaragua's most beautiful.

THE LEGEND OF CHICO LARGO

Over the years, this famous legend has taken two forms. In the first version, an old man by the name of Chico Largo lives in the wetlands of Charco Verde. There he appears to people at night and offers to make a deal with them: wealth and prosperity during the entirety of their lives, in exchange for their souls, which upon death, he converts into cattle. Many of the cows on the island, then, are the souls of Ometepe's previous generation, which opted for a life of decadence instead of hard work.

In the second version, the cacique Nicarao is buried with his throne made of solid gold along the edge of the Charco Verde. In this version, Chico Largo is a descendant of Nicarao and roams the area guarding and protecting Nicarao's tomb. Chico Largo, since he is already guarding the tomb, has now taken it upon himself to guard the forest, animals, and fish as well, and is the primary protector of Ometepe's wildlife.

Otherwise, in Charco Verde, Rubén Riveras will drop you off on the island in his motorboat and pick you up again later (or the next day) for about $15, depending on the number of travelers. But you can just as easily strike a deal with any of the locals in the small communities to the north of Moyogalpa, like Barrio de los Pescadores.

Valle Verde and El Tesoro del Pirata

The pirate's treasure is, in this case, an isolated retreat on a wide, black-sand beach rather off the beaten track. Reach the cove by hiking through the Charco Verde reserve or by getting off the bus at the entrance just beyond the community of San José del Sur, then walking 15 minutes or so from the highway, following the signs. **El Tesoro** (tel. 505/8832-2429) is located just far enough off the beaten track

to encourage the local wildlife to whoop it up for you. The view is excellent, as is the swimming and boating, and several readers claim they serve the best tasting fish on the island. Pay $25 for a cabana with air-conditioning and private bath, and $2 per person to camp with a $6 tent rental. Group discounts are available.

ALTAGRACIA

The second largest community on Ometepe and an important island port, Altagracia is more picturesque than Moyogalpa, but definitely plays second fiddle with regard to attractions and services. In 2000, *National Geographic* filmed a documentary about vampire bats here—and while there are indeed many vampire bats, they are a threat only to the local chickens, which the bats like to suck dry by hanging from the chickens' nerveless feet.

Sights and Entertainment

Altagracia's *fiestas patronales,* in celebration of San Diego, are held November 12–18. In addition to the traditional festivities, the **Baile de las Ramas** (Dance of the Branches) is a major component of the celebration. The dancers tear off smaller branches of the *guanacaste* tree, and hold them to their heads while dancing to imitate the worker *zompopo* (leaf-cutter) ants carrying leaves off to the ant hills.

El Museo Ometepe (open 9 A.M.–5 P.M. daily, $1) has a few exhibits of the flora, fauna, and archaeology of Ometepe, including statues and ceramic pieces unearthed around the island. The church courtyard makes for a peaceful retreat with a few interesting pre-Columbian stone idols for added irony. You might get yelled at by a group of bright green parakeets that make their home in the roof of the dilapidated old church (next to the freshly painted new church). Across the street in the central park, you'll find the **artesanía cooperative,** comprised of eight local artisans who take turns working in the shop. Some of the pieces are original and exhibit the pride that the islanders have for their home.

From the park, walk east down a sandy

LA ISLA DE OMETEPE

road about 30 minutes to the bay of **Playa Tagüizapa,** a fine sandy beach for swimming. You can pick up supplies in town for a picnic and make a lazy day of it. Located three kilometers north of the town of Altagracia, the port has boat service between Granada and San Carlos (Río San Juan). The road that leads to the port is shady and makes a nice, short walk—allow about 45 minutes each way. On the way, you'll pass Playa Paso Real, an out-of-the-way bathing beach you'll likely have all to yourself. If you're heading to the port to catch the boat to Granada or San Carlos, it's worthwhile to speak with the owner of Hotel Central. They offer pickup truck service to the port, so you don't have to carry all your luggage that far. Be aware that when the water is too rough, the boat may not show up at Altagracia, preferring to hug the eastern shore of the lake.

Accommodations

Altagracia's accommodations are all located within a block of each other, so feel free to walk around and compare before settling in. One of the cheapest and friendliest choices, **Hospedaje Ortiz** (a block or so from the central plaza) was recommended by several readers. More popular, **【 Hotel Central** (two blocks south of the park, tel. 505/2552-8770) is a traveler favorite, with a nicely furnished reading room, small garden, and friendly staff (though some have complained of overpriced tours and basic services). Expect to pay $6 per person for a private bath and fan, slightly less for a shared bath, and $7 per person for a private cabin out back.

Hotel Castillo (tel. 505/8475-7455, $4 pp shared bath, $10 private bath) is similar and sports one of the nicer bars in town. Across from the park, **Posada Cabrera** (tel. 505/8664-2788, www.posadacabrera.com, $5 pp) has a pleasant feel, nice staff, and a green backyard. The rooms, however, are extra small, and not as private (the walls don't go all the way up to the ceiling).

Try a homestay with a local family, courtesy of **La Peñita** (tel. 505/8972-6299, famrampaiza@yahoo.es, $3.50 pp). The friendly owner has bikes to rent and will take you on a guided tour of the island. To get there, take the bus from Altagracia to El Quino (at the fork for the isthmus) and walk 300 meters north. This is about as close as you can stay to El Ojo de Agua.

Services

The Camara de Turismo in the park has decent information about the island. The ENITEL phone office and the post office are found diagonally across from the park on the same corner as the Museo Ometepe. The Casa Cural, located on the south side of the park, has six computers and Internet service Monday–Friday. There's also one computer at Tienda Fashion, a block south of the park. You'll have no privacy there, as the computer is located in the middle of the store, but it's open late and on weekends. Check out the crafts while you're waiting.

The small Centro de Salud (on the southeast corner of the park, tel. 505/2552-6089) can treat patients 24 hours a day, but for serious injuries go to the hospital at Moyogalpa (get the owner of your hotel to take you in a vehicle).

【 EL OJO DE AGUA

Located near the town of Tilgue, on the northern part of the isthmus, El Ojo de Agua consists of crystal clear spring-fed waters captured in two natural, stone pools set in the middle of a gorgeous and colorful botanical garden. Swim in the revitalizing waters the way the Nahautls probably did, then climb out to drip-dry in the sun. It's essentially the only swimming hole on the island other than the lake itself, and the water is the cleanest you'll find anywhere. Your $2 entrance fee helps with maintenance, as does whatever you pay to take home some organic, herbal tea. Snacks are available at the little bar/shop, but nothing fancy.

【 PLAYA SANTO DOMINGO

Playa Santo Domingo is the narrow wedge of land that connects the volcanoes of Concepción and Maderas, the product of rich volcanic soil

© JOSHUA BERMAN

Playa Santo Domingo on Isla de Ometepe

that washed down from the slopes of both volcanoes over millennia, gradually connecting
the two islands. The several-kilometer-long
stretch of black sand on the northern part of
the Istián Isthmus has some of Ometepe's most
upscale (relatively speaking) accommodations.
The swimming can be nice, but with the near-
constant onshore breeze, the water is usually
choppy and it can get windy. If there are loads
of *chayules* (gnats) when you visit, consider
staying on another part of the island, away
from the water, where these harmless but annoying little bugs are nearly nonexistent. Also
note that in the rainy season water levels rise
and the sandy beach all but disappears.

Accommodations and Food

Rent a charming stone cabin at **☾ Villa
Paraíso** (tel. 505/2563-4675, www.hotelvil-
laparaiso.com.ni, $63–72). Rates are double for
rooms with private bath and air-conditioning;
suites feature air-conditioning, fridge, satellite TV, and hot water. The breezy waterfront
restaurant is fabulous. Call early for reservations as the place fills up quickly, especially on

weekends and holidays. Next door, **Hotel Finca
Santo Domingo** (tel. 505/8927-2019, $25–30)
is less exciting, and rooms are simple and uninspired though some are air-conditioned.

Two kilometers farther down the beach
toward Maderas **Casa Hotel Istiam** (tel.
505/2569-4276) provides enormous value,
and its beach is clean and pleasant. The rooms
are so-so but cheap ($5 pp shared bath, $8 pp
private bath) and the location is spectacular,
with an impressive view of both volcanos from
the second-floor deck. There is one $25 dou-
ble room with air-conditioning and private
bath. The service is friendly and the restaurant good. Make reservations in Moyogalpa
at Hotel Ometepetl as they sometimes fill up.
Camping is possible.

☾ RÍO ISTIÁN

The paddle trip in a kayak or canoe up the
Río Istián is best early in the morning or during sunset but is worthwhile at any time. You
slip into the still waters of a marshy isthmus
deep with shadow from the tree canopy and
raucous with the sounds of birds, all under the

HIKING OMETEPE'S VOLCANOES

Ometepe's twin peaks are a siren's call for many an intrepid backpacker, and hiking one or both is an intimate way to get to know the island. But do not underestimate the difficulty of the challenge before you: Both peaks are equally dangerous, for different reasons.

Volcán Concepción (1,610 meters) is the more arduous climb, and large parts of the hike are treeless, rocky scrambles. Don't be surprised if the volcano is off-limits the day you arrive, as Concepción is a quite active volcano, and has spewn gas and ash on several occasions in the past five years, as recently as December 2009. As such, the authorities prohibit climbs when the seismologists show the conditions aren't safe.

As you reach the volcanic cone, the wind that buffets you is cold until you reach the crater lip, where the volcano's hot, sulphurous gas pours forth (the clash of hot and cold air is responsible for the almost permanent cloud cover at the top of the volcano). On the off chance the clouds thin, the view from the peak is unforgettable.

Most travelers hike Concepción by way of the towns La Concha or La Flor, and there is an eastern approach from Altagracia that takes you through an impressive amount of monkey-inhabited forest before hitting the exposed section. Allow a full day for the hike: five exhausting hours up and four knee-shattering hours down. Take plenty of water, food, sun protection, and good shoes and socks to protect your feet.

Volcán Maderas (1,394 meters) is more accessible, and the volcano is dormant, if not extinct (in fact, there's a forested lake within the crater). It is thus more frequently hiked, but remains equally dangerous and is responsible for at least two deaths since 2005. Volán Maderas is a national park above 400 meters, and for good reason: It's really beautiful up there. When you reach the crater lip, the final descent down to the mist-swept crater lake requires a rope and should not be attempted without proper safety equipment – make sure your guide packs one.

The most commonly used trail to the top starts at Finca Magdalena; if you're not staying at the Finca Magdalena you must pay a trail fee to enter and pass through the coffee plantations. You'll pass a petroglyph or two on the way up. The trail, unfortunately, has seen better days. Lack of appropriate maintenance has made a knee-deep mud pit out of much of the upper stretch. Allow four hours to go up and two or three to come back down, and count on spending an hour at the crater lake (58 minutes of which you'll spend deciding whether or not to jump in the cold, mushy-bottom *laguna*). The other, more strenuous ascent leaves from Mérida. The first three hours are an almost vertical ascent, leveling off into the upper reaches that one hiker calls "enchanted." Hotel Hacienda Mérida offers this excursion, and can arrange transport back from Magdalena if you choose to descend the other side.

reflection of two volcanic peaks. **Caballito's Mar** (5 km from Santa Cruz, turn right at the signs and follow the dirt road to the lake, fernando@caballitosmar.com, www.caballitosmar.com, tel. 505/2451-2093 or 505/2961-7296) rents kayaks by the hour and offers a fun three-hour guided trip ($20) in which they'll point out the kingfishers, white herons, turtles, and caimanes (crocodiles). You can easily stay in their basic dormitory ($5 pp) or just have a meal (traditional Nicaraguan and lots of lake fish, about $3). You can also rent kayaks at **Hacienda Mérida** or Charco Verde ($5/hr). Allow half a day for the adventure, and bring sunscreen, snacks, and plenty of water. The shorter paddle to Isla el Congo, just offshore, is nice as well, but beware the monkeys!

◖ VOLCÁN MADERAS: SANTA CRUZ TO BALGÜE

Maderas is now officially a national park, which will hopefully encourage preservation of the thick forests. Maderas is a pleasant volcano to climb, since you hike in the shade, and

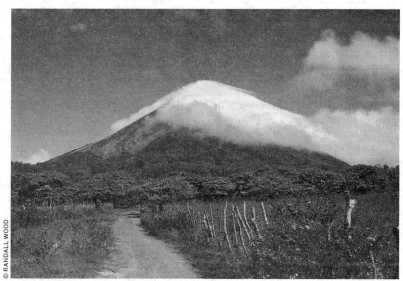

Volcán Concepción is a mile high and very active.

On either peak, a guide is *required*, and for very good reason: The "trails" as such are unmarked, and branch dozens of times. One death on Maderas was simply an experienced hiker who got lost in the crevices of the volcano's middle slopes and succumbed to dehydration. We recommend using a trained guide from the **Union Guias de Ometepe** (tel. 505/8827-7714, ugometepe@yahoo.com, www.ugometepe.com). Forming a professional collective has enabled the local guides to share knowledge, formalize their training, and get some sharp-looking uniforms to boot. You can hire a guide for $10-20 per group of five people, enriching your trip, giving something back to the community, supporting conservation efforts, and oh yeah, getting back down again safely.

is less demanding than its truly active twin, but a guide is now obligatory since a pair of hikers got lost and eventually perished on the mountain. But even if you're not a peak bagger, there's lots to do here, starting with a visit to the fields of old petroglyphs, a relic of the island's Nahuatl past; dipping into the natural springs at Ojo de Agua; sunning and splashing at the beach at Santo Domingo; mountain biking down the rutted roads to take a coffee tour, horseback ride, or kayak trip. In addition, a host of unique places to stay (many based on working farms, some using permaculture and principles of environmental sustainability) are fun and interesting.

Santa Cruz and El Madroñal
Its location at the intersection of two main roads makes **Rancho Santa Cruz** (tel. 505/8884-9894, santacruzometepe@gmail. com, www.santacruzometepe.com) an excellent base from which to explore in either direction, as your chances of catching a bus or taxi on this transportationally-challenged island

© RANDALL WOOD

double. Spacious rooms go for $10–25, nice dorms with good air circulation for $5 per person. The restaurant serves granola, yogurt, and pancake breakfasts for around $2 and a selection of vegetarian options including pastas and curries for $4–6 for lunch and dinner. You can rent bikes here for $5 a day, and they can arrange horseback riding on request.

Let the lapping waves of Lake Cocibolca rock you to sleep at **Little Morgan's** (tel. 505/8949-7074, $6–8 treehouse dorm beds, $30 private cabanas), named after the charismatic Irish owner's young son. Chill to the satellite tunes, play a game of pool, or simply hang out in one of the rancho's dreamy hammocks. From the village of Santa Cruz, a short walk down toward the water.

A 10-minute walk up the trail from the village of El Madroñal leads to **La Finca Ecologica El Zopilote** (tel. 505/8369-0644, www.ometepezopilote.com, $2.50–10 pp for camping, dorm beds, and private cabins), a hillside cluster of thatch huts and platforms run by a few peace-loving Italians and their pack of hound dogs. Meals are not provided, rather fix your own in the open-air communal kitchen; the compound has compost toilets, an artisan's workshop, and a clay oven for bread and pizza. Check out the organic products in the gift shop, from coffee to liqueur, and enjoy the permaculture plantation throughout the grounds. Tents for camping are also available. Volunteers willing to work on the farm for at least a week get a 20 percent discount and all the fruit they can eat. Pizza nights on Tuesdays, Thursdays and Fridays are a hit with expats and guests.

Balgüe

Balgüe is your base for hiking Volcán Maderas, a worthwhile endeavor, but it has increasingly good lodging of its own. The stalwart of course is Finca Magdalena up on the skirts of the volcano itself, with petroglyphs and a compelling history, but various international newcomers are providing a much greater range of options now.

Totoco Eco-Lodge (1.5 km up a steep hill from the secondary school in Balgüe, tel.

505/8425-2027, www.totoco.com.ni) is an ecologically-sensitive masterpiece. The property sits on a working 15-acre organic farm and was crafted of drought-resistant plants, compost toilets, passive cooling, and solar power. If "off the grid" means nothing to you, consider the awe-inspiring view of cloud-shrouded Volcán Concepción from your bedroom window. Four quirky cabins with private porches, quality mattresses, and hot water will set you back $77 plus tax and up; the budget minded can stay in the open palm-roofed dorms for $8 per bed. The restaurant serves delicious three-course meals and provides excellent service.

In the same spirit, but smaller scale and homier, are the cabanas at **Finca del Sol** (tel. 505/8364-6394, hotelfincadelsol.blinkweb. com, $37–47). The whole place is sun-powered and ecofriendly, including the composting toilets, and the Finca is overall, a bit less mainstream. Better yet, over a home-cooked meal, let your welcoming hosts Cristiano and Sheri tell you themselves about constructing by hand with natural materials, all without use of a vehicle.

Así Es Mi Tierra (tel. 505/8943-1997, www. mitierraometepe.com, $5 pp) in the town of Balgüe proper is a family-run *hospedaje* with seven clean rooms. Fernando and his family can rent you a mountain bike ($1/hr) or a horse ($4/hr), and can easily arrange transportation to all the local hot spots in their minibus.

At **Eduardo's Comedor** (located at the entrance to the elementary school) both vegetarians and meat lovers find fresh meals filled with love for $1–3.

Finca Magdalena

Just uphill from the town of Balgüe is the famed **Finca Magdalena** (tel. 505/8880-2041, www.fincamagdalena.com, $1.50 to string up your hammock or camp, $3 raised platform in a dorm, $8–15 private cabin, and more expensive cottages), a 24-family coffee cooperative established in the 1980s. The place tends towards austere, but welcoming and sincere. Everyone showers in the same bracing cold water piped directly from a spring up the slope,

NAHUATLS AND THE PETROGLYPHS OF OMETEPE

In the days of the Nahuatls, Volcán Maderas was called Coatlán, "the place where the sun lives," and Concepción was known as Choncoteciguatepe, "the brother of the moon," or Mestliltepe, "the peak that menstruates." In the lush forests of the lower slopes of the two volcanoes, the Nahuatls performed complicated rituals in honor of many different gods: Catligüe, the goddess of fertility; Ecatl, the god of air; Migtanteot, the god of death; Tlaloc, the god of soil; and Xochipillo, the goddess of happiness. The Nahuatl gods were all-powerful and vindictive, and spent their days in the land where the sun rises doing what all-powerful gods do best – feeding on human blood.

The concept of a soul was an important part of the Nahuatl belief system, as were the concepts of an afterlife and some form of reincarnation. Their calendar consisted of 18 months of 20 days each, for a total of a 360-day calendar year. They believed in a cycle of catastrophic events that recurred every 52 years, and according to that cycle the Nahuatls would store grains and water, in case this were the year.

Scattered around the island of Ometepe, but principally on the north and northeastern slopes of Volcán Maderas, are the statues and petroglyphs, carved around the year A.D. 300, that paid homage to the Nahuatl gods. Spirals are a consistent theme, representing perhaps calendars or the Nahuatl concept of time and space. It has been suggested the spirals may

Ometepe petroglyphs

also represent the islands themselves, or that the twin-spiral shape of Ometepe gave the island even more significance to the islanders, as it fit in with their ideas about the cosmos. More mundane images can also be identified in the carved rocks: monkeys, humans hunting deer, and a couple in coitus, suggesting Nahuatl wishes for prosperity and fertility, or just a bit of monkey business.

© POUTINE/COMMONS.WIKIMEDIA.ORG

and the evening meal is cooked over a wood fire. Horseback rides and coffee and petroglyph tours (45 min., $3–4 pp) are all availale, and you can purchase fresh roasted coffee and fresh honey—a good way to help support the farm. Magdalena is on the way up the trail to Volcán Maderas; guided trips leave pretty much every morning.

To get to Finca Magdalena, take the bus to Balgüe and follow the signs along the 20-minute walk up the road to the farm (arrive before dark), or take a taxi or minibus. Five daily buses depart the dock in Moyogalpa, the last at 3:30 P.M.

VOLCÁN MADERAS: MÉRIDA TO SAN RAMÓN

Some 250 families fish and farm on Ometepe's least-visited shoreline, but it remains the "dark side of the moon:" little visited but equally, if not more, compelling. Beyond San Ramón, the lonely east coast of Maderas is one of the most isolated spots in Nicaragua, connected tentatively by a poor excuse of a road with no bus service. The locals are not used to receiving guests. It's potentially feasible to circumnavigate the entire volcano on foot or on a mountain bike (about 12 or 6 hours, respectively). The coast of Tichana hides lots of unexplored areas, including, reportedly, caves full of paintings as well as some petroglyphs near Corozal.

Albergue Ecológico El Porvenir (tel. 505/8447-9466, $8 pp private bath) is a peaceful hillside retreat with modern buildings, screened windows, volcano views, and lush tropical grounds. It's less ecological than it pretends, but you will nonetheless awaken to the sounds of the jungle. Contact them directly, or make your reservations in advance through Hotel Central in Altagracia or Hotel Villa Paraíso on Playa Santo Domingo.

◖ Hotel Hacienda Mérida (tel. 505/8868-8973 or 505/8894-2551 www.hmerida.com, $6 dorm, $20–28 d with private bath, $3 pp campsite, plus tax) is a friendly lakeside compound where second-floor balconies have views of the volcanoes and the lake. They rent bikes and kayaks ($15 for the duration of your stay) and can arrange hikes, fishing trips, and horseback riding; breakfast and dinner buffets ($4.50 and 5.75 pp plus tax) are crafted with whole foods, many from the garden. Internet is available. The Nicaraguan owner, Alvaro Molina, speaks perfect English and is both passionate advocate for and walking encyclopedia of Ometepe social causes. A rigorous and none-too-obvious trail leads up to Maderas's crater lagoon from Merida; you can go down the way you came, or you can descend to the other side and emerge at Finca Magdalena or Finca Zopilote. But you absolutely must hire a guide, bring food and water, and get an early morning start: This a serious hike for pros only.

Despite the shabby exterior, travelers give good reviews of the food at **Restaurante El Pescadito,** just outside Hacienda Mérida. Huge plates of fresh fish or pasta will set you back $3–4. Service can be slow as this is a one-man band. The friendly owner has been known

to take repeat diners out on his boat to snag the catch of the day and then cook it up.

For more privacy and more money, try **La Omaja** (300 meters past Merida, tel. 505/885-1124, laomaja@hotmail.com, www.laomaja.com, $45). A bit isolated, it offers characterless cabins with panoramic lake views and all kinds of activities and services available.

Farther down the road is locally-owned **Monkey Island Hostel** (tel. 505/8844-1529 or 8652-0971, www.freewebs.com/monkeysisland, monkeysislandjancinto1@hotmail.com, $4–20), with friendly staff, boxy concrete rooms, and lousy feng shui.

Cascada San Ramón

The most popular attraction by far on Ometepe's south side is the stunning 180-meter Cascada San Ramón waterfall. The signs say it is a three-kilometer trail, but it's likely more than that: allow three hours minimum, as the three kilometers are vertical. You can drive a four-wheel drive vehicle part way up to the water tank to skip past

The San Ramón waterfall is worth the hike.

Ferries to Ometepe leave from San Jorge.

© RANDALL WOOD

the exposed water pipes and head straight to the prettiest section of the hike. Otherwise, walk through avocado, mango, and lemon trees and up to a small parking area and hydroelectric plant. Once you enter the lush canyon, the humidity rises. You may have to scramble over some river rocks and at times the trail seems to disappear before it emerges a few meters ahead. At the waterfall you can bathe in a shallow pool.

Maderas Rainforest Conservancy

Four kilometers up the road from Merida, in the tiny village of San Ramón, the Maderas Rainforest Conservancy (formerly the Ometepe Biological Field Station, Miami tel. 305-666-9932, info@maderasrfc.org, www.maderasrfc.org), is a facility visited by student groups and researchers from all over the world. In addition to being active in numerous forward-thinking conservation projects in surrounding communities, MRC operates a field school on the volcano's slopes for undergraduate and graduate students in primatology, ecology, bat ecology, botany, and other biological sciences. Tourists are welcome to sample the restaurant or stay at the station for a small fee.

GETTING THERE

Note that Lake Cocibolca can get rough when the wind is high, at which times the larger boats are more comfortable. Avoid the roughest seas by traveling early morning and late evening, and sit near the center of the ship where the rocking is slightest. Don't worry—when you pull into port, the men climbing the rails and jumping aboard are not pirates, they are taxi drivers in San Jorge or bag porters in Moyogalpa.

By Boat from San Jorge

Boats from San Jorge on the mainland sail to Moyogalpa daily. Thankfully, a few new safer boats have joined the old junky fleet. They compete to transport the island's plantain crop in addition to passengers.

The *Ferry Ometepe,* a big steel boat with radar and life jackets and from whose roof you can travel in the fresh air is one of the better old ships. A newer, larger, cheaper, and faster option than the old junk ferries is *El Che Guevara* (departure from San Jorge to Moyogalpa 7 A.M. and 4 P.M.; departure from Moyogalpa to San Jorge 8:30 A.M. and 5:30 P.M.). *El Che* charges $16.50 to bring a small pickup truck and $14 for a small car; motorbikes cost under $3.

Rey de Cocibolca, a 1,300-passenger, four-story boat built in the Netherlands, now plies the waters of Lake Nicaragua between San Jorge on the mainland and San Jose del Sur on Ometepe, a little town soon to become a big town thanks to the traffic. A one-way trip costs $2.50, any deck. This boat departs from San Jose del Sur to the mainland at 7:30 A.M. and 3:20 P.M.; from San Jorge to the island at 9:30 A.M. and 5:00 P.M. Bringing your vehicle costs less than $10 and the driver goes for free. For more information on the boat schedule, contact tel. 505/8691-3669 or 505/8833-4773.

The rest of the old San Jorge fleet ride lower to the water and thus provide a bumpier ride. These boats are independently owned and, unfortunately, rarely give honest information about the others; so if you're told, "The next boat doesn't leave for four hours," keep asking. Each company posts a sign with its own schedule; there is no main sign listing all the different times. **Volcano Lake Tours** (office near the port, tel. 505/8827-7714) will give you reliable information about the schedule.

By Boat from Granada and San Carlos

The **Empresa Portuario de Nicaragua (EPN)** ferry leaves Granada on Mondays and Thursdays at 3 P.M., arriving in Altagracia between 5 P.M. and 7 P.M. The ship then continues onward to San Miguelito on the southeastern lakeshore, arriving in San Carlos around dawn. You can usually stay on the boat until the Río San Juan boats begin operating at 6 or 7 A.M. (instead of having to get a room). An upper-deck ticket costs a couple dollars more and earns you more room to hang a hammock.

On the return trip, the ferry leaves San Carlos on Tuesdays and Fridays at 2 P.M., passes Altagracia at 11 P.M., and arrives in Granada at sunrise. The price for a one-way passage between Granada and Ometepe is $3, but when seas are high, the ship will skip Ometepe altogether, preferring to hold tight to the lee shore of the lake.

GETTING AROUND

Getting around the island is difficult, no matter how you slice it. You can take a slow, rickety, infrequent bus on the worst roads you've ever seen for under a buck, or you can shell out $25–35 for a taxi or microbus to take you to the sites. You can also rent a motorcycle or scooter, but aside from a few motorickshaws or scoring a ride by hitchhiking, there's not much in between. Once you've accommodated your stuff at your hotel, biking can be an enjoyable, cheap, and relatively fast way to get around the island if you take it easy, drink plenty of water, and don't mind riding a clunker. If you're traveling with a cell phone and speak Spanish, it can be helpful to get your taxi driver's number so you can call later and make arrangements yourself.

By Bus

Be very aware that buses are few and far between, especially on Sundays, which remain a tough day to get around the island in anything but a rented car, taxi, or by availing yourself of the services of your hotel.

In general, there's a bus in Moyogalpa to meet every boat. For the most up-to-date schedule, ask around the dock, or look for a posting in the tour offices or El Indio Viejo in Moyogalpa. Fully 90 percent of the buses leave the Moyogalpa dock, travel straight up the hill along the main street, stop at the park, then head east out of town on the road to Altagracia; the other 10 percent turn left, passing through La Flor and San Marcos on their way to Altagracia.

From Altagracia, buses depart for Moyogalpa and for the small towns of Maderas (Merida, San Ramón, Santa Cruz, and Balgüe). If you board a bus in Moyogalpa that's heading to Maderas, remember you'll pass through

Altagracia first, where you'll spend 30 minutes waiting for more passengers before continuing to Maderas. From Moyogalpa to Altagracia, it's approximately one hour, and from Altagracia to Balgüe it's another hour. The island is bigger than you think.

Three daily buses leave Moyogalpa for Merida at 8:30 A.M., 2:40 P.M., and 4:30 P.M.; from Altagracia buses depart at 7 A.M., 10:30 A.M., and 2 P.M. (these buses continue to San Ramón, returning the following day starting at 5:30 A.M.). From Merida to Moyogalpa, buses leave at 4 A.M., 8:30 A.M., and 3:30 P.M.

By Car

Either arrange a transfer with your hotel beforehand or call Berman Gómez (tel. 505/2647-5179), whose clients include the BBC. All of these operations are reputable and offer fairly creative trips. Most hotels will gladly help to arrange tours as well, getting you up the volcanoes or on waterfall hikes, horseback rides, kayaking excursions, and other area attractions. CITOMETEPE, the island's tourism commission, offers overview information at www.visitaometepe.com.

Rivas

Southern Nicaragua's most important town center, Rivas is a commercial center whose small population (under 50,000) helps it retain an old-world charm. Few travelers travel specifically to Rivas as a destination proper, but it remains an important companion town for San Juan del Sur, providing a better selection of medical, banking, and shopping services. Rivas is also the site of a Costa Rican consulate, in case you have immigration issues. Don't discount it as inconsequential however; it's one of Nicaragua's more pleasant cities, charismatic and enjoyable in its own right, and not lacking in historical sites worth visiting.

Rivas is often hot because of its low altitude, but a cool lake breeze from Lake Cocibolca makes it bearable. Rivas is known as Ciudad de los Mangos due to the abundance of the trees in and around the city; swarms of chatty *chocoyos* (parakeets) feast on the fruit, their calls filling the skies around sunset. Rivas was known as Valle de la Ermita de San Sebastián until 1717, when a delegation of pious villagers traveled to Guatemala, the capital of the republic at that time, to request their little town be declared a villa with the name of La Pura y Limpia Concepción de Nuestra Señora la Virgen María. Capitán General del Reino Francisco Rodríguez de Rivas granted the request, and to thank him, the villagers modified the name to La Villa de la Pura y Limpia Concepción de Rivas de Nicaragua. Thankfully for travelers and mapmakers, over time the name contracted to something shorter.

SIGHTS AND ATTRACTIONS

Rivas is small and easy to get around, and for about $1–3 dollars per hour, a pedal-powered *triciclo* will carry you around town among the different attractions.

🚩 Iglesia Parroquial de San Pedro

Rivas's obvious centerpiece is a well-loved historical monument repainted in 2007. Built in the 18th century, the Iglesia Parroquial de San Pedro has witnessed the California gold rush, William Walker, the Sandinista revolution, and the 21st-century real estate boom. As you take in the details of the church's pleasing colonial design, remember that every single gold rush–bound passenger that traversed Nicaragua in the days of Cornelius Vanderbilt's steamship line passed under its shadow. It is today, as always, a peaceful place to seek refuge; mass is held evenings around 6 P.M.

Other Churches and Museums

Four blocks west of the park at the town's center, the **Iglesia de San Francisco** was

RIVAS

© RANDALL WOOD

Rivas's cathedral, the Iglesia Parroquial de San Pedro, witnessed the California gold rush.

built in 1778 and was the first convent of the Franciscan friars. A beautiful statue commemorates the devotion of the friars to both God and their work. When they began construction of the nearby Bancentro, an underground tunnel was discovered that linked the Iglesia de San Francisco with the plaza (the open area adjacent to the central park's north side); the tunnel passes beneath the library (one door east of Bancentro). Researchers speculate it was probably dug at the same time as the church, meaning it was in place and probably used during the Battle of Rivas, when the plaza was the site of a military barracks.

Rivas is also the birthplace of several presidents of the republic, including Máximo Jérez (Liberal, governed from June 8, 1818 to August 12, 1881), Adén Cárdenas (Conservative, governed from March 1, 1883 to March 1, 1887), and most recently, Violeta Barrios de Chamorro (Coalition, governed from April 25, 1990 to January 10, 1997). Chamorro's childhood home is located across the street from the Iglesia Parroquial de San Pedro's south side.

Several direct descendants of William Walker also continue to reside in Rivas.

Rivas has its own history museum: the **Museo de Historia y Antropología de Rivas** (open 8 A.M.–noon and 2–5 P.M. Mon.–Fri., only in the morning Sat., foreign travelers $1), set on the western side of town in a 200-year-old house that was once part of a cacao and indigo plantation. Once known as the Casa Hacienda Santa Úrsula, on June 29, 1855, William Walker and his men were defeated here in a heroic battle Nicaraguans are still proud of. The Battle of Rivas, as it became known, was one of the first manifestations of Nicaragua's growing sense of independence in the late 19th century; in fact, the people of Rivas claim that "nationalism began in Rivas." The museum has a healthy collection of pre-Columbian pottery, as well as domestic utensils from the 18th and 19th centuries including kerosene lamps, silverware, and hand tools. The building itself evokes the lifestyle of the old farming community; more exciting are several old maps of the region. Some books are for sale.

LA ISLA DE OMETEPE

The **Monument to Emmanuel Mongalo y Rubio** marks the final resting place of a young Rivas teacher who lived here in the mid-1800s. Mongalo y Rubio gained his fame during the Battle of Rivas by setting fire to the Mesón (the museum building) where Walker and his men had sought refuge; as they abandoned the blazing building, they were captured or shot.

Another museum piece in its own right, the **Biblioteca Pública de Rivas** next to Bancentro is one of the oldest still-standing buildings in Nicaragua, dating back to at least the early 17th century. Among its various incarnations it was a secondary school founded in 1872 by Máximo Jérez and El Colegio de la Inmaculada Concepción. Still easily visible in the building is a stray bullet hole incurred during the Battle of Rivas.

At the southeast end of town not far from the road to La Chocolata, the Rivas **cemetery** is set on a little hill with a nice view of town and the surrounding hillsides. It's worth visiting in the late afternoon, as Rivas sunsets are often blazing washes of red and orange, thanks to the humidity from Lake Cocibolca.

ENTERTAINMENT AND EVENTS

The **Restaurante y Disco El Principe Numero Dos** (next to the baseball stadium on the highway to the border) is Rivas's most popular dancing nightspot, especially on Saturdays when you likely won't see any other gringos. The city's best bar is **Pipi's Bar** (across from the Texaco), serving appetizers and drinks starting at 5 P.M. Otherwise, enjoy the view of cloud-covered Volcán Concepción from the breezy second-floor patio of **Komalé** (from the BAC, two blocks south). With its creative decor, pleasant lighting, and music videos on a big screen, it is the hippest lounge in town.

No one enjoys baseball as much as the people of Rivas; at last count, there were 138 officially registered baseball teams and more than 3,900 registered players in the municipality, with stadiums or makeshift diamonds in every village in the department! Attending a Sunday afternoon game in Rivas's main stadium on the highway is a great way to experience the city and the energy of its people; tickets are $1, and in lieu of chili dogs, there are plenty of *vigorón* (fried pork and yucca) and enchiladas in the grandstand.

ACCOMMODATIONS

Few travelers find a reason to spend the night in Rivas, and the Ometepe-bound tend to prefer the lakeside places in San Jorge. But if you're visiting from San Juan del Sur, there's no reason not to spend the night.

Under $10

For budget travelers, **◖ Hospedaje Lidia** (half a block west of the Texaco station, tel. 505/2563-3477, $8 pp shared bath, $12 private bath) is the most popular and has a dozen clean rooms, including large rooms for up to five people. At the southeast corner of the church is a nice alternative, **Restaurante-Hospedaje El Español** (tel. 505/2563-0006, $10 pp), a pleasant corner place with a friendly and atmospheric bar and smoking room in the front *sala*. In the back are four simple rooms; each pair of rooms shares a bath.

Hospedaje Primavera (next to the Shell station, $5 pp private bath) is a bare-bones lodge catering mostly to working Nicaraguan expats on their way to and from Costa Rica. If you get stuck, you'll find a handful of similar, unremarkable but inexpensive ($5–7 pp) places to stay within a block or two of Primavera.

$50-100

Hotel Cacique Nicarao (a block west of the park, tel. 505/2563-3234, www.hotelnicarao-inn.com.ni, $69 includes tax and breakfast) is efficient and modern with cable TV, air-conditioning, Wi-Fi, a guarded parking lot, pleasant lobby, and attentive staff. You can arrange rides to San Juan del Sur and other parts here.

If you've got a car, outside the city limits and down the highway at the *empalme* (turnoff) to San Juan del Sur, you'll find **Hotel and Restaurant La Mar** (www.lamarlakeresort.

com, $60 plus tax, includes breakfast), with a unique lakeside swimming pool. Each large room has a front porch with terrific views of Ometepe's twin peaks. Major League pitcher Dennis Martinez owns the place, so it's decorated with lots of sports memorabilia.

FOOD

Buy fresh pastries and juice at **Repostería Don Marcos,** a block east of the park, an easy breakfast en route between San Juan del Sur and the boat to Ometepe. The best coffee in town can be had at **Repostería Ballesteros** (across from the Nicarao Hotel), where the outdoor seating lends itself to some quality people-watching and their pastries are a nationwide sensation.

Possibly the lowest-price lunch in town is **Soda Rayuela** (open 7 A.M.–10 P.M. daily), serving $1 sandwiches and burgers and $4 dishes. Across the street from the Iglesia San Pedro is **Pizza Hot** (closed Mon.) with outdoor tables and an **Eskimo** next door for dessert. In

the same price range is **Hotter's Pizza,** around the corner from the Texaco, with outdoor seating and karaoke some Wednesdays. During the evening, a number of typical *fritangas* set up shop in the plaza, and most of the bars listed in the *Entertainment and Events* section have reasonable food as well.

Pollo Dorado (closest to the center of town) and **Super Pollo** (near the market) sell chicken your way. On the southwest corner of the park is **Chop Suey** ($5–7 a plate), a Chinese place not far off the mark, though all the dishes have been subtly adapted to suit the Nicaraguan palate.

El Messon (south side of Iglesia de San Francisco), serves a decent Nicaraguan buffet lunch as well as *caballo bayo,* a hearty stew. The most upscale restaurant in Rivas is in the **Hotel Cacique Nicarao**.

SERVICES

Several well-stocked pharmacies in town make Rivas a good service stop for the San Juan del Sur beach crowd. **Farmacia María Inmaculada** (right across from the park on the side of the plaza, open 7:30 A.M.–7:30 P.M. daily) has a well-respected doctor on staff (consultation 2–4 P.M. Mon.–Fri.) and professional massage therapists. Another well-stocked pharmacy is the **Farmacia Rivas** (two blocks east of the park at the intersection of the boulevard, tel. 505/2563-4292).

The post office (a block south of the police station) has fax service and is open 7:30 A.M.–4:30 P.M. Monday–Friday and 7:30 A.M.–noon Saturday. Of the many Internet cafés in town, two of the most popular ones are one block south of the park.

There are several banks in town including BDF, Bancentro, Banpro, and BAC, all of which operate essentially on a schedule of 8:30 A.M.–4:30 P.M. Monday–Friday, 8:30 A.M.–noon Saturday.

The Costa Rican Consulate in Rivas offers help with immigration issues for Costa Rica-bound travelers. It's located about one kilometer west of town and is open 7 A.M.–5 P.M. Monday–Friday and 7 A.M.–noon Saturday.

© RANDALL WOOD

the local market in Rivas

GETTING THERE AND AWAY

Buses leave Managua's Roberto Huembes terminal for Rivas every 30 minutes. Several express buses depart in the early morning before 8 A.M. Express buses to San Juan del Sur and the border at Peñas Blancas will let you off on the highway at Rivas. They leave Huembes at 5 A.M., 8 A.M., 9:30 A.M., and 3:30 P.M.

A good way to reach Managua, Masaya, Carazo, and the Pueblos Blancos (such as Catarina) is to take one of the express minibuses, which leave from El Mercadito on the south end of town about once every hour ($2.50). Regular buses leave from the market on the northwest side of Rivas: every hour for Jinotepe and Granada, every 25 minutes for Nandaime, Masaya, and Managua. The last bus for Managua leaves from the Texaco station on the highway at 6 P.M. Four daily buses go to Belén and six for Las Salinas (9 A.M., 11 A.M., 12:40 P.M., 2:30 P.M., 4 P.M., and 4:30 P.M.).

To and From Costa Rica

Bus service to Peñas Blancas and the border begins at 5 A.M. and continues every 30–45 minutes. The last bus leaves Rivas at 5:30 P.M. (the ride takes less than an hour and costs less than a dollar). You can also share a *colectivo*. On the highway in the Supermercado Panamericana (next to the Texaco station), you can buy tickets for the TicaBus, which passes by Rivas each morning bound for Costa Rica between 7 and 8 A.M., and between 3 and 4 P.M. every afternoon bound for Managua. Buy your tickets the day before ($10–12 to San José, Costa Rica).

Taxis to San Jorge and San Juan del Sur

To San Jorge and the ferry to Ometepe, a taxi should cost you no more than $1 per person, whether you take it from the highway traffic circle or from Rivas proper. Ignore any taxi driver that tries to charge $2 or more, unless you're traveling after 10 P.M., when taxi prices go up. Taxis from Rivas to San Juan del Sur cost around $8 per person, or $1 if it's a *colectivo,* which only run during daylight hours.

Near Rivas

NANDAIME AND DOMITILA WILDLIFE RESERVE

Just south of where the highways from Granada and Carazo join to continue on to Rivas and the border, you'll pass by the midsize city of Nandaime, located on the Pan-American Highway in the shadow of Volcán Mombacho. This is a humble, unassuming pueblo with the most basic of traveler's amenities, a small-town tranquility, and a passion for music. Nandaime's most famous son is Camilo Zapata, a key founder of the Nicaraguan folk style, who composed the song, "El Nandaimeño." Nandaime is also home to three *chichera* groups, ragtag bands composed of a bass drum, a snare, cymbals, a sousaphone, and loud, clashing brass. Known as "orchestras," they participate frequently in parades and bullrings, and their music is happy, loud, and scrappy.

Just south of Nandaime, the private wildlife reserve of Domitila (tel. 505/8881-1786, www. domitila.org, $45 pp in the dorm, $65 private room; $5 pp for day-trippers) sits on 230 hectares of tropical dry forest and lakeshore. They have tree nurseries, hiking trails, and oodles of wildlife. Domitila is ecofriendly and uses composting toilets and its own wastewater treatment facility. You'll find comfortable, private cabins, complete restaurant service, and facilities for groups of up to 25 researchers, scientists, or travelers. The $45 per person rate includes three meals per day; gourmet lunch is $10. Call ahead to arrange one of their popular wildlife tours ($20 pp) for bird-watching, butterfly tours, or horseback riding. They also arrange luxury trips to the island of Zapatera, where hot meals are prepared and served to you on-site. The entrance is located five kilometers south of Nandaime (Km 72) on the road to Rivas; turn off the highway onto a dusty dirt road, which will lead you 10 kilometers past the Lagunas de Mecatepe to Domitila.

SAN JORGE

A traditional village with a strong Catholic spirit, San Jorge is primarily a port town and farming community that produces plantains. Nearby Popoyuapa, true to its Nahuatl-sounding name, cultivates cacao, the tree whose seed is used to produce cocoa and eventually chocolate, and which was once used by the Nicarao people as a form of currency.

The tiny lakeside port of San Jorge is your access point to La Isla de Ometepe and as such, most travelers breeze straight through it on the way to catch a boat. If you have an hour to kill before your ferry departs, there's no reason to spend it dockside sitting on your luggage. Some travelers even find San Jorge a pleasant place to spend a night, and the locals are turning out increasingly acceptable

hotel accommodations (mostly targeting the backpacker set) hoping that's exactly what you'll do.

Be advised that at certain unpredictable times of the year, a southern wind brings plagues of *chayules,* small white gnats that swarm the lakeside in San Jorge and eastern shores of Ometepe. They neither bite nor sting, but are relentless and always seem to wind up in your mouth.

Sights

Halfway down the long road to town, you'll pass under **La Cruz de España,** a graceful concrete arch that suspends a stone cross directly over San Jorge's main drag. This main street runs through town down to the water's edge and the docks. The monument commemorates—and is ostensibly built over the very place where—on October 12, 1523, Spanish conquistador Gil González Dávila and indigenous cacique Nicarao-Calli first met and exchanged words.

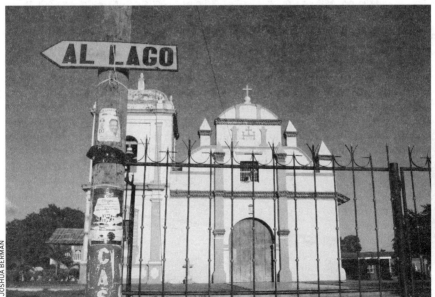

© JOSHUA BERMAN

In San Jorge, all signs point to the great lake.

LA ISLA DE OMETEPE

Across the street from the base of the arch is a mural commemorating the same event, with the words attributed to Nicarao: *"Saben los Españoles del diluvio, quien movía las estrellas el sol y la luna. Dónde estaba el alma. Cómo Jesús siendo hombre es Dios y su madre virgen pariendo y para qué tan pocos hombres querían tanto oro."* ("The Spanish know about the flood, who moved the stars, the sun, and the moon. Where the soul was found. How Jesus, a man, is God and his virgin mother giving birth, and why so few men wanted so much gold.") Many believe that the Spanish went on to refer to Nicaragua as The Land of Nicarao, which over time evolved into the modern word Nicaragua.

The squat **Iglesia de las Mercedes** is one of Central America's earliest churches. Built around the year 1575, it was renovated and repainted a bright yellow in 2001. Most tourists keep their bathing suits packed until they get to Ometepe, but San Jorge's kilometer-long **beach** is hugely popular among Nicaraguans, who flock there during Semana Santa to enjoy the lake and the awesome view of twin-peaked Ometepe on the horizon.

San Jorge celebrates its *fiestas patronales* in honor of their eponymous saint every year April 19–23 (the date changes to accommodate Semana Santa when necessary), at which time you can expect the beach to be packed. San Jorge usually has a parade or two during the celebrations, and there are performances of traditional dances, including **Las Yeguitas** (The Dance of the Little Mares) and **Los Enmascarados** (The Dance of the Masked Ones).

Accommodations and Food

If you missed the last boat to La Isla and don't feel like backtracking to Rivas, book one of the rooms at ❰ **Hotel Las Hamacas** (tel. 505/2563-0048, $30 d with private bath and fan, $40 with a/c, includes breakfast), no more than 100 meters west of the dock. Also consider **Hotel Restaurant Azteca** (from the dock, go two blocks past the castle, make a right, and go two more blocks, tel. 505/8879-9512, $20 d with a/c and TV). There is a nice restaurant plus a pool and pleasant common areas.

You won't go hungry in San Jorge's numerous food-and-drink joints lining the beachfront, but neither will you be surprised at the menu: chicken, beef, fish, fries, burgers, and sandwiches.

Getting There

Many tour operators in Granada now run shuttles straight to the dock for about $15. From Managua, take any southbound bus from the Huembes bus terminal to Rivas and get off at the traffic circle on the highway at Rivas. From the traffic circle in Rivas to the dock at San Jorge is four kilometers, accessible by Rivas buses once an hour ($0.25); they pass the traffic circle approximately 20 minutes after the hour. Unless you happen to be there right at that moment, however (or are traveling on an extraordinarily tight budget), take a taxi to San Jorge for $1 per person—ignore anyone who tries charging more. There is one Managua–San Jorge express, departing Huembes at 9 A.M., arriving in San Jorge at 10:50 A.M. The same bus departs San Jorge evenings at 5 P.M., arriving in Managua at 6:50 P.M.

SAN JUAN DEL SUR AND THE SOUTHWEST COAST

San Juan del Sur's crescent-shaped beach washed with the gentle, warm waves of the protected harbor have been attracting travelers for a long time. In the 1850s, this quiet fishing village experienced its first brief boom as a transport hub for gold rush pioneers crossing the peninsula on Cornelius Vanderbilt's passenger route. Here, North American travelers boarded the sailing ships to take them up the Pacific coastline to California and onward. This was also where many of William Walker's glory-seeking soldiers disembarked to join his ill-fated adventure. After the gold rush, the town sank into obscurity and tropical lethargy where it remained for a century-and-a-half.

At the turn of the 21st century, San Juan del Sur again grew in international popularity to the steady drumbeat of high-profile international press coverage declaring the area a real estate hot spot. The area attracted a frenzy of property pimps, land sharks, and a flock of checkbook-toting prospectors scouring the coastline for a piece of the pie. Some of the investment led to progress, new establishments, and healthy relationships between foreign investors determined to make money *and* a positive impact for their Nicaraguan colleagues and beneficiaries. But the economic growth was not without scuffles.

Meanwhile, sunsets continue to paint the silhouettes of fishing vessels in crimson, and the mood in San Juan del Sur is low-key and fun. The noon sun is scorching, so life is langorous and measured, spent swinging in breezy hammocks, enjoying fresh fish and cold beer at seaside, or splashing about in the surf.

© CHRIS SICILIANO

SAN JUAN DEL SUR

HIGHLIGHTS

Surfing: There's no denying San Juan del Sur has become a major surf center, drawing shredders and groms from all over. There are waves for all levels out here, and plenty of places that will give you your first lesson (page 133).

Sunset Cruise: San Juan del Sur's sunsets are spectacular year-round, and there's no better place to enjoy one than on

the water with a dozen friends and a glass of wine (page 135).

La Flor Wildlife Refuge: Even if you miss the spectacular nighttime turtle-nesting events, a simple walk along this protected beach and up the forested river is remarkable (page 148).

Playa Marsella: A gentle wave and a secluded beach make for all sorts of opportunities (page 150).

LOOK FOR **(** TO FIND RECOMMENDED SIGHTS, ACTIVITIES, DINING, AND LODGING.

San Juan del Sur

San Juan del Sur proper is a relatively small town; you could walk every street in a single morning. Most visitors spend at least two days and a night here, and if you start exploring the surrounding beaches and coves, beach lovers can stretch it into a full week, as can surfers. At a minimum, count on one full day wandering around town, one trip north to a nearby beach and another trip south to Playa el Coco or La Flor Wildlife Reserve; plan an extra half day for a canopy tour, sportfishing, or sailing excursion.

SIGHTS AND SPORTS

Of course, the main show in town is the brightly colored day's end over the languid harbor waves; San Juan sunsets can go on for hours; make sure you're on the beach as the setting sun drapes the fishing boats in shadow and the rock face of El Indio dims behind the evening. But there's a lot to do before day's end.

Next to the Casa de Cultura on the main beach drag are **volleyball** and **soccer** facilities; league games on weeknights. During the rest of

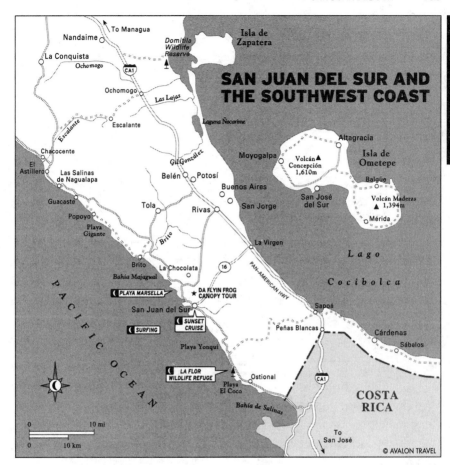

SAN JUAN DEL SUR AND THE SOUTHWEST COAST

the day, the Sports Park is open for (often competitive) pickup games. Otherwise, expect soccer games to be played on the hard sand beach at low tide on either end of the bay.

🄲 Surfing

Most surfers make base camp in San Juan del Sur and then drive or boat out to the better breaks, though a lot of beaches are now also developing accomodations of their own. Many of the best breaks are only accessible by boat. **Rana Tours** runs shuttles to the beach at Majagual in an authentic *panga,* leaving at 11 A.M. and returning at 4:30 P.M. ($10 round-

trip) and fishing and snorkeling expeditions ($35/hr, eight-person boat). Sign up at the kiosk in front of Hotel Estrella. But you can just as easily strike a deal with any local boat operator for a water taxi out to the other beaches.

An adequate selection of new and used surfboards is easy to find in San Juan. Local shredders Byron and Kervin López can be found in their shop, **Arena Caliente** (tel. 505/8815-3247, www.arenacaliente.com), next to the market. They'll rent you a board, drive you out to the beach and teach you the basics for $25. **Baloy's Surf Shop** (a block east of El Gato Negro) is owned by another pair of Nicaraguan brothers, who learned to surf on a secondhand board left behind by a tourist. They can arrange boards, gear, transportation, and lessons. **Action Tours** (tel. 505/8668-4407, www.actiontoursurfnica.com) runs private surfing, fishing, and chilling charters. The $220 full-day trip includes lunch.

Good Times Surf Shop (across from the casino, tel. 505/8675-1621, www.goodtimessurfshop.com) sells handcrafted boards manufactured in Nicaragua using renewable

materials, and can help you arrange for a repair if you mash up your board. They also offer boat trips to local surf breaks starting at $20 per person.

Chicabrava (tel. 505/8894-2842, www.chicabrava.com) is the first all-women's surf camp in Nicaragua, with both nightly and weekly rates at their beach house in town (drop in for a day's lesson and gear rental) and high-end, all-inclusive packages that cover lodging, food, equipment, six days of instruction, and

© JOSHUA BERMAN

San Juan del Sur and its perfect crescent bay

transportation. You can also stay at their flagship "cloud farm" nature retreat with many activities available.

◖ Sunset Cruise

San Juan Surf & Sport (20 meters west of the market, tel. 505/8984-2464) offers a sunset cruisein a fancy *panga* for $16 per person. Expect great photo ops, a merry crowd, and just a bit o' booze. Keep in mind that San Juan Surf & Sport can also take you fishing: Darío and his laid-back crew provide the equipment and will show you how to cast; you can keep any fish you catch.

Sailing and Diving

Gypsy Sailing (tel. 505/8608-9498, justin@ rootsengineering.com, $30–40 pp) offers all-inclusive half or full-day trips, or you can charter the *Pelican Eyes* yacht for an all-day jaunt (tel. 505/2563-7000, www.piedrasyolas.com, $90 pp) including lunch on a deserted beach and an open bar.

The Pacific lacks the visibility of the Caribbean waters, but fish are plentiful and there's a sunken Russian shrimp boat offshore, so it can be fun. The expert divers at San Juan's Nicaraguan owned and operated dive shop, **Neptune Watersports** (tel. 505/2568-2752, www.neptunenicadiving.com), will rent you gear and take you underwater ($85 for two tanks, $350 for open-water certification) if you already have your license and are an experienced diver.

Canopy Tour

Da Flyin Frog (tel. 505/8611-6214, daflyingfrog@yahoo.com, $30 pp, closed Sun.) is a 17-platform, two-kilometer canopy tour through the trees with great views of the ocean. It's located just outside town on the Chocolata road; arrange free transportation directly from the company.

Hikes

The statue of **Jesús de la Misericordia,** a 15-meter fiberglass thank-you note for the restored health of the gentleman who built

AFTER THE GOLD RUSH: THE FOREIGNER EFFECT IN SAN JUAN DEL SUR

From about 2003–2008, San Juan del Sur saw an explosion in foreign investment, property development, and tourism expansion that had no precedent. Old properties were scooped up, hotels and vacation homes constructed, and restaurants opened. Throughout the southwest corner of the country, scrublands were turned into investment properties and gated retirement communities under the mantra of "Nicaragua is the next Costa Rica!"

Then it ended with a whimper. In 2009, amid a global recession and inreasing uncertainty about Nicaragua's direction, the mood was sour and the verdict still out as to whether it was all worth it. The wave of investment was followed by foreclosures, half-built properties, and bitterness on both sides: Nicaraguans and foreigners.

On the Nicaraguan side are *campesinos* who hastily sold their undeveloped land at rockbottom prices. They then watched as their homesteads were turned into multi-million dollar investment properties. Some Nicas now work as guards and maids at the new places; others have taken advantage of the short construction boom. But not all of them. Meanwhile, to encourage tourism, the mayor's office criminalized the raising of livestock and chickens within city limits: reasonable at first glance, except that it's a law that impacts a lot of San Juan del Sur's poor right in the belly, and they're not happy about it.

On the North American side are the people who bought land during the frenzy but whose developments have not turned out as planned. In some cases, developers never connected water or power, nor built the roads they'd promised. Others blame the Nicaraguan government for suddenly enforcing forgotten taxes and the coastal law that prevents construction within 50 meters of the high-tide mark. Still others fell victim to contractors who ran off with prepayments without finishing the job and others whose workmanship was circumspect. Many investors have found that, far from being the next Costa Rica, Nicaragua was just too difficult to do business in, and they picked up and left.

The tension has boiled over in proxy battles, one of which was the case of Eric Volz, an American expat who was accused of killing his Nicaraguan ex-girlfriend, Doris Jimenez, in 2006. Evidence placing Volz in Managua at the time of the crime was rejected by the Sandinista judge in what observers called a "kangaroo court," while FSLN-organized mobs surrounded the courthouse bellowing for justice. Volz, who originally came to Nicaragua to edit a magazine called "El Puente" (as in "bridge" between Nica and gringo cultures) was declared guilty and was sentenced to 30 years – the maximum – in prison. After eleven months in the horrific Tipitapa prison, he was released and fled the country (Eric Volz tells his story in *Gringo Nightmare* [St. Martin's Press, 2010]).

For the moment, it seems both Nicaraguans and foreigners live in an uneasy detente, as some foreigners decide to pursue other interests and some have redoubled their efforts to be part of the local community. To the casual traveler, most of this will go unnoticed. But under the surface, the forces of globalization ensure that the battle between the haves and the have-nots will continue to be important.

–Jean Walsh contributed to this story.

Pacific Marlin, is easily reached via the gated driveway past the Pacific Marlin neighborhood or the ladder that winds its way from about 500 meters around the rocks on the northern point of the bay. The steep walk takes about 30 minutes each way and leads to one of the best overlooks of the bay. You can walk 90 percent of the way for free; pay $1 to access the summit. Beware the snarling dog. For a panorama from the **antennas,** take a bus toward Rivas and ask the driver to let you off at Bocas de las Montañas. From there, head through the trees and pastures to the breezy and beautiful *mirador* (lookout)—an hour each way.

Some 1,700-year-old **petroglyphs** are accessible via a 90-minute round-trip countryside walk beginning east of the Texaco station. Consider asking for a local guide. Take a left (north), pass the school, and walk through a gate after about 500 meters; find the farmhouse and ask permission to cut through. Follow the water pipes and the river until you find the stone with the carvings. Continue upstream to the (rainy season only) waterfall.

Mind and Body
Buena Vida Fitness Center (half block from El Gato Negro, www.buenavidafitness.com, closed lunchtime and Sunday) offers $5 yoga (mellow flow on Tues. and Thurs.), fitness and dance classes, and an assortment of free weights and machines. Find shiatsu massage ($20/hr), acupuncture, or chiropractic work at **Elixir** (next to the Casa de Cultura on the beach, tel. 505/8971-9393, closed Sunday).

Nica Yoga (www.nicayoga.com) offers daily yoga classes, individual guest accommodations, all-inclusive yoga retreats, and custom packages that include yoga and surfing and more (starts at $700). Packages include fine food, San Juan's largest outdoor wooden yoga floor, and a saline lap pool open to guests. The **Casa Tranquila Day Spa**, in the Pelican Eyes resort (tel. 505/2563-7000, reservations@piedrasyolas.com,), offers skin care, nail care, and salon services; an hour-long massage is $45. Call for appointments.

SHOPPING
During weekends, holidays, and cruise ship arrivals, street vendors—from Masaya and as far as Guatemala and Argentina—work the beachfront. **El Papagayo Artesanía** (closed afternoons) is French-owned with goods from around the world. Most everyday items, including fresh vegetables and those dollar flip-flops you've been looking for, can be purchased in or around the **Municipal Market** (center of town, open 7 A.M.–7 P.M.). On Saturdays an **organic farmers market** sets up across from the park.

ENTERTAINMENT AND EVENTS
San Juan del Sur's mellow, year-round party scene picks up around Christmas, New Year's Eve, and Semana Santa when the town is flooded with visitors. Managuan club owners set up beach discos during the high season. The rest of the year, the town's only disco, **Crazy Crab** (at the north end of the beach—take a taxi home at night), is open Thursday–Sunday (Saturday night is the best). San Juan del Sur's Bermuda triangle of bars, **Iguana, Marie's Bar,** and **Tsunami,** cater to locals and foreigners alike. Iguana's upper level heats up late night; Tsunami plays reggae. A bit farther down the strip is another enjoyable waterfont bar, **The Pier** with a more chill vibe.

San Juan del Sur's *fiestas patronales* are June 16–24, with bull riding, pole climbing, greased pig catching, and Coca-Cola chugging contests, followed by **Procesión de la Virgen del Carmen** on July 17. Locals parade the icon, the Patron Saint of Fishermen, through town and to the docks where waiting boats take her (and as many locals as possible) for a lap around the bay. On **September 2** the town commemorates the tidal wave of 1992, a 62-foot monster that swept across main street, destroying many structures (and farther up the coast, entire villages, like El Tránsito).

ACCOMMODATIONS
San Juan's lodging runs the gamut from grungy to luxe. The cheapest *hospedajes* are near the center of town, are Nicaraguan owned, and are usually extensions of someone's home. You may not encounter much of a "scene" at these places and a knock on the front door may be necessary if you return late at night. The beachfront road has a few nicer hotels and many of San Juan's restaurants and bars. It is safe to assume that nicer hotels have backup generators and water tanks, but you should still ask unless you don't mind the occasional candlelit bucket bath. Note: During the high season (New Year's and Easter) hotel prices double or even triple the rates listed below.

CRUISE SHIPS: *LOS CRUCEROS* COMETH

In 1998, the Holland America Line added San Juan del Sur as a port of call on several of their cruises. The announcement sparked hope in the people of San Juan del Sur, who began preparing their sleepy town to receive the thousands of cruise ship passengers scheduled to disembark.

After several years of regular biweekly stops however, whether or not *los cruceros* have benefited San Juan del Sur depends entirely on whom you ask. The well-to-do Careli Tour company, which enjoys a monopoly on the buses and guides who whisk passengers straight from the dock in San Juan to day trips in Granada or Masaya, isn't complaining. These passengers never set foot in San Juan proper, and the few hundred who decide to remain in town do not spend money in restaurants or hotels. A few bars have made a good business catering to thirsty crewmembers, but passengers themselves don't do much onshore imbibing or eating. The *ciclo* taxis and their drivers that cart passengers to and from the dock are imported from Rivas and few of the crafts vendors that display along the tree-lined beachfront strip are Nicaraguan. In fact, the majority of San Juaneños have not gained a dime from the arrival of the cruise ships and would only notice their absence by the lack of tinted-window bus convoys rumbling past their doors every two weeks.

Concerned cruise passengers should attempt to leave some dollars behind for someone other than their ship-sponsored tour operators, whether in San Juan del Sur or in other Nicaraguan cities they visit – and if you like what you see, come back and spend a night or two.

Under $25

La Casa Feliz (one block east of the market, tel. 505/8689-7906, www.lacasafeliz.com, $7 pp dorm) caters to surfers, offering a bunk, a key to the front door, kitchen, and bamboo showers. Surfboard rental and lessons are available on call; after the session laze around in their TV room or use their free Internet. This place could use a fresh paint job and a few night tables. Surfers also like to stay above the **Arena Caliente** surf shop (tel. 505/8636-1769, www.arenacaliente.com) and **Hostel Beach Fun** (tel. 505/2568-2441, $7 pp shared bath, $25 d with TV and fan, $10 more with a/c). The 16 rooms are small, but the owners are nice and the place is centrally located. You can rent a quad (don't even think of driving it on the beach) for $17 per hour and arrange rides to local beaches and trips to La Flor.

[**Hospedaje Don Wilfredo's** (25 meters east of El Timon, www.hospedajedonwilfredo.com) is a terrific value at only $6 pp with fan and private bathroom. The hostel is centrally located just steps from the beach. Ask for a room upstairs for good natural light and air flow.

Hotel Estrella (located where the market road meets the beach, tel. 505/2568-2210, hotelestrella1929@hotmail.com) was the first hotel in San Juan del Sur, constructed in 1929. Less glamorous than its glory years, Estrella is still the only place in town where you get an oceanfront balcony for $7 a person (so make sure you get one). Drawbacks include a surly manager, bats, and having to walk downstairs to use the 1929-era bathroom. Next door is the **Hostal Esperanza,** a chill work-in-progress right across from the ocean. Ten bucks gets you a thin mattress in a dorm room, use of the kitchen, and free Internet. Or string up a hammock in the patio next to the mango tree for $5.

Casa Oro (tel. 505/2568-2415, www.casaeloro.com) is a popular dorm-style youth hostel just west of the central park; bunk up in 8- or 12-person dorms for $8–9, $19 double with private bath plus $10 if you use the air-conditioning. They run three convenient beach shuttles daily, undercutting the competition Wal-Mart-style, to the chagrin of the smaller tour operators and taxi drivers. Guests love the daily surf report and travel info, lockers, TV lounge, and free make-your-own pancakes on the weekends.

Find a warm welcome, kitchen, and parking at **Rebecca's Inn** (25 yards west of the park, tel. 505/8675-1048, martha_urcuyo@yahoo.es, $16–20, all with private bath), run by Martha, who grew up in this house and can tell you about the local lore in English. Across the street, the **Posada Puesta del Sol** (tel. 505/2568-2532, lalacard98@yahoo.com, $10–15 d) has five simple rooms and gives deals to students studying Spanish in town. **Mama Rosa** has been welcoming foreigners into her home for eight years, mostly students from nearby Spanish schools. Clean, simple rooms with decent mattresses and newish sheets run $10 per person (with fan and shared bath).

Stay at **El Encanto del Sur** (75 meters south of the park, tel. 505/2568-2222, $20 d with fan, $30 with a/c,) for a traditional hotel on a quiet street with plenty of privacy. Tax, private bathroom, TV, and Wi-Fi are included.

$25-50

⬛ **Royal Chateau Hotel** (one block east of the market, tel. 505/2568-2551, www.hotel-royalchateau.com) is Nica-owned, and their friendliness, the security of the compound, private parking, a big wooden porch with traditional adobe-tiled roof, and a filling breakfast make the Royal Chateau an easy pick for the midrange hotels. Rooms run $46 double with fan, private bath, and TV, and $53 with air-conditioning, including tax.

Opened in 2009, **The Irish House** (two blocks north of the market, across from Gato Negro, tel. 505-8973-7855, irish.house2009@gmail.com, $50) offers Guinness at the downstairs pub and four apartments with TV, fan, kitchen, and safety box.

A few doors down, **Secret Cove Inn** (tel. 505/8672-3013, rjesq@aol.com, www.secretcoveinn.com, $28) is a little American-owned bed-and-breakfast with Wi-Fi, bicycles, and services like massage and manicures and pedicures for guests. One of the owners is a yoga instructor and can help you find classes; they also offer sailboat tours and weekly rates.

Azul Pitahaya (from the park, one block west, one block north, tel. 505/2568-2294, www.hotelazulsanjuan.com, $38) offers six spotless, brightly-colored rooms with cable TV, air-conditioning, and private bath with hot water; breakfast included.

Hotel El Pacifico (tel. 505/2568-2557, www.el-pacifico-hotel.com, $25 d with fan, $46 d with a/c, plus tax) is located across the river in the wealthy neighborhood of Barrio El Talanguera, well removed from the hustle and bustle of the city. Get there via the Chocolata road turnoff at the entrance to town or walk about 15 minutes across the amazing new, Golden Gate–esque suspension bridge at the north end of the beach. The nine remodeled rooms are comfortable, with private bath, parking, pool, Wi-Fi, cable TV, restaurant, and bar.

Lastly, for travelers less inclined to the beach-party scene, **Camino del Sol** (Km 137.5 Carretera San Juan del Sur, tel. 505/8400-0255, www.caminodelsol.com, $48 d) offers quality rooms in a quiet setting 3.5 km out of town, yoga classes, shuttles into town, and home-cooked meals ($7).

$50-100

Most of the places in this category include breakfast and free wireless Internet; you can also expect hot water and private bathroom, air-conditioning, and TV in your room.

⬛ **Hotel Villa Isabella** (across from the northeast corner of the Catholic church, tel. 505/2568-2568, villaisabellasjds.com) charges $75 plus tax for large rooms with private bath, air-conditioning, TV, heated pool, and $95–150 for family-friendly condos. This pristine, 13-room bed-and-breakfast is two minutes from the beach, and offers business services, full wheelchair accessibility, a huge selection of DVDs, and free calls to the U.S. or Europe. Their breakfast is no meager continental affair: homemade waffles, cinnamon rolls, banana pancakes, breakfast burritos, fresh fruit, and great coffee.

Frederica's B&B (waterfront, tel. 505/2568-2489, www.fredericasbandb.com) has a pair of

SAN JUAN DEL SUR

lovely, fully equipped doubles for $60. **Hotel Colonial** (half a block from the park, tel. 505/2568-2539, www.hotel-nicaragua.com, $54 d) has 12 rooms and decent parking; the lush interior garden is a lovely place to relax.

◖ **La Posada Azul** (half a block east of BDF bank, tel. 505/2568-2524, www.laposadaazul.com, $80–120) has lovely rooms and a small pool. Tasteful decor, lazily-spinning wicker ceiling fans, and classy wood-grained ambience echo the remodeled building's 90-year history.

A short taxi ride outside of town, in the Las Delicias neighborhood on the road to the southern beaches, is **Aventura Lodge** (tel. 505/8903-7622, www.aventurasanjuan.com, $70). Pretty but dark rooms have somewhat cheap mattresses and border a whimsical pool and lush garden courtyard. Beds in the quirky treehouse *palapa* are $20 a night and "jungle suites" start at $55; rates include a self-serve breakfast of yogurt, granola, and fruit. Mind the resident parrot, who can be delightful or annoying depending on what time you hit the sack.

Over $100

Pelican Eyes Hotel and Resort (tel. 505/2563-2110, www.pelicaneyesresort.com, $207–368) was one the first high-end resorts of its kind in Nicaragua, built on the hill above town offering fully equipped homes with kitchenettes and outdoor decks. Despite ongoing property disputes and management changes, the place trucks on. There are two bars, a world-class restaurant, and three infinity pools overlooking the ocean. Their **Bistro La Canoa** is one of the best places in town to enjoy a sunset; go for happy hour, otherwise a margarita can set you back $6.50. There's also an on-site spa and sailboat to charter.

The cocktails are cheaper and the pool is just as nice at **Villas de Palermo** (tel. 505/8672-0859, www.villasdepalermo.com, $149), in the hills outside of town. Stay the night in a handsome villa or just drop in for the day to take a swim and have a drink at the poolside bar and restaurant.

Built in 1902 and recently restored and splashed across the *New York Times* travel section, the ◖ **Hotel Victoriano** (tel. 505/2568-

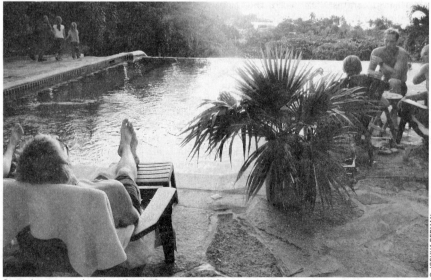

Sunsets are a main attraction in San Juan del Sur.

© JOSHUA BERMAN

2006, www.hotelvictoriano.com.ni, $140–180) has 21 rooms, giant four-poster beds, and all the amenities: little shampoo bottles, bathrobes, nice lobby, pool, air-conditioning, TV, hot water, private parking, and Wi-Fi. The hotel is located on the waterfront at the south end of town.

Long-Term Accommodations

Weekly or monthly rentals are easy to arrange, both in San Juan proper and in the hills surrounding the city. For the low budget set, most Spanish schools in town have packages combining lessons and a homestay, which can be arranged (whether or not you are attending class) for around $10 per day including three meals. Most places will cut you a deal if you stay more than a few nights.

For something fancier see **Vacation Rentals Nicaragua** (www.vacationrentalsnicaragua. com), **Vacation Rentals by Owner** (www. vrbo.com), or **Home Away** (www.homeaway. com), or stop by **Aurora Beachfront Realty** (tel. 505/2568-2498, U.S. tel. 323/908-6730). A fully furnished two-bedroom place goes for $800–1,200 per week and a big house is double that. Nearly all homes come with swimming pools and sweeping ocean views.

FOOD AND BARS
Cheap and Local

Fear not the municipal market: you can eat three tasty and filling *corriente* meals a day at one of the four counters inside for under $3. Evenings, try Juanita's **fritanga** on the street where the buses leave or walk to the southwest corner of the park for **Asados Vilma**, a.k.a. The Chicken Lady, with grilled meat, mountains of *gallo pinto,* and delicious *frescos* from $3.

Nearly every *hospedaje,* hotel, and beach restaurant makes a variety of breakfasts, usually for $2–3. Locally-owned *sodas* offer Nicaraguan standards for about $4.

Cafés and Bar Food

El Gato Negro (open 7 A.M.–3 P.M. daily) serves freshly roasted organic espresso and good breakfasts, including bagels and cream cheese, in a bookstore setting. **Barrio Viejo** (one block west of the bus stop) makes first-rate espresso drinks and serves breakfasts with coffee and orange juice starting at $2—a good deal.

A mellow bar with eclectic music, darts, and a great menu including a monster Philly cheesesteak, **Big Wave Dave's** is open early for breakfast, then serves bar food and drinks all day long, meals from $4. It's a good place to hang out at the ample horseshoe bar and chat with your compatriots. For dark beer, don't miss **The Irish House,** serving Guinness and probably more (we don't know; we never made it past the Guinness).

Seafood

A long row of virtually identical thatched-roof *rancho* restaurants runs along the central part of the beach, serving fresh fish dishes from $5 and shrimp and lobster dishes from $10–14 until 10 P.M. **Josseline's,** at the southern end, offers delicious fish dishes, a notable vegetarian soup, and a pleasant atmosphere. **El Timon** is a longtime favorite of Nicaraguans and tourists alike. Some say it has the best service of all the *ranchos;* it's also one of the most expensive.

At the south end of the bay or at **ExpoMar** (just east of BDF bank) you can buy grouper, swordfish, or red snapper fresh from the boat (they will fillet it for you), particularly on Wednesday and Saturday when the boats return from sea.

Bambu Beach Club (located at the far north end of San Juan del Sur's main beach, tel. 505/2568-2101, www.thebambubeachclub. com) is a Mediterranean-influenced restaurant with stylish decor and cool bathrooms. Serving seafood *bocas,* sandwiches, and entrées, it's also a full bar, relaxed beach hangout, seaside cinema, and acoustic concert space.

Italian

Mauricio's Pizzería (just west of the playground at the municipal park, tel. 505/2568-2295 for delivery, open from 5 P.M. daily) is easily one of the most popular restaurants in town, with great pasta and real Italian pizza by the slice, starting at $4.50 a pie. Ask Mauricio

downtown San Juan del Sur

© CHRIS SICILIANO

for a shot of his homemade *limoncello* after your meal.

Fine Dining

Bar y Restaurante La Cascada (in Pelican Eyes Hotel, tel. 505/2568-2511, $11–20) offers tables set above the village with a prime view of the ocean and sunset. The chef is world class, serving delights such as parmesan-crusted baked mahi over herb spaetzle. Breakfast and lunch start at $7; or just sample from the exotic tropical drink menu. Prices are in dollars, if that tells you anything.

C El Colibrí (one block south of the east side of the church, tel. 505/2568-2861, $7–12, no credit cards accepted) offers a reasonably priced assortment of delicious Mediterranean specialties in an unbeatable outdoor ambience. The menu goes from paella to polenta to chicken breast stuffed with walnuts, raisins, and basil in a red wine sauce, and don't miss the sangria. Reservations for large parties during the high season are recommended.

El Pozo (half a block south of the market, tel. 505/8806-5708, open from 6 P.M. Thurs.–Mon., $8–12) is a modern bistro featuring contemporary American dishes.

El Jardín (tel. 505/8880-4765, open 5–9:30 P.M. Wed.–Sun., $6–8) is located outside of town on the Chocolata road heading north, but is well worth the drive. They complement Asian fusion cuisine with an assortment of margaritas and fancy tequilas; leave room for the cheesecake.

INFORMATION AND SERVICES

From home, start at **www.sanjuandelsur.org.ni,** where many businesses listed here post their updated rates. The new **Municipal Tourism Commission** at the northwest corner of the park can provide information on activities, and free maps and flyers around town advertise local goings-on. Pick up a free copy of *Del Sur News,* a weekly bulletin of community news and events in English and Spanish, at many places around town.

The few pharmacies in town have limited supplies; for medical needs, the **Centro de Salud** provides free consultations 8 A.M.–7 P.M. Monday–Saturday, 8 A.M.–noon Sunday. However, for any serious medical concerns, plan a trip to Rivas, as the Centro is typically understaffed and crowded.

Nearly all of the nicer hotels (and some restaurants) accept major credit cards, but the three banks in town all have ATMs. BDF, located half a block from the Casa de Cultura; Banco ProCredit, one block west of the market; and Bancentro, next to Big Wave Dave's, all offer similar services but none will cash your travelers checks.

San Juan's handful of Internet cafés are slightly more expensive than other places in Nicaragua ($1 an hour) but are plentiful and easy to find. Cyber M@nfred, on the corner of the main street into town, has a generator and charges 50 percent more if you absolutely have to check Facebook while the power is out. Most bigger hotels offer free Wi-Fi.

Most of the nicer hotels provide laundry service, as will the inexpensive hotels if you strike a deal. If you'd rather go to an independent *lavandería* (laundromat) with modern machines, you'll find **Gaby's** (tel. 505/8837-7493) uphill from the market, charging $5 per load (wash, dry, fold). Gaby also gives massages.

GETTING THERE AND AWAY

The trip from Managua is about 2–2.5 hours in your own vehicle or express bus but nearly 4 hours in an *ordinario*.

To San Juan del Sur

From Managua, the absolute fastest way is by express shuttles that leave from the airport. **Adelante Express** (te;. 505/8850-6070, www.adelanteexpress.com) charges about $40 one-way, cheaper per person for groups. For guaranteed service make your reservation at least 24 hours in advance. **Nica Express** (tel. 505/2552-8461, info@nica-adventures.com, www.nica-adventures.com) also has comfortable, scheduled shuttles from San Juan to other cities.

By bus, regular express buses leave from Huembes market ($3–5 pp) about every hour around the middle of the day; the best and last one leaves at 4 P.M. Slow, crowded, *ordinario* service to Rivas from Huembes market in Managua operates 5 A.M.–5 P.M. The handlers at the Huembes bus terminal are unusually aggressive. They will grab your bags out of the taxi, push you onto a slow Rivas bus, claim it's an express, and then demand a tip. Read the windshield of the bus and ask the other passengers to verify.

Once in Rivas you can take a *colectivo* ($1.50 pp) or taxi ($7) the rest of the way to San Juan del Sur. *Colectivos* don't run after dark and taxi prices double because not even the most skilled drivers can see the potholes at night. And from Granada there are several shuttle services worth taking, all of which cost more than the bus but more than compensate in saved time and frustration.

To Managua and Rivas

Express buses leave from the corner in front of the market at 5 A.M. (this is the nicer *lujo* bus), 6 A.M., and 7 A.M. *Ordinarios* to Rivas and Managua leave every hour 5 A.M.–5 P.M. You can also catch a *colectivo* taxi to Rivas from 4 A.M. to about 3 or 4 P.M. and then catch any northbound bus toward Managua. The trip to and from Rivas takes about 30 minutes in a car; 45 minutes in a bus ($1).

Going to and from Costa Rica

From the Costa Rican border at Peñas Blancas, buses for Rivas leave every half hour. Get off at **Empalme la Vírgen** and flag a bus, taxi, or ride going between Rivas and San Juan del Sur. The beach is 18 kilometers due west of La Vírgen; taxis from the border to San Juan charge $11–20.

To the border at Peñas Blancas, get a ride to La Vírgen in a bus or taxi, then catch a lift south; the first Rivas–Peñas Blancas bus passes at 7:30 A.M. Or book a ticket with TicaBus (tel. 505/8877-1407) in Rivas. Also check with the shuttle services.

GETTING AROUND

You won't need a taxi to get around town (you'll only see them trolling for passengers to Rivas and the beaches): from one end of town to the other it's just a 15-minute stroll. Elizabeth's Hospedaje near the bus stop rents bikes.

To travel up and down the coast, you'll need a sturdy and preferably four-wheel drive car or a decent mountain bike and some stamina. Taxi

VOLUNTEERING IN SAN JUAN DEL SUR

If you'd like to spend some time working with the community, the environment, or the children of San Juan del Sur, there are numerous options.

Comunidad Connect (tel. 505/8853-8242, www.comunidadconnect.org) is a local nonprofit with a bilingual, multicultural staff, dedicated to supporting sustainable economic and community development in the area; they run the Sports Park by the beach, started a municipal recycling program in cooperation with the mayor's office, work with real estate agencies and developers to facilitate private sector donations to community projects, run a small business development initiative, and invite voluntourists like yourself to help with their projects. CC can arrange an all-inclusive homestay with a local family, volunteer projects, Spanish lessons, and excursions to their organic coffee farm. Contact director and long-time San Juan resident Jon Thompson (jon@comunidadconnect.org) to find out how to get involved – physically or financially.

The local book-lending project has been a smashing success in a country largely devoid of libraries that loan out books. The **San Juan del Sur Biblioteca Movil** (www.sjds-biblioteca.com), located across the street from the park, is the first lending library in Nicaragua and serves as the town library. Besides offering books and reading space to San Juaneños, it brings books to young and old in 31 outlying communities. The project was founded by Jane Mirandette (janem101@aol.com), the proprietress of Hotel Villa Isabella, and is supported by a nonprofit, the Hester J. Hodgdon Libraries for All Program (www.

librariesforall.org). Their Library in a Box program has helped initiate 30 other libraries in Nicaragua. Besides helping monetarily, tourists can volunteer by teaching English, organizing books, and reading to youngsters, or joining the staff on a visit to one of the rural schools. There is a formal volunteer program for librarians, library school students, and others held twice a year. Book donations are always welcome. Bring them with you or send Spanish-language books to the HJH Office at 1716 Del Norte Blvd., Loveland, CO 80538 (visiting Coloradans who bring a suitcase of books from Loveland get a free night at the Hotel Villa Isabella).

There are several opportunities to **teach English** in San Juan del Sur. At the Newton Montegri preschool, near the entrance to Pelican Eyes, track down the director Maria Luisa to work with four- and five-year-olds. Contact Heidy Herrera Obando (tel. 505/2568-2041 or 505/8924-6220, heidyho23@yahoo.com) to find out about opportunities to teach English at the library, which can provide teaching materials for other projects too. At the *instituto* (high school), you can teach English on Saturdays. Contact Director Rosa Elena Bello by calling 505/2568-2402 or 505/8858-0326. Finally, those wishing to arrange a longer-term experience in a rural setting, possibly staying with a family in the *campo*, can contact Mara Jacobsohn (tel. 505/8853-2767).

Fundación A. Jean Brugger (tel. 505/2563-7000 ext. 861, www.fundacio-najbrugger.org), founded in 1999, provides scholarships, uniforms, school supplies, and job training for promising local students. It also supports recycling and antilitter cam-

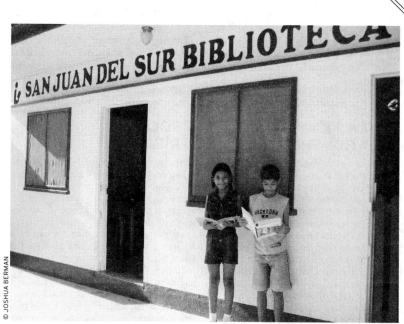

© JOSHUA BERMAN

Bring a Spanish-language book for San Juan del Sur's lending library.

paigns and a community art gallery, which hosts daily workshops for young and not-so-young artists. In addition, the foundation runs baseball camps for area youths, and hosts a popular monthly luncheon for senior citizens. Financial contributions are always needed and materials, such as school supplies, are appreciated as well.

San Juan del Sur has no fewer than five sister cities around the world: two in Germany, one in Spain, one in Norway, and one in Massachusetts. The **Newton-San Juan del Sur Sister City Project** (www.newtonsanjuan. org) sends brigades down twice a year (medical, dental, optical, construction, English instruction, etc.) and directly supports the library project. They also have an appropriate technologies workshop in which volunteers can help build and install improved stoves, latrines, and water filters. To make a tax-deductible contribution, send a check to Treasurer Don Ross, 211 Winslow Road, Waban, MA 02468. The local contact in San Juan is Rosa Elena Bello (rosaebel@ibw.com.ni).

drivers lounge around the market and can take you up and down the coast, but if you are going surfing for the day, you're better off catching a ride with one of the surf shops, or with the "gringo shuttles" from Casa Oro. Water taxis operate from in front of Hotel Estrella. Hotel Casablanca, on the central part of the beach, rents Alamo cars.

Arrange a **car and driver** in advance by contacting Ricardo Morales (2.5 blocks south of Hotel Villa Isabella, tel. 505/8882-8368, richardsjds@hotmail.com), a San Juan native with a few four-wheel drive vehicles and a great deal of local contacts and knowledge; he'll pick you up at the airport or in Granada.

¿PURA VIDA? NICARAGUA'S ROCKY RELATIONSHIP WITH COSTA RICA

Costa Rica is a wealthier, more politically stable country than Nicaragua. In his 1985 travelogue, *So Far From God*, Patrick Marnham called Costa Rica "the most European of the countries of the isthmus." To keep it that way, the Costa Rican economy is wholly dependent on low-cost Nicaraguan laborers for harvesting their sugarcane and coffee and filling the ranks of the construction workforce in urban centers. In an effort to control immigration, Costa Rican officials conduct regular roundups of illegal aliens, returning as many as 150 to Nicaragua daily. If you travel south into Costa Rica, you can expect patrolmen to stop and search your bus several times for illegals. Some estimates put the number of Nicaraguans living in Costa Rica at more than a million, but with the constant flux and large percentage of undocumented Nicas, no one knows for sure. The real number might be half that.

The tense relationship between these incongruous Central American neighbors loosely parallels the relationship between the United States and Mexico: namely, a massive flood of poor immigrants crosses the border into a more prosperous and stable nation and is subsequently accused of driving down wages, taking all the jobs, and straining social services without paying taxes. As the immigrants are darker skinned and easy to distinguish, they're easy to blame. Ask most Ticos (as Costa Ricans call themselves) about the issue and you'll likely get an earful of racist comments about Nicaraguans being "lazy, no-good, poor, and dirty." Oh yeah, they're "*Indios*," to boot.

Nicaraguans, for their part, generally mistrust Ticos and don't appreciate their arrogance. "The truth is," wrote none other than

Carlos Fonseca, founder of the FSLN, from exile in San José in 1960, that Costa Rica "doesn't even seem to be located next to Nicaragua – it is so totally different.... And even though this country is different from Nicaragua, and I am longing for a different Nicaragua, Costa Rica doesn't appeal to me, and I wouldn't want the Nicaragua of the future to be anything like Costa Rica."

Cultural tensions predate these new immigration issues; in fact, only 50 years ago, Ticos used to emigrate to Nicaragua to work on cattle farms. A hundred years before that, after helping to defeat William Walker's army in Rivas, Tico soldiers occupied southern Nicaragua, withdrawing only after being granted the Guanacaste Peninsula in an 1858 treaty. During the 1980s, U.S.-backed Contra forces illegally based operations in Costa Rica, prompting an irritated Costa Rican President Oscar Arías Sanchez to help negotiate an end to Nicaragua's conflict.

Costa Rica continues to press for a resolution to Nicaraguan immigration issues. Too much blustery rhetoric from Managua regarding other issues, like the sovereignty of the Río San Juan, may tempt the Ticos to crack down even more on illegal immigrants, something Managua would very much like to avoid. Even today, Nicaraguan immigrants have reported irregular and inhumane incarceration by Tico authorities, often for weeks at a time without formal charges (and sometimes without daylight, toilets, and food).

Rhetoric aside, the two neighbors desperately need each other. Perhaps pragmatism will win out over politics in the end.

Beaches South of San Juan del Sur

Between San Juan del Sur and Ostional on the Costa Rican border are a number of excellent beaches, and the Ostional bus will take you there, if you can afford to wait; otherwise, do like everyone else and bum a ride with someone with a vehicle, including the several shuttle options leaving from San Juan del Sur center. You'll first pass through Barrio Las Delicias, which includes San Juan del Sur's stadium and cemetery, followed by a fork in the road known as El Container. Turn right here to get to **Playa Remanso,** about a kilometer down a path infamous for robberies: Don't go alone. It'll take about 25 minutes to get there on rough dirt roads. This slow surf break is great for beginners, so expect to share it with all the new friends you met over beers last night. There's a shady outdoor bar right on the sand where you can purchase snacks and drinks at inflated prices. At low tide, look for bat caves, tidepools, blowholes, and various wildlife.

Walking 30 minutes south around the rocks brings you to **Playa Tamarindo,** followed by **Playa Hermosa** just under an hour later (it's a 20-minute walk from the bus stop at El Carizal, farther down the road toward Ostional). Ask in the surf shops in town about safety precautions and public access to these beaches.

A 30-minute drive south of town is **Playa Yanqui.** This powerful and fast wave that rolls into a giant beach was almost destroyed by one of the new developments when the owner decided to build a "viewpoint" going out into the sea. An effort by local surfers and activists prevented the construction and for now, this break remains one of the best in the area. Look for a sign at a fork on the main road before you get to the Yankee Beach development; go right and then left at another sign, then over a hill for a photo-worthy view of what awaits. Park at the small house on a hill at the south end of the beach for $3 to prevent theft. At low tide you can park right on the beach.

Places to stay in this area are limited. Carol and Alan rent out three cozy rooms at their charming

bed-and-breakfast, **Latin Latitudes** (www.latin-latitudes.com, $60–80). They've landscaped with native plants, used local construction materials and installed solar panels on the roof. **Orquidea** ($180, three-night minimum) is a high-end retreat with a luxurious pool perched atop the hills. Book in advance for both.

Lomas del Bosque (a few kilometers down the road to La Parcela, tel. 505/8376-7206) may be up and running by the time you read this. You can stay in a rustic cabin and wake up to the roosters while assuring your tourist dollars support the local community. Go horseback riding, butterfly-watching, and let your host, Don Miguel, point out the various tropical plants and crops. Some knowledge of Spanish would be helpful.

© JOSHUA BERMAN

There are countless bays and coves along Nicaragua's southwest coast.

PLAYA EL COCO

Eighteen kilometers south of San Juan, this jewel of a beach is great for swimming, fishing, and access to the turtles at La Flor; this is where you'll find **Parque Marítimo El Coco** (tel. 505/8999-8069, www.playaelcoco. ni), an extensive compound on a wide beach with a popular restaurant called **Puesta del Sol** (open 8 A.M.–8 P.M. daily) with meals from $7. Accommodations range from furnished apartments to fully equipped bungalows and houses; prices start at $80 and go to hundreds of dollars per night—weekend packages are very reasonable with a group of people. Houses have air-conditioning, satellite TV, hot water, and kitchen, and sleep up to eight people. You should come prepared with supplies; there is an on-site minimarket, plus bike rental, Internet, and a new conference facility.

◖ LA FLOR WILDLIFE REFUGE

One of the two Pacific turtle nesting beaches in Nicaragua, the park at La Flor is managed by the governmental environment agency MARENA. Foreigners pay $10 per person to enter, another $25 for a group for camping (bring your own gear). Make sure you catch one of the nighttime *arribadas,* or mass nesting events, that occur during the crescent moon from July to February. Casa Oro in San Juan del Sur runs shuttles during the season.

OSTIONAL

This picturesque bay and community at the extreme southwestern tip of Nicaragua is still more of a fishing town than a tourist destination, but curious visitors can seek out the rural tourism cooperative, **Community Tours** (tel. 505/8846-2272, communitytours@yahoo. es), for tours of the area and nearby bays— along with simple accommodations. All trips are about four hours and have a local guide, whether by boat or horseback. A portion of the profits goes toward 30 university scholarships for promising youths of the community. Buses from Rivas to Ostional pass through the San Juan del Sur market at 1 P.M., 4 P.M., and 5 P.M. (two hours to Ostional). They depart the center of Ostional at 5 A.M., 7:30 A.M., and 4 P.M., but confirm with the driver and anyone else you can find waiting around.

TURTLES

The Olive Ridley (or Paslama) sea turtle *(Lepidochelys olivacea)* is an endangered species well known for its massive synchronous nesting emergences. These seasonal occurrences, called *arribadas*, occur several times during each lunar cycle in the July-February nesting season and, at their peak (Aug.-Oct.), result in as many as 20,000 females nesting and laying eggs on a single beach.

In Nicaragua, the two beaches that receive the most turtles are **Playa Chacocente** and **Playa La Flor**, both on the southwestern Pacific coast. Playa La Flor, located about 15 kilometers north of the Costa Rican border and 18 kilometers southeast of San Juan del Sur, is a 1.6-kilometer-long beach that has been protected as part of a wildlife preserve. Hatchings have been less successful every year. Fly larvae, beetles, coyotes, opossums, raccoons, skunks, coatimundi, feral dogs, pigs, and humans all prey on Olive Ridley sea turtles in one form or another. High tides and beach erosion sweep away other eggs, and once they emerge from their shells, they are pounced on by crabs, frigate birds, caracara, vultures, and coyotes before they can reach the sea. Once in the water, they must still battle a host of predatory fish.

In general, females lay two clutches of eggs per season and remain near shore for approximately one month. The mean clutch size of the females differs from beach to beach but averages about 100 eggs; incubation takes 45-55 days, depending on the temperature, humidity, and organic content of the sand.

The *arribadas* and hatching events both occur during the night and witnessing these phenomena is an unforgettable experience. Tourism can protect the turtles, as it provides an incentive to continue protection efforts, but it can just as easily be disastrous (since the first edition of this book was published, the rangers have been permitting people to "swim with the turtles," an injurious practice). It is too easy to harass, injure, or frighten the turtles if you're not careful. Don't count on park rangers to tell you what's acceptable; use your common sense to respect this inspiring natural process and *please* pay close attention to the following rules during your expedition to the beaches of La Flor or Chacocente.

TURTLE-VIEWING ETIQUETTE

· Do not use your camera's flash when taking pictures of turtles coming out of the sea, digging a nest, or going back to the ocean – the light can scare them back into the ocean without laying their eggs. The only time that you can take a picture of them is when they are laying eggs; the flash will not disturb them as much, as they enter a semitrance state.

· Keep your flashlight use as minimal as possible; use a red filter over the lens or color it with a temporary red marker. If the moon is out, use its light instead.

· Do not dig out any nests that are being laid or are hatching.

· Do not eat sea turtle eggs, whether on the beach or in a restaurant. Despite their undeserved reputation as an aphrodisiac, the raw eggs may carry harmful organisms and their consumption supports a black market that incentivizes poaching.

· Do not touch, attempt to lift, turn, or ride turtles.

· Do not interfere with any research being performed on the beach (i.e., freeing hatchlings from nest boxes).

· If camping, place your tents beyond the vegetation line so as not to disturb the nesting turtles.

Shaya Honarvar, PhD,
Department of Bioscience & Biotechnology,
Drexel University, contributed to this piece.

Beaches North of San Juan del Sur

To get to Madera or Marsella, stop by any of the surf shops in San Juan. Rides cost $5 round-trip. If you're driving, access these beaches via the road to Chocolata, just east of the Texaco station. Much of this road served as the old railroad grade for a railroad never built. Seven kilometers along, turn left at Chocolata to a fork in the road: left goes to Marsella and Madera, right to Majagual. The drive out, on a newly-paved road through the ex-mayor's cattle ranch, is simply beautiful. It'll take you about 20 minutes to reach either beach.

⒞ PLAYA MARSELLA

This pleasant, breezy beach is one of the closest to San Juan del Sur and you can drive right up to the sand, making it a popular day trip for Frisbee throwers and sunset watchers. On the weekends a small restaurant on the beach serves ceviche, fried fish, and cold beer.

PLAYA MADERA

One of the most consistent, easy-to-access surf breaks from San Juan, Madera is enjoyed for its medium-speed hollow wave that breaks both right and left, best on incoming tides. There's parking right on the beach, and the place turns into a popular hangout around sunset. Surf shops bring groups here several times a day, so you won't be surfing solo.

Hospedaje los Tres Hermanos, a simple wooden bunkhouse with a kitchen, offers lodging right on the beach for $7 per person and cheap meals ($2 breakfast, $5 lunch), and rents boards by the hour.

A short walk north is **Hideout Surf Camp** (ddwysdwy@hyahoo.com, $10 pp dorm, $20 private room) followed by, another five minutes north along the beach, **Matilda's** (tel. 505/2456-3461 or 505/8818-3374, camping_matilda's@hotmail.com, $4.50 for a permatent, $8 dorm, $30 d private room with bath) right on the beach, perfect for swimming. **Buena Vista Surf Club** (tel. 505/8863-4180 or 505/8863-3312, www.buenavistasurfclub.com, $90 d) leans towards luxury and gets good reviews, located in the hills above Madera, from where you can watch the waves while doing yoga on an incredible wooden deck. About 1.5 km from the beach, **Mango Rosa** (tel. 505/8403-5326, www.mangorosanicaragua.com, $95 d) has a pool, volleyball court, hammocks, restaurant, and bar under a shady rancho. They've built with an environmentally friendly sewer system and are careful about energy use.

BAHÍA MAJAGUAL

Twelve rough kilometers from San Juan del Sur, this beautiful beach was formerly a peaceful backpacker-surfer retreat; it was purchased by investors and is now home to a 15-foot-tall cement wall surrounding their private property. The beach remains accessible, but the charm is gone.

© JOSHUA BERMAN

Playa Ocotál, as seen from the exclusive Morgan's Rock Hacienda & Eco Lodge

MORGAN'S ROCK HACIENDA & ECO LODGE

Playa Ocotál is the home of a much-hyped ecolodge at the vanguard of Nicaragua's upscale tourism market. **Morgan's Rock Hacienda & Eco Lodge** (tel. 505/8670-7676, www.morgansrock.com) is an exclusive resort surrounded by a 1,000-hectare reforestation project and an 800-hectare private nature reserve; its 15 elegant, hardwood cabins are built into a bluff above the crashing surf on the beach below. As few trees as possible were felled during construction, so you'll have to walk a 110-meter-long suspension bridge through a lush canopy to reach your cabin, which is the most luxurious and beautiful treehouse your childhood fantasies ever dreamed up. The structures—as well as the main lodge, which

features a gorgeous infinity pool—were designed with all local materials and feature ingenious architecture and attention to detail.

You're on vacation here, so no phones or Internet, but there's plenty to do: sunrise kayak tours of the estuary, tree-planting excursions, and tours of their shrimp farm and sugar mill, where they brew their own Morgan's Rum. More than 70 workers are employed to grow and produce much of the restaurant's vegetables, dairy products, herbs, and other needs. A cool $258 per person per night gets you a cabin, three meals, all you can drink of local, nonalcoholic beverages, and two tours a day. Prices vary by season, so call or email to reserve your room. The facilities and services are for guests only, so sorry, no day-trippers.

Tola and Pacific Beaches

Ten kilometers west of Rivas is the agricultural community of Tola, gateway to the steadily improving shore road and a string of lonely, beautiful beaches that make up thirty kilometers of Pacific shoreline. The word is out and land prices are rising but the beaches west of Tola are still far less developed than San Juan del Sur and retain some of their fishing village character. Tola is famous in Nicaragua as the subject of a common expression: *"Te dejó esperando como la novia de Tola"* ("He left you waiting like the bride of Tola"), which recalls the real-life soap opera of a young woman named Hillary, who, on the day of her wedding, was left at the altar at Belén while the groom, Salvador Cruz, married his former lover, Juanita.

In Tola proper, many travelers have stayed and worked with Doña Loida (an influential Sandinista leader, elected Mayor in 2004) of **Esperanza del Futuro** (tel. 505/2563-0482), who can help arrange cheap room and board from a week to six months. Her foundation provides education to local *campesinos* and provides a library, sewing co-op, and gardens; classes in guitar, agriculture, herbal medicine, and computers are offered. Find them on the road that leads from the park to the baseball field/basketball court, about 100 meters past the baseball field. There are a few decent eateries in Tola, the most popular of which is **Lumby's.**

PLAYA GIGANTE

North up the coast from San Juan del Sur, and an hour outside Rivas, Gigante is the first beach you come to after Tola and is named after the Punta Pie de Gigante (The Giant's Foot), the rock formation you'll see on the left side of the beach. The community of Gigante consists of a beautiful crescent beach, a few dozen poor homes occupied by about 500 locals—mostly fishermen—several restaurants and a few surf camps. Avoid this beach during Semana Santa, when it gets crowded with locals who camp out on the beach, get phenomenally drunk, and run cockfights.

Accommodations

Options for drop-in accommodations in and near Playa Gigante are sparse. **Hotel Brio** (tel. 505/8433-9737, www.hotelbrio.com, $20–30 with fan and private bath) sits atop a hill 300 meters back from the beach, with ocean views, a fresh paint job, and Wi-Fi. They also offer bunks for $14 a night with air-conditioning; this is your best bet for staying in a moderately priced room near Playa Gigante. They also have two 25-foot *pangas* for surfing and fishing tours. **Hotel Blue Sol** ($8 with fan) rents out a few rooms right at the beach but should be your last resort unless you like bedbugs. The restaurant is said to have the best tacos in town.

Giant's Foot Surf Lodge (tel. 505/606-9071, www.giantsfoot.com) rents out two adjacent beachfront lodges with air-conditioning, fan, and private bathroom; full capacity is 12 guests. Amenities include table tennis, a fire

a shuttle bus transporting people to the beaches

© JEAN WALSH

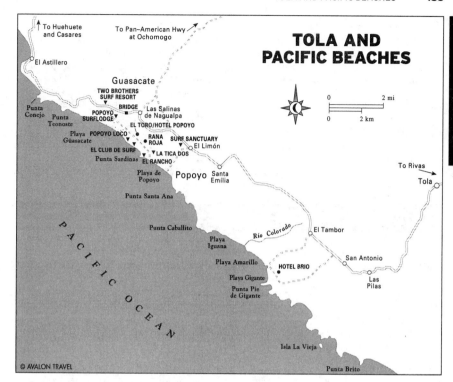

TOLA AND PACIFIC BEACHES

*Map labels:*
To Huehuete and Casares
To Pan–American Hwy at Ochomogo
To Rivas
El Astillero
Guasacate
TWO BROTHERS SURF RESORT
Punta Conejo
Punta Teonoste
BRIDGE
POPOYO SURFLODGE
Las Salinas de Nagualpa
EL TORO/HOTEL POPOYO
Playa Güisacate
POPOYO LOCO
RANA ROJA
SURF SANCTUARY
El Limón
EL CLUB DE SURF
LA TICA DOS
Punta Sardinas
EL RANCHO
Playa de Popoyo
Popoyo
Santa Emilia
Tola
Punta Santa Ana
Punta Caballito
Río Colorado
El Tambor
Playa Iguana
San Antonio
Playa Amarillo
HOTEL BRIO
Las Pilas
Playa Gigante
Punta Pie de Gigante
Isla La Vieja
Punta Brito
PACIFIC OCEAN
0   2 mi
0   2 km
© AVALON TRAVEL

pit, hammocks, DVDs, books, and board games. Weeklong packages cost about $1,300, everything included except your airfare; discounts are available in the off-season.

At **Dale Dagger's Surf Lodge** (Playa Gigante, tel. 505-8921-8694, Dale@NicaSurf. com, www.nicasurf.com), $1,450 a week gets you cushy digs, a ride from the airport, all meals, and unlimited trips to some of the best and least-known breaks in Nicaragua, returning to the luxury of air-conditioning, wireless Internet, and running hot water. Save a few bucks by staying in the dorm called **El Acopio** for about $60 per night. Dagger was the first foreign surfer to come to Nicaragua and scout the waves (he shipwrecked here in the 1990s and never left), and his knowledge of the coastline is unparalleled.

Momo's Camp (tel. 505/8990-1531, www. surfcamp-nicaragua.com), run by Vincent and Theresa, has all-inclusive packages for $750–1,500 per week with two daily boat trips to the best waves between Popoyo to the north and Manzanillo to the south.

Food

Two big, airy *ranchos* sit right on the beach: **La Gaviota** is famous for its *plato típico de Gigante* featuring seasonal seafood ($4–11). **El Mirador** prepares popular breaded fish nuggets *(deditos de pescado)*. Buy fresh seafood in the mornings from three local *acopios* (storage houses) and buy everything else from **Pulpería Mena.**

Getting There and Away

It's really best to have your own vehicle to reach Gigante. Otherwise, take the Las Salinas bus from Tola or Rivas and get off at the first entrance to Gigante. You'll have to walk or hitch about four kilometers to reach the beach. Taxis are few and far between, but anyone driving a pickup will probably let you hop in back. Only one bus a day goes all the way to Gigante; on the way home, a school bus departs in the morning for Rivas at around 5:30 A.M. ($1).

LAS SALINAS DE NAGUALAPA

Las Salinas is a humble fishing community whose lovely beach is popular among surfers. **La Tica** is its restaurant and *hospedaje*, where spartan rooms cost about $4 per person.

Nearby hot springs are worth exploring if you get sick of the beach (ask at La Tica for directions) but are also used by local families to wash clothing, so they're not exactly pristine.

The Surf Sanctuary (tel. 505/8894-6260, www.thesurfsanctuary.com) is a surf camp with restaurant, bar, TV, Internet, movies, and the works. For $60 per day, guests enjoy a private house with four beds, bath, hot water, air-conditioning, private porches, and pool; weeklong all-inclusive packages cost about $1,250 per person.

Guasacate and Popoyo

Guasacate, a huge stretch of gorgeous and mostly remote shoreline, is beautiful by any standard and for the moment, mostly undeveloped. Many of the restaurants and hotels in this area are European-owned, unlike mostly gringo San Juan del Sur, and relative to Playa Gigante, there's a better range of accomodations from weekly surf camps to midrange hotels to cheap crash-pad *hospedajes*. The entrance to Guasacate is 5–8 kilometers down the first left-hand road after crossing a bridge in Las Salinas. The road runs along the ocean until it dead-ends at Playa Popoyo, with a handful of hotels and restaurants sprinkled along the 12-kilometer stretch. If you're here, you're probably here to surf; in case of disaster, have Maximo (across from Rana Roja, tel. 505/8467-1798) fix your board, or take it to Popoyo Ding Repair/La Tiendita (tel. 505/8464 9563), a cute shop that repairs, rents, and sells boards and other handmade items, 200 meters down the road.

ACCOMODATIONS
Under $25

At the budget end of the spectrum is **(** **Popoyo Loco,** a funky surf shack right on the beach, offering a bed in a dorm with a thin mattress, fan, and shared bath for $5 per person. You won't find Internet or phone here, but feel free to use the kitchen. **La Tica Dos** (end of the road on the east side) is a two-story affair catering to surfers; $10 gets you a room, fan, private bath, and a few grunts from the unhelpful owner. Hotel Popoyo also has a few dorm beds at $14.

$25-50

El Club del Surf (tel. 505/8456-6068, www.elclubdelsurf.com) has Wi-Fi and five nice doubles with cable TV, air-conditioning, and private bath for $40; be sure to get a room facing the ocean. The restaurant features affordable Italian specialties and a variety of fresh salads (tuna, chicken, Caprese) and, of course, wine.

$50-100

On the left side of the road at the end of a short driveway, behind El Toro, sits **Hotel Popoyo** (tel. 505/8885-3334, www.hotelpopoyo.com) where a spacious room with a king-size canopy bed, plenty of windows, bamboo roof, air-conditioning, and cable TV goes for $89 including tax and breakfast. Pleasant and clean dorms are $14. There's a pool out back and a few hammocks slung under the *rancho*. Hotel Popoyo is closed the month of October.

Over $100

Popoyo Surf Lodge (tel. 321/735-0322, www.surfnicaragua.com) pioneered the local surf scene in the 1990s. The owner, JJ, is a ripping, born-again surfer who also preaches at the local church. Reservations and packages are available online; drop-ins (no surf pun intended) accepted in the off-season. About 300 meters from the beach, **Surfari Charters** (tel. 505/8874-7173, www.surfaricharters.com) specializes in all-inclusive surf and fishing trips; check their website for more information and captivating photography.

Across the street, **Two Brothers Surf Resort** (tel. 505/8877-7501, www.twobrothers-surf.com) offers more luxury, comfort, and security. Villas range $100–200 a night plus tax. The big one fits up to six people; the resort features a pool, lounge, hand-carved Indonesian temple doors and archways, locally crafted Granada floor tiles, fully equipped kitchens, air-conditioning, ceiling fans, and indoor and outdoor showers.

FOOD AND BARS

The most popular eatery in Guasacate is **El Toro** (behind Hotel Popoyo, east side of the road, tel. 505/8885-3334), with an airy dining area and a great selection of meatless treats such as gazpacho, hummus, pasta, and veggie burritos. Rum and cokes are $1 at their 4–6 P.M. happy hour. Just past El Toro, **Rana Roja** serves wood-fired pizza from 6–10:30 P.M., closed Monday.

Los Amores del Sol, or simply "el rancho" (at the end of the road), is a well-liked beachfront restaurant and full bar where you can watch the waves roll in or just enjoy the meticulously landscaped grounds. Breakfast is $3, lunch and dinner $4–10.

GETTING THERE AND AWAY

At least one bus a day leaves Roberto Huembes market in Managua bound for El Astillero via Ochomogo (not Tola). From San Juan del Sur or Costa Rica, you'll be driving through Rivas and Tola, following the signs to Rancho Santana, then continuing past this development's gates until you reach Las Salinas. Buses depart Rivas about every hour. A taxi to Guasacate from El Astillero costs $7, from Rivas $30. The road to the beach will take you past several austere salt flats, from which the nearby town of Las Salinas gets its name.

EL ASTILLERO AND BEACHES TO THE NORTH

Most of the little deserted beaches in the 10-kilometer strip between Las Salinas and El Astillero don't even have names. El Astillero itself is a fishing village full of small boats and is, in fact, the first safe boat anchorage north of Gigante. North of El Astillero, the road turns inland away from the coast. Accessing the beach anywhere along this area requires a boat and a lot of dedication. Ask around in El Astillero. There are plenty of underemployed sailors and fishermen that would be glad to strike a deal with you if you're interested in exploring the coastline.

REFUGIO DE VIDA SILVESTRE RÍO ESCALANTE-CHACOCENTE

One of the only Nicaraguan Pacific beaches where the Paslama turtle lays its eggs, Escalante-Chacocente Wildlife Refuge (tel. 505/2532-3293, www.chacocente.info) is a protected wildlife area whose beach provides habitat for numerous other species as well, including white-tailed deer, reptiles, and many interesting types of flora. There's lots to do, including guided wildlife tours, sportfishing, scuba diving, and projects with various local communities. Getting to Chacocente isn't easy which, for the sake of the turtles, is just as well. One early morning bus leaves Diriamba daily for Chacocente, spends the night, and returns to Diriamba before dawn the next day. Campers can bring their own tent or stay in the visitors center's wooden bungalows for only a couple of dollars. To get there, the turnoff from the Pan-American Highway is just south of the Río Ochomogo bridge, or take a taxi from Rivas (about $20 for the 90-minute ride).

Peñas Blancas and the Costa Rica Border

Peñas Blancas is the official border crossing into Costa Rica. Since 1999, this post has undergone massive construction and renovation, making it a nicer—and better organized—post than even Costa Rica's (although the Ticos have a cafeteria on their side, something still lacking on the Nica side of the border). A major effort is underway, with financing from the United States, to make this border crossing a bottleneck and entrapment point for drug traffickers headed north. Many of the buildings you see in the compound are inspection points for the hundreds of tractor-trailers that cross the border every day. Needless to say, this is one place you don't want to be caught smuggling furs. Sniffing dogs are common.

Border hassles can last anywhere from 1–10 hours! The longest waits happen at times when the hundreds of thousands of Nicaraguans living across the border are traveling to and from their country—this happens a week before and after Christmas, Easter, and any Nicaraguan election. The best time of day to cross is during the afternoon. Usually you can squeeze through in under an hour.

HOURS AND FEES

The border is open 6 A.M.–10 P.M. on all days, except Sunday when it closes at 8 P.M. There is a small fee for exiting ($2–4) and entering ($7–9) Nicaragua. Everyone traveling to the border on an international bus service like TicaBus or TransNica will pay $1 to the town government of Cárdenas before reaching the border, "just because."

Inside the customs and immigration building, find a branch of Bancentro, which can help you change money if necessary. Its schedule is generally tied to that of the border post itself.

PAPERWORK

Just a passport and some cash is all that's required of North American and European travelers, but don't forget to get stamped on both sides of the border to avoid subsequent headaches! To enter Costa Rica, Nicaraguan citizens must have a Costa Rican visa from the consulate either in Rivas or Managua. Upon entering Nicaragua, most North American and European travelers are granted a 90-day visa, with the exception of Canadian and Japanese citizens, who for some reason are only given 30 days.

By law, folks entering Costa Rica must have a ticket to leave the country. They usually don't check, as long as you're dressed like you have money. If they do, you lose your place in line and go to the table outside, where Transport Dendu will sell you an open-ended ticket from San Jose to Managua for $7.

ENTERING NICARAGUA WITH YOUR VEHICLE

If you are driving your own vehicle, the process to enter Nicaragua from Costa Rica is lengthy but usually not too difficult (rental vehicles cannot cross the border). You'll present your title (Titulo de la Propiedad), as well as your driver's license and passport. Get proper stamps from Hacienda (Timbres de Hacienda), and a property certificate from Hacienda. Also make sure you have a current tag and Tico insurance; all of this can be taken care of in the town of Liberia, just to the south. You will be given a temporary (30-day) permit to drive in Nicaragua that will cost $10—should you lose the permit, you will be fined $100. Travelers driving their own vehicles north from the border will be forced to pass through a dubious "sterilization process" on the Nica side, in which the exterior of the vehicle is sprayed with a mystery liquid to kill porcine and bovine diseases; it costs $1 and takes five minutes unless the line is long. Roll up the windows.

GETTING THERE AND AWAY

International bus services like TicaBus are popular ways to get across the border easily and comfortably, the best service being the new TransNica Plus, since you travel with 30 instead of 55 passengers. In many cases, the bus has a helper who collects your passports and money and waits in line for you. The disadvantage is that the bus won't pull away from the border post until every single traveler has had their papers processed, which can be time-consuming in some cases (waits up to four hours are not unheard of). More confident travelers like to take a Nicaraguan bus to the border, walk across to Costa Rica, and take a Costa Rican bus to San José, which is often faster. Express buses from Managua to Peñas Blancas depart Mercado Huembes at 5 A.M., 8 A.M., 9:30 A.M., and 3:30 P.M. Buses and microbuses leave the market in Rivas every 30–45 minutes. On the Costa Rican side, the last bus leaves the border bound for San José at 10 P.M. (about a six-hour ride).

CONTINUING INTO COSTA RICA

After crossing the border, you've got two choices: Buy a ticket to San José from the TransNica booth across from customs ($7 pp); the ride takes 6–8 hours, with departures daily at 5:15 A.M., 7:30 A.M., 9:30 A.M. direct, 10:45 A.M., noon, 1:30 P.M. direct, 3:30 P.M. , and 6 P.M. Or, get a Liberia–Pulmitan bus to Liberia ($1.50 pp, two hours, last bus at 5:30 P.M.). From Liberia, 14 daily buses go to San José ($4, 3–5 hours); buses leave every 20 minutes to the Nicoya Peninsula and its beaches. Liberia, the capital of Guanacaste, is also a good base for Santa Rosa National Park (where William Walker and company were resoundingly defeated) and Rincón de la Vieja National Park, with impressive volcanoes. In fact, Guanacaste used to belong to Nicaragua and some say it still feels connected, or at least socially and physically independent of Costa Rica proper. Many locals still have family in Nicaragua, and this is the only department with its own flag. You can overnight in **Hotel Liberia** (tel. 506/666-0161, www. hotelliberia.com, $5 pp with shared bath, $9 pp with private bath and really nice room) was highly recommended by several readers as safe, cheap, and clean.

LEÓN AND THE VOLCANIC LOWLANDS

Northwest of Managua are broad plains of peanuts, corn, beans, sorghum, and sugarcane. The fecund soils that make this the most agriculturally productive region in Nicaragua are a gift from the Maribio volcanoes, an uncommonly active and exposed chain of peaks and cones stretching from Lake Xolotlán to the Gulf of Fonseca.

Fire gives way to water, and the Pacific northwest coastline of Nicaragua includes some of the longest, most isolated stretches of sand in the country. There are coastal islands, endless estuaries, and virgin mangrove stands rich in marine life and waterfowl. Large tracts of this region are still difficult to access, but progress and paved roads are slowly creeping up on them.

You can't help but feel itinerant in León and Chinandega. Blame it on the heat—this is the driest, most scorching corner of the country. Volcanism seeps from the land in boiling mud pits, geothermal vents, and the occasional rumble. The ruins of León's first incarnation are a testament to the area's impermanence. This region suffered tremendously during Hurricane Mitch in 1998, when more than two meters of rain fell in three days. Nowhere in Nicaragua was the destruction as intense, and the still-visible landslide at Las Casitas is a silent reminder of the worst of it. For this, Leóneses and Chinandeganos know that life can be short and even violent, and should thus be enjoyed.

León is the principal city of the northwest, a colonial town with the architecture and

© JOSHUA BERMAN

HIGHLIGHTS

(León's Museums: Begin your art immersion at **La Casa de Cultura** and then continue around the corner to the fabulous **Centro de Arte Fundación Ortiz-Gurdián** (page 163).

(Volcano Boarding on Cerro Negro: Whether you go sitting down on a toboggan or standing up on a modified snowboard, hurling yourself down a steep pitch of tiny black pebbles on an active volcano is a scream (page 170).

(Las Ruinas de León Viejo: As old as Nicaragua's colonial history, this legitimate archaeological dig exposes the bones of Spain's earliest settlement (page 178).

(Las Peñitas Beach: Relaxing and peaceful accommodations at the ocean's edge all offer easy access to the impressive Isla Juan Venado (page 180).

(Padre Ramos Wetlands Reserve: If you're into isolated beaches and protected bird-filled estuaries, the bouncy trip north is worth it (page 193).

LOOK FOR **(** TO FIND RECOMMENDED SIGHTS, ACTIVITIES, DINING, AND LODGING.

languid lifestyle of centuries past. This bastion of liberal thought in Central America has narrow streets lined with cathedrals, universities, and cafés. For five hundred years, León's political history has consisted of long stretches of peace, punctuated by the staccato call of uprising, resistance, and war.

In contrast, Chinandega, Nicaragua's most northwestern city, is the agribusiness capital of the country, center for both the sugarcane and shrimp industries. Chinandega Department is also home to the Padre Ramos Reserve and the Cosigüina peninsula, whose beaches and surf are just beginning to be visited by foreigners.

PLANNING YOUR TIME

León is one of the few Nicaraguan cities with more attractions than you can see in a day. Plan on at least two to visit the museums and cathedrals of the city; another if you plan to hike a volcano, and another if you head to the shore. Las Peñitas, Isla Juan Venado, Padre Ramos, and other points outside León require more effort to get to but are excellent destinations for those traveling on a slightly slower schedule. It's worth slowing down in fact, so you can paddle boats through the estuaries and observe the wildlife (like nesting turtles on Juan Venado). There is plenty to do, whether you come for two days or two weeks.

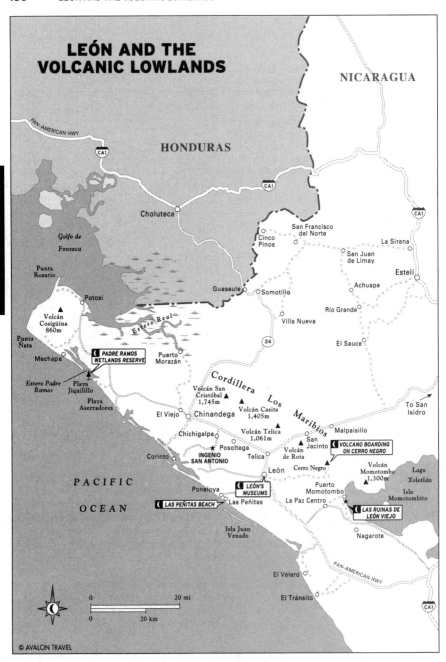

LEÓN AND THE VOLCANIC LOWLANDS

NICARAGUA

HONDURAS

Choluteca

Golfo de Fonseca

Punta Rosario

Potosí

Volcán Cosigüina 860m

Punta Nata

Mechapa

Estero Padre Ramos

Playa Jiquilillo

Playa Aserradores

Corinto

PACIFIC

OCEAN

PAN-AMERICAN HWY

CA1

CA1

CA1

San Francisco del Norte

Cinco Pinos

La Sirena

San Juan de Limay

Estelí

Achuapa

Guasaule

Somotillo

Río Grande

Villa Nueva

El Sauce

Estero Real

Puerto Morazán

24

Cordillera Los Maribios

Volcán San Cristóbal ▲ 1,745m

El Viejo

Chinandega

Chichigalpa

Posoltega

Telica

León

▲ Volcán Casita 1,405m

Volcán Telica 1,061m

San Jacinto

Volcán de Rota

Cerro Negro

Malpaisillo

To San Isidro

☾ PADRE RAMOS WETLANDS RESERVE

★ INGENIO SAN ANTONIO

☾ VOLCANO BOARDING ON CERRO NEGRO

Volcán Momotombo ▲ 1,300m

Lago Xolotlán

Isla Momotombito

☾ LEÓN'S MUSEUMS

Poneloya

☾ LAS PEÑITAS BEACH

Las Peñitas

Puerto Momotombo

La Paz Centro

☾ LAS RUINAS DE LEÓN VIEJO

Isla Juan Venado

Nagarote

El Velero

El Tránsito

PAN-AMERICAN HWY

CA1

0   20 mi

0   20 km

© AVALON TRAVEL

City of León

The principal metropolis of the low-lying Nicaraguan northwest, León has had several incarnations over the centuries. The Spaniards first built the city along the shores of Lake Xolotlán; they picked up and moved when Volcán Momotombo shook the ground beneath their feet. Modern León is at once a dusty provincial capital and an architectural delight; traditionally designed colonial homes, churches, universities, and an immense cathedral stand shoulder to shoulder in a tropical torpor that keeps city life to a low, but exciting hum. León is an easily walkable city, with a plethora of interesting cafés and restaurants, Latin America's largest cathedral, and an ambience quite unlike anywhere else in Nicaragua. Its longtime political rival, Granada, may have more fresh paint and international adoration, but León remains an irreverent, unique city where tourism is merely an afterthought, not a necessity.

HISTORY

The short-lived first city of León was a Spanish settlement founded by Francisco Hernández de Córdoba next to the indigenous village of Imabite on the shore of Lake Xolotlán in 1524. The Spanish were lousy neighbors. They immediately began to enslave the Imabite and doled out cruel punishments: Many natives met their ends at the jaws of the Spanish attack dogs. The old city was abandoned in 1610 when Volcán Momotombo erupted. They relocated alongside the indigenous village of Subtiava, which over the centuries was subsumed by the growing commercial center of León.

León was the capital of Nicaragua during Liberal governments several times before 1852. It has also been both a university town and a hotbed for leftist thought since colonial times. The Sandinistas found ready supporters here in the 1960s and '70s, and Somoza retaliated ferociously, even torching

LEÓN

León's many cathedrals are one reason to visit the city.

© JOSHUA BERMAN

LEÓN

CITY OF LEÓN

To Bus Terminal →

6 CALLE NE

CARNE ASADA ESTACION
OLD TRAIN STATION

5 CALLE NE

4 CALLE NE

3 CALLE NE

2 CALLE NE

HOTEL EUROPA

IGLESIA DE EL CALVARIO

Río Chiquito

HOTEL SAN JUAN DE LEÓN

IGLESIA DE SAN JUAN

IL CAPRICCIO

QUETZAL TREKKERS

HOTEL REAL

VIA VIA

HOTEL AMERICA

HOTEL POSADA DEL DOCTOR

CASONA COLONIAL GUESTHOUSE

IGLESIA LA RECOLECCION

GREEN PATHWAY TOURS

BIG FOOT

CINEMA

BAC

HOTEL LOS BALCONES

EL BUEN GUSTO

2 CALLE SE

3 CALLE SE

HOSTAL CASA LEONESA

CENTRAL MARKET

HOSPITAL

CASA PELLAS CAR RENTAL

AVENIDA CENTRAL

6 CALLE NO

1 AV NO

HOTEL LA PERLA

IGLESIA DE LA MERCED

CATEDRAL DE LEÓN

1 CALLE SE

HOTEL AUSTRIA

HOSTAL LA CLINICA

MUSEO DE LEYENDAS

RUINAS DE SAN SEBASTIÁN

Park

TIERRA TOURS

CASINO

PUERTO CAFÉ BEN LINDER

INTUR

RESTAURANTE FLOR DE SAGUANJOCHE

CAFÉ ROSITA

TAQUEZAL

BARBARO

ENITEL

LAUNDRY

HOSTALA LA CASONA

4 CALLE NO

2 AV NO

LAZY BONES

Parque Rubén Darío

DELICHAS TROPICALES

HOTEL EL CONVENTO

MUSEUM: LA CASA DE CULTURA

LIBRERIA DON QUIJOTE

MARCOLETA

TEATRO MUNICIPAL

CASA IVANA

3 AV SO

POST OFFICE

3 AV NO

CASA VIEJA CAFETÍN

INTERNET

CASA MUSEO RUBÉN DARÍO

MUSEUM: CENTRO DE ARTE FUNDACIÓN O-G

COCINARTE/VA PUES TOURS

4 AV SO

3 CALLE SO

4 AV NO

3 CALLE NO

SUPERMERCADO SALMON

1 CALLE NO

HOSTAL TORTUGA BOLUDA

CALLE CENTRAL

CALLE JOSÉ DE

2 CALLE SO

IGLESIA EL LABORIO

3 CALLE SO

5 AV NO

2 CALLE NO

LA OLLA QUEMADA

6 AV SO

To Subtiava and Poneloya buses

7 AV SO

© AVALON TRAVEL

200 yds

200 m

0

0

the central market and strifing peaceful demonstrations.

In September 1978, Sandinista forces attacked key locations in León, including National Guard installations at the famous XXI building. In response, Somoza bombed the populations of both León and Chinandega, and tortured or executed anyone suspected of sympathizing with the Sandinistas. Sandinista troops took León on June 4 after two days of vicious battle whose bullet holes remain to the present, as does local sympathy for the FSLN.

ORIENTATION

León is laid out in the traditional colonial grid system with the central park and cathedral at the center. It sprawls impressively in all directions. The main bus terminal and market are nearly a kilometer northeast of the main plaza, and Barrio Subtiava is 12 blocks due west. A *zona rosa* of sorts, is developing along 1 Calle SO as it extends westward from the southwest corner of the plaza. Most of the town's nightlife is condensed here; university campuses are primarily just north of the plaza.

SIGHTS
◖ Museums

León's museums are exceedingly eclectic, covering the political, natural, and all things cultural. Start at **La Casa de Cultura** (from the Iglesia San Francisco, one block north, 20 meters east, tel. 505 /2311-2116, open 8 A.M.– noon and 2–7:30 P.M. Mon.–Fri., until 6 P.M. Sat. and Sun.), housed in an old colonial home; enjoy a collection of artwork that includes a disparaging painting of Ronald Reagan and Henry Kissinger. Entrance is free. This is a good place to find out about all kinds of cultural classes and activities.

La Casa de Rubén Darío (tel. 505/2311-2388, open 8 A.M.–noon and 2–5 P.M. Tues.– Sat., 8 A.M.–noon Sun.) is a glimpse into León in the 19th century. Nicaragua's favorite son lived here with his aunt and uncle until the age of 14. Fellow poet Alfonso Cortéz later inhabited the same house as he battled insanity (the room he inhabited still has the iron

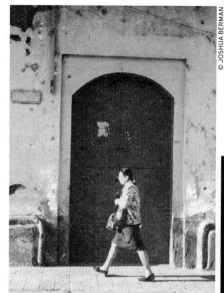

León has a slightly rougher look than its rival to the south, Granada.

bars he bent during one attempted escape). Darío's bed and the rest of the furnishings of the museum are typical of middle-class León in the late 19th century, as is the building itself, built from adobe with a clay-tile and cane roof. On display are original copies of his most famous works translated into several languages and copies of a magazine he published in Paris. The silver crucifix given him by Mexican poet Amado Nervos, correspondence from when Darío was the consul to Argentina and ambassador to Spain, and period coins and currency are also displayed; donations of $1–2 are accepted for the upkeep of the building.

A block west of the Parque Casa de Rubén Darío occupying two facing buildings, the **Centro de Arte Fundación Ortiz-Gurdián** (open 10:30 A.M.–6 P.M. Tues.–Sat. and 9 A.M.–5 P.M. Sun., $0.75 admission, free on Sun.) has reputedly the best collection of Latin American artwork in Nicaragua, with an emphasis on colonial America.

A WALKING TOUR OF CHURCHES AND RUINS

La Catedral de León is the largest cathedral in Central America and the modern city's focal point. One (probably apocryphal) story claims the architect accidentally switched two sets of plans while on the ship from Spain, and the larger of the two cathedrals, originally intended for Lima, Peru, was built in Nicaragua. The cathedral was constructed in 1747 at the request of Archbishop Isidoro Bullón y Figueroa and inaugurated in 1860 as a basilica by Pope Pius XI. It's an imposing and majestic baroque structure whose grandeur is magnified by the open space of the park in front of it. You can observe elements of late Gothic and neoclassical architecture, primarily from inside. Check out the paintings of the stations of the cross and the 12 apostles. The **Tomb of Rubén Darío** is a notable element of the cathedral – look for the golden statue of a lion. The cathedral holds the mortal remains of the musician José de la Cruz Mena and several religious figures. Look for the famous *Cristo de Pedrarias*, a painting that once hung in the cathedral of León Viejo. The particularly beautiful **Patio de los Príncipes** is a small courtyard of Andalusian design, with a fountain in the center and colorful beds of flowers. Ask in the INTUR office about **rooftop tours.** The conglomerate of white towers and domes that form the roof of the Catedral de León is fascinating in its own right – and the view of the city and nearby volcanoes is unsurpassed.

NORTH AND EAST FROM THE CENTRAL PARK

Iglesia de la Merced, 1.5 blocks north of the main cathedral, is the church considered most representative of León in the 1700s. It was originally built in 1762 by the Mercedarian monks, the first order of monks to arrive in Nicaragua during the years of the conquest. It is essentially baroque in style but has neoclassical elements in the front and colonial on the south. It faces a small but lovely park popular amongst León's skateboarders. Particularly attractive is the church's side bell tower.

Passing the Iglesia de la Merced and walking two blocks east along 2 Calle NE, you'll find the yellow **Iglesia de la Recolección** on the north side. This church has the most perfect baroque style of the León churches and a massive, functional bell tower. It was built in 1786 by Bishop Juan Félix de Villegas and is the only church in León constructed using carved stone.

From the Iglesia de la Recolección, continue one more block and turn north. Walk two blocks until you reach the picturesque **Iglesia de San Juan.** The old train station is a block farther north from the east side of the church. Built 1625–1650 and rebuilt in the 1700s, the Iglesia de San Juan's architecture is a modern interpretation of neoclassicism. This neighborhood of León will give you a good feel for what León was like in the 1700s: church, park, small houses of adobe using traditional *taquezal* construction techniques, and the nearby market.

Walking four blocks south down the same road, you'll find the **Iglesia del Calvario** on your left side. It is set at the top of broad steps on a small hill overlooking one of León's narrow streets. Renovated in the late 1990s, Calvario was built 200 years previous in a generally baroque style, but with neoclassical ornamentation in the front that reflects the increasing French influence in Spain in the 18th century. Inside are two famous statues known as *El Buen y el Mal Ladrón* (The Good and the Bad Thief).

SOUTH AND WEST FROM THE CENTRAL PARK

La Iglesia y Convento de San Francisco, three blocks west of the park on the north

from the roof of León's cathedral

side, and across the street from the Casa Museo Rubén Darío, contains two of the most beautiful altars of colonial Nicaragua. The church was built in 1639 by Fray Pedro de Zuñiga and rebuilt and modified several times afterwards, notably in the mid-1980s to restore the damage done to it during the revolution. Its small, tree-lined courtyard is a pleasant place to escape from the hot sun and relax.

Turning and walking a block south, you come to the unassuming **Iglesia de San Juan de Dios,** built in 1620 as a chapel for León's first hospital (now gone). Its simplicity and colonial style reflect the wishes of Felipe II when he designed it in 1573.

Two blocks farther south and one short block to the west is the **Iglesia del Laborío,** a graceful, rural-feeling church in the old mixed neighborhood of El Laborío. This church, one of León's earliest, formed the nucleus of the working-class neighborhood that provided labor to León's wealthy class in the 17th century. The street from Laborío east to the Ruinas de la Ermita de San Sebastián is known as **Calle la Españolita** and was one of the first streets built in León.

The **Ruinas de la Ermita de San Sebastián** consist of the shattered remnants of the outer walls, and inexplicably, the intact bell tower. The Ermita was built in 1742 on a site long used by the indigenous people for worship of their own gods. It suffered major damage in 1979 during Somoza's bombardment of León. El Museo de Tradiciones y Leyendas is across the street.

LEÓN

LOCAL GUIDES AND TOUR OPERATORS IN LEÓN

In addition to being rich in history, museums, cathedrals, and natural wonders, León is also blessed with an intelligent young crop of guides and creatively conscious tour operators, both locals and *extranjeros* who enjoy sharing their knowledge and love of the land. Most accommodations can also recommend a guide or company, but here are a few options to let you know who's doing what.

For city tours and day trips to nearby sites like León Viejo, San Jacinto Hot Springs, Isla Juan Venado, and others, you can start with **Julio Tours Nicaragua** (Calle Rubén Darío, one block east of the San Francisco Catholic Church, tel. 505/8625-4467, info@juliotoursnicaragua.com.ni, www.juliotoursnicaragua.com.ni). We've received rave reviews for Julio's relaxed, homespun services and highly recommend him.

Started by Barbados-born biology major Phillip Southan, **Green Pathways Tours** (tel. 505/2315-0964 or 505/8333-0898, greenpathways@gmail.com, www.greenpathways.com) is a self-described "association of naturalists and travelers" who are constantly asking the question, "Are the actions of my travels making a positive impact on the people and environment of the places I visit?" They focus on outdoorsy activities like volcanoes, local tours, and whale-watching (January-March); there is also a mouthwatering list of expeditions to far-flung corners of the country, including a kayak trip down the Río San Juan. They also offer important

traveler services like TicaBus tickets (office open 10 A.M.-6 P.M. daily) and beach house rentals.

Vapues Tours (Costado Norte, from Iglesia del Laborío, in front of Casa Cural, tel. 505/2315-4999, info@vapues.com, www.vapues.com), with an office across from the Iglesia del Laborío, offer a huge range of reasonably priced trips, plus shuttle services to other cities across the country. They can take you to Cosigüina, to Selva Negra, or to Granada and points south. They are also tied in with some community-based tourism efforts. **Tierra Tours** (1.5 blocks north of Iglesia de la Merced, tel. 505/2311-0599, tierratour@gmail.com, http://tierratour.com) has offices in Granada and León, and are highly recommended, along with Vapues Tours, for any number of trips. Both can take you on volcano or history tours and also offer countrywide all-inclusive packages, international bus tickets, and domestic flight booking. They also both produce excellent local maps which you can pick up around town.

For more eccentric, community-immersion tours, let Harrie from Holland, founder of **Nicaragua Así Tours** (tel. 505/8414-1192, www.nicasitours.com) take you to a cockfight, cow ranch, cooking class, or history tour. He likes to show visitors "more of Nicaragua than you can imagine exists." This generally means interacting with everyday Nicas, witnessing interesting community events, and will give you many opportunities to practice your Spanish.

El Museo de Tradiciones y Leyendas (Barrio Laborío, open 8 A.M.–noon and 2–5 P.M. Mon.–Sat., 8 A.M.–noon Sun., $1) celebrates Nicaragua's favorite folktales: the golden crab, La Carreta Nagua, the pig-witch, and La Mocuana. The building itself is the former XXI jail and base of the 12th Company of Somoza's National Guard. Built in 1921, **XXI** meted out 60 years of brutal torture. The mango tree that now shades this museum was planted by a prisoner and watered from the

same well that was used for electric shock and water-boarding sessions.

Murals

Many of León's colorful murals are products of the 1980s which have been painstakingly maintained. Other new ones still spring up each year. Perhaps the most famous is located across from the north side of the main cathedral—a long, horizontal piece telling the history of a proud and turbulent nation.

Starting on the left with the arrival of the Nahuatl, the mural traces the planned interoceanic canal, the exploits of William Walker, Sandino's battle with U.S. Marines, the revolution of 1979, and a utopian ending image of a fertile, peaceful Nicaragua; flanking a doorway across the street, Sandino steps on Uncle Sam's and Somoza's heads. One block to the west the CIA, in the form of a thick serpent, coils through the Sandinistas' agrarian reform, literacy campaign, and construction efforts, to strike at a Nicaraguan hand at the ballot box. The trend seems to be reviving in the 21st century; to wit, the intricate anticorruption mural on the basketball court.

Other Sights

The shady and pleasant **Parque Rubén Darío** (also known as Parque de los Poetas), a block west of the central park, pays tribute to four famous Nicaraguan writers, all sons of León: Azarías H. Pallais (1884–1954), Salomon de la Selva (1893–1959), Alfonzo Cortéz (1893–1969), and of course, the beloved Rubén Darío (1867–1916).

León's **Old Train Station,** built in 1884, was Nicaragua's first and most majestic. It has been rebuilt since being gutted by fire in 1956, now housing a boisterous market.

The creepy yet captivating **El Fortín de Acosasco** sits on a grassy hill just south of the city, providing phenomenal views of the entire Maribio volcano chain. Conservative president Sacasa built it in 1889 to keep an eye on the Liberals that would overthrow him four years later. Abandoned until Anastasio Somoza took interest and rehabilitated it, El Fortín has since served as both a military base and jail. It is presently abandoned once again, though the city has invested a small amount to seal off the dangerous dungeons and to slap on some fresh paint. From the Subtiava church, it's an easy 45-minute walk or $6 by taxi (don't walk alone): Go one block east and head due south up the hill along the shady dirt road. The panorama of the city is worth the walk (or taxi), though the stench and smoke from the nearby abandoned landfill can be a drag if the wind is blowing the wrong way (the city promises to cover it up soon).

Sights in Barrio Subtiava

The indigenous neighborhood of Subtiava (Maribio for "land of the big men") retains a trace of both its cultural identity and political autonomy. Besides the thrill of walking the streets of a village predating Columbus, note several interesting ruins here. Just about any of the microbuses that circulate through León will take you to Subtiava if you're not up for the 12-block walk.

La Catedral de Subtiava, beautiful in its aged simplicity, is second only to the Catedral de León in size and is the keystone of the community. Construction began in 1698 and finished 12 years later, but the indigenous inhabitants of Subtiava kept worshiping their own gods despite Spanish proselytism. In an effort to get the locals into the church, the Spanish mounted a carved wooden image of the sun representing the local god on the church ceiling, a compromise that left everyone satisfied, even if, during a church service the Spanish and locals were simultaneously worshiping different gods. The beautifully crafted sun remains, as do the immense wooden columns that evoke the kind of forest that surrounded León three hundred years ago. Next to the cathedral is the Casa Cural, which predates the cathedral of Subtiava by 160 years but was rebuilt in 1743.

Across the street from the cathedral on the north side is the **Museo Adiact** (open 8 A.M.–noon and 2–5 P.M. Mon.–Fri., 8 A.M.–noon Sat., $1–2 donation), a run-down but captivating museum that houses many of the area's archaeological treasures. Sadly, some of the better idols and statues were stolen in the late 1980s and sold to foreign museums.

Five blocks east of the cathedral's southern side is a small park dedicated to the last cacique of Subtiava, Adiact, and his daughter, Xochilt Acalt. From the cathedral of Subtiava, three blocks south and two blocks west is **El Tamarindón,** an enormous, gnarled tamarind

LEÓN

tree from whose branches the Spanish hung the last cacique.

There are two sets of ruins in Subtiava, **Las Ruinas de Veracruz** (one block west of the cathedral, set in high weeds) and **Las Ruinas de Santiago** (one block north of the cathedral on the other side of Calle Central, look for a small sign). The church at Veracruz was Subtiava's first, built sometime around 1560 and abandoned in the late 1700s due to its small size. The eruption of Volcán Cosigüina in 1835 caused its subsequent collapse. The church at Santiago, constructed in the early 1600s, is significant because its small square bell tower remains intact.

ENTERTAINMENT AND EVENTS
Bars and Discos

It's no surprise that a university town like León would have a thriving nightlife. And it's not just poor students here—there is plenty of money in town to support a semi-upscale nightlife. For student-centered beer gardens, roam the university area in the two blocks north of the main plaza. The nicest *discotecas* and bars are clustered on a single block called the *zona rosa* (a tongue-in-cheek swipe at Managua's more impressive and similarly-named hot spot), located on Calle 1 SO between Avenida 1 and Avenida 2. Walk west from the southwest corner of the main plaza.

Start at ◖ **Bar Baro** (one block west of the southwest corner of main plaza, tel. 505/2315-2901 or 8820-4000, open 8 A.M. to midnight daily, till 2 A.M. on weekends), a lively, high-ceilinged tavern where you can choose between a romantic loungy area, a quiet coffee patio, or a convivial bar-restaurant. The drink menu is the longest we've seen in the country, the food is excellent, and you can actually have a conversation with your friends without shouting!

For dancing, the best disco with the most varied music selection is **Oxigeno** (the sign says O2, open from 8 P.M. Wed.–Sat.), where things start picking up around 11 P.M. Or there are several other options on the same block, including **Liquid** (usually with a $5 cover charge), which

is also popular. **Dilectus** (south of the city center on the highway, tel. 505/2311-5439) is the fanciest and most expensive *discoteca* in town, with a fun crowd and well-mixed music; it's also an upscale and attractive restaurant with occasional live music and karaoke. Thursday is mariachi night and Friday is teen night; entrance fee is $2, but budget in a taxi ride home at the end of the night. Across from Parque La Merced, the **Don Señor** complex—disco, restaurant, downstairs dive, and upstairs patio lounge with a view of the nightlife—attracts the college crowd and foreigners. The disco is open from 8:30 P.M. Tuesday–Saturday, usually with a small cover charge ($2). The restaurant and the bars are open for lunch and dinner, and close late on Saturdays. The latest of the late-night options is **Salon Estrella** (one block south of La Iglesia de la Recolección) which lasts until 3 A.M. on the weekends.

Check out the fancy new casino across from Hotel La Perla, built with detailed attention to local architecture and modern casino offerings.

Live Music

Several bars and cafés host a weekly live music night. Friday nights at **Vía Vía** are a must; for current listings, can ask the folks at CocinArte (across from the north side of La Iglesia el Laborío). On Wednesdays, go to **La Olla Quemada** (a block west of Rubén Darío's House Museum) with a nice atmosphere and variety of performing artists. **Tequetzal** (half a block west of the central park) hosts live music on Thursday nights.

Cinema and Theater

León's small but modern **cinema** is in the Plaza Siglo Nuevo shopping center (from the cathedral, one block north, one block east, tel. 505/2311-7080). Look for the *cartelera* (schedule) at shops around the city for show times; tickets cost $4. **El Teatro Municipal José de la Cruz Mena** (one block south of the southwest corner of the central park, tel. 505/2311-1788) is the cultural heart of the city, open to the public for half-hour theater tours during the day with all kinds of events at night. Some big-name performers prefer León over Managua.

Special Events and Festivals

June 1 is the celebration of Somoza's defeat in León and August 14 is **La Gritería Chiquita,** when devout Catholics celebrate being spared from Cerro Negro's frequent eruptions. The first week of December is huge, with loud, firework-festooned celebrations of the Immaculate Conception. León celebrates its *fiestas patronales* on September 24 and the weeks surrounding it.

León's **Semana Santa** celebrations are acclaimed throughout Nicaragua as the nation's most lively. In addition to tons of food and drink, local artisans craft religious scenes in beds of colored sawdust worked painstakingly by hand.

SHOPPING

You won't find much in the way of traditional Nicaraguan crafts in León. For that, you still have to make it to the Huembes market in Managua, or to Masaya. You will, however, find plenty of used American clothes and old books, León's specialties. For books (and old Sandinista money), look for the sidewalk vendors near the plaza. The best shop is **Librería Don Quijote** (two blocks west of the park, open 8 A.M.–7 P.M. Mon.–Sat.), an interesting new and used book shop that sells many old Sandinista titles. For crafts, **Kaman,** just off the southwest corner of the plaza (open 9 A.M.–6 P.M. Mon.–Sat. with a break for lunch), has bead-making materials, bags and textiles from around Latin America, artsy postcards, and body piercing. There's a sprawling market near the bus terminal, or a smaller one immediately behind the cathedral with a selection for local shoppers, but not many crafts.

SPORTS AND RECREATION
Baseball

León has won more baseball championships than any other city in Nicaragua. Catch a game during the season (Jan.–May). Ask any taxi driver when the next game is and if he'll take you to the stadium on the edge of town.

© JOSHUA BERMAN

a used-book sale in León

LEÓN

Volcano Boarding on Cerro Negro

Careening down the black sands of Cerro Negro volcanic skree on a modified snowboard is León's most exciting outdoor adrenaline rush and with reason: the slope is a full 40° in places, and the ride is fast and hot. Stand-up boards get bogged down, but sitting down, you can build up some serious speed (Bigfoot has clocked clients at over 80 kph). Wear sturdy shoes, long pants, and long sleeves. Plan on a 60-minute climb and a 45-second descent in a hot, rugged landscape. Half-day trips run about $28 per person. The **Bigfoot** hostel runs daily trips which include an orange jumpsuit, goggles, gloves, and pads. **Vapues Tours** and **Tierra Tours** also make daily trips to Cerro Negro with experienced guides, and can pick you up and drop you off at your hotel.

At the entrance to Cerro Negro you will find a small information center, a *ranchón,* some bathrooms, and a friendly and informative local tourism cooperative called **Las Pilas-El Hoyo.** The $5 entrance fee goes to support conservation efforts and pays a portion of the members' salaries. Cooperative guides can take you on other hikes in the area, including the two taller volcanoes—El Hoyo and El Pilas—a nearby swimming hole, and a larger reservoir with some of the best views in the country.

ACCOMMODATIONS

When we wrote the first edition of *Moon Nicaragua* in 2002, we could fit every hotel option in León on one page. Today, dozens of hotels range from backpacker hostels to midrange and luxury hotels, and increased experience with foreign tourists is bringing the quality and the service up. You will sleep well here.

Under $25

The cheapest flop houses, often labeled *Abierto 24 Horas* (Open 24 hours) are located near the main bus terminal and are universally dismal in a potentially dangerous area; avoid them without hesitation.

Casa Ivana (across from the Teatro

surfing Cerro Negro

© JOSHUA BERMAN

Municipal's south side, tel. 505/2311-4423, $8 d) is the best Nicaraguan-owned option, with seven clean, quiet, safe rooms with private baths along a long garden in a family house. Around the corner, **Hostal La Clinica** (tel. 505/2311-2031, $5 in a dorm with fan, up to $25 with a/c) is another low-key, friendly, Nicaraguan-owned *hotelito* with a veritable jungle growing in the central patio. For a more Nicaraguan family-oriented, less meet-other-travelers vibe, check out **C** **Casona Colonial Guesthouse** (half a block west of the Parque San Juan, tel. 505/2311-3178, $15–25); its eight rooms with queen bed, private bath, hot water, and a fan represent one of the best bargains in León, complete with high ceilings, flower-filled courtyard, and beautiful wooden furniture.

The city's many international-oriented hostels each cater to a slightly different style: **La Tortuga Booluda** (1.5 blocks west from the San Juan de Dios church, tel. 505/2311-4653, www.tortugaBooluda.com) offers a breezy courtyard and has common hangout areas and a communal kitchen excellent for meeting other travelers. La Tortuga feels homey and prices range from $5 per dorm beds, to a small selection of rooms with private baths, $10–15; or choose the second-story en-suite with air-conditioning for $30. Features include a nice book exchange, billiards, coffee, Wi-Fi, and common-use kitchen. The only meal they serve is free pancake breakfasts for guests, a fun morning ritual.

Enter **C** **Vía Vía** (75 meters south of the Servicio Agrí cola Gurdián, tel. 505/2311-6142, www.viaviacafe.com) through its popular multicultural café and information area, then continue walking into a quiet, colonial-style patio where a small selection of dorms and private rooms surround a gorgeous garden. Two six-bed dorms go for $5 per person, and four rooms with private baths, high ceilings, and fans run $15–25. The building was reportedly built by an Italian in 1760 for his Nicaraguan mistress and her servants. Ask about Spanish classes and salsa dance lessons; also, expect your hosts to encourage you to get out and explore the area, as if you needed the encouragement.

Bigfoot Hostel (from Banco Procredit, half a block south, tel. 505/8917-8832, www.bigfootnicaragua.com, $6 dorm, $13 d) caters to backpackers, surfers, and anyone else who enjoys sipping a delicious mojito while seated in a small, footprint-shaped swimming pool. This is the biggest hostel in León, so expect a lively scene, but it doesn't get too crazy and is quiet after 10 P.M. The narrow but high hallways are dotted with events boards, rocking chairs, and clusters of barebacked travelers plotting their next move. Halls branch into multiple dormitories, common areas, and a mellow vegetarian eatery, the **Pure Earth Café.** Bigfoot offers lockboxes, a shared kitchen, laundry service, plus sign-up lists for the young owner's ecocentric tour company, Green Pathways. The hostel is ecofriendly, reusing shower water for the potted plants; they donate five *córdobas* from every mojito to a reforestation project (that's right, have another).

Centrally located two-and-a-half blocks north of Parque de los Poetas, **Lazy Bones** (tel. 505/2311-3472, www.lazybonesleon.com) offers $8 dorms and a handful of private rooms with fan for $19–28, some with shared bath. The kicker here is the pool, still a rarity in León hotels; seems to be a quieter option in this price range, offering free locker, breakfast, billiards, computers, and lounge space.

$25-50

Hotel San Juan de León (on the north side of the Plaza Iglesia San Juan, tel. 505/2311-0547, www.hsanjuandeleon.com, $40) has 20 smallish rooms with fan and private bath (a bit more with a/c) on two floors surrounding a tasteful courtyard and kitchen for guests' use. Breakfast is included. Another excellent, friendly family option in this range is **Hotel Real** (tel. 505/2311-2606, hotel.real@gmail.com, $45); 14 well-equipped rooms in a nicely furnished, comfortable home with Wi-Fi; be sure to compare several rooms to see what you prefer. Don't miss the lookout point upstairs.

HIKING THE MARIBIO VOLCANOES

Nicaragua has been called "a violent expanse of volcanic strength," and there is nowhere better to feel that force than on the hot, baked slopes of its mountains of fire. Start early and bring a minimum of three liters of water per person. None of these hikes should be attempted without a guide. Choose from a range of independent guides and well-established, insured tour companies like like Tierra Tours and Vapues Tours.

One freelance option is Flavio Parayón whose **Knowing Nicaragua** guide service (tel. 505/8880-8673, or 505/2311-4383, fparayon2003@yahoo.es) can get you up every peak in the area; contact him directly or at Vía Vía Hotel.

Quetzal Trekkers (1.5 blocks east of Iglesia de la Recolección, tel. 505/2311-6695, leon@quetzaltrekkers.com, www.quetzaltrekkers.com) is a remarkable, nonprofit, volunteer-run organization that specializes in volcano hikes, including overnight options. You'll probably get up before the sun to catch a local bus to the base of your hill. Your fee (only $25 per person per day) goes directly to **Las Tias,** a León nonprofit for local street kids and orphans, supporting them with academic and vocational opportunities, as well as a nutritional meal to all students. They are almost always looking for short-term volunteers (three-month minimum, intermediate Spanish required). If you are lucky enough to be in town during the full moon you will want to summit Volcán Telica at night with a well-experienced Quetzal Trekker guide.

MOMOTOMBO
1,300 meters, 8 hours round-trip
The quintessential cone-shaped volcano, Mo-motombo rises up from the shores of Lago Xolotlán in a particularly menacing posture – and history has proven that the menace is real. Momotombo is climbable, but it's not easy, especially when you hit the loose volcanic gravel that comprises the upper half of the cone. Your triumphant reward will be one of the best views possible of Lago Xolotlán without use of an airplane. From the Ruinas de León Viejo, head out of town to the main highway and turn right (north) along the highway. Follow that to the geothermal plant, where you'll have to convince the guard to let you through to hike. They're sensitive about people traipsing across their installation, so honor whatever promises you make.

TELICA
1,061 meters, 5-7 hours round-trip
Despite its tendency to spew ash over its namesake town, Volcán Telica makes for a good climb. Take a bus from León to Telica, then follow the road to the community of La Quimera and keep going until the road disappears beneath your feet and becomes the volcano. Alternatively, access the volcano from Santa Clara, the town adjacent to the Hervideros de San Jacinto.

CERRO NEGRO
675 meters, 2 hours round-trip
This is the most frequently active volcano in the chain (its last eruption was August 1999). The lowest and youngest of the Maribios, Cerro Negro rises like a black-sand pimple from the landscape, completely free of vegetation and scorching hot when there is no cloud cover. A road takes you from León to the base; from there, follow the makeshift

"trail," part of which will have you scrambling over awkward rocks and fighting surprisingly strong wind. The trail loops around the steaming crater, which the brave may enter at their own risk – if the gaseous wind blows across your path, move fast to get out of it. You can also descend into the second crater accessible from the summit, again at your own risk. Getting out of this one is much harder and much hotter, so make sure you are in good shape. Going down is easy – just run, skip, and hop down the back side or zoom down on a board. There are a number of approaches; the most common heads due east from León, near the town of Lechecuago. Leave early in the morning to beat the heat and avoid the afternoon thunderstorms. The metals in Cerro Negro attract lightning better than the taller volcanoes nearby, so don't test it.

LA CASITA
1,405 meters, 8 hours round-trip
Access can be very difficult because of property issues. Near the top of the climb, the guides will lead you into the saddle between La Casita and San Cristóbal and then to the peak of La Casita itself. There are some radio towers here, and the terminus of an access road damaged during the landslide. Though it's also possible to hike to the top along the slide itself, it's a treeless, sun-baked hike, not to mention possibly disrespectful to the thousands who remain buried beneath it. Although not as tall, La Casita offers a better view of Managua and the lake than San Cristóbal does.

SAN CRISTÓBAL
1,745 meters, 8 hours round-trip
This is the granddaddy of volcano hikes in the Pacific region; it's long but the grade is moderate and even easy compared to some of the hikes listed previously. You'll need a guide to help you wend your way through the myriad fields, farms, and fences that obstruct the path upward (and which change every planting season). Find your guide in Chichigalpa. Enrique Reyes and his brothers are experienced at leading trips up San Cristóbal, and can be found in the Barrio Pellisco Occidental, across from the Escuela Hector García. If they're not around, finding a guide in Chichigalpa is easy. Horses cost $2 a day, and you should pay the guides at least $8 per group.

COSIGÜINA
860 meters, 6 hours round-trip to edge of crater, 11 hours round-trip to crater lake
Literally, a walk in the woods and then you're at the vegetation-carpeted crater lip with crazy views. Start walking from Potosí, or rent horses. Head back along the road toward the community of La Chacara, where the slope of Cosigüina is most amenable for climbing. From the edge of the crater, you can see across the Gulf of Fonseca into El Salvador. There are competing claims about whether one can descend to the crater lake without the use of ropes. If you intend to descend the approximately 300 meters down to the crater lake, you should take 30 meters of good rope with you (you can purchase it in El Viejo or Chinandega) and consider a guide from La Chacara. Luís Mejía Castro in El Viejo (from the Cine Imperial, two blocks west, tel. 505/8886-5477) knows the Reserva Natural and its volcano intimately. Be careful: Careless hikers have died on this volcano.

The imposing 30-room compound of **Hotel Europa** (from the Iglesia San Juan, one block south and one east, tel. 505/2311-6040, heuropaleon@hotmail.com, www.hoteleuropaleon.com, $25–35) has been around since the 1960s, when it catered to the train passenger crowd. Recently remodeled and kept clean, it offers a restaurant, lounge areas, Wi-Fi, guarded parking, and its own water and electricity supply.

$50-100

Hotel Posada del Doctor (one block west of Parque San Juan, tel. 505/2311-4343, www.laposadadeldoctor.com, $45–60) offers 11 lovely, fully equipped rooms around a very bright and pleasant garden. In a converted colonial home, the **Hostal Casa Leonesa** (from the cathedral, three blocks north and half a block east, tel. 505/2311-0551, lacasaleonesa@gmail.com, www.casaleonesa.com, $55) has nine gorgeous rooms around a small pool and garden, each with air-conditioning, TV, hot water, and Wi-Fi. The beautiful common space makes you feel like Leónese royalty.

Expect old colonial stateliness in the 20 wood-adorned rooms at **Hotel Los Balcones** (three blocks east of the cathedral, tel. 505/2311-0250, www.hotelbalcones.com, $58). Upstairs rooms have small balconies overlooking the street, plus standard amenities: TV, air-conditioning (discount if you don't use it), hot water, and Wi-Fi. In the center of León, **Hotel Austria** (from the cathedral, one block south and half a block west, tel. 505/2311-1206 or tel. 505/2311-7178, www.hotelaustria.com.ni, $60) is a practical hotel with 35 spotless, modern, air-conditioned rooms with TV, phones, and hot water; continental breakfast and guarded parking for your vehicle. There is an on-site restaurant and comfortable space for relaxing or meetings.

The rooms at **Hotel La Perla** (1.5 blocks north of Iglesia de la Merced, tel. 505/2311-3125, www.laperlaleon.com, $80) are among the classiest we've seen anywhere in Nicaragua, combining old-style elegance and antiques with modern comforts like plasma screen TVs and Wi-Fi. This 150-year-old home was lovingly restored by owners with a passion for architecture and history. The two presidential suites sport mirrored dressers, king beds, and minibars, both on the second-story balcony with superb views of León's tiled roofs and churches. Hotel La Perla is also a veritable museum of fine art. Excellent breakfast and small pool for guests, plus a white-cloth restaurant with hearty fajita and pasta dishes.

Over $100

Hotel El Convento (next door to the San Francisco Church, tel. 505/2311-7053, www.hotelelconvento.com.ni, $112) offers bathtub-equipped rooms with lots of space and history. Parts of the hotel were built with stones used in the convent's original 1639 construction. From the beautiful centerpiece garden and fountain to the long, cool corridors adorned with art and antiques, El Convento impresses. In addition, the hotel offers business and conference services, a ballroom, a restaurant, and local tours for guests.

Long-Term Accommodations

A college town, León caters easily to those looking to stay on longer. Room for Rent posters are found easily around the universities and on bulletin boards of the main hostels. In general, expect to pay $150–200 a month for a room with shared kitchen and up to $400 a month for furnished apartments. Check with Jordan Clark (tel. 505/8672-3566, www.nicaraguarealestateleon.com) or Green Pathways Tours (www.greenpathways.com); both keep lists of long-term rentals in León and shared houses on the beach.

FOOD

León is slowly shedding its reputation for uninspired cuisine and lackluster restaurants. Though most Leónese eateries cater to the student crowd—i.e., *típica* (traditional), burgers, and pizza—new restaurants are starting to diversify the city's menu.

LEÓN

© JOSHUA BERMAN

Hotel La Perla in León is a class act.

Fritanga and *Comida Típica*

The best finger-lickin' *fritanga* in town is **El Buen Gusto** (a couple blocks east of the cathedral's south side, less than $4 a plate); mix and match from their sidewalk smorgasbord and hubcap grill between 10 A.M. and 10 P.M.; it's closed Sundays. The *carne asada* at the **Estación** offers strong competition for León's best *fritanga* crown; there you'll find several large grills serving mountains of *gallo pinto,* plantains, and fried cheese to an appreciative crowd. When in doubt—or on a Sunday evening when everything else is closed—head to the food grills behind the main cathedral.

Comedor Lucía (across from Vía Vía) specializes in the usual, but it's well done: solid traditional Nica dishes for about $3.

Cafés

Half a block west of the northwest corner of the central plaza, **C Cafe La Rosita** (in front of ENITEL, open 7 A.M.–9 P.M. Mon.–Fri.) is an excellent spot for espresso drinks, baked goods, sandwiches, and fast food. They also have Wi-Fi

and beer. Around the corner, headed north are several more tranquil, low-key places, including **Puerto Café Benjamin Linder** (Barrio Zaragoza, two blocks north of ENITEL, tel. 505/2311-0548, open 7 A.M.–3 P.M.), a coffee shop, juice bar, and Internet café; profits from the blind massage service help support local children with disabilities. The shop's name is a tribute to the only U.S. citizen killed in the Contra war.

Inside Bigfoot Hostel, the **Pure Earth Café** (tel. 505/8443-7516, open 7:30 A.M.–10 P.M., $3–5) is a cozy, all-vegetarian eatery serving fresh, healthy meals, juices, smoothies, and organic coffee. The name references the owner's Pure Earth Project, which promotes reforestation and a gardens-in-schools program. If you're sick of *gallo pinto,* the breakfast menu includes oatmeal, French toast, bagels, granola, and omelets; for lunch and dinner, think veggie burgers, quiches, panini, pasta, organic salads, and more.

To escape the León heat in a tropical, fruit-filled retreat, head just east of the Casa de

Cultura to **Delicias Tropicales** (tel. 505/2311-2818, open 7 A.M.–6 P.M. Mon.–Sat.). They use all-natural ingredients for their refreshing smoothies and juices and prepare filling sandwiches to order. **Il Capriccio** (tel. 505/2311-6339, open daily 9 A.M.–12:30 P.M. and 2–7 P.M.), located across from Quetzal Trekkers, offers some of the best Italian desserts and Nicaraguan coffee in town, plus a menu of sandwiches, salads, and pasta.

Pizza and Ice Cream

Enjoy pizza pies—and authentic Lebanese dishes—at **Restaurante Italian Pizza** (half a block north of the cathedral, tel. 505/2311-0857 delivery, open 9 A.M.–9 P.M. daily), about $10 for a large pie. The pizza at **Hollywood Pizza** (located in the movie theater complex, tel. 505/2311-0636, open 11:30 A.M.–9:30 P.M. Mon.–Fri., later on weekends) is less exciting but the air-conditioning provides a good respite. Both deliver.

León is hot, so ice cream takes on new significance. Start with any **Eskimo** outlet (or bicycle cart) in town for popsicles and cones; for something a little different, head to **Heladería La Michoacana** (located half a block east of Hotel Los Balcones), the first Nica distributor of the world-famous La Michoacana natural fruit pops *(paletas heladas),* which come in some incredible tropical flavors. Look for their street carts selling icepops and slushies *(granizados).*

Upscale Nica and International

Restaurante Taquezal (half a block west of the central park's southern end) has a pleasant atmosphere, a varied menu, and receives positive reviews from readers; typical dishes cost $5–9. Try the Nicaccino: cappuccino with a shot of Nicaraguan rum. On the other end of the block, you'll find 🄲 **Bar Baro** (one block west of the southwest corner of main plaza, tel. 505/2315-2901 or 8820-4000, open 8 A.M. to midnight daily, till 2 A.M. on weekends), a remarkable restaurant with old wooden beams, ceiling fans, and three different-themed dining areas in which to eat and lounge. The

THE LEGEND OF ADIACT AND THE TAMARIND TREE

Several competing versions of this tale have been passed down over three centuries of Nicaraguan history. When Subtiava was still a rebellious Native American village and the Spanish were trying to subdue its inhabitants, victory appeared in the form of a young woman named Xochilt Acalt (Flower of the Sugarcane). Her father was Adiact, the cacique of the Subtiava people and a ferocious warrior renowned for his victories in battle with the Spanish. But legend goes Xochilt fell in love with a young Spanish soldier. Some say the Spanish took advantage of the love affair to capture and hang Adiact; others say that when he learned of the illicit relationship, he hung himself in shame. Xochilt Acalt disappeared from town, and legend has it she too committed suicide (though some say she banished herself to Poneloya, where another tribe took her in). Either way, everyone agrees that the 300-year-old tamarind tree that still stands proudly in the center of Subtiava is where Adiact was hanged. To modern Subtiavans, the tree still represents the rebelliousness of the indigenous people and is a source of much community pride.

name comes from the common Nica expression "¡Qué bárbaro!" which means (more or less) "How awesome!" The menu is amibitious, offering both Nica and international comfort food with a flair, like steak and chicken dishes, burgers, bar appetizers, and pizza. Prices are reasonable from $6–15 per plate, and the drink menu of coffees and cocktails is the longest in the city.

The restaurant and coffee shop at **CocinArte** (across from the north side of La Iglesia el Laborío, tel. 505/8854-6928, 11 A.M.–10 P.M., $6–8) has an incredibly varied and creative menu, including Indian and mideastern dishes found nowhere else in Nicaragua, plus a small selection of chicken and traditional dishes for your carnivorous friends; most meals about $6. The reading and lounging space boasts chess boards and tasteful art as well.

The 🔲 **Mediterraneo** (half a block north of the Iglesia Guadelupe, open at 4 P.M. Tues.– Fri., at 11 A.M. weekends) is perhaps the best option for Italian dishes and pizza. Enjoy the pleasant green patio, nice art, and good service.

INFORMATION AND SERVICES
Tourism Information
The government **INTUR** office (from the central park, one block west and 1.5 north, tel. 505/2311-3682) has brochures, postcards, and updated bus schedules but will shrug their shoulders if you ask about anything beyond that. Go instead to the student-run **Information Office** (near the northeast corner of the plaza, tel. 505/2311-3992), which also offers mounds of brochures, plus a gang of eager UNAN co-eds waiting to help you with local information and maps—and practice their English. Both offices operate Monday–Saturday during normal business hours, including a two-hour lunch break. Also check in the Casa de Cultura for local tour services and classes, and nearly all the youth hostels maintain up-to-date bulletin boards.

Banks
Bancentro is only a block north of the cathedral, and most of the other banks in the city are clustered in the same area. ATMs are located one block east of the cathedral in the BAC (open 24 hours with guard, *córdobas* or dollars), at La Union Supermarket, at gas stations, and in Plaza Siglo Nuevo shopping center.

Medical Services
The hospital is in the center of León, one block south of the cathedral, though you're probably better off in one of the two private clinics with emergency rooms. On the block west of Café Puerto Benjamin Linder, Policlinica la Fraternidad (tel. 505/2311-1403) and Policlinica Occidental (tel. 505/2311-

2722) face each other from opposite sides of the street. Even there, on weekends and after normal business hours, they may not have a doctor on-site.

Internet
Internet cafés in León are too numerous to list; odds are you're standing within a block of one as you read this. But the better ones have backup generators to deal with power failures; it's worth asking if you are doing anything you can't afford to lose. Of note, **CompuService** (across from Policlinica la Fraternidad, open 8 A.M.–9:30 P.M. Mon.–Sat., 9 A.M.–6 P.M. Sun.) is air-conditioned with all kinds of fast services, including docks for laptops and cold beer from the restaurant next door. Also excellent, spacious, and well cooled is **Club en Conexion** (from the cathedral, three blocks north, half a block east, open 7:30 A.M.–9:30 P.M. Mon.–Fri., till 7 P.M. Sat.).

Mail, Phones, and Other Services
The **post office** (two blocks west and 1.5 north of Puerto Café Benjamin Linder, open 8 A.M.–5 P.M. Mon.–Fri., 8 A.M.–noon Sat.) deals with faxes as well as snail mail. **Agencia de Viajes Premier** (across from the Rubén Darío park, tel. 505/2311-5535) is León's only authorized UPS agent. International calls are extra cheap in León and can be made from most any Internet café.

Of the several huge supermarkets, the most central is **La Union** (a block east of the cathedral, open 7:30 A.M.–8 P.M. Mon.–Sat., 8 A.M.–6 P.M. Sun.).

Travel Agents and Tickets
Viajes Mundiales (from the cathedral, three blocks north, half a block east, tel. 505/2311-6263 or 505/2311-5920, viajesmu@ibw.com. ni, open 8 A.M.–noon and 2–6 P.M. Mon.–Fri., until 1 P.M. Sat.) is a full international agency and official representative of major airlines. Two blocks west is an authorized **TransNica** agency (tel. 505/2311-5219) with bus service to Costa Rica, Honduras, and El Salvador.

LEÓN

Agencia de Viajes Premier (by the Iglesia San Juan, tel. 505/2311-5535) is the authorized agent for La Costeña airline tickets, to plan your flight to the Atlantic coast or Río San Juan.

GETTING AROUND

To get anywhere within the city, taxis charge $0.75 during the day and $1.25 at night. Small city buses and converted pickup trucks also crisscross León and charge about $0.25; ask about your destination before getting on.

Don't miss León's answer to London's double-decker bus tours: **El Bus Pelón** (The Bald Bus) runs 30-minute rides around the city, weekends only, from about 5–10 P.M., sometimes featuring live *chichero* music. Line up at the southwest corner of the central park with your own booze. The locals love it.

Car Rental

The only official rental agency in León is Dollar, run out of the Casa Pellas dealership (tel. 505/2311-3371) in the southern part of town. You'll need a four-wheel drive if you're driving up to Cosigüina or on surf safari to coastal roads. They can order up special cars from Managua or Chinandega if you give them time, roughly $100 per day. You can also find individual cars and drivers for rent by inquiring through the main tour operators and your hotel.

GETTING THERE AND AWAY

From Managua, take an express *interlocal* from Mercado Israel Lewites; they cost about $1, take less than two hours, and depart every 40 minutes 5 A.M.–7:30 P.M. In León, the main bus station (La Terminal) is in the northeast corner of the city grid, where you'll find transportation to most points (except Poneloya and Las Peñitas—buses to these beaches depart from their own terminal in Mercadito Subtiava). Big, yellow buses and small, white *interlocales* depart all day long for both Managua and Chinandega, 4 A.M.–7 P.M. Traveling to Managua, you'll arrive at the UCA (best for Masaya and Granada connections) or Mercado Israel Lewites. There are also a few daily expresses to Estelí between 4 A.M. and 3:10 P.M. (depends on when they fill up) and to Matagalpa between 4:20 A.M. and 2:45 P.M.

If you'd rather not muck around with public transport, ask the tour providers and hostels in town about shuttle transport to Granada, San Juan del Sur, and other destinations.

International Buses

Most Central American bus routes include a stop in León. **TicaBus** (two blocks north of the San Juan church in Viajes Cumbia traveling agency, tel. 505/2311-6153, www.ticabus.com) offers buses to most Central American capitals and Mexico.

Near León

SOUTH OF LEÓN
◖ Las Ruinas de León Viejo

The sleepy ruins of Spain's first settlement in Nicaragua make for an easy and worthwhile day trip from León. Francisco Hernández de Córdoba founded the first León in 1524 and Pedrarias Dávila governed it. After two years, for reasons unknown, Dávila had Hernández de Córdoba decapitated in the town square. In 1610, Volcán Momotombo erupted, burying the site under ash. But León may have already been abandoned following a series of premonitory earthquakes that convinced the settlers to look elsewhere for a place to call home. (Momotombo has erupted several times since then, most recently in 1905.)

Dr. Carlos Tünnerman and a team from the National University (UNAN) first uncovered the ruins of old León in 1966, but in 2000, archaeologists found the remains of both Córdoba and Dávila and placed them in an onsite mausoleum. León Viejo is now a UNESCO World Heritage Site. The Nicaraguan Culture Institution has completed fascinating excavations

LEÓN

© RANDALL WOOD

the ruins of León Viejo

and has trained many local guides to take you around, most of whom are friendly, enthusiastic, and speak passable English. Entrance is $3, plus a small fee to take photographs or video.

The ruins are located just adjacent to Puerto Momotombo; turn off the highway at La Paz Centro (at the statue of an indigenous warrior). The site is open seven days a week, 8 A.M.–5 P.M. (till 4 P.M. on Sundays, hours are strictly observed by bribe-resistant guards). Most people go on tours organized by their hotel or tour company in León, but you can do it by yourself as well: Catch a bus from León to La Paz Centro, then take either an 8 A.M. or 11 A.M. bus to the ruins; last return bus from the ruins is 3 P.M. For more info, call 505/2222-2905, ext. 112, for the Palacio Nacional de la Cultura in Managua.

Volcán Momotombo and Momotombito Island

Volcán Momotombo is the most challenging Pacific volcano to climb, and it is one of Nicaragua's more active volcanic peaks. While the small town of El Cardón, on the other side of Volcán Momotombo is closer, the town itself is difficult to get to from the highway.

Momotombo's little sibling, the island of Momotombito was once a pre-Columbian religious sanctuary, when the islet was called Cocobolo. Today, it is an uninhabited natural reserve of tropical dry forest. First, head to the town of Puerto Momotombo, where for the right price, many fishermen would be eager to transport you the 25 kilometers along the north shore of Lake Managua to the island. Bring water and supplies to last two days in order to camp on the island, and don't pay your boatman until he returns to take you off the island. The island reportedly contains petroglyphs and the faintest remnants of the previous civilization who would be horrified to see what has become of their precious lake.

Nagarote

About halfway between Managua and León, the historic village of Nagarote (Chorotega for "the road of the Nagarands"), whose claim to fame is an enormous old *genícero* tree dating to the time of Columbus, whose broad branches shade the small market. The tree and a statue of Diriangén are two blocks north and one block west from the central park. The Casa de Cultura is located one block south of the tree. Nagarote is also nationally renowned fo dr its *quesillos,* a snack of mozzarella-like string cheese, sour cream, and onions wrapped in a hot tortilla. Enjoy them at any of the roadside restaurants that cater to León–Managua travelers, many of whom plan their trips around a stop in Nagarote for cheesy goodness.

BEACHES WEST OF LEÓN

Only a 20-minute drive toward the coast from León (on a new road completed in 2009), Poneloya has been a playground of the Leónese elite for generations. Nearby Las Peñitas is better developed for foreign travelers who come looking for beginner surfing waves and nature excursions into the Isla Juan Venado Wildlife Reserve. During Semana Santa, hotels at both beaches swell to capacity and double their rates.

Las Peñitas is more popular among beginner surfers, since the waves are a bit mellower and there are many boards for rent. It's a rare exception along this stretch of Nicaragua's Pacific shoreline, where the waves are less forgiving than the beaches around San Juan del Sur; they break faster and and with more force, and the currents are stronger. Poneloya in particular has a vicious undertow that makes it dangerous for casual swimmers; bathers die every year.

Exactly halfway to the coast from León, look for the turnoff for **Rancho Los Alpes** (Km 100.5, León–Poneloya road, tel. 505/8803-7085, rancholosalpes@gmail.com), an old-style ranch house with nice rooms filled with handmade furniture and interesting antiques. This is an excellent spot for groups, with service and tour opportunities, excellent food and barbecues, as well as horseback riding and other day trips to beaches and volanoes.

Poneloya

The road from León splits when it reaches the coast, the right fork placing you in Poneloya. The *estero* here is safer than the ocean, a fact not overlooked by lots of children who come to splash around. **Hotel La Posada de Poneloya** (150 m west of the entrance on right-hand side, tel. 505/2317-0378, tel. 505/2311-4612, posadadeponeloya@yahoo.com, $60 d) is the only hotel in town, remodeled in 2010 and now offering 15 rooms with private bath, fan, and

air-conditioning. It's simple and not quite on the beach, but essentially clean. A better option is a five-minute boat ride away, on Isla Los Brasiles. There, the **Surfing Turtle Lodge** (tel. 505/8640-0644, www.surfingturtlelodge.com, $8 dorm, $35 d rooms) has one dormitory and several rooms, plus surfing lessons and rentals, horseback riding, biking, yoga, massage, fishing, and salsa dance lessons.

For food, **El Pariente Salinas** is the only restaurant in the middle of Poneloya. A better option is to walk north up the beach to La Bocana, where you will find a group of restaurants, all of which let you choose a fish to befried whole. The last one, **El Chepe,** is the best, and the only establishment in the area that accepts credit cards.

◖ Las Peñitas Beach

Traveling several kilometers south along the coast will bring you to a series of accommodations that make up Las Peñitas, presented here in the order from north to south. **Playa Roca** (three miles south of Poneloya, tel. 505/8858-3656, www.playaroca.com, $6 dorm, $15–40) has two dormitories, eight cozy rooms, and a popular bar-restaurant open till midnight on weekdays and 2 A.M. on weekends. The view of the rocks and the waves is one of the best on the beach and the large *pasillo* (patio) is ideal for reading, playing pool, and watching the sunset.

Hotel Suyapa Beach (tel. 505/8317-0219 or 505/8885-8345, frobertoreyes@yahoo.com, www.suyapabeach.com, $21–45) is a modern, well-kept hotel and restaurant with 22 rooms around a small pool. The food and service is here is reportedly the best on the beach.

French-owned **Hotelito El Oasis** (tel. 505/8839-5344, aixpat426@hotmail.com, www.oasislaspenitas.com, $6 dorm, $15 d) has reasonable rates, spacious rooms, and slow service. But what's the rush? Rooms have fans and private baths. Enjoy the small *rancho* and hammock area with a great second-story view of the beach. Like most other places on the beach, they rent surfboards and can arrange tours of Isla Juan Venado or Spanish lessons

($4/hour). Around the corner and past the local bars of Los Cocos and El Calamar, you'll find the Canadian-owned **La Samaki.net** (tel. 505/8640-2058, $20), with simple concrete rooms, a small pool, Wi-Fi ($3/hr), and nice kite surfing instruction and rentals. They serve different vegetarian options, including Indian curry. **Restaurante y Cyber Manojito** (tel. 505/8669-9467, reynercalderon@yahoo. es), offers seafood, cocktails, surf lessons, and local tours.

At the end of the road, **Hotel de la Playa Barca de Oro** (tel. 505/2317-0275, tortuga@ ibw.com.ni, www.barcadeoro.com) remains the clear favorite among travelers, with its range of accommodations from $6 dorm to $20 double cabanas; includes fan, mosquito net, and private bath (you can fit up to four people in a $30 cabana). Food is fantastic. La Barca looks directly out to the northern tip of Isla Juan Venado, only 100 meters away across a protected lagoon. They can help you arrange all kinds of local (and inland) excursions. You can also rent kayaks, horses, sportfishing guides, and locals for a massage or pedicure.

Getting There and Away

Buses for Poneloya leave every 45 minutes from the Subtiava Mercadito, from early in the morning until 6 P.M. They stop first in Poneloya, idling for 10 minutes, then continue to Las Peñitas; the trip to the end of the road at Barca de Oro takes about 30 minutes with the new road. You'll save time if you take a taxi from León (about $8–10, not bad if you have three or four people to split the cost). The last bus back to León leaves Barca de Oro at 6:30 P.M., so you can easily do a day trip and end up back in your colonial room in León for dinner.

Isla Juan Venado Wildlife Reserve

The 21-kilometer strip of tropical dry forest, mangroves, and inland estuary south of Las Peñitas provides habitat for hundreds of species of migratory birds, as well as crocodiles and other wetland creatures, and is also an important nesting beach for sea turtles. The park is named for a man who, in colonial times, made his living hunting deer on the island and selling the meat in the market of Subtiava.

Many León-based tour operators run trips to Isla Juan Venado, but you can just as easily strike a deal with one of the many boatmen in Las Peñitas to explore the endless, tree-lined channels. Arrange your trip at least one day in advance, especially if you plan on a sunrise excursion, when you'll see the most wildlife (late afternoons are good, too). Take sun protection and lots of water. You'll need to purchase tickets at the ranger station/youth club ($2 pp includes life vest), a two-story house 100 meters down the beach from Barca de Oro. The youth club helps with reforestation of the mangrove forests, turtle monitoring, and other types of ecological research in cooperation with the organization FUNDAR. Like many protected areas in Nicaragua, Isla Juan Venado is comanaged by the local community and an NGO, in this case LIDER. This is one of the most successful examples of the COMAP (co-management) program in Nicaragua, and the ranger station can be a good source of information on this topic, as well as other issues concerning the flora and fauna of the reserve. They can also arrange boat trips to the island for $50 per group of up to 14 or $20–30 for a smaller boat with one of the community members. Also available are nighttime turtle-viewing trips (seasonal) for $10 and mandatory guided camping also for $10. Some of the hazards in the reserve include caimans, bees, snakes, and crab and turtle egg hunters frustrated by poverty, so bringing a local guide is a really good idea.

You can also access the reserve from the rustic community of Salinas Grandes on the south side of the island, where you can rent kayaks and stay in beachfront *ranchos* at **Rigo's Guest House** (tel. 505/2311-3306 or tel. 505/8647-3146, rsampson@ibw.com.ni). Make arrangements at least one week in advance to make sure that Rigo is ready.

Puerto Sandino

This nondescript fishing village and port town, about 45 minutes southwest of León, receives both Hugo Chavez's oil shipments and a tiny trickle of surfers seeking local waves. Infrastructure for tourists is extremely limited (there is one hotel in town, a few eateries, and 80 percent unemployment).

El Velero and El Tránsito Beaches

Local surf information (there are several world-class waves in the region) is fiercely guarded by those in the know. Beaches south of Puerto Sandino have enormous potential for tourism, and a few surf tour providers operate out of nice homes along the coast. One of those is **Surf Tours Nicaragua** (tel. 505/8440-4123, nicanicolas@gmail.com, www.surftoursni-caragua.com), offering all kinds of activity-based, all-inclusive packages. They also run the **Nicaragua Eco-Hotel** in El Transito (Carretera Vieja a Leon-Managua, Km. 44, tel. 505/8387-9394, info@NicaraguaEcoHotel. com, www.NicaraguaEcoHotel.com, $80).

South from León, the gorgeous two-kilometer stretch of white-sand beach known as **El Velero** (The Sailboat) has tremendous tourist potential but instead is simply occupied by summer homes for wealthy Leóneses. Buses for Puerto Sandino and El Velero leave from the station at León. The limited options for travelers are not cheap and have fallen into total disrepair, an ignoble end to one of Herty Lewites's more ambitious tourism projects in the 1980s. It's better to visit for the day.

A quiet fishing community 60 kilometers from Managua along the old highway to León, **El Tránsito** was devastated by the tidal wave of December 1992. The Spanish helped them recover and built what is now the new town on the hills above the old one, which was at the shoreline. The swimming here can be a bit tricky, as there's a strong undertow that will pull you north along the cove, but walk south along the shoreline to see the rock formations and popular swimming holes behind them. These rocks run parallel to the shoreline and buttress the full blow of waves. Splash around in one of them at high tide, when the waves strike the rocks and rush up and over in an exhilarating saltwater shower. Ten minutes'

walk north along the shoreline takes you to the wreckage of **El Balneario,** an old abandoned vacation spot. Enjoy cheap, cold beer and fresh fish on the south end of the village. Buses leave Managua every afternoon from Mercado Israel Lewites at 11:15 A.M., 12:40 P.M., and 2 P.M. Buses leave El Tránsito every day at 5 A.M., 6 A.M., and 7 A.M.

NORTH OF LEÓN
Los Hervideros de San Jacinto

On the southeast flank of 1,060-meter Volcán Telíca, Los Hervideros de San Jacinto are a warren of boiling mud pits and thermal vents which have formed a veritable martian landscape not far from León. The vents testify to the region's geothermal electric potential, an opportunity that has not gone unnoticed by potential foreign investors—some Israeli—that continue to explore the idea of producing energy from the vast reserves that are forming the vents. One visitor called it "Yellowstone without fences" and loved interacting with the children guides; others thought it was boring. To get there, take a bus from León bound for Estelí, San Isidro, or Malpaisillo and get off at the town of San Jacinto (approximately 25 kilometers from León). The entrance is marked by an enormous arch and a posse of women and children selling "artifacts" from the hot springs. Entrance is $1, and the park is open 7 A.M. to 5 P.M. The boys will offer to guide you around for $1 or less, which is worth it, considering the danger of falling into a scalding mud bath. Community-based tourism projects and trail improvements are in the works, as is a new hotel.

El Sauce

In the foothills of the Segovia Mountains, about a 90-minute drive northeast of León, the village of El Sauce (rhymes with WOW-seh) was once the eastern terminus of the railroad that received inland-grown Nicaraguan coffee bound for the port at Corinto. In the 1800s, caravans of mules lumbered into town laden with thousands of pounds of coffee beans. El Sauce has since faded into a sleepy cowboy village whose pride and joy is a breathtaking colonial church built in 1750 in tribute to the patron saint, El Cristo Negro de Esquipulas (the Black Christ). El Sauce celebrates its *fiestas patronales* on January 18 and attracts a massive pilgrimage (as many as 25,000 people!) from all over Nicaragua to view the Black Christ icon.

El Sauce makes a fine first stop on pueblo-hopping routes toward Achuapa, San Juan de Limay, and Estelí. There are a couple of places to eat in town, and several simple *hospedajes* for lodging: try **Hotel Blanco** (tel. 505/2319-2403) or **Hotel El Viajero** (tel. 505/2319-2325, $3 shared bath, $5 private bath and TV). If you're gong to stay here though, a better option is to sample El Sauce's unique community-based tourism project, administered by the **Associación Turistica de El Sauce** (one block west of the bus station, tel. 505/2319-2213 or 505/8907-9645, visit.elsauce@gmail.com). They can rent bicycles ($5 a day, $2 for two hours), and provide local history tours by teenagers who are forming their own company, Sauce Tours. Ask to see the church, the railroad line (with great views), swimming holes in the river,

farm tours, and more. They also manage the Casa Huespedes guesthouse program, where you can stay in a local home for $16 a night (three meals included) or $11 a night with just breakfast.

Their most spectacular offering is an overnight excursion to **Los Altos de Ocotal** (note: this is a local mountain peak, not the northern town of Ocotal), run by a rural tourism co-operative in Las Minitas, about 17 kilometers from El Sauce (steep road, takes about an hour, four-wheel drive necessary; contact Los Altos at 505/2319-2213 or 505/8907-9645 , or directly at altos.de.ocotal@gmail.com). One reader told us that "the most spectacular view I've seen so far in Nicaragua" is from El Ocotal. Stay with a host family for about $6 a night. There are hiking trails, horseback riding, and different tours to learn about the *campo* lifestyle, coffee production, and forest conservation, all in gorgeous pine forest (tours are only $2–$4 per person). Pick up some organic coffee and export-quality pine needle baskets. You can also go to the cooperative in a *ruta* (small truck) that leaves the bus station everyday at 2 P.M. and comes back to El Sauce at 7 A.M. for $1 per person each way.

Chinandega

Chinandega, a provincial capital grown out of the agriculture business, is the last major town before the Güasaule border with Honduras, and also the gateway to Nicaragua's distant corner of the Gulf of Fonseca. It's a town you'll get to know well if you are stocking up for a visit to the desolate coastline or the unvisited crater wall of Volcán Cosigüina. It's also the undisputedly hottest corner of the nation.

The same threatening volcanoes that loom over the city of Chinandega and its surrounding plains are also responsible for the high fertility of the soil. This attracted the Nahuatl, who called their new home Chinamilt ("close to cane"). Chinandega

suffers the same poverty as the rest of the nation, but also boasts a prosperous community of old and new money, based primarily in sugar, bananas, peanuts, sesame, soy, and shrimp. Cotton used to be the number-one cash crop in the 1960s, but the deforestation and agro-chemicals essential to its production caused monumental environmental damage, like poisoned aquifers and toxic soil, still affecting life to this day. The agricultural activity of the region and proximity to the northern borders and Port of Corinto make Chinandega Nicaragua's most important agribusiness center.

Did we mention that it's hot in Chinandega? It's so hot in Chinandega, expect to break a

CHINANDEGA

To El Viejo
To Cosiguina

Río Acome

To Guasale and Honduras
To León and Managua
To Corinto

CALLE CENTRAL

ROTONDA LOS ENCUENTROS
TEXACO STARMART

ESSO-ON THE RUN
BUS TERMINAL
MERCADO EL BISNE

IGLESIA EL CALVARIO
HOTEL EL CHINANDEGANO

LAS TEJITAS
RASPADOS CHOPY

CENTRAL MARKET
HOTEL GLOMAR

SELECTO SUPERMARKET
POST OFFICE
INTUR

HOTEL SAN JOSÉ
INTERNET
LOS BANCOS
CORONA DE ORO
LAUNDRY
IGLESIA GUADELUPE

MERCADITO
ENITEL
CASA GRANDE
CONSULATE OF SALVADOR
PALI
HOTEL COSIGUINA
LIBRARY
KODAK
FUNDACION COEN
BAC

IGLESIA SANTA ANA
Central Park
LA PARILLADA
PIZZA HOT
IGLESIA SAN ANTONIO

POLICE STATION
HOSPITAL
TICABUS
INTERNET
CONSULATE OF HONDURAS

0   400 yds
0   400 m

© AVALON TRAVEL

© JOSHUA BERMAN

The San Cristóbal Volcano lords over the scorching streets of Chinandega, occasionally powdering them with a layer of white-gray ash.

sweat in the shower. This is what it feels like to be a rotisserie chicken. You can easily see Chinandega's colonial churches and central market in a couple of hours before stopping to catch your breath. Keep your wits about you, as the areas south of center can be a bit dangerous due to the presence of *pandillas* (street gangs).

ORIENTATION

Chinandega's two hubs of activity are the area surrounding the Mercado Bisne (from the English word business), and the town center, or simply, *el centro*. The Mercadito is located two blocks north of the central park, and the Central Market a few blocks east of the park, along the Calle Central. La Rotonda los Encuentros and the Texaco StarMart are both important reference points you'll pass on your way into town. Everything is walkable, but drink lots of water. Taxis are plentiful and cost $0.40 within city limits; *ruta* buses are $0.10.

ENTERTAINMENT AND RECREATION

For dancing, especially on Saturdays, the **Dilectus Disco** (located just east of town on the road to León) is popular with well-off locals, but also overpriced and ridiculously loud. If you prefer a looser, younger crowd and still want air-conditioning, try **Montserat** on the highway to Guasaule (Wednsedays are mariachi nights) or better still, **La Terraza** (on the road to El Corinto), which has an open-air *rancho;* it's very pleasant, with dancing on the weekend, decent food, and a clean swimming pool!

VOLUNTEERING

Stop by the office of **Fundación COEN** (tel. 505/2341-2906, www.fundacioncoen.org), half a block south of INISER, where arrangements can be made to work with children with disabilities or with chemotherapy patients. For other local volunteer opportunities, contact Vittoria Penalba in Managua (tel. 505/2266-5401 ext. 115, vpenalba@fundacioncoen.org).

ACCOMMODATIONS
Under $10
At less than $5 a night, **Hotel Chinandega** is the best dump in town: centrally located, 15 rooms, relatively clean, and only slightly depressing and dingy.

$10-25
Hotel Glomar (a block south of the central market, tel. 505/2341-2562) has 13 passable doubles for $17–25; the place is clean enough, a few rooms with air-conditioning. Similar accommodations are in the **Casa Grande** (tel. 505/2341-0325, $12–18); there's free laundry service, and the friendly owner, Don Alvaro, can help organize volcano expeditions.

$25-50
◀ **Hotel El Chinandegano** (tel. 505/2341-4800, hotelchdgano@turbonett.com.ni, $31) offers 11 rooms with air-conditioning, private bath, breakfast, phone, and Wi-Fi; also laundry, parking, and lovely, bird-filled common spaces. Centrally located 75 meters north of *la esquina de los bancos,* **Hotel Los Balcones** (tel. 505/2341-8994, www.hotelbalcones.com, $35–45) is another excellent option, offering similar services to its sister hotel of the same name in León.

Over $50
The plushest digs in the city center are at **Hotel Cosigüina** (located half a block south of *la esquina de los bancos,* corner of the banks, tel. 505/2341-3636, $55 plus tax) with air-conditioning, hot water, and private bath. They also rent cars and serve food and drinks in the Fumaroles Restaurant. **Hotel Los Volcanes** (Km 129.5, Carretera a Chinandega, tel. 505/2341-1000, $69), has 30 relatively plush rooms with basic business services, located right on the highway, but only two kilometers from the city center.

FOOD
You won't go hungry in Chinandega, with choices ranging from every type of street food imaginable staring at you from thousands of coolers, stands, and baskets all over town, to the *comida corriente* in any of the markets (meals for less than $2) to a host of expensive restaurants. Good Salvadoran *pupusas* are found in the central park. Or head to Calle Central, seven blocks east of the park, to **Las Tejitas** (open evenings). This may be the best *fritanga* in Nicaragua, a bold statement indeed, but so say the stream of regular clients. Sit outside on the sidewalk and enjoy a heaping plate of juicy roasted chicken, *gallo pinto, tajadas* (fried plantain chips), and any number of deep-fried delicacies, all for under $3, drink included. Another good *fritanga* is **La Parrillada** (about 100 meters south of Palí, tel. 505/2341-3745, open all day long) with free delivery and buffet, grill, fry, and rotisserie options.

If you can find **Raspados y Soda "Chopy"** (located around the corner from El Chinandegano) the sugar buzz from the traditional shaved ice might snap you out of the heat coma. The best Chinese food, and in an air-conditioned setting, is **Hong Kong,** 2.5 blocks east of the Esso station. More Nicaraguanized Chinese food at **Corona de Oro** (a block and a half east of Iglesia San Antonio), with large portions (about $5) and good service.

Many fancier restaurants abound along the highways in and out of town, including **Restaurante Los Vitrales** at Hotel Los Volcanes (Km 129.5, Carretera a Chinandega, tel. 505/2341-1000, $8–11), open Sunday–Thursday 6:00A.M.–11:00 P.M., till midnight on weekends. Options include juicy bacon-wrapped filet mignon and other fare. Cheap, greasy gringo fare is plentiful, including a Jerry's Subs and Pizza in the StarMart and all kinds of junk food and sandwiches at On the Run. **Sport Burger** (tel. 505/2341-3264) or **Pizza Hot** (tel. 505/2341-8730) will deliver great and greasy food right to your hotel.

INFORMATION AND SERVICES
INTUR (block and a half south of Selecto, tel. 505/2341-1935, chinandega@intur.gob.ni) maintains an office full of brochures and has a staff who are surprisingly helpful as long as you sign in. For shopping, you won't find any

local crafts in this town (please let us know if you do) but there are two fully stocked supermarkets: El Palí in front of the park, and El Selecto, 3.5 blocks farther east.

The police occupy the entire block along the west side of the central park, and the hospital is right across the street to the south. Money changers work the streets near the central market, and most of Chinandega's banks are clustered on *la esquina de los bancos* (corner of banks), two blocks east of the park.

The post office is 3 blocks east of the park and 1.5 north. Also, the TicaBus agent will send FedEx packages via their Managua office. The ENITEL phone office is one block east of the park—look for the giant red and white tower. ATMs can be found at Banco America Central (BAC), as well as at StarMart and On the Run.

Chinandega's abundant cybercafes are in constant flux, though you'll want to seek out the ones with air-conditioning, such as the one located one block north of the corner with all the banks. For laundry, head to Lavamatic Express (north of Iglesia Guadelupe, tel. 505/2341-3319, 7 A.M.–9 P.M. Mon.–Sat., 8 A.M.–5 P.M. Sun.).

International Consulates
The Consulate of El Salvador (tel. 505/2341-2049, open 8 A.M.–2 P.M. Mon.–Fri.) is two blocks north of *la esquina de los bancos*. When applying for a visa, leave your passport before 11 A.M. The Honduras Consulate (tel. 505/2341-0949, open 8:30 A.M.–4:30 P.M. Mon.–Fri.) is across from ENITEL. The Costa Rica Consulate (tel. 505/2341-1584, open 8:30 A.M.–5 P.M. Mon.–Fri., until noon Sat.) is located half a block north from Banpro.

GETTING THERE AND AWAY
The main bus station is at Mercado Bisne, just past Rotonda los Encuentros. From La Rotonda, highways run north to Somotillo and the border with Honduras at Guasaule, southeast to León and Managua, south to Corinto, and three daily buses to Matagalpa. Service to Managua, León, and the border runs 4 A.M.–7 P.M. daily. A second bus station located at El Mercadito (just north of the central park) provides service to all points north: El Viejo, Jiquilillo, Potosí, Cosigüina, and Puerto Morazán.

Car rentals starting at $35 a day are available at the Avis office in the Hotel Cosigüina and Budget in Hostal Las Mañanitas. There is also a Dollar office at Casa Pellas.

Even though there is a TicaBus agency in town, those traveling north into Honduras or El Salvador will have to go to Managua to catch the bus, which no longer stops in Chinandega. Be advised: Any foreigner who enters El Salvador must have a visa. Get yours at the Salvadoran Consulate. Contact tour companies in León for the latest.

Near Chinandega

EL VIEJO
Only a few kilometers west of Chinandega, El Viejo is a cheerful town of some 50,000 Viejanos. Less service-oriented than its big neighbor, El Viejo can still launch you on your next adventure. El Viejo is much older than Chinandega. Originally an indigenous community called Tezoatega, for the fierce cacique who once ruled it, the town was renamed for the old Spaniard who arrived in 1562 carrying a sacred image of the Virgin Mary. According to legend, when the Spaniard tried to sail back to Spain, the Virgin created a hurricane so that she would be returned to her new home in Nicaragua. The old man complied, and the image soon became the most important Virgin Mary in the country. Her fame has lasted through the centuries, and in 1996 the Pope himself recognized her when he came to declare El Viejo's church a Basilica Minor. The church is impressive and worth your time to visit.

LEÓN

VOLCÁN CASITAS AND HURRICANE MITCH

On October 30, 1998, the quiet municipality of Posoltega (whose Nahuatl name, Posolitecatl, means "neighbor of the boiling place") was catapulted into a horrendous sort of fame as the site of one of the worst naturally caused disasters in Nicaragua's history. After Hurricane Mitch dropped two meters of rain in just three days, the southwest flank of Volcán Casitas transformed into a gigantic wave of mud and rock more than three meters high and nearly 1.5 kilometers wide. The communities of El Porvenir and Rolando Rodríguez were instantly consumed by the very soil on which they were built. Some 2,500 people immediately lost their lives, and those who were not buried lived through the horror of losing nearly everything and everyone in their lives. Immediate relief efforts were held up by the political shenanigans of President Alemán, who stalled help to the Sandinista leadership of Posoltega.

A survivor told one Witness for Peace volunteer, "You should have seen how the children, the little ones, fought to survive.

People were pulling themselves up out of the mud naked, completely covered in mud. They looked like monsters in a horror movie. All you could see were their eyes. Children didn't even recognize their own parents. For days we could hear the ones who were still half-buried crying for help."

More than a decade later, the slide is still clearly visible from the León-Chinandega highway. International efforts helped construct several new communities for survivors, despite reports of disappearing relief funds reminiscent of Somoza's postearthquake "emergency committee." The new suburban communities, however, provided no means of production for a people accustomed to living off the land. Many were psychologically devastated and eventually made their way illegally to search for work in Costa Rica.

The entire slide area has been declared a national monument, and a memorial plaque personally delivered by U.S. President Bill Clinton can be visited in the Peace Park on the highway, near the turnoff for Posoltega.

Buses arrive half a block north of the basilica, across the street from the market where you'll find the cheapest eats. Buses called *interlocales* back to Chinandega leave from the basilica, one block west of the park, and run until about 11 P.M.

Entertainment and Accommodations

Nightlife in El Viejo is exciting and sometimes downright rowdy. Local volunteers say it's all "beer and bark" though, and everyone makes up and shakes hands the next day. Just north of the basilica is the clean and well-liked **Tezoatega** (well known even in León), with good food and service, lots of music (including mariachi night Thursdays). **La Piscina,** two blocks north of the basilica and half a block east, is almost as good, with dancing Thursday–Saturday. Their swimming pool costs $0.75 to use all day.

El Viejo's *fiestas patronales* are the week of December 6, with firework-spitting bulls every night, culminating in the **Lavada de la Plata,** when even the president and national ballet often show up to help wash the church silver. There is no lodging in El Viejo save a few motels of ill repute: Stay in León instead.

CHICHIGALPA

Set in the middle of hundreds of square kilometers of sugarcane, Chichigalpa's **Ingenio San Antonio** is Nicaragua's largest and most powerful sugar refinery, and more importantly, the Compañía Licorera, Nicaragua's alcohol monopoly and source of all the Toña, Victoria, Flor de Caña, and Ron Plata you've been drinking. The two companies belong to the wealthy Pellas family, who founded the sugar refinery in 1890 and have produced sugar and liquor ever since (except 1988–1992 when the Sandinista government briefly expropriated it—the Chamorro government subsequently returned it).

As alcohol is a mainstay of Nicaraguan culture and legend, the refineries and distilleries have been important parts of Nicaraguan life for more than a century. Arrange a tour of the cane processing facilities and Flor de Caña distillery by calling the plant in advance (tel. 505/2343-2344, try asking for Simón Pedro Pereira) and requesting a guided tour. At the moment, there is no charge for the tour, but neither are there free samples.

CORINTO

Nicaragua's primary port complex is the reason for Corinto's existence, linking Nicaragua with the shipping lines of the Pacific. Corinto is 20 kilometers southwest of Chinandega with a couple of halfway decent beaches and a small range of simple hotels and seaside restaurants. Corinto's 20,000 inhabitants live on 49 square kilometers of what is actually a barrier island, connected to the rest of Nicaragua by two small bridges.

The Spanish first made use of the harbor in the 1500s, but didn't completely conquer the region until 1633, when an armada of 26 ships, 500 Spaniards, 227 horses, and 2,000 slaves arrived, swiftly defeating Tezoatega's troops and taking many of them as additional slaves. The original port, placed at El Realejo (which still exists as a faint shadow of its former self), was transferred closer to the ocean at Corinto in 1858 after mangroves and sediment had choked the waterways.

In 1875, Corinto's wooden pier linked to the railroads transporting coffee from El Sauce to Corinto. At the harbor, ships took it to the United States and elsewhere. A railroad constructed during Zelaya's presidency further expanded the port and its strategic significance.

In 1912, nearly 3,000 U.S. Marines landed in Corinto in response to Benjamin Zeledón's revolution, beginning what would be a 20-year occupation of Nicaragua. In October 1983, CIA operatives stole into the harbor under cover of night, where they mined the harbor and blew up several oil tanks on the docks. The

economic and psychological damage strained an already suffering Sandinista government, but the "covert" operation, when publicized later, earned the Reagan administration international condemnation and the ire of the American public.

From 2000–2001, the Alemán administration revitalized the port and dredged the harbor with project financing from the World Bank in order to increase export production. Corinto remains a vibrant coastal community with all the headaches and spice of a port town.

Sights and Entertainment

Playa Paso Caballo is located on the northern tip of the island, and all buses from Chinandega pass by here before continuing to the center of town. Be careful, as the rip currents are notoriously strong, and keep a close eye on your possessions on these beaches. Several *ranchos* on the beach provide shade, food, and alcohol, but a growing number have succumbed to the beach erosion that began when a spooky, wrecked tanker that had been there for years was finally scrapped.

In town, what was once the **Old Railroad Terminal and Customs House** is now a museum in tribute to the old train, well worth a visit. Two discos, **Ali Baba** and **Centauro,** are on the road between town and the northern beaches.

Festivals

If you are in the neighborhood around the weekend that falls closest to May 3, don't miss the **Féria Gastronómica del Mar** (Seafood Festival), where you can try more than 100 different Corinteña recipes with fresh fish, shrimp, and other local delicacies. The festival takes place in the central park, 10 A.M.–3 P.M. Saturday and Sunday.

Accommodations, Food, and Services

The family-run **Hospedaje Vargas** (about a block west of the Texaco station where buses arrive, $6/s shared bath, $8/s private bath) is simple and has fans in all 10 of its rooms.

Hospedaje Luvy (1.5 blocks west of the central park, tel. 505/2342-2637, $11 with fan, shared bath) is similar. All 10 rooms in the **Hotel Central** ($40 with a/c, private bath, cable TV) enjoy a view of Corinto's dock operations.

As always, your best bargain is the *comida corriente* in the town market. Otherwise, numerous *cafetíns* dot the town and a row of restaurants flank the town beach. **Restaurante Costa Azul**, **El Peruano**, and **Restaurante New Orleans** all have typical meat and seafood dishes starting at $5. They are pleasant, breezy, open-air *ranchos* with views of the harbor and islands; hours are casual and all are easy to find, just head downtown and ask. Also consider **New Orleans** (one block east of the minisupermarket), run by a returned Nica who spent ages in New Orleans, Louisana's French Quarter. Free crab soup for serious drinkers.

The best restaurant in town is on the main road to Chinandega, near the bridge (from which you can jump into the water)—it's called **El Español** and the owner makes a mean sangria. **Corinto Online** (half a block north of the park) will connect you to the Internet for $2.50 per hour. Getting to and from Corinto is a snap from Chinandega's Mercado Bisne, or by hitching from the Rotonda.

Northwest Coast and Cosigüina Peninsula

This magnificent volcanic knuckle juts into the Golfo de Fonseca, providing stunning scenery, untouched wetlands, long unspoiled beaches, and massive peanut farms. This part of the country was too hot and isolated for most tourists until very recently when parts of the main access road were improved and foreigners began investing in land and hotel projects. Although a trip to the scenic crater that makes up the highest point of Reserva Natural Volcán Cosigüina is the centerpoint of a trip to this area, you can also ride horseback, explore, fish, or just lounge on the beach.

VOLCÁN COSIGÜINA NATURAL RESERVE

Not only does this nationally protected reserve provide incredible views from the volcano's rim, but the dense vegetation inside the crater is home to a rare scarlet macaw population. Most hikes and horseback trips to the rim begin 15 kilometers past Potosí in the community of El Rosario; the park's official ranger station, comanaged by a nonprofit organization called LIDER, sits below the volcano and is the best place to begin your exploring. LIDER links tourists with a community tourism organization called Centro Ecoturístico de Aguas Termales, which offers two-day, one-night all-inclusive visits to the reserve during which you will take a horse ride up to the crater rim, take boat rides past mangrove forests, go on hikes, and cook (yourself) in the hot springs—all for $60 which goes to support the community and the comanaged conservation efforts. Contact Irving Caballeros at the LIDER office in El Viejo (tel. 505/8625-4607, turismocosiguina@yahoo.com).

Potosí

This poverty-stricken coastal village on the east coast of the peninsula was a trading port with El Salvador until the Contras blew it up in the 1980s. Authorities have yet to reestablish regular El Salvador–Nicaragua ferry service, but a new dock was being built in 2009, so it's possible. In the meantime, if you can find a local licensed captain you can make your own way to El Salvador, either to the port city of La Union or the tourist beach at Tamarindo, where you can find hotels, basic services, and buses to the capital. You'll need to stop by the lonely immigration office at the end of a dirt path to get your passport stamped and pay the exit fee. The ride is less than an hour, there is no set fee.

On the road toward Potosí, at the tiny village of La Piscina, is an interesting community-

© JOSHUA BERMAN

LEÓN

The land around Volcán Cosigüina is used mostly for cattle and peanuts.

based tourism effort called **Ramsar Lodge** (www.ramsarlodge.com), located near a cemented-in hot springs and providing primitive wood-and-thatch huts with communal hangout area. Ramsar is for adventurous, open-minded backpackers who aren't afraid to sweat or sign up to milk cows, make tortillas, and so on. For details, inquire at Vapues Tours in León.

A few more kilomters up the road, as you enter Potosí, look on your right for the very reasonable, locally owned **Hotel Brisas del Golfo** (tel. 505/2231-2238, $15) with five clean, private rooms with fan at a very reasonable price. Don Rafael Castro and his wife can prepare you three meals a day and help organize your volcano expedition.

If you're on the peninsula in May, ask about the three-day festival on Meanguera, an El Salvadoran island that allegedly allows unchecked passport access during the fiesta. You can reach Potosí at the end of a three-hour bus ride from Chinandega; about six buses leave daily and cost under $2 each way.

El Hostal Hato Nuevo Private Nature Reserve and Ranch

North of El Viejo, just past the community of El Congo, but before you reach the volcano is **El Hostal Hato Nuevo** (tel. 505/8865-9683, www.hostalhatonuevo.com, $69); look for a steep driveway on the right. This totally unique, elegant stone home in the middle of the forest has seven comfy rooms and an old-ranch feel with plenty of shade and hammocks. The owner, Mareano, is a native of Chinandega who has studied art in London and Mexico City and whose custom-crafted paintings and furniture fill the place. He's a wonderful cook too, so even if not spending the night, try calling ahead for a relaxing meal. Located on a 600-plus-acre natural reserve, there are nature trails, horseback riding, and wetlands, beach, and volcano expeditions available.

Mechapa Village and Redwood Beach

This tiny fishing village on the Pacific coast of Volcán Cosigüina fronts a long, gorgeous, nearly-empty beach which stretches north-west to the cliffs at Punta Ñata (travel to the cliffs by horseback or car at low tide only). Ask for Captain Odel Yoel Gaitán, an experienced sailor who'd be happy to take you fishing or surfing in his *panga*. There are few services in the area and only one place to stay: **Redwood Beach Resort** (tel. 505/8996-0328, U.S. tel. 800/583-4289, info@rbrmechapa.com, www. redwoodbeachresort.com, $135–150), an iso-lated, American-owned beach retreat especially popular with foreign diplomats and well-off Nicaraguans.

The rate includes three solid meals, most of which are fresh from the sea; cheaper rates with fewer meals or during low season are available. The eight cabanas are wood-constructed, el-evated one-room structures with fan, optional air-conditioning, private bathroom, and com-fortable porches only meters from the pound-ing surf. RBR has the only Wi-Fi service for miles around. You can laze around the beach, hunt *moro* crabs, and a lot more. A planned sister property will offer campsites with basic

services ($5 pp), including a brick grill to cook fish; cheap ($10 pp) backpacker lodging in basic plank and thatch huts. To get there, one bus a day leaves Chinandega at 1:30 P.M. for the three-hour ride to Mechapa; it departs the village the following morning at 4 A.M. A more pleasant option is to travel by vehicle to Jiquilillo then arrange with the Redwood folks to be picked up by boat.

JIQUILILLO AND PADRE RAMOS

Less than a one-hour bus ride from El Viejo, **Playa Jiquilillo** is on a northwest-pointing peninsula of beaches which make this area ei-ther a beautiful day trip or an extended, lazy stay, paddling through the wetlands and lazing on the beach. Avoid the area during Semana Santa, when it's overrun. The area remains de-serted and undeveloped. Five buses make the daily round-trip from Chinandega to Jiquilillo, starting at 7 A.M. last one at 4:30 P.M. The bus to Jiquilillo continues up the coast, through the Los Zorros barrio, and arrives at the end

the peaceful Rancho Esperanza on Jiquilillo beach

of the road in the community of Padre Ramos. A simple fishing village of some 150 dispersed families, Padre Ramos is the gateway to the neighboring protected wetlands, and consequently the site of several grassroots tourism projects. Lately, unusual high tides have been washing away large chunks of the gorgeous beach up and down the peninsula. The best local cooks are Doña Widia and Don Pablo—just ask for them.

In peaceful, rural **Padre Ramos,** there is a family-run hostel behind the school, just 50 meters from the beach and 100 meters from the estuary; the place was started with the help of its sister hostel, La Tortuga Booluda, in León (inquire there for more info). Simply tell the bus driver to let you off in front of Doña Reyna's house, and she and her seven granddaughters will make you feel like you are part of the family. Dine at **Bar Zulema** or **Don Roque's** traditional *ranchos* on the water's edge. You can get a quick boat ride to the community of Venecia across the estuary, where you'll find long stretches of utterly deserted beach. The entire area is a breeding ground for sea turtles, the eggs of which are laid and hatch between November and January.

Accommodations and Food

Things are still very basic in this area. **ᙅ Rancho Esperanza** (tel. 505/8680-0270 or 505/8879-1795, rancho.esperanza@yahoo.com, www.rancho-esperanza.com, $8–10 pp) is a unique, community-centric operation offering a cluster of bamboo huts and dormitories with sand floors and grass mats; only $4 to pitch a tent or hammock. There is electricity and fans, lockboxes, books, surfboards, a community garden, and games. Experience low-impact natural living with projects that actively benefit the village like a kids' club and community center. Ask about special rates for volunteers (two-week minimum, some Spanish required). The hostel offers great local food ($3–4 per meal) and will organize excursions to nearby Padre Ramos estuary and Volcán Cosigüina.

A bit farther up the beach, **Rancho Tranquilo**

(tel. 505/8814-2245 or 8968-2290, $6 dorm, $20 private hut) has beachside bamboo-thatch huts with cement floors, mosquito nets, and shared toilets and showers. Features include a good learning beach for surfing, open *rancho* right at the waterline, primitive veggie living. Ask about English-teaching and Spanish-learning opportunities. Around the corner, on the estuary-side of the peninsula, **Hotel Los Zorros** (tel. 505/8688-0878, $30) has five rooms lined up on the calm water and a breezy, stilted restaurant with stunning views, fried fish, and cold beers. They offer the only area deep-water sportfishing trips.

Guides

For guide services, **Eddy Maradeaga** (tel. 505/8371-6761) is available for mangrove tours by boat, hiking, or horseback riding. Eddy is one of the most engaged community members and is very knowledgeable about the local ecosystem and conservation efforts. He is working with a group of local students to develop a community-based tourism program for Padre Ramos.

ᙅ Padre Ramos Wetlands Reserve

Relax in the gentle waters of this protected estuary, laze in a hammock under the shade of a nearby *palapa,* or be lulled to sleep on a deserted starlit beach. Padre Ramos is a little-visited part of Nicaragua that will reward you with an expanse of serene coastline and an overflowing supply of hospitality, wilderness, community, and culture.

The estuary is a decidedly mellower place to swim than the ocean and is home to all the wildlife—especially birds—you could hope to see. Check out the visitors center when you arrive to ask about fishing and boat trips into the wetlands.

One of the best, most silent ways to explore Estero Padre Ramos is by sea kayak, paddling amongst the birds, sea turtles, and mangroves that inhabit this rich environment. **Ibis Exchange** (tel. 505/8961-8548, U.S. tel. 415/663-8192, www.ibiskayaking.com) has

© JOSHUA BERMAN

one way to explore the wetlands on the Cosigüina Peninsula – on horseback

new, safe boats, professional guides, unique expeditions, plus delicious meals, kayak gear, and camping equipment for day tours and overnight adventures. Trips cost $35–120 per person. All ages and skill levels are welcome. Ibis Exchange offers eight-day package tours that include León, Estero Padre Ramos, and Juan Venado Nature Reserve. Contact Ibis's local contact (tel. 505/8460-4854).

Puerto Morazán and Estero Real

Here's a chance to forge a trail on your own: The decrepit inland port town of Puerto Morazán is the gateway to the magnificent and sinuous Estero Real Wetlands Reserve, whose mangrove-filled estuary provides habitat for countless marine species and birds. The estuary is gorgeous, even if its "protected" status has been largely ignored by government officials and the shrimp industry over the years. Morazán has not always been so poor. During World War II, Morazán's port, railway terminus, and customs office saw the movement of tons of cargo bound for European

and North American destinations. When the war ended, so did Morazán's brief prosperity, and when Volcán Chonco erupted, damaging the railroad tracks, the final nail was put in Morazán's coffin. During Hurricane Mitch Morazán flooded so severely only the church steeple appeared over the surface of the water. Shortly after Mitch, the community rebuilt itself on its original site, disregarding the humanitarian assistance community's plan to relocate the community to higher ground.

Take a bus from El Viejo and ask around for a local guide or boat driver. The mayor's office may help guide you in the right direction. You won't be disappointed by the extraordinary variety of wildlife, nor by the amazing view of Volcán Cosigüina.

PLAYA LOS ASERRADORES

Playa Los Aserradores is quiet and desolate, with impressive surf good only for experienced wave-shredders. Beginning surfers will have better luck at nearby Aposentillo and Bahía Santa Maria.

Stay at **Hotel Chancletas** (tel. 505/8868-5036 or 505/8879-0014, surfingnorthernnicaragua@msn.com, www.hotelchancletas.com, $10 pp dorm, $35–85 for nicer rooms, with or without a/c), perched on a grassy rise. Activities include surfing, fishing, hiking, horseback riding, or relaxing in a hammock. Chancletas has a full bar and restaurant for when the tides aren't perfect. Miami native and owner Shay O'Brien is a great source of information and can point the way to nearby breaks.

There are two daily Los Aserradores buses, leaving from the Mercadito in Chinandega. Buses leave Chinandega around 12:30 P.M. for these areas and return the next day at 5 A.M.

This area is also home to Nicaragua's only luxury yacht-docking option, **Marina Puesta del Sol Resort** (www.marinapuestadelsol.com, $185), an incongruous multi-million-dollar, 600-acre development with gorgeous suites, and a dockside restaurant, all with stunning views over the estuary to the San Cristóbal volcano. They have a beach area and pool for events. The rooms are well equipped and nicely laid out. The restaurant offers a huge menu, including sandwiches for $6–9 and seafood entrées for $12–23. The Marina hosts the Flor de Caña International Fishing Tournament during the first weekend of December.

Getting Around North of Chinandega

Access this area on the Nic-12 highway, most of which was paved with financial support from the American government in 2009. There's no real coastal road to area beaches, only side spurs from Nic-12. Some of the side roads are in better condition than others. Four-whee drive is still necessary to explore this area. Buses to Cosigüina's scattered northern villages and beaches leave from Chinandega's Mercadito and make stops in El Viejo before continuing northwest. Many of these destinations only have bus service once a day, which means you'll be making an overnight trip if you don't have your own wheels. Most visitors either rent a vehicle or arrange a transfer with their hotel.

HONDURAN BORDER AT EL GUASAULE

Located about 1.5 hours north of Chinandega, El Guasaule is the principal Pacific-side border crossing with Honduras. It is six kilometers beyond the town of Somotillo, where you'll find a large number of trucker and traveler services. At the actual border, there is a Bancentro branch and some basic food services. Reach the migration office at Guasaule by calling 505/2346-2208.

El Guasaule is open 24 hours, and there is always heavy truck traffic and road repair problems on the Nicaraguan side. It costs $2 to leave Nicaragua and $7 to enter the country. Just a passport and some cash is all that's required of North American and European travelers.

If you are driving your own vehicle, the process to enter Nicaragua is lengthy, but usually not difficult. You must present the vehicle's title, as well as your own driver's license and passport. You will be given a temporary (30-day) permit to drive in Nicaragua, which will cost you $10—should you lose the permit, you will be fined $100.

There are numerous and regular buses traveling between the Bisne Terminal and El Guasaule, and the main international bus lines (TicaBus, etc.) heading to Honduras and El Salvador pass through Chinandega on their way to the border.

ESTELÍ AND THE SEGOVIAS

As you travel north and up out of the sultry Pacific lowlands, your introduction to Nicaragua's hilly interior begins with the Sébaco Valley, green with rice, carrot, and onion fields. From there, the Pan-American Highway struggles upward to the pleasant city of Estelí, "Diamond of the Segovias," then continues through mountains and valleys dotted with rural villages whose inhabitants are proud to call themselves *norteños*. Most folks here get along by subsistence farming and ranching, while cash crops like tobacco and coffee also define the land; a few communities boast talented artisans in pottery, leather, and stone. Underneath the north's gentle exterior of pine trees and tended fields are minor ruins of ancient cities, deep pools and cascades, and rugged communities of farmers and cowboys.

The north of Nicaragua is poorer than the rest, and suffers acutely from drought, poor soils, and deforestation: Nowhere else is the six-month dry season so intense. The challenging living conditions however make for a hardy and hardworking people, quick with a smile or a story. The curious and unrushed traveler will not regret breaking away from the highway and going deep into this northern countryside.

PLANNING YOUR TIME

If you've only got a day and a night, spend them in the city of Estelí, Nicaragua's capital of tobacco, to sample world-renowned cigars and admire the town's inspiring collection of murals. With a second day, the bird-watcher, hiker, and historian should focus on nearby attractions like the Estanzuela waterfall, the lodge and trails

© JOSHUA BERMAN

HIGHLIGHTS

◖ **Estelí Cigar Factories:** Cigar aficionados know Nicaragua better than most, and the local factories are proud to invite you in for a glimpse at the smokes that rival even Cubans (page 203).

◖ **Custom Cowboy Boots:** They're custom made from high quality leather, so don't leave Estelí without a pair for long rides into the wild or just dancing, northern-style (page 207).

◖ **El Salto Estanzuela and Reserva El-Tisey:** Visit Estelí's premier swimming hole and ecolodge, where you can hike, ride horses, or just jump in for a swim (page 212).

◖ **Miraflor Nature Reserve:** This is the best place in Nicaragua to get back to nature and spot the elusive quetzal or other exotic wildlife (page 214).

◖ **San Juan de Limay:** Rumble over the mountain pass and down into the valley to seek out one of the famous soapstone workshops (page 219).

◖ **Iglesia de Nuestra Señora de la Asunción:** Ocotal's church has seen it all, and even withstood the world's first air-raid bombing in the 1930s (page 222).

◖ **Grand Canyon of Somoto:** The nicest swimming hole north of Estelí is also a great example of responsible community-run tourism (page 226).

LOOK FOR ◖ TO FIND RECOMMENDED SIGHTS, ACTIVITIES, DINING, AND LODGING.

at Tisey, or the orchid-rich broadleaf forest reserve of Miraflor. With a little more leisurely pace however, you can easily spend another day exploring Miraflor. Or spend it getting a feel for the *campesino* lifestyle by spending a lazy afternoon in any of the small northern towns off the Pan-American—like Condega, La Trinidad, or Pueblo Nuevo—or find yourself in the highland border towns of Ocotal or Somoto. If you're really curious, go deeper still, by traveling long loops eastward to Jalapa and Quilalí, or to Cusmapa, the highest town in Nicaragua.

HISTORY

The Spanish conquistador Francisco Hernández de Córdoba personally founded the city of Segovia on the banks of the Río Coco where it met the Jícaro, and the first settlers began exploring for veins of gold in the nearby hillsides. But the Spanish abandoned this early settlement and moved farther north along the Río Coco. The Xicaque, Miskito, and Zambo tribes attacked the new settlement with growing ferocity, however, strengthened and emboldened by shiny new firearms from

ESTELÍ AND THE SEGOVIAS

HONDURAS

0   10 mi
0   10 km

Teotecacinte

Jalapa

Murra

Santa
María

Las
Manos

Cerro Mogotón
2,107m

Cordillera Dipilto y Jalapa

Santa Clara   Ciudad Sandino

San Fernando

Susucayan

Macuelizo

Ocotal

Ciudad Antigua

IGLESIA DE NUESTRA
SEÑORA DE LA ASUNCIÓN

Quilalí

Totogalpa

San Juan
del Río Coco

GRAND CANYON
OF SOMOTO

Telpaneca

Palacagüina

Río Coco

Somoto

Yalagüina

PAN-AMERICAN HIGHWAY

El Espino

Ducualí Grande

Pueblo Nuevo

CA1

Las Sabanas

Condega

San Sebastián de Yalí

Cinco Pinos

San José de
Cusmapa

CA1

MIRAFLOR
NATURE RESERVE

La
Concordia

San Rafael
del Norte

San Francisco
del Norte

SAN JUAN
DE LIMAY

La Sirena

Río Estelí

Jinotega

CUSTOM COWBOY BOOTS

CIGAR FACTORIES

Estelí

Somotillo

Achuapa

EL SALTO ESTANZUELA
AND RESERVA EL-TISEY

Santa Cruz

To Matagalpa

Villa Nueva

Río Grande

La Trinidad   San Isidro

San Nicolas

El Sauce

Sébaco

To Chinandega

CA1

To Managua

To Léon

© AVALON TRAVEL

the British, and English pirate Henry Morgan later sailed up the Río Coco and reduced the city to rubble. The Spanish moved west to the present village of Ciudad Antigua, which became the Segovian capital despite continued attacks. Not until the early 19th century did the little village of Ocotal begin to assume any importance, when the Catholics transferred valuable religious artifacts to the new church of Nuestra Señora de la Asunción. The faithful followed the relics westward, and Ocotal began to grow.

In the early 1930s, General Sandino and his men were firmly entrenched in the mountains north of Ocotal, and the American government, intent on capturing him, sent in the Marines. Based in Ocotal, they scoured the countryside around Cerro Guambuco and built the country's first airstrip in Somoto, from which they launched strikes on the city of Ocotal, the first city in the history of the world to experience an air raid. During the 1980s, much of the conflict between Sandinistas and Contras took place in the same area, fiercely punishing outpost towns like Jalapa.

City of Estelí

Spread across a flat valley 800 meters above sea level, Estelí is an unassuming city whose 110,000 merchants, ranchers, artists, and cigar rollers are prouder than most. In Nahuatl, Estelí means something like "river of blood," an apt moniker for an area so saturated with Sandinista rebels in the days that led up to the 1979 revolution that Somoza carpet-bombed the city (ask locals where to find *la bomba*, a relic from the air strikes). But these days, most Estelíanos live a bucolic life of farming and commerce.

ORIENTATION

Buses to Estelí will deposit you in one of the two bus terminals (Cotran Sur and Cotran Norte) on the east side of the highway, and express buses bound farther north for Ocotal and

© RANDALL WOOD

a street corner in Estelí

ESTELÍ AND THE SEGOVIAS

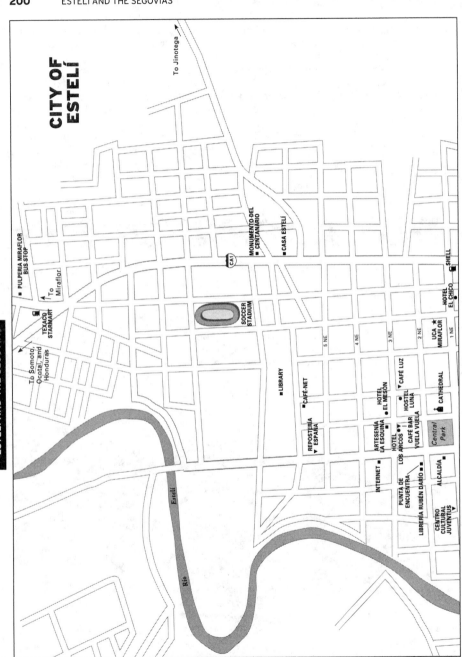

CITY OF ESTELÍ

To Jinotega

PULPERIA MIRAFLOR BUS STOP

To Miraflor

TEXACO STARMART

To Somoto, Ocotal, and Honduras

MONUMENTO DEL CENTANARIO

CASA ESTELÍ

CAT

SOCCER STADIUM

LIBRARY

5 NE

4 NE

3 NE

2 NE

1 NE

CAFÉ-NET

REPOSTERÍA ESPAÑA

ARTESENÍA LA ESQUINA

HOTEL EL MESÓN

CAFÉ LUZ

HOSTEL LUNA

HOTEL LOS ARCOS

CAFÉ BAR VUELA VUELA

UCA MIRAFLOR

CATHEDRAL

Central Park

INTERNET

PUNTA DE ENCUENTRA

LIBRERÍA RUBÉN DARÍO

ALCALDÍA

CENTRO CULTURAL JUVENTUS

Estelí

Río

HOTEL EL CHICO

SHELL

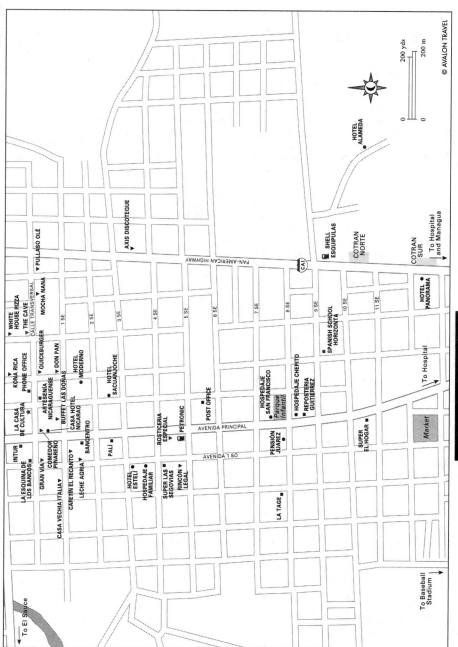

ESTELÍ AND THE SEGOVIAS

© AVALON TRAVEL

200 yds
200 m

To Hospital
and Managua

HOTEL ALAMEDA

SHELL ESQUIPULAS

COTRAN NORTE

COTRAN SUR

To Hospital

HOTEL PANORAMA

AXIS DISCOTEQUE

PULLASO OLÉ

WHITE HOUSE PIZZA
THE CAVE
CALLE TRANSVERSAL
MOCHA NANA

PAN-AMERICAN HIGHWAY

CAI

1 SE

2 SE

3 SE

4 SE

5 SE

6 SE

7 SE

8 SE

9 SE

10 SE

11 SE

SPANISH SCHOOL HORIZONTÉ

KONA RICA
PHONE OFFICE

QUICKBURGER
DON PAN

HOTEL MODERNO

HOTEL SACUANJOCHE

HOSPEDAJE SAN FRANCISCO
Parque Infantil

HOSPEDAJE CHERITO

REPOSTERÍA GUITIÉRREZ

LA CASA DE CULTURA

ARTESENIA NICARAGUENSE
BUFFET LAS DOÑAS

CASA HOTEL NICARAO
BANCENTRO

ROSTICERÍA ESPECIAL
PETRONIC

POST OFFICE

AVENIDA PRINCIPAL

INTUR

LA ESQUINA DE LOS BANCOS

GRAN VÍA
COMEDOR PINAREÑO

CASA VECHIA ITALIA

CAFETÍN EL RECANTO
LECHE AGRIA

PALÍ

AVENIDA 1 SO

PENSIÓN JUAREZ

HOTEL ESTELÍ
HOSPEDAJE FAMILIAR

SUPER LAS SEGOVIAS
RINCON LEGAL

LA TAGE

SUPER EL HOGAR

Market

To Baseball Stadium

To El Sauce

THE CHILDREN'S MURAL WORKSHOP

In 1987, in response to a request for help from community leaders in the struggling Barrio Batahola in Managua, three former art students began teaching mural workshops to children. The program was a success and two years later, the three muralists passed their roles on to other youth in Managua and moved to Estelí to continue their program. The idea was to empower the people while at the same time reclaiming Nicaraguan culture and promoting the participation of children in society. They found that painting murals was an empowering achievement for the participants, and the creation of the murals was invariably tied to further community activities and social work (and lots of pretty pictures to look at).

Today, the mural project is known as the **Fundación de Apoyo al Arte Creador Infantíl** (FUNARTE), a nonprofit, nongovernmental organization run by a group of young adults who grew up through the original mural workshops. They offer weekly painting workshops to hundreds of Estelíano children for free and give special workshops for imprisoned teenagers and children with disabilities. The murals depict their history, culture, and the daily reality in which they live.

There are well over 100 murals in Estelí, the majority of which were painted by participants of FUNARTE's workshops. The murals are best viewed and photographed in the late afternoon sun, as many of the best are on west-facing walls. The paintings are everywhere, but take special note of those on the Alcaldía (mayor's office), Casa de Cultura, and in and around the Parque Infantíl (nine blocks south of the main plaza). Also, be sure to get a good look at the long, horizontal mural on the wall of the army base along the Pan-American Highway, just south of the main bus station.

To visit FUNARTE's headquarters (tel. 505/2713-6100), walk four blocks south from the southwest corner of the plaza, then two west to reach the main workshop, itself covered in powerful paintings; continue another block west, turn right past the mural depicting the book *The Little Prince,* and make your next left to arrive at the offices and classroom.

Somoto will drop you off at the nearby Shell Esquipulas. In either case, take a cab to the central park ($0.50) to start your exploration. Estelí is quite possibly the only city in the country to name avenues (north-south) and streets (east-west), a system ignored in lieu of the tradition of counting blocks from known landmarks.

The two avenues that border the park, and one additional avenue on either side, make up the bulk of the commercial district. Avenida Central, on the west side of the park, hosts the greatest number of businesses and restaurants.

You're essentially safe in Estelí, but exercise more care here than elsewhere. In the barrios east of the highway and west of the river be especially cautious.

SIGHTS AND RECREATION
El Parque Central
Estelí's central **park** is a hub of mellow activity and a magnet for local characters. Buy an ice cream cone, kick back on a bench, and watch it all swirl by. The **Iglesia de San Francisco** was built in layers starting in 1823. It began as nothing more than a humble adobe chapel with a straw roof. Rebuilt in 1889 to a grander scale and given a roof of clay tiles with a baroque facade, the church was later redesigned as a modern building, with stately columns, a neoclassic facade, and twin bell towers topped with crosses.

La Galería de Héroes y Mártires
Located half a block south of the church, La Galería (tel. 505/8419-3519, 505/2713-7763, open 8 A.M.–5 P.M. Mon.–Fri., donations accepted, call ahead if other times are needed for groups and speak to Guellermina "Mina" Meza) is only one of the projects of the Association of Mothers of Heroes and Martyrs of Estelí, a support group of 300 women who lost children during the

battle against Somoza's National Guard. The musem also offers Spanish classes for individuals or for families. The gallery itself is a single room in what was once one of Somoza's jails, filled with memorabilia from the days of the revolution—photos of Estelí as an urban battleground, quotes from Sandino and Che Guevara, weaponry and shell casings, and portraits of young men and women killed in action, sometimes accompanied by uniforms and other personal effects.

Connected to the Galería, you'll find the less powerful, but still interesting **Museo de Historia y Arqueología** (open 9 A.M.–noon Mon.–Fri., closed Wed.), with a small display of petroglyphs, artifacts, and revolutionary photos.

Still in the same building, on the south side, the **Casa de Cultura** offers a series of music, art, and dance classes to the public; the Casa also often has a display of local artists in its spacious lobby. The entire block used to belong to a prominent Esteliano family before it was confiscated by the Sandinistas.

Yoga

If you want to study a traditional form of hatha yoga from a guru-trained Nicaraguan yogini, be at **Licuados Ananda's** (one block south of the central park, next to the Casa de Cultura) 10 minutes before 6 A.M. or 6:40 P.M. Mon.–Fri. with a towel or mat. Classes have monthly and individual charges. Or ask Doña Edith in the Hospedaje Familiar about classes in yoga and eastern medicine.

◖ Estelí Cigar Factories

In the past Estelí cigar factories were often closed to the casual visitor, unless you sought permission from distant owners. Today, many offer tours either to individuals or with a local specialized tour guide; the local INTUR office and the information desk at Casa Estelí can provide a comprehensive list of factories offering tours. A simpler option is to contact Leo Flores (tel. 505/8415-2428, leoafl@yahoo.es), a certified tour guide and expert in the cigar making process. Make sure to call Leo in advance to arrange the tours.

ESTELÍ AND THE SEGOVIAS

© JAMES SAVAGE

Puros, or cigars, grown and rolled in Estelí are acclaimed around the world.

SMOKIN' NICARAGUA

There is history in that cigar you're smoking – stories hidden among the tightly packed folds of tobacco and along the delicate veins of its wrapper leaf. As you light the *puro* in your hand and watch it turn into ash and smoke, take a sip of rum and ponder the unique legacy of the Estelí cigar industry.

It all began with the 1959 Cuban revolution, when capitalist Cuban cigar lords found their businesses liquidated into the new socialism. These artisans of the finest cigars in the world quickly gathered illicit caches of the precious tobacco seeds their families had been cultivating for centuries and fled to Miami. From there, it was only a couple of years before they discovered Nicaragua. One grower told *Cigar Aficionado* magazine that Cuba and Nicaragua "have the most fertile dirt in the world for tobacco. It's almost like God said, 'I'm going to pick these two countries and I'm going to use them for tobacco.'"

And so the core of the old Cuban cigar aristocracy moved to Estelí and, with their precious seeds from the homeland, began turning out world-renowned cigars once again. They endured another popular revolution in 1979, the ensuing civil war and land redistribution, and then survived the cigar boom and bust of the 1990s, followed by the waters of Hurricane Mitch that tore through their fields in 1998. But the business is sunk deep into the rich soil, and the handful of familial cigar dynasties that first came to Nicaragua 30 years ago are still here, and still rolling world-class cigars.

Most of the tobacco fields and giant wooden drying barns are found across the Estelí valley as it runs north away from the city, as well as in many upper reaches all the way to Jalapa. In Estelí there are about 10 serious cigar producers, a few of which will let travelers in their doors for an informal tour and perhaps a taste test. Most businesses are *zona franca* (free-trade zone), however, which prohibits them from selling their product within Nicaragua. Don Orlando Padrón, head of Cubanica Cigars, keeps the doors to his Estelí factory shut for another reason: to protect the trade secrets that produce one of the most internationally acclaimed cigars in the world, El Padrón.

Some of the other heavy hitters are Latin Tobacco, Estelí Cigar, Tabacalera Perdomo (formerly Nick's Cigars), Plasencia, and Nicaraguan American Tobacco (NATSA). Don Francisco's Tabacalero Santiago is the newest

Empresa Nica Cigars (around the corner from the COTRAN Sur, tel. 505/2713-2230) will also allow curious visitors to come inside and take pictures of their rollers. You'll smell the tobacco from blocks away. They are famous for the *padron,* a cigar manufactured using organic tobacco that has received international awards and acclaim.

Tabacalero Santiago (tel. 505/2713-2230) gained fame with endorsements from Arnold Schwarzenegger, Bruce Willis, and Charlie Sheen—and a contract to provide cigars to the Playboy mansion. The owner's family won its first cigar factory in a poker game in Cuba shortly after World War II. Now with a factory in Panamá as well as Estelí, don Francisco provides Churchills, Figurados, Magnums, El Presidentes, and other brands to a global market.

Tobacos de Estanzuela/TESA (two blocks west of El Buen Sabor, tel. 505/2714-1800 or U.S. tel. 205/265-6703, tesa@munditel.com.ni) can offer a close up view of a small family-run operation which also specializes in carpentry. Kick back, spend some time, and hear the stories from Alan Arguello Kuper, the owner and designer of the furniture.

For an all-inclusive package where you can stay as close as possible to the production facilities, you may try contacting **Drew Estate** before you travel (U.S. tel. 786/581-1810, www.drewestate.com). They have a small all-inclusive hotel and provide Cigar Safari tour company, one that grows and rolls organic tobacco. The factories are scattered across Estelí, and unless you've got pretty good Spanish, bring a translator. Although the main tourist office will tell you all the factories in Estelí offer tours, hospitality varies widely. Don Francisco's production manager can arrange a tour if arranged a day in advance, and Don Kiki, of Estelí Cigars, sometimes gives casual tours, maybe even a cup of Cuban coffee and a smoke.

Cigar making is a proud family tradition here and elsewhere in the world, and there's no denying the craftsmanship of a fine cigar. But as the blunt you're smoking burns lower, and the heat of the cherry seeps into the leaf between your fingers, consider the yang side. Organic tobacco is grown in Nicaragua, but barely; most production employs massive quantities of chemicals, which invariably find their way into the earth, the water, or the lungs, hands, and feet of the workers. Tobacco handlers often absorb the toxic elements of the leaf, and although at least several of Estelí's factories have impressive, airy environments for their workers, conditions for the rollers are often no better than the worst sweatshops. And the history burns on.

© JAMES SAVAGE

tobacco harvest near Estelí

ESTELÍ AND THE SEGOVIAS

packages. Drew Estate is known for producing more eclectic types of cigars with names such as Acid, Ambrosia, Chateau Real, and Isla del Sol.

Others in the area which may or may not be available for tour with a local guide and advanced notice are Plasencia and My Father Cigars.

As with a fine cigar, if you choose to take a tour, or venture out on your own, make sure not to rush. The process of producing a well-made cigar is as enjoyable as smoking one. Make sure to block out lots of time and head in with a "go with the flow" attitude. Most establishments have been making cigars for many generations and are very proud to share their stories for all truly interested.

ENTERTAINMENT AND EVENTS

Estelí's festival season is clearly December, when practically the whole month there is some sort of activity including the famous *Hípica* (horse parade) and Purisima celebrating the Virgin Mary with free take-aways at every house.

Bars and Disco

Estelí has quite an eclectic nightlife considering it is far from any beaches or larger cities. It has a little something for everyone from dive bars, mixed local and foreign crowd scenes, salsa, and live music.

The **Rincón Legal** (200 meters south of the Hospital San Juan de Dios, near El Chaman) is the brainchild of Frankie Legall and is a bar-shrine to the FSLN and Cuban Communist Party; Carlos Mejía Godoy plays here when in town, and this is the home turf of many artists—and a place for wandering lefties to toast the light arms and photos of Carlos Fonseca on the wall. **El Punto de Encuentro** (40 meters west of the northwest corner of the central park) features a mellow hangout in the hidden patio/garden for enjoying cheap eats and drinks.

In the same area you will also find the very popular **Rancho Bar El Semáforo** which is perfect for large groups and especially lively on Saturday; when its two large dance floors attract a mixed crowd. Just before Semáforo is **El Chaiman,** also large with a thatched roof and a jungle motif, with live music every once in a while and definitely more of a local crowd. For good local live music and great food try Ixcoteli Bar and Restaurant or Friday nights at Mocha Nana Café. To just sit back and catch up on conversation, go to Habana Sports Bar. Take a taxi to the south side of town and spend an evening just walking from one to the other.

For dancing, **Axis Discoteca** on the Pan-American Highway towards the center of town has a spacious dance floor and a party that lasts well past midnight. But a newer and hipper place is ◖ **The Cave Club** (adjacent to Whitehouse Pizza near the cathedral, tel. 505/2713-2116) with three levels of bar and a truly cavelike basement disco that really thumps.

Karaoke is as popular as ever in Nicaragua and Estelí keeps pace. **La Confianza** (from Payless, 1.5 blocks north) is the place to be for beers, talking, and catching interesting regulars. The atmosphere allows for talking but also boasts lots of space and karoke. **Be Lounge** has karaoke during the week but the weekends are usually crowded with the younger Estelíanos. **Las Vegas** is often a late-night stop, open until 6 A.M. with a small dance floor that alternates from karaoke to disco music in a black-light room of Las Vegas kitsch.

SHOPPING

Provided you're not interested in fruits and vegetables (in which case you want the *mercado* on the south end of Estelí), the entire length of Avenida Principal is lined with boutiques whose shop girls might whistle and catcall to entice you into their stores softly asking *"¿Que busca, amor?"* ("What are you looking for, my love?") as you walk by.

Guitarras y Requintas el Arte (from Camera de Commercio, two blocks west, tel. 505/2713-7555) sells handmade guitars, mandolins, and *guitarrónes* (the bass guitar used by mariachis).

Bookstores

The tiny **Librería Leonel Rugama** (on Ave. Principal, across from the Kodak) is a bookshop run by the famous poet-martyr's parents. Rugama's dramatic death at the hands of Somoza's National Guard is legendary: Cornered in a building in Managua, the young soldier single-handedly held off a contingent of guardsmen while Carlos Fonseca escaped through the sewers. Ordered to his knees by the Guardia, he was commanded, *"¡Rindase, Sandinista!"* ("Surrender, Sandinista!"). Rugama retorted, famously, *"¡Que se rinda tu madre!"* ("Let your mother surrender!") before he was shot. Otherwise, **Mocha Nana** has a small English language bookstore, where no one has to surrender at all.

Artesanías and Local Crafts

Two shops—**Artesanía La Esquina** (one block north of the cathedral, tel. 505/2713-2229) and **Artesanía La Sorpresa** (one block south of the cathedral, tel. 505/2713-4456)—each have a huge selection of Nicaraguan arts and crafts from all over the country. In general, prices are cheaper in the Managua and Masaya markets, but for locally produced items, like soapstone carvings and Ducualí pottery, these are good places to shop. Artesanía La Sorpresa also has a small section with herbal medicines. **Café Luz,** the sister restaurant to Hostel Luna, the only *hostal* in Estelí, has a

© RANDALL WOOD

Seek out leather crafters in the blocks around the market of Estelí.

number of talented local artists selling their arts and crafts products. Casa Estelí near the Tip Top on the Pan-American highway is another interesting location for buying your unique Nicaraguan souvenirs.

◖ Custom Cowboy Boots

Estelí is the place to buy handmade **leather goods** like belts, saddles, and cowboy boots: Find them all along the southern half of Avenida 1 SO. A pair of quality cowhide boots (or deerskin or snakeskin, the latter of which might get confiscated at your home customs office) go for $60–100 and take a week to make when custom fit to your foot. Order a pair on your way north and pick 'em up on the way back to Managua.

ACCOMMODATIONS
Under $10

Estelí's least expensive lodging is on the south side of town by the Parque Infantíl. **Hospedaje Chepito** (one block south of the park, tel. 505/2713-6388, $4) is a favorite with the backpacker set, with passable rooms and shared

cold-water bath. A better choice is **Hospedaje Sacuanjoche** (2.5 blocks south of ENITEL, tel. 505/2713-2862), a family run and peaceful lodging. A bit closer to the action, **Hospedaje Familiar** (half a block north of Super Las Segovias, next to the Tip Top distributor, tel. 505/2713-3666, $10–13) is run by Edith Valenzuela Lopez, a tried-and-true Sandinista with more than 33 years of hosting *internacionalistas;* rooms have private bath and TV.

$10-25

◖ **Hostel Luna** (one block east and one block north of the cathedral, tel. 505/8441-8466, www.cafeluzyluna.com) is run by British expat Jane Boyd, offering dorm beds for $10 and private rooms for $20. Breakfast is served at **Cafe Luz** across the street where you can hang in the garden hammocks. Jane is a valuable source of knowledge on activities in the area and can help arrange anything from a trip to Miraflor, a cigar factory tour, or a walking mural tour with a local guide. The eight rooms at **Hotel El Mesón** (one block north of the cathedral, tel. 505/2713-2655, $23–27) have private bath

STONE MAN: A CHAT WITH ALBERTO GUTIERREZ

Self-taught sculptor Alberto Gutierrez, at nearly 70 years old, has done hundreds, if not thousands of carvings and sculpting of the rocks on his family farm. He says he started his art based on a dream he had when he was nine years old on the night of his birthday. An angel visited him in his sleep and laid out the plan for all the sculptures he has created. Alberto says he didn't think much about the dream until many years later when he began having problems controlling his drinking. He visited a priest and asked for guidance on how to manage alcohol. The priest gave him the advice to find something to occupy his time. So, Alberto picked up a piece of metal and began carving. In a short while he had formed a perfectly proportioned elephant about three feet tall protruding out of the rock face. He kept going.

You can visit Alberto. He'll most likely offer you a tour. Being very spiritual, he has hundreds of interpretations of Jesus, and small versions of churches he has created. His inspiration also includes Nicaraguan poets, self-portraits, quetzal birds, and eagles. Although each one may seem the same to the uncommon visitor, Alberto will be sure to tell you each story and why that particular carving is unique.

Beyond his artistic abilities, Alberto lives in one of the areas with the best views of the mountains surrounding Estelí. As you walk, he will stop to point out the beauty and give you a sense that he himself is noticing it for the first time, although he has had over 9,000 visitors to his home since 2004 (you will be asked to sign his guest book so he can remember your visit.)

Alberto Gutierrez also has hundreds of varieties of orchids, pineapples, bananas, and medicinal plants. He will rattle off the names of each one faster than Bubba in Forrest Gump. You will always leave with a gift of whatever he has in season of oranges, bananas, pineapples, or some type of other plant.

VISITING THE ROCK SCULPTURE GALLERY

Make sure to wear comfortable shoes, be in good enough shape for a decent hike, and carry a long-sleeved shirt, jacket, or something to keep warm and block the wind. It can get surprisingly chilly at the farm. About 1.5 kilometers down the road toward La Garnarcha from Eco-Posada Tisey, you will come across a sign that says Ministerio del Ambiente Y Los Recursos Naturales Area Protegida Tisey-Estanzuela. Stop and admire the spectacular view for a moment then pass through the gate just down the hill. Most likely it will feel like trespassing on private property, but it's okay. Follow the main trail and ask the local farmers along the way if needed. Just keep walking down the hill.

---

and fan (a few with a/c); this place is quiet and clean, and the hot water makes January mornings a lot more bearable. They have parking, a bar and restaurant, a garden, a travel agency, car rental, and will change travelers checks. Not far away, **Hotel Moderno** (one block east of the park and two blocks, tel. 505/2713-2378, $30) consists of 11 rooms—all with private bath, hot water, TV, and fan—surrounding a shaded courtyard, conference room, bar, and restaurant.

$25-50

The gorgeous **Hotel Los Arcos/Café Vuela**

Vuela (one block north of the cathedral, $40–75) is run by a Spanish development organization in a charming colonial edifice. All profits go toward development activities like their schools, continuing education programs, and street children. If you're more interested in a relaxing evening than a night in town, **Hotel Cualitlán** (from COTRAN Sur, two blocks south, four east, and one north, tel. 505/2713-2446, $50) is a walled-in guesthouse compound unlike any other in Estelí. It has a verdant sitting area with a tree-canopy roof, soothing music, and a creative menu geared to the international

© RODNEY MCDONALD

Alberto Gutierrez welcomes visitors to his remote, open-air studio.

After crossing a cow pasture and continuing on a well worn trail, you will see another state sign that says "Bienvenidos A Galeria Esculturas En Piedras." Cross over the wooden bar used as a gate and start calling out. Eventually someone will come either by your voice or the sound of the barking dogs, which will have picked up on your presence way before anyone else. Alberto will never ask for any money for the visit, but the experience may move you to make a donation, which is welcome.

Contributed by Rodney McDonald.

traveler. Choose one of several delightfully appointed cabanas—something like Swiss chalets—set around the lush tropical courtyard, all with hot water and cable TV. They have two rooms that can house up to six for $20 per person, all with breakfast included.

Long-Term Accommodations

All of the Spanish schools have networks of families accustomed to housing foreigners for a weekly or monthly rate. Doña Edith at the **Hospedaje Familiar** offers extended room-and-board deals, starting at $150 a month. **Centro Cultural Juventus** (tel. 505/2713-3756) can offer housing for visiting students or those in language school. For house and apartment rentals, call **Bienes Raices Gomez** (tel. 505/2713-3835).

FOOD

The Esteliáno diet is hardy and satisfying, but simple. Local venues tend to mostly serve steaks, fried chicken, and bowls of soup big enough to drown in. The nicest restaurants are found in the town's upscale hotels and on the blocks around the park. Many of the places where locals eat are in the *Entertainment and Events* section.

Bakeries and Cafés

There is an excellent Spanish bakery, **Repostería España**, 3.5 blocks north of the central park, and a German one, **Repostería Alemán**, behind the cathedral. (| **Mocha Nana** with a new location (half a block from the Parque Infantíl on the Avenida Central, tel. 505/2713-3164, mochanana@hotmail.com, 9 A.M.–7 P.M. Mon.–Sat.) is a perfect afternoon respite from the sun; in addition to fine cappuccinos, mochas, coffee, and espresso they have bagels, waffles, and a small English language bookstore and trade library.

Licuados Ananda has health foods, yogurt, natural juices, and fruit smoothies in a patio surrounding a pool. Try the vegetarian *nacatamales,* veggie burgers, and sandwiches. They also have educational opportunities on many facets of eastern and natural medicine. Also now open for dinner until 7 P.M.

The menu is simple, healthy, and homegrown at (| **La Casita** (across from La Barranca, south entrance, tel. 505/713-4917, casita@sdnnic.org.ni). Yogurt, home-baked breads, fresh cheeses, vegetables, granola, juices, and coffee drinks are all served in a pleasant garden atmosphere along the shore of a babbling brook. It's on the Pan-American Highway a few kilometers south of the city, and is open 1–7 P.M. Monday, 7 A.M.–7 P.M. Tuesday–Saturday, and 9 A.M. –7 P.M. Sunday—closed first Monday of every month. Take an *urbano* bus to the new hospital, then walk south around the bend in the road; or hail a taxi for about $1.50—it's well worth the trip. In addition to featuring wonderful food and mellow music, La Casita sells local crafts and plants, including herbs, ornamentals, and much much more.

Juventus Centro Cultural (two blocks west of the central park's southwest corner, tel. 505/2713-3756, open 9 A.M.–6 P.M. Mon.–Sat.) is situated on top of the hill that drops down to the river, making for great panoramas of the river and mountains to the west as you enjoy *licuados,* granola, open-face swiss and brie sandwiches, and hot drinks.

Fritanga and Comida Típica

For low cost and finger-lickin' goodness, the many *fritangas* and pizza trucks in the park and scattered around are hard to beat. For excellent *empanadas* step across the street from La Galería de Héroes y Mártires at night. Also easy on the wallet is **Don Pollo's** fried chicken, one block north and half a block east of the cathedral. **Cafe Luz,** one block east and one block north of the church, serves a variety of international and *comida típica* fare that is particularly appealing to the *gallo pinto*–weary traveler.

Leche Agria (2.5 blocks south of *la esquina de los bancos*) serves excellent *quesillos* (cheese and tortilla snack), juices, and cheeses.

Pupusas are traditionally from El Salvador but have been adopted to the Nicaraguan culture as well. If you are in the mood for some great local food at an amazingly cheap price, try the little grill located behind the Hotel Estelí named **Pupusas Nicaragua,** by far the best in the country. There is no official sign, just look for the garage door painted with a Pepsi sign. At $0.50 per *pupusa* it makes a great way to fill up on local flavor at hardly any expense.

Comedor Popular La Soya (Ave. Principal, 2.5 blocks south of the park), true to its name, serves soy-based meals and soy milk drinks. For an excellent local breakfast or quick lunch for under $4, try Cafetin **El Recanto** two blocks south of the park. For quick and tasty lunch at the park, try **Delicias Loco** which offers a plate at lunchtime for about $2.50 including a drink or hamburgers and tacos at night. For some of the best pizza in the country visit **Dough Pizza,** located on the highway just north of Tip Top. If you prefer quick good quality pizza by the slice, try **Fresh Pizza La Segovia** (2.5 blocks south, tel. 505/8853-8023).

For a bit of a splurge, try (| **El Pullazo Olé** (open 5–10 P.M. daily, $4–9) and join the fierce Nicaraguan competition for the best beef in the nation; they also serve fantastic sausages and desserts.

International

La Gran Vía (just south of *la esquina de los bancos,* closed Sun.) serves Chinese meals from $4.

For excellent Cuban cuisine try El Rincón Pinareño (tel. 505/2713-4309, 505/2713-0248) located two blocks south of the cathedral. It is a family-run establishment, serving authentic food served in an impeccable atmosphere. For Italian, try **Casa Vechia,** one block south then one block west of *la esquina de los bancos.*

INFORMATION

Casa Estelí (tel. 505/2713-4432 or 505/2713-2584, casaesteli@nortedenicaragua.com, www.nortedenicaragua.com) is a highly informative tourist office with maps, translators, Internet access, and an on-site café as well.

INTUR's Estelí office, (located half a block south of Edificio Gloria, tel. 505/2713-6799, www.intur.gob.ni, open 8 A.M.–1 P.M. Mon.–Fri.) was recently revamped. It is filled with brochures of all the northern regions and has helpful, trained staff to point you in the direction of reliable guides. The public **library** (four blocks north and one east of the central park, tel. 505/2713-7021, open 8 A.M.–noon and 2–5 P.M. Mon.–Fri.) is in a huge, brand new building built with foreign donations.

SERVICES
Emergencies

El Hospital Regional de Estelí (tel. 505/2713-6300) is located just south of the city, but for minor cuts and bruises, Avenida Principal's many private clinics are a better option. The police station (tel. 505/2713-2615) is located on the main highway, toward the northern exit.

Banks and Exchange

There are three respectable banks at *la esquina de los bancos* (the corner of banks), one block west and one south of the park; Bancentro is 2.5 blocks south on Avenida Principal. All have ATMs, as does the Texaco station on the northern border of the city. The travel agency in Hotel Mesón changes travelers checks, as do most of the banks. The street money changers, a.k.a. *coyotes,* are safe to use and often give you a better exchange rate than the banks. You'll usually find bunches of *coyotes* at various corners of Estelí: near the old hospital, the Petronic

gas station on the Avenida Principal, and the corner close to Quesillos y Leche. These will be the gentlemen usually sitting on the corner holding or shaking loads of money in mysterious dark sunglasses. Don't let their appearance sway you. They will have certification to show they are legit.

Mail and Phones

The post office is open 8 A.M.–4:30 P.M. Monday–Friday and and closes for lunch noon–1:30 P.M. The Farmacia Corea (Petronic El Carmen, one block east, half a block south, tel. 505/2713-2085) offers mail and package service, as well as money transfers. ENITEL (one block south of the church and half a block east, tel. 505/2713-2222) is open 8 A.M.–8 P.M. Monday–Friday and 8 A.M.–5 P.M. Saturday.

Internet

There are several Internet cafés any direction within two blocks of the park, open generally 8 A.M.–9 P.M. Monday–Saturday, 8 A.M.–6 P.M. Sunday. Estelí@Net (one block south of the park on Calle Transversal near Farmacia Estelí) is the most convenient and comfortable, and air-conditioned. Cyber Place (one block north of the park from the traffic light) is also decent.

GETTING THERE AND AWAY

Express and ordinary buses for Estelí leave from Managua's Mayoreo terminal. Seven *expresos* per day pass Esteí bound for Managua, making stops along the highway. If you're arriving from Honduras, buses leave frequently daily from Somoto and Ocotal, the last one leaving at 5 P.M.

From Estelí, *ordinario* buses leave the COTRAN Norte at regular intervals for Ocotal, Somoto, and points north 4 A.M.–5 P.M.; they leave COTRAN Sur for Managua, Matagalpa, León, and Yalí. Ocotal *expresos* stop off at the Shell Esquipulas approximately every hour on the half hour.

From COTRAN Sur there are dozens of daily buses to both Managua and Mataglapa, leaving from the wee hours until 6 P.M.; three express buses to León depart before 7 A.M., plus a few daily microbuses to León (they leave when they fill up, and competition is fierce).

GETTING AROUND

Estelí is a long city; you can cut short the walking by hopping a cab for the fixed price of $0.30–$0.60 anywhere in the city (except La Casita restaurant on the south side of town). *Urbano* buses ($0.25) are safe to ride and run a big loop around the city, including up and down the main avenues and nearby barrios.

Travel Services and Car Rental

Agencia de Viajes Tisey (in Hotel El Mesón, tel. 505/2713-3099, fax 505/2713-4029, barlan@ibw.com.ni) is a modern and professional agency that deals with airlines, international reservations, and Budget rental cars.

Casa Estelí (on the Pan-American Highway, 20 meters south of the *monumento centenario*) has a Budget rental car office, with four-wheel drive trucks for about $60 per day. The **Dollar car rental agency** is located with the Toyota dealer on the highway with economy sedans for $35 a day and pickup trucks for $60 a day.

Near Estelí

◖ EL SALTO ESTANZUELA AND RESERVA EL-TISEY

Estelí's most famous swimming hole, this is a gorgeous 15-meter, rainy season–only cascade you can swim behind, plunging into a cold, shady pool, all smothered in colorful native flora and fauna. It's just southwest of the city. You can hike to the waterfall from the highway. The road to Estanzuela leaves the Pan-American just south of the new hospital and is sandwiched between two *pulperías* where you can stock up for the journey. This is the terminus of the *urbano* bus routes which start at the central park, or take a taxi from the city center for about $0.50. The five-kilometer walk should take 60–90 minutes each way. It's an easy hike, but with lots of ups-and-downs. Otherwise, hop a bus for the 20-minute ride (buses leave COTRAN Sur at 6:30 A.M. and 1:30 P.M.). Before you reach the hamlet of Estanzuela, look for a gated road on your right; the waterfall is at the bottom of a hill after the first two dilapidated wooden homes of the village. Villagers charge 30 *córdobas* ($1.50) to hike down to the falls. Head downward for about 10 minutes until the track veers steeply down to the left. If you take one of the side trails to the left now it will lead you to the top of the falls. Before the

road turns to the right again, take the path in front of you straight down to the falls, there is a large sign for the Ministerio del Ambiente. You should now be able to hear the falls.

mountain scenery in Reserva El-Tisey

Reserva El-Tisey

Down the same road as the waterfall, the 9,344-hectare co-managed Reserva El-Tisey makes available a rustic ecolodge, fields of organic vegetables, a network of hiking trails, and trips on horseback, not to mention spectacular panoramas: From the top of Tisey on a clear day, you can make out the Pacific coastal plain and the entire chain of volcanic peaks from Cosigüina to Lake Managua and Momotombo, the Estelí valley, and north to the mountains of the Segovias on the horizon. The reserve has an office in Estelí (tel. 505/2713-3918) and an office in Managua (tel. 505/2249-6039).

Start by settling in at **Eco-Posada Tisey** (tel. 505/2713-6213 or 505/8836-6021), which charges $3 per person for communal living, $10 for a double bed and some privacy, and $1.50 per meal. They will find you guides, rent horses, or show you around the organic farm that stocks most of Managua's supermarkets with fresh veggies. There's more to see there than you'll likely have time for, so plan a few days at least. One trail climbs to a lookout (1,300 meters) where you'll enjoy the phenomenal view and the falls. The folks here can show you some of the reserve's other highlights, like the septuagenarian sculptor who picked up hammer and chisel to absorb some of his nervous energy when he quit drinking, or the bat cave, local hangout for more than 10,000 winged friends (hint: bring a hat). Closer to the lodge, taste fresh cheeses and vegetables, or spend a night in the farming community of La Garnacha. To get there, catch a bus to El Jalacate.

La Ganarcha is the heart of Reserva El-Tisey; the only way to get here is to hike or hire a truck from Eco-Posada Tisey. The biological station is the headquarters for the reserve where you can get maps, talk with the rangers, and arrange for guides. There are five-person cabins here with fantastic views of the surrounding forest and hills for $10 per night, or dormitory lodging for $3–5 per night. Food can be arranged with a local family for usually around $5 a day. There are many marked trails that leave from either the biological station, or the guest quarters—one heads due west from the station and winds through rocky hillsides and pine forest to several highpoints with views of the volcanoes to the west. Winds stir the trees and the smell of pine needles is everywhere.

LA TRINIDAD

Just as the Pan-American Highway begins its curvy climb into higher altitudes, midsize La Trinidad, named for the three hills that surround it, is a festive village of bread bakers, bus drivers, musicians, and cowboys. Its unhurried and friendly populace can often be found hanging out in the well-tended central plaza—kept green even in the height of the dry season. The Catholic church, although decidedly ugly by Latin American standards, may be worth a visit during mass to hear the dueling mariachi choirs. La Trini's rip-roaring *fiestas patronales,* celebrating La Virgen de Candelaria and Jésus de Caridad, occur during the last week of January and roll raucously into the first week of February, with a famous *hípica* (horse parade) that attracts riders from all over Central America.

Take a walk up to the old **Spanish cross** or west up the river valley road to the **Rosario shrine**—allow about an hour each way. The hill to the east of the highway is the legendary Mocuana, with its caves of witches, gold, snakes, and a tunnel to Sébaco, if you believe everything you hear.

Hotel y Restaurante Tzolkin (tel. 505/2716-2124 or 505/8437-6067, winstonmairena@yahoo.com, $15–20) is located just off the southwest corner of the park, serving dinner for less than $4. Otherwise dine at **Don Juan's Las Sopas,** on the southern outskirts of town; this is a popular stopover for Pan-American commuters and truck drivers, with an open-air patio and a fantastic menu of soups—including *huevos de toro* (bull balls), ox tail, and chicken soup.

◖ MIRAFLOR NATURE RESERVE

More than a trip into Estelí's misty mountains, a visit to Miraflor is a trip backward in time. Perhaps this is what Costa Rica's Monteverde was like 40 years ago before it was populated with four-star resorts and laced with splinter-free wooden walkways. Miraflor is unabashedly rustic, natural, and unpretentious. Declared a protected natural reserve in 1990, this rudimentary tourist infrastructure was developed by locals, with their own sweat and labor and in the absence of any external help.

Miraflor as an entity is a little vague. There's no town, per se, or even a real center. Rather, the 5,000 Mirafloreños live dispersed throughout the 206 square kilometers of the reserve in a geographically dispersed but socially united community. The Miraflor Reserve is privately owned, cooperatively managed in many parts, and almost entirely self-funded by associations of small-scale producers. Most notable among these is the UCA Miraflor (or in full, the Union de Cooperativas Agropecuarias Héroes y Mártires de Miraflor)—not to be confused with the University of Central America—an association of 14 small farmer

MIRAFLOR NATURE RESERVE

© AVALON TRAVEL

SWAMP THINGS: LEGENDS OF THE MIRAFLOR LAGOON

La Laguna de Miraflor is, compared to other *lagunas* (lakes) in the country, a mere puddle, whose marshy banks are crowded with vegetation and birdsong. Its fame lies not in its grandeur, but in its myth. There are at least five legends surrounding the lagoon, stories passed down over the years that have smothered the 10-hectare body of water in a shroud of mystery as thick as the white clouds sweeping over its surface.

The most famous of these legends is the **Ramo de Flores.** Every Thursday of Semana Santa (Holy Week), a cluster of beautiful flowers rises to the surface of the lagoon and circulates around and around. The flowers, say some, are bringing a message to the people that they should unite. The name Miraflor (flower view) comes from this legend, and variations tell of a tiny dancing prince in the middle of the flowers and dwarfs bearing the flowers to give to local girls.

Also well known is the story of the **Ciudad Perdida** (The Lost City). Only the oldest of Mirafloreños know of the hidden entrance, but everyone knows of the vast fields of exotic fruit-bearing trees in the city at the bottom of the lagoon (which, by the way, has been measured at 27 meters deep, plus three meters of sediment).

One can eat all they want when in the city, but if they try bringing the fruit back to the surface world, they will not be allowed to pass.

Every now and then, the water of the lagoon turns jet black; evidence, say some, of the giant **black serpent** that lives in the water and occasionally stirs up the sediment on the bottom. The snake may or may not have something to do with the lagoon's vengeful nature, punishing anyone who speaks disrespectfully of it or disbelieves its power. One unfortunate young man did so while swimming in the middle – he had barely spoken his blasphemy when a whirlpool formed, sucked him under, and then spit him back up, whereupon he apologized profusely and pledged his eternal respect for the enchanted waters.

Just across the road, the **Laguna de Lodo,** or Lagoon of Mud, has its share of legends as well. The mud pond is half the size of its counterpart and lies above the subterranean river that feeds the main lagoon. One day, a local *leñador* (lumberjack) was working near the Laguna de Lodo and dropped his axe into the mud, which promptly swallowed it up. He cried and cried and cried, until his axe finally rose to the surface...with a head and blade of shining gold.

cooperatives and 120 families living within the protected area. UCA Miraflor is primarily an agricultural credit and loan institution, but it has also tackled issues and begun programs, such as community health and education, organic agriculture and diversification of crops, cooperative coffee production, gender and youth groups, and conflict resolution. Tourism, Miraflor's greatest potential, was just an afterthought.

Visiting Miraflor

Start with a call or visit to the UCA Miraflor office in Estelí (from the cathedral three blocks east, half a block north, tel. 505/2713-2971, miraflor@ibw.com.ni, www.miraflor.org, open 8 A.M.–12:30 P.M. and 2–5 P.M. Mon.–Fri.). They will present your options and help arrange lodging, tour guides, horse rental—taking care to distribute guests fairly among the various families who have agreed to host guests. Expect to pay $15–25 per service requested.

Sights and Attractions

Miraflor has something for everyone—nature lovers, hikers, social justice workers, organic farmers, artists, horse lovers, orchid fanatics, birders, and entomologists—each of whom will find their own personal heaven here. You can certainly visit parts of

Miraflor in a day trip from Estelí, but read on and consider experiencing the unique accommodations.

Every attraction in Miraflor is privately owned, often by poor *campesinos*. Your financial support leads to the continued preservation of these magnificent forests, because, "hey, this would be a great place to chop down the trees and plant some beans."

The community of La Fortuna has a small museum that they are trying hard to improve which has indigenous relics from the area and articles from the war. It is a great place to get out of the weather in the rainy season.

Fauna: The distinct bird species number 236, belonging to 46 different families which inhabit or fly through these mountains—that's nearly 40 percent of all bird species in the country, including four species of the elusive quetzal *(Pharomachrus mocinno)*, toucans, the *ranchero (Procnias tricaruntulata)*, with its three dangling chins, and the Nicaraguan national bird, the *guardabarranco*. Miraflor is also one of your best chances to spot coyotes, sloths, deer, howler monkeys, or one of six different feline species, not to mention raccoons, skunks, armadillos, and exotic rodents.

Orchids: Miraflor is one of the richest and most unexplored orchid-viewing regions anywhere. Among the more than 300 identified species is an enormous colony of *Cattleya skinniri* (the national flower of Costa Rica), not to mention scads of bromeliads and a museum of other orchids from throughout the reserve.

Hikes and Adventure: Short hikes are possible through any of the hundreds of pockets of forest, but ask your guide to take you on one of the more adventurous trips. Although difficult to access, the 60-meter waterfall at **La Chorrera** is one of the wildest spots in the reserve. **The Caves of Apaguis** were dug in pre-Columbian times by gem seekers and have been occupied ever since by *duendes* (dwarves), as any local will inform you. The mature cloud forest of **Bosque Los Volcancitos** is Miraflor's highest point at 1,484 meters and is known habitat for howler monkeys and quetzals. If the monkeys don't snatch away your

binoculars, expect fantastic views from El Tayacán, Cerro Yeluca, Cerro El Aguila, La Coyotera, and Ocote Calzado. Furthermore, the forests are replete with mysteries, such as the **casa antigua,** a 1,200-year-old foundation in the Tayacán area, surrounded by dozens of other unearthed *montículos* (mounds). Archaeologists haven't even begun to investigate the rest of them.

The lagoon in Miraflor is a great place to pass time, maybe stop for a great lunch. If you are lucky, you will get a chance to see monkeys in the area, but don't leave your food for long or it may become theirs.

Progressive Agriculture: If you enjoy inspired agriculture and alternative farming practices, the *campesinos* at Miraflor will gladly show you their cutting-edge lifestyle, including organic compost, natural pest management, watershed protection, live fences, crop diversification, soil management, reforestation, worm farming, and environmental education. In addition, Miraflor's small-scale, fair trade, organic coffee cooperatives and cupping lab (in Cebollál) are among the nation's finest.

What to Bring

At 1,400 meters above sea level, Miraflor is remote, cloud-covered, and sometimes downright chilly. Be prepared for inclement weather (buy a sweatshirt at one of Estelí's millions of used-clothing stores) and bring your own bottled water if you're concerned. A flashlight or candles will be helpful on that midnight walk to the latrine.

Accommodations and Food

Accommodations are all well kept, but primitive; some do not have electricity. Start with a call or visit to the UCA Miraflor office in Estelí (from the cathedral three blocks east, half a block north, tel. 505/2713-2971, miraflor@ibw.com.ni, www.miraflor.org, open 8 A.M.–12:30 P.M. and 2–5 P.M. Mon.–Fri.). They will present your options and help arrange lodging, taking care to distribute guests fairly among the various families who have agreed to host guests. Expect to pay $13–17 per person per night, with all meals included. The UCA Miraflor–affiliated lodging is distributed between four main communities, and they'll ask you to pick a zone: either the cloud forest with the communty of La Rampa, the middle zone (best for birders as it has more species diversity) with the communities of Sontule and El Cebollál, or the low, dry zone with the communities of Coyolito and La Pita.

Campesino Homes: This option features a network of families trained in the subtle art of entertaining picky travelers; their homes, while clean and well maintained, are usually quite rustic. Lindos Ojos is affiliated with the UCA Miraflor, but handles its own business. Ask about package trips that include meals, guided hikes, and organic agriculture demonstrations.

Getting There and Away

Until the road from Estelí is finally paved, expect bumps, dust, and mud on the slow ride into the hills. There are four buses a day from Estelí: two leave for La Pita from Pulpería Miraflor by the Texaco Starmart at the north end of town (6 A.M. and 1 P.M.). The buses to Sontule and La Perla leave from COTRAN Norte at 2 P.M. and 3:40 P.M. The UCA Miraflor office may also be able to arrange transport.

Returning to Estelí, buses depart La Pita at 8:10 A.M. and 3 P.M., from Sontule at 8 A.M., and from La Perla at 7:30 A.M. The bus from Yalí passes by La Rampla at 7 A.M., 11 A.M., and 4 P.M. Hitching in this remote area of the Estelí countryside is very difficult, as there are not many rides.

CONDEGA

The 9,000 inhabitants of the Tierra de los Alfareros (Land of the Potters) eke out a living raising cattle, corn, and beans as did the Nahuatl centuries before. Truckloads of pre-Columbian pottery have been dug out of area cornfields, and the tradition lives on today with a women's pottery cooperative in Ducualí Grande. Before the revolution, only three *terretenientes* (landowners) owned all the land from Condega to Yalí. Condegans proundly supported the Sandinistas, which led to lots of harassment from Somoza's National Guard (Commandante Omar Cabezas once hid out for months with his troops in the mountains outside Condega, reportedly in a cave near El Naranjo). In 1979, the Sandinista government confiscated those properties and redistributed them to the locals.

Contra soldiers found easy pickings in the unprotected farms of the Canta Gallo Mountains east of Condega, where several major skirmishes took place during the 1980s. Most locals can tell you some of the horror stories. In 1998, Hurricane Mitch destroyed more than 200 homes and two of the three local industries (a cigar box factory and a tannery).

Sights

Toward the end of his grip on power, Somoza took to strafing the northern regions with his air force. When, on April 7, 1979, the Sandinistas downed one of his planes, it was considered a major victory and huge morale booster. Follow the dirt road behind the cemetery, then 100 meters to the top of the hill to the **downed airplane**—now a monument—complete with a simulated airport control tower viewing platform. In the course of a recent restoration however, the original blue and red dot, symbol of the Somoza Air Force, was replaced by the stars and bars of the U.S. Air Force. Ignorance or revisionist history? You make the call.

The **Casa de Cultura** is a former command post of the National Guard. In its **musical instrument workshop** you can order a custom-made guitar, *guitarrón,* or violin. Among other attractions, the **Julio Cesár Salgado museum** (open 9 A.M.–5 P.M. Mon.–Fri., reading room open 1–5 P.M. Mon.–Fri.), named after the town's first archaeologist, has a collection of pre-Columbian ceramic work that local farmers have unearthed. Take in some baseball weekends at the ball field just north of town, or catch the *fiestas patronales* on May 15, traditionally the first day of the rainy season—a double cause to celebrate in this rain-starved region. A couple of blocks north of the town square and half a block toward the river (east) is a **cigar factory,** where you can ask to see the process and buy fresh *puros* cheaply.

The **Taller de Cerámica Ducualí Grande** is an artisan's workshop founded in the 1980s with the help of a Spanish volunteer; the 13 workers continue to create charming ceramics using the simplest of wheels and firing the pieces in a woodstove. Pottery costs about $1–7. To get there, take a bus north about two kilometers and get off where a large concrete sign points west to the workshop. Follow that road one kilometer across the bridge and through the community of Ducualí Grande. Turn left when you see the small church, and look for the white sign on the right side.

Venecia Coffee Farm Homestay and Hiking

The Sandinistas created Venecia in the 1980s to house the local coffee cooperative workers. The Contras attacked it relentlessly, burning it mostly to the ground once. These days, the **Los Alpes de Canta Gallo** is an ecotourism facility with a network of hiking trails that wind through the pines and coffee plantations between San Jerónimo and Venecia. Two-day, one-night packages ($30 pp including transportation from nearby El Bramadero, local family homestays, and some time on the coffee plantation) are available through the **Oficina de Nueva Esperanza Cooperativa** (tel. 505/2715-2036, alpes90@yahoo.com) or **Julio Cesar Muños** (tel. 505/2715-2271, reservalindavista@gmail.com). For simple lodging rather than a homestay, the **Estancia El Naranjo** near Venecia (tel. 505/2715-2020 or 505/8662-6221) will accomodate you in private cabins with bath and hot water or in three dormitory-style rooms for about $15 per person.

Accommodations and Services

Pensión Baldovinos (south side of the park, tel. 505/2715-2222, $10) has six simple double or triple rooms with shared bath and decent meals. A town landmark for decades, it closed unexpectedly in 2009—perhaps

temporarily. Next door, **Hospedaje Framar** (tel. 505/2715-2393, $4) is newer and clean, offering seven rooms with shared bath; doors close at 10 P.M.

Belgian-Nicaraguan **Rincón Criollo La Gualca** (tel. 505/2715-2431) has cheap rooms with shared bath for $6, or $13 double with private bath. **Hostal and Mirador La Granja** (half a block east of the park by the catholic church, tel. 505/2715-2357, $10 pp) has private bathrooms. Their balcony offers a splendid view. **Campestre La Granja Hospedaje** (from Instituto Marista, one km east, tel. 505/2715-2521, $10 pp) is in a beautiful location with lots of greenery and a pool.

Getting There

Any bus that travels between Ocotal, Somoto, or Jalapa and Managua or Estelí can drop you off on the highway in front of Condega, a two-block walk from the center of town. Or take the Yalí–La Rica buses from Estelí (5 A.M.– 4:10 P.M.). Make sure to ask if the bus goes through Condega, as there are two routes to Yalí. Express buses will let you off on the highway by the cemetery; *ordinarios* will let you off in front of the park. From Condega, walk out to the Instituto on the highway to try to catch north- or south-bound *expresos,* or wait for slow buses at the park.

PALACAGÜINA AND COFFEE COOPERATIVE

The town of Palacagüina is best known as the pastoral setting for Carlos Mejía Godoy's revolutionary religious anthem, "Cristo de Palacagüina," in which Jesus is born *"en el cerro de la iguana, montaña dentro de la Segovia."* In the song, the Christ child's *campesino* parents, Jose and María, are dismayed when, instead of becoming a carpenter like his father, he wants to be a guerrilla fighter.

One of Nicaragua's largest fair trade coffee cooperatives, **PRODECOOP** is comprised of 2,000 coffee-growing families; they export as many as 30,000 *quintales* (100-pound bags) a year. PRODECOOP can house and feed up to six guests in brand-new accommodations atop the cupping lab overlooking the drying beds, which bustle with activity during the harvest. There is also a swimming pool and a 360-degree view of the surrounding hills. For reservations, contact their office in Estelí (75 meters west of *la esquina de los bancos,* tel. 505/2713-3268, www.prodecoop.com). The coffee compound is between Palacagüina and the northern exit to the highway.

Most *ordinario* buses (not *expresos*) traveling between Estelí and Somoto or Ocotal pass through Palacagüina. If you take an *expreso,* the walk from the highway into town will be long and dusty, but there are usually taxis waiting for just a few *córdobas.*

PUEBLO NUEVO

First inhabited in 1652, Pueblo Nuevo is one of the few northern towns that was not affected much by the Contra war. There are about 3,000 folks in town and another 19,000 living off the land in the surrounding countryside. Pueblo Nuevo honors San Rafael Arcángel during the week leading up to October 24.

Doña Selina will rent you a room in her house, feed you, and should be able to help you find a local guide to go hiking in thte surrounding hills or to view some of the organic agriculture by the river. One nice hike is to the community of Pencal, across the river and about 1.5 hours each way. You can also stay in the farmhouse/*hospedaje* Finca La Virgen. While in Pueblo Nuevo, take a look at the infrequently visited **Museo Arqueológico** (next to the phone office, tel. 505/2719-2512, open 8 A.M.–noon and 2–5 P.M. Mon.–Fri.) in the Casa de Cultura, exhibiting pottery, old farm implements, and archaeological pieces found in the area.

Twelve kilometers west of town on the road to Limay, you'll find **El Bosque,** an archaeological dig site where the bones of several mastodons, glyptodons (predecessors to modern armadillos), and early ancestors of the horse species have been uncovered. At 18,000–32,000 years old, the bones are considered one of the oldest archaeological sites in the Americas. Closer to the surface, remnants of Paleolithic weapons were discovered on an upper stratum of soil.

Buses leave Estelí twice a day at 11:45 A.M. and 3:10 P.M., leaving Pueblo Nuevo at 6:30 A.M. and 8:30 A.M.; ask in the park about transportation that continues farther west into the country.

SAN JUAN DE LIMAY

Since 1972, Limay's claim to fame has been its *marmolina* (soapstone) sculptors, trained by a priest named Eduardo Mejía so they could improve their living conditions. Padre Mejía helped the new artists mine the soapstone from nearby Mt. Tipiscayán (Ulúa-Matagalpa for "mountain of the toucan"), develop their talent, and market their beautifully polished long-necked birds, kissing swans, iguanas, and Rubenesque women. After the revolution, minister of culture Ernesto Cardenal, helped the sculptors organize a short-lived cooperative. A core of local carvers still lives and works in Limay, and

© JOSHUA BERMAN

soapstone sculptures from San Juan de Limay

you can watch them work and purchase some pieces with little effort. In town, just ask for the *artesanos de piedra*.

Nearby Río Los Quesos meanders outside the city limit. Ask a local kid to show you the Poza La Bruja swimming hole, ringed with pre-Columbian petroglyphs. Find a place to bed down for the night at **Pensión Guerrero** (a pink corner building located one block north of the Catholic church, $2.50 s). Limay is part of a sister-city program with Baltimore, Maryland.

San Juan de Limay is a 40-kilometer bus ride from Estelí that traverses a 1,000-meter mountain pass through coffee fields. Buses follow two routes to Limay (via La Shell and via El Pino) and leave Estelí's COTRAN Norte at 8:45 A.M., 9:15 A.M., 12:15 P.M., and 2 P.M.

Ocotal

Built on a thick bed of red sand and surrounded on all sides by mountains draped with green Ocote pines, Ocotal is the last major settlement before the Honduran border at Las Manos and the unbroken wilderness that stretches eastward to the Caribbean. Since 2000, it has seen a lot of development: Formerly sandy streets are now paved. There are two big supermarkets, San Judas and Palí, both located just north and west of the park.

The feeling of Ocotal is one of progress. For most travelers, Ocotal may be nothing more than a place to sleep before hitting the border—but for many coffee growers and subsistence farmers, Ocotal is still "the big city" for supplies and business. And in many ways, Ocotal marvelously represents the kind of quiet, steady growth that goes unnoticed until you've been away for awhile and then takes you by surprise. Steadily, Ocotal is reinventing itself as a great place to do business. Here you are indeed getting close to the frontier however, and you only have to head a mile out of town in any direction before you are back to the rutted dirt roads, soporific cow towns, and sweeping valleys that make Nicaragua at once so charming and so challenging.

ORIENTATION

Buses will deposit you at the COTRAN bus station located within the "new market" to the south of the city about one kilometer from the central park. Two main *entradas* (entrances) to the city, one from the south, and another from the highway to the west, lead straight into the town center. If you enter from the west, pause at the top of the monument to San Francisco to appreciate the layout of the city before continuing into town. Most of the commercial activity occurs between the park, the market, and around the Shell station on the highway. Ocotal is walkable but has numerous taxis anyway.

Saint Francis looks over the northern city of Ocotal.

OCOTAL

To Las Manos and Honduras

To Jalapa

To Macuelizo

HOTEL SAN MARTÍN
RESTAURANTE KILIMANJARO
HOTEL BEL RIVE
SHELL
HOTEL FRONTERA
POLICE STATION
SUPER SAN JUDAS

MARKET

▼ BUFFET LINDA VISTA
BANCENTRO
PALÍ
ALCALDÍA
BANCPRO
CASA DE CULTURA
Central Park
◖ IGLESIA DE NUESTRA SEÑORA DE LA ASUNCIÓN
MONUMENT TO SAN FRANCISCO ★
LLAMARADAS DEL BOSQUE (BUFFET)
LLAMARADAS DEL BOSQUE HOTEL
HOSPITAL
LA YUNTA
DISCO SKY DANCING ▼
EL VIAJERO
MI HOTELITO
LA ESQUINITA ▼
■ INTUR

Río Dipilto

BUS STATION ■
New Market
▼ LA CABAÑA
● HOTEL BEN MORAL

0   400 yds
0   400 m

Río Coco

TURISTICO EL KRIQUE ■
To Estelí and Managua
▼ LA QUINTA

© AVALON TRAVEL

SIGHTS AND ATTRACTIONS

◖ Iglesia de Nuestra Señora de la Asunción

Start with this three-naved church in the center of town. Construction began in 1804, and the northern bell tower (the left one) wasn't completed until the 21st century! Two centuries of inhabitants have taken the liberty of scratching their names into its soft adobe walls, including U.S. Marines in the 1930s. The church looks out over Ocotal's **central plaza,** one of Nicaragua's most gorgeous. Shady and green, it fills up in the evenings with sparrows and gossiping *campesinos.*

Las Kariamba de Fortileza

South of town and across the river is the museum built to commerate the battles of Sandino and his army against the "Yanquis." Completed in 2009, it is less inspiring than the view of Ocotal it commands, as it is perched on the top of a hill.

Half a block west of the park's southwest corner (across the street from Restaurante Llamaradas del Bosque), the **Casa de Cultura** boasts an impressive collection of photos of gringo military defeat and General Sandino's resistance. Yes, "boast" is the right word there. Ironically, the Marines lodged their troops in the Casa de Cultura as well as most buildings surrounding the park during their stay in Ocotal.

ENTERTAINMENT

Centro Turistico El Krique (open 11A.M.–7 P.M. weekdays, 11 A.M.–10 P.M. weekends closed Wed.) is a bit out of the way: just after the bridge over the Río Coco walk one kilometer east on the dirt road. You will not be alone here, as its two very well-maintained swimming pools, games, and sporting equipment, trampoline, and soccer field are Ocotal's equivalent of the local country club. Eat here for about $8 after your swim.

Ocotal's two discos compete for crowds Friday–Sunday. **Discoteca Infinito** (four blocks north of the cathedral) currently has the advantage over **Disco Sky Dancing** (three blocks south and one block west of the central

park). Ocotal celebrates its *fiestas patronales* August 14–15, when you can expect to find Ocoteleños blowing their hard-earned cash on horse shows, live music, gaming tables, and the like.

ACCOMMODATIONS
Under $10

Ocotal has nearly a dozen cheap and spartan *hospedajes.* Backpackers will do fine in secluded ◖ **El Viajero** (seven blocks north and one block east from the bus station, tel. 505/732-2954, $10), offering TV, private bath, and Internet. A recent remodeling including an addition of 10 rooms also provides rooms with higher amenities for up to $20. It's quiet and clean, and the service is exceptionally friendly in an area not really accustomed to tourists.

$10-25

A favorite among travelers is **Llamaradas del Bosque** (south side of the park, tel. 505/732-2643, $18), a good value for the money. **Hotel Bel Rive** (west side of the highway across from the Shell, tel. 505/732-2146 or 505/732-3249, $15) has doubles with private bath, phone, TV, fan, and parking. This is a big step up in quality.

Mi Hotelcito just a few of blocks west of the main square and seven blocks east from the bus station (half a block east of the Hotel Viajero) is a great no-frills but very clean option with rooms varying in size and shape for $7–16 including TV, private bath, and hot water. Breakfast, lunch, or dinner served upon request for just a few dollars.

Just about one kilometer from the COTRAN on the first entrance to the city you see is the **Hotel Ben Moral,** a favorite for quality and price with rooms ranging $13–25, including private bath, phone, TV, air-conditioning, hot water, and Wi-Fi.

Over $25

Ocotal's finest is **Hotel Frontera** (just east of the Shell station, tel. 505/732-2668, $45) with private bath, phone, and TV, plus a slick poolside bar, conference room, parking,

Internet, restaurant, and pleasant airy porches overlooking the city and mountains. More expensive rooms are by the pool, cheaper rooms are in the back.

FOOD

The menu in these parts is chicken, steak, and fish, and we usually recommend avoiding the fish this high in the mountains. **[C Llamaradas del Bosque** (on the south side of the park, open 6:30 A.M.–8 P.M. Mon.–Sat.) is a favorite, serving three meals buffet-style for around $2, and its breakfasts are renowned for the city's best coffee.

La Merienda (one block east and one south of Hotel El Viajero) serves meals in a would-be disco atmosphere. **La Yunta** (one block east and one south of Hospedaje El Viajero, closed Mon.) is higher quality and pricier, with live music many Thursdays and karaoke on the weekends. **Gigis** (just south of the park, tel. 505/2732-2967, 11 A.M.–10 P.M., closed Wed.) has burgers and pasta served by a Nicaraguan who spent years in New York. He makes a mean steak sandwich—recommended. **La Cabaña** (adjacent to Hotel Ben Moral, tel. 505/2732-2415) has good food in a pleasant atmosphere for under $8, with entertainment and dancing on the weekends.

La Esquinita (5 blocks south of the park, 7:30 A.M.–3 P.M.) is immaculately clean, with generous portions for about $5.

For great food and an amazing view of Ocotal head out of town just a few kilometers toward Estelí to **Roca Dura** (tel. 505/8853-7696 or 505/8834-6949, open 10 A.M.–11 P.M. Mon.–Thurs., 10 A.M.–12:30 A.M. Fri.–Sun.) for chicken, steak, burgers, and a truly impressive view. A taxi there will run you about $1,

or $0.25 by bus, daytime. This place is rapidly becoming the weekend party spot.

INFORMATION AND SERVICES

The Ocotal INTUR office (from the central park, three blocks south, one block west, one block south, tel. 505/732-3429, open 7:30 A.M.–4:30 P.M. Mon.–Fri., 8:30 A.M.–12:30 P.M. Sat.) is better than most regional branches. They train waiters and hoteliers, and organize cultural exchanges with other parts of Nicaragua. Bancentro and other banks are located one block west and one north of the park. The post office (open 8 A.M.–noon and 2–5 P.M. Mon.–Sat.) is one block south of the cathedral and one east. ENITEL (open 7 A.M.–5 P.M.) is two blocks north of the park. Find a cybercafe across from the police station, or a half-block west of the northwest corner of the park. In either you'll pay about $0.75 per hour for dog-slow connections.

If you'd like a friendly, ebullient, bilingual **local guide** to accompany you to the Grand Canyon of Somoto or other local attractions, call Sarahi Sofia Gutierrez Gomez (tel. 505/8900-9733, sofiagomez1984@yahoo.com), world-renowned tourist guide, translator, and Nicaraguan traveler.

GETTING THERE AND AWAY

At least 11 express buses leave Managua's Mayoreo terminal for Ocotal, stopping along the highway in Estelí to pick up additional passengers. Sixteen buses ply the route between Somoto and Ocotal daily, 5:45 A.M.–6:30 P.M. If you miss the *expreso* buses, there are countless additional, painfully slow ordinary buses from Mayoreo.

Near Ocotal

SANTO DOMINGO

Just shy of Totogalpa is **El Centro Solar** (Km 212.5, tel. 505/8333-0197, www.grupofenix. org), a sustainable energy workshop building and selling solar energy equipment designed for Nicaragua. Use of solar energy is more uncommon than you'd think, and the team is happy to show you around; soon they may even be able to cook you a meal in their solar kitchen, but they'll accept your volunteer help right now.

MOZONTE

An easy 60-minute walk from Ocotal, Mozonte, of largely indigenous descent, is notable for its workshops of potters who produce ceramics from a particularly fine clay. You can spend the better part of a morning (start walking early to avoid the heat) in Mozonte admiring the craftsmanship of these potters. Both the **Centro de Artesanías** and the **Centro de Artesanía Ojos de Mujer** exhibit a variety of ceramic pieces for sale.

CIUDAD ANTIGUA

Ciudad Antigua was the second Spanish attempt to settle Nueva Segovia (the remnants of the first settlement, built in 1543 at the bequest of then-governor Rodrigo de Contreras, are called Ciudad Vieja, and can still be seen near Quilalí at the junction of the Jícaro and Coco Rivers). The wooden church doors still bear the scorch marks of one attempted sacking of the city by pirates. You can pore over some well-loved religious pieces and a few historic documents and other colonial structures that survived the onslaughts of the 19th century at the **Museo Religioso de Ciudad Antigua** (next to the Iglesia Señor de los Milagros, open 8 A.M.–4 P.M. Mon.–Fri.). Two buses a day depart from Ocotal at 7 A.M. and noon.

MACUELIZO

If sitting in a completely undeveloped, natural hot spring appeals to you, grab a *camión* at the Shell station and settle in for the 90-minute ride for a day trip to **Macuelizo Termales.** Find a guide in town.

SAN FERNANDO AND PICO MOGOTÓN

San Fernando is a notably picturesque village of thick adobe-walled homes set around the town park and **Templo Parroquial.** Its 7,000 inhabitants live on more than 200 individual coffee farms and produce an estimated 25,000 *quintales* of coffee annually. More famous than its coffee, however, are its inhabitants, who since the colonial days have been a little lighter-skinned and a little more Spanish-looking. Many have blue or light brown eyes. How do they do it? Well, just don't ask about those last name combinations: Herrera-Herrera, Urbina-Urbina, and Ortez-Ortez, though many attribute the blue eyes to the town's occupation by the U.S. Marines 1927–1931. Life revolves around coffee in San Fernando, and many homes double as coffee-processing mills *(beneficios).*

You can stage a hike to Pico Mogotón, Nicaragua's highest point (2,106 meters) from San Fernando, but even from there, Mogotón is 20 kilometers away. A better hike is to the **Salto San José,** where water rushing off the Dipilto mountain range cascades into a small pool. Take a bus to the community of Santa Clara and get off across from the ball field, turn left (north), and walk the 6–8 kilometers to the river. To be sure of the trail, hire a local kid for some food and a couple *córdobas* to take you. They all know the way and might even jump in for a swim with you.

CROSSING THE BORDER AT LAS MANOS

The Honduran border is 24 kilometers north of Ocotal, and open 24 hours. You will be charged $2 to leave Nicaragua and $7 to enter (or $4 exit, $9 entry after normal business hours or on weekends). There are several small eating booths, two places to change money, and not much else. Fill out the immigration form at the little grey building and walk 100 meters farther down the road to the immigration building to pay and get your exit stamp. Honduran buses to Danlí stop running after 4:30 P.M. To get to the border from Ocotal, buses leave 5 A.M.–4 P.M. ($0.50), or take a cab (around $4–6, depending on how hard you bargain). You should not need another visa for Honduras thanks to Nicaragua's participation in the CA-4 Border Control Agreement of 2006.

JALAPA

Tucked back in one of Nicaragua's farthest populated corners, Jalapa enjoys a cool, moist microclimate suitable for the production of tobacco and vegetables which its drought-stricken neighbors could only hope for. Only four kilometers from the border, it is surrounded on three sides by Honduras and only surpassed in its remoteness by nearby border outpost Teotecacinte. That isolation made Jalapa prime stalking ground for Contra incursions from three nearby bases in Honduran territory—Pino-I, Ariel, and Yamales. The city of Jalapa was flooded with refugees from farming communities farther afield in response to Contra attacks like that of November 16, 1982, when a Contra unit kidnapped 60 *campesinos* at Río Arriba. Muddy and isolated, Jalapa is a peaceful and laid-back place these days, most concerned with good tobacco and coffee harvests. The whole town comes to life every year at the end of September for the **Festival de Maíz** (Corn Festival). Look for local *artesanía* of baskets made of coiled and lashed pine needles. **Grupo Pinar del Norte** has lots of fine examples of this unique craft.

QUILALÍ

Starting in the 1930s when Sandino dug into the area of El Chipote and held off the U.S. Marines, Quilalí has been bloodied by decades of battle. But the town remains steadfastly anti-Sandinista to this day and is home to both El Chacál (José Angel Talavera) and El Chacalín (Alex Talavera), the leaders of the Resistance Party (made up of ex-Contras). Upon entering town, you'll notice Quilalí is surprisingly well developed, courtesy of international aid money destined to support the Sandinista government's opponents. Look for U.S. Army tin cups, knives, and mosquito nets in town, relics from the intense military training given to local Contras in the 1980s. The area is also well known for its marijuana production. A recommended read if you travel this area is *White Man's Burden* by William Easterly, who uses the town of Quilalí as a case study for the effectiveness of development assistance.

The road to Colina La Gloría offers beautiful views of surrounding mountains and passes at least two swimming holes, one each in the Río Jícaro and Río Coco. **Hospedaje Tere** (on the main street) costs $4 a night and is the cleanest place in town. Several informal, family establishments, including **Comedor Jackson and Sholla,** serve typical food for about $3 a plate. Quilalí has a very good hospital supported by Médicos sin Fronteras, and standard services like ENITEL and Correos.

Four buses a day leave Ocotal via Santa Clara. The first one is at 5 A.M. From Estelí, five buses depart (5:45 A.M.–1:40 P.M.) for a five-hour bone-cruncher through San Juan del Río Coco and onward to Wiwilí.

ESTELÍ AND THE SEGOVIAS

Somoto

Located on the south side of the Pan-American Highway as it veers westward toward the Honduran border at El Espino, Somoto is an average-size city of 15,000 and capital of the department of Madriz. Tucked into the Cordillera de Somoto at 700 meters above sea level (the highest point of this range is Cerro Tépec-Xomotl at 1,730 meters), Somoto enjoys a fresh climate most of the year. Originally named Tépec-Xomotl, or Valley of the Turkeys, Somoto is known today more for its donkeys, *rosquillas* (baked corn cookies), and blowout carnival each November. A tributary of the Río Coco traverses the city.

U.S. Marines built an airstrip here, three blocks south of the park (now lost forever under a modern development), to try out a military technique they'd just invented: the air strike. They used the base in Somoto to bomb Ocotal in the 1930s in a failed attempt to root out General Sandino. These days, the Ciudad de Burros has not much more to offer than a quiet evening in its quaint and friendly park and a pleasant, village ambience.

SIGHTS AND EVENTS

La Parroquia Santiago de Somoto is one of Nicaragua's oldest churches. Construction began in 1661, some 86 years before León's great cathedral. If you're around Somoto on the eighth of any month, consider joining the religious masses on their pilgrimage to the tiny community of **Cacaulí**, all hoping for a glimpse of the Virgin Mary. Ever since she appeared to a young farmer named Francisco in the late 1980s, thousands of people have arrived to try to repeat the miracle. They each carry a clear bottle of holy water, which they hold up to the sun at exactly 4 p.m. The Virgin— not parasites—should appear in the water. Whenever the eighth falls on a Sunday, the believers turn out in larger numbers.

Somoto's *fiestas patronales* fall on July 15–25, but the town is more famous for the **carnival of November 11** (or the second Saturday of the month), when it celebrates the creation of the department of Madriz in 1936. All of Nicaragua's best party bands make the trip north, each setting up on one of seven stages— plus mariachis, dance parties, and the standard bull- and cockfighting. As for nightlife, try the **Hotel Bambú,** on the highway just east of the bus terminal.

Pass through the **Mercado Municipal 19 de Julio** to rub shoulders with the locals, mostly farmers. Or check out the two scenic view overlooks: The first is just west of the city and offers a quick, easy walk and a rewarding view. The second, **Mirador de Canopy Castillo** (tel. 505/8648-1452), has a small café and a four-cable canopy tour that looks steeper than it should be: Be cautious.

◖ GRAND CANYON OF SOMOTO

"Discovered" only in 2006, Somoto's best swimming hole permits you to float through limpid, cool pools penned between the lush vegetation of the canyon walls, home to cliff bats and rare birds. The deep pools are separated by shallow sections and so preclude boating. Rather, spend all day splashing from pool to pool. Bring a picnic and plastic bags to keep things dry.

This is possible as a day trip from Estelí, though it's nearly three hours each way to get there and the last express bus back to Estelí leaves at 3:30 p.m. Catch a bus to Somoto, then another to El Espino (every 45 minutes or so), getting off at *entrada para Cañon de Somoto* (25 minutes from Somoto). About 200 meters down the path is a gate and cabin, with guides who can offer you anything from a 5–6 hour guided hike ($20) to a rented inner tube for floating the canyon ($6). See www.namancambretours.com for more, as this destination is evolving fast.

ROSQUILLAS SOMOTEÑAS

© RODNEY MCDONALD

Rosquillas, as seen baking in a clay oven, are best eaten with black coffee.

Although *rosquillas* are baked in adobe wood-burning ovens all over Nicaragua, Somoto is particularly renowned throughout the country for the quality of this baked treat. The *rosquilla* is a crunchy ring of salted corn-dough baked with cheese. When they're not baked the traditional way, you'll find them as flat, molasses-topped *ojaldras* or thick nugget-pockets called *pupusas*. Serve them up with a cup of steaming hot, black coffee, still fragrant with smoke from the wood fire, and enjoy: The two tastes naturally complement each other. The two main producers in town are **La Rosquilla Somoteña Betty Espinoza** and **Rosquilla Garcia,** both two blocks west of the COTRAN on either side of the street. *Somoteñas* are the most famous regional variety of *rosquillas* – if you're traveling anywhere else in the country, they make a cheap, simple gift, greatly appreciated by any Nicaraguan.

ACCOMMODATIONS AND FOOD

The **Hotel Panamericano** (on the north side of the park, tel. 505/722-2355, $6–15) has hot water and additional amenities in a variety of rooms; there are a few interesting animals in captivity here. Reinel Mendoza Gradiz (tel. 505/2722-2340 or 505/8817-1096, reymen2008@hotmail.com) gives tours, including of the canyon.

The **Hotel Colonial** (half a block south of the church, tel. 505/722-2040, www.hotelcolonialsomoto.com, $25) has a new restaurant and large patio, rooms with private bath, cable TV, and parking, with breakfast included. **Hotel El Portal del Angel** (one block west, one south of the police station, tel. 505/2722-0244, portalhotel@yahoo.com, www.hotelportaldelangel.com) was constructed in 2008 and has sumptuous rooms starting at $35, a restaurant, and an upstairs bar with a nice view of the mountains.

Comedor Soya (on the plaza) serves soy with a smile; all kinds of surprising and cheap meals available. For excellent juice drinks, snacks, and fries, check out **Café Santiaguito** (1.5 blocks south of the church). The market is full of other delicious treats, all of them fried.

Comedor Bamby (2.5 blocks west from the Enitel office, 8 A.M.–8 P.M. Mon.–Sat.) is a great place for lunch on just a few dollars. A lunch buffet is served 11 A.M.–2 P.M., or until they run out of food. Many working people in Somoto frequent the spot, so it pays to get there early.

The Almendro (across from the Colonial, open 10 A.M.–9 P.M. daily) was mentioned in a Mejía Godoy song *("el almendro de donde la Tere")* and has nicer meals from $5.

INFORMATION, SERVICES, AND TRANSPORTATION

There is a bank across the street from the Alcaldía. The post office is across from the Hotel Colonial, and ENITEL is behind the church (open until 5 P.M.). A modern health clinic, Profamilia, is two blocks south of COTRAN and open 24 hours a day. Buses to Somoto from Estelí run every hour 5:30 A.M.–5:20 P.M. There are also regular express buses from Mayoreo in Managua.

EL ESPINO BORDER CROSSING

The least used border crossing in Nicaragua, El Espino is open 24 hours. To get there from

Somoto is known as "The City of Burros."

Somoto, take one of the regular buses ($0.50) that head toward El Espino, or chip in for a cab (about $4). It's a 40-minute ride from Somoto. At the crossing, you first receive and fill out an immigration form at the booth next to the steel railroad crossing–style gate, then proceed 100 meters up to the little building on the right where you'll pay $2 to exit ($4 after hours) or $7 to enter ($9 after hours). Continuing bus service into Honduras is just over the hill and runs until 4:30 P.M. You should not need another visa for Honduras thanks to Nicaragua's participation in the CA-4 Border Control Agreement of 2006.

© RANDALL WOOD

THE MATAGALPA AND JINOTEGA HIGHLANDS

As you turn eastward from the Pan-American Highway and begin the gradual climb upwards, the character of the Matagalpan and Jinotegan highlands will attract your attention immediately. This rugged, determined region of blue-green hillsides, sometimes thickly forested mountains, and small, farming villages of adobe homes and clay-tile roofs is unlike anywhere else in the country. As highlands go, Nicaragua's center is not that high, rising to barely 2,000 meters above sea level, but after visiting the torrid plains around Granada and Managua, the relatively cool air and the smell of pines will be a welcome surprise. The temperatures favor vegetable production, though many quiet valleys are still thick with corn and red beans. They also favor the production of coffee and east of Matagalpa, the rumpled landscape of hardwoods and coffee plants dominates. Coffee's preference for shade has encouraged the preservation of much of this region's forests, and the mornings resonate with birdcall and the bellow of the howler monkeys.

Matagalpa is the more elegant and historical of the region's two big cities, with a gargantuan cathedral and several big, shady parks. A city draped over the curves of more than one hill, your legs will quickly notice the changes in altitude as you explore. Jinotega is farther north into the mountains, higher, and smaller. Emphasizing its sense of isolation are the green walls of the valley that cradles it; even the cathedral in the town's center is dwarfed by the immensity of nature in its lush plaza. Jinotega remains somewhat of a cowboy town,

© JOSHUA BERMAN

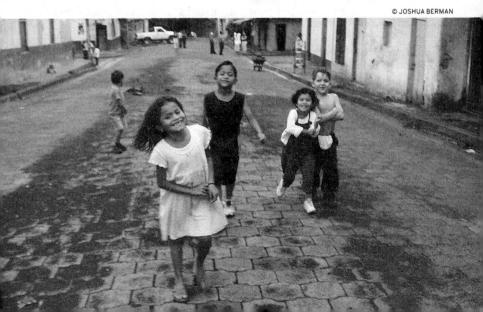

HIGHLIGHTS

◖ **Parque Darío:** End your self-guided walking tour of Matagalpa City here, in this shady plaza where you can watch the world go by and listen to the deafening calls of the birds in the treetops (page 237).

◖ **La Catedral de San Pedro de Matagalpa:** One of the north's finest structures, this gorgeous cathedral can be spotted from anywhere in town (page 240).

◖ **Grupo Venancia:** Rub shoulders with Matagalpa's enlightened citizens and visitors while you enjoy stimulating theater and great music (page 241).

◖ **Finca Esperanza Verde:** Call ahead to reserve space at this award-winning ecotourism effort in the hills above San Ramón, with hiking trails through area coffee farms and deep, fertile valleys (page 251).

◖ **La Sombra Ecolodge:** Hardwood forest and coffee intermingle at a lovely forest lodge perfectly situated for forest excursions to the remarkable Peñas Blancas (page 252).

◖ **Hotel de Montaña Selva Negra:** A hotel quite unlike any other, Selva Negra has enough farm tours, mountain hikes, good food, and quiet, peaceful relaxation to rest any weary soul (page 254).

LOOK FOR ◖ TO FIND RECOMMENDED SIGHTS, ACTIVITIES, DINING, AND LODGING.

the uncouth little brother of more cultured Matagalpa. Jinotega feels like the end of the road, the gateway to the thousands of remote kilometers that separate the Atlantic coast from the rest of Nicaragua.

Both Jinotega and Matagalpa suffered mightily during the revolution and ensuing Contra war. But today's *norteños* work their farms without the fear of war, bending their backs instead in the struggle against rural poverty, drought, and the whims of the world coffee market. That said, a new group by the name of Fuerza Democratica Nicaragüense (FDN) has arisen here in opposition to Daniel Ortega's perceived growing autocracy.

In general, residents of Matagalpa and Jinotega are accustomed to adversity and live bright, intense lives. Spending time among them will give you a perspective you won't find in the more frequently visited corners of Nicaragua.

PLANNING YOUR TIME

Two or three nights is sufficient for seeing Matagalpa and Jinotega, but allow an extra day or two if you plan to explore any of the surrounding countryside. Those looking for a peaceful mountain retreat often spend 2–3 nights at either Hotel Selva Negra, Finca Esperanza Verde, or with a homestay program run by a coffee cooperative. Combining such

THE MATAGALPA AND JINOTEGA HIGHLANDS

MATAGALPA

a trip with a night or two in the city can easily consume five or six days—more if you visit the more remote communities.

HISTORY

Periods of tremendous violence and warfare have racked the mountainous north for over a century. In the early 1930s, Augusto César Sandino fought U.S. Marines and the National Guard here; 40 years later, young revolutionary Sandinistas faced Somoza's National Guard in several bloody battles, particularly in the region of San José de Bocay, Matiguás, and Bilampi. Far more devastating than either of those conflicts, however, were the 1980s, when Matagalpa and Jinotega (along with the RAAN, or North Atlantic Autonomous Region) experienced the worst of the war between the Sandinista military and Contras. Travelers along the region's few roads were frequently ambushed and soldiers from both sides raided villages as a matter of course. Farmers learned to tend their crops with rifles slung over their shoulders.

Peace swept the region at the start of the 1990s and the past decade has transformed Matagalpa and Jinotega into an agricultural powerhouse. Gone are the thousands of cold, wet, and hungry guerrilla soldiers that muddily marched through these hills. Some of the same rugged trails are now popular with campesinos and foreign travelers intent on visiting coffee cooperatives, climbing mountains, and swimming in waterfalls.

The Road to Matagalpa

The highway from Managua climbs from the verdant plains of sugarcane and rice up through a series of plateaus with long horizons and broad panoramas before reaching the long mountain valleys that characterize the north. Most travelers take an express bus straight through most of the landscape and beeline for the mountains, but Matagalpa's dry lowlands hide a few interesting places if you have your own vehicle.

LA CASA-HACIENDA SAN JACINTO

A must-see on the high school curriculum of all Nicaraguan history students, the Casa-Hacienda San Jacinto, located about 35 kilometers north of Managua along the Pan-American Highway, merits its own roadside statue. The monument guards the turnoff to the battlefield of San Jacinto and depicts a defiant Andrés Castro standing atop a pile of rocks. This is the site where, in 1856, the Liberals—supported by William Walker and his band of filibusters—and Conservatives battled fiercely. Conservative Andrés Castro, out of ammunition, picked up a rock and hurled it at the enemy, killing a Yankee with a blow to the head and becoming a symbol of the Nicaraguan fighting spirit that refuses to bow to foreign authorities.

Three kilometers east of the highway (a flat, 20-minute walk), the museum at the restored San Jacinto ranch house is run-down and little visited except by occasional hordes of high school students. For $1 admission, you can explore the period relics and admire the displays. If no one's manning the ticket window, just shout until the caretaker rides her bike down from the main building. Bring water: There are no facilities at the site itself, and just one mediocre restaurant at the highway turnoff.

LA LAGUNA DE MOYOÁ AND LAS PLAYITAS

After conquering the first big ascent on the highway from Managua (known as Cuesta del Coyól), you'll be greeted by the Laguna Moyoá (Nahuatl for "place of the small mosquitoes") on the west side of the highway and the swampy Laguna Tecomapa to the east (unless it is a dry year, when both disappear). Geologists believe they are the remnants of the ancient Lake of Sébaco, a giant reservoir that formed the heavy clay soils of today's Sébaco Valley. A tectonic shift ages ago sent the Río Grande de Matagalpa flowing eastward toward the Atlantic instead of into Lake Xolotlán through Moyoá, and the lake gradually disappeared. It experienced a brief revival during Hurricane Mitch, when Lake Moyoá rose to the edge of the highway and Tecomapa became a legitimate lake through which wading cattle grazed.

Moyoá was once home to the Chontaleña people, and it is possible that they had a fixed settlement on the island in the lake. Some clay pottery has been uncovered from the A.D. 500–1500 period, which would indicate they at least frequented the site, probably to fish and hunt.

The locals do a good business catching fish out of Moyoá—mostly *mojarra* and *guapote*—both very good for eating, and both of which you'll see held up on strings along the side of

© JOSHUA BERMAN

Matagalpa, the Pearl of the North, is nestled in the highlands.

the road. To visit the lake, stop in at Comedor Treminio and ask for Anita Vega or Humberto Treminio, the owners of the land that borders the lake. You can eat your meals at their establishment, and strike a deal with them for the right to camp out on their land. Try the shady grove down at the end of the road that leads to the lake. Birds you might see at Moyoá include *playeritos, piches, zambullidores,* and several types of heron.

CIUDAD DARÍO

Named after the prized poet of Castilian literature, Ciudad Darío was known by the indigenous name of Metapa until 1867 when Rubén Darío was born. Today, a battered but handsome brass statue of the author stands at the southern approach to the city.

Darío's primary attraction is the unassuming **Casa Natal Rubén Darío** (along the main street in front of the ENITEL building, 8 A.M.–12:30 P.M. and 2–5 P.M. Mon.–Fri.). Darío was born here and then moved to the city of León shortly afterward to live with relatives. The eastern part of the house has been converted

into a small amphitheater for the presentation of cultural shows.

For a plate of *gallo pinto,* hit the **Comedor Clementina** (from the mayor's office, two blocks north and half a block west) for a hearty beef soup or her famous chicken and *ayote* (a type of squash). There are plenty of fresh fruit juices to sip while you wait for your meal and try to talk with her pet parrot, who speaks Italian (so she claims!). A half a block east from Clementina's is a big *fritanga* that opens up around 6 P.M., $1–2 a plate.

Restaurante El Coctél (from the Pulpería Masaya, go west one block and north a half block) likes to serve crowds coming out of the museum, and specializes in *carne a la plancha;* a bit pricier than the other options in town—you can pay more than $7.50 for some things—but it's one of the few restaurants with a real ceiling overhead. The favorite restaurant among the NGO and businessperson crowd is **Doña Conchi's** (a block north of the Shell station toward the north end of town), a relatively upscale place with a full menu ranging $2–8 per dish.

MATAGALPA

Express buses between Managua and points north save an hour off the trip by not entering Ciudad Darío. So, if you're headed there by bus (from Managua's Mayoreo terminal), make sure to take an *ordinario*. Any local bus leaving Matagalpa or Estelí headed to Managua will go by way of Darío.

THE LEGEND OF CIHUACOATL

At the edge of the Río Viejo, there was once a powerful community ruled by a mighty cacique. His wife was considered the most beautiful woman in the country, but she made regular suspicious trips down to the river with great quantities of carefully prepared foods: beverages of seeds and berries, and birds prepared with spices and grains. One day, one of the cacique's men decided to follow the woman down to the river to see what she did. There, he watched as the woman sat calmly on a rock at the river's edge and struck the palm of her hand against the water's surface several times with a sharp smacking sound. From out of the ripples on the water's surface emerged a giant snake, which rose halfway out of the water and placed its head on the woman's beautiful smooth thighs. She fed the snake, its head resting on her lap, and afterwards the two made love at the water's edge. Then the serpent slithered back into the river, down to its underwater cave, and the woman gathered her things to leave.

The cacique's servant ran quickly back to tell the story, trembling as he related the infidelity to the cacique. When the woman returned home, her husband, in a jealous rage, killed the woman with a single stroke of his knife. The snake, upon realizing his lover had been slain, agitated the river with its tail, causing it to rise up violently and destroy the entire community. The goddess Cihuacoatl (Snake Woman) has been worshipped ever since by the Nahuatl people in the area.

Near Ciudad Darío

Anyone between the ages of 7 and 15 will know exactly how to help you find the following historical and geological destinations in the Darío neighborhood of Santa Clara, located about one kilometer east from the town's park (not far from the Carlos Santí baseball stadium).

To get to the **petroglyphs,** start at Darío's mayor's office in the park and head east toward the stadium at the top of a hill (0.5 km). On the other side of the stadium is a school for deaf children. Beyond that, the paved road will turn to dirt as you enter Barrio España. There is a *pulpería* on the corner where you can get directions to the petroglyphs, less than a 30-minute walk.

La Posa de Las Yeguas (The Mare's Pool) is a deep spot in the creek where, supposedly, women who weren't faithful to their husbands were turned into mares and went to live. Several rocks there bear petroglyphs and more modern graffiti. It is said the friars of old would go to meditate at **La Cueva del Fraile** (The Friar's Cave), not far from La Posa de Las Yeguas.

SÉBACO

The name Sébaco comes from the Nahuatl name Cihuacoatl (the "snake-woman"). In 1527, the Spanish founded the city they called Santiago de Cihuacoatl on the banks of the Río Viejo alongside the indigenous settlement of Cihuacoatl, capital of the Chontales people. But when a major flood put the town under water in 1833, Sébaco was moved to the hill east of town, where the remnants of Sébaco Viejo can still be found: The **Templo Viejo** houses a simple collection of archaeological artifacts, including pieces of pottery and ceramics, some small statues, and a wooden carving of the deity Cihuacoatl. When they moved, the residents of Sébaco packed up their buildings piece by piece and transported the materials to the new location, where they reconstructed the buildings to approximately their original form. Since then, the houses slowly crept down the hill and back to the water's edge, waiting for history to repeat itself.

And that's exactly what happened. In 1998, Sébaco was hit so hard by Hurricane Mitch it became one of the primary obstacles separating Managua from the north. The large bridge at the south end of town resisted the floods of the Río Grande de Matagalpa, but the river overflowed its banks just south of the bridge and sliced a new channel through the road hundreds of meters wide. The combined torrent swelled into a deadly wall of water that ripped through Ciudad Darío.

No matter where you travel in the north of Nicaragua, at some point you'll pass through Sébaco. Located right where the highway splits to take travelers to either Estelí and the Segovias (fork left) or Matagalpa, Jinotega, and the northeast (fork right), Sébaco, a.k.a. La Ciudad de Cebollas (City of Onions), is known throughout the region for its lively roadside commerce. If you're traveling at night, Sébaco is a sudden blast of streetlights, traffic, and bustle after two hours of darkness since Managua.

While travelers are more typically interested in the Texaco station's restrooms, most Nicas pick up fresh produce—carrots, beets, and of course, onions at one of the many identical stands on the true roadside market. Sébaco's aggressive road vendors will scale the side of your bus and display their goods through your window (hope you don't mind a faceful of carrot tops). If you have a long bus ride ahead of you, this is a good place to pick up bags of fruit juice, snacks, or veggies which make good gifts for your Nicaraguan hosts.

Accommodations and Food

Although there are a few cheap but unimpressive places to crash in town, you'd be much wiser to continue to Matagalpa or Estelí, either about a 45 minute drive away. The dozens of decent roadside restaurants offer similar menus of chicken, tacos, beef, and sandwiches.

◖ El Sesteo is the best sit-down spot, with uniformed waiters, an air-conditioned *sala,* and array of steak, chicken, and seafood dishes. On the east side of the intersection across from the triangle, the cheaper **Sorbetería Mac-et** serves sandwiches, hot dogs, light lunches, fruit juices, and ice cream. Sébaco also has several banks, a telephone office, and a private health clinic.

CHAGÜITILLO

About two kilometers north of Sébaco along the highway to Matagalpa, Chagüitillo is a small community with access to several dozen pre-Columbian petroglyphs scratched into the stone walls of a canyon just outside the village. The site **Apamico** is named in Nahuatl for "place of the monkeys." Relics depicting monkeys, shamans carrying human heads, and hunting scenes line the banks of the Aranca Burba stream. The locals can easily help you find the two streambeds and show you the petroglyphs; both sites are an easy walk from the center of town. Particularly good guides are Orlando Dávila and Melvin Rizo, who speaks some English. Dávila lives in front of the school whose tall green wall is painted with representations of the petroglyphs; Rizo lives a block or two closer to the highway.

In town, find the *pulpería* run by Bernabe Rayo (located on a side street off the main road through town). Chagüitillo is the source of a water project for the city of Matagalpa, and engineers digging the trenches for the pipelines have unearthed many additional artifacts. Some are scattered amongst the many houses of the community, but Rayo has done an admirable job of collecting some of them and trying to form a small community museum out of the pieces. You can support him by purchasing something from his store. He's got an interesting collection of old ceramic pots, cups, and small statues, plus some larger pieces he's reconstructed from the shards.

MATAGALPA

Matagalpa City

The department of Matagalpa is the most mountainous in Nicaragua, and its capital city remains true to form. As you walk up and down the steep streets, you'll realize the city is draped like a blanket over the rolling valley floor beneath it. Nicknamed La Perla del Septentrión (The Pearl of the North), Matagalpa's true precious stone is a ripe, red coffee bean, the production and harvest of which is essential to the region's—and the nation's—economy. Matagalpa enjoys clean, mountain air, but water is another story. Radically depleted by deforestation and human contamination, clean water is in dreadfully short supply here. During the driest times, city officials cope with the problem by implementing draconian rationing schemes. The surrounding mountains have been mostly scraped clean of trees, but during the wet season, they turn emerald green and remain so throughout the Christmas season, when the coffee harvest turns the city of Matagalpa into a lively center of coffee pickers, prospectors, packers, and processors.

Nahuatl influence is more prominent in Matagalpa than elsewhere, particularly in regional vocabulary, which retains much pre-Columbian vocabulary. The Nahuatl word *chüisle*, for example, is used instead of the Castilian *quebrada* for stream. The city's central office for the region's indigenous community settles land disputes and other issues. Modern-day Nicaraguan politicians prize Matagalpa because its high population can often swing the vote, but tourists will prize Matagalpa as a welcome respite from the heat of the lowlands, plus a chance to sip the best coffee in the world while plotting forays deeper into the mountains. Ignore the inflated population sign as you enter the valley—the latest figures put Matagalpa's urban population at just over 100,000.

HISTORY

The beautiful valley where the city of Matagalpa now sits was already a cluster of Nahuatl communities—including Solingalpa and Molagüina, which still exist today—when the Spanish first set eyes on it. Nahuatl traditional histories don't include any stories of their people having arrived in this valley—as if they have always been here. Long before it was called the Pearl of the North, Matagalpa was known as the City of Ten in Nahuatl, in reference to the 10 small settlements within the valley. The name is also attributed to the powerful cacique Atahualpa, who governed the area during the time of colonization (Solingalpa was his wife).

The Spanish established a camp alongside the Nahuatls around 1680. Some powerful Spanish families made up the first settlers; their last names are still common in the region: Alvarado, Castañeda, Reyes, Rizo, Escoto. They set up extensive cattle ranches and planted fields before coffee was even a dream. In 1838, the area was named Departamento del Septentrión, and in 1862, Matagalpa was elevated to the status of city. Even with that status, the city of Matagalpa was of far less economic importance to the nation than Sébaco.

That changed in the second half of the 19th century when Matagalpa saw a flow of German immigrants. They had not arrived in Nicaragua to plant coffee, as is commonly believed, but to develop the gold mines in the east. Once established in Nicaragua, however, they quickly realized how perfect the climate was for the cultivation of coffee and their interest switched to the crop that would define Nicaragua's economy for the next 150 years. Matagalpa had developed a new reason for being, and coffee has been the focus of Matagalpa ever since.

Today, several problems constrain Matagalpa from the prosperity it enjoyed in the 19th century. Most critical is the lack of potable water—even the Chagüitillo water project may provide water for no more than 10 years—but developing rural roads and dealing with the growing solid waste problem will both be necessary before Matagalpa returns to its status as a pearl.

© JOSHUA BERMAN

Matagalpa's steep streets lead straight into the rugged countryside.

SIGHTS
◖ Parque Darío

Grab a bench in Parque Darío and buy a crushed ice *raspado* to enjoy while people-watching. There are probably more trees jammed into the park's tiny confines than any other in Nicaragua, and come sunset the branches fill with thousands of birds. A permanent fixture in the park is a vendor with rows and rows of handmade ceramic piggy banks for sale, none of which costs more than $1.

Churches and Museums

El Templo de San José de Laborío sits at the edge of the Parque Darío at the south end of town. It's probably as old as the colonial presence in Matagalpa, but no one is quite sure exactly when it was built. It was rebuilt in 1917 on top of its old foundation, but underneath that foundation are the ruins of another that date to at least 1751, and possibly a bit earlier. In 1881, an indigenous uprising used the church as its garrison.

Matagalpa was the birthplace of the founder of the FSLN, Carlos Fonseca. The house he was born in has been converted into a museum. Known as **La Casa Cuna Carlos Fonseca** (one block east of Parque Darío's south side, tel. 505/2772-3665, open 8 A.M.–noon and 2–5 P.M. Mon.–Fri., small donation), the tiny corner building has the original brick floors, mud walls, and tile roof, as well as an interesting assortment of documents, photos, and memorabilia, including Carlos's typewriter and his gear from military training in Korea.

The history of **La Iglesia de Molagüina**, found in the center of the city, has been forgotten. It was probably constructed between 1751 and 1873, though those dates have been questioned by historians. Simple and monastic, it is a well-used and well-loved church: Molagüina is home to a Catholic order of nuns and the College of San José.

Museo de Café (located on the main street two blocks east of the mayor's office, across from Teatro Perla, open 8 A.M.–5 P.M. Mon.–Fri., closed for lunch, open Sat. mornings) displays some interesting murals and photographs from Matagalpa's history, plus a small

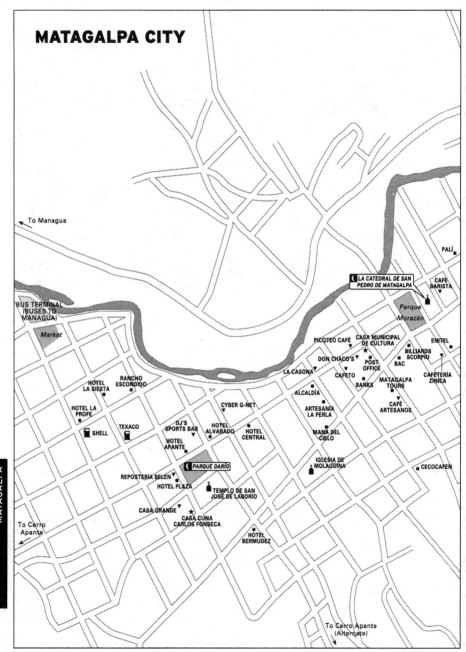

MATAGALPA CITY

To Managua

PALÍ

LA CATEDRAL DE SAN PEDRO DE MATAGALPA

CAFÉ BARISTA

BUS TERMINAL (BUSES TO MANAGUA)

Market

Parque Morazán

PICOTEO CAFÉ

CASA MUNICIPAL DE CULTURA

ENITEL

DON CHACO'S

POST OFFICE

BILLIARDS SCORPIO

BAC

HOTEL LA SIESTA

RANCHO ESCONDIDO

LA CASONA

CAFETO

BANKS

MATAGALPA TOURS

CAFETERÍA ZINICA

ALCALDÍA

HOTEL LA PROFE

CYBER G-NET

ARTESANÍA LA PERLA

CAFÉ ARTESANOS

SHELL

TEXACO

DJ'S SPORTS BAR

HOTEL ALVARADO

HOTEL CENTRAL

MANA DEL CIELO

HOTEL APANTE

IGLESIA DE MOLAGUINA

CECOCAFEN

REPOSTERÍA BELÉN

Parque Darío

HOTEL PLAZA

TEMPLO DE SAN JOSÉ DE LABORÍO

CASA GRANDE

CASA CUNA CARLOS FONSECA

To Cerro Apante

HOTEL BERMUDEZ

To Cerro Apante (Alternate)

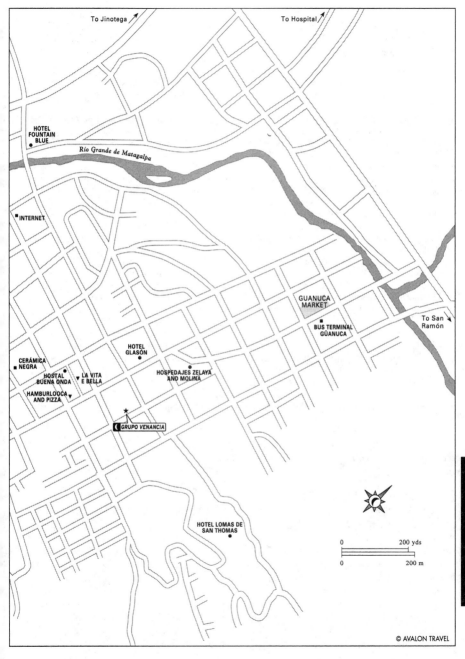

To Jinotega

To Hospital

HOTEL FOUNTAIN BLUE

Río Grande de Matagalpa

INTERNET

GUANUCA MARKET

BUS TERMINAL GÜANUCA

To San Ramón

HOTEL GLASÓN

CERÁMICA NEGRA

HOSTAL BUENA ONDA

LA VITA E BELLA

HOSPEDAJES ZELAYA AND MOLINA

HAMBURLOOCA AND PIZZA

GRUPO VENANCIA

HOTEL LOMAS DE SAN THOMAS

0   200 yds
0   200 m

MATAGALPA

© AVALON TRAVEL

LA RUTA DE CAFÉ: COFFEE TOURISM IN THE NORTH

Today, both international coffee merchants and *café-turistas* can travel a circuit of coffee cooperatives scattered through the mountains of Jinotega, Matagalpa, and the Segovias. As a participant in this Ruta de Café not only will you sample coffee in special cupping labs, you'll also visit coffee-growing families and their farms, which are often magical cloud forests shrouded in cool mists; you can stay for a couple of hours or a couple of days, living with the families, eating meals with them, picking coffee, and learning about all stages of the process. As a *café-turista,* you'll experience the communities of real people who have been behind every sip of coffee you've ever taken. What's more, you will learn why the quality of a coffee is inextricably tied to the quality of life of those that produce it, as well as the quality of the environment in which they live. Finally, you will learn what organic, bird friendly, and fair trade-certified coffees are (visit www.transfairusa.org and www.globalexchange.org for details).

To experience the most activity, be sure to arrange your visit during the peak of the harvest, usually mid-December–February. Make your arrangements in advance with the ecotourism project of **CECOCAFEN** (Center of Northern Coffee Cooperatives, tel. 505/2772-6353, turismo@cecocafen.com), whose main office in Matagalpa city is located two blocks east of Banco Uno. They can arrange anything from an afternoon coffee cupping at their Sol Café *beneficio* (coffee-processing mill) to a day trip, visiting some of their farmers, to a multinight excursion, staying in *campesino* homes and touring their farms (or even putting some work in during the harvest). Trips include transportation and food, and hikes (with pickups) can be arranged between towns. Prices fully depend on the trip. Or consider a stay at **Finca Esperanza Verde** (www.fincaesperanzaverde.org), an acclaimed accommodation and working organic coffee farm, located outside San Ramón.

In Jinotega, **SOPPEXCA** (Society of Small Coffee Producers, Exporters, and Buyers, tel. 505/2782-2617, soppexcc@tmx.com.ni) is eager to serve as your tour guide of the region, arranging any number of hikes, trips, and homestays among its growers in the surrounding hills. Their office and cupping lab is located in Jinotega, one block west of the Ferretería Blandón.

There are also several welcoming coffee cooperatives in the hills north of Estelí with similar tours available.

collection of indigenous artifacts. The museum is currently going through a complete remodeling.

◖ La Catedral de San Pedro de Matagalpa

At the northeastern end of town, La Catedral de San Pedro de Matagalpa was a disproportionately large cathedral—the third largest in the nation—when it was built in 1874, reflecting the opulence of Matagalpa at the time. The cathedral is built in the baroque style, with heavy bell towers set at both sides and an airy, spacious interior. It's the most prominent building in town and is easily visible from the hillsides north of town on the road to Jinotega.

The cathedral's interior is crisp and cool, tastefully adorned with bas- and medium-relief sculpture, carved wood, and paintings. Mass is held nightly at 6 P.M.

El Castillo del Cacao

The Castle of Chocolate (tel. 505/2772-2002, www.elcastillodelcacao.com) is the Willie Wonka factory of Nicaragua, located 500 meters north of the Las Marias Esso station, about a five-minute cab ride from the city center. Here you can tour the factory, visit a chocolate museum, and learn about the production of organic chocolate in Nicaragua. Nicaraguan cacao is known as a *landrace,* or a traditional variety almost identical to pre-Columbian cacao.

It has a rich, complex, nuttier flavor than the heavily cultivated and hybridized strains grown elsewhere in the world. To get the best tour of the factory go in the afternoons.

Cemeteries

There are two adjacent cemeteries on the hillside east of the city, about a 30-minute walk from town. One is for locals and one for foreigners, a rare arrangement in Nicaragua. Both contain headstones hand carved from dark rock, something seen only in Matagalpa. Buried in the cemetery higher up on the hill in the local section is one of the most famous casualties of the 1980s war: Benjamin Linder. An American, Linder was an avid juggler and unicyclist, and his headstone reflects those passions, along with some doves, the symbol of the peace he never lived to see.

ENTERTAINMENT AND EVENTS

Matagalpans celebrate their *fiestas patronales* on September 24, and the anniversary of their becoming a city on February 14. Every September there is a rowdy country fair that brings in crowds from the north and east, and cattle traders from all over the country. This is the best time of year to catch Matagalpa's traditional music of polkas, mazurkas, and *jamaquelos,* performed by the roving street bands that play at restaurants.

The **Academía de la Danza de Matagalpa,** under the able direction of Marcos Valle who studied modern dance in Spain, puts on dance presentations several times a year. If there's going to be a show, they advertise it at the Casa Municipal de Cultura, next to the fire station.

Local radio stations include Radio Norteña, FM 94.1; Radio Stereo Apante, FM 94.9; and Radio Yes, FM 90.1. The latter has several programs for a rural audience, including impersonations, jokes, and news commentary. Their morning news program is worth a listen in the early hours of the day while you're taking a cold-water mountain shower. A women's co-operative runs the show at FM 101.7.

Grupo Venancia

Grupo Venancia (1.5 blocks south of La Iglesia de Guadalupe, tel. 505/2772-3562, www.grupovenancia.org, open Thurs.–Sat.) is a convivial open-air bar surrounding a stage and sometimes dance floor. They host music, dance, theater, artsy international films, and both local and global activism. The place is renowned for its free shows every Saturday night. Grupo Venancia is also a nonprofit women's group that can probably be called ground zero of Nicaragua's feminist movement. It was founded in 1990 and in addition to the gathering space, runs urban and rural workshops on women's rights and domestic violence. Ask about their published materials, ways to volunteer, and try to catch their Saturday morning radio show, "La Hora Lila," on Radio Yes (FM 90.1) at 8:30 A.M.

Nightlife

There's no doubt that the Matagalpinos like to shake their boots as much as other Nicaraguans, though they prefer *ranchera,* merengue, and Reggaeton over salsa. Matagalpa's various *discotecas* may be open Thursday–Sunday nights, in general, but the only consistently happening night—with guaranteed crowded and electric dance floors—is Saturday. For dancing, **Las Tequilas,** just past the Hora del Taco restaurant on the left if heading out of town toward Managua ($2 or less taxi ride from downtown), is popular, as is **El Rancho Escondido,** which also offers *corriente* meals for less than $2. The newer **Hot Dance** is popular among a younger crowd. More mature revelers and couples enjoy the hassle-free dance floor at **Rincón Paraíso.**

For a friendly testosterone-filled cantina atmosphere, order a few liters at **El Rincón Nica,** sometimes with live music on Fridays, located near Rancho Escondido. Open all week for mediocre lunch and dinner, **La Casona** comes alive as Matagalpa's premiere Friday night fiesta, with live music in a crowded, open-air back patio.

The bohemian hang of choice is **Cafe Artesanos** (a half-block up from BAC next

MATAGALPA, WATER, AND THE LEGEND OF THE SERPENT

Matagalpa is a water-stressed city. In some neighborhoods, the water pressure is only turned on once a day; in others, Matagalpinos are forced to walk to distribution points to fill up containers from tanker trucks. You may see these trucks along the city streets in the early mornings, when everyone comes out with buckets and pans to get what water they can.

At the same time, there's more water in Matagalpa than some people know what to do with. Time and time again, shallow excavations in the city for routine projects have turned up a moist layer of earth just several meters below the surface. When a well-loved priest died in the 1990s, his tomb was dug underneath the floor of the cathedral. Before they had finished digging, the hole had begun to flood. Studies have determined the water under the city of Matagalpa isn't exploitable in quantities great enough to supply the city, and so other alternatives are being developed.

Much of Matagalpa's limited water supply comes from the forested hillsides that surround the city, hillsides that are rapidly being stripped of their timber. Matagalpinos speak of an old legend: The hill known as Apante, just southeast of the city, was said to be an enormous upwelling of water trapped within a pocket of soil and rock. Within the water lived a great snake. One day the snake began to shake, and the hillside began to crumble, threatening to unleash a massive landslide upon the residents of the city. In despair, they turned to the Virgin Mary for protection. Mary fought the snake and subdued it by planting its tail underneath the foundation of the church of Molagüina in the center of the city.

But the snake grows stronger each day . . . when it finally has enough strength to break free, it will shake its tail again, causing the hills to crumble and collapse upon the city. If the deforestation of the hillsides surrounding Matagalpa continue, this prophecy may very well come true.

---

to Matagalpa Tours, tel. 505/2772-2444), sometimes with live music from around the country.

A lively drinking spot (across from UNAN, a university) is **Café Bar Las Anotoychas Casa de Los Hijos del Maíz** (open 5 P.M.–midnight Mon.–Fri. and 11 A.M. Sat. for lunch). Expect live music on Saturday evenings.

Madre Tierra (one block south and 2.5 blocks west from Parque Darío) is run by a pair of Italians serving simple dishes and appetizers; they host occasional live music and foreign films, with funky cushions, couches, and high benches to perch on. You'll recognize it by the massive red painting of an ancient earth mother.

SHOPPING

The north's famous black pottery—darkened by a particular firing technique—is unique in Nicaragua, where pottery is typically a natural reddish-orange color. Find it for sale throughout the city. Multiple shops bearing the name **Cerámica Negra** are spread throughout the city, offering similar selections, but if you are looking for a specific location, a kiosk is located in Parque Darío. Even La Vita e Bella restaurant offers an excellent variety of ceramics and jewelry.

You'll find a great selection of local crafts at **Centro Girasol** (a bright yellow corner building right across the first bridge as you enter Matagalpa from Managua, tel. 505/2772-6030). They've also got local jams, honey, coffee, and yogurt.

HIKING AND TOURS

Start by picking up a map at the **Centro Girasol** (a bright yellow corner building right across the first bridge as you enter Matagalpa from Managua or two blocks south and one west from the COTRAN Sur, tel. 505/2772-6030). The *Treasures of Matagalpa* map costs less than $2, benefits local children with disabilities, and outlines a number of walks, offering guide service as well.

Matagalpa Tours (a half-block east of BAC, tel. 505/2772-0108 or 505/2647-4680, www. nicaraguatravels.net) is a guide service, travel agent, and backcountry outfitter, run by a Dutch expat and his Nicaraguan wife who manage the on-site Spanish language school. Let them arrange a variety of packages, shuttle service from Granada, homestays, Bosawás treks, coffee plantation tours, and community tourism. Anywhere from $15 per day to $60 per day depending on the extent. Arien has explored, hiked, and camped throughout the Matagalpan countryside and has even drawn a number of trail maps. The Bosawás tours are major wilderness excursions that need to be arranged long in advance. Granada shuttles cost $25 per person. Inside the office is a great local crafts shop run by a local women's organization called Zona Franja.

Hiking Cerro Apante

Immediately recognizable by the cluster of antennas on its peak, Cerro Apante (1,442 meters) towers above Matagalpa. Officially, it is a nature reserve, though most of its steep flanks are privately owned, covered by thick vegetation and a handful of small farms. Apante is a well-preserved piece of tropical humid forest that contains decent stands of oak and pine, as well as several hundred types of wildflowers. It is protecting an important source of water for the city (*apante* is Nahuatl for "running water"). It is crisscrossed with many small trails that lead to its streams and lagoons, all of which are easily accessed by foot from the city. In an effort to provide more funding to protect the natural resources of Nicaragua, the county has now implemented a fee of 30 *córdobas* ($1.50) to enter the park.

The two routes to the top both begin by standing at the northwest corner of Parque Darío (in front of Hotel Alvarado). Walking south on the *calle principal* will take you up to the Apante neighborhood on the edge of town (also serviced by the Chispa–Apante

Rapibuses). Continue up the road, keeping the summit to your left and continually asking if you're on the right track to *el cerro*. From the same corner in town, travel due east up a road that climbs steeply, eventually deteriorating into a rutted road. The road switches back a few times, ending at a hacienda atop a saddle in the Apante ridgeline. From there, find a footpath to the top. The actual summit is off limits, and is guarded by a caretaker and his dog, but the nearby ridge enjoys a breathtaking view of its own. You can link the two hikes into a three-hour loop; bring lots of water for the trail.

ACCOMMODATIONS
Under $10

Hotelito Reposado (located two blocks east of the northeast corner of Parque Morazán) offers simple rooms from $7 shared bath to $10 private bath. However, you're better off choosing from the many options along the *calle principal* and, in particular, the few places around the Parque Darío.

Hotel Plaza (on the south side of Parque Darío, tel. 505/2772-2380) has been a stalwart in the Matagalpa lodging scene for decades. The 18 rooms range from $2.50 cubby holes with shared bath to $10 doubles with private bath, TV, and fan. On the west side of Parque Darío, **Hotel Apante** (tel. 505/2772-6890) charges $7.50 per person for shared bath, fan, and TV in its bright, clean rooms. **Hotel La Siesta** (one block south and 2.5 blocks west of Parque Darío, $7 pp shared bath) is a family-run place with a quiet coffee balcony; the seven rooms range from singles to quadruples.

One of the best, safest budget options is **⬛ Hotel Alvarado** (across from the Parque Darío's northwest corner, tel. 505/2772-2830 or 505/2772-2252, $8 pp), run by a friendly Christian doctor couple who run a pharmacy downstairs. Ask for one of the top-floor rooms which boast private bathrooms, a breeze, and views of the city and mountains from the small balconies. If their eight rooms are full, ask about their other location across town.

MATAGALPA

BLACK GOLD: THE STORY OF NICARAGUAN COFFEE

In 1852, Germans Ludwig Elster and his wife Katherina Braun were passing through Nicaragua on their way to the California gold rush. They never made it to California, but they did find gold. Rather, Katherina did.

While crossing Nicaragua, Ludwig met many disheartened travelers returning home from failure in California. He and Katherina decided to cut their journey short and look for gold in the mines of San Ramón, Matagalpa. While Ludwig worked the taxed gold deposits of Matagalpa, Katherina Braun established a home garden and planted some of the coffee beans they'd picked up in Managua. Her discovery – that Matagalpa's climate and soils were just right for the cultivation of the bitter but full-bodied arabica coffee bean – dwarfed the importance of San Ramón's gold mines and changed the course of Nicaragua's history.

Coffee fever gripped Matagalpa in the 1880s, and the Nicaraguan government, eager to capitalize on the crop, threw its weight behind the Germans. Laws were passed encouraging young Germans to immigrate to Nicaragua. One such law gave them free land to work; many of these family farms are still operating today.

At first, coffee was shipped in bean form through the port of Corinto, around Cape Horn to European importers in Bremen and Hamburg. By 1912, though, the Nicaraguan German community had established their own processing plants where they milled and processed the coffee beans. They used a new "wet" method that stripped the beans of their pulp over grated steel cylinders. Today, more than 40 wet coffee mills, plus thousands of micromills on individual farms process coffee throughout the nation.

FROM MATAGALPA TO MOCHACCINO: HOW NICARAGUAN COFFEE IS PROCESSED

One of the truly unique aspects of Nicaraguan coffee, besides its exceptional quality, is how much of the process is performed on the farm, before the product is shipped elsewhere. This is a significant difference from the routine adopted by Costa Rican coffee growers, most of whom send off their harvest immediately after picking.

Also, an increasing number of small-scale Nicaraguan coffee farmers are learning to recognize and judge the quality of their product and eliminate the middlemen, or *coyotes*, who have traditionally taken the lion's share of coffee profits. One tool that allows them to do this is the cupping lab – a specially equipped kitchen where Nicaraguan cooperative members are trained to grind, brew, and rate their own coffee using internationally recognized criteria. One of the key figures in the cupping lab project was Paul Katzeff, CEO and roastmaster of Thanksgiving Coffee Company (www.thanksgivingcoffee.com).

But before you cup it, you must grow, harvest, and process it. Following are the steps involved:

1. Coffee berries are picked during the harvest months December–February. The fleshy berries are red and yellow and called *café en uva* (meaning grape or cherry coffee).

2. The berries are de-pulped, i.e., the fleshy covering is removed. This is done the same day they're picked to prevent fermenting, which would affect the flavor. This is either done dry or while they're suspended in water ("wet processing").

3. The coffee beans at this stage still have a mucilaginous coating on them. The beans are allowed to sit for 24 hours to allow the coating to ferment, facilitating the removal of the mucilage.

4. After 24 hours, the beans are soaked in water and stirred with wooden paddles. The mucilaginous coating dissolves. During this stage, the good beans sink to the bottom of the vessel, and the bad beans float to the surface, where they're removed.

5. The beans are now called *café en pergamino* (parchment coffee). Small growers sell their

© JOSHUA BERMAN

Café oro starts off as red or yellow fleshy berries.

beans to the coffee cooperatives at this point. They still have a hard shell around them.

6. The beans are laid out in the sun on broad concrete slabs to dry and raked continuously to prevent burning.

7. When the beans reach 12 percent humidity, they are stored for around one month in a cool, semi-dark building. During this time, the coffee beans' flavor is enhanced.

8. When ready for shipping, the beans are milled to remove the hard shell. What is left after milling is the familiar coffee bean, in two halves. At this stage, the coffee is considered *café oro* (gold or green coffee).

9. The beans are sorted. All broken, burned, or blackened beans are removed by hand. The beans are packed in 150-pound burlap sacks and sent to the port of Corinto for international shipments.

10. The green coffee beans are roasted, ground, and bagged. In Nicaragua, you can find these at co-op headquarters or any local supermarket.

GOOD BEANS: WHAT MAKES GOURMET COFFEE

As much as 80 percent of Nicaraguan cooperative-produced coffee can be considered "quality coffee" because it fills the following internationally recognized requirements:

- They are arabica beans (not robusta) grown at an altitude of 900 meters or higher.

- Consisting of big beans, the lots are aromatic, well sorted, and free from broken or burned beans and small stones.

- Beans are given one month to sit during processing and are not de-hulled until just before shipping.

- Beans are transported in sealed containers.

- Beans are adequately stored by the purchaser.

- Upon roasting, the beans are sealed immediately in special one-pound vacuum-packed bags that prevent the introduction of light, air, and moisture, but permit carbon dioxide to escape.

- The consumer can buy the coffee in whole-bean form, not ground.

$10-25

◖ **Hotel Fountain Blue,** a.k.a. Fuente Azul (third entrance to Matagalpa just west of the bridge, or from Salomón López 1.5 blocks west, tel. 505 /772-2733), has a dozen practical rooms—$21 double with private bath, hot water, TV, and fan or $10 per person for smaller rooms with shared bath. This place is quiet and comfortable, with a pay phone, Internet, free coffee, continental breakfast, and guarded parking.

The choice of many visiting Nicas, **Hotel La Profe** (across from Shell El Progreso gas station, tel. 505/2772-2506) offers rooms for $10–15; ask for the quiet rooms in the back. North along the *calle principal,* **Hotel Central** (across from the Supermarket Matagalpa, tel. 505/2772-3140) has doubles from $11, or pay $19 for private bath and fan. The rooms are secure and clean, but a bit musty in the rainy season.

A peaceful respite in the heart of Matagalpa, **Hostal La Buena Onda** (the name roughly means "good vibes," tel. 505/8720-1468, labuenaonda.matagalpa@gmail.com, www. labuenaondamatagalpa.com, $10–30) is located 2.5 blocks east of Union Fenosa, walking distance from the best attractions and food in the city. The new hotel occupies a large, revamped two-story house where travelers can lounge in the garden patio hammocks and take in the surrounding mountains from the upper balcony. There are five communal rooms, each with bathroom, hot shower, and handcrafted wooden bunk beds. There is also a private room with bath and air-conditioning ($35). You also have free coffee and tea from the adjacent **Artesanos Café Bar,** free Wi-Fi, book and DVD library, laundry service, an extensive all-day brunch menu, and afternoon cocktails. Meals are available for $2–$7. *Buena onda,* indeed.

$25-50

Hotel Lomas de San Thomas (350 meters east of Escuela Guanuca, tel. 505/2772-4189, www.hotellomassnthomas.com, $35–75) lords over the city, a mustard-colored, three-story establishment on a breezy hill just east of town. The 25 rooms have private bath, hot water, TV, and telephone, many with an excellent balcony. There is also a bar and restaurant on-site. It gears itself for business conventions and the NGO crew, offering secretarial services, conference rooms, fax, Internet, and a tennis court. To get there, leave the highway at the third entrance to Matagalpa and pass straight through town following the signs. At the eastern edge of Matagalpa, turn left and climb the hill on a cobblestone road to the hotel.

FOOD
Coffee Shops and Cafés

There is no shortage of coffee up here where it's produced: ◖ **Cafeto** (half a block west of Citibank, open 9 A.M.–9 P.M. Mon.–Sat.) never fails to impress, with hot and cold sandwiches, paninis, salads, waffles, smoothies, and ice cream.

Sniff around just east of Bancentro, and you will surely catch a whiff of warm, fresh breads and pastries wafting out from the **Panadería Belén** (open 8 A.M.–6 P.M. Mon.–Sat.). **Repostería Gutierrez** (one block east and half a block south of the southeast corner of Parque Morazán, open 7 A.M.–8 P.M. daily) is a favorite among locals, with savory, cheap Nica dishes. On the corner of Parque Darío, **Mus Manni** (open 6 A.M.–8 P.M. daily) also has great bread and pastries. **Coffee Shop Barista** (right behind the cathedral, open 8 A.M.–9 P.M.) offers the full barista experience plus pastries and sweets.

◖ **Cafe Artesanos** (a half-block up from BAC next to Matagalpa Tours, tel. 505/2772-2444, open 8 A.M.–noon and 3 P.M.–midnight daily) is one *norteño*'s cathedral to coffee. Propietor Noel Montoya offers a close look—and taste—of Nica beans at their best, and is happy to introduce you to the art of roasting and brewing. Mix the black liquor with Flor de Caña. In addition to coffee, Artesano's is one of the most relaxing hangouts in the city. It's open for breakfast and dinner and is especially soothing in the morning. The place features local artists' paintings and murals on the walls of an old colonial building.

Comida Típica

Local snacks and simple dishes are Matagalpa's specialty. As always, there's tasty street food in both parks, and as always, it's *vigorón* or *chancho con yucca* (both include pork and yucca served on banana leaves). However, during the lunch hour, several *fritangas* at Parque Morazán serve a more robust menu.

One of the friendliest and most famous *comedores* is █ **Don Chaco's** (1.5 blocks east of the Alcaldía, open 7:30 A.M.–9 P.M. Sun.–Thurs., 7:30 A.M.–5 P.M. Fri.), where in addition to heaping plates of *comida típica* (with great veggie options), you'll find a delicious *batido* (smoothie) menu of fruits, vegetables, and even soy milk. If you prefer buffet, lunchline style, with a smorgasbord of Nica food lined up in front of you, the ragingly popular **Mana del Cielo** (located 2.5 blocks south of the banks) will satisfy; it's owned by a retired baseball player who played in Nica's pro leagues for a number of years.

To taste the sweet goodness of Matagalpa's best *güiríla* (a sweet-corn pancake wrapped around a hunk of salty *cuajada* cheese, about $0.35), you'll have to brave the chaos of the crowds that cluster around the smoky stands across the street from Palí.

Everybody loves Don Tano's **Picoteo Café** (located just east of the post office, open 7:30 A.M.–10 P.M. daily), serving chicken, burgers, pizza, and lots of beer. The walls are covered with platitudes painted on wooden plaques; most dishes run around $2.

Pique's (not far from the Parque Morazán) is a stylish Mexican joint, with dishes in the $2–4 range. Their *chalupas* and mole are especially good, and the atmosphere is relaxing.

La Casona (on the main drag, across from the mayor's office) offers a lunch buffet and a variety of bar-type foods for $3–4. It's open 9 A.M.–11 P.M. daily or later on weekends when it turns into a popular bar. Look for the big 7-Up sign outside. **Cafetería Zinica** is summed up best by the proprietress: "We don't have a menu. We just serve hamburgers—the best damn hamburgers in the country." Actually, they do have a menu and serve several other things, including fresh fruit juices. Super-clean, the place is named after the Matagalpa town where Carlos Fonseca, founder of the FSLN, was killed by Somoza's National Guard.

Finer Dining

One of the cornerstones of Matagalpa's dining scene, █ **La Vita e Bella** (tel. 505/2772-5476, vitabell@ibw.com.ni, 12:30 P.M.–10:30 P.M. Tues.–Sun.) is tucked into an alley in the Colonia Lainez, serving Italian and vegetarian dishes, and desserts that will make you glad you found the place. This is possibly the best restaurant in the city for non-chicken and non-beef dishes; entrées are under $4, large pizza $6, and there's an excellent wine selection.

There are three notable restaurants on the highway to Managua, all on the right-hand side as you leave town, a few kilometers south of the first entrance to Matagalpa. **La Hora del Taco** (open 11 A.M.–11 P.M. daily) offers the same finger-licking Mexican menu as its Managua counterpart, with an added outdoor balcony looking out into the Valle Las Tejas; margaritas are $2, and the $4 fajita plate is to die for.

Around the next bend in the highway, **El Pullazo** (open for lunch and dinner) just might serve you the best piece of beef tenderloin you'll taste in Nicaragua, but they won't tell you their secret recipe. They have a few other beef dishes too, but no one orders them. Your *"pullazo"* of meat (a vulgar play on the word for injection) is accompanied by a sweet *güiríla* pancake and hunk of *cuajada* cheese. Wash it down with a beer and you're only $7 in the hole.

Popular with locals for special occasions, **Parradea** (open 7 A.M.–11 P.M. daily, $5–15), 75 meters north from the Shell at the Virgin, offers seafood, steaks, and even such delicacies as bull testicle soup, as well as *comida típica* breakfasts.

There's also the **Sacuanjoche Restaurant and Bar** at the Hotel Lomas de San Thomas, offering standard fare like steaks, fajitas, shrimp dishes, and salads (entrées $4–9), a ceramic shop, and taxi service ($1 to or from the town center).

Casa Grande (one block south of the Iglesia San José, tel. 505/2772-0988, 11 A.M.–midnight daily). At $10–20 a meal, it's expensive, but shows in the quality of the food. Their famed *Metro* is a meter-long tray of meat, feeding six people for about $25. Enjoy your meal on a lovely balcony that overlooks the hillsides and the city while taking in a fresh breeze.

SERVICES
Emergencies
All emergency services are covered in Matagalpa—fire (tel. 505/2772-3167), police (tel. 505/2772-3870), and hospital (tel. 505/2772-2081). The hospital is located at the north end of town on the highway to San Ramón. But you'll get better medical treatment at the Clínica Maya Flores.

Banks
There are a half-dozen banks in Matagalpa—BAC, Banpro, Banexpo, Banco Caley Dagnall, Bancentro, and Banco Mercantíl—and a fistful of money changers that hang out around the southeast corner of Parque Morazán. The banks are mostly clustered in a three-block strip, starting at the southeast corner of Parque Morazán. Nearly all have ATMs.

Internet
The fastest, most advanced cybercafe in town is **Matt's Cyber** (located two blocks north of Parque Darío, open 8 A.M.–10 P.M.). **CyberCafe Downtown** (a half-block west of the southwest corner of the Parque Darío, open 8:30 A.M.–8 P.M. Mon.–Sat., 10 A.M.–7 P.M. Sun.) is popular and fast. Walking north on the *calle principal,* about halfway to Parque Morazán, you'll find **NetCom** just past La Casona; it provides decent service, and is open 8 A.M.–9 P.M. daily, closing a bit earlier on Saturday and Sunday (8 P.M. and 7 P.M. respectively). One of the fastest servers in town is at **Cybercafe Matagalpa** (a half-block north, one block west from the Palí supermarket, across the street from Mi Favorita store, open 9 A.M.–9 P.M. daily, to 7 P.M. Sun., about $2 an hour), with cheap membership deals available.

OPPORTUNITIES TO VOLUNTEER

At least 16 Matagalpan organizations accept volunteer help from time to time if you'd like to make this your home for a few months or more. The **Movimiento Comunal** (tel. 505/2772-3200) deals with indigenous rights issues and fights against water privatization. **La Casa de la Mujer Nora Hawkins** (tel. 505/2772-3047) promotes social programs that benefit women. The **Comunidad Indígena** (tel. 505/2772-2692) is rather disorganized but well intentioned and could certainly use your assistance if you can find a way to be useful. **Habitat for Humanity** (located two blocks east and half a block north of the Deportiva Brigadista, tel. 505/2772-6121) has built several housing settlements in the area and continues to be active. Ask about volunteer opportunities at **Matagalpa Tours** or **Centro Girasol.**

Mail and Phones
Correos de Nicaragua Matagalpa (tel. 505/2772-4317, open 8 A.M.–12:30 P.M. and 2–5:30 P.M. Mon.–Fri., 8 A.M.–1 P.M. Sat.) is located one block west of Parque Morazán, tucked into a side street that runs south from the main drag. Fax, phone, and mailbox services are available.

There are a number of card-based public phones and BellSouth posts all over town, especially along the main *calle principal,* and the main ENITEL building (open 7 A.M.–9 P.M.) is located to the east of Parque Morazán (look for the big antenna jutting out from the city skyline). Cheap, web-based international call service is available at all three Internet places.

Laundry
A block and a half east of the Cancha Brigadista is a washer and dryer for rent. It's open 8:30 A.M.–5 P.M. Monday–Saturday and charges $4 a load, including wash, dry, and fold.

Haircuts

The male hairdressers at **Max Salon** (across from the cinema) are proud, flamboyant, and terribly excited to give you a makeover; let them pamper you with a new 'do, pedicure, and manicure, as they chat away and laugh; expect U.S. or European quality ($8 for a cut and dry, more for coloring and highlights). For a simpler, more old-fashioned cut, try the old-school barber shop next to Mana del Cielo, where a cut and straight-edge shave costs under $4.

GETTING THERE AND AWAY
From Managua

Express buses from Managua leave the Mayoreo bus terminal every hour 5:30 A.M.– 5:30 P.M. The ride takes two hours and costs about $2.50. If heading north from Granada or Masaya, you can bypass Managua by grabbing one of two direct buses from the Masaya bus terminal, leaving at 5 A.M. and 6 A.M. and taking less than three hours (these are full-size buses and run every day except Thursday and Sunday).

From Other Cities

From León, there are two daily expresses, leaving at 4:30 A.M. and 2:45 P.M.; this ride takes less than three hours and costs about $2.50 per person. Matagalpa-bound buses leave every half hour, starting about 5 A.M. from both Estelí (last bus leaves at 5:45 P.M.) and Jinotega (last bus leaves at 7 P.M.). There is one direct bus from Chinandega to Matagalpa, leaving at 5 A.M.

Leaving Matagalpa

Matagalpa has two bus terminals—which one you head to depends on your destination. At the south end of town, the **COTRAN Sur** (tel. 505/2772-4659 or 505/2603-0909) services Managua, Estelí, León, Masaya, and Jinotega. There's a public bathroom there ($0.10) and several small eateries.

Express buses to Managua depart every hour 5:15 A.M.–5:15 P.M. Nonexpress Managua-bound buses leave every half hour 3:30 A.M.–6 P.M. Direct buses to Masaya leave at 2 P.M. (daily except Thursday and Sunday).

To León via San Isidro and Telíca, there are two daily expresses, leaving at 6 A.M. and 3 P.M. There are also *interlocales* minivans that leave whenever they fill up; or take any bus bound for Estelí, get off at the Empalme León, and catch a bus to León (departing just about every 20–30 minutes).

There is a constant flow of buses to Estelí and Jinotega, leaving every half hour 5 A.M.– 5:40 P.M. (Estelí) and till 6 P.M. (Jinotega). One daily direct bus to Chinandega leaves Matagalpa at 2 P.M.

At the north end of town, the **COTRAN de Guanuca** services the interior of Matagalpa, including El Tuma–La Dália, San Ramón, Río Blanco, Muy Muy, and Bocana de Paíwas. The ride to San Ramón takes about 45 minutes. Road conditions in these areas are bad in the dry season, horrible in the rainy season when bus service sometimes slackens. Buses to points east depart approximately every 15 minutes to an hour until around 4:30 P.M.

GETTING AROUND

Matagalpa is a perfectly good city for walking, except for all those hills, where you'll sweat out all that *fritanga* grease; the taxi fare within town is $0.35. City buses ply three different routes back and forth across town, and cost about $0.10. Particularly useful is the bus route called El Chispa.

Car Rental

Prices are standard. Budget (tel. 505/2772-3041 or 505/2266-6226, reserve@budget.com.ni) has a small lot at the La Virgen Shell Station, just as you enter town from the south. Dollar (tel. 505/2772-4100 or 505/2772-4640, $40/ day) has an office in the Toyota dealership.

East of Matagalpa

Segmented by dozens of rivers—some of which are impassible in the wet season—and bereft of roads throughout much of the area, the lands east of Matagalpa made good training grounds for the guerrillas that followed Fonseca into battle against Somoza's troops in the 1970s. Thirty years later, the population has grown but the wild and rugged landscape is as impenetrable as ever. The mostly undeveloped hillsides that stretch from Matagalpa to the Honduran border vary from dense tropical jungle to pine forest to shallow, bushy hillsides.

Heading into the geographic heart of the nation, the traveler encounters broad hillsides of shiny coffee bushes beneath shady canopies, plots of corn and beans, and small communities of tile-roofed adobe houses sitting among the rugged mountains that are the eastern reaches of the Cordillera Dariense. The *campesinos* in the folds of these mountains live much the way they have for centuries, even as governments, revolutions, and natural disasters have swirled violently around them.

The major communities of the east, Río Blanco, Matiguás, and Muy Muy, serve as commercial and transportation centers for the region, and they offer rudimentary accommodations for the traveler. But don't expect any luxury rides here: The roads east of Matagalpa are some of the most neglected in the country, notably the stretch between Siuna and Mulukukú, which is practically impassable during the wettest months of the year. That said, you will be traveling through some of the most beautiful—and least visited—parts of Nicaragua.

SAN RAMÓN

Only 12 kilometers from Matagalpa, the village of San Ramón is nestled in a lovely valley at the base of several steep hills. Founded in the late 1800s, San Ramón got its start around the La Leonesa and La Reina gold mines, and today is a peaceful, friendly hamlet, about five blocks square and surrounded on all sides by green farms and forests penetrated by a number of roads and trails. San Ramón has two parks, a health clinic, a gas station, and a number of nonprofit and coffee-related administrative offices. Because of sister-city relationships with Catalan (Spain), Henniker (New Hampshire), and Durham (North Carolina), small groups of wandering foreigners are not uncommon and San Ramón adeptly hosts both foreign groups and individuals in one of several guesthouse and homestay programs.

Use San Ramón as a more rural alternative to Matagalpa (travel to and from the city is a cinch), or sample one of the short local excursions, such as the walk to the La Pita coffee cooperative. On the way, you'll pass the 100-year-old ruins of the Leonesa mine, overtaken by moss, ferns, and giant ceiba trees. **Cesar Davila** (work tel. 505/2772-9734 or cell 505/2478-3519) has a privately owned nature preserve that he has reforested practically right in San Ramón. Cesar, an ex-soldier, is full of stories of the war, and has knowledge about forestry, birds, and herbs. He has built a trail across his lands for a half-hour hike to the point of the cross above San Ramón with beautiful views of surrounding hills.

El Suena de la Campagna (fundacionla-campana@gmail.com)—located just down from the gas station, across the creek at the bridge and on the left—is not only a hostel but a Spanish NGO that supports work with children with disabilities in San Ramón as well as a Casa de Cultura. The hostel has 11 rooms from dormitory accommodations for $10 per person to $25 for a private matrimonial. The restaurant has excellent *comida típica,* laundry service, library, Internet, 24-hour reception, and trails on the property. Stay as a guest or get involved in some of the projects.

Find the office of Finca Esperanza Verde (an ecoresort outside town) by walking east from the Shell station past the police station, and through a small gate at the dead end. This is the place to inquire about the **Club de Guías** (trained young guides, $10/day, some with English) and the local **Casa de Huespedes** or guesthouse system (tel. 505/2772-5003, U.S. tel. 919/489-1656, fincaesperanza@gmail. com), which offers a secure room, private bath, and three meals for $15 a day.

There are no true restaurants in San Ramón, but plenty of more casual eateries, including tasty *comedores* along the sidewalk across the highway from the Shell station. **Doña Nelys Arauz** serves heaping plates of originally styled Nica food for under $2.

Buses to and from San Ramón are frequent, leaving the Guanuca terminal every hour or more 6 A.M.–7 P.M., in addition to the many other eastbound buses that pass through San Ramón on their way elsewhere. A cab from Matagalpa costs about $3 per person, if you're interested in day- or night-tripping into the city of Matagalpa.

FINCA ESPERANZA VERDE

Although its office and many of the community programs it supports are in the village of San Ramón, Finca Esperanza Verde (FEV, tel. 505/2772-5003, www.fincaesperanzaverde.org) is its own destination. A cool, green getaway 18 km east of San Ramón and 1,180 meters above sea level, travelers will find a range of peaceful accommodations, as well as beautiful sunsets, delicious food, and a menu of educational and recreational activities. FEV is closely associated with the Durham, North Carolina–San Ramón Sister City Project.

The open-air lodge and cabanas have wide, west-facing vistas, surrounded by shade-grown, organic coffee plantations and second-generation cloud forest, through which winds an impressive and varied trail system; hike it on your own or, to see more of the 150 species of birds, howler monkeys, numerous orchids, and medicinal plants, hire one of the farm's guides ($7/hr, per group, well worth it if you speak Spanish, or want to help them learn English).

FEV's property features several waterfalls, a butterfly house and breeding project (tours $6 pp), and a delicious spring-fed, potable water supply. From November through February,

pick, process, and sort the coffee beans, then follow the coffee to Matagalpa where it is sun dried, sorted, graded, cupped, and exported. The farm's all-Nicaraguan staff enjoy teaching visitors about coffee and are proud that their care of the farm makes it a home to hundreds of species of birds, butterflies, mammals, trees, and orchids. Other possible activities include a cooking demonstration and class, and a folk music concert. Or just relax on the hammock terrace watching the jungle and the sunset.

The lodge and cabins, built of handmade brick and other local materials, can accommodate up to 26 people and are equipped with solar electricity, flush toilets, sinks, and warm sun showers. There is a range of accommodations—bunks cost $15 per person, and a private cabin for two with a view, $75, all with private toilet (the bigger your group, the better the deal). Meals ($9) include fresh juices, fruits, vegetables, and eggs from neighboring farms, and of course, homegrown organic coffee. A gorgeous camping area features tent sites and a roofed picnic table in the middle of a coffee and banana grove ($6 pp, bring your own gear). You can book a variety of package tours, and get a detailed breakdown of pricing at their website.

If you have a vehicle with moderate clearance (and four-wheel drive for the rainy season), FEV is a 40-minute drive from San Ramón. Follow the road to Yucúl, then turn left and follow the signs to the *finca*. By bus, take the Pancasan–El Jobo bus from the COTRAN Guanuca terminal in Matagalpa, and get off in Yucúl past San Ramón; then follow the signs to FEV, a beautiful 3.5-kilometer uphill walk that should take under an hour. Don't forget a long sleeve shirt and a rain jacket.

RÍO BLANCO AND CERRO MUSÚN

Cerro Musún, one of Nicaragua's youngest and least visited parks, encompasses the 1,460 meter peak of the same name and is still the haunt of some of Central America's more elusive mammals, like the puma. In 2004, however, Musín ("water mountain" in Nahuatl) lived up to its name when heavy rains caused several of its lower slopes to collapse, destroying several hillside communities in a massive mudslide.

The town of Río Blanco is your jumping-off point for hikes in this tremendous reserve area. Rest up at **Hotel Bosawas** or **Hotel Nicarao** (both $15 s with a/c and TV) before tackling hikes up to the seven waterfalls or the peak itself. Your hikes start at the FUNDENIC guide station (about one km out of town), where you can hire a guide to lead you through the reserve (about $6/day).

While you're in town, check out the statues in the Catholic church, artifacts from the pre-Columbian civilizations that occupied these lands. They left behind some petroglyphs at the river's edge (visible only during the dry season). Start searching near the red hanging bridge on the exit to Barrio Martin Centeno.

Two express buses leave for Río Blanco from Managua's Mayoreo terminal around noon; additional service is available from the COTRAN Guanuca in Matagalpa.

BOCANA DE PAÍWAS AND MULUKUKU

Bocana de Paíwas has a *hospedaje* and several restaurants, including the well-liked **Restaurante Mirador,** located on a long peninsula overlooking the Río Grande de Matagalpa. This is also the site of some pre-Columbian petroglyphs, tucked into the rocks alongside the Río Grande de Matagalpa.

Mulukuku was founded primarily to support a Sandinista military base in the 1980s, but quickly became a refugee center for those fleeing battles farther north; today's descendants of that time live in a humble but vivacious village on the edge of the mighty Río Tuma.

Mulukuku is well known for one of its expat residents, Doña Dorotea, a nurse born in 1930, who's lived and worked in the community for decades. Because of her work with Sandinista charities, she became a target for former president Alemán's political mischief and blind personal vengeance—he even ordered her deported after falsely accusing her of performing abortions. Over a period of several weeks in 2001, Dorotea's fellow townspeople rallied behind her as Alemán continued threatening to throw her out of Nicaragua and she pleaded that she had nowhere else to go. Though she was never deported, she spent several frustrating years hassling with her residency permit and is finally back in Mulukuku and continuing her work; Alemán was never asked to explain.

◖ LA SOMBRA ECOLODGE

Intimately connected to the Contra war of years past, El Tuma–La Dália are local commercial centers serving the local farming region. Both host resettlement camps where Contras gave up their weapons in exchange for a piece of land to farm. The La Sombra Eco-Lodge (tel. 505/22455-3732 or 505/22468-6281, sombra_ecolodge@yahoo.es, www.lasombraecolodge.com, $30–40) is an ecotourist facility set in a private forest reserve on about 200 hectares of shade-grown coffee and hardwoods. Stay in their enormous, wooden lodgehouse, with spacious balconies overlooking the greenery, where the price includes three meals and coffee, tours, and a guided trip to Peñas Blancas—well worth it, and the guides do a commendable job of interpreting the local ecosystem for you. They also lead guided trips on horseback, and more.

About 10 kilometers (15 minutes) southwest of La Dália, Piedra Luna is a rainy season–only swimming hole formed by the waters of the Río Tuma swirling around a several-ton rock sitting midstream. The swimming hole is easily seven meters deep, and local kids come from all over to dive off the rock into the pool. How did the rock get there? Ask the locals, who will relate the fantastic legend of the spirits that carried it there from someplace far away.

SANTA EMILIA AND EL CEBOLLÁL WATERFALL

The farming community of Santa Emilia is marked by a left turn at about Km 145; a bit farther, you'll find a 15-meter waterfall

© JOSHUA BERMAN

El Salto de Santa Emilia

spilling impressively into a wide hole flanked by thick vegetation and a dark, alluring rock overhang. The falls are known alternately as Salto de Santa Emilia and Salto el Cebollál. Access is just beyond the Puente Yasica, a bridge at about Km 149; look for a small house and parking area on the right, where a soft-drink sign reads Balneario El Salto de Santa Emilia. You'll be asked to pay a $1 parking fee unless you're just jumping off the Tuma–Dália bus.

PEÑAS BLANCAS

Located on the road that leads between El Tuma–La Dália and El Cuá, the cliffs of Peñas Blancas (1,445 meters) are several hundred meters high and carved out of the top of a massive hillside. This is unquestionably one of the most stunning natural sights in northern Nicaragua and the widely respected Gateway to Bosawás. At the top of the cliff is a waterfall, gorgeous and little known, even by Nicaraguans who live outside of the immediate area. The cliffs and waterfall are easily visible from the highway, next to property owned by Alan Ball. He's currently developing hikes and tours to the waterfall, but you can be proactive and get there yourself by asking around.

Getting there by yourself requires some effort—it's much easier to rely on a local provider like La Sombra Ecolodge in Tuma–La Dalia. Take the El Cuá–Bocay bus from Matagalpa (leaves Guanuca station at 7 A.M.), and about an hour after La Dália get off at the entrance to the reserve and Centro de Entendimiento con la Naturaleza. From there, ask for the best route to the falls. The hike is only possible in the dry season, and there is no well-established trail to the falls. The walk is worth it, as you'll pass through a series of humid forest ecosystems of orchids and mossy trees. Near the falls, the wind is full of spray. The hike up and down can be done in two hours but expect to get extremely muddy and wet. A Matagalpa-bound bus will pass the entrance to the reserve at 2 P.M. Peñas Blancas is run by a *cooperativa* and costs about $5 to go up with a guide. There are screened-in cabins for hikers that want to stay the night.

THE OLD MATAGALPA-JINOTEGA HIGHWAY

The sinuous mountain road between Matagalpa and Jinotega is considered one of the most scenic roads in all of Nicaragua. The road was first opened around 1920 by the English immigrant and coffee farmer Charles Potter for use by mules and wagons taking coffee from his farm to Matagalpa. No small feat of engineering, the road had to negotiate over 100 curves, the worst of which was the Disparate de Potter (still legendary). A stubborn old man, Potter built his road in spite of the naysayers, and it's said he used the road to carry a piano—strung atop two mules—all the way to his farm.

The long valley panoramas are often breathtaking: Momotombo and the Maribio volcanoes are visible when the sky is clear. You'll pass neatly arranged coffee plantations shaded by windrows of cedar and pine, banana trees, and canopies of precious hardwoods. There is also an endless succession of vegetable and flower fields, and roadside stands that sell farm-fresh goods. Should you take the express bus, you'll miss the opportunity to stop and take photographs, buy fresh vegetables, and hike into the coffee plantations. But if you drive, you may need to concentrate on the road so much that you'll miss the scenery. Jinotega and Matagalpa are the two most copious producers of vegetables in Nicaragua, and a set of small farm stands along the road are evidence of the rich harvests of this area. Whether you want to eat them or just photograph them, the stacks of fresh cabbage, carrots, broccoli, radishes, beets, lettuce, squash, and greens are a culinary feast for the eyes. The stands are typically run by the family's older children, who might just sweet-talk you into making a purchase.

◖ HOTEL DE MONTAÑA SELVA NEGRA

Hotel de Montaña Selva Negra (tel. 505/2772-3883/5713, reservaciones@selvanegra.com, www.selvanegra.com) has been an anchor in Nicaragua's tourism scene since well before there ever *was* a tourism scene. With a name meaning Black Forest, it remains popular for

MATAGALPA

© JAMES SAVAGE

Hotel de Montaña Selva Negra is one of Nicaragua's most established tourist destinations.

people looking to hike, dine, and monkey-watch, though San Ramón and La Sombra now provide some healthy competition.

The resort is, at its heart, a coffee farm by the name of La Hammonia, owned and run by Eddy Kühl and Mausi Hayn, third- and fourth-generation German immigrants and members of the founding families of the country's coffee industry. The farm—considered one of the most diversified in Central America, and winner of the 2007 Sustainability Award from the Specialty Coffee Association of America—is based on the German tradition of chalets set around a peaceful pond with access to short hiking trails up the adjoining 120-hectare hillside and along its ridge. Rooms run from $8 for a spot in the youth hostel to $35 for a double overlooking the lake, or $60 for a private bungalow. There are larger bungalows for groups and families. The restaurant serves hearty, home-cooked meals using organic ingredients produced entirely on the farm; you'll dine on a gorgeous outdoor patio overlooking the water. Needless to say, the coffee is superb and fresh (and sold at Whole Foods Market in the United States). The entrance to Selva Negra is marked by an old military tank on the side of the road, a relic from the revolution and painted over with the rainbows of Doña Violeta's UNO coalition in the early 1990s.

Selva Negra is a birder's paradise with some 200 species of birds that have been identified. You can see a list of identified bird species on their website, and try to spot them with one of the professionally trained bird guides. Tours of the coffee farm, flower plantations, the cattle, and livestock start at 9 A.M. and 3 P.M.—in Spanish, English and German when Mausi is available. Almost everything on the farm is recycled even down to using the plastic bottles as pest control. The tour is an amazing education in permaculture and innovative organic

a chapel at Selva Negra

© JAMES SAVAGE

methods. Or you can easily rent a horse for the day and ride the many roads that crisscross the plantation on your own. In 2000, the Kühls built a gorgeous, orchid-adorned stone chapel for the wedding of their daughter, and they now rent out the facilities—chapel, horse-drawn carriage, and fresh-cut flowers—for guests who come to get hitched.

Expect to have a chat with the owners while you're there—Eddy is a wealth of knowledge, a prolific writer, and a well-loved amateur anthropologist; many of the family's ideas have come from the suggestions and talent of the guests who visit them. Especially charming is the original *finca* house built by Otto Bosch in 1893. Also, you can arrange tours and buy their coffee from their daughter's U.S. coffeehouse in Atlanta, Georgia: Java Beano (www.javabeano.com).

MATAGALPA

Jinotega City

When walking the cobbled streets of Jinotega, you can't help but feel you're at the edge of the world, with all kinds of unknowns in the hills to the north and east. In fact, hundreds of kilometers of wild, lush mountain country beckon to the east. East of the city the pavement stops, the roads turn rutted and bumpy, bus service is less frequent, and the accommodations dwindle—at least the kind where they leave a mint on your pillow and fold the edge of the toilet paper into a little triangle. But the immense department of Jinotega is comprised of hundreds of small communities and thousands of farmers who make their livelihood in the hills around them—including many who have barely ever traveled beyond this land in their lives. Jinotega is replete with fragrant valleys of orange groves, white corn, plantains, sweet vegetables, and a whole lot of cattle. But in between the small farms, Jinotega is open space—virgin forest, small freshwater lagoons, stately mountain ranges, and some of the loveliest rivers in Nicaragua, including the mighty Río Coco (which forms the northern border of the Jinotega department) and the Río Bocay, one of the Coco's most important tributaries.

Jinotega, or La Ciudad de las Brumas (The City of Mists), is the watering hole and commercial center for the department of the same name. Farmers from the north and east inevitably find their way here to do their business and trading, and Jinotega City has built itself into a clean, prosperous community around the business needs of those farmers. It's a working town whose streets are lined with cobblers, tailors, barbers, blacksmiths, watch repairmen, and merchants that deal in housewares, veterinary supplies, saddles, cowboy hats, firearms, auto parts, and an endless stock of farming tools. It's a town very much in tune with the rugged and self-sufficient life of the Nicaraguan *campesino,* and you will learn much just by wandering its streets among such hardy characters. Jinotega, your gateway to the wide-open expanses of the east, is at once charming and thrilling. As late

as the mid-1960s, it wasn't uncommon to find wild monkeys in the old-growth park canopy of *lechito* trees.

Travelers enjoy Jinotega because its high elevation (a full kilometer above sea level) gives it a pleasant climate, especially nice in the picturesque setting. Jinoteganos themselves are at once friendly and aloof—they might leave you to your own, but if you make the effort to talk to them, you'll find them warm, open, and full of country hospitality.

HISTORY

The name Jinotega is said to come from the Nahuatl name Xilotl-Tecatl ("place of the jiñocuabo trees"; also translated as "the place of the eternal men and women"). Indeed, the natives who lived in this peaceful valley enjoyed healthy and prosperous existences and were known to live to more than 100 years of age. Today's department of Jinotega was in those days the border between two diverse indigenous peoples: to the north, in the Bocay region, lived the Chontales (Kiribie) people, and near the present-day city of Jinotega, the Chorotega. They were an agricultural people who lived off small plots of corn, beans, cacao, roots, tubers, and fruit orchards. They wove their own clothing from wood and cotton fiber, as well as animal skins tinted with plant extracts. In the late 18th century, the Spanish chose to inhabit the southern part of Jinotega, forcing the indigenous peoples to move north. The community of Jinotega was officially recategorized as The Valley of Jinotega in 1851, and as a city in 1883.

For better or for worse, nearly every major armed uprising in recent Nicaraguan history began in the Jinotega department. The young Sandinistas first took to the hills here to battle squadrons of the National Guard in the 1960s, and when the Sandinistas took power, the first groups of Contras took to the hills, again in Jinotega. At the end of the Contra war, the two groups that refused to lay down their weapons

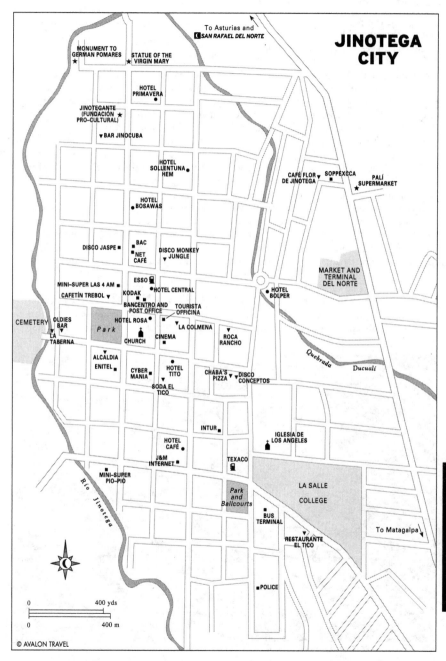

JINOTEGA CITY

To Asturias and
SAN RAFAEL DEL NORTE

MONUMENT TO
GERMAN POMARES ★

STATUE OF THE
VIRGIN MARY ★

HOTEL
PRIMAVERA ●

JINOTEGANTE
(FUNDACIÓN ★
PRO-CULTURAL)

▼ BAR JINOCUBA

HOTEL
SOLLENTUNA ●
HEM

CAFÉ FLOR
DE JINOTEGA ▼

SOPPEXCCA ■

PALÍ
SUPERMARKET ★

HOTEL
BOSAWAS ●

DISCO JASPE ■

BAC ■
NET ■
CAFÉ

DISCO MONKEY
JUNGLE

MARKET AND
TERMINAL
DEL NORTE

MINI-SUPER LAS 4 AM ■

ESSO ▣
KODAK ●
HOTEL CENTRAL

HOTEL
BOLPER ■

CAFETÍN TREBOL ▼

BANCENTRO AND
POST OFFICE ■

TOURISTA
OFFICINA

CEMETERY

OLDIES ▼
BAR ■

Park

HOTEL ROSA ●

CHURCH ✝

LA COLMENA ▼

ROCA
RANCHO ▼

LA
TABERNA

Quebrada

Ducualí

CINEMA ■

ALCALDIA ▼
ENITEL ■

CYBER ■
MANIA

HOTEL
TITO ●

CHABA'S ▼
PIZZA ▼

DISCO
CONCEPTOS ■

SODA EL
TICO

INTUR ■

HOTEL
CAFÉ ●

IGLESIA DE
LOS ANGELES ⛪

J&M ■
INTERNET

TEXACO ▣

MINI-SUPER ■
PIO-PIO

Río Jinotega

Park
and
Ballcourts

LA SALLE

COLLEGE

To Matagalpa

BUS ■
TERMINAL

RESTAURANTE ▼
EL TICO

POLICE ■

0   400 yds

0   400 m

© AVALON TRAVEL

and accept the peace treaty (the Recompas and Recontras) fled back into the mountains of Jinotega to keep up their fight.

For most of the 1990s, remnants of fighting groups, like FUAC, plagued certain wilder areas of northeastern Jinotega, hassling the peace-loving Jinotegan farmers trying to raise crops and their families at the same time. Jinotega was possibly the worst-affected department in Nicaragua during the 1980s, as Contras and Sandinistas fought each other on the mountain roads and the deep valleys. In those days, there was only one bus per day between the city of Jinotega and Managua (as compared to one every hour now), and travelers intent on driving their own vehicles ran the daily risk of being ambushed, robbed, raped, or killed. Since the 1980s, Jinotega has voted steadfastly against the Sandinistas, who they claim are responsible for 10 years of devastation. The survivors of the generation that was marched off to the mountains as machine-gun fodder are resentful and frustrated now, robbed of their adolescence, and desperately trying to make a decent, honest living off the land.

ORIENTATION AND GETTING AROUND

Jinotega occupies the bottom of the steep-walled bowl formed by the mountains that surround it on all sides. The highway passes along its east side, and the cemetery is at the western edge. It's a city with a pleasant, cool climate and not too much vehicular traffic, both of which make it a pleasurable city for walking. There are no city buses, nor is there need for them.

There are several taxi cooperatives that circulate the city streets and that will take you across town for $0.35. But Jinotega isn't a big place, and the temperature never gets hot enough to be unpleasant. You should be able to walk anywhere you need to go.

SIGHTS AND ATTRACTIONS

There are few traditional tourist sights in Jinotega, but lots to see and do. Jinotega

The drizzly streets of Jinotega, the City of Mists.

© JOSHUA BERMAN

MATAGALPA

was the scene of a few ferocious battles during the revolution years, and it was down by the riverside in Jinotega where much-loved Sandinista commander **German Pomares** (a.k.a. El Danto) was killed in battle. Pomares and his troops had fought many battles against Somoza's National Guard and had been instrumental in the operation that led to political prisoner Daniel Ortega's release from jail. His sacrifice has not been forgotten, and a very carefully maintained red-and-black memorial marks the spot where he was killed.

Don Pilo is a second-generation medicine man who lives in an unknown location in the mountains west of Jinotega city. Twice weekly, he climbs down out of the mountains with his bags of herbs and potions and sets up camp at the cemetery to sell them. He's a well-loved town character who some put off as a charlatan, and others consider a true magician and physician. Regardless, both rich and poor wait for him Tuesdays and Fridays to see if he can cure their ills, from intestinal parasites and coughs to bad marriages, naughty children, and spurned lovers. And you don't need a prescription, just a strong stomach. The cures are all natural and brewed out of the stronger medicinal plants of the region, plus bark, moss, and sometimes even soil.

The town **cemetery** is an interesting place to wander. The graves started at the entrance to the cemetery and have worked their way south over time. The victims of the war in the 1980s are located at the south end of the plot. Some of the older gravestones are particularly ornate and well crafted in stone.

Festivals and Celebrations

Jinotega's *fiestas patronales* begin on May 1 and continue through May 15. You can expect to see folks from all over the north of Nicaragua showing up for the occasion. The *fiestas patronales* of San Juan de Jinotega are June 24. In addition (perhaps just to round out the year with parties), the Aniversario de la Creación del Departamento de Jinotega is celebrated on October 15.

ENTERTAINMENT AND NIGHTLIFE

The best bar in town, and a common expat hangout, is **La Taberna** (on the right just before the cemetery gate, open daily except Mon.) serving food, booze, and a list of unique cocktails. This place takes the cowboy motif to an extreme with a woven bamboo roof and barstools with saddles. However, the carefully partitioned and cozy feel lends a romantic air. Also a friendly bar, **Roca Rancho** (a couple blocks east of the park across from the Beneficio Ducalí, tel. 505/2782-3730, open noon–midnight daily) is a unique space where the beer flows smoothly and you sit in a kingly, high-backed bar stool.

There are two small discos in town. Start with the tried-and-true **Conceptos,** not far from the center of town, formerly a house but was converted into a dance hall with a house-party feel. Newer and more modern **Monkeys Jungle** is a half-block north of the downtown Esso in an old theater. For a surprising scene ("reminiscent of Los Angeles in 1982," wrote one reader), the **Oldies Bar** features music from the 1970s and '80s; food is served, and the lighting and bright white decor combined with occasional dry ice create a serious *Saturday Night Fever* set (open 2:30 P.M.–1 A.M., closed Tues.).

SPORTS AND RECREATION

Basketball is the game of choice in Jinotega, and there are pickup games most evenings on the *cancha* (town court). Jinotega has an active youth league and both women's and men's teams; the players are better than you'd expect, if you're thinking about getting in a game.

Hikes from Town

The western wall of the Jinotega valley makes a popular climb for a Saturday morning. Start at the cemetery and work your way upward to Peña de la Cruz, where the cross is planted. Depending on how ambitious you are, the hike is 30–90 minutes, and you'll be rewarded with an impressive view of the city and the verdant

MATAGALPA

valley of Jinotega. The cross isn't the original— locals say its predecessor was bigger and "better"—but the modern cross is illuminated, thanks to an electric cable that climbs the same steep hillside you just did. Look for the shining beacon of Christianity at night from the city. During misty nights, it's particularly eerie, emitting a diffuse white glow through the mists.

The eastern wall of the valley is steeper and longer, and there are no trails. That doesn't stop many locals from making their way to the top for a look around. Plan on two hours for this one. The easiest way to do it is the steep, windy dirt road that climbs abruptly out of the city and snakes its way to the top of the ridge. By road, it's around an hour on foot, but it's still not an easy walk, as the road is exceptionally steep. Watch your step on the loose gravel.

ACCOMMODATIONS

Keep in mind that until recently, Jinotega's chief clientele were the small-scale farmers of the east who come in for weekends at a time to see a dentist, sell some corn, and have their boots fixed. They don't require many luxuries and don't want to waste too many *córdobas* while they're in town, as evidenced by all the under-$2 *hospedajes* that spot the neighborhood around the market. The following are some more "upscale" options. As you choose your lodging, remember to ask about hot water: This is about the only area in Nicaragua where you'll want it.

Under $10

Hotel Rosa (tel. 505/2782-2472) is the oldest gig in town, and a hundred years ago, when it first opened its doors, it was the only gig in town. Its 19th-century feel remains in massive wooden beams, simple rustic rooms, and a laid-back atmosphere. Somewhat dark and dingy, the 30 rooms cost $2–3 per person.

El Hotelito (just east of the park, next to Sopas Coyote's Bar, tel. 505/2782-2079) has 10 rooms with tiled floors, comfy-looking beds, and shared baths for about $4 per person. It

closes its doors at 10 P.M.; knock to be let in after hours.

Toward the north end of town, but still in a quiet residential area, **Hotel Primavera** (tel. 505/2782-2400) is run by a family that expects you to behave; 28 small rooms set around a courtyard are nothing special, but they're clean, simple, and cheap—$3.50 per person. There are rooms with private bath for a relatively steep $10. Inside the family's living room, there's a pay phone available. The doors close at 10 P.M. and don't open until morning—make sure you're on the right side of the door and mind the sign "No Women of Bad or Dubious Conduct."

$10-25

Hotel Central (only a block from the park, tel. 505/2782-2063, $14) is indeed central and features a massive lobby leading back to 23 well-lit rooms not much larger than their beds. There are nice rooms upstairs with cable TV, private bath, and hot water; meals are available at the dining room for around $2 each. Both the hotel and restaurant are closed Sundays. **Hotel Fuente** (located on the south side of the El Carmen Shell station, tel. 505/2782-2966, $12) has 13 clean but loudly-furnished rooms with old art deco furniture, private baths, hot water, and TV. The owner tries very hard (there's even a suggestion box in the hallway!).

Hotel Sollentuna Hem is owned by a Swedish-Nica woman (the name is Swedish for "home of the green valley"). In business since 1988, the hotel has 17 different rooms (Scandinavian clean, with a unique, mismatched style) with private baths and hot water for $8–25. Meals, $2 breakfast and $3 lunch and dinner, are available, and she can accommodate vegetarians. Complete laundry service is also offered, as are tours of her farm on the outskirts of town.

Four kilometers outside of town on the old road to Matagalpa is a truly unique escape called **Biosfera Hospedaje Montañero Lodge** (tel. 505/8698-1439, info@hijuela. com, http://hijuela.com/diversion/cabanas. html, $5/s dorm beds, $40). Foreign owned, the lodge offers rustic but comfortable accommodation and camping, home-cooked exotic meals (Indonesian, Mediterranean), motorcycle or horseback tours, camping, hiking, and so on. Expect to roll up your sleeves and work, but you'll get a discount and maybe have some fun.

$25-50

Jinotega's classiest accommodations, the 【 **Hotel Café** (one block west, a half-block north of the Texaco station, tel. 505/2782-2710, www.cafehoteljinotega.com, $60) stands heads and shoulders above the rest with its 16 tidy, comfortable, and tastefully decorated rooms, taking up two stories and surrounding a lush garden and spiral staircase. The rooms feature private baths, hot water, cable TV, telephones, desks, and air-conditioning; minisuites for a few bucks more, continental breakfast included. You'll find valet parking and laundry service. Hotel Café accommodates groups and has a conference room, business center, and some great views of the surrounding city and countryside, as well as Jinotega's nicest restaurant and bar. Hotel staff can assist in planning your visit and tours of the area.

FOOD

Meals are simple but hearty in this neck of the woods. There are no real fine dining options (except in the Hotel Café). After dark, the streets fill with *fritangas,* and families open their front doors to create cheap eateries in their living rooms and front parlors. You can eat your way to greasy happiness for under $2 with no effort at all. Start at the southeast corner of the park and troll the two main streets through a sea of enchiladas, *papas rellenas* (stuffed and fried potatoes), and *gallo pinto* (the national dish of rice and beans).

Soda El Tico, a local lunch favorite, is just east of the park and has a clean and inexpensive lunch buffet and simple menu. Meals go for around $3–7. **Cafetería Trebol** is a popular, charming option with a simple menu of burgers, chicken, and sandwiches; located on the north side of the park, this is a great place

to enjoy a hot chocolate or *café con leche* with a plate of French toast. It's open for breakfast at 8:30 A.M., 11 A.M. on Sunday.

Look for **Chaba's Pizza** (2.5 blocks east of the park, next door to Dance Magic, tel. 505/2782-2692, open 11 A.M.–10:30 P.M. Tues.–Sun.), serving a variety of thin-crust pies for $7–11, delivery service anywhere in town. You'll find excellent, reasonably priced meals and a friendly open-air atmosphere at **Roca Rancho** (tel. 505/2782-3730, open noon–midnight daily); local volunteers rave about the jalapeño steak here.

Restaurante La Colmena (The Beehive) is one of the nicest restaurants in town with a menu of beef, chicken, and fish ($5–9); good service; and a pleasant atmosphere. But a close rival is the **Restaurante Borbón** at the Hotel Café, with sandwiches and meals $6–12, and a full wine and foreign drink list at the bar; the chicken cordon bleu is spectacular.

As you enter town from Matagalpa look for the corner building on your left before you get to the Texaco. About 15 minutes on the highway before Jinotega is **La Perrera,** a bar and restaurant owned by an American-trained chef.

For baked goods hit **Repostería Silvia** next to the BAC, and be sure not to miss 【 **Cafe Flor de Jinotega,** located next to the Soppexcca coffee exchange, a small-scale coffee producers' cooperative. Here you can have a cappuccino as good as any in Nicaragua, check out educational displays on coffee and coffee economics, and check out packages as they're sold in the U.S. Hit it before or after you get on the bus for the hinterlands at COTRAN Norte.

INFORMATION AND SERVICES

One locally produced online portal is **www. jinotegalife.com.** Also check out the **Alianza Turistica,** one block east and one block south of the church.

Not only does Luis Lautaro Ruiz (tel. 505/2782-4460, lautaror@ibw.com.ni) seemingly know all there is to know about his native Jinotega and the surrounding mountains,

MATAGALPA

he speaks some English and is a professional writer, film producer, musician, and clown. He is a flexible freelance tour guide and will charge comparable prices to guides in Managua ($15–20 a day). He also claims his house, located a half-block north of the Escuela Mistral, is a museum.

Banks

There's a bank on practically every corner in Jinotega. All the major players are present—Banpro, Bancentro, BAC, and more. Bank hours are standard; check your firearm at the door, please. The most reliable ATM is found at BAC, 1.5 blocks north of the central park.

Internet

Rates are standard at about $0.75 per hour. **Cybermania,** across from Soda El Tico is the largest in town with the fastest connection. **J&M Internet Café** (three blocks south of the park) has five machines, and a scanner and CD burner are also available. **NetCafe** (across the street from Restaurante/Disco Jun Shan, open 8 A.M.–10 P.M. daily) has speedy service.

Phone and Mail

The ENITEL office is located just north of the park along the main street. It's open 7 A.M.–5 P.M. daily. The post office (open 8 A.M.–4 P.M.) is a bit hard to find: It's tucked into a business complex behind Bancentro. As you're facing the front door of the bank, look for a sidewalk that leads behind the building to the offices that are part of the same complex. A fax machine is available.

GETTING THERE AND AWAY

Buses at the Terminal del Sur head south to Matagalpa and Managua, including several express buses that make one stop along the highway at Matagalpa without entering the city itself, then continuing straight on to Managua. Express buses to Managua ($4) leave every hour, and more express buses are being put into service every day, so ask ahead of time to find out what your options are. These buses may or may not make a brief stop along the highway

at Matagalpa before continuing straight on to Managua (3–4 hours).

To Points South

The bus terminal (actually, just a parking lot) is located across from La Salle (a Catholic high school). Several eateries line the road behind the station, where you can relax and wait for the bus to leave, as the terminal doesn't have any facilities for passengers. Buses to Matagalpa leave every half hour 5 A.M.–6 P.M. (the trip takes one hour). Buses leave for Estelí from the COTRAN Norte on a long, roundabout overland route that may require making a connection in La Concordia or San Rafeal del Norte. It is much easier to get to Estelí by simply taking any Managua bus to Sébaco, and transferring to a north-bound bus heading to Estelí, Ocotal, Somoto, or Jalapa.

To Points North and East

Buses at the Terminal del Norte go to points inland in Jinotega and beyond, including El Cuá, San José de Bocay, San Rafael del Norte, and Wiwilí. This is where the adventure starts, and the rugged conditions at the terminal should prepare you mentally for what awaits you inland: mud, livestock, and a lot of friendly people moving sacks of produce, selling grains and cheap merchandise, and laughing. There are five express buses for Estelí, 5:15 A.M.–3:30 P.M. There are 10 regular buses for San Rafeal del Norte, starting at 6 A.M. with the last bus at 6 P.M. Regular buses for Wiwilí leave between 4 A.M. and 1:15 P.M. (seven hours). Regular service to El Cuá–Bocay begins daily at 4 A.M. for the four-hour trip. There is regular service to Pantasma about once per hour (two hours) until 4:40 P.M. Pantasma buses go past Asturias and the dam at Lago Apanás.

The northern terminal also has regular bus service to San Sebastián de Yalí and La Rica, via San Rafael del Norte and La Concordia, from where you can get back-road bus service to Estelí—a fun way to make a loop through some really beautiful country.

The Frontier: Beyond Jinotega

EL VALLE DE TOMATOYA

Located just north of the city of Jinotega on the road to San Rafael del Norte, this is the home of a women's cooperative that produces the region's famous black pottery. The production of black pottery is a little more intricate than other types of ceramic arts, and these women have produced some very beautiful pieces of art, including faithful replicas of some pre-Columbian designs. **Grupo de Mujeres de Las Cureñas** has some fine pieces for sale.

Along the highway is **El Centro Recreativo de Tomatoya,** a bathing area created by damming up the San Gabriel stream. Your host, Blanca Dalla Torre, regularly empties out the pool and lets it refill with fresh water. Drinks and snacks are available, as well as a complete selection of beer.

LAGO DE APANÁS AND THE MANCOTAL DAM

Lake Apanás is the largest artificially constructed body of water in Nicaragua. Luís Somoza Debayle's administration created it in 1964 by damming the Río El Tuma, flooding the broad valley just north of Jinotega, which until that time was pasture, small farms, and an airstrip that serviced the north of Nicaragua. Today, Lake Apanás is a long, irregularly shaped lake. It feeds the twin turbines at the Planta Hidroelectrica Centroamérica, which produces 15 percent of the nation's hydropower (downstream along the Río Viejo, the same water passes through the turbines at Santa Bárbara and Lago La Virgen, which produce an additional 15 percent). Apanás is not a typical reservoir; unlike many hydropower plants that are located at the dam itself, the Planta Centroamérica is located at the upstream end of the lake, so keeping the lake full is essential. The water passes underneath the highway through massive steel pipes where it drops and passes through the turbines. The hydropower project actually forces the water to change watersheds: Water from the Río El Tuma watershed is discharged into the tributaries of the Río Viejo, where it flows south to Lake Xolotlán (Managua) instead of the Atlantic coast.

Hurricane Mitch nearly sent the whole works downstream in 1998, when waters overtopping the "morning glory" spillway (the concrete structure that looks like a flying saucer on its head in the middle of the lake), flowed through the secondary spillway under the bridge, and down a long stair-step energy dissipater. The volume of water rushing through the channel quickly eroded it away along with all of its concrete, nearly destroying the dam itself and nearly causing a wall of water that would have raged for hundreds of kilometers downstream. The loss of the lake would have been economically catastrophic, affecting irrigation, fishing, and hydropower production, not to mention the loss of life and property downstream on the Río El Tuma. The government has been negotiating since 1999 to find a way to repair the spillway and return the dam's safety structures to normal, while the IMF and World Bank have been trying to privatize the whole system.

To get to the dam, take any bus headed toward Pantasma and get off at Asturias (60–90 minutes from Jinotega). The highway crosses the dam, so you'll know when you've arrived. The lake itself is picturesque, but equally impressive are the remains of the damaged spillway. On the lake side of the road are the remains of an old military base built in the 1980s to prevent Contra troops from destroying the dam. (The Planta Centroamérica is a highly sought Contra target in the 1980s and was similarly tightly guarded to prevent its destruction. Some land mines still litter the hills around the hydropower plant.)

You can fish here, for giant tilapia and guapote, or take a dip. There are several grassy areas at the lake's edge where you can jump in the surprisingly cold water of Apanás. From the dam, walk along the highway in either direction and choose your place. The lake is safe—there are no underwater structures or water intakes to be afraid of, and the water is quite deep and refreshing. Obviously, stay away from the spillover drain.

LAGO ASTURIAS AND THE EL DORADO DAM

The El Dorado dam was completed in 1984 and filled in in 1985 as a supplement to the Mancotal Dam. Water is captured in Asturias and pumped up to Apanás, where it flows through the turbines for energy production. Anglers in the know realize that Asturias is home to some monster freshwater fish. To get there from the Mancotal Dam, walk back toward the city of Jinotega about one kilometer to the first major intersection. That road descends quickly past a few coffee farms and small farming communities to the El Dorado Dam.

El Dorado also experienced severe damage during Hurricane Mitch. As you look at the lake, imagine that the same massive deluge that destroyed Mancotal's spillway also flowed through that placid little lake and out the other side—then appreciate how fortunate it is to have withstood the hurricane.

There's a little grassy hill on the upstream side of the dam where you can pitch a tent and do some fishing. If you'd like to try to hitch a ride with all your catch, occasional vehicles transit this road—mostly old IFAs and pickup trucks—bound for the communities east of El Dorado.

SAN RAFAEL DEL NORTE

This remote, cloud-shrouded town has a cool climate and is surrounded by green hills year-round. To know San Rafael is to know history. A visit to the **General Augusto César Sandino Museum** (right off the park) gives you a sample of the small town's pride at having served as the proving grounds for the general's legendary battles with the U.S. Marines in the 1930s. Sandino's wife was a San Rafaelina, and Nicaraguan folk musician Carlos Mejía Godoy wrote moving lyrics about love and war in Sandino's hills there.

There are some precious swimming holes around San Rafael, the easiest of which to access are in the two creeks that meet at **Los Encuentros** restaurant, a 10-minute walk on the road to Yalí. You can also hike into the gorge that runs on the north edge of town; descend from the Hospedaje Rolinmar, and then start upstream to where cold water rushes out of a narrow canyon.

La Iglesia de San Rafael del Norte is more impressive than you'd expect for such an out-of-the-way town; some call it the most beautiful church in all of Nicaragua. Pastel-colored windows admit a calming light in which to view the many bright murals, reliefs, and shrines. Many locals distinguish between Sandino the man and Sandinismo as practiced by Daniel Ortega. Look closely at the inside left wall of the church, where a painting of the devil implies that Daniel has betrayed the ideals of Sandino.

The church was a project of Italian priest Odorico d'Andrea who gave much more than that to this town. From his arrival in 1953 to his death in 1996, Father Odorico achieved virtual sainthood among the people of San Rafael and surrounding communities. His image, a smiling man in plain brown robes, can be seen in nearly every home, business, and vehicle in the town. Among his achievements are a health clinic, library, several neighborhoods for the poor, and the renovation of the church. Odorico's soul has multiplied posthumously; many believe he performed miracles and that his body has not decomposed. You can check for yourself at its resting place, called the **Tepeac,** on the hill overlooking the town. Ascending the stairs, you'll pass the 12 stations of the cross until you reach the shrine on top where the tomb lies—as well as gorgeous views. An impressive stand of old trees shades the hilltop. Virgin pine forests carpet the countryside.

There are great eats at **Doña Chepita's,** and there are two places to stay: **■ Hotel Casito San Payo** (2.5 blocks north of the park) is a cute family-run place that doubles as a local watering hole. A room will run you $10 and

BEN LINDER (1959-1987)

As the only reported incident in which a United States citizen was killed by Contra soldiers, Benjamin Linder's death had enormous repercussions, stemming primarily from the fact that he was shot with weaponry purchased by his own government, and by soldiers carrying out a hotly contested policy of violence supported by the same government. Linder's death was elevated to the status of martyrdom by those that shared his values. He was one individual in a huge wave of international supporters of the Sandinista revolution, leftists from Europe and North America who saw a chance to take part in the real-world political laboratory of Nicaragua. Some came to make a stand against the policies of the Reagan administration; some to physically help as development workers, teachers, and coffee pickers; and some came simply to experience the new world order at ground level.

Oregon native Ben Linder graduated from the University of Washington in 1983 with a degree in mechanical engineering, and because he believed in the ideals of the revolution, came to Nicaragua like thousands of other *internacionalistas* to help the revolution reach the poor. He moved to Nicaragua shortly after graduation, where he shared a small apartment in the capital and worked for the electric company. In his free time he would delight the Nicaraguan children by dressing up in a clown suit and rubber nose and pedalling around on a unicycle.

In mid-1985 Linder moved to Jinotega to help install a minihydroelectric plant in the town of El Cuá. This was an area overrun with raiding Contra, and the danger in the region was real. But rather than avoid the danger, his engineer's passion for solving problems led him farther into the bush, to San José de Bocay, to repeat the success he'd had at El Cuá. Bocay was even farther out of Sandinista control than El Cuá, and the Contra were everywhere. On April 28, 1987, Linder and a crew of Nicaraguans went into the field to build a small concrete weir that would measure the flow in a stream Linder thought would be a good site for a hydroelectric plant. His crew crossed paths with a squadron of Contra that

had been stalking Sandinista supporters. He, and several others with him, were assassinated at point blank range by a bullet to the temple.

The political repercussions were enormous and the Sandinistas, the Contras, and the U.S. government all angrily accused each other. Though the Contras claimed that Linder had been dressed in combat uniform, was carrying a weapon, and that Linder's team had fired the first shots, the evidence did not support it. That an American had been killed in Nicaragua, with a bullet also paid for by the American people, resonated deeply.

Linder was buried in a small, neat grave in the Matagalpa cemetery. Today, his legend and inspiration live on; if you wander through the peaceful community of San José de Bocay, you'll notice the town has been electrified, courtesy of the Benjamin Linder Mini-Hydroelectric Power Plant, constructed after his death. The Benjamin Linder School is down the road, and one of Bocay's more newly settled neighborhoods was christened Barrio Benjamin Linder.

In the early 1990s, when the Sandinistas handed power over to Doña Violeta's administration and it became obvious the great socialist revolution of the 1980s was not to be, most of the international crowd packed up and returned home, but what Ben Linder set out to do – bring progress and hope to the people whose lives are the most difficult – is an ideal that did not die with the revolution.

Today, the Asociación de Trabajadores de Desarrollo Rural Benjamin Linder (The Benjamin Linder Association of Development Workers) continues to do what Linder was doing the day he was killed: build small-scale hydroelectric plants to promote rural development. The association is located 25 meters south of the Hotel Bermúdez in Matagalpa (tel. 505/2612-2030) and is managed by Linder's coworker Rebecca Leaf. To learn more about Ben, visit the Quaker House in Managua, the Ben Linder Café in León, or read the book *The Death of Ben Linder: The Story of a North American in Sandinista Nicaragua* by Joan Kruckewitt (Seven Stories Press, 2001).

MATAGALPA

you can get meals here as well. **Comedor y Hospedaje Aura** (on the main street east of church) is a typical Nicaraguan *hospedaje* catering more to the traveling *campesino* than foreign traveler.

Near San Rafael del Norte is the ecotourism project **Finca el Jaguar** (tel. 505/2279-9219, www.jaguarreserve.org), a 105-hectare stretch of land, of which 60 percent is cloud forest. The *finca* was established to monitor over-wintering survival of migratory birds, and now offers a variety of lodging options. They require reservations at least 10 days in advance—a unique way to get under the forest canopy.

Buses pass through San Rafael del Norte regularly on the route between Jinotega and San Sebastián de Yalí/La Rica. There is also one express bus to Managua that leaves at 4:30 A.M., passes through Jinotega at 5:30 A.M., and continues south through Matagalpa to Managua. The same bus leaves Managua at 3 P.M. and retraces the route to San Rafael del Norte, arriving sometime after 7 P.M.

EL CUÁ, SAN JOSÉ DE BOCAY, AND AYAPAL

Two-and-a-half hours outside of Matagalpa, El Cuá is best known for Benjamin Linder, the only known American casualty of the Contra war. El Cuá and San José de Bocay are illuminated by minihydroelectric power plants he helped design and implement. Both towns were completely enveloped in conflict during the 1980s, overrun first by Contras and then by the FSLN. Today it's a logical place from which to hike, or just visit, the Peñas Blancas.

Of El Cuá's three *hospedajes,* travelers prefer **Hotel Chepita** (tel. 505/2784-5158 or 505/8437-1531, reservaciones@hotelchepita.com, www.hotelchepita.com), run by an affable, anglophone Nicaraguan woman by the name of Josefa. She has 16 rooms at $8 single, $16 double, with fan, TV, and Internet access.

There's one *hospedaje* in Bocay, a few small eateries, and a gas station.

Ayapal is a small community on the banks of the Río Bocay. From here, you can hire boats to take you downstream to several Miskito communities (not cheap), or visit the surprisingly expansive **Cuevas de Tunowaiam,** a sandstone cave structure north of San José de Bocay. Guides are available through Hotel Chepita in El Cuá.

WIWILÍ

The upstream capital of the Río Coco region lies snug near the Honduran border and a long, bumpy, five-hour slog north of Jinotega. Wiwilí is a mestizo town, meaning it's of Spanish, not indigenous origin. Waspám, 550 kilometers downstream, is the other anchor at river's end, and is mostly indigenous.

Wiwilí is split by the Río Coco which runs through the middle of town. Several hundred inhabitants of Wiwilí lost their lives to the river during Hurricane Mitch, and political fallout outlasted the storm. Post-Mitch, the two sides of the community went their own separate ways to find international aid, and subsequently decided to become independent. While they retained the same name, Wiwilí on the north side of the river is now part of the department of Madriz, while Wiwilí on the south bank remains part of Jinotega. Both are important port towns with access to the deep waters of the Río Coco.

Local coffee cooperative members can lead individuals or groups on community-led tours to nearby Kilambé National Park and other surrounding treasures. This is some truly wild country and we've only heard of a couple of souls who have attempted the epic six-day trip downstream to Waspám, braving crocodiles, bandits, and drug smugglers; there are reportedly guides that will take you on rafts, camping along the river, and hanging out with wandering, dugout canoe–paddling fishermen, known as *nomados* by locals.

There are a few decent *comedores* and two accommodations in Wiwilí: **Hotel Central** charges $3 for a bed with shared bath, or $19 double with private bath. **El Hotelito** has standard singles with shared bath for less than $4.

boat traffic on the Río Bocay

WAMBLÁN

Wamblán saw some ferocious battles during the 1980s. The last part of the drive to Wamblán is notable for a stunning descent into the city along a mountain ridge. If your trip happens to coincide with the end of the day, the long mountain shadows falling into the ridges will ensure you never forget the moment you entered Wamblán. Those pleasant memories will hopefully outlast your memory of the town's one unpleasant *hospedaje*.

CHONTALES AND THE NICARAGUAN CATTLE COUNTRY

East of Lake Cocibolca lie hundreds of thousands of hectares of rolling hillside in a broad ecological transition zone where undulated, scrubby pastureland gradually unfolds into the pine savannas and wetlands of the Caribbean coast. Less populated than the Pacific region, Chontales and Boaco residents are easily outnumbered by their cattle, and in reality it's the cattle that make this area famous; Chontales ranches produce more than 60 percent of Nicaragua's dairy products, including dozens of varieties of cheese and millions of gallons of milk.

This entire regions is firmly off the beaten path, so expect to be the only tourist for miles in most of the towns and sights in this chapter. Overall, Boaco is less well-to-do and less enticing than relatively upscale Juigalpa, which dwarfs it in every sense. Boaco makes a reasonable base for treks or drives into the hills between Boaco and Matagalpa Departments. Juigalpa is a much bigger and much more important urban center that remains an overgrown cowboy village. Here you'll rub shoulders with cowboys and *campesinos* sporting their cleanest boots on their twice-a-month trip to the city to pick up supplies, strike a few deals, and do their errands.

Juigalpa's patron saint celebrations in mid-August are among the best in Nicaragua and draw a crowd from as far away as Managua to enjoy the elaborate bull-riding competitions, horsemanship contests, and traditional dances, all under the magnificent backdrop of the Amerrisque mountain range. These mountains remain little explored, and the continual

HIGHLIGHTS

◖ **San José de los Remates and Esquipulas:** These backwoods cowboy towns offer a great opportunity to hike, ride horses, see petroglyphs, and cool your heels in a waterfall (page 277).

◖ **Santa Lucía:** The most charming and picturesque of Boaco's mountain villages, Santa Lucía is rich with gorgeous mountains, river valleys, and opportunities to hike (page 279).

◖ **Museo Arqueológico Gregorio Aguilar Barea:** This warehouse of statuary is filled with treasures the Chontales carved long before Columbus (page 281).

◖ **Juigalpa *Fiestas Patronales*:** Juigalpa throws a cowboy party unsurpassed in the nation. Join Juigalpans for rodeo, mechanical bull-riding contests, and down-on-the-farm good times (page 283).

◖ **Punta Mayales Nature Reserve:** This isolated peninsula jutting into Lake Cocibolca is a fine example of rural tourism (page 285).

LOOK FOR ◖ TO FIND RECOMMENDED SIGHTS, ACTIVITIES, DINING, AND LODGING.

discovery of ancient Chontal statues and sculpture imply the grandeur of the mysteries this area still retains.

PLANNING YOUR TIME

Many travelers treat this whole region as an uninteresting and unavoidable expanse to be traveled through as quickly as possible en route to Nicaragua's Atlantic coast, but the flavor of Chontales and Boaco play no small part in the flavor of Nicaragua as a whole—from the cowboys, to the wide open sky, to the pre-Columbian relics and the small-town lifestyle. Travelers who tire of the Granada hype and the overwhelming presence of other foreigners will be amply rewarded with a trip to Chontales.

How much time you'll need in this region depends on your inclination for adventure and ability to forgo some creature comforts.

You could easily spend a day and a night in one of many quiet agrarian towns like Boaco, Camoapa, and Cuapa. The attraction is simply a bucolic, rural lifestyle. Most towns in the area have some sort of basic accommodation and small local sites of historical, cultural, or geologic interest. Add an additional day if the bouldering and hiking opportunities at Cuisaltepe or Cuapa whet your appetite, and another day on horseback in San José de los Remates (you can even continue on the high road to Matagalpa).

HISTORY

The lands now known as Boaco and Chontales were first settled by the Chontal people (not their own name for themselves—the word is Nahuatl for the "mountain people," implying "savages" or "foreigners"). Less is known

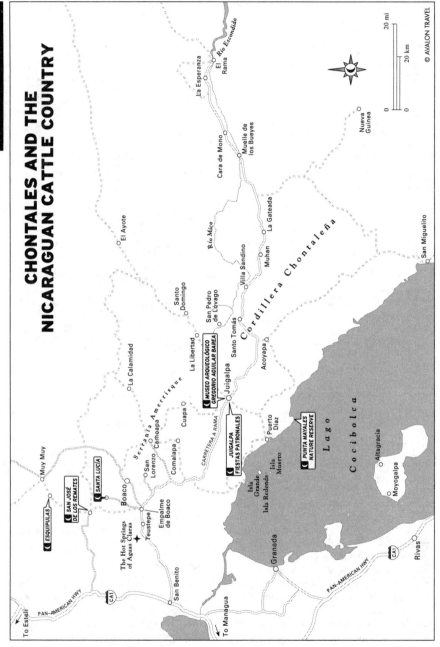

CHONTALES AND THE NICARAGUAN CATTLE COUNTRY

© AVALON TRAVEL

about them than the Nahuatl, but we know the Chontals were responsible for much of the statuary and stone monuments unearthed over the past decades in the Amerrisque mountain range north of the highway.

The first Spanish settlements of El Corregimiento de Chontales suffered often at the hands of aggressive Miskitos and Zambos (and the British who armed them to do so), whose frequent attacks devastated 7 out of 12 Spanish settlements. In 1749, Camoapa, Boaco (today Boaco Viejo), and Juigalpa were attacked; the towns were nearly destroyed and the churches burned to the ground. Boaco's then-governor, Alonso Fernández de Heredia, returned the aggression, leading an excursion that returned with more than a hundred Miskito prisoners. The settlers reestablished their communities eight kilometers to the south. Nothing remains of Boaco Viejo today. From 1750 to 1760, these same indigenous groups attacked Juigalpa, Camoapa, Lóvago, Lovigüisca, Yasica, Guabale, Santa Rosa, and nine other communities. In 1762, Boaco was reestablished by Father Cáceres, who was killed shortly thereafter by yet another Miskito

attack. In 1782, the church in Juigalpa was—you guessed it—burned to the ground.

As the threat of attack diminished, the lands east of Lake Cocibolca were developed into extensive cattle ranches. Coffee was introduced around the Boaco area, but before long its production had been pushed up into the better lands in northern Boaco and southern Matagalpa. Cattle quickly became the economic mainstay, followed by the extraction of gold from the mines at La Libertad and Santo Domingo.

The social and economic reorganization of the Sandinista years earned the unbridled antipathy of the people of Chontales and Boaco, who were generally frontier-minded people uninterested in government regulation. As their lands were confiscated and reorganized, they naturally had more sympathy for the Contra forces, whom they clandestinely supported throughout much of the 1980s. Much of the violence of the 1980s occurred in the towns that border both sides of the highway and inland. Since the 1990s, both departments have voted against the Sandinista party with overwhelming margins.

Boaco

Nestled snugly in a 379-meter-high notch in the Amerrisque mountains, Boaco is a departmental capital, an agriculture center whose soil struggles to support both cattle and corn, and a commercial center beset with poverty. Modern Boaco (the city's name is a combination of Aztec and Sumu words that mean "land of the sorcerers") is the third city to bear the name: In the 18th and 19th century, two previous Boacos were built and destroyed in the same place. In 1749, an expedition of Zumos, Miskitos, and Zambos armed with English rifles sacked the original Boaco, killed the priest, took several females hostage, and burned the town to the ground. The settlers started over along the edge of the Río Malacatoya in what's now the town of Boaquito, and in 1763, due to a brutal outbreak of cholera and the difficulties

the land presented for agriculture, moved to the present site of Boaco. By the 19th century, Boaco was a cow town, though residents raised several crops, including *cabuya,* for making rope, to sell in the markets of Masaya, a four-day mule-drawn wagon trip.

The modern city of Boaco began on a hilltop and crept down the hillside into a valley, earning the nickname The City of Two Floors. During the Contra war, Boaco was spared from direct battles, but in the hillsides that surrounded the city, Contras and Sandinistas fought skirmishes in Muy Muy, San José de los Remates, and San Francisco. The violence dislodged countless *campesinos,* all of whom eventually found their way to the city of Boaco seeking refuge. Many decided to stay, and Boaco has swelled over the past

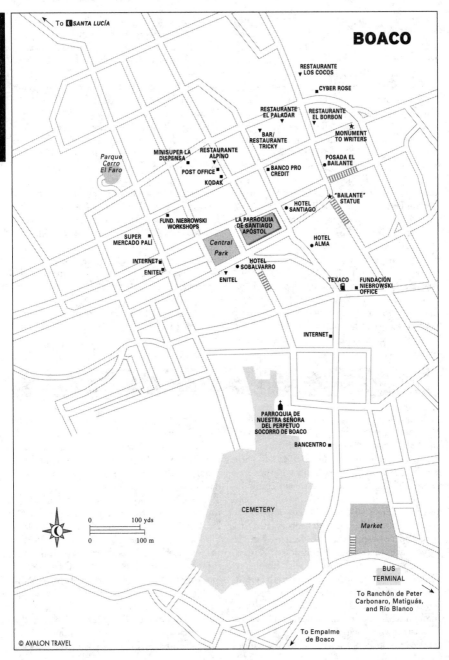

BOACO

To SANTA LUCÍA

RESTAURANTE LOS COCOS

CYBER ROSE

RESTAURANTE EL PALADAR

RESTAURANTE EL BORBON

BAR/ RESTAURANTE TRICKY

MONUMENT TO WRITERS

MINISUPER LA DISPENSA

RESTAURANTE ALPINO

Parque Cerro El Faro

POST OFFICE

BANCO PRO CREDIT

POSADA EL BAILANTE

KODAK

"BAILANTE" STATUE

FUND. NIEBROWSKI WORKSHOPS

HOTEL SANTIAGO

LA PARROQUIA DE SANTIAGO APÓSTOL

SUPER MERCADO PALÍ

Central Park

HOTEL ALMA

INTERNET

HOTEL SOBALVARRO

ENITEL

ENITEL

TEXACO

FUNDACIÓN NIEBROWSKI OFFICE

INTERNET

PARROQUIA DE NUESTRA SEÑORA DEL PERPETUO SOCORRO DE BOACO

BANCENTRO

CEMETERY

Market

0   100 yds

0   100 m

BUS TERMINAL

To Ranchón de Peter Carbonaro, Matiguás, and Río Blanco

To Empalme de Boaco

© AVALON TRAVEL

© ROMAN YAVICH

Boaco is a city of two levels and a lot of stairs.

20 years, faster than it can provide for its new inhabitants, most of whom occupy neighborhoods of small concrete homes around the outskirts of the city.

Boaco was an inspiration to several notable Nicaraguan authors and scholars, four of whom—Diego Sequeira, Antonio Barquero, Hernan Robleto, and Julian N. Guerrero—won the Nicaraguan Rubén Darío prize for literature. A monument in their honor, just east and north of the park, overlooks the city from a sort of balcony.

Boaco's best mayor was a man of the cloth, Father Niebrowski of Poland, who arrived in 1916. While preaching to an underserved community, Niebrowski took it upon himself to better their lot in life and used his determination and practical know-how to bring Boaco into the modern world. Niebrowski built a cinema, a brick factory whose bricks he used to rebuild the church, and a small hydropower plant on the Río Fonseca, which provided electric light to the city for the first time. Niebrowski also established the first hospital,

the first community music band, and countless other things that contributed to Boaco's social welfare. To this day, the Niebrowski Foundation is active in the city and provides for small programs in the Boaco area, while the church, factory, and hydropower plant have all faded into memory.

SIGHTS

Boaco's patron saint is Santiago Apóstol, and the *fiestas patronales* in his honor are particularly interesting and historic. The festival lasts the entire month of July, during which time the saint's statue is paraded daily from one neighborhood to the next. The crux of the ceremony is July 23–25 when the procession is accompanied by dancers whose performance tells an elaborate tale of the expulsion of the Moors from Spain.

A statue located one block east of the church represents a dancer, complete with snake stick in one hand and brass knuckles in the other. Boaco's churches neatly serve the residents of Boaco's two levels without their having to traipse up and down the hill. In the lower half, the **Parroquia de Nuestra Señora del Perpetuo Socorro de Boaco** is an elaborate nontraditional church whose architecture is nearly Greek orthodox. A statue of the Virgin Mary keeps watch over the earth from its starched white rooftop. Inside, statues of Jesus and the Virgin Mary line up side by side with the carved stone statuary of Boaco's Chontal and Sumu ancestors, an intriguing compromise between the religions of new and old.

The freshly painted **Parroquia de Santiago Apóstol,** located at the top of the hill, has been a Boaco landmark since the mid-1800s. Mass is held every day, plus several on the weekends, when the ringing of the church bells fills the town square and scatters the pigeons.

Boaco's highest point is **Cerro El Faro,** the lighthouse without a sea. A concrete pedestal and tower, the Faro offers a good view of the city and the valley of the Río Mayales. Technically, the tower is open all week, but the caretaker closes it when he pleases. Underneath is the town convention center and

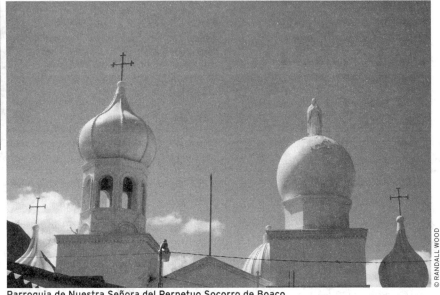

© RANDALL WOOD

Parroquia de Nuestra Señora del Perpetuo Socorro de Boaco

a popular gymnasium. Evenings, the Faro is one of Boaco's more popular places to steal a few kisses.

ENTERTAINMENT AND NIGHTLIFE

Boaco's sole disco is **El Ranchón de Peter Carbonaro,** a kilometer or two out of town along the highway to Muy Muy. Its relaxing atmosphere is perfect for a drink and some traditional Latin music: salsa, *cumbia,* and merengue are popular—and the occasional Mexican *ranchera* cowboy song. By 10 P.M., the dance floor is packed, especially when there's live music. Take a taxi for $1. There are many bars in town offering cheap beer and a relaxed atmosphere until about 11 P.M.

ACCOMMODATIONS

Many of the hotels and *pensiónes* near the bus terminal and along the main road of Boaco's lower level do a brisk trade in prostitution and romantic getaways for young couples and should be avoided. Because of Boaco's constant

water problems, ask about reserves and be prepared to grin and bear it with a manual (i.e., bucket) shower if need be. At the south edge of the park, 【 **Hotel Sobalvarro** (tel. 505/2542-2515, $10–25) has been lodging travelers and passers-through since before the revolution and still retains the faded charm of yesteryear. It has a few rooms with air-conditioning in a once grandiose building of wooden rooms set around a courtyard with a balcony overlooking the lower half of town.

Another good budget option is **Posada San Francisco** (tel. 505/2544-2018, $12) offering clean private rooms with air-conditioning. Near the stoplight, just where the steep road turns nearly vertical, **Hotel Alma** (tel. 505/2542-2620, $8–20) has clean rooms with either private or shared bathroom, plus a good view.

Posada El Bailante (tel. 505/2542-2380, info@posadaelbailante.com, www.posadaelbailante.com, $20–25) is another easy recommendation. It's down the block from the dancer's statue, and offers cable TV, Wi-Fi, and air-conditioning in all 22 rooms. At **Hotel**

Santiago (tel. 505/2542-4915, hotelsantiago@ aol.com, $11–26) English-speaking Carlos David offers eight rooms in an old building with a homey atmosphere. Ask about visiting his nearby cheese and coffee farms and horseback riding.

FOOD

Pastries and snacks are for sale in the park, they go well with a shake from Hotel Sobalvarro—where you can also grab a sandwich or burger, all served on the best front porch in the city. Several restaurants on the top floor of Boaco

EMPALME DE BOACO'S FIELD OF DREAMS

In 1990, a North American traveler named Jake Scheideman fell ill during an ambitious bicycle tour of Central America and was taken in by a family at Empalme de Boaco. They befriended this complete stranger and helped him until he was healthy and ready to continue his travels. In 1998, after Hurricane Mitch, Scheideman returned to Nicaragua after many years of having been away, wanting to do something for the community that had taken care of him when he was ill. He asked what they would like, and all they wanted was a place to play baseball.

The ballpark, constructed in Empalme de Boaco (the intersection of the road to Boaco) took more than two years to complete but is now the best of its kind east of Lake Cocibolca; games are Saturday and Sunday afternoons in season.

The project has expanded past baseball fields, building 65 homes, a high school, and a community center, and they're still going, pushing for higher education and economic development in the area. They are always looking for volunteer Spanish-speaking teachers and computer experts. Contact Jake and friends to participate, donate, or learn more through the website of his bike shop in Northern California: www.sthelenacyclery.com or www.casanica.net.

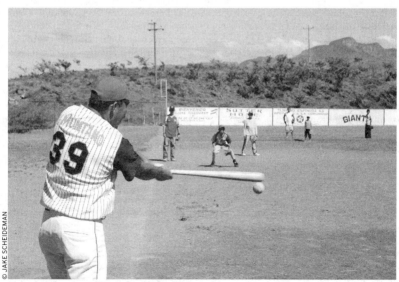

© JAKE SCHEIDEMAN

Dreams became reality in Empalme de Boaco.

serve traditional Nicaraguan dishes, burgers, sandwiches, and similar, of which, the least expensive is **Restaurante Maraíta,** also a popular drinking hole.

American-owned **The Pizza Place** (75 meters west of BanPro, tel. 505/8885-6636, open 3 P.M.–10 P.M. Tues.–Thurs., noon–10 P.M. Fri.–Sun.) has burgers, pasta, and a "big meat pizza" with ham, pepperoni, bacon, and hamburger. A little pricier than the others but still reasonable, **Restaurante Alpino** hits the spot with great beef *churrasco* ($8) and seafood. Locals and foreign NGO workers like **Restaurante Borbon,** which is known for its *pollo al vino* and pork chops, among other classics, for around $3–5 a dish, plus huge glasses of *fresco* (juice) served on a breezy balcony overlooking the hills. **Restaurante Los Cocos** (a block farther north on the same street) is cheaper but equally tasty and has a nice back patio lined with trees and plants.

SERVICES

There are two banks in Boaco. In the lower part, Banpro is located on the main street. In the upper part, ProCredit is a block north of the back side of the church. Western Union is near the market, open 8 A.M.–4:30 P.M. Monday–Saturday. One of the better Internet joints is Cyber Rose (near the writer's monument), which has six computers and a nice smoke-break balcony. The post office is 1.5 blocks north of the church on the left side. There's a pay phone out front (open 8 A.M.–5 P.M. Mon.–Fri., until noon Sat.). ENITEL is located across from the cathedral's northeast corner (open 8 A.M.–9 P.M. Mon.–Fri.).

GETTING THERE AND AWAY

Buses to Boaco leave every 30 minutes or so from the Mayoreo terminal in Managua. From Boaco, the most comfortable way to travel to Managua is by microbus. Two leave each day from the terminal, at 6:30 A.M. and 12:30 P.M. ($2). Regular buses leave every 30 minutes for Managua until 5:40 P.M.

Five buses leave each day for Santa Lucía, 10:30 A.M.–5 P.M. (one hour). Buses bound for Río Blanco (three hours) and Muy Muy leave 5:50 A.M.–5 P.M. For traveler masochists, the 12-hour Boaco–Siuna kidney-bruiser will take you over some of the worst dirt roads in the nation.

NEAR BOACO
The Hot Springs of Aguas Claras

Locals say the *aguas termales* at Aguas Claras are heated by an underground volcano, probably not too far from the truth, given Nicaragua's seismicity. In 2000, an entrepreneur channeled the geothermally-heated waters into pipes and a series of conrete pools protected by palm-thatch roofs. The resulting **Aguas Claras Hot Springs and Hotel** and resort complex (tel. 505/8856-7306) has six pools available to the public and another two reserved for hotel guests. All pools are clean and professionally maintained. The water isn't boiling hot, but it's extraordinarily warm, and is therefore more enjoyable at night. While you lounge in the pool, you can order from an extensive menu of traditional Nicaraguan food and drink. The hotel features 17 private rooms with air-conditioning for $23–46. Just coming in for the day costs about $1; credit cards are accepted for hotel and restaurant expenses, but not the entrance fee.

During Semana Santa and weekends in the dry season, the hotel can fill quickly, so make reservations. The *aguas termales* are located seven kilometers west of Empalme de Boaco and are tough to reach by public transportation.

Hike to La Cebadilla

Around the turn of the 20th century, a farmer from the mountain town of Cebadilla was surprised to see the Virgin Mary appear before him amongst the rocks where he was tending his cattle. The site has been treasured by the locals ever since.

La Cebadilla is no easier to get to than it ever was, and if you're interested in a hike through an out-of-the-way corner, try walking up the mountain to La Cebadilla. At one

© RANDALL WOOD

leisure time in Chontales

time a small chapel was erected in honor of the Virgin, and there was a small well where it was said the water was blessed. Today, the chapel has mostly fallen to bits.

The day hike starts 1.6 kilometers east of Empalme de Boaco, where on the south side of the highway there's a dirt road leading south to the community of Asedades and a steel sign with a picture of the Virgin Mary and the words La Cebadilla. The road leads south one kilometer to Asedades, a poor community of adobe houses, flower gardens, and rocky fields. It's imperative that you find a guide in Asedades to take you up the mountain to La Cebadilla. There are many small footpaths that lead up the hill, but they intertwine and none is more obvious than the others. The walk up the hill will take you between three and four hours—take water and food and make sure you have something to share with your guide. The walk back to Asedades can take 2–3 hours. Your guide will recommend that you stay at the top of the hill through midday and do your walking in the cool of the afternoon.

At La Cebadilla, you may or may not have visions of the Virgin Mary, but you will certainly have a fantastic view of the valley below and the hills of Boaco to the east, sometimes all the way to Lake Nicaragua.

☾ San José de los Remates and Esquipulas

These picturesque cowboy towns can be the backdrop to your guided horse tours and hikes to local waterfalls. Catch a ride to **Cerro Cumaica Natural Reserve** from either town. The weather here is usually a perfect 20°C (70°F) with a slight breeze almost year-round. Consider visiting both of these towns on the back road to Matagalpa. The bus trip is bumpy but the views are grand. One of the main attractions is the "original black Jesus." In fact, thousands of national and international pilgrims descend each year on Esquipulas during the *fiestas patronales* (January 14–15) to catch a glimpse of their saint icon, **El Señor de Esquipulas,** housed in one of the best kept churches in Nicaragua. Locals believe that only due to the power of their patron saint was the town spared from all the wars that over the centuries had engulfed the surrounding hills.

In **San José de los Remates,** Jorge Isaac

HIKES IN THE BOACO AREA

HIKING MOMBACHO

In the early 1900s, Nicaraguans from Granada transferred their homes and possessions to Camoapa to try growing coffee on the area's hillsides. They chose the slopes of one mountain in particular because of its rich soils and named the peak Mombacho, in memory of their Granada homeland. Camoapa's Mombacho is a forested mountain with a rocky protuberance jutting out of the top. It is lined with several coffee plantations and a handful of radio towers and makes a pleasant day hike from Camoapa. Long ago, Mombacho was the site of a moonshine distillery, the products of which were sold under the name Mombachito.

Hiking the hill is significantly easier than hiking Cuisaltepe and offers a beautiful view of Camoapa's open ranges. From Camoapa, the road to Mombacho can be accessed by the Salida de Sangre de Cristo (Sangre de Cristo is the name of a church found along the first part of that road). From ENITEL in the center of Camoapa, walk six blocks west, crossing over a small bridge and arriving at the public school. Turn right at the school and head north until you see the Iglesia de Sangre de Cristo. Continue on that road until you reach Mombacho. The hike from town takes 3-4 hours. There's a dirt road that leads up Mombacho from Camoapa to the radio towers. In Nahuatl, *mombacho* means "steep," so be prepared.

HIKING PEÑA LA JARQUÍNA

At the entrance to Camoapa on the southeast side of the highway (to your right as you head toward Camoapa) is a broad, rocky cliff face at whose base is a hardwood forest. This is Peña la Jarquína, named after a prominent local family. It's an easy 90-minute hike from the entrance to Camoapa, around the back side of the hill to the top. Skilled climbers might find it makes a suitable technical ascent; the rock is solid and has plenty of cracks – and is almost assuredly unclimbed.

HIKING CUISALTEPE

Unless you breezed by it on the midnight bus to El Rama, Cuisaltepe inevitably caught your eye: a massive, rocky promontory that juts out of the hillside between San Lorenzo and the entrance to Camoapa. Approaching it from the west, its silhouette resembles the tip of an upturned thumb, pointing in the direction of the highway. In Nahuatl, Cuisaltepe means "place of the grinding stone"; it was a good source of the volcanic rock the indigenous peoples used for making long, round stone implements with which to grind corn into dough. Cuisaltepe was the home of the last cacique of the region, Taisigüe.

Hiking Cuisaltepe is no casual endeavor. More than 300 meters high, much of the south side of the rock is a series of vertical crevasses and overhangs and much of the rest of it is prohibitively steep. However, there is one summit approach – from the north side of the rock – which you can reach from Camoapa. Hike with caution. The climb takes around six hours round-trip, but adjust that estimate according to your own hiking ability. You should

(tel. 505/2542-2359) will help you find accommodations in the 10-room town hostel (hot water) or with a local family. Also look for Doña Rosinda (from ENITEL, half a block east), who is involved in the San José tourism committee and can help you get horses, guides, or maps. The view from Cruz del Milenio is worth the walk: On a clear evening, you can see the lights of Granada and Cerro Negro in León.

Nearby **Esquipulas,** in Matagalpa department, is similar, but has its own charm, waterfall, and friendly tourism committee representative: Doña Berena (tel. 505/8426-8238 or tel. 505/2772-9262, berenatellez@gmail.com). She can arrange visits to Salto de Limon in the nearby Cumaica Nature Reserve, petroglyph walks, and all-inclusive tourism packages with rural, cultural, and historic elements in and near Esquipulas. Ask about Cerro El Padre (a giant granite rock on top of a large hill) and the *miradores* (viewing points) that some of the locals

© RANDALL WOOD

Cuisaltepe's imposing rock face

have good shoes, as much of the route is loose, slippery gravel.

Your point of entrance is the road to Camoapa. Any bus traveling between Managua or Boaco and the east will take you there, leaving you at Empalme de Camoapa (also called San Francisco) along the highway. A better option is to take a direct bus to Camoapa, 10 of which leave per day from Managua (five on Sundays). From the highway, the road that leads to Camoapa climbs 25 kilometers. Get off the bus before you reach Camoapa at Km 99, where a small turnoff to the west leads to the community of Barrio Cebollín with a little red bus stop at the entrance. Access to the summit is neither obvious nor easy, and involves climbing partway up, crossing the small forest in a notch in the hillside, then climbing the ridge to the summit. You can find guides in Barrio Cebollín in the first house on the left after you pass the school (the house nearest the utility pole). Euclídes and brothers know the mountain well and climb it periodically.

are putting up in their backyards. Don't ask about the *cususa*, corn mash moonshine as clear as water and as strong as gasoline. The area is famous for it.

For food, try **El Quelite** or **El Campero,** both on the main street. **El Hotelito** (near the park, tel. 505/2772-9132, $11) has seven cozy rooms.

Four buses leave Teustepe daily and a direct bus from Managua's Mayoreo terminal leaves daily at 12:30 P.M. ($2).

Santa Lucía

The town of Santa Lucía was created in 1904 by decree of President José Santos Zelaya in an effort to concentrate the dispersed and poorly administered farming communities of the hillsides north of Boaco. Its well-planned and organized beginning boded well for Santa Lucía which, a century later, remains a picturesque and enchanting mountain village in a valley ringed by green mountains.

Santa Lucía itself doesn't have hotel rooms or

fancy restaurants but travelers sometimes come for the scenery around Cerro Santo Domingo, the long rocky precipice of Peña La Brada, and **Las Máscaras** petroglyphs in the valley of the Río Fonseca. For hikes in the Santa Lucía area, Osmin is the right gentleman to accompany you. He can be found in the ENITEL office, where he works—he's a fun tour guide.

Nearby **Salto de los Americas** is a seven-meter waterfall with a deep pool, located a short walk up the river off the road to Boaco. There are several families of monkeys that live in the area. **Peña La Brada** is a cliff edge outside town, with an amazing panoramic view of Boaco and beyond.

There are no official accommodations in Santa Lucía, but the **Comedor Santa Lucía** will put you up and feed you in a pinch. More good food can be found in the *comedor* in the park, which specializes in grilled meat. A direct bus leaves from Managua for Santa Lucía at 10:30 A.M. ($1.50), bypassing Boaco entirely. The same bus leaves Santa Lucía for Managua early in the morning.

Camoapa

A cow town of 13,000 set in the mountains east of Boaco, Camoapa got its name from a Nahuatl phrase that can be translated as either "place of the parrots, place of the dark rocks," or "place of the yams." (How's that for precision?) Once an indigenous community ruled by the cacique Taisiwa, it was later absorbed by the Spanish settlers and incorporated under the name San Francisco de Camoapán.

Today, besides its renowned dairy production, Camoapa is best known to Nicaraguans for its production of woven straw hats. In the 1960s, a school for promoting the art of weaving was formed, and the art passed through several generations; there are still several hundred weavers in Camoapa. The hats they are known best for are created from intricately and tightly woven strips of fibrous white *pita* and are sold all over Nicaragua's craft markets.

Camoapa's economy is largely dependent on

three dairy cooperatives, whose employees like to have a good time on the weekends when they return from their farms and ranches outside of town to party and relax. Camoapa's *fiestas patronales* begin on October 2 in honor of San Francisco de Asís, with bull riding, cattle contests, and the like. Camoapans boast that they have the toughest bulls and best horses around. Other weekends, the disco at **Atenas** is the place to be, unless you're a true cowboy, in which case the party is at **La Asociación** (Asogacam) out by the ballfield: beer, mariachi music, and the occasional brawl (what did you expect?).

Stay at 🄲 **Hotel Las Estrellas** (seven blocks east of the church's north side, tel. 505/849-2240, $10–13), a former auto-hotel turned honest, which offers the best value rooms in this price range. Smaller but closer to town along the main road, **Hotel Taisiwa** has 11 rooms for $5 with private bath. In addition to **Atenas** solid meals are found at **Camfel** (one block west of the church's north side), a clean place run by seven women; and **Bosquecito** (just down the road that leads to Comalapa), a restaurant filled with potted plants and flowers.

Buses from Managua to Camoapa depart Mayoreo Monday–Saturday, starting at 4:30 A.M. and running through 4:10 P.M. The Sunday schedule provides fewer buses. Buses to Managua depart from the shady side of the church (whichever side that is as the day progresses), Monday–Saturday beginning at 6:25 A.M. and running through 5 P.M. There is a minibus that shuttles between the Empalme del Camoapa (San Francisco) and Camoapa, but it's irregular. A ride between the two points will cost you $0.50.

Comalapa

In 1752, Friar Morel de Santa Cruz visited Comalapa and said, "This is a town of Indians located in a land that's stony, mountainous, and fenced in by hills. Its church is of straw, reduced and indecent, lacking a vestry, but possessing an altar . . . 100 families and 484 persons both Indian and Ladino." Comalapa is largely the same 250 years later, though the church is now a quaint stone structure. Access to Comalapa is through Camoapa, 20 kilometers down the road. There is one bus per day, leaving Camoapa at 6:30 A.M. The same bus leaves Comalapa at 4 P.M. At other times of the day, hitch a ride with pickups traveling between the communities, or try hiking a piece of the road.

Juigalpa

The last big settlement on the road southeast to El Rama (or south to San Carlos and the Río San Juan), Juigalpa is a prosperous city of some 70,000 cattle ranchers and farmers. Juigalpa bears the traces of its indigenous roots in elaborate statuary and other archaeological pieces still being discovered in the mountains east of town. Juigalpa in Aztec means "great city" or "spawning grounds of the black snails." Its first inhabitants were likely the Chontal, displaced from the Rivas area by the stronger Nicaraos. They resisted the Spanish occupation fiercely in the 16th century, rising up no fewer than 14 times to attack the installations of the colonial government.

Upon Nicaragua's independence, the land that comprised Chontales and Boaco was controlled by Granada. In 1858, the Department of Chontales was formed. In the 18th and 19th centuries, travelers bound for the gold mines of Santo Domingo and La Libertad crossed Lake Cocibolca, landed in Puerto Díaz, and spent a night in Juigalpa before proceeding.

SIGHTS AND ATTRACTIONS
◖ Museo Arqueológico Gregorio Aguilar Barea
Juigalpa's most interesting attraction is the Museo Arqueológico Gregorio Aguilar Barea, an airplane hangar–like building housing a collection of more than a hundred examples of pre-Columbian statuary uncovered in the folds of the Amerrisque mountain range. Ranging 1–7 meters tall, the pieces are reminiscent of totem poles, elaborately carved in high- and low-relief, with representations of zoomorphic figures and humans (the latter often clutching

knives or axes in their hands, or presenting their arms folded across their chests). The statues, thought to be 1,000 years old, were the work of the Chontal people, driven to the east side of Lake Cocibolca by the more powerful Nicaraos some 1,500 years ago.

Unlike the Nahuatl and Nicarao, relatively little is known about the Chontal culture and its statues, more of which are continually being discovered in the Amerrisque range. The museum was built in 1952 by the well-loved former mayor of Juigalpa, Gregorio Aguilar Barea. It also exhibits Nicaraguan coins from across two centuries, gold figurines, original paintings by the museum's namesake, and several historical paintings and photographs. The museum is open 8 A.M.–noon and 2–4 P.M. Monday–Friday, and only in the morning on Saturday; closed Sunday. The entrance fee is less than a dollar. The building has an open front, so even if the gate to the museum is locked, all the statues can be seen from the street.

Parque Palo Solo
The view from the park at the north end of town, Parque Palo Solo, is elevated above the surrounding streets, giving the impression of looking over the bulwark of a fortress. The fortress feeling isn't entirely accidental: Juigalpa was built at the top of the hill to offer it some means of defense from the Miskito and Zambo peoples who once raided it from those same mountains 200 years ago. The park was built by Mayor Aguilar Barea in the 1960s and named after the one tall tree that dominated its center. The tree has since been replaced by a fountain adorned with images of the mainstays

CHONTALES

JUIGALPA

To Amerrisque

To Managua

Río Mayales

PETRONIC

RESTAURANTE LA CAZUELITA

PUNTA MAYALES OFFICE

INTERNET

SHELL

CAFETÍN

MUSEO ARQUEOLÓGICO GREGORIO AGUILAR BAREA

PARQUE PALO SOLO

ENITEL

INTUR

HOTEL CASA COUNTRY

BURGER HOT

PALI

HOTEL EL BOSQUE

RESTAURANTE BELLA VISTA

ESSO

BANCENTRO

7/24 CASA DE QUESO

BUS TERMINAL

POST OFFICE

HOTEL EL NUEVO MILENIO/ HOTEL EL REGRESO

HOTEL/SPA LAS MIRADAS

KODAK

CHURCH

TEXACO

PANADERÍA ALLISON

FARMACIA LA SALUD

Park

CENTRO DE SALUD

LAB LAFAYETTE & SALAZAR

BANPRO

SÚPER SAN ANTONIO

BDF

LA EMBAJADA

PIZZA ITALIANA

CEMETERY

ESKIMO

Old Market

ZOOLÓGICO THOMAS BELT

To Puerto Díaz

HOSPITAL

LA QUINTA

Río Mayales

To El Rama

New Market

RESTAURANTE EL TONGA

BASEBALL STADIUM

0   200 yds
0   200 m

© AVALON TRAVEL

of the Chontales economy: corn and cattle. A restaurant at the edge of the park serves fancy lunches and dinners.

Juigalpa's other park, in the center of town, is an orderly and clean place, whose statue of a boy shining shoes was made by a former mayor who spent his early years earning money as a shoe-shine boy; the statue bears the inscription: "Hard work dignifies a man."

◖ Juigalpa *Fiestas Patronales*

Juigalpa's *fiestas patronales,* August 11–18, attract visitors from the entire nation and even Honduras and Costa Rica. Much of the festivities take place on the north side of town in the Plaza de Toros, but you'll find parties, bull riding, rodeos, and horseback games all over the place at all times. In one of these, called the *carrera de cinta,* mounted riders gallop underneath a wire from which is suspended a small ring. If a rider successfully puts a pencil through the ring at full gallop, he can present it—and a kiss—to the woman of his choice among the contestants vying to be queen of the festival. The woman who receives the most rings is crowned the queen.

ENTERTAINMENT AND NIGHTLIFE

The best disco in town is **La Quinta** (out on the highway, Saturday night only). Second best is **Caracoles Negras** (a half-block south of the Petronic station along the highway, formerly Hotters), which picks up the slack on Sunday night and appeals to the cowboy crowd more than La Quinta.

Toward the center of town, **Casa Bravo Club** is an upscale pool hall behind tinted glass and in the comfort of an air-conditioned hall. Near the park, **7/24** is brash and nonstop, with a giant projector screen, and a menu based on local cheeses for snacking. The baseball field is located by the river at the south end of town in Barrio Paimuca; games are on Sundays.

ACCOMMODATIONS

Many of Juigalpa's cheapest *hospedajes* are intended to be occupied one hour at a time;

travelers should avoid these, as well as two otherwise obvious places to the west of the park, Hospedaje Angelita and Hospedaje Central.

Rather, stay to the east (rear) side of the church. **Hotel El Regreso** (the one-story establishment, tel. 505/2512-2068, $5 pp shared bath) has 18 clean rooms, and a friendly owner. The room closest to the street is a bit noisy. Immediately next door, **Hotel El Nuevo Milenio** (tel. 505/2512-0646, $10 shared bath, $13 private) has 22 not-so-clean rooms, but also a pleasant balcony overlooking the street.

◖ **Hotel Casa Country** (Parque Palo Solo at the north end of town, tel. 505/2512-2546, $20) has nine very nice rooms on the second story of a gorgeous colonial-style house, all with private bath, air-conditioning, and TV.

Hotel La Quinta (tel. 505/2512-2574, hotellaquinta@hotmail.com, $15–20) farther east along the highway, almost directly across from the hospital, has 38 rooms, some with air-conditioning; great place to crash if you are raging at the on-site disco, which is only open on Saturdays.

The fanciest place in town, with the best view bar none, is ◖ **Las Miradas Hotel & Spa** (next to 7/24 restaurant, tel. 505/2512-4525, hotellasmiradas@hotmail.com, $50 includes breakfast). You'll find the most stunning view in the city, luxury accommodations (hot water, a/c, Wi-Fi), a hair salon, massage studio, private barbecue lounge, small gym, and a glass-wall sauna with that same five-star view. Las Miradas only has four rooms, so make reservations. Ask Doña Edelmira about the *guardabarrancos* that nest in the hotel wall.

FOOD

Juigalpa has a variety of food—often at reasonable prices—naturally, with massive quantities of beef and dairy on the menu. Case in point: **La Embajada** (difficult to find, but everyone knows it, just ask around). The only thing on the menu at this hole in the wall is meat, ordered by the pound (about $4). The "Meat Lady" has a secret marinade recipe she learned from her grandmother and is currently passing down to her granddaughter. It's served with salty *cuajada* cheese and tortillas. Native Chontaleño Daniel Ortega has been known to make an appearance here, and it is also frequented by the bigwigs of Chontales.

La Cazuelita (three blocks east and two north from the Esso) sells a remarkable barbecue-chicken sandwich (less than $3 with fries). This newly remodeled, air-conditioned restaurant is popular with Peace Corps volunteers and well-off Juigalpans for its excellent Nicaraguan food, all of which you can sample via a *surtido* ($11, serves 2–3).

Right across from the cathedral is **7/24 Casa de Queso,** offering cheeseburgers, Nica-Chinese cuisine, and a good assortment of cheese. There are a few more places in and near the park, and for good, fresh bread and pastries, stop by **Panadería Allison** (open 5 A.M.–7 P.M. daily). They have a refrigerator full of cold milk to wash it all down.

On the highway in front of the Esso station, **Restaurante Tacho** has great chicken and steak at moderate prices ($3–5) in a pleasant atmosphere. Roving bands of mariachis frequent the place, which has a mostly male crowd. Across the street, and next door to the Esso, is **Bella Vista,** serving up a large choice of meat ($5–7) with a dance floor open till 2 A.M. on the weekends. For more upscale dining, try **Restaurante La Tonga,** with plates from $5 and up, and, of course, Juigalpa's favorite, **La Quinta,** with a juicy *churrasco.*

SERVICES

For Internet, check behind the Texaco station or just walk around town. There is an ATM located off of the central park outside the Banpro. The post office is located down the street from the church, and ENITEL (open 8 A.M.–noon and 1:30–5:30 P.M. Mon.–Sat.) is four blocks north of the park. The INTUR tourist office, located a block east of the museum, can provide you with brochures and recommendations on where to stay and what to do.

One of the better pharmacies in town is Farmacia La Salud (at the northwest corner of the park, tel. 505/2512-0932). **Hospital La Asunción** (on the southeast side of town along the highway) doesn't have very good

Chontales is filled with small villages and sacred Catholic shrines.

facilities. A better option for travelers is the **Lab Lafayette & Salazar** (two blocks west of the park, tel. 505/2512-2292), a private clinic and doctor's office. There is a Centro de Salud across the street from the church, which is open 8 A.M.–9 P.M. Monday–Friday and 8 A.M.–1 P.M. Saturday–Sunday.

The old movie theater is now a Palí grocery store; Supermercado San Antonio has a better selection and is locally owned.

GETTING THERE AND AWAY

Microbuses to Managua depart from the north or east side of the church at 6 A.M. and 1:40 P.M. (2.5 hours). The larger buses depart Juigalpa from the cramped bus terminal in the market, which at the time of publication was being rebuilt. Ask around to be sure from where your bus departs. Buses leave hourly for El Rama, 4:30 A.M.–1:30 P.M. and every half hour to Managua, 4 A.M.–5 P.M. You'll also find daily service to Nueva Guinea until 3:20 P.M., to Boaco (via Camoapa and Comalapa), and other local destinations.

NEAR JUIGALPA
Puerto Díaz

It's a short but uncomfortable ride from Juigalpa down to the village of Puerto Díaz, a sleepy lakeside town of fishing families that pretty much live off what they catch. Puerto Díaz doesn't have any facilities for travelers but is worth a day trip on a lazy Saturday to see how the "far" side of the lake (i.e., the world across the lake from Granada) lives. Buses leave from Juigalpa three times a day at 5 A.M., 2 P.M., and 5 P.M. From the bus terminal, they cross the highway at the Esso station before working their way slowly down to the shoreline.

◖ Punta Mayales Nature Reserve

Located an hour from Juigalpa, Punta Mayales is home to 250 species of birds including owls and hawks; mammals like porcupines, anteaters, sloths, and monkeys; and an incredible assortment of flora with a backdrop of Lake Cocibolca and the Isla de Ometepe and

Zapatera volcanoes. There are three cabins of various sizes and tents for camping, plus five trails, ranging 1–3 kilometers, and each offering a unique view of the peninsula.

Stop in the Juigalpa office (near ENITEL, tel. 505/2512-2322, arbagar@yahoo.com) to arrange a day trip or an overnight stay. Camping is $12 with breakfast; cabins cost $50 per person a night, which includes three meals, guided walks, and an aquatic tour down the Mayales River and out into the lake. If you'd just like to visit for the day, entrance is $2, a land tour is $6 with the option to take horses, and the river tour is $5. Snake shows and caiman-watching trips are easily arranged.

Balneario El Salto

Somewhat neglected and a bit dirty these days, Juigalpa's favorite swimming hole is located an easy two kilometers out of town on the highway to Managua. Look for the big blue sign on the northeast side of the highway; the falls are located a scant 100 meters from the highway. El Salto is formed by a concrete dam that causes water to pool up in a natural reservoir. In the dry season, there's no waterfall at all, though the swimming hole remains quite deep. In the rainy season, the water from the Río Mayales tumbles first over the concrete dam and then through a gorge of enormous boulders carved into fantastic shapes by the flowing water.

The near shore gets littered with the remains of old picnics after major holidays (like Semana Santa, when the place is packed), but the far shore is tree lined and grassy. Consider swimming across to the far side and watching the local kids turn somersaults off the wooden-plank diving boards. There is supposedly a $1 fee to get in, but the locals have skirted the fee for so long by entering downstream and walking up the streambed that, with the exception of Semana Santa, no one seems to try to charge any more.

Cuapa and the Monolith of Cuapa

Tiny, isolated Cuapa, once just another anonymous farming town in the foothills of the Amerrisque mountain range, gained an awful

© RANDALL WOOD

Balneario El Salto

sort of notoriety during the 1980s, when it came to represent the worst of what the Contra war had become. In 1985, Contras attacked and took control of Cuapa, holding it for several hours. They captured the Sandinista mayor Hollman Martínez but later released him when the townspeople pled for his life. Twelve other Sandinista activists, sent from the capital to work in Cuapa, weren't so fortunate: The Contras marched them out of town and executed them at the roadside. When the Sandinista military got wind that Contras occupied the town, they dispatched a truckload of 40 soldiers to defend the town. Contras ambushed the vehicle along the road to Cuapa, killing nearly all of them. A small roadside monument bearing the Sandinista flag commemorates both the civil servants and the soldiers killed during the war.

Cuapa is famous among devout Catholics. In late 1980 and early 1981, the Virgin Mary appeared several times—bathed in radiant light and dressed in pure white—to local farmer Bernardo Martínez. She told Martínez she had a message for the world and for Nicaragua: "Don't preach the kingdom of God unless you are building it on earth. The world is threatened by great danger." She later asked for prayers for unbelievers and for peace on earth. Devout Catholics were overjoyed at the appearance of the Virgin, but even that moment became rapidly politicized in the toxic climate of the 1980s. Some claimed her message was a coded recrimination of the Sandinista government, and the Sandinistas responded by clamping down on all press coverage of miracles not previously accepted by the Vatican. An elaborate and well-maintained statue and sign greet you at the entrance to Cuapa with Bienvenido a la Tierra de María (Welcome to Mary's Land). Believers from all over eastern Nicaragua flock to Cuapa on May 8, the anniversary of the day the Virgin first appeared. (Read a fascinating fictionalized account of the events surrounding the apparition in Silvio Sirias's novel, *Bernardo and the Virgin*.)

Whether you've come to see the shrine to Mary or to climb the impressive, needlelike

HIKES NEAR JUIGALPA

EL MONOLITO DE CUAPA

The Cuapa Monolith is a 75-meter-high chunk of granite that projects like a giant needle out of a field, as though it dropped from the sky and pierced the ground; it's first visible on the bus ride to Cuapa.

Climbing El Monolito isn't easy, but it isn't impossible either. It's a hike, not a technical rock climb. The locals in Cuapa know all the trails that lead there, and any young *campesino* will be glad to show you the way to the top to see the cross. From the town of Cuapa, it's a 2.5-hour hike to the top, including several extremely steep sections. Hike with good shoes; locals recommend not climbing it on particularly windy days. Ask around for Nicolas, an English-speaking resident of Cuapa (originally from Bluefields), who can be a guide. He runs a tire repair shop next to Parque Zapera.

SERRANÍA AMERRISQUE

A powerful backdrop to Juigalpa, the Amerrisque mountain range forms a rocky backbone to the history of the city. Most of the archaeological pieces in the Juigalpa museum were unearthed in the Amerrisques, and countless other sites have yet to be explored. Although the area is undeveloped for tourists, the rocky peaks make a tempting hike and the locals claim the east side of the range contains several caves.

Your starting point is the road called the Camino de la Vaticana, built by Rome and Holland in the late 1990s. It will lead you nine kilometers east toward the range and the tiny farming community of Piedra Grande. From there, you can strike into the hills to explore. You can try hitching a ride out there to trim down the flat, boring part of the hike, but it won't be easy, as traffic along the road is sparse at best. There are few communities along its length. Consider hiring a pickup truck in town; a group of five travelers offering $15–20 might be able to convince someone to drive them out there. Try to swing a deal for the ride back while you're at it.

Daniel Molina can serve as a guide (tel. 505/2512-2940). He is a young man who speaks English and can arrange a trip out to the mountains, where he'll help you find a local guide to show you the trails.

monolith outside of town, Cuapa isn't a bad place to spend the night. One option for the climb is to arrive in the evening, spend the night at Cuapa, and set off to climb the monolith the following morning. You can find accommodations and meals at **Restaurante Hospedaje La Maravilla,** with rooms in the $1–3 range. The hotel fills up the week of June 19–27, when Cuapa celebrates its patron saint, San José.

Six buses leave Juigalpa for Cuapa every day, starting at 6 A.M. and the last departing at 6 P.M. Buses from Cuapa to Juigalpa leave from the town center every day, 6 A.M.–4:30 P.M.

Thermal Vents at Agua Caliente

While eastern Nicaragua lacks the volcanoes of the Pacific horizon, it too was formed volcanically and the hot springs are evidence that under the surface, even quiet old Chontales is bubbling and tectonically active. When they're hot they're hot, but when they're not, a trip out to the hot springs at Agua Caliente yields nothing more than a trickle of water seeping out of the side of the creek bed. When they're active, however, expect torrents of bubbles gushing out of the creek bed in water too hot to touch.

To get there, take the Camino de la Vaticana as though you were going to the Amerrisque mountains, but take the first major left-hand turn instead; Agua Caliente is 4.8 kilometers down the road. You'll know you've reached the site when you get to a relatively new school building followed immediately by a streambed. The hot springs are located about 100 meters upstream from where the road crosses the stream.

La Libertad and Santo Domingo

These two pueblos have been the site of small-scale gold mining for well over a hundred years. British mining engineer Thomas Belt was surveying in the Santo Domingo area when he wrote his book, *A Naturalist in Nicaragua*, in 1874. The mines were run by a Canadian organization that ceased activities around 2000. The curious may be interested in poking around either town, both of which, though run-down and slightly decrepit, still very distinctly bear the traces of a small boomtown atmosphere. La Libertad is the birthplace of president Daniel Ortega as well as Nicaragua's outspoken and politicized Catholic archbishop Miguel Obando y Bravo.

Nueva Guinea

This region is nearly as off the beaten path as you can get in Nicaragua. Technically, the town of Nueva Guinea is part of the RAAS (Southern Atlantic Autonomous Region), but it is more easily accessed from the Rama Highway and Juigalpa than Bluefields and the Río Escondido. A full 293 kilometers southeast of Managua, Nueva Guinea lies in the tropical, humid, rolling lowlands that stretch toward the Caribbean. It's one of the rainiest corners of Nicaragua, receiving an average of 8,000 millimeters (yes, that's eight meters) of rainfall each year, but that varies from town to town, based on the forest cover of the area. In terms of population, it is the second largest municipality in Nicaragua, with a de facto population of 120,000 people, many of whom technically live in the municipality of Bluefields but whose transport and public services are provided via Nueva Guinea.

In the 1960s, Nueva Guinea was a rich, dense, tropical rainforest with a wide variety of animal life, but since then, due to poor public policy, misguided development projects, and inadequate agricultural practices, much of the territory has been transformed into barren, useless pasture. Forested areas include the land that borders the Reserva Indio-Maíz and the Reserva Natural Punta Gorda. Even that land is in the process of being slowly and illegally colonized and exploited, and poor farmers in desperate need of land overwhelm the capacity of the Nicaraguan government to prevent their homesteading.

Nueva Guinea was founded as part of U.S. President John F. Kennedy's Alliance for Progress, a program meant to defuse demands for land reform across Latin America in the wake of the Cuban revolution and the postcolonial struggles in the rest of the world. Original settlers were given one *manzana* of land (about one hectare) in the urban center, and 60 in the countryside. The same program was applied to help victims of natural disasters—victims of both the Managua earthquake of 1972 and the eruption of Cerro Negro near León in 1973 were shipped out to Nueva Guinea. In the 1980s, the area was a hot spot of Contra activity under the command of Edén Pastora's group, ARDE, based across the Costa Rica border.

These days, farmers in the area of Nueva Guinea live in some 140 neighborhoods and produce an uninspiring variety of the same thing everyone else does—corn, beans, and rice—plus ginger. Nueva Guinea is a wild place, with horses parked outside of bars and people walking their pigs or herding cattle down main street. The town of Nueva Guinea has few facilities, but the curious traveler may appreciate visiting a place so out of the way.

SIGHTS AND ATTRACTIONS

For the extreme wilderness adventurer, Nueva Guinea is also your base for exploration of two of Nicaragua's most pristine nature reserves—**Punta Gorda** and **Indio-Maíz**. Retrace the steps of colonial Spanish captains, Calero and

Machuca, who sought the best route to the Caribbean coast through the communities of Puerto Prinicipe, Atlanta, and others, concluding in the coastal community of Punta Gorda. Arrange for a guide at the mayor's office. Less demanding is the one-hour hike to the falls at **Salto Esperanza:** Take the bus to the community of Esperanza and ask around.

At **Finca La Esperanzita,** you can glimpse an organic agriculture project where small farmers are growing cacao, vanilla, pepper, and several species of tropical hardwoods. They'll gladly provide you with a tour of the facilities, including a coffee-, cacao-, and cinnamon-processing plant run by World Relief one block south and one block east of the hospital.

ACCOMMODATIONS AND FOOD

There are three options in Nueva Guinea. **Hotel Nueva Guinea** (on the main drag, tel. 505/2575-0090, hng2007@gmail.com,

$10–25) has a variety of rooms, some with air-conditioning, cable TV, and bath. Newer, quiet **Hotel Miraflores** (300 meters south of URACCAN, tel. 505/2575-0039, $10) has good mattresses. Backpackers tend to settle for **Las 24 Horas Hospedaje** (municipal market 1.5 blocks north, across from the police station, $2.50 pp).

Llamas del Bosque (next to the Esso station) serves the best meal in town for about $5. Sit poolside at **Ranchón Kristofer** (three blocks north of the park) or join the crowd on the dance floor. **Comedoría Dalili** (across from the mayor's office) is the least expensive *comedor* in town; less than $1 for a meal.

GETTING THERE AND AWAY

Buses leave for Nueva Guinea from Managua's Mayoreo terminal approximately every hour for the six-hour trip on an entirely paved road. In your own vehicle, it takes as little as three hours.

SOLENTINAME AND THE RÍO SAN JUAN

The Río San Juan carries the waters of Lake Cocibolca to the Caribbean through a lush landscape of extensive nature reserves and broad cattle ranches. Five hundred years ago, the Spanish, intent on piercing the Central American isthmus, focused their efforts on the Río San Juan, which nearly connects the two sides of Central America, save a thin strip of land. In 1524, Hernán Cortés wrote King Carlos I of Spain, "He who possesses the Río San Juan could be considered the owner of the World." The strategic and economic importance of this region has not diminished since.

The principal settlement in the area, San Carlos, is transforming from edgy port town to quaint destination and you'll inevitably pass through it on the way to various adventures.

The town is thick with itinerants, rowdies, farmers, fishers, swindlers, and you. Offshore, the Solentiname Archipelago is a quiet group of islets as pertinent to the revolution years as to Nicaragua's prehistoric past, and a center of production for some of the country's most gorgeous paintings.

Or, take a wooden boat down the river towards the Atlantic, a sun-baked ride back through time. El Castillo, one of Spain's most permanent colonial legacies, remains little changed from the 17th century and the days of marauding pirates. From there, downstream fishing village follows pasture follows rapids until you reach San Juan de Nicaragua, the little town where it all began and where it all ends, remote and untamed.

It's not easy to get to the Río San Juan, and

© DAVID WEBSTER SMITH

HIGHLIGHTS

** La Isla Elvis Chavarría:** One of the Solentiname archipelago's jewels, La Elvis features a museum, a hiking trail, an arboretum, and a wonderful host community of farmers, fishers, and artists (page 304).

** Los Guatuzos Wildlife Refuge and Centro Ecológico:** This is one of the best places in the south to get down and dirty with nature; start by identifying a few of the 389 species of tropical birds (page 306).

** Sábalos Lodge:** Bamboo, thatch, lazy afternoons, and the burbling river – this lodge

is close to the jungle and far away from everything else (page 311).

** El Castillo:** The mighty embattlements of this historic mud-river fortress have watched over the river since the days pirates prowled the Spanish mainland (page 311).

** San Juan de Nicaragua:** Remote and thick with history, San Juan de Nicaragua is an adventure in itself; the local blue lagoon swimming hole is dramatic and an easy dugout-canoe ride away (page 314).

Isla de Zapatera

Isla de Ometepe

El Almendra

Palos Ralos

0   20 mi

0   20 km

Rivas

San Juan del Sur

La Isla Elvis Chavarría

San Carlos

Sábalos Lodge

Caribbean Sea

COSTA RICA

El Castillo

Los Guatuzos Wildlife Refuge and Centro Ecológico

San Juan de Nicaragua

Río San Juan

LOOK FOR TO FIND RECOMMENDED SIGHTS, ACTIVITIES, DINING, AND LODGING.

tougher still to get around, but everyone agrees that things are rapidly changing for the better, due in large part to a $14 million tourism development plan called La Ruta del Agua, the effects of which you'll see as soon as you step onto the refurbished dock or recently paved airstrip at San Carlos. This region isn't part of the casual traveler's itinerary, but if you can invest a little more time than usual, the dramatic landscapes and remoteness of this region will impress you, and the tourism potential here is enormous.

PLANNING YOUR TIME

It's wise to allow a full week for exploration of this region. Make your plane reservation from Managua to San Carlos early, as seats fill up fast. In general, expect about 25 percent higher costs for most goods in this isolated region (35 percent more on Solentiname). Make use of your time in San Carlos to find updated boat schedules, make contact with downstream river lodges, and stock up on snacks and supplies. Public transportation is both slow and capricious, but inexpensive. You are better off hiring

SOLENTINAME AND THE RÍO SAN JUAN

© AVALON TRAVEL

a boat and driver or making arrangements with a tour company, which will affect your budget by an order of magnitude (organizing a group of like-minded travelers to share costs is one way to offset the price).

You could make it to Solentiname and back in two days if the stars align, but boat schedules will make it more likely three or four. It's only a day more to see El Castillo, which you should not miss. Don't head farther downstream than El Castillo with fewer than four days including flights to and from the region.

HISTORY
Colonial Times to Independence
The mouth of the Río San Juan, choked with labyrinthine estuaries, had eluded explorers for years, including Christopher Columbus, who failed to find it in 1502. The Spanish founded Granada in 1524. In 1539 Spanish explorers finally reached the Atlantic by sailing downstream from Granada. This made Granada Spain's first quasi-Atlantic port in Central America. To consolidate their hold on the river, the Spaniards began persecuting the indigenous people living along its banks and on the Solentiname Islands.

In 1567, the first Spanish trade expedition set sail from Granada: three ships laden with agricultural products for Panamá. They made it as far as the Caribbean, where English pirates plundered the vessels and fed the surviving sailors to the sharks. Tension and conflict between European nations over the next 300 years led to a virtual state of war between Spain's colonial holdings in Nicaragua and English, Dutch, and French pirates whose respective governments encouraged them to give the Spanish hell. Until the Spanish improved their fortifications along the Río San Juan, the pirates were disastrously successful at sacking and burning Granada, which suffered repeatedly. By 1724, however, a dozen fortresses guarded the river and the pirates' pillaging came to an end.

Throughout the 19th century, the Río San Juan grew in importance for commerce and for its value as a shortcut through the isthmus

for foreigners traveling between New York and California, the most famous of whom was Mark Twain who passed in 1866 on Cornelius Vanderbilt's steamship route. After dreams of a cross-isthmus canal petered out and Vanderbilt's steamship business came to a halt, the river slipped back into bucolic obscurity for a century.

The Contra War
As a sensitive border area during the 1980s, the Río San Juan was a southern front for Contra forces, particularly for the Alianza Revolucionaria Democrática (ARDE), under the leadership of Edén Pastora, a.k.a. Comandante Cero, who fought on the southern front years after the CIA stopped supporting him. Troops from both sides planted fields of antipersonnel mines, and entire communities evacuated the war zone, fleeing south to Costa Rica or west to other points in Nicaragua. The population of the region dropped to fewer than 40,000, then nearly doubled in the 1990s as people returned with new families, stressing already environmentally sensitive land.

The Río San Juan Today
In spite of relentless "El Río San Juan is ours!" chest thumping up in Managua, the Nicaraguan government has traditionally ignored the people of this region, spurring tens of thousands of Nicaraguans emigrate to Costa Rica, legally and illegally, in search of work and better living conditions. For those Nicaraguans living along the river, most television and radio stations come from Costa Rica, as do some schools and health services. Many towns—especially San Juan del Norte—use the Costa Rican *colón* instead of the *córdoba*. Increased government attention has begun to improve the area, helped in part by wealthy Managua legislators purchasing land along the river for their own use and development. But the greater force has been private development of tarpon fishing lodges, eco-resorts, and similar, providing needed jobs and economic stimulus in a region otherwise limited to cattle raising.

SOLENTINAME

CANAL DREAMS PAST AND PRESENT

After realizing the coveted natural water passage across America was nonexistent, geographers discovered that the lowest point along the entire north-south American divide – from Alaska to Tierra del Fuego – is found in Nicaragua. The fact that it is possible to go no higher than 40 meters above sea level in crossing from the Pacific to the Atlantic Ocean has maintained a fierce interest in the building of an interocean canal there since the early 1500s.

U.S. Army engineer Colonel Orville Childs carried out the first systematic study of the canal route in 1852, at the invitation of U.S. millionaire Cornelius Vanderbilt, who, three years earlier, had set up a transisthmus transit route across Nicaragua to carry gold prospectors between California and New York.

The original Childs proposal, designed to move sailing ships from ocean to ocean, was followed by another half-dozen U.S. Army and Navy surveys over the next 100 years, with the greatest interest occurring at the turn of the century. At this time, Panamá and Nicaragua were vying for the construction of a U.S.-controlled Pacific-Atlantic canal. After intense lobbying by promoters of both projects, the U.S. Congress finally opted to buy out the bankrupt French company that had already started building the Panama Canal.

The 1914 Bryan-Chamorro treaty, signed by the U.S. and Nicaragua in the year the Panama Canal opened, gave the United States exclusive rights – in perpetuity – to build a canal through Nicaragua. Two further U.S. Army studies for a Nicaraguan canal were commissioned by Congress during the 20th century, one in 1929-1931 for a deep-draft canal similar to that in Panamá, and another in 1939-1940 to build a shallow-draft barge canal. However, despite wartime fears of damage being caused to the Panama Canal, the U.S. Congress never saw sufficient economic merit in either variant to approve construction funds.

The Bryan-Chamorro treaty was abrogated in 1970, at around the same time as containerized cargo traffic began to grow exponentially in international maritime trade. These facts, together with the signing of the Carter-Torrijos treaty in 1979, which would hand over the Panama Canal to Panamá at the end of 1999, spurred renewed interest in the Nicaraguan canal.

During the Sandinista period, a proposal was made by a Japanese consortium to construct a canal that would accommodate ships

San Carlos

Surrounded on three sides by a watery horizon, San Carlos's sky is frequently pierced by bright rainbows sparked by afternoon showers. San Carlos, a town of about 10,000 people founded in 1527, is one of the oldest towns on the continent, and has served as a raucous and spirited way station for many travelers over the centuries. San Carleños are a lively bunch. Many were born elsewhere in the country and ended up here on their way to somewhere else—field hands on their way to Costa Rican harvests, border soldiers on leave from remote posts, and lake and river merchants trading with Chontales cattlemen.

All foreign travelers in the Río San Juan region are obliged to pass through San Carlos, the departmental, economic, and transport hub of the region. The city has cleaned up its act and greatly improved in the last few years, with a new waterfront park, new bus station, improved airstrip, and an increasing number of services (the region's first ATM was installed in 2009). In the words of one reader: "It's a bustling, cheerful place, and in spite of the odd rough spot, it may be the cleanest city four times the size of the largest that can squeeze through the locks at Panamá. The Sandinistas were busy fighting the Contra war, with their economy in tatters, and the proposal never prospered.

In the 1990s, two "dry canal" projects surfaced (CINN and SIT-Global), with proposals to build high-speed, transisthmus railways connecting ports on both oceans, which would transport containers on specialized railcars between ships berthed at either terminal of the railway. The routes are being proposed as a potential alternative to the Panama Canal and the U.S. transcontinental rail system, both of which are becoming increasingly congested for the east-west container trade between Asia and the East Coast of the United States. The construction cost has been estimated at $1–2 billion.

In 1999, Nicaragua's National Assembly approved a 30-year concession to a private company named EcoCanal for the construction of an inland waterway to permit the navigation of shallow-draft barge traffic along the Río San Juan from Lake Cocibolca to the Caribbean. Although not an interocean project as such, the $50-million waterway could be converted to one with the excavation of the 18-kilometer stretch of land between the Pacific Ocean and Lake Cocibolca – at an additional cost of some $300-400 million.

Politicians from the two leading parties, the Liberals and Sandinistas, have also revived variants of the 1980s Japanese proposal for building a huge, post-Panama canal, with a price tag in excess of $20 billion.

Until now, recent proposals have been paralyzed by a lack of venture capital to finance full feasibility studies, necessary to convert them into bankable projects for construction. Until such studies are completed, doubts will persist over their economic and environmental viability. Nonetheless, despite potential backing from U.S. investors, the Nicaraguan government has been unwilling to lend its wholehearted support to the project, and instead continues to talk of an interocean rail and pipeline project, possibly financed by Venezuela. This, together with President Ortega's rhetoric about "U.S. imperialism," has made EcoCanal investors nervous and unwilling to commit.

Contributed by Tim Coone, a journalist who has lived and worked in Nicaragua since the Revolution years.

---

in Nicaragua." Indeed, there are garbage cans on every corner, street sweepers, and newly painted homes, giving San Carlos a whole new look and feel.

ORIENTATION AND GETTING AROUND

The main center of San Carlos is only about a dozen city blocks, all south of the central park on the flank of a hill looking south over the water. The waterfront can be a little confusing, especially if you find yourself in one of the narrow market aisles, but all in all, there's not much actual "town" in which to get lost. Main Street runs along the waterfront, from which the city sprawls northward along the muddy highway to the hospital and airport. If you are landing at the airstrip, grab one of the rickety four-wheel drive taxis to take you the couple of kilometers into San Carlos—the five-minute ride costs less than $1. The bus station is more or less in the town center, across from the gas station and docks. Arriving by boat dumps you right in the middle of the *malecón*.

SIGHTS AND ENTERTAINMENT

The old **Spanish fort,** agressively restored in recent years, enjoys a nice view overlooking the town and lake. Its cultural center and library were founded with Cuban support—to wit, countless volumes of communist propaganda—and has since been supported by the Netherlands. At the *mirador,* you'll find old

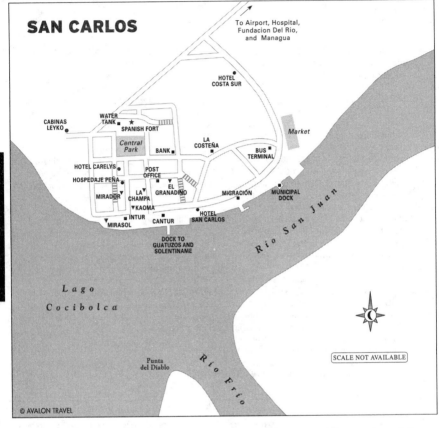

SAN CARLOS

To Airport, Hospital,
Fundacion Del Rio,
and Managua

HOTEL
COSTA SUR

CABINAS
LEYKO

WATER
TANK

★ SPANISH FORT

Central
Park

LA
COSTEÑA

Market

BANK

BUS
TERMINAL

HOTEL CARELYS

POST
OFFICE

HOSPEDAJE PEÑA

EL
GRANADIÑO

MIGRACIÓN

MUNICIPAL
DOCK

MIRADOR

LA
CHAMPA

KAOMA

INTUR

CANTUR

HOTEL
SAN CARLOS

MIRASOL

Río San Juan

DOCK TO
GUATUZOS AND
SOLENTINAME

Lago
Cocibolca

Punta
del Diablo

Río Frío

SCALE NOT AVAILABLE

© AVALON TRAVEL

cannons, a romantic sunset setting, and one of the nicest restaurants in town.

For nightlife, locals make their way to **La Champa,** a bar so popular, its name has become a verb among locals (as in, "Let's go *champear!*"). **El Bocano** is newer and located just north of the water tower. Bars line most streets throughout town, with the rowdiest ones down by the waterfront; try the **Granadino** or the **Kaoma** for a mellower vibe. The annual **sportfishing competition** in September is a big deal for Nicaraguan anglers and attracts crowds from across the nation for prizes like outboard motors and more. Enjoy the *fiestas patronales* on November 4. Most radio stations in the area are Costa Rican and feature Spanglish reggae and *soca.*

ACCOMMODATIONS

San Carlos's half-dozen greasy *hospedajes* on the main drag charge as little as $3 per person, but you get what you pay for. If you're short on cash, or just into slumming, try **Hospedaje Peña** (a block back from the water, tel. 505/2583-0298, $4 pp) a cheap but relatively secure dump with 10 rooms and streetside balcony.

A better bet is to walk 200 meters north of the bus station to **Hotel Costa Sur** (tel. 505/2583-0224, orlando104@hotmail.com, $7–12); rooms are clean and far quieter than

© DAVID WEBSTER SMITH

San Carlos has been investing in its tourism industry, including a new waterfront, or *malecón*.

the budget options in town. The owners can arrange day trips to Solentiname and other sites; they are part of a local tour guide effort and can recommend unique tours throughout the area.

Hotel Carelys (a half-block south of the park, tel. 505/2583-0389, $15) is also known as Aquiles or Doña Coco. Its 14 rooms are the cleanest and most pleasant in the city and include private bath, fan, and complimentary drinking water, and old magazines in Spanish. Another popular choice is the **Cabinas Leyko** (two blocks west of the church, tel. 505/2583-0354, leyko@ibw.com.ni, $18–40). Its 22 somewhat damp and dark rooms start with a simple double with fan, but they have some higher-end alternatives with air-conditioning and cable TV as well—have a close look at the room first.

FOOD

The row of *comedores* alongside the bus station offers the best cheap meals in town ($2 for a big plate). Otherwise, **El Granadino** serves chicken plates from $4, fish from $5. Its food is the

best in town though slow to get to your table. Down the block, popular **Kaoma** has a similar menu but better service with prices starting at $7; it's open late on weekends. **The Mirador,** aptly named for the landmark on which it sits, has good food and pleasant lake views from the outside seating area. Try the jalapeño steak and imagine shooting cannonballs at pirates. Just below the cannons in the same area is the less impressive **Mirasol,** with similar fare.

Look for a new restaurant, art gallery, and souvenir shop called **El Güegüense** (tel. 505/8460-3504), quickly becoming an inexpensive gathering spot for both locals and tourists, also offering lots of local information.

INFORMATION AND SERVICES

INTUR (near the park, tel. 505/2583-0301, riosanjuan@intur.gob.ni) may be able to help you arrange for special transport and can provide a brochure or two about the region. Directly in front of the same dock is the office for CANTUR, which when staffed can provide information on public boat schedules, contacts

SAN JUAN'S STEAMERS: CORNELIUS VANDERBILT'S NICARAGUAN VENTURE

Entrepreneurs and fortune-hunters heading to California in the famed '49 gold rush found it easier to traverse Central America than to brave the long, perilous overland trek across the United States. American businessman Cornelius Vanderbilt formed the first company that provided passage between New York and San Francisco via Nicaragua. The 45-day trip from New York to California cost $145. Vanderbilt made the first successful voyage himself in 1851. Upon reaching the Nicaraguan shore at Greytown in great, square-rigged clipper ships, passengers boarded side-wheeled *vapores* (riverboats), including the 120-ton iron-hulled *Director* and the smaller *Bulwer*, which worked different stretches of the river (to get around unnavigable rapids, passengers disembarked and transferred to the next upstream ship). The second leg sailed past San Carlos, then traversed the lake to the town of Virgen; there, passengers boarded horse carriages and traveled overland to San Juan del Sur where another clipper ship took them to California.

The route was an immediate success, and by 1853, Vanderbilt's company could scarcely provide enough ships to meet the demand. Vanderbilt's company remained uncontested and by 1854, had transported more than 23,000 passengers between New York and California. Business was booming along the route, which now included a short railway to avoid the rapids at El Castillo. San Juan del Norte became a rip-roaring port town with 127 foreign consulates and embassies, and a stream of adventuring gringos, foreign investors, and New Orleans whores, prompting U.S. envoy E. G. Squier to remark on the town's "general drunkenness and indiscriminate licentiousness."

The most famous of Vanderbilt's passengers was also one his biggest critics: After Mark Twain made the voyage in 1867, he took Cornelius to task in "An Open Letter to Commodore Vanderbilt." In it, he complained about the wretched quality of the steamship line. More of Twain's comments on Nicaragua are found in a posthumously assembled collection called *Travels with Mr. Brown*.

The boom lasted another half century, fueled after the end of the gold rush by the prospect of an interoceanic canal. The dream all but died when the bid went to Panamá in 1902, and communities up and down the Río San Juan began to wither. Outside San Juan del Norte, the remains of an old iron steamdredge stand in the shallows of the river where it foundered, testament to the boldest of dreams and the still-unwritten future of transoceanic shipping in Nicaragua.

To learn more about this fascinating chapter of Río San Juan history, read *Tycoon's War: How Cornelius Vanderbilt Invaded a Country to Overthrow America's Most Famous Military Adventurer,* by Stephen Dando-Collins (Da Capo Press, 2008).

---

for private services, and a list of tours offered on Solentiname. The kiosk selling tickets near the entrance to the municipal dock can provide the balance of the updated boat schedules.

Tour Guides

Most river lodges and hotels can arrange daily trips and activities, or hire a local guide in San Carlos. Ronny Zambrana of **Ryo Tours** (tel. 505/8828-8558, ryobigtours@hotmail.com, www.ryobigtours.com) is part of a growing group of professionally trained young Nicaraguan guides. Many national tour operators based in Granada and Managua offer package trips to the Río San Juan region.

To paddle the Río San Juan and camp along its banks, contact Green Pathways (in León tel. 505/2315-0964, www.greenpathways.com) and ask about their 12-day Río San Juan kayak expedition (minimum of three people and two weeks advance notice).

Emergency

The police station (tel. 505/2583-0350) is located three kilometers from the center of San Carlos on the road to Managua. The fire station can be reached by calling 505/2583-2149. Hospital Luis Felipe Moncada (tel. 505/2583-0238 or tel. 505/2583-0244) is north of town on the highway; or try the Centro de Salud (505/2583-0361). San Carlos's medical services may be okay for minor problems, but for any real emergencies, you're better off chartering a boat south to the hospital in Los Chiles, Costa Rica (one hour or less by boat) or trying to get a flight back to Managua.

Communication

There are cheap Internet cafés all over town; start near the park. You can make phone calls from most Internet places, and both Nicaraguan cell phone companies offer service around San Carlos.

The San Carlos post office (located a block south of the park, tel. 505/2583-0276, tel./fax 505/2583-0000, open 8 A.M.–5 P.M. Mon.–Fri., 8 A.M.–1 P.M. Sat., closed for lunch) receives and sends mail via the daily La Costeña flights. Carlos Reyes (near Hospedaje Peña, tel./fax 505/2583-0090) can also receive a fax for you.

Banks

You still need lots of cash down here. San Carlos got an ATM in 2009—the only one in the region—but it's heavily used, so don't rely on it. Some of the main area lodges take credit cards: always confirm. Banco de Finanzas (one block east of the park, tel. 505/2583-0144, open 8:30 A.M.–4 P.M. Mon.–Fri., until noon Sat.) will exchange dollars, but will not deal with travelers checks, Costa Rican *colónes,* or credit-card cash advances. There are plenty of *coyote* money changers down by the Migración office, trading *córdobas,* dollars, and *colónes.* Otherwise, head for the Western Union just southwest of the church.

NICARAGUA'S FAMOUS FRESHWATER SHARK

How the *Carcharhinus leucas* became the only shark in the world able to pass between saltwater and freshwater is a fascinating story. After thousands of years of hunting in the brackish outflow of the Río San Juan, Nicaragua's freshwater sharks made their way up the river and formed a healthy population in Lago de Nicaragua. The tale continues with the arrival of humans and their role as both victims and hunters of Nicaragua's bull shark, told in full in Edward Marriott's 2001 book, *Savage Shore.* Indigenous tribes on Ometepe worshipped the shark, sometimes feeding their dead to it. This fear and reverence only faded when the Asian market for shark-fin soup helped to create an industry around harvesting the famous fish, culminating in the late 1960s, when Somoza's processing plant in Granada butchered up to 20,000 sharks a year. Today, the only freshwater shark in the world is seldom seen, although it is still inadvisable to swim in the waters near San Juan del Norte.

GETTING THERE AND AWAY
By Air

This is the recommended way. There are two daily 50-minute flights from Managua on weekdays, one at 8 A.M. and one at 1:30 P.M. The view as you arc over the lake and volcanoes is stunning. Only the morning plane leaves on Saturdays and just the afternoon plane makes the flight on Sundays. The return flight departs San Carlos immediately after landing and unloading. The round-trip costs $120. Contact La Costeña in Managua (tel. 505/2263-2142). In San Carlos, the La Costeña office is run by Doña María Amelia Gross out of her home (one block west of the BDF bank, tel. 505/2583-0271). Always reserve your spot as far in advance as you can, as flights fill up fast. Getting on the waiting list and trying to go stand-by works more often than you would think for a 12-person plane.

By Land

While a highway project connecting Managua and San Carlos is in the works, for now the second half of the journey remains rough. Buses leave Managua's Mayoreo market, starting at 5 A.M. with the last night bus leaving at 6:30 P.M. The first of the seven buses to Managua is at 6:30 A.M., the last at 10 P.M. The 300-kilometer trip costs under $10. In San Carlos, buses for all destinations leave from the terminal near the municipal dock. If driving on your own, be sure to have a spare tire and jack, plus water and provisions, as you will need all of them.

By Boat to Granada and Ometepe

There are three weekly boat runs between Granada's municipal dock and San Carlos. The older ferry leaves Monday and Thursday at 2 P.M., making stops at Altagracia, Ometepe at 6 P.M. and Morito and San Miguelito before arriving in San Carlos around 6 A.M., $10 for padded first-class seats with air-conditioning, and hard wooden seats below. There is also a VIP suite for $110. The same boat departs San Carlos bound for Granada on Tuesdays and Fridays at 2 P.M.; be there at least an hour in advance to get your ticket. This boat passes Ometepe around 1 or 2 A.M., where you can get off at Altagracia. The boat gets crowded at times, especially around Semana Santa, when the hot easterly winds chop the lake into steep swells, and the voyage degenerates into a 16-hour puke-fest. Get there early and be aggressive to stake your territory topside. At other times of the year, the ride is long but generally pleasant, and sailing west is always easier than sailing east.

A third boat, the *Barco Turistico,* leaves Granada Fridays at 7 P.M., stopping only in Altagracia, then arriving in San Carlos the following morning at 6 A.M. It departs San Carlos Sunday evening at 6 P.M.; cost is $20 for first

© DAVID WEBSTER SMITH

Depart at the San Carlos dock for the Solentiname Islands and trips down the Río San Juan.

class (includes coffee and drink service), $13 for economy. For more info, contact Empersario Portuario (tel. 505/2583-0256).

By Boat Down the Río San Juan

All boat tickets are sold at the Empresario Portuario (tel. 505/2583-0256, open 7:30 A.M.–5 P.M. Mon.–Sat., but hours vary to match boat schedules) on the main drag toward the gas station. Inside the little shack you'll find up-to-date schedules and advance ticket sales for its fleet of *lanchas*. All boats for El Castillo also stop in Boca de Sábalos. The first boat leaves San Carlos at 6:30 A.M., the last one at 4:30 P.M. Four slow (2–3 hours) boat trips to El Castillo depart daily, costing $4, faster boats $11.

Boats to San Juan de Nicaragua (San Juan del Norte) are less frequent. Only two boats make the trip, one fast and one slow. They leave on Tuesdays and Fridays and come back on Thursdays and Sundays. The slow boat ($13, 12 hours) leaves San Carlos at 6 A.M. and San Juan del Norte at 5 A.M. The fast boat ($25, 6 hours) leaves an hour after the slow boat.

Arrange private boat trips at the Venta, INTUR, or directly with a *panguero* (private boat owner). Armando Ortiz's Viajes Turisticos (one block from the Western Union, viajesturisticosortiz@hotmail.es, tel. 505/2583-0039)

also specializes in private tours and transfers. Rising gas prices make chartered trips hundreds of dollars. As the demand for transportation continues to grow and shift, so do boat schedules. Always check departure times at the docks well in advance, and be sure to get a second (and third) opinion.

RÍO FRÍO BORDER CROSSING

Boating south into Costa Rica begins with a visit to the *migración* office, located on the *calle principal* in San Carlos, on the waterfront near the park with a line that forms before 7 A.M. The office is open 8:30 A.M.–6 P.M. daily. There are usually three or four boats to Los Chiles, starting at 10:30 A.M. The hour-long chug up the Rio Frío to Los Chiles, Costa Rica costs about $10 each way. To enter Nicaragua costs $7.

Once in Los Chiles, Costa Rica Migración is located 200 meters up the road from the dock, where you *must* get stamped. Daily direct buses depart for the five-hour trip to San José, about $8. Boats leave Los Chiles to San Carlos throughout the day (or, when there aren't enough people, not at all, forcing you to spend the night in Costa Rica). Note: Be aware that a second town by the name of Los Chiles is about two hours northeast of San Carlos, in Nicaragua. Be sure to distinguish between the two when asking for directions.

The Solentiname Islands

The 36 volcanic islands in southern Lake Cocibolca have a long history of habitation; signs of its original residents are abundant in the form of petroglyphs, cave paintings, and artifacts. The name Solentiname comes from Celentinametl, Nahuatl for "place of many guests."

The islands are of volcanic origin with rocky, hard-to-farm soils. More effort is going into avocados these days. Somoza's logging companies deforested most of the archipelago, and Boaco cattlemen cut the rest to make pasture. In the last three decades, however, much of the forest

has been allowed to regenerate, and the rebirth has attracted artists and biologists from all over the world. Fishing, of course, remains a mainstay of the islanders' diet.

Today, 129 families (about 750 people) share the archipelago with an amazing diversity of vegetation, birds, and other wildlife. Solentiname's most unique and well-known attraction is the creativity of its inhabitants, a talent Padre Ernesto Cardenal discovered in 1966 when he gave brushes and paint to some of the local *jícaro* carvers. Cardenal, recently returned from a Trappist monastery in

SOLENTINAME

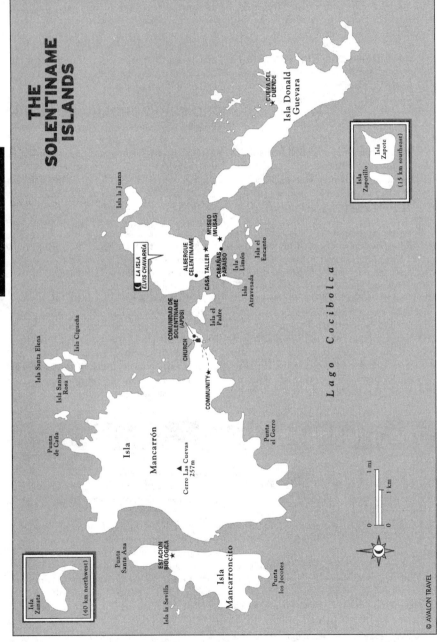

THE SOLENTINAME ISLANDS

Isla la Juana

Isla Santa Elena

Isla Santa Rosa

Isla Cigüeña

Punta de Caña

Isla Mancarrón

Cerro Las Cuevas 257m

COMUNIDAD DE SOLENTINAME (APDS)

CHURCH

COMMUNITY ★

Isla el Padre

LA ISLA ELVIS CHAVARRÍA

ALBERGUE CELENTINAME ★

CASA TALLER ●

MUSEO (MUSAS) ★

CABAÑAS PARAISO ●

Isla Limón

Isla el Encanto

Isla Atravesada

CUEVA DEL DUENDE ★

Isla Donald Guevara

Punta el Gorro

Lago Cocibolca

Punta Santa Ana

ESTACION BIOLOGICA ★

Isla la Sevilla

Isla Mancarroncito

Punta los Jocotes

Isla Zanata (40 km northwest)

Isla Zapotillo

Isla Zapote (15 km southeast)

0   1 mi
0   1 km

© AVALON TRAVEL

Kentucky in the late 1960s, formed a Christian community in Solentiname and stayed on Isla Mancarrón to work and write for the next 10 years (he is locally referred to as "El Poeta"). Under his guidance, the simple church at Solentiname became the heart of Nicaragua's liberation theology movement, which represents Christ as the revolutionary savior of the poor. It inspired Carlos Mejía Godoy to write "La Misa Campesina" in 1972. Masses were communal, participatory events, and Cardenal's book, *The Gospels of Solentiname,* is a written record of the phenomenon, with transcriptions of a series of *campesino*-led services throughout the 1970s.

On October 13, 1977, a group of anti-Somoza Solentiname islanders staged a daring and successful assault on the National Guard post in San Carlos. Somoza retaliated by torching the islands. In 1979, Ernesto Cardenal, now the Sandinista Minister of Culture, formed the Asociación Para el Desarollo de Solentiname (Solentiname Development Association, or APDS). Under APDS, much of what had been destroyed was rebuilt, and the arts continued to flourish and receive much attention from the rest of the world. Today, there are no fewer than 50 families who continue to produce balsa-wood carvings and bright "primitivist" paintings of the landscape and community.

ORIENTATION AND GETTING AROUND

Essentially, only the four largest of the nearly three dozen islands are inhabited: Isla Mancarrón, Isla Elvis Chavarría (a.k.a. Isla San Fernando), Isla Donald Guevara (a.k.a. Isla la Venada), and Isla Mancarroncito. Only the first two have services for tourists. If you are on a budget, getting around the islands will be your biggest challenge, especially considering that the *colectivo* water taxis only run twice a week, ensuring a minimum stay of three days. To get around, you can either catch a free or discounted ride in someone's *panga,* or you can rent a dugout canoe or rowboat and do some paddling.

SOLENTINAME

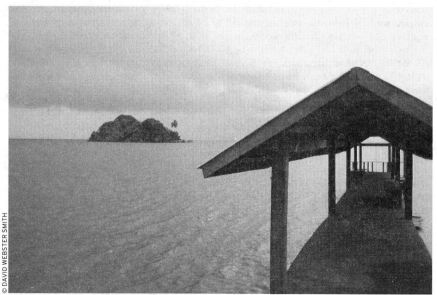

© DAVID WEBSTER SMITH

The Solentiname archipelago is a magical place.

MANCARRÓN

The biggest (20 square kilometers) and tallest (at 257-meter Cerro las Cuevas) island, Mancarrón is populated by 34 families—about 200 people. The "town" of Mancarrón, built up in the 1980s, is simply a cluster of houses, a health center, school, and *pulpería*, five minutes up the muddy path from the dock. **Casa Taller de la Cooperativa** has a large collection of works by artists from different islands. The cooperative shares the profits from the individual sales. Much of the rest of the island is off-limits and has supposedly been purchased by cattle ranchers from Boaco, though conspiracy and corruption theories abound.

Ernesto Cardenal's project began in the 1960s in the church, which he reconstructed and designed. It is unlike any house of worship you've ever seen, featuring children's paintings on the whitewashed adobe walls, a unique crucifix sculpted by Cardenal, and an altar decorated in pre-Columbian style. The nearby APDS compound includes a library, a museum, an art gallery, a display of indigenous artifacts, and an eclectic collection of books in a variety of languages, including the complete works of Ernesto Cardenal, who still maintains a residence in the APDS compound. There are other works on liberation theology, plus the original primitivism painting by local resident Eduardo Arana that helped start the whole project. Ask if they can show you the 1970s BBC video documentary about the Solentiname Islands.

Accommodations and Services

A local collective of families offer **homestay accommodations;** go to the community center and inquire at **Hostal Familiar El Buen Amigo** (tel. 505/8869-6619, $6 pp). One of the rooms has a private bath and meals run $2–3. Next door, **Villa Esperanza** has a few rooms for $25 per person, including three meals.

On the hill, **Hotel Mancarrón** (reserve through Solentiname Tours, tel. 505/8421-5689 or 505/227-09981, info@solentiname-tours.com, $50) is a fenced-in miniresort with 15 basic rooms, a bar, and a restaurant. The property is at the center of a long, contentious battle over its ownership and even once evicted El Poeta from the premises—it's sometimes open and sometimes closed. There is Internet access in the island library.

◖ LA ISLA ELVIS CHAVARRÍA

"La Elvis" owes its name to a young martyr who participated in the 1977 raid on San Carlos and was subsequently captured and killed by the National Guard. The island has a health center, a school (Escuela Mateo Wooten, named after the Peace Corps volunteer who led its construction in the mid-1990s), a museum, and a hiking trail.

El Museo Archipiélago de Solentiname (MUSAS) (at the top of the steep path out of town, open 7 A.M.–noon and 2–5 P.M. Mon.–Sat., $2) was built in September 2000 to preserve and display the natural and cultural heritage of the Solentiname Islands and its people. The flowers along the path on your way up were planted to attract butterflies and hummingbirds. Inside, local artists have painted scenes of the islands' early history. Also find interesting maps of the area, archaeological information, and a display of traditional fishing techniques and the balsa-wood carving process. Behind the museum are a natural medicine garden, arboretum of 42 tree species, a model organic avocado and balsa-wood plantation, and a weather station.

The Fundación MUSAS (made up of six community leaders, the Italian NGO ACRA, and several other organizations) also organizes environmental education workshops in the island's school and supports a number of research projects in the area. The museum is open daily, but if you find it closed, ask around for Socorro, the local curator, caretaker, and key master. For more information, contact ACRA in the Managua office (tel. 505/2249-6176, musasni@yahoo.com).

At the peak of the dry season (March—April), **La Cueva del Duende** becomes accessible. It is usually underwater, and is an important archaeological site that the islands'

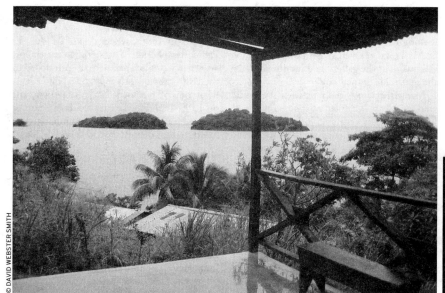

© DAVID WEBSTER SMITH

view from the *museo* on La Isla Elvis Chavarría

past inhabitants believed to be the entrance to the underworld. They painted faces to represent their ancestors, believed to reside there, and left other markings including a female fertility figure. The cave is located on the nearby Isla Donald Guevara, but you can arrange the tour with CANTUR here.

Accommodations

Doña María Guevara has been running the **Albergue Celentiname** (tel. 505/8893-1977, celentiname7@yahoo.es, $50 for a double room, rate includes breakfast, lunch, and dinner) since 1984 on a beautiful point at the western edge of the island. She and many of her family members are painters, participating in Cardenal's project since its earliest days. All of the electricity in the hotel is solar generated. The eight cabanas have capacity for up to 25 people, all with private bath. There is a picturesque porch, a bar, and a *comedor.* The flower-framed views are priceless. Kayaks and fishing gear are available for rent. Try to make reservations in advance if possible. They can help arrange for transportation when it's available, but expect round-trip transportation from the island to run upwards of $120.

Several hundred meters east, with his own dock on the southern shore of the island, **Don Julio** rents three rooms in his rustic and comfortable, lakefront homestead for $6 per person. Don Julio's brother, Chepe, runs transport to and from San Carlos and can arrange custom trips. Their sister Doña Maria Magdalena Pineda has her own hotel another couple of minutes east along the shore: **Cabañas Paraíso** (tel. 505/2278-3992, gsolentiname@amnet.com.ni, $35 d with three meals and private bath) also has a *comedor,* rents kayaks, and offers tours around the island and beyond. They also have an office in San Carlos and a gallery in Managua, plus excellent local guides.

DONALD GUEVARA, MANCARRONCITO, ZAPOTE, AND ZAPOTILLO ISLANDS

Also known as Isla la Venada, or "La Donald," Isla Donald Guevara's namesake was martyred alongside his *compañero* Elvis Chavarría. La Venada is home to Rudolfo Arellano, one of the original artists from the islands. His family has a total of seven artists now who exhibit their work at the gallery and family house on the south side of the island.

Mancarroncito is the most well preserved, wild, and least inhabited of the main islands. Its steep, thickly vegetated hills rise to a 100-meter peak. The newly opened **Estación Biológica** is run by a local NGO, Fundación del Río, and offers lodging for up to 12 people at $21 per person including three meals and guide services around the reserve. Make reservations in advance by contacting Fundación del Río in San Carlos (tel. 505/2583-0035, fdrio@turbonett.com.ni).

Zapote and Zapotillo are the two closest islands to the mainland and are both owned by APDS, which has essentially decided to leave them alone. Zapote is a key nesting area for a variety of birds and turns into a whitewashed, foul-smelling squawk-fest in March and April, when some 10,000 breeding pairs build nests there. Observe the reproductive mayhem from your boat only, as landing there disturbs the birds. Smaller Zapotillo has less bird activity and a more sordid history, involving a fruit farm, an orphanage for boys, and a pedophile Evangelist priest who was eventually chased into Costa Rica, barely escaping with his life.

ISLAS EL PADRE AND LA ATRAVESADA

Located just off the western tip of La Elvis, El Padre island became a howler monkey sanctuary when a single breeding pair introduced in the 1980s subsequently reproduced into a family of some 50 members. Isla la Atravesada, just off La Elvis and to the east of Isla el Padre, is owned by a North American but inhabited by Solentiname's densest crocodile populations.

TOUR PACKAGES

The same foundation that runs the museum on Isla Elvis Chavarría has also arranged a fully-guided, four-day exploration of the entire Solentiname archipelago and the Río Papaturro in Los Guatuzos, including all its natural, archaeological, and cultural attractions. See also tour guides in San Carlos, including **Transporte San Miguelito** (tel. 505/8828-6136, anyeljba@yahoo.es).

GETTING THERE AND AWAY

From San Carlos, boats depart on Tuesday and Friday at 1 P.M. for the two-hour trip to the archipelago (about $2 pp). The return trip leaves Solentiname on the same days at 5 A.M., arriving in San Carlos in time to catch the boat to Managua. Should you want to leave the islands at any other time, a private boat starts at about $100. CANTUR can also arrange transportation to Los Guatuzos or San Carlos.

Near San Carlos

◖ LOS GUATUZOS WILDLIFE REFUGE AND CENTRO ECOLÓGICO

The 438-square-kilometer strip between Nicaragua's southern border and Lake Cocibolca is a protected wetlands and wildlife reserve replete with myriad species of animals and inhabited by some 1,700 fishermen and subsistence farmers in 11 small communities. The locals are descendants of the Zapote and Guatuzo (or Maleku) peoples as well as the mestizos who arrived in the late 19th century to cultivate rubber. These same *huleros* reverted to the slave trade when the world rubber market crashed, selling Guatuzos for 50 pesos a head to the gold mines of Chontales. Today, only a handful of full-blooded Maleku exist, mostly over the border in Costa Rica.

In the 1930s, settlers introduced cacao to the region, which, because of the crop's need for shade, preserved much of the area's original forest canopy. When plummeting

All three of Nicaragua's primary species have been sighted throughout the Los Guatuzos Wildlife Refuge.

© DANIELLE VAUGHN

The research center and guest facilities are located 40 kilometers from San Carlos, up the Río Papaturro, which drains the slopes of Costa Rica's northern volcanoes. The narrow river's fauna-rich jungle gradually swallows you as you approach the community of Papaturro.

Accommodations

Research station, nature center, and isolated backpacker's hideaway, the **Centro Ecólogico** has two eight-bed dorms at $11 a night, plus campgrounds (tents and sleeping pads for rent). Arrange your meals in advance in the nearby village for about $4.

Arrange birding safaris, fishing trips, kayak excursions, nighttime wildlife safaris, boat trips in the wetlands and lake, and tours of local villages (most tours cost $11 pp). A multiplatform suspension canopy bridge allows for incredible bird and wildlife viewing in the upper reaches of the rainforest. There is also an orchid display of over 100 species including the tiniest one in the world, a butterfly farm, a turtle nursery for export to the pet industry, and a caiman nursery for scientific research, export, and tourist adrenaline production. The center also has a conference room, workshop facilities, and support for anyone coming to do field research (GPS equipment, bird nets/traps, and field assistants). They will gladly work out deals for researchers and students. Your host and guide, Armando, offers rubber boots for the mud, and an incredible wealth of knowledge from over 13 years of working in the jungle. Bring quick-drying clothes and adequate protection from the sun, rain, and especially bugs.

For more information or reservations contact FUNDAR in Managua (tel. 505/2270-5434, centro.ecologico@fundar.org.ni, www.fundar.org.ni) or Armando Gómez (tel. 505/8674-3559 or tel. 505/8677-8082). In San Carlos, FUNDAR works out of the Amigos de la Tierra office (inside the Red Cross building, tel. 505/2583-0139); they can help arrange transport to Los Guatuzos or down the river to El Castillo.

Another excellent option is only a five-minute boat ride from San Carlos but in

cacao prices and a deadly fungus wiped out the industry in the 1970s, hardwood logging ensued. Only military conflict in the 1980s stopped the logging, but it also drove nearly the entire population of Los Guatuzos into Costa Rica. When families returned in the early 1990s, the area's ecosystem was still largely intact, and the new government quickly acted to protect it from destruction.

Today, residents count on the richness of their natural surroundings to attract visitors and scientists. No fewer than 389 species of birds have been observed here, and between February and April, flocks of migratory species fly through in spectacular concentrations. Los Guatuzos contains dense populations of crocodiles; caimans; feral pigs; jaguars; and howler, white-faced, and spider monkeys. This is also home to a rare, ancient species of fish called the gaspar *(Actractoseus tropicus),* a living, armored relic of the Jurassic age that uses its snout and fangs to eat other fish, crabs, and even small turtles.

a world of its own. **Hotel La Esquina del Lago** (tel. 505/8864-1665 or 505/8688-0961, www.riosanjuan.info, $20–35 d) is a jungle lodge which grew from a French expat's world-class sportfishing trips and area nature tours. Despite cold water, bugs, and broken fixtures, the rooms are homey and charming. Access is only by boat, and the spot feels incredibly remote, with views of surrounding volcanoes and the lake and all kinds of tours and water activities, specializing in birding, kayaking, and fishing adventures. They offer all transfer services, boats for your use, 24-hour electricity, Internet, and package deals with meals included.

Getting There and Away

From the west dock near the CANTUR kiosk in San Carlos, *colectivos* leave for Papaturro at 7 A.M. Monday, Tuesday, and Thursday; the four-hour trip costs $3.50 a person and stops at the small island of Chichicaste where fried fish and soup are available for about $1. The same boat returns to San Carlos the day after arriving, leaving Papaturro at 7 A.M. Or you can rent a private *panga*—which costs $120, but can take up to 10 people to Los Guatuzos in only 1.5 hours.

ESPERANZA VERDE

Also a part of the Guatuzos Reserve, this 5,000-hectare protected area is part of an effort to reforest and protect the overgrazed watershed of the Río Frío and the Río San Juan. From the dock of Esperanza Verde and the military post walk 500 meters downstream to the **Centro de Interpretación Ambiental**

Konrad Lorenz, and a row of six guest rooms with 20 beds ($40 pp with transportation and food); inquire about special rates for NGOs, students, and Nicas. The barren area immediately surrounding the guest facilities is uninteresting, but a 40-minute walk up the road brings you straight into the heart of the rainforest—monkeys, 200 species of birds, giant spiders, and potentially even pumas. There are a total of three trails and numerous aquatic trips. Contact Leonel Ubau with FUNDEVERDE in Hotel Cabinas Leyko in San Carlos (tel. 505/2583-0354, fundeverde@yahoo.es). Located 15 minutes from San Carlos, take any *colectivo* heading up the Río Frío toward Los Chiles.

NORTH OF SAN CARLOS
San Miguelito

A peaceful, lakeside community, San Miguelito has an interesting Casa de Cultura and access to the island of El Boquete. You can also venture up various rivers, into local wetlands, or over to Solentiname. In town, stay at **Hotel Cocibolca** (tel. 505/2552-8803, $12), a tranquil hardwood building of 16 rooms, all with shared bath, and incredible sunset views of Ometepe's silhouette. Just outside of town, the **Finca el Cacao** (tel. 505/8414-9927) offers a more bucolic stay, with cow-milking, crocodile-searching, monkey-watching, and similar, plus three meals a day for $35 per person. One daily direct bus leaves Managua's Mayoreo at 7 A.M.; in San Carlos, ask at the bus station. You can also take the slow boat from Granada and get off in San Miguelito before it reaches San Carlos.

Down the Río San Juan

The 190-odd-kilometer journey to the sea takes you down the broad, lethargic Río San Juan through forests and isolated cattle farms. You'll have the opportunity to stop in several villages, isolated clusters of stilted homes, or in one of several river resorts and research stations. There are a few minor *raudales* (rapids) where the channel suddenly narrows, including the infamous **Raudal el Diablo** in front of El Castillo. Enormous, silver *sábalos reales* (tarpon) are often seen rising just upstream from these fast waters. Downstream of El Castillo, things become decidedly wilder, especially on the Nicaraguan side, where the enormous Gran Reserva Río Indio-Maíz spills over the left bank. Finally, you'll reach San Juan del Norte, with all its ghosts, and a long sandbar, beyond which lies the Caribbean. (Note: In the following section, the terms "river right" and "river left" refer to a boater traveling downstream).

BOCA DE SÁBALOS

A two-hour *lancha* ride from San Carlos brings you to this town, six kilometers upstream of El Castillo. Boca de Sábalos is a working town of about 1,200 souls, located at the mouth of one of Río San Juan's nearly 1,000 tributaries. Boca de Sábalos has more bars, *hospedajes,* and places to eat than El Castillo, and is actually the de facto seat of the El Castillo municipality (it was transferred here from El Castillo temporarily during the war, and then never moved back).

Sights

Don Julio Murio (across from the big bar on the walkway leading north from the dock) speaks English, organizes tours on Río Sábalos, and rents canoes and kayaks for $5 per hour without a guide and $10 per hour with a guide. He can also arrange an all-inclusive adventure kayaking trip to San Juan del Norte ($250 pp)

public transportation along the Río San Juan

© DAVID WEBSTER SMITH

SOLENTINAME

SAN JUAN DEL WHAT?

Sometimes knowing a place's name is all you need to understand its history. San Juan del Sur is an elegant example. The story begins in the 16th century. Spanish explorer Diego de Machuca first reached the mouth of the winding river the Spanish called *el desaguadero* (the outlet or the drain) on June 24, 1538, feast day of Saint John the Baptist. They added "del Norte" to denote the North Sea (the Atlantic), as it was known at the time (the Pacific was the South Sea).

Rodrigo de Contreras, Nicaragua's first Spanish governor, renamed it San Juan de la Cruz in 1541, upon establishing the area's first military garrison. And so it ostensibly remained for the next 300 years, except that owing to the proliferation of Spanish San Juans around the Caribbean, traders began calling it San Juan de Nicaragua. In 1796, the Spanish declared San Juan de Nicaragua a Free Port, which the British, slowly expanding their Atlantic Coast protectorate, must have found amusing: Soon it would be theirs alone.

In 1821 Central America declared its independence from the Spanish crown, and in the ensuing power vacuum, the British took possession of the Atlantic coast with the assistance of their well-armed allies, the local Miskito Indians. At first the British helped the Miskitos take control in 1841 in return for the right to explore. In gratitude, the Miskito King Mosco renamed the town in honor of the Jamaican Governor, Sir Charles Edward Grey, who became the de facto governor of the British protectorate.

Greytown, as it was now called, grew to be the eastern terminus of one of the most popular interoceanic trading routes, and the English sent in the army to occupy the settlement in 1848, now far too important for indigenous control. Cornelius Vanderbilt's steamships made Greytown into a booming port town that received thousands of interoceanic visitors each year. During this period, Greytown was destroyed twice, once by the American Navy and once by flooding in the Río San Juan. But before it could fully recover the steamship line closed down, gold rush traffic trickled off, and the world forgot about the little town at the end of the river and end of the world.

San Juan del Norte has essentially remained in that condition ever since, but its name continues to change. During the jingoistic war of words with Costa Rica over ownership of the river, President Arnoldo Alemán renamed the town San Juan de Nicaragua in 2002, a name often ignored by many people and mapmakers.

Contributed by Roman Yavich, former Fulbright scholar and Nicaragua tourism expert; Roman co-founded ComunidadConnect.org, a nonprofit organization based in San Juan del Sur.

or take you on one of the 10 tours designed by the Sábalos tourism collective.

El Quebracho Wildlife Reserve, located in the part of the biosphere reserve allocated for ecotourism development, has two trails (one of which is self-guided) through a wildlife-rich setting. The reserve can accommodate up to 25 people for $20 per person including three meals, and guides can be hired for $10 per day (discounts for groups larger than 10). Count on spending the night, as its isolation makes day trips challenging. Make arrangements at the office of Fundación del Río (a block south of the *alcaldía* in Sábalos, tel.

505/2583-0035), which owns and operates the reserve or the main office near the hospital in San Carlos.

Hire a vehicle to take you to the shady, pleasant 2,000-hectare **African palm plantation,** about a half hour outside of town, one of only two such operations in Nicaragua. Before being purchased by the Chamorro family, it employed hundreds of locals.

You can also hike down the Río San Juan to the 100-year-old, half-buried hulk of the **steamship wreck.** To go tarpon fishing, get a permit from the town MARENA office (hook only, no spears), and then hire a guide and boat to take you to just above the Toro Rapids, less than five minutes down the Río San Juan.

Punto Lodge is open 2 P.M.–midnight daily for music and drinking, as are several smaller and noisier establishments.

Accommodations

Walking up from the dock, you'll first come to beautiful hardwood **(Hospedaje Katiana** (tel. 505/2583-0178, $7), offering a variety of 14 rooms, some with private bath, all in a nice homey setting. Next door, **Hospedaje Clarissa** ($4 pp, mosquito net, fan, shared bath) has 11 rooms and one of the most popular eateries in town. Across the street, the **Hotel Central** ($3 s with fan) is inexpensive but basic and not quite as nice.

(Hotel Sábalos (tel. 505/8659-0252 or 505/2271-7424, www.hotelsabalos.com.ni, $36 includes breakfast) is located across the way at the confluence of the Río Sábalos and the Río San Juan, built on a big dock over the water. The view from the deck might be the best in the entire Río San Juan area. Also enjoy hot water, private bathrooms, classy accommodations, and a *panga* that can take you on tours around the area. Arrange a ride across the river to the hotel at their family's store next to Hospedaje Katiana on main street.

Getting There and Away

Six boats make the trip to El Castillo from San Carlos and back every day (reduced service on Sunday), stopping at Boca de Sábalos and the lodges upon request.

OTHER RIVER LODGES

(Sábalos Lodge

A one-time amphibian farm, growing everything from poison dart frogs to snakes for export to the United States, Sabalos Lodge (tel. 505/8850-7623, Managua tel. 505/8823-5514 or 505/2278-1405, sales@sabaloslodge.com, www.sabaloslodge.com, $35–70, includes breakfast) now focuses on tourism, with 10 riverside bamboo and wood cabins with thatched roofs, hammock lounge, and a dining area. The meals and the service are excellent, $5 for

breakfast and $10 for lunch and dinner (huge portions). Hiking trails and inner tube floats are available, plus three *pangas* for pickups from San Carlos and tours to the sunken ship, nighttime caiman-watching, and more; also tours to Indio-Maíz biological reserve, kayaks, and horses. The lodge is a five-minute boat trip (or 15-minute walk) downstream from Boca de Sábalos.

The lodge is associated with the private nonprofit, nonpartisan **San Juan Rio Relief** (sanjuanriorelief@cox.net, www.sanjuanriorelief.org), a team of dedicated people from the U.S. and Nicaragua who came together in 2003 with the goal of bringing free medical healthcare to the people of the Río San Juan.

Montecristo River Resort

Located downstream from Boca de Sábalos on river right (before reaching El Castillo), Montecristo (tel. 505/8649-9012 or 505/2583-0197 in San Carlos, montecristoriver@yahoo.com, www.montecristoriverlodge.com, $65 all-inclusive) is a calm, riverside resort offering sportfishing, birding, hiking trails, horseback riding, and tours of local cacao farms and reforestation projects; a variety of rooms on a neatly kept compound and private nature reserve of 120 acres. They can also get you to area reserves and Solentiname. Your all-inclusive package includes three meals, horses, boats, and other activities; ask about discounts.

(EL CASTILLO

The fortress of El Castillo de la Inmaculada Concepción de María was strategically placed with a long view downriver, right in front of the shark- and crocodile-infested Raudal el Diablo (still a navigational hazard). Now dark, moss-covered ruins, the Fortress of the Immaculate Conception is the one place in this region you should not miss.

The town (pop. 1,500) has neither roads nor cars—reason enough to visit. Its residents work on farms in the surrounding hills, fish the river, commute to the sawmill in Sábalos, the palm oil factory up the Río San Juan, or one of the new resorts up and down the river. In between

SOLENTINAME

harvests, a lot of folks cross illegally into Costa Rica—an easy 45-minute walk. El Castillo celebrates its *fiestas patronales* on March 19.

History

Ruy Díaz, on the first Spanish exploration of the river in 1525, built the first fortification in 1602, on a section of the river he called "The House of the Devil." In 1673, Spain commissioned the building of a new fort, which, when completed two years later, was the largest fortress of its kind in Central America, with 32 cannons and 11,000 weapons. Granada, at long last, felt safe.

But in 1762 Spain and Britain began the Seven Years War, prompting the governor of Jamaica to order an invasion of Nicaragua. An expedition of 2,000 soldiers took all the fortifications until they reached El Castillo, where a massive battle commenced on July 29. Rafaela Herrera, the 19-year-old daughter of the fort's fallen commander, Jose Herrera, seized command of her father's troops and succeeded in driving off the British, who retreated to San Juan del Norte on August 3.

Eighteen years later, 22-year-old Horatio Nelson entered the Río San Juan with a force of 3,500 men. He captured the fortification at Bartola on April 9, and then, two days later, El Castillo via a surprise, landside assault. Nine months later sans reinforcement, the soon-to-be Lord Admiral Horatio Nelson and his handful of surviving soldiers—all rotting from sickness—pulled out and went home.

Visiting the Fort

Celebrating 500 years in the Americas, the government of Spain restored the fortress at great cost, building both a historical museum and lending library, plus the nearby school and Hotel Albergue. The museum (open 8 A.M.–noon and 1–5 P.M., $2) is pertinent and interesting, showing the history of the fortress and a collection of arms and other items dating as far back as the 1500s, including a pile of cannon balls and early rum bottles. A nearby *mariposario* (butterfly farm) was also built by the Spanish, although much more recently.

The town of El Castillo is only reachable by river.

© DAVID WEBSTER SMITH

Fishing, Hikes, and River Tours

Asociación Municipal Ecoturismo El Castillo (AMEC) can help with boat rental ($10 per hour for two people) and fishing (rods and lures for $5 per day, $10 to replace a lost lure), or charter fishing (from $140 per day). These prices keep rising as El Castillo becomes more popular, so be sure to check at the *caseta* near the dock.

The AMEC *caseta* can also help you arrange full- or half-day river and tributary tours and hikes, jungle tours (popular, $75–90 for up to six people), canoe trips ($10 pp for two people), horseback tours ($15 pp), or a nighttime caiman-watching tour ($45 for a group of four). Unfortunately smaller groups pay the same minimum price.

Accommodations

Most *hospedajes* are downstream from the dock. The ones closest cost $4 a night but don't offer much. On a side street there's **Nena Lodge and Tours** (tel. 505/8419-8158, nenalodgeandtours@yahoo.es, www.nenalodge.com, $10), with 10 rooms and a streetside balcony, and **Hotel Richarson** (tel. 505/8644-0782, $15). The most comfortable of the budget options is **Casa de Huespedes y Restaurante El Chinandegano** (tel. 505/2583-0191, $4 pp shared bath, $2 extra private bath).

The two-story, wooden ◖ **Hotel Albergue El Castillo** (tel. 505/8924-5608, minar.calero@yahoo.com, $15 pp) was built in 1992 with the help of the Spanish government. Its comfortable double balcony overlooks the town, the river, and rapids beyond. It sleeps up to 35 people, with shared bath, and the $15 per person price includes an excellent breakfast, bottomless cup of coffee (legitimate coffee, not instant—a rarity in these parts), and 30 minutes of Internet time. The bar and restaurant are roomy and classy.

Hotel Victoria (tel. 505/2583-0188, $20 pp includes breakfast) is newer and cleaner than some of the cheaper hotels, and has hot water. Many of the rooms have bunk beds, however, and most have shared baths. Victoria is at the very end of the road leading downstream from the dock.

Travelers on a larger budget will want to treat themselves to **Posada del Rio** (on the left side of the walkway down from the dock, tel. 505/8616-3528, $70, includes breakfast). In Granada, Hotel Colonial is owned by the same family, and the luxury is similar. The rooms are well decorated and all have private balconies overlooking the water, private state-of-the-art bathrooms, hot water, and air-conditioning. Laundry service available.

Food

There's delicious and frighteningly large river shrimp at **El Cofalito** and steaming bowls of soup at **Soda Conchita,** served on a nice second-story deck. **El Chinandegano** is the best value ($2 for basic meals), but there is lots of similar fare down by the dock. **Border's Coffee** (open 7 A.M.–10 P.M. daily), located across the dock from El Cofalito, has an espresso machine, tasty pastries and desserts, fresh juices and milk shakes, all in a great ambience.

Information and Services

The tourist *caseta* in front of the dock is actually a group operation known as the Asociación Municipal Ecoturismo El Castillo (AMEC) and headed up by a guy named Cofal. AMEC is constantly working on an updated list of local guides, boat services, and has compiled a series of hikes and other things to do while in town; contact them via the phone at the Albergue (tel. 505/8892-0195). The most reliable phone in town is the satellite phone at the Albergue, but you can also ask to borrow someone's cell phone and pay them a dollar or two.

Getting There and Away

Lanchas colectivas (to El Castillo $3.50, three hours or $1.50, five hours) depart San Carlos daily at 8 A.M., 10 A.M. (fast boat), noon, 2:30 P.M., 3:30 P.M., and 4:15 P.M. (fast boat). The last fast boat makes part of the journey after dark, which is more dangerous. Returning boats leave for San Carlos from 5 A.M.–2 P.M., with two fast boats at 5:30 A.M. and 11 A.M.

SOLENTINAME

To go downstream, ask around the dock or at the Albergue. Boats for San Juan del Norte pass through on Tuesday and Friday around 9 A.M. They head upstream on Thursday and Sunday, passing El Castillo in the early afternoon. It costs $11 to get to San Juan del Norte from El Castillo and $17 on the fast boat, which is more than worth it for the six hours it saves you.

REFUGIO DE VIDA SILVESTRE RÍO SAN JUAN

This two-kilometer-wide belt that follows the north side of the river is part of the **Río Indio-Maíz Biosphere Reserve,** a 3,618-square-kilometer virgin rainforest, inaccessible to all but the most persistent scientists armed with a permit from the MARENA office in Managua. The first access point to the Refugio is just six kilometers downstream of El Castillo (or about three hours by boat from San Carlos). The western border of the reserve is made up by the Río Bartola at its confluence with the Río San Juan. Arrange a hike through the local MARENA post, with AMEC in El Castillo, or at the ecolodge and research station, **Refugio Bartola** (tel. 505/8880-8754, refugiobartola@yahoo.com, $50 pp with breakfast). There are 11 rooms here on the corner of the protected area with wonderful views of the river. The compound and natural history museum is surrounded by rainforest and fueled by solar energy but is difficult to contact: You may need to wait until you're in El Castillo.

Farther down the river you can access the Refugio de Vida Silvestre Río San Juan through any of the army posts including Boca San Carlos, Sarapiqui, and Delta. Do not expect much more than a place to pitch your tent and friendly, if camouflaged, company.

◖ SAN JUAN DE NICARAGUA

Still commonly referred to by its previous name, San Juan del Norte, this settlement near the mouth of the river is located 100 winding kilometers beyond El Castillo. This hot, historic village in Nicaragua's extreme southeast corner is inhabited by about 900 residents. Sir Charles Grey, governor of Jamaica, first seized the land for the English in 1848 and built the rowdy port of Greytown, which lasted about 150 years. When the British pulled out, it melted into a forgotten backwater, and these days nothing but a historic cemetery of segregated plots with both British and American headstones remains.

Present-day San Juan lies hidden in the brackish swamps at the confluence of Río Indio with the Río San Juan. San Juan del Norte suffered during the Contra war in the 1980s, during which time Hurricane Joan also flattened it. In the 1990s, Comandante Cero returned to torch it to the ground "just because."

Sights and Tours

The most popular attraction in town is the **colonial cemetery,** a short boat ride away across the mouth of the river. At the time of publication the dock at the cemetery was in bad shape, which made landings a bit difficult. Just beyond is the Caribbean, often rough and not suitable for swimming. Rather, the locals prefer to *costanear* (walk the coast), which occasionally yields treasure (and cocaine—be careful). Don Enrique (of Hotelito Evo) offers several tours around the area including the largest coconut farm in Central America, sportfishing, and visits to the indigenous Rama Kay community. His son Raul is an INTUR-certified guide, which gives him access to the Río Indio-Maíz reserve. A two-day trip for four people, including hiking to hot springs, sleeping in hammocks, food, transportation, and a visit to an indigenous village costs $350. Contact Don Enrique or Raul at Hotelito Evo.

Across the river from San Juan del Norte, the Blue Lagoon or La Laguna Azul is a small pool of clean, blue water surrounded by coconut palms and lush vegetation. Doña Angela's children (their house is next to the *ranchón*) can take you over for about $5 in a dugout canoe; for another $5 continue on to the beachfront.

Accommodations and Food

There are several decent options. We like the ▐ **Hostal Hotelito Evo** (located on the fourth walkway parallel to the river, tel. 505/2583-9019 or 505/8624-6401, evohotel@yahoo.es, $12) has seven clean rooms, three with a private bath. Also try **Hotel Paraíso Virgen** ($18), another relatively clean and secure option, located south of the main dock with comfortable rooms and 24-hour lights and water.

The all-wood **Hospedaje Anderson** (third walkway, tel. 505/2414-1368, $7) is basic but adequate. Otherwise try the thatched-roof cabins in **Cabinas El Escondite** (tel. 505/2414-9761, $10 pp with private bath) owned by a Caribbean-Cajun Rastafarian. To find Rasta's *cabinas* ask around near the military post at the north end of town, or walk down the third walkway until it ends and turn left.

Hedley Acton Thomas Barss, a.k.a. Chalí, is the end of earth's most popular bar. For dancing some *soca*, at almost any time in the day or night, it's **Bar y Discoteca Tropical,** located at the very southern end of the first walkway. For food, try **Doña Marta,** across the street from Chalí, **Soda El Tucán,** near the center of town, or **El Ranchón,** at the southern end of town.

Services

Services are limited, and so is the water and power supply. There is public Internet access in the library and mayor's office (*la alcaldía,* tel. 505/2583-9018).

Getting There and Away

The easiest way to get to San Juan del Norte is to take the long boat ride downriver from San Carlos. A variety of *pangas* now make the trip nearly every day of the week, much less limiting than it once was, but the schedule is still in flux. The slow boat takes at least 11 hours, and costs $13 each way. The fast boat costs $25, and takes half the time. Buy your downstream ticket at the San Carlos municipal dock the day before your trip.

Rumors about scheduled weekly boat service between San Juan del Norte and Bluefields are finally true. Two San Juan del Norte–based boats, *Virgo I* and *Virgo II,* make weekly passenger runs, departing San Juan del Norte on Wednesdays and Saturdays at 8 A.M. for the three-hour ride over open ocean ($30 pp). Contact Silvio Reyes Arragón (tel. 505/8411-1887) or Señora Rosario García (in San Juan del Norte, tel. 505/8691-6421) to verify this information, and please send us a report if you successfully make the trip. The boats are not big, so expect a lot of painful slamming up and down; sit in the back for smoothest ride.

The Río Indio Lodge

Since 2002, the multimillion-dollar, five-star Río Indio Lodge, a self-described ecotourism and sportfishing resort (Costa Rica tel. 506/2231-4299, U.S. tel. 866/593-3168, reservations@bluwing.com, www.bluwing.com), Costa-Rican owned and operated, has run fancy fishing trips on this Nicaraguan river. This place is geared to the luxury adventure traveler: A night in one of the 34 rooms will run you about $200 per person. Activities include guided fishing trips, bird-watching, kayaking, hiking, and visits to nearby Laguna Silico.

SOLENTINAME

BLUEFIELDS AND THE CORN ISLANDS

The Atlantic coast of Nicaragua is a land unto itself. It extends eastward from the Amerrisque mountains, down the rivers Coco and San Juan, descending through pine savannahs to mangroves and estuaries, and finally the Caribbean. Culturally, Nicaragua's vast semi-autonomous Atlantic regions are influenced more by the English than the Spanish and ethnically, more by indigenous and African blood than by mestizos (though the "Spanish," as western Nicaraguans are known, are quickly moving in and catching up).

The vast majority of Nicaragua's 450 kilometers of Atlantic coastline are unexplored, undeveloped, and unapproachable. Writer Edward Marriot called it "Nicaragua's jungle coast. Not the 'Caribbean'—despite cartographers' insistences—but, deliberately, the 'Atlantic.'...this was the Atlantic coast, with its mangrove swamps and alligators, hurricanes and stiff westers that washed up bales of high-grade cocaine, shrink-wrapped for export."

The Atlantic coast is languid and lazy, but it's got an edge too—in the form of bitter poverty and drug-related danger. It also has sultry mangrove estuaries, white, sandy beaches, and a relaxed lifestyle. The warm, humid breezes smelling of coconut palms and vegetation is a nice break from the dry, dusty highlands. Bluefields is a quintessential Caribbean port town, with enough fresh seafood to wear you out, an oppressive afternoon sun, and a no-hurry attitude. Corn Island and Little Corn Island are another scene altogether: the soft sand beaches and rustling palm fronds of your most primitive

HIGHLIGHTS

◖ Palo de Mayo Festival: Sensual and rhythmic, Bluefield's joyous May Day celebration is one of the flashiest shows in the country (page 320).

◖ Pearl Lagoon: The quiet lanes of this waterside village beg to be explored. Follow them all the way out to the beach (page 332).

◖ Wawachang and Khaka Creek Reserve: Few foreigners have yet ventured up the Wawachang River to this guesthouse and forest reserve, one of Nicaragua's newest community-based ecotourism ventures (page 334).

◖ Picnic Center Beach: This Corn Island classic is an uninterrupted crescent of white-sand hedonism; a wonderful beach and a bed await (page 340).

◖ Little Corn Island Diving: Snorkel, swim, or scuba to visit the reefs and marine life just offshore of Little Corn Island (page 344).

LOOK FOR ◖ TO FIND RECOMMENDED SIGHTS, ACTIVITIES, DINING, AND LODGING.

Caribbean fantasy, plus an isolated feeling that's hard to find elsewhere.

PLANNING YOUR TIME

If you lay in a good stack of books, a bottle or two, and a jug of sunscreen, you could spend weeks on Nicaragua's right coast, exploring the islands, reefs, bays, and broad pine savannahs and villages along the coastline. Corn Island is worth a night or two unless you really crave remoteness, in which case you should beeline to Little Corn, the more rustic of the pair, where 2–4 days will provide ample opportunity to dive and explore the reefs. Remember that everything except seafood is more expensive here—expect to pay 2–3 times more than you would on the Pacific side for lodging, beef, beer, and soft drinks. If you're

traveling overland from Managua, schedule in one day for the trip and another to recover in Bluefields. Otherwise, take an afternoon flight to Bluefields and spend the rest of the day poking around the city.

A night or two in both Bluefields and Pearl Lagoon is enough to get a basic taste of Creole culture, but if you have time, you can take a cooking class, sign up for Creole and Garífuna dance lessons, meet natural medicine doctors, poke around the two universities. Or head north on the early morning *panga* to Wawachang and the Khaka Creek Reserve. Spend a couple of days hiking, exploring the fauna and flora, and meeting local farmers. Then catch the twice-weekly *panga* back down the river to Orinoco, the Nicaraguan home of the Garífuna. Spend a day trying local foods

BLUEFIELDS

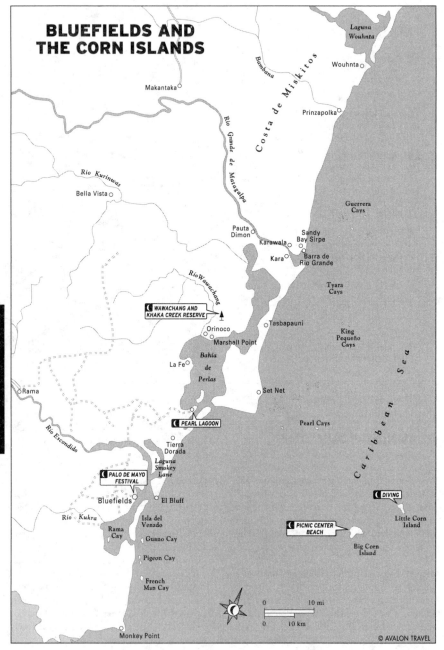

BLUEFIELDS AND THE CORN ISLANDS

Laguna Wouhnta

Wouhnta

Makantaka

Costa de Miskitos

Bambana

Prinzapolka

Rio Grande de Matagalpa

Rio Kurinwas

Bella Vista

Guerrera Cays

Pauta Dimon

Sandy Bay Sirpe

Karawala

Kara

Barra de Rio Grande

Rio Wawachang

Tyara Cays

WAWACHANG AND KHAKA CREEK RESERVE

Orinoco

Tasbapauni

King Pequeño Cays

Marshall Point

La Fe

Bahía de Perlas

Set Net

Rama

PEARL LAGOON

Pearl Cays

Rio Escondido

Tierra Dorada

Laguna Smokey Lane

PALO DE MAYO FESTIVAL

Caribbean Sea

Bluefields

El Bluff

DIVING

Little Corn Island

Rio Kukra

Isla del Venado

PICNIC CENTER BEACH

Rama Cay

Guano Cay

Big Corn Island

Pigeon Cay

French Man Cay

0   10 mi

0   10 km

Monkey Point

© AVALON TRAVEL

and listening to village elders tell their unique history on a front-porch step. See if anyone wants to walk up to Marshall Point with you. A couple of days later, hop back on the (also twice weekly) *panga* and stop in Pearl Lagoon for as long as you desire.

When to Go

The Atlantic coast receives 3,000–6,000 millimeters of rain annually (with the higher levels falling in southern RAAS), making it among the wettest places on the planet. The rainy season is punctuated by hurricanes in September and October and can extend well into December, sometimes longer. The end of December is marked by cool, "Christmas" winds. Most visitors come during the period between late January and April when things are generally dry and sunny. The biggest crowds arrive for Christmas, Semana Santa (the Holy Week before Easter), and during various regional fiestas, when making reservations is a good idea.

Safety

A note on safety: International drug trafficking continues to impact the Atlantic Coast of Nicaragua, including Bluefields and the Corn Islands, which have, at times, seen incidents of both petty crime and more serious assault against tourists. We no longer recommend exploring too far off the beaten track in this region; stay in groups, especially on beaches, and keep your wits about you.

HISTORY

The Atlantic coast of Nicaragua was originally populated by native Miskito, Mayangna (Sumu), and Rama people, who settled along the rivers and coastline and lived on fishing and small-scale agriculture. Columbus mentioned the area when he cruised by in 1502, but throughout the 16th century, its general inhospitality kept it free of foreign influence.

Spanish friars hoping to Christianize the Mayangna, Tawaka, and Miskito were killed immediately, and Spain subsequently lost interest in this part of Central America. That made it attractive to English and Dutch pirates, like Abraham Blauveldt in the 1630s, whose name in English, Bluefields, came to represent the bay and later the coastal city that emerged.

In the 1700s, the English organized the Atlantic coast into a British protectorate, establishing "Miskito Kings" whom the British educated and maintained in power. Throughout the 1700s, England armed the Miskito and Sambo people, and encouraged them to raid nearby lands, including Spanish territories in inland Nicaragua, where the bellicose Miskitos reached as far as Nueva Segovia and Chontales.

German Moravian missionaries integrated with Atlantic coast communities beginning in the early 1800s; their legacy is a largely protestant population and distinct, spartan churches. In 1860, the British departure was followed by the advent of American businesses, which established timber and banana company camps all along the Atlantic coast. Bluefields became a thriving commercial center with regular steamship connections to New Orleans, Baltimore, Philadelphia, and New York.

Such was the state of Bluefields and the Atlantic coast when President José Santos Zelaya ordered its military occupation in 1894. General Rigoberto Cabezas sailed down the Río Escondido in February, deposed the Miskito government, and officially united Nicaragua from Atlantic to Pacific for the first time. But once united to Spanish-speaking Nicaragua, Managua felt free to tax and ignore the Atlantic coast, and Zelaya and successors roundly abused indigenous rights for centuries. The foreign companies began to withdraw, and Sandino and his anti-imperialist troops brutally attacked those tempted to linger. In the aftermath and right up to the present, the Atlantic coast has decayed into a state of corruption, financial mismanagement, and poverty.

Costeños were decidedly apathetic about their supposed Sandinista "liberation" in 1979 and many were hostile to it after major FSLN errors in the region. Since the Contra war ended, Spanish-speaking Nicaraguans have arrived en masse, putting the black and indigenous populations in the minority for the first time ever. Considering their long-held isolation and resistance to the Managuan government, this is no small change. Tensions rise as these new "Spaniards" (as Costeños have always referred to mestizos) seek housing and employment, and at the same time, attempt to import their language, music, food, and other cultural aspects to their new home.

Bluefields

Bluefields is a rich waterfront melting pot of nearly 50,000 souls, many of whom make a living in the fishing and timber industries, or working on cruise ships, where their bilingual skills are prized. The city has never been connected to western Nicaragua's highway system and can be reached only by water or air. Bluefields Bay remains an important Atlantic port, and the city itself is the capital of the RAAS and home to several universities. Despite all the activity, unemployment is acute and drugs and crime are on the increase. Bluefields's primary attraction is its Creole culture. Do not miss the Palo de Mayo celebrations, an exuberant and erotic calypso-inspired dance and music event, unique to the city and celebrated fervently throughout the month of May.

ORIENTATION AND GETTING AROUND

From the Bluefields airport take a taxi for the several-kilometer approach to town for the fixed price of $0.50. Overlanders traveling from El Rama will arrive by *panga* at the municipal wharf downtown. Parque Reyes is located three blocks west of the waterfront road. Bluefields is small enough that you should need a taxi only to go to the extremes of town—the URACCAN campus at the north and the airport at the south, or when you feel unsafe. Two nearly identical bus routes run 6 A.M.–7:30 P.M. Get on and off where you like for $0.25.

SIGHTS AND ACTIVITIES

Bluefields does not offer much in the way of sightseeing, but if you're up for a stroll, there are a few places to visit. Start at the red-roofed **Moravian church,** built in 1848 with English, French, and Caribbean influence, the first of its kind on the Central American coast. About a block and a half west, the whitewashed wood and stained glass **Catholic cathedral** is captivating, airy, and modern.

The Historical Museum of the BICU university is worth a visit (located in the CIDCA building, on the second floor) if you'd like to learn more about Bluefields. They have a collection of historical objects and fascinating photos of Bluefields before Huricane Joan, the last Mosquito King, and many more.

◖ Palo de Mayo Festival

Also known as the *¡Mayo Ya!* festival, Bluefields's May Day celebration is unique in Central America. In North America, this

---

CRAB SOUP!

Be here at the end of August (27-28) for the **Crab Soup Festival,** a commemoration of the islanders' emancipation from British slavery in 1841. The governor of this then-British protectorate, sitting miles away in Kingston, Jamaica, was authorized to pay slave owners compensation for the loss of their "assets," while the newly freed slaves scrambled to put together a meal out of what was most handy – crabs. Be sure to catch the crowning of Miss Corn Island, Miss Coconut, and Miss Photogenic.

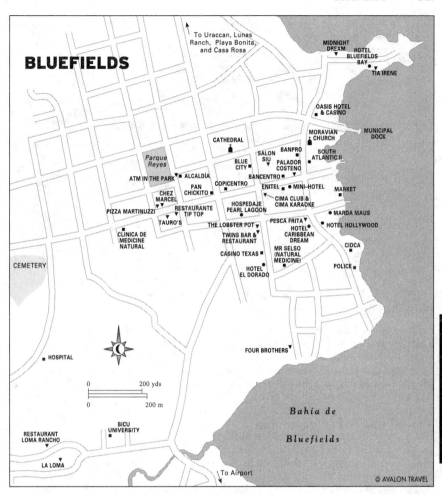

BLUEFIELDS

To Uraccan, Lunas Ranch, Playa Bonita, and Casa Rosa

MIDNIGHT DREAM
HOTEL BLUEFIELDS BAY
TIA IRENE

OASIS HOTEL & CASINO

MUNICIPAL DOCK

MORAVIAN CHURCH

CATHEDRAL

Parque Reyes

SALON SIU
BANPRO
SOUTH ATLANTIC II
BLUE CITY
PALADOR COSTEÑO

ATM IN THE PARK
ALCALDÍA
COPICENTRO
BANCENTRO
ENITEL
MINI-HOTEL
MARKET

PAN CHICKITO
CHEZ MARCEL
CIMA CLUB & CIMA KARAOKE

PIZZA MARTINUZZI
RESTAURANTE TIP TOP
HOSPEDAJE PEARL LAGOON
MARDA MAUS

TAURO'S
THE LOBSTER POT
PESCA FRITA
HOTEL HOLLYWOOD

CLINICA DE MEDICINE NATURAL
TWINS BAR & RESTAURANT
HOTEL CARIBBEAN DREAM
CIDCA

CASINO TEXAS
MR SELSO (NATURAL MEDICINE)

CEMETERY

POLICE

HOTEL EL DORADO

HOSPITAL

FOUR BROTHERS

0   200 yds
0   200 m

BICU UNIVERSITY

Bahía de

Bluefields

RESTAURANT LOMA RANCHO

LA LOMA

To Airport

© AVALON TRAVEL

BLUEFIELDS

pagan-rooted party is about springtime, fertility, and the reawakening of the earth after a long winter. In Bluefields, May falls on the cusp of the rainy season, and the entire month is a bright burst of colors, parades, costumes, feasting, and, most importantly, dancing around the maypole. Every night is a party, and the festival comes to a rip-roaring peak at the end of the month with the celebracion of the tululu dance, starting in Old Bank and parading through Beholden, Pointeen, Central, and Cotton Tree neigborhoods.

In English and Nordic tradition of the 19th century, on the first of May young men and women would collect freshly cut flowers. This was known as "going-a-maying." A long, straight pole was set in the center of town and decorated with the fresh flowers and colored ribbons anchored to the top of the pole. The celebration ushered in the spring and expressed hopes for happiness and a good harvest.

How the Palo de Mayo got to the Atlantic coast of Nicaragua remains a mystery, though it very probably passed directly from England

approaching Bluefields by water

© JOSHUA BERMAN

during the years the Atlantic coast was an English protectorate, possibly by way of Jamaica, where it evolved into something more Caribbean and erotic. To date, the Palo de Mayo is celebrated in such disparate locales as Austria, Spain, and amongst the Wenda and Galla people of Africa.

In Bluefields, the Palo de Mayo refers to the month-long celebration in Bluefields, Pearl Lagoon, and the Corn Islands, and also the name of a dance and style of music. The dance has gotten progressively more sensual in recent decades—sometimes appearing as simulated sex on the dance floor (more conservative Costeños have started a movement to return the dance to its more respectable origins).

Other Festivals

The biggest show in town is Palo de Mayo, but since the 1950s, when Bluefields adopted the patron saint of the city of Masaya, **San Jerónimo** is honored each September 30 with fireworks and celebration. These festivities roll right into the city's birthday celebrations

which last throughout the month of October. October 30 is the anniversary of the 1987 passage of the Autonomy Law; its commemoration features cuisine competitions between all the ethnic groups. This is a great time of year to sample the foods of the coast, learn about the autonomy process (and its history), and meet community leaders and politicians.

Sportfishing

For professional catch-and-release river and deep-sea fishing (and wildlife tours) contact Gerald Lewis and the **Casa Rosa Lodge** (local cell 505/8832-4269, toll-free 912/275-5485, randyrosa97@hotmail.com, www.rumbleinthe-jungle.net). For $350 a day per person, you get a large room, all meals, guide, boat, and gear. Bar drinks and tip not included.

The Oasis Hotel & Casino hosts the **Annual Oasis International Fishing Tournament** (www.fishbluefields.com, $70 pp to enter) in late March that brings the best Nica and international anglers to compete in the tarpon, snook, and open categories.

"HOW YOU MEAN?"
A FEW CREOLE EXPRESSIONS

Put your Spanish dictionary away in Bluefields – you're in Creole country! Creole is a complete language system, currently being documented by the Institute of Linguistic Promotion, Investigation, and Rescue of the Culture (IPILC) at the University of the Autonomous Regions of the Atlantic coast of Nicaragua (URACCAN). Popular books are being written to teach Creole students to read and write in their first language. The campaign slogan is: *Kriol iz wi langwij, mek wi rait it!* (Creole is our language, let's write it). At times, the rhythms of the Costeño tongue are difficult to understand, but not so tough to speak. And, of course, coastal communication slides easily in and out of English and Spanish. For instance, *"Dem aprovecharing beca dem mama no de"* means "That person is taking advantage of the fact that his mother is not home." Listen for the following expressions – and try them out, if you're feeling up for it.

Creole	English
"She done reach Raitipura."	She arrived at Raitipura.
"How you mean?"	Explain that please.
"No feel, no way."	Don't worry, it's okay.
"I no vex."	I'm not angry.
"Dat nasty."	That's awesome!
"That ain't nothing."	Thank you.
"Check you then."	Goodbye.
"Make I get tree o dem."	Give me three of those.
"She feel fa eat some."	She's in the mood to eat.
"He own"	His.
"It molest we."	It bothers us.
"Nice."	"It's all good," or goodbye.
"Uno jus keep walking."	You all just keep walking.
Wabool	Cassava pounder, or penis
Coco	Coconut, or vagina

Thanks to "Dr. G.," a.k.a. Georgie Cayasso, Bluefields native and distinguished Creole linguist.

ENTERTAINMENT AND NIGHTLIFE

You'll hear the reggae bumping wherever you go, from dance hall, roots, *soca, punta,* and Palo de Mayo to reggae *romantica,* and of course, long sets of Bob Marley. Interestingly, the Atlantic coast's second favorite is American country music, which locals proudly call their "coastal music."

To safely sample the nightlife of Bluefields, we recommend arriving to the club before 10 P.M. and leaving by midnight, before the crowd gets drunk and dangerous. For dancing, **Four Brothers** (six blocks south of the park, open 9 P.M.–4 A.M. Thurs.–Sun.) has been the heart of the Creole social scene since the 1990s. Expect a small, cramped juke joint with a wooden-plank dance floor and ice-cold beer. You'll need that beer to help you master the sensual Caribbean "hug-up" grind.

Cima Club (half a block up from Bancentro on the left, 2nd floor) draws a lively Creole crowd with its intimate dance floor; upstairs, **Cima Karaoke** offers louder music, a spacious dance floor, a longer bar, and a more diverse crowd (both are open seven days a week). **Midnight Dream** (Barrio Pointeen, two long blocks from the Moravian Church, open daily), popularly known as Baghdad, is owned by former mayor and town celebrity "Lala," a.k.a. Lawrence Omeir. This is a prominent drinking and dancing social center with a dark, open-air bar and dance floor with a view of the bay.

Radio

Soak in the culture with programs like *Roots Rap Reggae* (9 A.M. on Radio Zinica, 95.9 FM), *Energía Volumen* (4–6 P.M. on Radio La Morenita, 102.1 FM), and *Caribbean Breeze* (1 P.M. on Radio Punto Tres, 90.7 FM). Radio La Costeñísima plays regular sets of Miskito music (101.1 FM). Hear the Voice of America daily at 6 A.M. on Radio Bluefields Estereo (96.5 FM), followed by a country music show. On 97.7 FM, Radio Riddim hosts Creole talk radio programs about local politics and autonomy, as well as good reggae and dance hall music.

SHOPPING

Visiting the town market on the municipal dock is a dark, damp experience, with cramped stalls in an ugly metal building, but it's interesting nevertheless, especially if you need to stock up on homemade cheese and bun. **Joyeria y Artesania Gutierrez** (Barrio Central in front of the SOS Farmacia) sells Caribbean-inspired wood carvings, which you'll also find at some hotel shops. **Julio Lopez,** a Garífuna originally from Orinoco (Barrio 19 de Julio, in front of INAFOR) and **Leo Bolanos Padilla** (Barrio 19 de Julio, *"contiguo donde fue la cocotera,"* or "next to where the coconut trees used to be," tel. 505/2572-0070) are renowned local artisans. **Mr. Rene Hodgson** (tel. 505/2572-1658) is a talented, self-taught Creole painter and local Adventist pastor whose work is frequently displayed at the Bluefields Bay Hotel.

ACCOMMODATIONS

Bluefields is more dangerous than other Nicaraguan cities, and the city is grimy and less sanitary in general—just get an eyeful of all the dirty water and mangy mutts slithering down the roads. So this is one place where "roughing it" in the cheapest flophouses (there are a few obvious ones near the dock) is asking for trouble. If you do decide to go for one of the budget hotels, assess both its security measures and the kind of people hanging around. Insist on either a window with screens and a mosquito net. Avoid the Pension Lopez, famous for drunk men and hourly room rentals.

Under $25

Hospedaje El Dorado (Barrio Punta Fría, across from the Cruz Lorena, tel. 505/2572-1435, $6–10) is one of your best options if you are determined to stick to a strict budget. The hotel offers relatively clean, well-maintained rooms with private bath and cable TV. **Lobster Pot** (on the main drag in Barrio Central, no phone, $6–$8 pp) is owned by a Creole-speaking, Cayman Islander who runs a large establishment that rents many of its rooms to permanent guests. The clean rooms with a shared bath are better than some other run-down places but that's about it. **Hospedaje Laguna de Perla** (Barrio Central, across from the UNAG, tel. 505/2572-2411, $5) offers very basic rooms with fan, "but we don't accept drunks or scandalous behavior, and you cannot come in past midnight."

Mini-Hotel Central (Barrio Central, across from Bancentro, tel. 505/2572-2362, $15 with fan, $20 with a/c) has been a mainstay of Bluefields since 1983 and its 10 rooms are nearly always booked. It has a popular restaurant and outside veranda, and clean, well-maintained rooms with private bath and cable TV.

Under $25-50
Bluefields Bay Hotel en Casa URACCAN (tel. 505/2572-2143, www.bluefieldsbay.galeon.com, $28) is on the water, away from the hustle and bustle of the central barrio, yet still within walking distance of central town. It's a uniquely Costeño establishment that helps fund university programs and has clean, comfortable rooms; hot water, air-conditioning, simple meals available.

Hotel Caribbean Dream (Barrio Punta Fría, 30 meters south of the main market, tel. 505/2572-0107, $27) offers spacious, well-appointed rooms with private bathroom, closets, cable TV, new air-conditioning units, hot water, Wi-Fi, an on-site restaurant, a bright atmosphere, and an upstairs veranda.

Gran Hotel Anabas (Barrio Central, next to Radio Zinica, tel. 505/2572-1144) is a step up from Mini-Hotel Central, plus hot water, ceiling fans, and better beds but no wireless Internet. **Hotel South Atlantic II** (Barrio Central, next to the gas station Levy, tel. 505/2572-1022, $25–45) is a friendly, centrally located, Creole establishment, popular with Nicaraguan business travelers. They offer a safe environment and well-maintained, spotless rooms with air-conditioning, cable TV, hot water, and an on-site restaurant and travel agency.

Over $50
Oasis Hotel (on the corner near the municipal wharf, tel. 505/2572-2812, reservations@ oasiscasinohotel.com, www.oasiscasinohotel. com, $75–90 pp plus tax, includes breakfast) was opened in 2005 by a North American businessman who also owns the two casinos in town (one of which is on-site). This is the classiest hotel in town, with both carpeted and hardwood floors, Wi-Fi, and good views. The handful of spacious rooms have lovely bathrooms, minibars, safe, TV, and air-conditioning; there are a few larger suites, and the top floor is a ridiculously huge presidential apartment with a hot tub overlooking the bay; it used to belong to a foreign playboy.

FOOD
Caribbean Baked Goods
Start at the Bluefields Bay Hotel, where you'll find **Ms. Emma Rose's** baked goods; for a delicious, filling afternoon snack, arrive around 3 P.M. to place an order for a loaf of her famous bun, the official sweet bread of the Atlantic coast, often with raisins, coconut milk, and hand-ground cinnamon and nutmeg. Pick it up between 4–5 P.M. Fridays she also makes a mean "patti"—a spicy beef empanada.

Soro (Barrio Central, across the street from Galileo) sells a variety of typical Nicaraguan and Costeño baked goods. Try the moist Coco Cake for a true coast snack: grated taro with coconut milk, cinnamon, nutmeg, and sugar. For savory small loaves of coconut bread, bun, soda cake (coconut bread with ginger and sugar), and *pico* (bread with sugar and cheese), go to the woman who is in front of Pan Chickito (also known as Mercadito Mas y Menos) in Barrio Central.

Breakfast
One of the only establishments serving pancakes, sausage, and eggs is **Salon Siu** (across from Blue City, open daily at 7 A.M. for under $3). But **Bluefields Bay Hotel** features the best Costeño breakfast in town with coffee and tea, fruit, eggs, and fresh, warm coconut bread for $2.

SEA TO SOUP: ATLANTIC COAST COOKIN'

Atlantic coast cuisine is marked by its simplicity and freshness. That lobster on your plate was probably picked off the ocean floor this morning; the fish were swimming hours ago. The only way you'll get fresher fish is by cooking it on the ship – or eating it raw: **ceviche** with lime juice, tomato, and onion. Seafood on the Nicaraguan Atlantic is cheap by international standards, delicious by anyone's standards, and well worth the wait (most Bluefields restaurants are slow, even by Nicaraguan standards). If your travel complaints don't evaporate in the garlicky steam of lobster under your nose, then you obviously are going to need to spend another couple of days.

Start off with **yellowfin, snapper,** or **sea bass,** grilled or fried. **Conch,** when tenderized correctly, is soft and delicate, less briny than other seafood but with a soft texture. Or enjoy a lobster *al vapor,* bulging with delicate, white meat you can pull from the shell with your fingers, drenched in butter and lime.

Mixed soup is served in a helmet-sized bowl choked with crab, lobster, conch, and fish. Not hearty enough? Then reach for **rondon,** or rundown, a thick stew of fish (or endangered turtle), vegetables, and coconut milk thickened with starchy tubers and plantains. In August, don't miss the Corn Island **Crab Soup Festival,** when Costeños cook tons of soft crabmeat into a festival you won't forget. Atlantic coast crabmeat is particularly soft, with a delicate flavor unique to the tropics.

You don't have to stick to seafood to eat well on the Atlantic coast. Even the *gallo pinto* tastes better here: That's because it's cooked in sweet coconut oil. Between meals, fill up with **coco bread** – football-sized loaves of soft, rich wheat flour cooked up with coconut and served hot out of the oven. Another treat is kind of like cinnamon rolls but without the cinnamon: hot coconut **bun** is sweet and sticky.

Creole cooking means coconut in your *gallo pinto* and a heavy plate of *rondon.*

© JOSHUA BERMAN

Street Food and *Frito*

In Bluefields, Creole *fritanga* (usually just $1) features stewed chicken with a savory brown and salty sauce, served in a small, plastic bag with *tajadas* and Creole cabbage salad. Try **Mr. William's** shop, Thursday–Sunday, located to the left of Four Brother's disco (which also sells good *frito* and soup Thurs.–Sun.).

The mestizo version of *frito* consists of fried or slow-roasted chicken plus all your favorites from Spanish-speaking Nicaragua. Try **Comedor Arlen** (Barrio Central, right across the street from the well-known Galileo store), or on the corner across from the Texas Casino. Enchiladas that cost $0.25 and cheap beef tacos are on the menu at **Pulpería El Guayabo.**

Inexpensive Eateries

🍸 **Bar Tauro's** (Barrio Central, next to the Tip-Top) is a tiny place well loved for loud music and a good menu, including *rondon* (rundown) soup for less than $4. It's known also by the name of the new owner, Bam Bam. **Mini-Hotel Central Café** offers a wide range of well-prepared Nicaraguan and Costeño dishes at reasonable prices.

Irie Foods & Honey Sweets (10 meters down from the Obelisco Monument, open 10 A.M.–10 P.M. daily, tel. 505/8929-4382) offers classic Creole kitchen featuring stew beans and dumpling, rundown, and coconut rice and beans for under $8.

Try **Pizza Martinuzzi** (next to Parque Reyes), whose local 'za comes pretty close to the real thing.

Upscale Restaurants

Twins Seafood and More (Barrio Central, next to Texas Casino) is the new, hip restaurant in town, specializing in seafood, vegetarian, and salads. After 4 P.M., the bar and dance floor upstairs are popular with the moneyed Creole crowd. **Loma** (near BICU) is another semi-elegant option with a view from your table, a longer menu, and steeper prices. Feel free to drink the ice (they have a water purification system for ice and fresh drinks), in a delicious piña colada or a fresh fruit punch.

🍸 **Tía Irene Bar and Restaurant** is located over the water below Bluefields Bay Hotel; its one-of-a-kind view of the bay and reliable quality have kept this restaurant a local favorite from the time it was known as Manglares. **Lunas Ranch** is a well-known restaurant in the newer part of town (Barrio Loma Fresca, almost across from URACCAN). Decorated with the traditional thatched-roof design, the restaurant offers great food, mid-range prices, and a very professional staff. **Chez Marcel** is another longtime standby, especially if you're craving a steak, located near Pizza Martinuzzi.

Playa Bonita (jeanlouis.vigo@gmail.com) was opened in 2007 by a French–Bluefields couple and offers a varied menu in an open-air, waterfront setting in Barrio Loma Fresca; take a taxi. **Casa Rosa Lodge** (www.rumbleinthejungle.net), a small, family-run restaurant specializing in seafood, is located next to Playa Bonita and also on the waterfront.

INFORMATION AND TOUR GUIDES

The INTUR office (tel. 505/2572-1111) can't hold a candle to CIDCA, the Research and Documentation center for the Atlantic coast (affiliated with the UCA, 50 meters north of the police station, open 8 A.M.–5:30 P.M. Mon.–Fri., with a break for lunch). CIDCA makes available to the public a wide selection of materials about Caribbean cultures and languages, including several Miskito-only publications.

The best Bluefields tour guide is **Kenny Siu** (tel. 505/8837-2861, ksiu2000@yahoo.com), a Corn Island native who teaches tourism at the university. Kenny is a wealth of contacts and information; he worked with a Travel Channel film crew when *Bizarre Foods with Andrew Zimmern* came to film in Bluefields.

SERVICES
Emergency

The fire department (tel. 505/2572-2298) is just north of the Moravian church; the police (tel. 505/2572-2448) are on the same side of the street, three blocks south; and the Red Cross (tel. 505/2572-2582) can be found in Barrio Fatima. Hospital Ernesto Sequeira (tel. 505/2572-2391 main switchboard or 505/2822-2621 emergency) is located about five, long blocks south and west of the park.

Phones and Mail

The Claro phone office is located next to Mini-Hotel Central (open 8 A.M.–5 P.M. Mon.–Fri., 8 A.M.–noon Sat.). The post office is half a block west of the Texas Casino building, and the two Western Union offices are located one and two blocks east of the park.

Banks and ATMs

Banpro is the older of the two banks on the Atlantic coast and is located in front of the Moravian Church. Bancentro is located just around the corner on Calle Cabezas. Both are open 8 A.M.–5 P.M. Monday–Friday and 8 A.M.–noon Saturday. Money changers are on the corner between the two banks and are both safe and useful.

Both banks now feature 24-hour ATM service, though the one at Banpro dispenses the money in much more reasonable denominations (100 *córdoba* vs. 500 *córdoba* bills, which can be hard to change in Bluefields). The town hall (or Palacio) also has a 24-hour ATM booth, located just east of the park, across the street.

Internet

Bluefields has faster Internet access than much of western Nicaragua. For the best chance of securing a decent computer without a long wait, check out the original Bluefields cybercafe, **Copicentro.** Another good option is **Blue City,** run by Mark Narcisso, who spent part of his childhood in the U.S.; it offers a nice atmosphere, many computers, air-conditioning, beverages, CD burning, printing, and a music studio (same basic hours as TechHouse). All offer Internet access for about $0.75 per hour and international phone calls to the U.S. for about $0.10 per minute.

© RANDALL WOOD

Nicaraguan puddle-jumpers fly daily between Managua and the Atlantic coast.

GETTING THERE AND AWAY
By Land

The overland route is no longer the heroic journey it once was before they repaved the highway to El Rama in 2002–2003, but you'll still need some stamina and patience. Most people leave Managua for El Rama at night, then board a predawn *panga* and soak up two hours of fresh air during a sunrise trip down the Río Escondido to Bluefields (bring a sweater for both parts of the trip). This route is cheaper than flying, and also offers you a true appreciation for Nicaragua's sheer girth—and the Atlantic coast's geographical isolation.

Buses to El Rama leave from Managua's Mayoreo terminal (tel. 505/2248-3005) daily at 3 P.M. and from Mercado Ivan Montenego (tel. 505/2280-4561) daily at 9 P.M. Call ahead for seats. Express buses don't linger in Juigalpa or stop along the road, shaving two hours off the trip. All boat transportation to Bluefields is found at the Rama municipal wharf: *pangas* cast off from the dock as they fill up, 6 A.M.–4 P.M. (1.5-hour trip to Bluefields, $11

pp). There are several larger ships that carry freight and passengers between El Rama, Bluff, Corn Island, and Puerto Cabezas, but they are slow. They leave El Rama every Tuesday and Saturday at 11 A.M. (call the *Captain D* at 505/8661-7201).

By Air

La Costeña offers regular, daily flights between Bluefields, Managua, and Big Corn Island. The trip from Managua to Bluefields takes about one hour and costs $83 for a one-way ticket ($127 round-trip). To fly directly from Managua to Corn Island will cost you $107 ($165 round-trip). The flight from Bluefields to Corn Island costs $65 ($99 round-trip). It is easy to buy a Managua–Corn Island round-trip ticket with a stopover in Bluefields on the way to Corn Island for $197. Buying an "open" ticket means no dates are fixed, so you can arrange your onward flight by calling or visiting the airport, or by dealing with a ticket broker in town (South Atlantic II hotel is a good one, or look for the Costeña and Atlantic signs elsewhere).

© RANDALL WOOD

El Rama's international port

AFRICAN-DERIVED SPIRITUAL PRACTICES OF THE ATLANTIC COAST

A distant cousin to the voudoun ("voodoo") of Haiti and Benin, **Obeah** refers to sorcery, folk magic, and other religious practices brought by Central and West African slaves to the Americas. Using herbal teas and baths, charms, amulets and prayer, Obeah is best described as a method of communication with the supernatural world, and a means of calling on metaphysical powers through shamanistic rituals.

Obeah was frowned upon by Christian missionaries and slave masters, resulting in the awkward Christianization of modern Obeah: Many African deities now bear the names of Catholic saints. Obeah is most commonly used in the West Indies, but is widely practiced in Caribbean and Latin American nations whose African descendants have maintained a connection to this aspect of their ancestry, including the Creole, Garífuna and Miskito people on Nicaragua's Atlantic Coast.

Contrary to popular belief, Obeah is not always used for negative purposes. In fact, often times Costeños pay a practitioner to heal a medical, emotional, or spiritual problem; to influence events in a person's favor; to achieve success in a particular endeavor; or to find out the answer to an important question (such as who is my husband sleeping with, who stole my cows, etc.).

However, amongst the Miskito and Afro-Caribbean peoples negative Obeah is not unheard of: Locals will even resort to Obeah revenge rather than the police department. Whether you personally believe in Obeah or not, on the Atlantic Coast you are entering a world where the practice and the belief of Obeah are a large part of the culture, and every Costeño believes, just a little, in its power.

When visiting the Caribbean coast of Nicaragua, there is no need to fear Obeah (unless you take away another's lover)! Moreover, the way that most Costeños approach Obeah is indicative of their overall spiritual perspective on life. For example, in Creole culture, there is a strong nine-day ritual that follows a person's death: As soon as the person is pronounced dead, word begins to spread amongst the Creole community. The family's closest friends and family quickly arrive at the house to clean, cook, and receive the multitudes that will soon come to accompany the family during their grief. This set-up occurs 24 hours a day (though most people come at night) and appears to be like a party without the music – crowds of people eating, drinking rum, and talking. On the ninth night, the night before the person is finally buried, a very specific ritual occurs: The same close friends and family of the deceased go through the house and remove all bed linens, tablecloths, and curtains. At midnight, all present sing to the spirit of the deceased to signal that it is now time to ascend to heaven. It is widely believed that failure to perform this ritual will cause the spirit of the dead person to wander the earth as a miserable ghost, causing trouble, harm, and sometimes death to the living.

For more information check out the novels and memoirs of Jamaica Kincaid, or *Vampire The Masquerade, Unburnable,* and *Brown Girl in the Ring* by Nalo Hopkinson.

In Bluefields, Mr. Selso (tel. 505/8845-4137 or 505/2572-2176) is a traditional and fascinating Miskito **"Bush Docta"** and Obeah practitioner who is highly sought after for spiritual, emotional, and medical issues that doctors trained in western medicine have been unable to resolve.

The small Clinica de Medicina Natural en Terapias Alternative (Barrio Teodoro Martinez, Avenida Cabeza, in front of Escondite bar, open 5:30–8 P.M.) is a **natural medicine** clinic offering beach flower therapy, healing massage, and medicinal plants.

Contributed by Phoebe Haupt-Cayasso, trip leader and experiential learning consultant with a decade of experience working with students in Bluefields and Atlantic coast communities.

By Boat

Passenger-boat traffic to El Rama, Pearl Lagoon, Orinoco, and Pueblo Nuevo (up the Wawachang River) originates from the main municipal dock. Pay the $0.10 entrance fee at the first window (pays for their cable TV connection). Trips to El Bluff ($2 each way) originate at a much smaller MINSA dock next to the municipal market (inquire at the market). Old cargo-passenger boats leave three times a week for Corn Island. If you choose this route instead of flying, take lots of water, sun protection, a barf bag, and a sense of humor. The *Captain D* reportedly makes monthly runs to Puerto Cabezas around the middle of the month (about $35, 12 hours), but we've never heard of anyone making this trip.

Rumors about scheduled weekly boat service between Bluefields and San Juan del Norte to the south appear to finally be true. Two boats, *Virgo I* and *Virgo II* are currently making weekly passenger runs from the Bluefields municipal dock on Thursdays and Sundays, departing at 8 A.M. for the three-hour ride over open ocean ($30 pp). Expect an uncomfortable, rough ride. Contact Silvio Reyes Arragán (tel. 505/8411-1887) or Señora Rosario García (San Juan del Norte tel. 505/8691-6421) to verify.

Near Bluefields

EL BLUFF

Once connected to the mainland before 1988 when Hurricane Joan breached the bar, El Bluff is an industrial platform that happens to be adjacent to a gorgeous little Caribbean white sand beach. Reconnected in 2006 by pedestrian walkway, El Bluff makes an exotic day trip for Bluefielders tired of the "big city," but only attracts the most adventurous foreigners. El Bluff remains an important port, deepened in the 1980s by Bulgarian cooperation and currently in search of private investment to build out Nicaragua's ties with the eastern U.S. and Europe.

Hire a Bluefield *panga* to get to El Bluff (from the MINSA dock next to the municipal market in Bluefields for $1.50, 30-minute ride, embarking as soon as they fill up with 12 passengers. The last boat returns to Bluefields around 4 P.M.). From Hotelito El Bluff, walk out the main entrance of the hotel, take your first left onto a paved path and follow it through a residential area until it ends (about 10–15 minutes). Keep going straight for about 200 meters at which point you will be able to see the beach.

There's no reason to stay here, as Bluefields has better options. But for the determined, **Hotelito El Bluff** (tel. 505/2577-0059, $5) is located right next to the park, with basic rooms with cable TV and fan. Skip the hotel restaurant in lieu of **La Casona Bar and Restaurant** (open Tues.–Sun. nights), located along the paved path towards the beach.

RAMA CAY

Fifteen kilometers south of Bluefields is Rama Cay, ancestral home of the Rama people. About 800 souls live on this small island. According to historians, the Rama people are originally descended from the Chibchas and Aruac Rama from the Amazon basin; several oral histories explain how the Rama came to occupy this isolated island at the end of the 17th century. Rama culture is now disappearing: Only a small handful of elders still speak the language.

A tour of the island is sometimes available to visitors for $3 ($6 if you want lunch). Getting to Rama Cay is an easy $6 *panga* ride from Bluefields; it takes about an hour to cross the bay.

RESERVA SILVESTRE GREENFIELDS

On the outskirts of Kukra Hill, Reserva Silvestre Greenfields (tel. 505/2278-0589 or

505/8434-4808, info@greenfields.com.ni, www.greenfields.com.ni) is a protected reserve, characterized by its scenic beauty, silence, and proximity to nature. Privately managed as an ecotourism business, you can hike more than 25 kilometers of trails, canoe through jungle watercourses, or rest and enjoy the silence surrounded by lush vegetation. Price includes lodging, meals, and guided tours. You can make this a day trip (no lodging, no meals) for $15 per person or $50 per group (up to six persons), and enjoy excursions with guides by foot or canoe, the botanical park, the bathing pier, and more. All trips must be previously arranged and reservations need to be received at least four days in advance.

KARAWALA AND SANDY BAY

Sandy Bay, located three hours north along the Caribbean coast, is one of the only Miskito communities accessible from Bluefields, and nearby Karawala is the last indigenous Ulwa site in the world (the Ulwa are related to the Mayangna but have distinct cultural characteristics and language). The boat ($17 one-way) to both places leaves the *muelle* (dock) in Bluefields on Mondays and Fridays at 10 A.M.—or whenever they fill up; it returns on Wednesdays and Fridays. There's not much to do in Sandy Bay for nonanthropologists, although the beach is nice. Karawala, however, is situated between pine forest and mangrove swamps and offers world-class tarpon fly-fishing. In town, you'll find basic accommodations and simple meals. Sand flies in both places can get pretty bad, so be prepared with long pants and baby oil.

◖ PEARL LAGOON

Tucked away one lagoon north of Bluefields, Pearl Lagoon (Laguna de Perlas) is a small community whose natural splendor is a welcome respite from Bluefields. Its sandy streets are easily explored on foot. This little village gives access to local Miskito communities and the enchanting Pearl Cays. The locals earn their living from the water—you'll see boats of the five companies that deal in fishing and fish processing tied up along the docks or moored in the lagoon. Denmark and Norway have been active in the economic development of the region, constructing municipal piers in Pearl Lagoon, Haulover, Tasbapauni, Kakabila, Brown Bank, and Marshall Point to assist local fishermen in getting their catch to market.

Sights and Entertainment

Don't miss the **"the great gun,"** as the locals lovingly call the iron cannon mounted in front of the municipal dock and surrounded by a lovely garden. Embossed with the seal of the British empire and the year 1803, it dates back to the protectorate. The clean architectural style of the most eye-catching building in town, the whitewashed **Moravian church,** was typical of the period. Attending an evening service there is memorable (dress appropriately).

Don't miss a night of reggae at one of Pearl Lagoon's several small ranches, or clubs, the most popular of which is **Cultural Vibrations** (known locally as Stiff Cock, seriously).

Pearl Lagooners love baseball, and compete on teams with names like the Buffalos, Mariners, Young Stars, Hurricanes, Sweet Pearly, First Stop, Young Braves, and the Haulover Tigers—watch them battle it out at the stadium on Saturdays and Sundays September–January.

Accommodations

The best of the family-run guesthouses is ◖ **Green Lodge Guesthouse** (tel. 505/2572-0507, $15), a pleasant place on the main drag. **Hospedaje Ingrid** (tel. 505/2572-1777, $8) has a quiet veranda with hammocks and chairs. It's located towards the back of Pearl Lagoon, to the left of the stadium in Barrio 4th of May. All rooms have private bath and some have TV. Right on the main drag in front of the dock, the **Sweet Pearly's** (tel. 505/2572-0520, $10–13) is another standby with 11 small, clean rooms with fans, plus bar, restaurant, and ice-cream parlor downstairs.

Casa Blanca Hotelito y Restaurante (tel. 505/2572-0508, $10–30) is clean, well liked, and run by a Danish-Creole couple intent on making your trip pleasurable.

© RANDALL WOOD

the Moravian church in Pearl Lagoon

Food

Miss Betty's Bread Shop is the place to go for pastries, juices, and sweets. The **Green Lodge** serves fresh, well-prepared food; their plate of the day costs $3–5, though breakfast is cheaper. **Hospedaje Ingrid** and **Cool Spot** also offer good cooking from $3. The basic **Pearl Paradise** is on the second story of the building adjacent to the municipal dock.

◀ **Queen Lobster Restaurant** (100 meters north of the municipal dock, open 10 A.M.–11 P.M. daily, $6–12) has a tranquil setting on the lagoon and serves mostly seafood and mixed dishes.

The **Casa Blanca Hotelito y Restaurante** has the most varied menu in town, served in a pleasant ambience, though a few readers have complained about unfriendly service. Shrimp dishes start at $5 and lobster at $7.

Services

The ENITEL office and a police post are in the center of "town" by the wharf. The health clinic is a few blocks south, to the right of the Moravian church. Four pharmacies can take care of basic medical needs. For more serious medical emergencies, you will be strapped into a *panga* and rocketed off to Bluefields. With that in mind, stay safe.

Getting There and Away

The *panga* trip up the Río Escondido and then north through a complex network of waterways to Pearl Lagoon is a beautiful ride that takes under an hour and costs $7 each way. On the way, you'll pass several shipwrecks, and the active dock at Kukra Hill, named after a long-assimilated cannibalistic tribe. Go to the municipal dock in Bluefields around 7 A.M. to sign up for the Pearl Lagoon *panga*. Boats leave as soon as they have 20 passengers, all day until 3 P.M. The last *panga* back from Pearl Lagoon leaves between noon and 3 P.M. but won't leave if the boat isn't full.

THE PEARL CAYS

Most of the 18 specks of land that make up the Pearl Cays archipelago remain untouched and relatively accessible, though a few cays are being built up by wealthy foreigners, and controversy over their ownership and development is building. The cays (pronounced "keys") are six kilometers east of a small Miskito coastal village called Set Net. Hire a boat from Pearl Lagoon and enjoy the ride through the harbor, into the open Caribbean, then up the empty coastline to the cays.

So far, the Pearl Cays have zero tourist facilities (though one resort has come and gone, and more may follow), so bring water and your Gilligan's Island survival kit to be safe. Arrange a trip through La Casa Blanca or Hospedaje Ingrid in Pearl Lagoon. A round-trip *panga* ride to the Pearl Cays can cost $150–300, so the more people chipping in, the cheaper it'll be. If you find yourself sharing one of the islets with local fishermen cutting down coconuts and telling fishing stories over a fire on the beach, feel free to strike up a deal for some fresh seafood for the grill.

VILLAGES NEAR PEARL LAGOON
Awas
The town of Pearl Lagoon sits on the southeast side of a small prominence jutting out into the bay. Walk west from the town (to the left of the dock) to get to the broad, shallow lagoon-beach community of Awas. This half-hour walk down a flat, sandy road will cross a saltwater estuary and a small footbridge. When you get to the Miskito community of Raitipura (Miskito for "on top of the cemetery"), turn left and follow the road to Awas. Rent a small palm-thatch hut from one of the locals for $2–4, kick back, and relax. Take advantage of the new **Bar and Restaurant Tropical View,** built out over the water.

Tasbapauni
Farther up the coast, on the Caribbean side of the land, is the community of Tasbapauni (two hours from Pearl Lagoon), set on a thin strip of land right between the Caribbean and the lagoon, close to the Man of War Cays. There is one place to stay: **Mini Hotel, Bar & Restaurant Yadosh** (tel. 505/2572-9080,

$10) with seven rooms with private bathrooms; the restaurant offers a wide variety of seafood. Beware of the sand flies when the breeze is not blowing (same with visiting Set Net). From Bluefields, you can go directly here via *panga* for $13 each way.

Pueblo Nuevo
To hear the Bluefielders tell it, Pueblo Nuevo, 45 minutes up the Wawachang River just to the west of Orinoco, is home to farming families that began slashing and burning back in the Pacific, and mowed their way east until they hit the Atlantic. FADCANIC is here teaching organic farming and forest management in order to save the only remaining tropical forest in the region. Catch the Pueblo Nuevo *panga,* departing Bluefields on Sundays and Wednesdays ($12 pp each way), and returning on Mondays and Thursdays. He passes Wawachang and the Khaka Creek Reserve on his way to Pueblo Nuevo. It's harder to catch *at* Pueblo Nuevo, when it might already be full. Either way, reserve your return seat in the boat on your way upstream.

◖ Wawachang and Khaka Creek Reserve
Located about a kilometer up the river from Wawachang, Khaka Creek Reserve is the epitome of the local, grass-roots ecotourism movement which is providing alternate means of subsistence in a delicate ecosystem. Run by FADCANIC, new, modern tourist facilities allow you to take advantage of this wilderness area, from hiking trails to eight cabins and trained guides knowledgeable in local flora and fauna.

An all-inclusive package (food, lodging in the guesthouse, and trail guide) costs $30 per night plus $24 for round-trip transportation to and from Bluefields. The center is ideal for ecological research and is equipped with solar energy, Internet access, screened windows, and purified water. The guesthouse offers seven rooms that can accommodate 25 people, one with a double bed and private bath. To pay for your services separately, it's $15 per night for lodging, $2.50 per meal, and $5 for the services of a local trail guide for half a day ($10 full day). Contact them via the Wawachang Center (tel. 505/2572-2386, mruizg1964@hotmail. com). To arrange your trip from Bluefields, stop by the FADCANIC office, located just up from Mini-Hotel and speak with Reynaldo, Silver, or Marcos (or any of the Agro-Forestry or Wawachang staff).

The whole Wawachang region is serviced by the Foundation for the Autonomy and Development of the Atlantic Coast of Nicaragua (FADCANIC). Founded by a small group of passionate Creole leaders in the early 1990s, FADCANIC manages a number of successful development programs, financed largely by the Norwegian government and various NGOs. The **Wawachang Center for Sustainable Agro-Forestry Development** is FADCANIC's largest microcredit program. Stop by it to visit the Agro-Forestry high school and walk the fields, seedling nursery, and model farm.

ORINOCO AND MARSHALL POINT

Orinoco is the southernmost home of the Garífuna people, a distinct ethnic group with strong West African roots unique to Central America. On May 18, 2001, UNESCO proclaimed the Garífuna language, music, and dance a "Masterpiece of the Oral and Intangible Heritage of Humanity." Their dancing, drumming, and singing manifests strongly African roots. Try to visit on November 19, the Garífuna Arrival Day in Nicaragua and National Day for the Garífuna People, featuring talented Garífuna singers, drummers, and dancers from the coast, as well as from Belize, Honduras, and Guatemala.

Marshall Point is a typical, small Creole community. You can reach Marshall Point by going to Orinoco and then walking or hiring a *panga* to take you around the corner. Do not walk alone. Tip: Grease the edge of your shoes with a thick line of Vaseline as you arrive in Orinoco and Marshall Point, as grass lice can be abundant.

Try to sample some *fufu*, a cassava dish common throughout West Africa, or the Garífuna *ereba* or *bami*, flat bread also made from cassava. Invite community leaders Frank Lopez, Ramon Martinez, and Fermin Gonzalez to lunch to hear about the history and culture of the Garífuna and Orinoco. You may extraordinarily witness a *walagallo*, or *dugu*, ceremony, a healing ritual that has been known to bring people back from the brink of death. The spirit of an ancestor appears to someone in a dream, giving the specific recipe for that particular *walagallo*. Dancing, singing, and sacrificing of chickens then continues until the dying person gets up from the sickbed to start dancing, signifying to the crowd that he or she has been cured.

Accommodations and Food

The only lodging option in Orinoco is the **Hostal Garifuna** (tel. 505/8927-0123 or 505/8648-4985, www.hostalgarifuna.com, $8–16), a nice, new guesthouse with seven large rooms and a pleasant area for relaxing. Arrange to eat your meals at the hostel to experience authentic Garífuna cooking. The owners can help direct all your activities and transport in the area.

Getting There and Away

From the municipal dock in Bluefields, take a *panga* ride up into the Laguna de Perlas (the water body, not the town) to Orinoco and Marshall Point. The famous "hardway *panga*" ($11 one-way) leaves Bluefields on Mondays, Thursdays, and Saturdays, and returns to Bluefields on Mondays, Tuesdays, Thursdays, and Fridays. You can sometimes catch this boat from Pearl Lagoon, depending on whether or not they filled up with passengers in Bluefields. You can also rarely catch the Pueblo Nuevo boat.

EL RAMA

At the eastern terminus of the highway from Managua, El Rama straddles the frontier between Atlantic and Pacific more perceptibly than any other Nicaraguan town. A longtime

THE ROAD
TO EL RAMA

If you've got a few extra days to spare, consider the overland route to Bluefields from Managua. The road is in better condition than it ever has been and takes you through some out-of-the-way corners of the country.

During the 1980s, the highway from San Benito (Managua) to Rama, known as the Rama Highway, was a hotly contested military prize. At stake was control of the port at Rama, through which Managua received much of its oil and supplies from the Baltic states and the Soviet Union. The Contras finally succeeded in capturing the highway in 1987 with a massive offensive of 2,500 troops, who laid waste to government buildings in La Gateada, Santo Tomás, and San Pedro de Lóvago and demolished five bridges, all but the crown jewel – the bridge at Muelle de los Bueyes which, standing 150 meters high over the Río Mico, remains the highest and most irreplaceable bridge in Nicaragua. The highway, a pothole-ridden disaster by the end of the war, was completely resurfaced during 2002–2005.

Between Villa Sandino and La Campana are hundreds of pre-Columbian petroglyphs in situ, around which the **Parque Arqueológico Piedras Pintadas** (tel. 505/8850-2121, $3 entrance fee) was developed in 2008 with help from Finland. From Villa Sandino it's 20 minutes by bus but you can easily walk it. Stay in Villa Sandino at **Hotel Santa Clara** (tel. 505/2516-0055, maisalar@hotmail.com) where you'll find rooms for $20 with air-conditioning and hot water, $15 with fan; or the more economical **Hospedaje Chavarria** across from the Medical Center.

people who once inhabited the shores of the Siquia, Rama, Escondido, and Mico Rivers. The inhabitants of today's El Rama, however, are the progeny of immigrants from Chontales, Boaco, and Granada, all of whom swarmed here in the late 18th century to take advantage of the boom in the wood, rubber, and banana trade. Before 1880, the original port of El Rama was located on the southwest shore of the Río Siquia but was relocated to the present location due to the unbearable mud, floods, and swamps that plagued the original location.

While Nicaraguans from all over the country resented the stringent rationing of food and basic goods during the war years of the 1980s, no one was more indignant than the people of El Rama, whose international port was where the millions of metric tons of military hardware were brought onshore from Eastern-bloc freighters to be shipped up the Rama Highway to military bases around the nation. In the 1980s, while locals were forming lines to receive a half-bar of soap and one pound of rice, they watched steel-armored convoys of tanks, fighter planes, and trucks full of rifles, grenades, and antipersonnel land mines pass through their town bound for the battle lines. Short of the trenches of the front line, nowhere was the military buildup—and the irony of the shortage of basic goods—more obvious.

El Rama, though wholly dependent on the river, is also at the mercy of it. El Rama has been under water several times, including during Hurricane Joan, when for three days the only thing seen above the surface of the boiling, muddy waters of the swollen Río Escondido was the church steeple. Deforestation upstream means the river floods more and more frequently these days, and with less advance warning. An electronic system of flood warning devices was installed along the river in 2000 to give residents a chance to evacuate.

Sights and Activities
The typical traveler spends no more than 15 minutes in El Rama between the time he

riverine port and trader town, El Rama is a melting pot of some 50,000 people, where mestizo cattle traders meet Caribbean steamer captains, and dark-skinned Creoles mix with "Spaniards" from the Pacific.

The name Rama is a tribute to the Rama

or she gets off the bus and onto a boat to Bluefields. But should you find yourself stuck here, you may find El Rama to be worth a second look, and even useful as the base for an expedition or two. The folks at El Rama are interested in developing a tourism infrastructure; they just don't know how to do it yet (the first step should be to pick up all the garbage).

Any adventuring you do in the region will require ingenuity and patience. Divided by rivers and swamps, the lands around El Rama are teeming with places to explore and look for wildlife. **Los Humedales de Mahogany** is a wetlands reserve important for the reproduction of local species. It's a 4–5 hour trip by boat downstream in the direction of Bluefields along the Mahogany River near the entrance to the Caño Negro (Black Creek). **Cerro Silva** was declared protected in 1997; it's located 2.5 hours along the Río Rama in the direction of San Jerónimo. Once you disembark from your boat, it's a 2.5-hour hike from the river's edge to the park; find a guide in San Jerónimo to lead you there.

The falls of **Salto Mataka** are found along the Río Siquia, 2.5 hours from La Esperanza (the town with the big bridge, just west of El Rama). Also located near La Esperanza is **El Recreo,** a popular swimming hole three kilometers north of town.

Accommodations

Hotel Johana (tel. 505/2517-0066, $2 pp) is better than nothing, but there's a floor-thumping *discoteca* downstairs. A bit cleaner and far quieter is **Hospedaje García,** with singles for $3, double beds for $5, and fancier rooms on the second floor with air-conditioning and a view of the river for $11. Or try **Hospedaje Solidaridad Tres Rios** (a few hundred meters up from the dock, on the left along the main drag, $2–3) with very basic rooms, run by a nice family.

◖ **Eco Hotel El Vivero** (Km 291 on the highway from Managua, tel. 505/8617-6001, ecohotelvivero@hotmail.com, $13–25) is a quiet, peaceful place within a private reserve, located two short kilometers from the city of El Rama. The wooden cabins and decent meals have been recommended by several readers.

Food and Services

Restaurante El Expreso is slow anyway, but serves good seafood, soups, chicken, and steak. Across from the market, **Antojitos Mexicanos** is popular with the locals for Mexican dishes and beer. The **Eskimo** sells sandwiches in addition to ice cream. A good *fritanga* sets up shop evenings near the market (approximately across from Antojitos Mexicanos).

The ENITEL and post office are located across the street from each other. ENITEL is open 7 A.M.–9 P.M. Monday–Saturday. For late-night phone calls, try the Pepsi booth on the street that leads to the municipal pier (i.e., the pier with boats for Bluefields). There's a phone there that the owner will let you use. **Farmacia El Carmen** (open 8 A.M.–1 P.M. and 2–6:30 P.M. Mon.–Sat.) is well stocked with medicines, sanitary supplies, and more.

Getting There and Away

Buses to El Rama leave from Managua's Mayoreo terminal (tel. 505/2248-3005) daily at 3 P.M. and from Mercado Ivan Montenego (tel. 505/2280-4561) daily at 9 P.M. Call ahead for seats. Choose an express bus, since they don't linger in Juigalpa or stop along the road, shaving two hours off the trip. All boat transportation to Bluefields is found at the municipal wharf: *pangas* cast off from the dock as they fill up, 6 A.M.–4 P.M. (1.5-hour trip to Bluefields, approximately $10 pp). There are several larger ships that carry freight and passengers between El Rama, Bluff, Corn Island, and Puerto Cabezas, but they are slow. They leave El Rama every Tuesday and Saturday at 11 A.M. (call the *Captain D* at 505/8661-7201).

Big Corn Island

Eighty-three kilometers due east of Bluefields Bay's brackish brown water, the Corn Islands are a pair of Tertiary-period volcanic basalt bumps in the Caribbean. Formerly home base for lobster fishermen and their families, the islanders are increasingly turning to tourism for their future. How well the fragile island ecosystem will support it will determine the fate of the islands.

Big Corn Island is 10 square kilometers of forested hills, mangrove swamps, and stretches of white coral beaches. The mangrove swamps and estuaries that line several stretches of coastline are crucial to the island's water supply, and the islanders have fiercely resisted attempts by foreign investors to drain or fill them. The highest points are Quinn Hill, Little Hill (55 and 57 meters above sea level, respectively), and Mount Pleasant (97 meters).

Of the six sea turtle species swimming off Nicaragua's shores, four live in Caribbean waters. On land, Corn Island boasts three endemic species of reptiles and amphibians, all threatened by the continued swamp draining.

Like many Caribbean islands, time is measured "since the last hurricane," which at press time, was Hurricane Ida on November 5, 2009. It toppled power lines, coconut trees, houses, churches, and schools; the waves and wind smashed boats as well. Reconstrunction began immediately.

HISTORY

Pirates on their way to maraud the coast of Central America and Nicaragua's Río San Juan first visited here in the 16th century, sometimes by accident after the reefs tore the bottom of their ships open. But Corn Island was inhabited long before that by the Kukras, a subtribe of the Mayangnas whose penchant for consuming the bodies of their enemies inspired the first English visitors to call them the Skeleton Islands. The Kukra were eventually assimilated into the Miskitos. Nowadays, the native Creole population shares the island with an increasing

number of menial laborers from the mainland, who have overtaken the Creoles in number and have increased the island's total population to nearly 12,000 people.

Native islanders are direct descendants from several of the more infamous European pirates, as well as English royalty and plantation owners—don't be surprised if you meet people with names like Kennington, Quinn, Dixon, or Downs.

ORIENTATION AND GETTING AROUND

From the new airport building, it's a five-minute taxi ride ($0.75 by day, $1.50 by night) to almost anywhere on the island, though buses circulate about twice per hour ($0.35). A walk to Brig Bay, which is the "downtown" area, is around 2.5 kilometers or 20 minutes. A paved road circumnavigates the island and bicycles can be hired at some hotels, including Hotel Morgan or Corn Island Car Rentals. The municipal docks are in Brig Bay with *panga* service to Little Corn.

DIVING

Three distinct layers of reef, composed of more than 40 species of coral, protect the north side of the island. Though the diving and snorkeling are impressive (divers regularly see nurse sharks, eagle rays, and lots of colorful fish), the reefs closest to shore have deteriorated over the past decades, victims of overfishing, predatory algae (which grow as a result of increased nutrient levels in the water from sewage runoff), sedimentation, storm damage, and global warming.

Blowing Rock is a rock formation with lots of color and dozens of varieties of tropical fish. The island's only dive shop, **Dive Nautilus** (tel. 505/2575-5077, divechema@yahoo.com, www. divebigcorn.com) offers scuba gear and the dive-master services of "Chema" Ruiz, a jolly Guatemalan with a wall full of framed scuba diplomas and a full-service, modern dive shop:

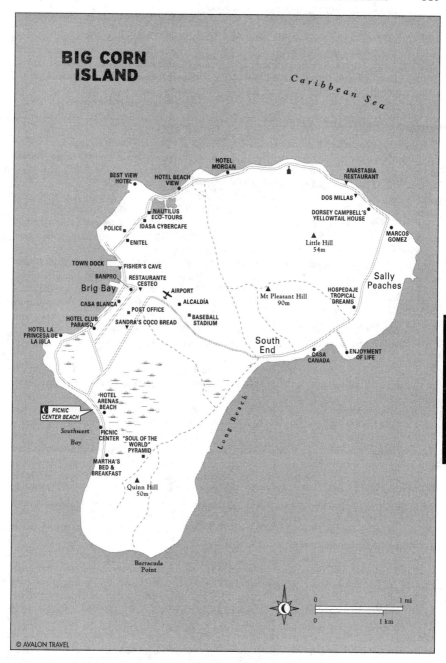

BIG CORN ISLAND

Caribbean Sea

BEST VIEW HOTEL
HOTEL BEACH VIEW
HOTEL MORGAN
ANASTASIA RESTAURANT
DOS MILLAS
NAUTILUS ECO-TOURS
DORSEY CAMPBELL'S YELLOWTAIL HOUSE
POLICE
IDASA CYBERCAFE
MARCOS GOMEZ
ENITEL
Little Hill 54m
TOWN DOCK
FISHER'S CAVE
Sally Peaches
BANPRO
RESTAURANTE CESTEO
Brig Bay
AIRPORT
Mt Pleasant Hill 90m
HOSPEDAJE TROPICAL DREAMS
CASA BLANCA
ALCALDÍA
POST OFFICE
HOTEL CLUB PARAISO
SANDRA'S COCO BREAD
BASEBALL STADIUM
South End
HOTEL LA PRINCESA DE LA ISLA
CASA CANADA
ENJOYMENT OF LIFE
PICNIC CENTER BEACH
HOTEL ARENAS BEACH
Long Beach
Southwest Bay
PICNIC CENTER
"SOUL OF THE WORLD" PYRAMID
MARTHA'S BED & BREAKFAST
Quinn Hill 50m
Barracuda Point

0   1 mi
0   1 km

BLUEFIELDS

© AVALON TRAVEL

$75 for an introductory course, $60 for a two-tank dive, $250 for open-water certification, or $90 for two dives at Blowing Rock.

A few sandy stretches of beach along the north shore allow you to get into the water. One good one is in front of Dorsey Campbell's Yellowtail House.

SIGHTS

The incongruous **Golden Pyramid** on the top of Quinn Hill was built in 2006 by the Soul of the World society, a group whose members believe Quinn Hill is one of eight spots in the world where the vertices of a cube—with a diameter the same as the earth itself, and placed inside the Earth's orb—intercepts the land surface of the globe. Got that? The other vertices are found in the Cocos Islands (Indian Ocean), Hawaii, Santiago de Compostela (Spain), South Island (New Zealand), Buryat (Siberia), Tierra del Fuego (Argentina/Chile), and the Kalahari desert (Namibia).

◖ Picnic Center Beach

The most popular swimming beach, South West Bay is a long, golden crescent of soft sand and turquoise water, with a smattering of cheap restaurants and not-so-cheap hotels. Or go to **Long Beach,** just as pretty, but a bit rougher and with fewer services.

Other Activities and Events

For a walking adventure, tackle the shore between Marcos Gomez's hotel and the South End Cemetery in Sally Peaches, or break a sweat on the hike up Mount Pleasant where the view from the top of the old lighthouse tower is well worth the effort. A path leads up to Mount Pleasant opposite the **Casa Canada.** When you reach the local school, take the path that winds up behind the school to the left.

Weekends, the islanders dance to island rhythms at **Reggae Palace,** just south of the docks in Brig Bay, and at **Nico's** in the South End. Corn Islanders are serious about their **baseball:** A league of eight teams (including two from the Little Island) play in the quite-nice stadium east of the airport.

ACCOMMODATIONS

Traditionally more expensive than elsewhere in Nicaragua, stiff competition on Corn Island has kept prices reasonable. There are now at least two dozen hotels and guesthouses on Big Corn Island; many small ones come and go. Following is the cream of the crop.

Under $10

Practically the only place on the island with a room for less than $10 is **Hospedaje Angela** (across from the bank, tel. 505/2575-5134, $7).

$10-25

For $10, you can stay with the impressive family of **Marcos and Jeanette Gomez** (tel. 505/2575-5187) who rent clean, safe rooms out of their house or additional outbuildings. Nearby **Dorsey Campbell's Yellowtail House** ($10) offers two self-catering private cabins plus boat or accompanied dive trips from the shore out to the reefs ($10 per hour). Dorsey knows the reefs better than anybody. No meals, but Seva's Dos Millas is conveniently right around the corner.

$25-50

◖ **Hotel Morgan** (north end, near the brewery, tel. 505/2575-5052, kerrygean.morgan@gmail.com, $25–40) on the north side has six cabins with simple rooms with air-conditioning, fridge, TV, and private bath. They serve three meals a day in the restaurant, or climb the stairs to the open-air balcony for drinks and a top-notch ocean vista. **Hotel Best View** (tel. 505/2575-5082, $30) is less fancy, with a nice second-story balcony overlooking the water.

$50-100

◖ **Paraíso Beach Hotel** (tel. 505/2575-5111, info@paraisoclub.com, www.paraisoclub.com, $45–70), tucked away on its own grounds in Barrio Brig Bay, has 14 recently renovated cabana-style rooms with private baths, and fan or air-conditioning, including a honeymoon suite. Laundry service, plus food and drink service to guests on the nearby beach; snorkeling trips on their boats are also available, and Swedish massage (starting at $20). Under Dutch management since 2005, the hotel offers excellent service and the restaurant, though expensive, has the best menu on the island (breakfasts from $4 and $5 burgers, all the way up to the $17 surf and turf) and is open till 10 P.M.

Locally owned, wonderfully clean **South End Sunrise Hotel** (three minutes from the airport, tel. 505/8828-7835, www.southend-sunrise.com, $35–55) has 15 double rooms with air-conditioning, TV, and hot shower; nice beach area nearby.

The **Picnic Center Hotel & Restaurant** (tel. 505/8420-6186, $50) enjoys the best uninterrupted crescent of white sand on the island; rooms are a little overpriced for quality of the services, though they are well equipped with air-conditioning, TV, queen-size beds, and private baths and superb hot showers. The restaurant is an enormous, palm-thatched open-air patio.

Arenas Beach (tel. 505/2575-5223, info@arenasbeachhotel.com, www.arenasbeachhotel.com, $90) has 26 rooms and large, clean, and well-equipped bungalows with deck verandas, all finished in tropical timber, on the same South West Bay. It has a bar on the beach, and next door you can rent golf carts to tour the island.

La Princesa de La Isla (tel. 505/8854-2403, info@laprincesadelaisla.com, www.laprincesadelaisla.com, $55–70) is a secluded and recently remodeled beachfront hotel at Waula Point, run by a very amiable Italian and his family, who offer excellent cuisine. It is at the south end of Brig Bay and accessed by a beach road that passes by the shrimp processing plant.

Over $100

C Casa Canada (tel. 505/8644-0925, Canada and U.S. tel. 306/861-9224, casacanada@canada.com, www.casa-canada.com, $109) has a superb location at South End overlooking a turquoise bay and reef. The resort is classy and luxurious, from sumptuous towels and hot showers to the minibar, cable TV, air-conditioning, fridge, and coffee machine. Each cabin features king-size beds and overstuffed sofa and chairs. Dip in the infinity pool, or explore the beach and rocks. The restaurant serves excellent seafood and strong coffee at breakfast.

FOOD

Outside the hotels, there are very few restaurants. One exception is **Fisher's Cave,** adjacent to the docks, with a breezy deck. **C Seva's Dos Millas** (Two Miles) on the north side of the island has seen better times, but still serves reliably tasty seafood and ice-cold beer. A meal at **Anastasia's by the Sea** will convince you lobster tastes best by the water. Meals are served in a building on stilts directly over the water. A couple of hundred meters south of Brig Bay town, **Comedor La Rotonda** makes a mean *gallo pinto* with toasted coco bread for $2.

Fill up on **coconut bread,** which usually comes out around midday. Ms. Sandra, 50 meters south of the Banpro building (look for a small roadside sign), bakes the best coco bread on the island, as did her mother.

INFORMATION AND SERVICES

Before you go, check for updates and announcements at www.bigcornisland.com, which has updated listings of all the island's businesses. Big Corn has no post office. Cell phone services are available from the two main local carriers, Movistar and Claro, or roaming from your own phone. Internet is available at most of the hotels on the island or Idasa Ciber Café (100 meters down the road from Nautilus Dive Shop, tel. 505/2575-5082, open 8A.M.–noon and 1:30–6 P.M. Mon.–Fri.) offers Internet services, as well as national and international phone calls. ENITEL (the phone office) is north of the docks and around the corner.

Banpro is the only bank on the island, occupying a new building in Brig Bay, at the corner where the road turns parallel to the runway; they have the only ATM on the island. Dive shops and larger hotels take credit cards, but some only take Visa; check before you go. There is a small and improving hospital with limited ability.

Corn Island Car Rentals (next to Arenas Hotel, tel. 505/8643-9881 or 505/8413-9553, nestort0110@hotmail.com) offers golf carts, scooters, bicycles, and boat rides; they have diving and fishing gear also.

GETTING THERE AND AWAY
By Air
La Costeña offers several daily flights to Corn Island from Managua (which stop in Bluefields). Round-trip flights from Managua to Corn Island are about $165 round-trip. Call the following numbers for an updated schedule:

Managua: 505/2263-2143 or 505/2263-2142, fax 505/2263-1281

Bluefields: 505/2572-2500
Corn Island: 505/2575-5121

By Boat
The quickest ride is the Rio Escondido boat, which leaves the municipal dock in Bluefields to Corn Island on Wenesdays and returns on Thursdays from Corn Island's municipal dock to Bluefields, $10 one-way. The *Captain D,* a larger, smaller craft, leaves Bluefields (El Bluff, actually) bound for Corn Island on Wednesdays and returns Sundays. It's a 4–6-hour, sun-baked trip. Contact the Emusepci office just inside the gates of the municipal dock for current ship schedules (open 7 A.M.– 5:30 P.M.), or call their office in El Rama (tel. 505/2572-1467). The same ship can take you upriver to El Rama—or, if the stars align in your favor, to Puerto Cabezas.

Little Corn Island

A humble, wilder version of Big Corn, "La Islita" is a mere three square kilometers of sand and trees, laced with footpaths and encircled by nine kilometers of coral reef. Little Corn is a delicate destination, visited by an increasing number of travelers each year. There are clever accommodations for several budgets here to meet the demand, but rough boat transport from Big Corn—an experience one traveler likened to pursuing a *narco-panga* across 15 kilometers of open swell—will help hold the masses at bay. Bring a flashlight, your snorkel gear, and a good book.

Note that Little Corn Island is irregularly policed by volunteers and has experienced a handful of violent attacks on tourists in recent years. The security situation is sometimes better, sometimes worse, so be sure to ask your hotel for the latest news—and advice on staying safe. Above all, don't walk alone on the beaches, or at night.

ORIENTATION AND GETTING AROUND
Unless you make special arrangements with your *panga* driver to take you elsewhere, you will be let off at the southwestern-facing beach, where you'll find a cement sidewalk that runs the length of the village. This is called the "front side" by islanders and is the center of most social activity.

Walk north along that sidewalk to the school, baseball field, and phone office before the road deposits you in the unsavory barrios where migrant workers camp out in huts of black plastic and corrugated steel. Turn right at the school for the walk up to the lighthouse and the north side of the island, or follow the red muddy track from Miss Bridget's place through forests and swamps to the north beach and Derek's place. Just south of the dive shop is another muddy track that leads across to the "breezy side" of the island and the Casa Iguana.

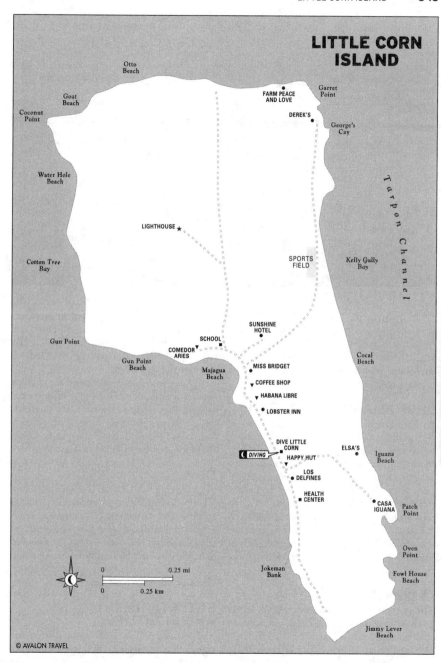

LITTLE CORN ISLAND

Otto Beach

Goat Beach

Coconut Point

FARM PEACE AND LOVE

Garret Point

DEREK'S

George's Cay

Water Hole Beach

Tarpon Channel

LIGHTHOUSE ★

Cotton Tree Bay

SPORTS FIELD

Kelly Gully Bay

Gun Point

SUNSHINE HOTEL

SCHOOL

COMEDOR ARIES

Gun Point Beach

Majagua Beach

MISS BRIDGET

Cocal Beach

COFFEE SHOP

HABANA LIBRE

LOBSTER INN

DIVE LITTLE CORN

DIVING

HAPPY HUT

ELSA'S

Iguana Beach

LOS DELFINES

HEALTH CENTER

CASA IGUANA

Patch Point

Oven Point

Jokeman Bank

Fowl House Beach

Jimmy Lever Beach

0   0.25 mi

0   0.25 km

© AVALON TRAVEL

© RANDALL WOOD

the view from Casa Iguana

Circumnavigating the island on the beach is ill-advised, as the sandy shoreline is interrupted by long, rocky, impassible sections, both at Goat Beach and the southern tip of the island. Elsewhere, there are long sandy stretches of beach to enjoy and explore.

SPORTS AND RECREATION

Beach hikes, snorkel excursions, and lots of time reading and swinging in your hammock will fill your day. **Casa Iguana** offers fishing, snorkeling, and picnic trips, and most of the beachfront hotels have snorkel gear for rent. For a rewarding hike, walk to the school, turn right and follow the sidewalk to its end; then follow the footpath up and to the left to reach the **lighthouse** (about 20 minutes from the waterfront), perched on Little Corn's highest peak. You can climb up to get a view of the entire island.

Diving

The island's bigger scuba shop, **Dive Little Corn** (www.divelittlecorn.com), operates out of a wooden building just south of the new pier on Pelican Beach. They offer morning and afternoon dives for novice through advanced divers, night dives by appointment, hourly and all-day snorkel trips, PADI certification, and kayak rentals. Hotel Delfines also has **Dolphin Dive.**

Most dives around the island are shallow (less than 60 feet), but a few deeper dives exist as well. Little Corn's delicate reef system is unique for its abundance of wildlife and coral formations—these include overhangs, swim-throughs, and the infamous shark cave.

Fishing

Within a couple kilometers of shore, you'll find schools of kingfish, dolphin, amberjack, red snapper, and barracuda. Fly fishers can catch tarpon and bonefish right from the beach, or Casa Iguana will take you out for $59 a person. Boat trips can also be arranged with a number of locals, or at Hotel Delfines—ask around on the front side for a good deal.

ENTERTAINMENT AND NIGHTLIFE

The best place on the island to sip a drink and enjoy the gorgeous waterfront view of the big island on the horizon is **Habana Libre,** owned by a Cuban transplant to the island ("I married an islander. Everyone here has the same story," laughs owner Ronaldo). They offer the best *mojito* on the Atlantic coast, with mint fresh from the garden. The bar is also home-base for the Island Braves baseball team. The **Happy Hut** is another option, a reggae-colored building on the front side, which is a grinding good time on weekends.

ACCOMMODATIONS

A variety of accommodations are available on Little Corn, from palm-thatch huts to cabins to conventional hotel rooms with color TVs. **Guess House Sweet Dreams** ($15 pp) is an ordinary *hospedaje* with nothing-special rooms. Another budget option is **Sweet Breeze** (from $10 pp), a locally run establishment and backpacker favorite with cabins made from traditional bamboo and palm thatch, and hammocks slung from the coconut trees just meters from the shoreline (five minutes' walk north from Casa Iguana). It is run by several Miskito families with surprising skill in the kitchen.

© RANDALL WOOD

Fishing is the mainstay of the Atlantic coast economy.

Get back to nature (that's why you came to Little Corn, after all) at **Derek's Place** (dereksplace@gmail.com, www.dereksplacelittlecorn.com). Derek has been here for years and his original backpacker desert island getaway continues to evolve. You can still camp if you want ($4), or shack up in a thatch hut ($14) or in raised cabins with electricity and breezy porches looking over the reef ($45–85). Delicious international meals are available, as are snorkel trips and transfers.

Hotel Los Delfines (tel. 505/8892-0186 or 505/2285-5239, hotellosdelfines@hotmail.com, www.hotellosdelfines.com.ni, $20–60) has 18 air-conditioned concrete and glass bungalows on the water. They'll be glad to arrange trips for you and private boat transport from Big Corn. Local-owned **Sunshine Hotel** (tel. 505/8883-9870, $45) is rather quiet. A bit simpler but still breezy and clean, **Hotel Lobster Inn** (tel. 505/8847-1736, $20) has basic rooms with private bath and fan, and a full menu in the restaurant downstairs.

Casa Iguana (casaiguana@mindspring.com, www.casaiguana.net, $35–75) is a cinch to recommend: Located on the cliffs of the southeast, breezy side of the island, Casa Iguana consists of raised, wooden cabins clustered around a communal, hilltop lodge where guests gather to eat, drink, and listen to the waves. The 15 cabins are a clever compromise between rustic simplicity and comfort, and include soft mattresses, outdoor showers, private, breezy porches with hammocks, and shelves full of books. Join the other guests each morning for breakfast, lunch, and each evening for happy hour and family-style dinner, frequently the day's catch. Casa Iguana provides snorkel gear rental, fishing trips ($59 a person), and satellite email.

Little Corn Beach & Bungalows (tel. 505/8333-0956 or 505/8662-7033, info@littlecornbb.com, www.littlecornbb.com, $48–85) is impressive: Their eight bungalows have private bathroom and small kitchen, just steps from the water. Co-owner/architect, Scot Smyth (winner of an Innovative Builder of the Year Award from the Northern Colorado homebuilders association) has ensured his ecofriendly design includes shower water from rooftop rain barrels, and coming soon, wind and solar power. The owners have sponsored several veterinary clinics on the island resulting in the spaying and neutering of hundreds of pets; ask how you can help.

Hard to find but worth the effort, **Farm Peace Love** (paola@farmpeacelove.com, www.farmpeacelove.com) offers rich, fresh Italian and Caribbean dinners from local ingredients ($18 prix fixe) and also a classy guest suite for $70 per couple (or three people), including breakfast. They also have a fully-equipped cottage with bedroom, living room with futon, and full kitchen; it costs $85 a night for up to three people (five-night minimum). Get your boat to drop you off to avoid the 45-minute overland trek. Ask about weekly and monthly rates, or low-season discounts May–October. Reservations are required; snorkeling and horseback riding available.

FOOD

Nearly every accommodation offers meals. **Elsa's Great Food and Drinks** offers just that, but slowly, in a beachside barbecue setting on the east side of the island. On front side, **Bridgett's First Stop Comedor** is a good choice for home cooking. **Hotel Lobster Inn** is more formal and offers chicken and steak as well. Knock on the door at the blue house past the school to inquire about coconut bread.

Located on the trail that divides the island, Rosa's Restaurant and Store, serves tasty made-to-order meals all day. Breakfast is around $4, and lunch and dinner are $6. Good menu options for vegetarians and vegans, including delicious curry.

Italian native Paola Carminiani will cook a legitimate three-course Italian (or Caribbean) meal with fresh ingredients, $18 a person at her place, **Farm Peace Love** (paola@farmpeacelove.com, www.farmpeacelove.com). Contact her at least one day in advance.

SERVICES

The ENITEL office (open 8 A.M.–5 P.M. Mon.–Fri.) is the yellow building with the satellite dish, across from the big blue *acopio*. You can find a wimpy health clinic just south of the Hotel Delfines. Anything more complicated requires a *panga* ride back to the big island, or even Bluefields. You'll find the Idasa Ciber Café in the Delfines Hotel (open 11 A.M.–7 P.M. Mon.–Sat.), with Internet and telephone service.

GETTING THERE AND AWAY

Sometimes one, sometimes two scheduled *pangas* ply the route between Corn Island and Little Corn Island ($6 each way, 40 minutes) and are coordinated with the departure and arrival of the two rounds of daily flights. Boats depart from Big Corn Island (pay a $0.20 harbor tax) at about 9 A.M. and 4 P.M.; boats depart Little Corn Island at 7 A.M. and 2 P.M.

The trip to Little Corn is often choppy and rough, especially when the seas are up. During the windiest time of year (December–April), if it gets too rough, the port authority can stop shuttle service until conditions are safer. You can expect to get wet regardless the weather. Also, the *panga* drivers sometimes enjoy racing their friends, tipping a cold one before getting behind the wheel, and gunning it on waves to catch mad air. Seats in the front afford a more violent bashing; seats in the back are prone to more frequent splashes of spray. The *pulperías* across from the dock on Big Corn sell heavy, blue plastic bags that fit over a backpack for less than $1—an essential investment for keeping your gear dry. Alternatively, rent your own boat and driver, which runs $70–90 each way. Smooth-drivin' Charlie, on Little Corn, provides this service; he can be contacted through any of the hotels there.

A number of larger fishing boats travel between the islands, and these may agree to take on a paying passenger. See Miss Bridgett for the day's schedule. Ask about *The Adventurer* and the *San Nikolas*, freighters which makes regular trips between the islands.

PUERTO CABEZAS AND THE RÍO COCO

Isolated from the rest of Nicaragua by vast tracts of inaccessible forest and coastline, Puerto Cabezas (Bilwi) and the Río Coco watershed are remote, wild, and unique. Spanish-speaking Nicaragua has always felt nationalistic about its right to alternately claim and ignore this far-off corner of the country. Managua has incited neighboring Honduras over the subtleties of the border, yet the only road to Puerto Cabezas degenerated into bumpy oblivion decades ago, making Puerto somewhat of an island in itself. Tourism is undeveloped throughout this region, which for some travelers, makes it all the more enticing.

This is far and away the most indigenous region of Nicaragua, where Miskito is heard more than Spanish. At first glance, Puerto Cabezas and the Río Coco might have the air of a drowsy backwater unchanged through the centuries, but to the contrary, the area is affected by many modern issues, including drug trafficking, global lobster prices, and international development projects.

The Río Coco is Central America's longest river and the cultural and spiritual heart of the Miskito people, who live a rather traditional lifestyle on both banks of the waterway. The whole region burned white-hot during the revolution years, and the scars run deep, but these days the rhythm of the days revolves around fishing and farming, as it has for centuries.

Inland, the "mining triangle" is composed of the three pueblos of Siuna, Bonanza, and La Rosita. The area no longer produces the quantity gold or guerilla warriors it once did, but there is yet a pioneering feel to the area,

HIGHLIGHTS

◖ **Puerto Cabezas's Old Pier:** Any farther east and you're in Barbados. This old dock is the heart of the town and a picturesque look at the 19th century (page 350).

◖ **Moravian Churches:** The Moravian religion took root early in Nicaragua's Atlantic Coast and remains an important influence. Join a Sunday church service given in the Miskito language: only here! (page 350)

◖ **Tours to the Miskito Communities:** Nicaragua's indigenous fishing communities are practically a country unto themselves and AMICA, an association of indigenous women, will take you there (page 361).

◖ **Waspám:** This is the spiritual home of the Miskito people and gateway to Central America's longest river, the Río Coco. It's about as rough and remote as you can get in Central America (page 362).

◖ **Bosawás Biosphere Reserve:** No corner of Central America is wilder or less explored than this unbroken stretch of cloud forest (page 366).

LOOK FOR ◖ TO FIND RECOMMENDED SIGHTS, ACTIVITIES, DINING, AND LODGING.

which is still host to a Canadian gold mining company and a few casinos in the town of Bonanza. This area is also the jumping-off point for the country's most rugged adventure, an expedition into the sprawling and untamed Bosawás Reserve.

PLANNING YOUR TIME

It's safe to say Puerto Cabezas, the mining triangle, and the indigenous communities along the Río Coco don't figure prominently into the travel itineraries of many, so if you're traveling here, chances are you are an aid worker, gold miner, or documentary filmmaker and already have your itinerary planned. Though it's easy enough to hop a puddle jumper in Managua for an hour-long flight to Puerto,

Siuna, or Waspám, you should always plan more time than you think you'll need when traveling in these areas. Perhaps a few days in Puerto with a few days allowed to head up the coast or to nearby villages.

HISTORY

The Mayangna inhabitants that settled in Puerto Cabezas gave it the name Bilwi, in reference to the great quantity of *wi* (leaves) and the equally great number of snakes *(bil)* hidden in the foliage. Renamed in the early 1900s after the general that President Zelaya sent out to the Atlantic coast to unify the nation, Puerto Cabezas—like much of Nicaragua's Atlantic coast—has seen more glorious days. Its zenith was probably at the start of the 20th century, when Puerto was the center for exportation of Atlantic coast lumber and mineral products, including gold from the mining triangle. Its airstrip was, in 1964, the longest in Central America. Testimony to the wealth of Puerto Cabezas during the lumber boom is the enormous wooden dock that juts into the Atlantic, built in the mid-1940s out of locally cut hardwoods.

Somoza was well liked in Puerto and the northeast. Puerto locals fondly recall the times Tacho would arrive on the Atlantic coast in his private plane, barbecuing with the locals and telling jokes. Somoza had largely left the Atlantic coast to its own devices and Costeños generally viewed the goings-on in Managua as news from a foreign country. When the Sandinistas arrived to unite the country after taking power in 1979, the revolution collided with a growing sense of Native American autonomy worldwide. Originally intending to work with the Sandinistas, indigenous leaders soon disputed Sandinista authority to rule the Atlantic coast. The Sandinistas retaliated by forcing the relocation of entire Miskito communities and razing the villages, ostensibly to deny support to Contras. Ten thousand Miskito villagers resettled in refugee camps, while another 40,000 Miskito and Mayangna escaped over the Río Coco to Honduras, some of whom returned as Contras themselves. In 1985, Minister of the Interior Tomás Borge conciliated, and the Río Coco communities have slowly rebuilt their original villages in the delicate autonomy now granted to the two departments of the Atlantic coast.

While a significant number of Puerteños work in government jobs—Puerto is not only the departmental capital, but also the center of the indigenous community's government—several thousand workers were laid off when the Chamorro government replaced the FSLN, and the city has never quite recovered. Puerto Cabezas is largely a coastal backwater and commercial hub for the northeast. Its small economy is based on commerce—particularly of lobsters, wood, fish, and transport. The Nicaraguan military maintains a naval base here, from which it patrols the northern Atlantic coast and Miskito Cays. There are scattered jobs in the timber and fishing industries, and many people looking for a legitimate way to earn a living.

Today, life struggles on, with a wary eye on the future. Tankers from Venezuela and Curaçao periodically pull up at the dock to replenish the town's supply of petroleum, and a Louisiana-based engineering company continues to fuss with plans to build a modernized port complex complete with grain silos, a power plant, container storage, industrial cargo cranes, and facilities for deepwater tankers. In the meantime, Puerto Cabezas continues to experience a two-headed wave of immigration: poor Miskito families from the Río Coco area in search of a better life, and wealthy families from Managua who are starting businesses and buying beachfront properties.

Puerto Cabezas (Bilwi)

Far away from everything, Puerto Cabezas (usually referred to as just "Puerto" or "Port") is connected to Pacific Nicaragua only by semi-passable, seasonal roads. Most travelers fly to this outpost city from Managua.

It is entirely possible that you'll be the only traveler in this town of about 50,000 inhabitants, but enough foreign volunteers and missionaries have passed through that you won't draw too much attention. In Puerto, most streets are nothing more than streaks of bare red earth connecting neighborhoods of humble wooden homes set on stilts. It's a glimpse of many worlds, with Miskitos tying wooden canoes alongside steel fishing boats at the pier. It's an easy walk from anywhere in town to the water's edge, but there are no real recreational beaches, and the water is shallow and rocky. The Mayangna inhabitants named it Bilwi, because the leaves *(wi)* were full of snakes *(Bil)*. These days you should worry less about serpents than the increasing drug traffic slowly impacting the social norms of the region: You are closer to trouble here than elsewhere, because of that same remoteness.

SIGHTS AND ATTRACTIONS
◖ Old Pier
The old wooden pier is the mainstay of the town and certainly worth a look. Built in the 1940s of precious woods culled from the nearby forest, the pier has been on its last legs for years due to extensive hurricane damage, saltwater, and old age. Tied up there are usually a motley crew of old fishing freighters, Miskito double-ended sailboats, and small fiberglass *pangas*. The pier is beautiful during the day, but dangerous at night.

◖ Moravian Churches
Puerto is more Moravian than Catholic, and its quaint churches betray the region's separate

history. In Barrio El Cocal, in the northern part of town, the **Moravian church** is the only place on earth you can hear service given in Miskito (Sunday mornings only). You may also visit the Moravian church and school in the center of town, and the **Catholic church** replete with stained glass; the remnants of the former Catholic church stand behind it.

Other Sights

Near the center of town is an interesting house/museum/hotel, the **Casa Museo** (entrance $1), commemorating the life and work of Judith Kain Cunningham, a local painter who passed away in 2001. A prolific artist, her subject matter was the Río Coco and the Miskito communities of the Waspám. Also on display are works of macramé, sculpture, artifacts celebrating local indigenous movements, and more.

At the north end of town just past Kabu Payaska restaurant is **La Bocana,** a sandy Atlantic coast beach that is unfortunately getting a bit dangerous, so enjoy its tranquil beauty from afar.

YATAMA AND THE STRUGGLE FOR INDIGENOUS SELF-DETERMINATION

Fraught with frequent reversals and setbacks, the struggle of Nicaragua's indigenous people for human rights, electoral privileges, and autonomy has never been easy. The Somoza government was popular in the Atlantic coast primarily because Anastasio and his sons largely ignored non-Spanish-speaking Nicaragua. The Miskito people of Puerto Cabezas fondly recall the days when Tacho would fly into the northeast for a visit, accompanied by tons of fresh meat he would distribute. To this day, Tacho is popularly associated with summer barbecues and relative isolation. The Sandinistas, however, paid quite a bit of attention to the Atlantic coast.

The FSLN came to power just when a sense of unity and independence was growing among the Miskito people. The new government gave the native peoples a unique opportunity to press for their own interests and historic demands. The Sandinistas moved quickly to attempt to incorporate the indigenous movement into their own organizational structure, but soon learned the Miskito people were not even remotely interested in being a part of any group led from Managua. The indigenous peoples of the Atlantic coast instead organized themselves into the political group MISURASATA and renewed their fight for self-determination.

The Sandinistas blundered badly in their early years on the Atlantic coast. Attempts to break up indigenous patterns of life and form state-sponsored cooperatives, mandates on which crops were to be planted and for how much they would be sold, and expropriations of foreign-owned companies alienated the indigenous peoples of the Atlantic coast from the start.

The Sandinistas met the growing resistance with violence and repression. Labor strikes and other organized disruptions led to a massive increase in government military presence, and, in 1981, more than 30 Miskito leaders were rounded up and arrested on the grounds that they were inciting the indigenous peoples to rise up against the Nicaraguan state. Whether the charges were true or not, the arrests cemented the Miskito's mistrust of the new government into hatred and many communities packed up and moved across the Río Coco to Honduras, where the Contras tried to win them over. The rancor was mutual: The Sandinista government broke ties with MISURASATA, forcefully relocated the remaining Miskito villages to refugee camps outside of Puerto Cabezas, and burned the old villages to make sure roving bands of Contras couldn't make use of them.

Against insurmountable odds, MISURASATA leaders, like the controversial Brooklyn Rivera, hoped to convert the entire Atlantic region into an autonomous, self-governing reserve for indigenous peoples. Sandinista minister of state Tomás Borge offered them instead a few concessions that, when accepted, eventually helped to restabilize the region: a limited form of autonomy and self-policing and the chance to return to their ancient homelands. In 1987, after just over two years of consulting with the Atlantic coast communities, the government went a step further in reaching out to the indigenous peoples of the coast: They signed into law an autonomy statute.

The statute reshaped the Atlantic coast like nothing else had since the days of the British. It guaranteed self-rule and first-class citizenship for all minority groups on the Atlantic coast without sacrificing their cultural roots or identities. The statute permitted them to use their own languages, common land, and have a say in the development of the Atlantic coast's natural resources. The statute called for two 45-member coastal governments to be formed, one each for the northern and southern regions, responsible for governing trade, the distribution of goods, and the administration of health and education. The statute's one weakness was its flexibility, which opened the door for internecine feuds and leadership rivalries among the Atlantic coast peoples.

The Miskitos, who eventually found their way into the ranks of the Contras during the 1980s, organized themselves into a group called Yatama (Yapti Tasba Masraka Nanih Aslatakanka, or Sons of the Mother Earth). With the advent of the Chamorro government, the Yatama Contras generally disbanded and turned in some of their weapons in exchange for land to farm. Yatama made the conversion from armed movement to political party. Chamorro's effort to stabilize the region, plus her government's respect for the newly created autonomous regions earned her the respect of the indigenous peoples.

In contrast, the government of Arnoldo Alemán apparently tried to set the indigenous movement back a hundred years, causing the entire political climate in Puerto Cabezas and the Atlantic to become more tense as a result. Not lost on the indigenous peoples of the Atlantic coast is the auspicious fact that Alemán was of the same political party as Zelaya, who integrated the Atlantic coast at gunpoint a century ago. The now infamous "Pact," in which the Sandinista and Liberal parties essentially divided the government between themselves, imposed election criteria that makes it nearly impossible for small or new parties to get a foothold in the elections.

During the departmental elections of 2000, violence erupted when Yatama was completely excluded from appearing on the ballot or taking part in the elections. Representatives of Yatama vowed that unless they were permitted to participate in the municipal elections, there would be no elections. The military was sent to Puerto Cabezas and bullets flew in armed confrontations with protesters. Several people were killed. During the elections, there was significant Miskito abstention, resulting in the election of a Sandinista mayor.

Yatama supporters accused Alemán of trying to politically eradicate the indigenous community, abandoning the Miskito, Mayangna, and Rama peoples to continued poverty and exploitation. The Bolaños government (2002–2007) largely ignored Yatama, whose leaders were subsequently wooed into an alliance with the Sandinistas for the 2006 Presidential and National Assembly elections. Brooklyn Rivera now serves as a deputy in the National Assembly for the FSLN, and Steadman Fagoth, another of the former Contra Miskito leaders, now heads the Fisheries Ministry in the Sandinista government. This political about-face is so complete, Sandinista cadres on the Atlantic Coast complain that Yatama has effectively displaced them in regional governments. How long it will be before the FSLN feels it has to retake control remains to be seen; the FSLN has never been comfortable for too long with independent-minded allies. This story is far from over.

© RANDALL WOOD

the old Catholic church in Puerto Cabezas

The **URACCAN** campus is located a few kilometers down the road out of town. There's a good library there, as well as people with a wealth of information about the area.

ENTERTAINMENT AND EVENTS

Karaoke Payito is a small, low-key bar with a proclivity for 80s and 90s music and cold beer without the booming sound systems that prevail in most of Puerto's discos and bars. Climb to the second floor of **Mirador Kabu Yula,** a friendly bar with views of the bustling dock. On the east side of the park, **The Flipper Bar** is an old Caribbean classic with $0.50 beers in the pool hall out back.

For dancing, the **Malecón** is Puerto's overall most happening nightlife venue, with inside and outside tables overlooking the beach and two dance floors that start throbbing on the weekends. **Disco María** (two block west of the park) rules the disco scene but there's *reggetón* at **El Rincón** (north of town just past the Petronic gas station). *Soca* and salsa beats throb

at **Disco Zaire,** and a group of other discos that surround the park.

Semana Santa in Puerto Cabezas is an unforgettable event during which many overseas Puerteños try to return home. The town sets up dozens of thatch *ranchos* at La Bocana beach, and the 24/7 party lasts at least a week: food, drink, music, and nonstop Caribbean grinding.

ACCOMMODATIONS
Under $10

Family-run **Hospedaje Britton** (Calle Central, across from the Moravian Church, tel. 505/8450-8504, elvinkind@yahoo.com, $5) has 10 rooms with shared bath and fan, plus two cabins for $15 (ask about monthly rates), all set on a couple acres of tropical fruit trees. Norton the owner can arrange everything from day trips to swimming holes on the Rio Tuapi to sailboat tours and lobster dives; he loves to talk about Nicaragua, knows where absolutely everything is, and speaks English, Spanish, Miskito, and Creole.

Hospedaje Wangki (Calle del Aeropuerto, next to CSE, tel. 505/2792-1545, $7—$13) has 15 decent rooms, your choice of shared or private bath with or without air-conditioning. Breakfast available. Try your luck at the **Hospedaje Mar Azul** (half a block west of the *alcadía,* tel. 505/8844-8546, $7), though some readers have complained about its shabby facade and depressing location.

$10-25

Hotel Casa Museo (tel. 505/2792-2225, casamuseojudithkain@hotmail.com, www.casamuseonicaragua.org, $12–27) was built in and around the Judith Kain Cunningham museum; a handful of accommodations on wooden stilts with bright, well-appointed rooms surrounds a central garden with sprawling comfy sofas, tables, benches, and other sitting areas. The on-site café serves breakfast and lunch as well as coffee and sodas throughout the day.

Hotel Triple H (tel. 505/2792-1615, $15–20 includes breakfast) is a new hotel in Barrio Cocal, across from Kabu Payaska. Six bright

PUERTO CABEZAS

THE ATLANTIC COAST DRUG TRADE

Long the territory of pirates plying the waves in tall ships, the hidden and sparsely populated rivers, cays, and lagoons of Nicaragua's Atlantic coastline are a favorite haunt of South American cocaine merchants and their local cronies. During the 1980s, each Atlantic coast community had a Sandinista police force and a boat to patrol the coastal waters and estuaries. Succeeding governments pulled the police out to save money and, in the vacuum of power, the Atlantic coast became a lawless and virtually unpatrolled haven. Colombian drug runners would land onshore to refuel their boats and consolidate, divide, and distribute their merchandise. The Nicaraguan military's meager resources have been a poor match for the well-equipped drug boats sporting 250–500 horsepower engines with the latest in GPS, radar, and weaponry.

It's a well-known fact that many drug boats pass through the wilds of the Miskito Cays, an archipelago of islets, mangrove swamps, and trackless lagoons where the police have found stashes of gasoline. Other points of entry to Nicaragua include Cabo Gracias a Dios and the Río Coco, the city of El Rama, the Río Escondido, the northern half of the Pearl Lagoon, Corn Island, and the community of Sandy Bay. Some traffickers purchase gasoline from willing locals, paying with bales of high-grade, uncut product; this devastating introduction of cocaine and crack has threatened to unravel the social fabric of many coastal communities.

Sometimes drugs come to shore when Colombian traffickers transiting Nicaraguan waters jettison their cargo into the sea when threatened with boarding or capture, either abandoning it entirely, or circling back later, using their ample knowledge of the Atlantic currents to predict where the packages will turn up on the beach.

In early 2001, three Colombians turned up dead in the coastal community of Sandy Bay, with no explanation; supposedly, they were assassinated by Yatama for trying to hook the locals on their product, which they were offering at ridiculously low prices. In 2004, hired gunmen burst into the police station at Bluefields, blowing away six officers in a carefully planned hit. And in 2009, a plane full of coke dropped from the sky, crashing near Waspám in the north. By the time the authorities arrived, the plane was empty, and nobody knew a thing.

Since the new Nicaraguan police chief, Aminta Granera, a one-time trainee to become a nun, was appointed at the end of 2006, the war against the drug barons has turned serious. The police and military presence on the Atlantic coast has increased dramatically and major busts are becoming a weekly occurrence.

In 2009, Nicaraguan soldiers occupied several villages in the area in search of Colombian drug traffickers, with whom they eventually engaged in deadly firefights. Rioting subsequently broke out in Puerto Cabezas after indigenous leaders accused Nicaraguan soldiers of using drug searches as a pretext to destroy property, steal, and even kill local Miskito citizens (charges the government denies).

Travelers should expect police to thoroughly inspect bags at every dock and airport in the area.

and clean rooms have air-conditioning and private bath; Internet in reception. **Hotel Pérez** (tel. 505/2792-2362, $11–22) has eight rooms set in an old wooden house on the main drag, some with air-conditioning, all with private bath and use of the kitchen.

$25-50

El Cortijo (tel. 505/2792-2340, $27) is on the main drag, a block south of the mayor's office with air-conditioning, private bath, and cable TV. **❰ El Cortijo 2** (tel. 505/2282-2223, $25) is classier and more elegant, two blocks away and sitting atop a bluff over breaking surf. Guests here enjoy stained hardwood interiors, a wonderful ocean-facing deck, garden, and a semiprivate beach at the bottom of the stairs.

SPINY LOBSTERS AND PUERTO'S DIVERS

During my first trip to Nicaragua in the spring of 2007, I had no agenda, no contacts, and I made up my itinerary as I went. After a few weeks of traveling, I ended up on Big Corn Island where, over a lobster dinner, I first learned about the socioeconomic issue that would develop into a three-year documentary film project called *Mi Aldea, Mi Langosta* (My Village, My Lobster).

BACKGROUND

I met with several people on Big Corn Island who educated me about the lobster "situation." I learned about the bends, how diving for lobster is crippling and killing men and destroying families. I came to understand the environmental impact of the industry, as lobsters were disappearing at an incredible rate and continue to do so to this day. People informed me about the economic travesty as well, as the price paid per pound had been dwindling over the years, and was expected to continue to decline well into the future. Since I had my camera with me, it made sense to record interviews with people in the community.

Lobster is red gold in and around Puerto Cabezas, providing over $40 million dollars of income for the north Atlantic coast of Nicaragua. Several methods of lobster fishing exist in Nicaragua. Commercial trapping, the method used by fishers in Canada and the United States, requires setting metal mesh traps. Commercial diving, however, is more common on the Miskito coast of Nicaragua and Honduras. It is also the cause of most cases of decompression illness in Nicaragua's lobster divers, a sickness caused by numerous and sequential immersions to unsafe depths, which exists in epidemic levels in this isolated corner of the country.

A smaller percentage of Nicaraguan divers follow the artisanal method, diving to lesser depths with a simple hook, fins, mask, and a glove. Artisanal fishermen trap and free-dive in small groups, taking smaller quantities of lobster than their commercial counterparts. They work mostly off the Moskito Keys and Corn Islands, either free diving or compressor diving (breathing through a regulator and hose connected to an onboard compressor), but in 2011, a new law prohibiting compressor diving will have an enormous impact on artisanal divers. Besides the divers who will be put out of work, there are thousands of other people including, amongst others, boat deck hands, assistants, food providers, and mechanics, all who will also be seeking alternative ways to earn a living.

I returned to Puerto Cabezas in August 2007, this time with a plan. My goal was to meet those individuals who were heavily engaged in the industry as well as those seeking to remedy the problems which arose as a result of the diving. I was fortunate enough to meet Martha Downs, an activist with disabilities fighting for equal rights for the others with disabilities, including divers. Several divers with disabilities and their families also welcomed me into their homes as they went through physical therapy and decompression

Over $50

[K] **Hotel Monter** (tel. 505/2792-2669, hotelmonter@gmail.com, www.hotelmonternicaragua.blogspot.com, $54) is a class act, centrally located above the Supermercado Monter and across the street from the baseball stadium. They're the only hotel which offers airport transfers. Breakfast and Internet are included, rooms with balconies are nicest; all have private bath, air-conditioning, and fans.

FOOD

Puerto has a good selection of simple *comedors*, typically offering barbecue beef and chicken. **Asados Corner** is only open on weekends and is run out of the family's home. **Asados El Patio** is open noon–midnight Wednesday—Sunday. There is always a line in front of the grill at **Comedor Aqui Me Quedo**, kitty-corner from the central park. Nearby, you can order one-dollar tacos and a milk shake at **La Esquinita del Sabor** (across from the *alcaldía*), chamber sessions. I also felt that this was an important opportunity to explore the interdependent relationships between the Nicaraguan Atlantic coast and the United States, since 95 percent of all lobster caught in Nicaragua is fed to American consumers in restaurants including Red Lobster and other popular seafood chains.

A LITTLE HISTORY

The Nicaragua diving industry can be tracked to the civil war of the 1980s, when a Sandinista scorched-earth policy forced the relocation of many Miskito people from their ancestral homeland along the Río Coco to camps closer to Puerto Cabezas. This provoked many to flee from Nicaragua. While some men began training with the Contras in Honduras, others traveled to the north to find work. Miskito men, already familiar with catching lobsters by free diving, gravitated toward the established commercial lobster diving industry in Honduras, which by the 1980s had already incorporated the use of SCUBA, a practice absent in Nicaragua at that time. With the end of Sandanista rule in 1990, these men returned to Nicaragua, bringing with them the acquired practice.

That's how Nicaraguan commercial lobster diving was born. Over the years, the fleet of commercial boats has increased to match the growing consumption of warm water lobsters. The Atlantic lobster count itself, however, has dwindled exponentially, failing to match the consumer need. As a result, fishing boats are forced to travel to increasingly deeper waters,

forcing divers to plunge to dangerous depths for longer periods. So long, in fact, that it quickly became a common sight on the north Atlantic coast to see men in wheelchairs or bedridden after suffering decompression sickness; commonly called the bends. Without proper treatment and rehabilitation, decompression sickness leads to paralysis, and even death.

ABOARD THE *SPANISH LADY*

I returned the following two summers to Puerto Cabezas, adding production crew members and eventually boarding the *Spanish Lady*, a 60-foot converted U.S. shrimping boat, loaded to the brim with 65 fishermen, support staff, and our crew. We lived and filmed for a little over a week on the boat, sleeping on roach-infested, filth-ridden, oil-slick decks. It helped us get a better perspective on the lives of the divers as well our own. Each diver was armed with a hook, dilapidated fins and mask, and five tanks of compressed air, sufficient for 10-15 dives per day.

The story of Puerto Cabezas' lobster divers is a complicated one – we hope to tell it from as many sides as possible. It is a story of life at sea and on shore, of how the community is shaped by the diving and disabilities, and about the equal rights movement within. Watch *Mi Aldea, Mi Langosta* and visit www.nomading.com or our Facebook site for updates.

Contributed by Joshua Wolff, Nomading Films, www.nomading.com.

---

a favorite *comedor* serving three square meals a day. If for some reason you find yourself out, about, and hungry between the hours of 9 P.M.–3 A.M., stop by **Karen's Fried Chicken.** Karen, a Miskito woman, has been frying chicken at her street stand half a block up from the northeast corner of the park for ages, and whatever hour of the night, you'll wait in line behind a crowd of locals.

At the **MiniSuper,** grab a stool at the counter, or out on the patio for a cheeseburger

and fruit drink ($3 for a meal). The owner, a nice guy with impeccable English, retired in 2009 from working cruise ships out of the southern United States. For traditional local food, **Paulina's Kitchen** ($3–5) is only open for lunch 11 A.M.–2 P.M.; try the *gallo pinto* with coconut, *rondon*, and other regional meals.

There are a handful of nicer restaurants throughout town, all offering essentially the same menu of shellfish, fresh fish, soups, beef, and chicken. At the north end of town, the best meal in the city is at **❰ Restaurante Kabu Payaska** (Sea Breeze), serving seafood on a beautiful grassy lawn overlooking the ocean; $6–8 for lobster, shrimp, or fresh fish. **Miramar** is a little cheaper and closer to the center of town, with a nice view as well (dancing here on weekends makes some people think of it only as a disco).

There are two good restaurants near the airport: **Famahi** ($6–10). They are open for three hearty meals a day; their breakfast and house *mondongo* (tripe soup) is their specialty. **El Esteliano II** ($6–10) is a local favorite which blasts country and *ranchero* music all day long; they have excellent *carne a la plancha,* fish, shrimp, lobster, pork, and beef dishes.

INFORMATION

For a taste of life in Puerto and Nicaragua's northeast, tune in to one of the local radio stations for news and commentary—even more interesting if you speak Miskito. Radio Miskut (104.1 FM) has lots of Miskito music and other programming. Radio Van (90.3 FM) presents itself as "The Voice of the North Atlantic," but throws in a cheesy *ranchera* song now and again just for good measure.

SERVICES

Supermercado Monter has a surprisingly full repertoire of canned and dry goods, fresh foods, and basic housewares. The post office (open 8 A.M.–noon and 1:30–5 P.M. Mon.–Fri., until noon Sat.) is located two blocks northeast

---

HEALTH AND SAFETY CONCERNS IN THE RÍO COCO REGION

Due to its low, wet geography, the Río Coco area is particularly prone to malaria and dengue fever outbreaks. All travelers here should ensure they're taking a prophylaxis to prevent malaria, as well as standard precautions to prevent being bitten by mosquitoes, i.e. keep your skin covered, try to stay indoors around 5 P.M., and use repellent and a mosquito net. A major issue is the availability (or lack) of medical facilities and supplies in the region.

At the same time the Río Coco is venerated by local communities, it is also the public toilet for most of the communities that line its shores. Don't be surprised to see someone scooping a bucket of river water out for cooking just downstream of someone defecating. Although the water is usually treated with chlorine, you should pay extra attention to the food and beverages you ingest, and especially all water and water-based drinks. Treat all water with iodine pills or a portable water filter before drinking. That goes double any time you are downstream of Waspám. If you are not carrying bottled water from Managua, it is recommended that you use a good water filter. While it is possible to purchase bottled water in Waspám, the supply is not always guaranteed, so don't rely on it.

This health warning needs to be taken even more seriously since Hurricane Felix devastated the northeast part of the country in August 2007. Flooded latrines have contaminated wells and various disease vectors have multiplied alarmingly.

In addition, the Río Coco was a heavily mined area in the 1980s. Though the land mines have largely been cleared away, known mined areas still exist and have been cordoned off with ribbon or wire. Ask the locals before you go wandering too far from the road or riverbank. Additionally, the locals took care of some land-mine clearing operations themselves, to speed the process of returning to their homes, by scooping up the mines and throwing them into the river. Some of them probably settled down into the mud, and others were carried downstream. Be wary at all times.

Finally, the entire Atlantic coast is experiencing the effect of drug trafficking from Colombia, and the Río Coco area provides particularly good hiding spots. The delta at Cabo Gracias a Dios is a known point of entry for small smugglers who take advantage of the almost total lack of police vigilance there.

You can catch boats heading north from Puerto Cabezas.

of the park. The phone company, ENITEL (open 7 A.M.–9:30 P.M. Mon.–Fri.) is located a block southeast of the park

Both banks in town have ATMs. Bancentro (a block south of the *alcaldía*) and BanPro (across from ENITEL, tel. 505/2792-2211, open 8 A.M.–4:30 P.M. Mon.–Fri., till noon Sat.) sometimes have long lines—bring a good book.

For Internet, the café two buildings down from the MiniSuper has the best connection, newest computers, and air-conditioning. Also check email at Bilwinet (behind the Pegatel), the place with air-conditioning right across from the mayor's office and next door to Casa Museo. Bilwi Internet is down the block from Cifra. The run-down municipal hospital is a block from the bus terminal.

GETTING THERE AND AWAY
By Air
The La Costeña flight from Managua takes about 90 minutes and costs about $150 round-trip. From Bluefields, it's about one hour and $100. There are three or four scheduled flights a day to and from Managua, and one daily from Bluefields. La Costeña can be reached at 505/2282-2255 or 505/2282-2586. Always confirm flights beforehand; reservations or advanced ticket purchases are recommended. If you need to make changes to flight reservations it is best to do this at the local office.

By Land
Oh you are a brave soul indeed! Two daily buses (9 A.M. and 1 P.M.) make the arduous 24-hour journey from Managua, through Nicaragua's muddy interior. The municipal bus terminal in Puerto Cabezas is located on the western edge of town. Puerto buses leave Managua's Mayoreo terminal, or you can piece the trip together from Jinotega's north terminal on a bus bound for Waslala; from there, you board a second bus to Siuna, and then another to Puerto Cabezas. There's an alternate road from Matagalpa to Siuna by way of

A FEW MISKITO PHRASES

The Miskito language doesn't use the vowel sounds "e" (as in bread) or "o" (as in boat), which makes it a flowing, rhythmic language of "a," "i," and "u," as in the following sentence, which exhorts the locals not to let the Yellow Coconut Virus infect the coconut plantations: *Coco lalahni taki pruiba sikniska alki takaskayasa.*

Here are a couple of words you might come across during your travels in the northeast.

English	Miskito	English	Miskito
Hello	*Naksa*	Dirty	*Taski*
Goodbye	*Aisabi*	Clean	*Klin*
What is your name?	*Ninam dia?*	Meat	*Wina*
How are you?	*Nahki sma?*	Chicken	*Kalila*
Fine	*Pain*	Rice and beans	*Rais n bins*
Bad	*Saura*	Fish	*Inska*
Sick	*Siknis*	Small boat	*Duri*
Thank you	*Tingki pali*	Lagoon	*Kabu*
Food	*Plun*	River	*Awala*
Toilet	*Tailit*	Birds	*Natnawira nani*
Water	*Li*	Parrot	*Rahwaa*

Río Blanco and Mulukuku. Both roads are largely impassable during the wet season. We received this report from a reader who found his own route: "I've just come by bus from León to Puerto Cabezas. At each stop I took the next bus that was going in the right direction [east]. From León to Matagalpa, then Río Blanco, then Santa Rita (overnight), then Siuna, Rosita, Sahsa (overnight), and finally to Puerto Cabezas . . . It's not for everyone, but I'm thrilled with the close look I've gotten at the heart of Nicaragua."

By Boat

When asked about ship service to points south, one official said, "There used to be two [boats making the run] but the other boat sank." The one left is the *Captain D* (tel. 505/8661-7201), which does a quasi-monthly run to Big Corn Island (12 hours overnight, about $40), continuing to El Bluff and El Rama (another six hours, after a layover in Big Corn to unload freight. Ask at the municipal dock; usually leaves around the middle of the month.

GETTING AROUND

Puerto Cabezas has no bus system, though the mayor's office is trying to put a couple of local city buses in place. In the meantime, Puerto has an astounding number of taxis (many of which are pirate cabs without plates, but you can use them too). The price is fixed at about $0.50 per person to go anywhere in town, a bit more to go from the airport to the pier or bus terminal.

NEAR PUERTO CABEZAS

Tuapí, just 10 kilometers north of Puerto, has a popular swimming hole on the banks of the eponymous river. Buses leave for Tuapí several times a day from the terminal in Puerto. It's also possible to travel by boat north or south along the Atlantic coast to visit Miskito communities.

Traveling Along the Coast

For points north, make arrangements with a boat owner at the old dock in Puerto Cabezas. You'll have better luck in the early mornings when the boats are setting out for a day's fishing. Someday, travelers will have interesting adventures in the gorgeous beachfront community of Sandy Bay (two hours from Puerto Cabezas) and the Miskito Cays (two hours across the open sea from Sandy Bay), but as of press time, both locations are known rendezvous points for drug runners and other dangerous types.

For points south, take a bus or taxi ($3.50 per person) to the community of Lamlaya; or hop a bus or truck in front of Hotel El Cortijo for $0.50. From there, boats leave daily for Wawa and Karata between noon and 1 P.M., charging $3 one-way for a *panga,* and $2 for a "punkin" local boat (which takes twice as long). Or hire a boat to Prinzapolka, quite possibly the single hardest destination to reach in Nicaragua and the statistically poorest community in the nation. You should have a basic command of Miskito to visit these communities on your own, both to avoid suspicion and to be able to communicate.

◖ Tours to the Miskito Communities

Hurricane Felix pummeled many Miskito communities in 2007 and recovery has been slow. Most people are friendly, living in very rustic circumstances. **Norton Perilla** (tel. 505/2450-8504, elvinkind@yahoo.com), an American expat, can arrange day trips to the mainland Miskito communities of Tuapí and Boom Serpi.

© JAMES SAVAGE

church in the Miskito community of Boom Serpi

The best way to visit local indigenous communities is with **AMICA** (Asociación de Mujeres Indígenas de la Costa Atlántica, one block south of the baseball stadium, tel. 505/2792-2219, asociacionamica@yahoo.es), an organization making an effort to promote the empowerment and development of women along the northern Atlantic coast. AMICA gives training in gender development, reproductive health, leadership, and AIDS, plus the laws that affect indigenous women. AMICA offers trips to the Miskito communities of Haulover, Wawa Bar, and Karata, with homestays, nature tours, and dance or cultural presentations. Accommodations aren't as rustic as you'd think—including box spring mattresses and towels. Prices depend on recent transport costs; renting a boat adds considerably to the cost (about $65 pp per night, meals around $2, all negotiable depending on the number of people and number of nights). In all cases, it's crucial to call at least three days ahead.

Waspám and the Río Coco

◖ WASPÁM

Waspám, in the far northern reaches of the Miskito pine savanna and at the edge of the mightiest river in Nicaragua, is the gateway, principal port, and economic heart of the Miskito communities that line the banks of the Río Coco. It is, in itself, a difficult place to get to, yet it is really the first step of the voyage to places even farther away still. The communities here would prefer to be left to their own ways, but this has not been the case, and the Miskito peoples of the Río Coco suffered more than most during the 1980s, including a massive relocation that is still cause for resentment.

Waspám is not expecting travelers. You will find no package tours here, no one hawking T-shirts, real estate, or their new bed-and-breakfast. Rather, you will be immersed in a community that lives in a very traditional way, that retains a strong cultural identity despite growing mestizo influence, and that is prepared to show you exactly what it is, not what it expects you are expecting.

The Miskito people live largely off the river, fishing for small freshwater species, and off their small, neatly tended fields of corn, beans, and even upland rice. Their version of the ubiquitous tortilla is a thick, wheat-flour cake, which is fried in coconut oil. Starch makes up the rest of the diet along the Río Coco, including tubers like *quiquisque* (taro) and yucca. *Rondon* is a fish stew (and along the Río Coco it will be made of fish, not turtle, like on the coast), and the *gallo pinto* is cooked in coconut milk. Wild game also finds its way onto the menu; don't be surprised to find boar, deer, and armadillo.

Waspám proper has a few paved streets but little traffic to speak of, a point in its favor. It also has a growing solid waste problem (the bane of every rural community's early development). Once you have gotten a feel for town, a trip up the Río Coco is the natural way to glimpse the communities—usually just a couple of families living together—that make up the Miskito landscape. This endeavor is neither cheap nor easy, but you will find it rewarding, more so if you can speak enough Miskito to speak with the locals. In fact, some basic Miskito is nearly obligatory throughout your exploration of this region.

Accommodations and travelers' facilities in the traditional sense of the word are practically nonexistent. The chance to visit this frontier—and it is truly frontier—to live and travel amongst the Miskito people, and to feel the spiritual power of the mighty Río Coco should not be missed.

The Miskito people are reserved but friendly—once you've broken the ice, you'll find them helpful and inquisitive. They're also more conservative than other Nicaraguans, so leave the short shorts and bikini tops back home. Most Miskito people speak Spanish as a second language and practically no English at all. Foreigners who speak languages other than Spanish or Miskito will inevitably be called Miriki (American). Even Nicaraguans from the Pacific region are considered foreigners and are referred to as mestizos.

Accommodations

Accomodations are frequently basic, but reasonable (you might want to bring your own mosquito net here).

C Las Cabañas has rooms from $3–$10 double depending on how much comfort you'd like, but at the top end even have cable TV. **El Piloto** ($25) is located at the north end of main street, about two minutes from Wangki. They have air-conditioned single rooms with private bathrooms and a kitchen area with meals available.

Located right across from the airport is **Hospedaje Rose.** In the main house, all the rooms have private bathrooms and 24-hour electricity; three meals are available, as well as Internet and satellite TV. Rose also has a small movie theater, and the town's only

Internet connection is hers as well, adjacent to the *hospedaje.*

Hotel Manguito is the best of the low-end, with no telephone, but basic rooms starting at $5 double, cleaner than you'd expect but also only bucket showers. If you get stuck, **Vanessa's** (across from the ENITEL tower), **Wangki Tangni** (towards the south end of the airstrip), or a no-name place overlooking the river will also do in a pinch, though they have little to recommend them.

Food

There are several small eateries in town, most serving rice and beans accompanied by a hunk of meat, sometimes fish. You can ensure fish—or shrimp—for dinner by arranging beforehand with the restaurant where you intend to eat later that day. Vegetables are scarce and any salad usually consists of cabbage and some tomatoes in vinegar; eggs are usually available as well. Ask to try some *wabul,* a thick, warm, green banana drink, which has many variations. Coconut bread can usually be found at the market during the evening, when it's still warm from the oven, or in the early morning. You can find something to eat at **Comedor La Esperanza** currently, though other places appear sporadically and then disappear after a few months in business. Expect an enormous, generic meal for about $3. Travelers also report delicious coconut bread on sale streetside, evenings.

Information and Services

The ENITEL phone office (open 8 A.M.–noon and 1–5 P.M. most weekdays, until noon Sat.) is located just west of the Rotonda Centroamerica. The post office—a private home with a Correos de Nicaragua sign posted out front—is along the airstrip.

There is a local, underequipped police station in town and a health clinic with very basic services. The Catholic church has a private clinic with slightly better service and more supplies; in case of an emergency go to the convent and tell the nuns. One of the attending doctors speaks good English.

Getting There and Away

La Costeña (tel. 505/2263-2814) pilots radio ahead to have someone shoo the cattle away. Daily morning flights leave Managua most of the week; the flight is about 90 minutes long over some of the most exotic scenery in Nicaragua; $97 one-way ($149 round-trip).

Land transportation to Waspám can be arranged in Puerto Cabezas. The grueling bus trip takes 5 hours when the road is in good condition and it isn't raining; in the rainy season the trip can take as long as 12 hours. Two or three daily Waspám-bound buses leave Puerto at the crack of dawn and cost $10; get there early for the 6 A.M. bus. The following day, the same buses leave Waspám at the crack of dawn bound for Puerto Cabezas. Because all the buses leave their respective starting points in the morning, day trips are impossible.

Additionally, there's a truck that leaves Puerto Cabezas every morning between 5 and 6 A.M.—a lumbering, diesel-belching IFA—and many opt to travel with El Chino Kung Fu, a local character with a decent pickup truck who makes regular trips between Waspám and Puerto Cabezas. Ask around and try to form a group to share the costs. Bear in mind that hitchhiking runs the danger of being an unknowing accomplice to transporting narcotics.

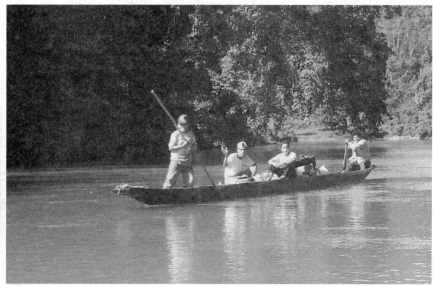

© RANDALL WOOD

traveling on the Río Coco

RIVER TRIPS FROM WASPÁM

Waspám is your gateway to the Río Coco, and small boats—fiberglass *pangas* and dugout *batu* canoes—are your means of transport. One local volunteer recommends the *panga* trip to San Carlos, which has a simple *hospedaje*. In the upriver villages located between Waspám and Leimus, visitors are not common and facilities are somewhere between limited and nonexistent. Don't plan on staying overnight or finding food for sale.

Nothing is easy or cheap, by the standards of travelers accustomed to the prices of the Pacific side. In general, expect to pay $35–100 per person per day for boat transportation along the Río Coco, which includes the boat, the gasoline, and the boatman. The dream adventure is a trip all the way up to Wiwilí, the upstream port town. El Bailarín makes the trip from time to time, but charges $1,000 round-trip per person for the extended 550-kilometer voyage one-way.

Two tributaries to the Río Coco, the Yahuk and the Waspuk, are both home to waterfalls the locals say are beautiful places to visit, but make for long trips. To visit the Yahuk, for example, you'd have to hire a boat for two days. The first day, you can motor up the Río Coco to the Yahuk and continue upstream to the falls, then spend the night in San Carlos, and return the following day. The Waspuk falls are reportedly a site of religious significance to the Miskito people. The trip is just upwards of 130 kilometers in each direction.

TRIPS BY LAND FROM WASPÁM

Travel is difficult, transportation infrequent, and food and lodging service nonexistent. If necessary, you can try arranging a meal with a local family, for which you'll pay. There are two local villages that are close to Waspám: Kisalaya (five kilometers) and Ulwas (three kilometers, a 30-minute walk through pleasant country). Locals will point you in the right direction. Bilwaskarma (10 kilometers, approximately a 90-minute walk from Waspám) is a pleasant village with a small health center that was a world-famous nursing school before the conflict of the 1980s.

Siuna and the Mining Triangle

In the heart of the mining triangle, Siuna is a town of about 12,000 people, which is the best point of entry for the Bosawás nature reserve. It is also home to a growing number of Mayangna Indians who have gradually migrated from the Atlantic coast and the Río Coco. Throughout the mining triangle (the term refers to the towns of Siuna, Bonanza, and Rosita), roads, power supply, and water systems are unreliable, and the towns are filled with drunks and cowboys. Sound like a good time? There are cheap places to stay and eat in all three towns, and Bonanza has a working Canadian-owned gold mine and a dozen depressing casinos. Each town also has a handful of natural attractions nearby and local guides to get you there. The Bosawás reserve, to the north, is one of the largest expanses of wilderness in Central America.

HISTORY

In the early 20th century, Siuna was a bustling mining town that drew workers from as far away as Jamaica. But in 1968 the foreign companies closed the mines (Yamana Gold out of Toronto, Canada has recently taken a renewed interest). Distant and poorly patrolled, the whole triangle made an easy target for Contra operations during the 1980s, and indeed several serious skirmishes took place in the region. When the war ended, an uneasy peace ensued, for the entire area was peppered with land mines, now lost or abandoned, and many well armed but still unemployed men gave up guerilla warfare for a life of petty banditry.

Regaining a sense of civility took more than a decade. There have been no attacks on foreigners with the 1999 exception of Manley

PUERTO CABEZAS

Guarducci, a Canadian mining engineer who was kidnapped and held for ransom for five weeks before being released unharmed.

ACCOMMODATIONS AND FOOD

Hotel Siu (Barrio Sol de Libertad, from the police station, one block west and one south, tel. 505/2794-2028, $25) has nice rooms and tasty meals; **Los Chinitos** (tel. 505/2794-2038, $7–12) is also clean and well recommended with a nice wooden deck and lounging area and a range of 15 rooms.

Doña Azucena (across from Los Chinitos, Barrio Luis Delgadillo) serves an especially good breakfast featuring eggs any style, fresh bread, and coffee. **La Terraza** serves basic meals, and also run an Internet café next door. **Las Praderas** (Barrio Campo Viejo, near URACCAN, $6–9) is recommended for dining; or rub elbows with the cowboys over steaks at **El Machin.**

Not surprisingly, beer joints are everywhere. Locals prefer **El Secreto** (right on the landing strip in the center of town), a gritty disco that seems to be full all weekend; eat at the *fritanga* right outside.

🅲 BOSAWÁS BIOSPHERE RESERVE

Located 350 kilometers north of Managua, the 730,000 hectares of forest, mountains, and rivers collectively known as Bosawás are located within the municipalities of Waspám, Bonanza, Siuna, El Cuá–Bocay, Wiwilí, and Waslala. Although inhabited by some 40,000 widely dispersed people (more than half of whom are Mayangna and Miskito), most of Bosawás remains unexplored, unmapped, and untamed. Its name is derived from the region's three most salient features: the Río Bocay (BO), Cerro Saslaya (SA), and the Río Waspuk (WAS).

It's the largest uninterrupted tract of primary rainforest north of the Amazon, and besides unparalleled stretches of cloud forest, Bosawás contains tropical humid forest, rainforest, and a wealth of disparate ecosystems

that vary in altitude from 30 meters above sea level at the mouth of the Waspuk River to the 1,650-meter peak of Cerro Saslaya. Bosawás is a Central American treasure, an immense genetic reserve of species that have vanished elsewhere in Mesoamerica, including jaguars, rare small mammals, 12 kinds of poisonous snakes, and many bird species, including the gorgeous scarlet macaw and 34 boreal migratory species.

Bosawás was designated a protected reserve in 1997, but where there is no money, there is little enforcement and few rangers—there are many more desperately poor who continue to make a living from this ancient land. In many cases, this translates into slash-and-burn clearing of the forests and the continual push of the agricultural frontier, mostly for subsistence. The 1.8 million acres of protected area was declared a part of the Nature Conservancy's international Parks in Peril program in 2001.

Visiting the Reserve

To do anything in Bosawás, you *must* receive permission (at time of printing, free). Talk to the Bosawás Office (at central park near the stadium, not far from Hotelito Los Chinitos, tel. 505/2794-2036) who will help arrange a guide. The MARENA office in Managua can also help (tel. 505/2233-1594). Guides are both obligatory and absolutely necessary and cost about $7–12 per day plus food. You may be convinced to hire two guides for your trip, a recommended safety and comfort precaution.

There is also a park office in Bonanza (tel. 505/8497-0258 or 505/2794-0109), located a mile or so out of town, and can help you find local trails and guides.

Unless you have months to explore the reserve, you'll have to pick and choose from various possible destinations. Get off the bus at Casa Roja (1.5 hours from Siuna) to stage an ascent of Cerro Saslaya (4–5 days); or continue to Santa Rosita (2.5-hour bus ride) for a two-hour hike to the river or trailhead to Cerro El Torro (4–5 days). Waslala is a 4–5 hour ride from Siuna and home to the original tomb of

Carlos Fonseca (his remains were moved to Managua after the revolution's victory).

Be advised: Any trip in Bosawás is a serious backcountry undertaking and should not be attempted without proper supplies, some wilderness experience, a tolerance for dampness and discomfort, and a basic survival instinct. You should already have supplies like water bottles, a mosquito net, and some kind of pump or purifying tablets for water (start your hike with at least three liters in your bag; a fresh source is available in the park), a brimmed hat, sunscreen, sturdy shoes, and a medical kit. Additional supplies that can be purchased in Siuna include rubber boots (for snakes and knee-level mud), four yards of heavy black plastic for a roof in the jungle, a piece of plastic or waterproof cover for your backpack, a machete, a hammock, extra rope, and food.

Take a local bus to Rosa Grande, then walk or rent a horse ($5 per day) to Rancho Alegre. From there the journey is a challenging one-hour hike through the community of Rancho Alegre to a series of waterfalls at Salto Labu. Another hour hike up a steep path leads you to Mirador, a lookout and an incredible view of an absolutely stunning waterfall before you reach the primary forest on the path into Bosawás.

BACKGROUND

The Land

The largest and lowest Central American country, Nicaragua is a nation of geographical superlatives. Located at the elbow where the Central American isthmus bends and then plummets southward to Panamá, Nicaragua is almost dead center between North and South America. Part of a biological corridor that for millions of years has allowed plant and animal species from two continents to mingle, it boasts an extraordinary blend of flora and fauna.

In the 16th century, Nicaragua's geographical beauty enchanted the conquistadores, who reported, "The Nicaraguan plains are some of the most beautiful and pleasant lands that can be found in the Indies because they are very fertile with *mahicales* and vegetables, *fesoles* of diverse types, fruits of many kinds and much cacao."

Nicaragua is roughly triangular in shape and dominated by two large lakes in the southwest. Its 530-kilometer-long, northern border with Honduras is the longest transect across the Central American isthmus. To the south, the southern shore of the Río San Juan defines the better part of the Nicaraguan–Costa Rican border. Wholly within Nicaragua, the San Juan has been a continual source of conflict with Costa Rica to this day, whose attempts to navigate and patrol the river have been met aggressively by the Nicaraguan government.

© JOSHUA BERMAN

To the east and west lie the Caribbean Sea and the Pacific Ocean, respectively. With 127,849 square kilometers of land area, Nicaragua is approximately the size of Greece or the state of New York. But Nicaragua has lost some 50,000 square kilometers to her neighbors over the past several centuries: the eastern third of what is now Honduras, as well as the now–Costa Rican territories of Nicoya and Guanacaste, plus the Caribbean island of San Andrés.

Administratively, the nation is divided into 15 units called *departamentos,* and two vast autonomous regions on the Atlantic coast known as the North and South Atlantic Autonomous Regions (RAAN and RAAS). The departments, in turn, consist of 145 municipalities. The two autonomous regions elect their own officials on a separate electoral calendar. Nicaragua's three largest cities are Managua, León, and Granada, followed by Estelí, Masaya, and the remaining department capitals.

GEOGRAPHY

Nicaragua's favorite nickname, "The Land of Lakes and Volcanoes," evokes its primary geographical features: two great lakes and a chain of impressive and active volcanoes. Nicaragua's water and volcanic resources have had an enormous effect on its human history, from the day the first Nahuatl people concluded their migration south and settled on the forested shores of Lake Cocibolca (Lake Nicaragua) to the first Spanish settlements along the lakes to the many as yet unrealized plans to build a trans-isthmus canal.

Geologic History and Formation

The isthmus now known as Central America took shape 60 million years ago (MYA); Nicaragua's northern third is geologically the most ancient. In the area of Telpaneca and Quilalí, rocks dated at 200 million years old are thought to have once been part of a small Jurassic-Cretaceous continent that included the modern-day Yucatán Peninsula in Mexico and the Antilles Islands. To the south, what are now Costa Rica's Talamanca Mountains formed an archipelago of isolated volcanoes.

During the Tertiary period (65–1.7 MYA), intense volcanic activity and erosion produced large amounts of sediment and volcanic flows that accumulated underwater.

At least two periods of intense volcanic activity: one in the Eocenic-Oligocenic epoch (55–25 MYA) formed the lesser features of Nicaragua's central highlands, and a second in the Miocene (25–13 MYA) produced the larger mountains in Matagalpa and Jinotega. Eleven million years later, shifting tectonic plates in the Pacific and Caribbean lifted the seabed, forming the Pacific region.

When the Cocos plate slid under the Caribbean plate, the main volcanic mountain range running northwest–southeast across the Pacific plains blistered to the surface. Ocean water from the Atlantic rushed in along a broad sunken valley of the Pacific plate now known as the Nicaraguan Depression, and pooled, forming the lakes. Some geologists believe the Atlantic and Pacific actually connected at this point in time and were later cut off by volcanic sedimentation. Erosion began pulling material from the landmass outward to the sea, building up Nicaragua's Pacific region and gradually forming the Atlantic coast.

Plate tectonics theory, in spite of being widely accepted since the 1960s, is most frequently criticized for its failure to adequately explain the geology and geography of several regions of the world, including Central America. It is highly probable that our concept of the geological events that formed Central America will change as geologic science progresses. Regardless of the mechanism, however, convergence of the plates ensures crustal instability, which manifests itself in frequent volcanic and earthquake activity in all of Central America, and especially in Nicaragua.

Volcanoes and Mountain Ranges

Nicaragua has about 40 volcanoes, a half dozen of which are usually active at any time, whether venting light, clouds of gas or actually erupting. Running parallel to the Pacific shore, Nicaragua's volcanoes are a part of the Ring of Fire that encompasses most of the western

HURRICANE MITCH

It was late October 1998, and the rainy season had been reduced to sporadic drizzle, just right for the red beans that were slowly gathering strength in the fields. The newspapers mentioned a hurricane forming in the Atlantic, but Nicaragua seemed spared when the storm, called Mitch shifted to the north instead of making landfall on the Caribbean coast.

Instead, on October 28, rain began to fall steadily from a leaden sky over most of Nicaragua. Mitch had come to a near complete stop off the north coast of Honduras, and thick gray arms of clouds swept in long spirals across the entire Central American isthmus, greedily gathering strength from both the Caribbean and Pacific Ocean, while winds around the eye of the hurricane reached 290 kilometers per hour. The rains fell day and night for seven days. The country roads of red earth turned muddy, then became dangerous rivers of coffee-colored water coursing through the center of towns, while cattle that had been left in the fields found high ground or were drowned and swept away. Swollen to 10 times their normal size, Nicaraguan rivers flared over their banks, tearing out trees, snatching away homes, and breaking apart (or just tearing around) every bridge in their path. On October 29, the electricity failed in most of the north as power lines fell and poles were swept away. In Sébaco, the Río Viejo and the Río Grande de Matagalpa, which normally pass within a kilometer of each other, rose and combined before tearing through Ciudad Darío.

The waters of Lake Xolotlán rose three meters over the course of three days. Overtopping the basin, the waters barreled through the old, dry channel of the once-intermittent Río Tipitapa, raising the level of Lake Cocibolca and the Río San Juan; the town of Tipitapa, built in the low saddle between the two lakes, was completely inundated. On the Pan-American Highway, the enormous bridge that crossed over the Tipitapa River was damaged, then destroyed, and finally carried away completely. By October 30, the entire northern half of the country was isolated: Major bridges had been demolished in Sébaco and Tipitapa, and every bridge without exception between León and Managua had been destroyed.

But Mitch was cruelest in Posoltega, Chinandega, where the equivalent of a full year's rainfall came down in under four days. The intense rains filled the crater of Volcán Casita with rainwater, and at 2 P.M. on October 30, the southwest edge of the crater lip tore away, unleashing a deadly avalanche of mud, water, and rock 1.5 kilometers wide and three meters high on the three small communities below. Thousands died immediately, as the mudflow poured southwest more than four kilometers to the highway, crossed it, and continued southwest into the town of Posoltega. In the aftermath, there was no hope of recovering or even identifying victims.

By the time the rains finally stopped, Hurricane Mitch had reduced Nicaragua's GDP by half and destroyed more than 70 percent of the country's physical infrastructure. Hundreds of health clinics and more than 20,000 homes were carried away, and arable farmland was reduced by 11,550 hectares. Overall, economic losses sustained by this already poor nation were around $1.5 billion. Mitch also opened up political and social scars less obvious than deforested hillsides. Under duress, political divisions reopened as relief money poured in and politicians – particularly President Alemán – struggled to divert it for their own interests.

Though the press called Mitch "the storm of the century," scientists estimate it was much more severe even than that and declared it the most deadly storm event in at least 200 years. However, the hundreds of millions of dollars of aid money that poured into Nicaragua in the aftermath have provided Nicaragua with a much-needed opportunity to strengthen and rebuild, and much effort has gone into ensuring that the Nicaraguan government and people are more capable of dealing with future disasters through training programs, flood-warning detection systems, computer models, and more. These are crucial to Nicaragua's future well-being, because Hurricane Mitch will surely not be the last storm to wreak havoc in Nicaragua.

Nicaragua is known as "the land of lakes and volcanoes."

coast of the Americas, the Aleutian Islands of Alaska, Japan, and Indonesia. The Maribio (Nahuatl for the "giant men") and Dirian volcano ranges stretch nearly 300 kilometers from the Concepción and Maderas in the middle of Lake Nicaragua to Cosigüina, which juts into the Gulf of Fonseca.

The first volcanic event in recorded history was a major eruption of Volcán Masaya in the early 1500s. The lava formed the present-day lagoon at the base of the mountain. Another great lava flow occurred in 1772, leaving a black, barren path still visible today where the Carretera Masaya highway crosses it. In 1609, Spanish settlers abandoned the city of León when Momotombo erupted. And in January of 1835, Volcán Cosigüina violently blew its top, hurling ash as far away as Jamaica and Mexico, covering the area for 250 kilometers around the volcano in ash and burning pumice and forcing the entire peninsula into three days of darkness. All this volcanic activity is responsible for the exceptional fertility of Nicaragua's soils, most notably the agricultural plains around Chinandega and León.

Volcán Masaya is the most easily accessed of Nicaragua's volcanoes and boasts a paved road leading right to the lip of the crater. Volcán Masaya is actually formed of three craters, the largest of which, Santiago, is the only crater in the Americas that contains a visible pool of incandescent liquid lava in its center. The visibility of this lava fluctuates on a 30-year cycle and was best seen 1965–1979.

Climbing a few Nicaraguan giants is a great way to experience Central America. San Cristóbal is the highest peak, at 1,745 meters. A smaller peak adjacent to San Cristóbal, Volcán Casita still bears the immense scar of the landslide that buried thousands in an avalanche of rock and mud during Hurricane Mitch—and trembled briefly again in January of 2002. Isla de Ometepe's twin cones are popular for hiking and easily accessible. No matter where you hike, always hire a guide, as several foreigners have gotten lost and perished while peak bagging.

Momotombo, San Cristóbal, and Telíca are the most active peaks and are prone to emit plumes of poisonous gases, smoke, and occasionally lava. La Isla de Ometepe's Volcán Concepción (1,610 meters) last blew its top in 2005 and 2007. The other half of Ometepe (Nahuatl for "two peaks") is Volcán Maderas (1,394 meters) which sleeps, its crater drowned in a deep lagoon that feeds a thriving jungle.

Volcán Telíca, just north of León, erupts approximately every five years, while gas vents at its base churn out boiling mud and sulfur. Neighboring Cerro Negro is one of the youngest volcanoes on the planet: It protruded through a farmer's field in the middle of the 1800s and has since grown in size, steadily and violently, to a height of 400 meters. Cerro Negro's last three eruptions have been increasingly powerful, culminating in 1992 when it belched up a cloud of burning gases and ash seven kilometers high, burying León under 15 centimeters of ash and dust. Eight thousand inhabitants were evacuated as the weight of the ash caused several homes to collapse. Volcán Momotombo's (Nahuatl for "great burning peak") perfect conical peak is visible from great distances across the Pacific plains, as far away as Matagalpa. Momotombo is responsible for approximately 10 percent of Nicaragua's electricity via a geothermal plant located at its base. It hasn't erupted since 1905, but Momotombo remains a monster whose menace is taken quite seriously. In April 2000 it rumbled long enough to get Managua's attention, then quieted back down (for now).

A popular day trip from Granada is the cloud forest park and coffee plantations of Volcán Mombacho (1,345 meters), a dormant volcano whose explosion and self-destruction formed the archipelago of *isletas* in Lake Cocibolca. Mombacho took its modern shape in 1570 when a major avalanche on the south slope opened and exposed the crater, buried an indigenous village of 400 inhabitants in the process.

Three lesser mountain ranges dominate Nicaragua's center and north: the Cordilleras Isabelia, Huapi, and Chontaleña. These three ranges radiate northeast, east, and southeast, respectively, from the center of the country, gradually melting into the lowland jungle and swamps of the Atlantic coast. Their half-dozen prominent peaks were the scene of intense fighting during several conflicts in Nicaraguan history. Nicaragua's highest point, Cerro Mogotón, at 2,107 meters, is located along the Honduran border in Nueva Segovia.

Lakes and Lagoons

Two lakes, Cocibolca (Lake Nicaragua) and Xolotlán (Lake Managua), dominate Nicaragua's geography, occupying together nearly 10 percent of the country's surface area.

Lake Xolotlán, although broad (1,025 square kilometers), is shallow with an average depth of only seven meters. It reaches its deepest—26 meters—near the island of Momotombito. Lake Managua is, for the most part, biologically dead, after a century of untreated human waste and extensive dumping of industrial wastes during the 1970s, including lead, cyanide, benzene, mercury, and arsenic. The tremendous opportunities for tourism, recreation, and potable water for human consumption that a clean lake would facilitate have led to an ambitious plan to detoxify Xolotlán. Backed by loans from Japan and the World Bank, the project has already begun collecting and treating Managua's sewage and, gradually, cleansing the lake itself in water treatment plants on the lakeshore. See the result for yourself on a booze cruise from Managua's Malecón.

Lake Cocibolca is the larger of Nicaragua's two lakes and one of Nicaragua's greatest natural treasures. At 8,264 square kilometers and 160 kilometers long along its axis, Lake Cocibolca is nearly as big as the island of Puerto Rico and lies 31 meters above sea level. It's also deep—up to 60 meters in some places, and relatively clean. The prevailing winds, which blow from the east across the farmlands of Chontales, make the eastern part of Cocibolca calm and the western half choppy and rough. A massive pipe system is presently being designed which, if built, will carry drinking water from

Cocibolca to Managua to help meet the needs of the capital's rapidly growing population.

Nearly a dozen stunning lagoons mark the maws of ancient volcanic craters. Around Managua are the Nejapa, Tiscapa, and Asososca lagoons. West of Managua, the picturesque twin craters of Xiloá and Apoyeque form the Chiltepe peninsula. Near Masaya, the 200-meter-deep Laguna de Apoyo was formed sometime in the Quaternary period (1.6 MYA) by what is thought to be the most violent volcanic event in Nicaragua's prehistory. Not far away is Laguna de Masaya, at the base of the volcano of the same name. Other gorgeous lagoons flank Volcán Momotombo in the craters of the Maderas and Consigüina volcanoes.

Rivers

To the original Spanish settlers in Granada, the Río San Juan was the elusive "drain" of Lake Cocibolca; since then, the possibility of traveling up the Río San Juan, across Lake Cocibolca, and then by land to the Pacific Ocean has made the San Juan the most historically important river in Nicaragua. In the years of the gold rush, thousands of prospectors navigated up the Río San Juan en route to California; some made the return trip laden with riches, others with nothing. These days, several sets of rapids and decades of sedimentation reduce its navigability, exacerbated by shifts in the riverbed from occasional earthquakes. Cattle ranches and small farms primarily producing basic grains line both shores (farmers on the southern shore identify more closely with Costa Rica and even use its currency).

Formed by the confluence of three major rivers—the Siquia, Mico, and Rama—the Río Escondido is the principal link in the transportation corridor from Managua to Bluefields and the Atlantic coast. Produce and merchandise (and busloads of travelers) reach El Rama and then proceed down the Escondido. The Escondido and its tributaries are important to the cattle industry in Chontales, but massive deforestation along its banks have unleashed dangerous floods that frequently put the river port of El Rama under water.

The 680-kilometer-long Río Coco is the longest river in Central America, fed by headwaters in both Nicaragua and Honduras. Also known as the Río Segovia or its indigenous name Wanki, the Coco traverses terrain that varies from several minor canyons to vast stretches of virgin forest. The indigenous Miskito people, for whom the river bears great spiritual significance, live in small communities along its shores.

The Estero Real (Royal Estuary), at 137 kilometers in length, is the most consequential body of water on the Pacific coast and is one of Nicaragua's best places to spot waterfowl. It drains most of northwestern Nicaragua through extensive mangroves and wetlands to the Gulf of Fonseca and is the nucleus of extensive shrimp-farming operations.

Soils

In the Pacific region, the volcanic soils are highly fertile and mineral-rich. The mountainous north and central regions of Nicaragua are

A trip to Nicaragua is not complete without a visit to the *campo*, or countryside.

less fertile basalt, andesite, and granite-based soils, and their steeper slopes are prone to erosion and soil degradation. The better soils are usually found alongside rivers where deforestation and fierce storms such as Hurricane Mitch (1998) haven't carried it away, stripped it of its nutrient value, or buried it under thick layers of sand. In the north and northeast towards the Caribbean, the weak, quartz-based soils can bear little more than thin stands of white pine. The Sébaco Valley, thought to have once been the bed of an immense lake, has thick, black clay soils that impede the production of corn or beans but greatly facilitate wet rice farming.

CLIMATE

Located between 11 and 15 degrees north latitude, Nicaragua's tropical climate ranges from 27–32°C (81–90°F) during the rainy season, and 30–35°C (86–95°F) in the dry season, but varies remarkably by region: In the mountains of Matagalpa and Jinotega, the temperature can be 10°C cooler, while in León and Matagalpa, they can be 10°C warmer, making ordinary travelers feel like glazed chickens roasting over the coals. Nicaragua's *invierno* (winter, or rainy season) lasts approximately May–October, and *verano* (summer, or dry season) lasts November–April: rain during these months may mean just a quick shower each afternoon, or a deluge that goes on for days. As you travel east toward the Atlantic coast or down the Río San Juan, the rainy season grows longer and wetter until the dry season only lasts the month of April.

Flora and Fauna

Nicaragua's variety of ecosystems, and its position at the biological crossroads between North and South America and between the Atlantic and Pacific Oceans have blessed it with an astonishingly broad assortment of vegetation and wildlife.

FLORA

Of the world's known 250,000 species of flowering plants, an estimated 15,000–17,000 are found in Central America. Nicaragua is home to some 9,000 species of vascular plants, many of medicinal value. But outside a few protected areas, conservation efforts are half-hearted or underfunded, and even protected areas are under intense pressure from the agricultural frontier and the scattered human settlements grandfathered within the confines of the reserves.

Trees

The *madroño (Calycophyllum candidissimum)* is Nicaragua's national tree. The hills south of Sébaco form the southern limit of the pine family found on the continent; south of Nicaragua,

the pines are out-competed by other species. At the turn of the millennium, Nicaragua's forest area measured 5.5 million hectares, the majority of which is broadleaf forest, followed by pine *(Pinus caribea* and *P. oocarpa)*. At altitudes greater than 1,200 meters, the forests also include the conifers *P. maximinoi* and *P. tecunumanii*. A full 2.5 million hectares of forest are classified as commercial timber forest. Though often privately owned, the Nicaraguan government regulates exploitation of forest products (and not infrequently simply sells the forests for its own profit).

Principal Ecosystems

Nicaragua's varied topography and uneven rainfall distribution, not to mention the presence of tropical reefs, volcanoes, and volcanic crater lakes, result in a phenomenal diversity of terrain and ecosystems. Watch prairie grasslands melt into rolling hills into near-desert into craggy mountain ranges whose peaks are draped in cloud forest on any trip. You can burn your feet on an active volcano's peak and cool your heels in ocean surf the same day. Nicaragua's higher peaks are isolated ecosystems in their own right and home to several endangered as well as endemic species, and the streams, rivers, and two very different coastlines furnish myriad other distinct ecosystems. In general, the land is comprised of the following ecological zones:

Pacific Dry Forest: The lowlands of the Pacific coast, specifically the broad, flat strip that borders the Pacific Ocean from sea level to approximately 800 meters in altitude, are a rain-stressed region dominated by thorny, rubbery species. The region typically receives less than 2,000 millimeters of rain per year. Both trees and non-cactuslike plants in this ecosystem shed their leaves in the middle of the dry season in preparation for the rain, and burst into flower in April or May.

Upland Pine Forest: With the exception of the slopes of several Pacific mountains, namely San Cristóbal and Las Casitas in Chinandega and Güisisíl in Matagalpa, the majority of Nicaragua's pine forests are found in the north near Jalapa and Ocotal. Pines particularly thrive on poor, acidic soils, which erode easily if the area is logged.

Lower Mountainous Broadleaf Forest: Nicaragua's higher peaks are cloud covered for most of the year and home to a cool, moist biosphere, rich in flora and fauna. Most of these areas are the more remote peaks of Matagalpa and Jinotega, like Kilambé, Peñas Blancas, Saslaya, and Musún. It's easier to enjoy this ecosystem on the beautiful and easily visited peaks of Volcán Mombacho near Granada, and Volcán Maderas on Ometepe.

Caribbean Rainy Zone: The Atlantic coast receives rain throughout nearly 10 months of the year and the humidity hovers around 90 percent year-round. Most of the Atlantic coast is covered with tropical forest or even lowland rainforest, with trees that often reach 30 or 40 meters in height. In the north along the Río Coco are the remains of Nicaragua's last extensive pine forests *(Pinus caribaea),* presently subject to intensive logging by national and international concessions.

FAUNA

Nicaragua is home to a great deal of exotic wildlife, much of which—unfortunately— you'll only see for sale on the sides of the highways and at intersections in Managua, where barefoot merchants peddle toucans, reptiles, ocelots, parrots, and macaws. This is a considerable, largely unchecked problem, more so because, of the animals that are captured for sale or export in Nicaragua, 80 percent die before reaching their final destination. To view fauna in their natural habitat involves getting out there, being very, very quiet, and looking and listening. Most critters are shy and many are nocturnal, but they're out there. To date, 1,804 vertebrate species, including 21 species endemic to Nicaragua, and approximately 14,000 invertebrate species have been defined. However, Nicaragua remains the least-studied country in the region. Excursions into the relatively unexplored reserves of the north and northeast will surely uncover previously undiscovered species.

Mammals

One-hundred seventy-six mammal species (including sea life) are known to exist in Nicaragua, more than half of which are bats or small mammals, including rodents. Of the at least three endemic mammal species, two are associated with the Caribbean town of El Rama—the Rama squirrel *(Sciurus richmondi),* considered the tropical world's most endangered squirrel due to reduced habitat, and the Rama rice mouse *(Oryzomis dimidiatus).*

Nicaragua is also home to six big cat species, but there's no guarantee they'll be around for long. All six are listed as endangered, most seriously of all the jaguar and puma. Once common, both require vast amounts of wild hunting territory. In the Pacific region, isolated communities on the higher slopes of some forested volcanoes like Mombacho may remain, but they have not been seen. In the Atlantic region, small communities of cats eke out their survival in the dense forests of the southeast side of the Bosawás reserve. These species are unstudied and untracked, and are presumably preyed upon by local communities. The smaller feline species like ocelots and *tigrillos* have fared better. Though they are largely trapped in the central forests, the latter at least makes a decent living preying on farming community chickens.

There are three kinds of monkeys in Nicaragua: the mantled howler monkey *(Alouata palliata),* known popularly as the *mono congo;* the Central American spider monkey *(Ateles geoffroyii);* and the white-faced capuchin *(Cebus capucinus).* Of the monkeys, the congo is the most common: One thousand individuals roam the slopes of Mombacho alone. You can also find them on Ometepe and the mountains of Matagalpa, particularly Selva Negra. Howler monkeys are able to project their throaty, haunting cries to distances as great as several kilometers. They eat fruits and leaves and spend most of their time in high tree branches. The threatened white-faced capuchin lives in the forests in southeastern Nicaragua and parts of the Atlantic coast. But the spider monkey has nearly been eliminated and is the most threatened of the three.

The Baird's tapir is present in very small numbers in eastern Nicaragua; several communities of this three-toed ungulate inhabit Bosawás, but this species is threatened with extinction. The agouti paca (a large, forest-dwelling rodent known in Nicaragua as the painted rabbit), the white-tailed deer *(Odocoileus virginianus),* and the collared peccary *(Tayassu tajacu),* a stocky piglike creature with coarse, spiky fur, though abundant, are under much pressure from hunters throughout northeastern Nicaragua. You may still see an agouti or peccary east of Jinotega if you're lucky.

Aquatic Life

A wide variety of both saltwater and freshwater species of fish, take advantage of the two large lakes, two ocean coastlines, and numerous isolated crater lakes. Among Nicaragua's many saltwater species are flat needlefish *(Ablennes hians),* wahoo *(Acanthocybium solandri),* three kinds of sole, spotted eagle rays *(Aetobatus narinari),* the Gill's sand lance *(Ammodytoides gilli),*

two kinds of moray *(Anarchias sp.),* croakers *(Bairdiella sp.),* triggerfish *(Balistes sp.),* hogfish *(Bodianus sp.),* eight kinds of perch *(Diplectrum sp.),* sea bass *(Diplectrum sp.),* and a dozen kinds of shark, including blacktip *(Carcharias limbatus),* great white *(C. carcharias),* silky *(C. falciformis),* and spinner *(C. brevipinna).*

Among the freshwater species are needlefish *(Strongylura sp.),* grunts *(Pomadasys sp.),* introduced tilapia *(Oreochromis aureus),* catfish *(Hexanematichthys sp.),* mojarra *(Eucinostomus sp.),* and snook *(Centropomus sp.).* Some species of cichlid *(Amphilophus sp.)* found nowhere else in the world swim in Nicaragua's varied crater lakes.

At least 58 different types of marine corals have been identified in the Atlantic, specifically in the Miskito Cays, Corn Island, and the Pearl Cays. Nicaragua's most common coral species include *Acropora pamata, A. cervicornis,* and *Montastrea anularis.* Brain coral *(Colypophylia natans)* and black coral *(Antipathes pennacea)* are common. Studied for the first time in 1977 and 1978, the shallow reefs of the Pearl Cays contain the best coral formations in the nation, but are now threatened by the enormous sediment load discharged by the Río Grande de Matagalpa.

The manatee *(Trichechus manatus)* is an important species currently protected by international statutes. You may see it at the mouth of the Río San Juan and in the coastal lagoons, notably in Bluefields Bay. In 1993, the freshwater dolphin *(Sotalia fluviatilis)* was first spotted in Nicaragua and since then has been occasionally sighted in Laguna de Wounta, despite conjecture that this species' northern range was Panamá.

Birds

Many thousands of bird species migrate through the Central American biosphere corridor. To date, 676 species of birds in 56 families have been observed here, the more exotic of which you'll find in the mountains of the north and east, and along the Atlantic shore (check out the bird list of Martinez Juan Carlos, 2007, for details). Nicaragua has no endemic bird species of its own, but hosts 87 percent of all bird species known. The most exotic species known to reside in Nicaragua is also its most elusive, the quetzal *(Pharomacrus mocinno),* known to inhabit highlands in Bosawás, Jinotega, and Matagalpa, especially along the slopes of Mt. Kilambé, and in Miraflor in Estelí.

Nicaragua's elegant and colorful national bird, the *guardabarranco (Momotus momota),* is more easily found than you'd think. The Guardian of the Stream (as its Spanish name translates) can be found catching small insects in urban gardens in the capital. It is distinguished by its long, odd-shaped, iridescent tail, which it carefully preens to catch the eye of the opposite sex. The *urraca* is a bigger, meaner version of the North American blue jay, with a dangly black crest on the top of its head. It's one of the larger of the common birds in Nicaragua and scolds humans from the treetops. Though the *urraca* are everywhere, a particularly sizeable population patrols the slopes of Ometepe's twin volcanoes and Las Isletas by Granada. Also in Las Isletas, look for the brightly colored oropendolas *(Psarocolius wagleri)* that hang their elaborate, suspended bagnests from the treetops around the lakeshore.

Reptiles

Of the 172 reptile species in Nicaragua, nearly half are North American, found in Nicaragua at the southern limit of their habitat. Fifteen species are found only in Central America and another five are endemic to Nicaragua.

Nicaragua's several species of marine turtles are all in danger of extinction. The Paslama turtle *(Lepidochelys olivacea)* in the Pacific and the Carey turtle *(Eretmochelys imbricata)* and Green turtle *(Chelonia mydas)* in the Atlantic are protected, and much effort has gone into setting aside habitat for them, particularly nesting beaches. However, the struggle is fierce between those who aim to conserve the turtles and those who'd like to harvest their eggs, meat, and shells. There are approximately 20 beaches in the Pacific whose conditions permit the nesting of these turtle species, most of which play host to only occasional nesting

Nicaragua is home to more than a few IOUs (insects of unusual size).

© JEAN WALSH

events. But two beaches, Chacocente and La Flor on the Pacific coast, are the nesting grounds of the Paslama turtle and experience massive annual egg-laying events between July and January (primarily during the first and third quarters of the moon). In them, 57,000 and 100,000 turtles crawl up on the moist sand at night to lay eggs. It's a safety-in-numbers survival strategy—only 1 out of 100 hatchlings makes it to adulthood. Armed guards on these beaches do their part to make sure the youngsters make it to the sea instead of the soup.

Alligators, crocodiles *(Crocodilus acutus),* caimans *(Caiman crocodilus),* and the *Noca* turtle *(Trachemys scripta)* are frequently seen along the Río San Juan and some larger rivers of Jinotega. The *garrobo* is a bush lizard the size of a small house cat you're more likely to see suspended by its tail on the side of the road than in the wild. Poor *campesino* children hunt and sell them to passing motorists who take it home and make an aphrodisiac soup from the meat. Similarly, the *cusuco (Dasypus novemincinctus)* is a type of armadillo with plated sides and sharp-clawed feet, commonly found in drier areas of the countryside.

Amphibians

Sixty-four known species of amphibians, four of which are endemic, live in Nicaragua's humid forests and riversides. They include the Mombacho salamander *(Bolitoglossa mombachoensis)*, the miadis frog, the Cerro Saslaya frog *(Plectrohyla sp.)*, and the Saslaya salamander *(Nolitron sp.)*.

Insects

Each of Nicaragua's different ecosystems has a distinct insect population. Estimates of the total number of species reach as high as 250,000, only 1 percent of which have been identified. Notable species to seek out are several gigantic species of beetles, including *Dynastes hercules* (found in cloud forests); several species of brilliant green and golden Plusiotis (found in Cerro Saslaya and Cerro Kilambé); the iridescent blue butterfly *Morpho peleides,* common all over the country, and its less common cousin, *M. amathonte,* found at altitudes of 300–700 meters, especially in the forests of Bosawás. Nocturnal moths like the Rothschildia, Eacles, and others are common. For more information about bug hunting in Nicaragua, you'll want to contact Belgian entomologist Jean-Michel Maes (www.bio-nica. info, jmmaes@ibw.com.ni), who, with nearly 20 years of research experience in Nicaragua, knows his stuff. He runs the entomological museum in León (normally closed to the public), and sells a CD-ROM entitled *Butterflies of Nicaragua* ($30). There is an increasing number of *mariposarios* (butterfly farms) in Nicaragua, notably in Los Guatuzos, Papaturro, El Castillo (Río San Juan), and San Ramón (Matagalpa).

National Parks and Reserves

Nicaragua's complex system of parks and reserves encompasses more than two million hectares. The Sistema Nacional de Areas Protegidas (SINAP) is made up of 76 parks, reserves, and refuges classified as "protected" by the Ministerio del Ambiente y los Recursos Naturales (Ministry of the Environment and Natural Resources, or MARENA). Of these, many are privately owned land, which strains enforcement of their protected status. That, combined with MARENA's paltry resource base and budget, has led to the decentralization of park management. Since 2001, MARENA has been experimenting with the co-management model in six natural reserves, handing natural-resource management responsibilities over to local NGOs who work with the communities within the areas to create sustainable alternatives to natural resource use and ecotourism infrastructure. Co-management is a novel, ongoing experiment, and while it has been surprisingly successful in some areas, the great majority of protected lands in Nicaragua remain unmanaged, unguarded, and completely undeveloped for tourism. They are sometimes referred to as "paper parks," existing only in legislation and studies, not in reality. The Río Estero Real, a wetlands preserve in the northwest corner of the country, is one of those, where half of the "protected" territory has been granted to private shrimp farmers who have eliminated most of the mangrove swamps and lagoons where shrimp once bred naturally, replacing them with artificial breeding pools.

Remoteness and neglect provide meager protection to some regions, but more frequently Nicaragua's richest treasures succumb to foreign and national cattle, logging, and mining interests. *Campesino* populations given little incentive or education to better manage the land are equally destructive. Worst of all are the cases where the government "protects" a territory where people have been living traditionally for generations. They are suddenly expected to drastically alter their fishing, hunting, and planting patterns to protect a "park" that is and always has been their homeland. That has been the experience in the Bosawás Biosphere Reserve, where Mayangna and Miskito people were not consulted during the planning of the reserve and have consequently fought against new regulations that interfere with their traditional lifestyle.

Conversely, Fundación Cocibolca, managing La Flor, has both staffed the reserve with local residents and turned to them for input on how to run it. Tourism can go a long way toward bolstering local incentive to protect—rather than consume—the natural world.

The following is a selection of some of the more accessible (or just spectacular) of Nicaragua's protected areas.

NATIONAL PARKS
Volcán Masaya

Nicaragua's best-organized and most easily accessed park features a paved road to the crater, a museum, interpretive center, and paid guides to lead you through more than 20 kilometers of nature trails. Declaring the 5,100 hectares that surround Volcán Masaya a national park was one of President Anastasio García Somoza's last moves before he was deposed in 1979. The park's extensive lava fields are home to coyotes, *garrobo* lizards, white-tailed deer, and *cusucos*. A rare variety of sulfur-tolerant parakeets inhabits the inside of the crater's walls.

Zapatera Archipelago

Thirty-four kilometers southeast of Granada on the western side of Lake Nicaragua is an archipelago formed by Zapatera Volcano (629 meters) and the eight islets that surround it. Although owned by private landholders, the islands gained national park status in the 1980s in recognition of their immense natural, cultural, and historical value, and the government subsequently took control over much of the land. The islands still contain virgin forests and lovely shorelines, but are perhaps most famous for their pre-Columbian statuary, many of which are displayed in the Convento San Francisco in Granada. Isla Zapatera and

© RANDALL WOOD

Volcán Masaya

surrounding islets, like Isla de la Muerte, were at least used for ceremonies and rites, though they may have also been burial sites. In addition to the statues are extensive petroglyphs that date from contact with the first Spaniards.

BIOLOGICAL RESERVES
Miraflor

Draped with Spanish moss and carpeted with orchids and lush vegetation, the more than 5,600 hectares of the Reserva Natural Miraflor are one of the most important natural cloud forest reserves in Nicaragua. The area is entirely privately owned and managed by several farmer associations and *campesino* cooperatives. This is one of few places in Nicaragua to spot the exotic, elusive quetzal, but up to a third of Nicaragua's bird species can be observed here as well.

Río Indio-Maíz

Close to 4,000 square kilometers of jungle pressed between the Indio and Maíz Rivers make up La Gran Reserva, which abuts two additional protected areas, the Punta Gorda Nature Reserve to the north, and the Río San Juan Wildlife Reserve to the south. Together, the reserves are part of the Biósfera del Sureste de Nicaragua, an immense territory dedicated to the preservation of animal and plant species along with their natural ecosystems in the Río San Juan watershed. The reserve is one of the few remaining areas in the Americas where you can experience virgin tropical humid forest as it was 200 years ago. It is one of the last refuges in Nicaragua for ocelots and other big cat species, but its remoteness has made inventorying the wildlife challenging and little is known about its interior.

Cayos Miskitos

Defined as all the cays and small islands found in a 40-kilometer radius from the center of Isla Grande in the Atlantic Ocean off Puerto Cabezas, plus a 20-kilometer swath of shoreline from Cabo Gracias a Dios to the south, the Reserva Biológica Cayos Miskitos has important economic and cultural significance to the Miskito people, who depend on it for fish and shellfish. The Cayos Miskitos are an ecological treasure whose impenetrable lagoons, reefs, mangrove forests, and swamps are home to marine turtles, manatees, dolphins, and several types of endangered coral species. The mangrove forests give shelter to bird species, such as *pancho galán, garza rosada,* and the brown pelican. Substantial petroleum deposits lie below the continental shelf in the Cayos Miskitos area, so the management of the region will warrant much caution and a careful balance. In the meantime, the cays' most immediate threat is drug traffickers, who use the area as a lair.

WILDLIFE RESERVES
Río Escalante-Chacocente

Named for the peculiar smell of *choco* (rotting turtle egg shells after a hatching), the Refugio de Vida Silvestre Río Escalante-Chacocente encompasses 4,800 hectares of dry tropical forest along the edge of the Pacific Ocean. The area was declared a reserve primarily because of its importance as the nesting ground of the endangered tora and Paslama turtles, incredible multitudes of which crawl up on the beach each year to lay eggs in the sand. Exotic orchids, like the *flor de niño* and *huele noche* fill the nocturnal air with a sweet, romantic fragrance. But Chacocente is also home to important forest species, mangrove systems, and the "salt tree." Check the treetops for howler and white-faced monkeys, and keep an eye peeled for the many reptiles, pelicans, white-tailed deer, and *guardabarrancos* that are watching you from the forest edges.

La Flor

This southern Pacific beach, a gorgeous white sandy crescent at the edge of an 800-hectare broad strip of tropical dry forest, is one of the most beautiful beaches in Nicaragua. Thousands of Paslama turtles beach themselves here annually to nest and lay eggs, one of just a handful of beaches in the world that witness such a spectacle. Many *garrobo negro,* iguana *verde, lagartijas,* monkeys, coyotes, raccoons, and skunks (some of which prey on the turtle eggs) also make their home in the reserve. The skies at La Flor are full of bird species that make their homes in the relatively intact dry forest: *urracas, gavilanes caracoleros, chocoyos, querques, garzas,* and *sonchiches.*

Los Guatuzos Wildlife Refuge

The 43,000 hectares of protected wetlands that separate the southern shore of Lake Cocibolca from the Costa Rican border are a remnant of a Sandinista-era wildlife reserve called Sí-a-Paz (a play on words meaning yes to peace). Los Guatuzos preserves both the spirit and the wildlife of the reserve and offers valuable habitat to hundreds of different species, plus several small border settlements of people.

NATURAL RESERVES
Volcán Cosigüina

In the farthest northwestern corner of Nicaragua, more than 12,000 hectares of the Cosigüina peninsula have been declared a natural reserve. The area has been quietly revegetating itself since the volcano's massive eruption in 1835, predominantly as dry tropical forests of *genícero, tempisque,* and *guanacaste* trees. Its nearly inaccessible crater has become the home to spider monkeys, coyotes, black iguanas, white-tailed deer, and coatis, but more obvious to the naked eye are the hundreds of bird species, notably the scarlet macaw. Climbing the volcano—no easy feat—offers a phenomenal view of the crater lake (which began filling after the eruption 150 years ago), the Gulf of Fonseca, and beyond.

Isla Juan Venado

Much more than a sandy barrier beach island, Isla Juan Venado contains 4,600 hectares of estuary and coastline along the Pacific coast west of León. Its vegetation is successional, going from mangroves at the water's edge to inland dry tropical forest. Isla Juan Venado is rife with bird species due to the estuary system—its mangroves are home to the nests of thousands of parrots and herons—as well as crabs, mollusks, and more than 50 species of mammals and reptiles.

Volcán Mombacho

A scant 41 kilometers from the lowland heat of Managua is an otherworldly island of cloud forest atop an ancient and dormant volcano. Volcán Mombacho's lower slopes are devoted to agriculture, cattle raising, and coffee production, but its upper third—above 800 meters—is a spectacular, misty wildlife and cloud-forest reserve. Mombacho is managed by the Fundación Cocibolca, which has done an admirable job of constructing trails and low-impact guest and research facilities. Mombacho is home both to several endemic species of butterflies and the endemic Mombacho salamander.

Chocoyero-El Brujo

The closest natural reserve to Managua, Chocoyero–El Brujo makes up for its small size with the sheer quantity of *chocoyos* (parakeets) that inhabit its cliff caves. There's no excuse for not exploring Chocoyero–El Brujo some lazy afternoon at sundown when the skies fill with the ruckus of thousands of squawking green *chocoyos.* Chocoyero is set in a semihumid forest of stately *pochote, tigüilote,* and cedar trees, and in addition to its famous birds, provides habitat for several types of owls, monkeys, and squirrels.

Estero Padre Ramos

In the northwest corner of the department of Chinandega, Estero Padre Ramos is a mangrove forest reserve with more than 150 bird species, and untouched, pristine beaches as far as the eye can see. The fingers of the estuary are a sea kayaker's dream, or you can try the local *botes.*

Other Reserves

There are many more nature reserves, typically small and designated as such in an attempt to protect a very specific resource. In addition to those mentioned previously, there are 11 reserves that protect volcanic or coastal lagoons,

16 that protect specific peaks, such as Kilambé and Pancasán, six that protect volcanic complexes, such as San Cristóbal or Pilas–El Hoyo, plus dozens of others.

BIOSPHERE RESERVES

Nicaragua's two biosphere reserves were indirectly based on a model proposed for protecting several vast areas in the southeast United States. The strategy is to create a central "nucleus zone," with wilderness status totally preventing human activity. The nucleus is then surrounded by various levels of buffer zones with increasing, but still regulated, resource exploitation permitted as the distance increases from the center. That's the intention, anyway. The virgin lands of Bosawás and the Río San Juan areas have long served as "safety valves" for Nicaragua's expanding population, accommodating *campesinos* as they look for new forestland to clear and farm. Several hundred *campesino* families currently inhabit the Bosawás reserve, and in the absence of regulation, more will surely follow.

Located in the remote north-central wilds of Nicaragua, Bosawás is the largest continuous expanse of virgin cloud forest in Central America. In the extreme southeast of Nicaragua, the Refugio de Vida Silvestre Río San Juan stretches from El Castillo southeast to the Atlantic Ocean along the north edge of the Río San Juan. In addition to the river itself, an important part of the reserve are the four interconnected lagoons at the river's mouth and their related pools, all of which are crucial habitat for manatees and several other mammals.

PRIVATE RESERVES

A handful of protected areas are privately owned. Reservas Silvestres Privadas (Private Wilderness Reserves) are entirely private landholdings granted protected status through the SINAP project. Interested landowners must meet a number of criteria and present an approved management plan. Such reserves are usually near other parks or reserves, contain substantial vegetation and wildlife, and are often a part of some biological corridor. At this early point in the game, they are in varying stages of developing their tourism infrastructures. The original six private reserves are Montibelli near Chocoyero, Domitila outside Nandaime, La Maquina on the road to the coast from Diriamba, Toromixcal in San Juan del Sur, César Augusto in Jinotega, and Greenfields near Pearl Lagoon. Look for them in the appropriate regional chapters.

Environmental Issues

Nicaragua's environmental issues betray a rat's nest of bigger problems, from politics, land rights, and population pressure to war and natural disasters. The remedies are anything but simple.

The primordial environmental concern is the rapid loss of forests—at the rate of 150,000 hectares per year. Some analyses indicate Nicaragua's timber reserves will be completely depleted by 2015, but the extent of the risk is disputable, as the calculations rely on figures collected in the 1970s.

The great majority of country-dwellers cook on *leña* (firewood), so increasing population expansion into previously unsettled lands has boded poorly for forests. Population pressure and the swelling cattle industry have pushed the agricultural frontier inward from both the Atlantic and Pacific sides of the country, reducing Nicaragua's forests by 4.6 million hectares from 1950 to 1995. On the Atlantic coast, much of the hardwood logging is happening at the hands of U.S., Canadian, and Asian companies that have negotiated lucrative timber concessions with Nicaragua's successive cash-strapped governments.

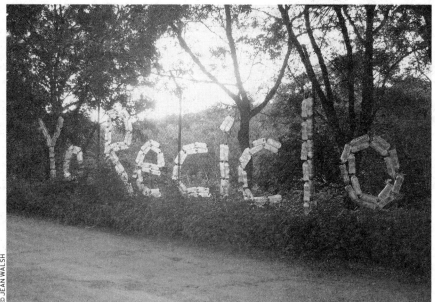

© JEAN WALSH

Solid waste disposal (especially of plastic water bottles) is a huge problem in Nicaragua; one recycling program in San Juan del Sur is doing something about it.

Nueva Segovian pine forests are under further ecological pressure from pine bark beetles, a major outbreak of which decimated 6,000 hectares across the north 1999–2001, particularly the area around Jalapa. The beetle attacks both young and mature pines weakened by fires, resin harvesting, and poor management, boring into the tree to feed on the resin between the wood and the bark. At the start of each rainy season, young beetles disperse and fly longer distances. The infestation can spread up to 20 meters per day, that is a full kilometer in just under two months.

Deforestation exposes fragile tropical soils to rainfall, leading to erosion, contamination and elimination of water sources, and outright microclimate changes. This is the case in much of Nicaragua, where within one human generation, rivers and streams that were once perennial now flow only sporadically, if at all. As any *viejito* will tell you, "it doesn't rain as much as it used to." On the Pacific coast, decades of chemical-intensive agriculture and wind erosion have caused the loss of once-rich volcanic soils as well. In general, the entire Pacific, central, and northern regions of the country are at immediate risk of sustained soil erosion.

Sustained efforts are underway to attack the problem from all sides, from environmental education of children to active replanting of hillsides, to the introduction of less-destructive agricultural techniques.

History

PRE-COLONIAL YEARS

A Caribbean coastal people known as *Los Concheros* (the shell collectors) are the first evidence of human settlement on Nicaraguan soil 8,000 years ago. Two thousand years later humans living on the southern shores of Lake Managua left their footprints in drying mud in an archeological site called *Las Huellas de Acahualinca*. Agriculture began around 5,000 years ago with the cultivation of corn, and pottery making followed 2,000 years later.

Sometime in the 13th century, the Chorotega and Nicarao people, under pressure from the aggressive Aztecs in Mexico, fled south through the Central American isthmus, led by a vision of a land dominated by a great lake. The Chorotegas settled on the shores of Lake Cocibolca and around the volcanic craters of Masaya and Apoyo, and the Nicaraos farther south.

COLONIALISM (1519-1821)

In July of 1502 on his fourth and final voyage, Christopher Columbus (Cristóbal Colón in Spanish) skirted Nicaragua's Mosquito Coast, then continued on to South America. Seventeen years later, the conquistador Pedro Arias Dávila returned under orders from the Spanish crown to explore the land bridge of Nicaragua. Indigenous leaders Nicarao and

A BRIEF HISTORY OF U.S. INTERVENTION IN NICARAGUA

In President Teddy Roosevelt's addition to the Monroe Doctrine of regional dominance, he proclaimed that the United States, by virtue of its status as a "civilized nation," had the right to stop "chronic wrongdoing" throughout the Western Hemisphere. Subsequently, the so-called Roosevelt Corollary was used to justify troop deployment to Latin America 32 times between the end of the Spanish-American War and the years of the Great Depression. President William Howard Taft provided further rationalization for aggressively dominating Latin America with his Dollar Diplomacy, an unabashed strategy to advance and protect U.S. businesses in other countries. Nicaragua, which had been host to U.S. fruit, mining, and transportation interests since the 1850s, was a frequent recipient of such foreign policy.

U.S. Marines landed at least seven times during the aforementioned period, and spent a total of 21 years occupying Nicaragua. Official reasons for these visits included "pacification of Nicaragua," "prevention of rebellion," and, of course, "protection of U.S. interests and property." It would be unfair to call these visits uninvited, since nearly all were ostensibly serving the purpose of one or more Nicaraguan parties, usually the Conservatives.

The following is a more detailed list of gringo interventions.

1853: Washington sends U.S. Navy commander George H. Hollins to Greytown to extract an apology from local British officials for having insulted U.S. diplomat Solon Borland. Those responsible were nowhere to be found, so, reports a U.S. Marine Corps historical website, "Hollins' only alternative was to bombard the town, and this he tried to do in the most humane manner possible." Hollins allowed 24 hours for evacuation, then commenced firing. "At 0900 on 13 July, 177 shells plowed into Greytown. That afternoon a landing party of Marines and seamen completed the destruction of the town." Humanely, of course.

1853-1856: U.S. citizen William Walker usurps power and declares himself president of Nicaragua; he is briefly recognized by Washington before the other Central American nations

Diriangén engaged them in a brief battle. But irregardless, Francisco Hernández de Córdoba arrived soon after to establish Spain's first settlements in the new land. Córdoba settled Granada alongside the Chorotega communities on the banks of Lake Cocibolca, and forging farther inland and up the Tipitapa River, the settlement of León on the western shores of Lake Xolotlán. Nicaragua remained a part of Spain's overseas possessions for the next 300 years under the governance of the colonial capital in Guatemala.

INDEPENDENCE, WILLIAM WALKER, AND THE U.S. MARINES (1821-1937)

Central America won its independence from Spain in 1821, and for a short time remained united as the five provinces of the Central American Federation. The belief that Europe would act militarily to return the former colonies to Spain forced the United States to issue the Monroe Doctrine in 1823, declaring the New World off limits to further European colonization and interference, paving the way for two centuries of political domination in Latin America. The Central American Federation was short-lived, however: When Nicaragua withdrew from the federation in 1838, the remaining states opted to become individual republics as well and the federation dissolved.

Newly independent Nicaragua was anarchic for years, dominated by the independent, feuding city-states of León and Granada until 1845 when a national government was finally agreed upon (the political rivalries that endure to this

---

briefly unite, drive him out, and eventually execute him by firing squad.

1894: The U.S. Marines under Lieutenant Franklin J. Moses have a monthlong occupation of Bluefields.

1896: From May 2-4, when fighting near Corinto "endangers American holdings," 15 Marines, under First Sergeant Frederick W. M. Poppe, and 19 seamen land in Corinto and stand guard in a "show of force."

1898: As President Zelaya extends his tenure for still another term, the local U.S. consular agent requests the U.S.S. *Alert*, at anchor in the harbor of Bluefields, to stand by in case of an attack on the city. On the morning of February 7, the U.S. flag on shore rises "union downward" over the consulate, signaling a force of 14 Marines and 19 seamen to land; they withdraw the following day.

1899: Another display of force lands, this time with a Colt automatic gun "to prevent both rebels and government troops from destroying American property."

1910: Marines and Navy vessels concentrate in Nicaraguan waters and land in Bluefields and Corinto on May 19 "to guard American property."

1912: Nicaraguan president Adolfo Díaz requests the support of U.S. forces. The United States complies when the U.S.S. *Annapolis* arrives in Corinto, deploying a contingent of naval officers to Managua on August 4. Three companies of marine infantry also land and are transported to Managua by train.

1927-1933: President Coolidge sends Marines to find Sandino and "gun the bandit down." They fail.

1981-1990: The CIA runs a secret command operation directing and financing Contra forces in their attempt to topple the Sandinista government. U.S operatives carry out supply and intelligence activities, train commanders and soldiers, plant harbor mines, and sabotage Sandinista holdings.

All citations from "Marine Corps Historical Reference Series, The United States Marines in Nicaragua," by Bernard C. Nalty, Historical Branch, G-3 Division, Headquarters, U.S. Marine Corps, Washington, D.C.

day). In the early 19th century, export of cacao, indigo, and cattle allowed the landed and merchant classes to accumulate considerable wealth at the expense of the Native Americans and landless class. A nascent liberal class grew in León inspired by the French and American revolutions that sought for more equal distribution of wealth.

Nicaragua's unique geography has inspired multiple plans for a transcontinental-canal, even today. During the California gold rush (1849–1856), prospectors transited Nicaragua courtesy of steamship baron and businessman Cornelius Vanderbilt's Pacific Steamship Company, then operating in Panamá. Travelers bound for California sailed up the Río San Juan and across Lake Nicaragua to the small port at San Jorge. There, they were taken by horse cart 18 kilometers across the narrow isthmus through Rivas to the bay of San Juan del Sur. Ships waiting in the harbor then carried the travelers north along the Pacific coastline to California. Vanderbilt dredged the channel of the Río San Juan and built roads, railroads, and docks on both coasts to accommodate the traffic. At about that time, the Leóneses, embroiled in a bitter battle with the Conservatives of Granada, enlisted the help of William Walker, an American filibuster who eventually installed himself as president of Nicaragua, razed the city of Granada, and caused a whole lot of trouble.

Though the relative peace of the 30-year Conservative period fostered many advances in infrastructure and technology, including the Granada—Corinto train and the telegraph, Nicaragua remained several decades behind its neighbors in coffee exportation and the economy mostly stagnated. The bourgeoisie became restless and rebelled, installing Liberal General José Santos Zelaya as president. Zelaya was a fierce nationalist who, among other things, reclaimed the Atlantic region at gunpoint from its British occupants (the two administrative units of the Atlantic coast bore Zelaya's name until the 1990s). Zelaya furthermore rejected Washington's proposals to build a cross-isthmus canal through Nicaraguan territory while courting Great Britain to finance the construction of a transcontinental railway.

The United States, which since 1904 had been building the Panama canal, was unimpressed by the nationalist leader and his railway proposal and in 1909, sent the U.S. Marines to secure Zelaya's ouster. The U.S. intervention reestablished the Conservatives in power until 1912, when Liberal and nationalist Benjamin Zeledón led another rebellion. This time the U.S. Marine occupation happened on a much larger scale: 2,700 marines landed at Corinto and took immediate control of the railways, ports, and major cities.

Nicaragua became subject to the United States financially at about this time, as U.S. financial institutions began to quietly acquire coffee-export businesses and railway and steamship companies, easing Nicaragua into a credit noose. Under the watchful eye of the U.S. Marines, governmental control was handed over to the Conservatives, whom Washington thought would more faithfully represent U.S. business interests. But the Liberals staged 10 uprisings between 1913 and 1924, all of which the U.S. military quelled.

In 1924, Conservative President Bartolomé Martínez instituted a novel form of government—a power-sharing arrangement between the Liberals and the Conservatives at the local level. The United States withdrew Marines in 1925 but they were back within the year. No sooner had power sharing begun than ambitious Conservative Emilio Chamorro staged a coup d'état, seized power, and sparked the Constitutional War. The United States stepped in to prevent the imminent takeover by the Liberals, but because the Conservatives had discredited themselves, the United States was unable to simply hand the power back to them. The deal they worked out was known as the Espino Negro Pact (named after the town where it was signed; Spanish for Black Thorn). It was a crucial moment for the Liberals. One of their generals, Augusto C. Sandino, was opposed to the pact, and fled with his men to the northern mountains to start a guerrilla war in opposition of the continued presence of the United States in Nicaragua. The leader of the Constitutional Army was forced to declare, "All my men surrender except one."

The U.S. military tried unsuccessfully to flush Sandino from the mountains despite drastic measures like the aerial bombing of Ocotal, so in 1933, Washington tried a new approach. Withdrawing U.S. troops from Nicaragua, the United States formed a new military unit called the National Guard and placed young Anastasio Somoza García at its head.

During the presidency of Juan Bautista Sacasa, Sandino enjoyed overwhelming support in Nicaragua's northern mountains as he was perceived to have successfully accomplished both the repatriation of both U.S. armed forces and the removal of Conservative oligarchy from power. But he represented a major threat to Somoza's political and military ambitions. In February of 1934, President Sacasa invited him to Managua to negotiate an agreement. When Sandino left the presidential palace that night, several National Guard members ambushed and assassinated him on the streets of Managua. The National Guard immediately swept the northern countryside subsequently, destroying cooperatives, returning lands to their previous owners, and hunting down, exiling, imprisoning, or killing Sandino's supporters.

THE SOMOZA ERA (1937-1979)

General Anastasio Somoza García overpowered Sacasa in 1937; his enormously wealthy and powerful family dynasty would permanently reorient and dominate Nicaraguan politics for the following 42 years. Nicaraguans and foreigners to this day refer to the nearly continuous succession of three Somoza presidents as one all-powerful "Somoza." The Somozas were wily politicians with a near-genius for using existing political conflicts to their personal advantage; they were also expert practitioners of a favorite trick of Latin American dictators, *continuismo,* in which a puppet leader would be elected but resign shortly afterward, handing the power back to the Somozas. Five

such "presidents" were elected during the 42-year reign of the Somozas, not one of which lasted longer than three years. The Somozas maintained a strong foothold in the national economy as well by manipulating government licensing requirements and importing duty-free goods with the complicity of the National Guard. If there was money to be made in any economic sector, the Somoza family quickly came to control it. They extracted personal income from public utilities and the financial sector, monopolized the cotton industry when it surged in the 1950s and, later, meat, shrimp, and lobster export in the 1960s and 1970s. They owned the nation's prime food-processing industries; sugar refining; cement production; the cardboard, tobacco, and recording industries; and sea and air transport. In fact, by the late 1970s, the Somoza family owned just about everything in Nicaragua worth owning.

Born in San Marcos, Carazo, and educated in Philadelphia, Anastasio Somoza García ascended rapidly through the military. The Roosevelt administration overlooked his rapacious greed, questionable politics, and strong-handed military tactics in exchange for a Central American ally. World War II was an economic windfall for Nicaragua—and Somoza's industries, which exported raw material—but just in case, Somoza declared war on Germany and Japan as a pretext for confiscating the valuable German-owned coffee land. Somoza García's administration oversaw construction of the Chinandega–Puerto Morazán railway, Managua's city water system and International Airport, and the Pan-American Highway. Popular frustration at his heavy-handedness grew until 1956 when, at a celebratory ball in the Social Club of León, poet, political idealist, and frustrated nationalist Rigoberto López Pérez shot him.

Anastasio's son Luís Somoza Debayle, a.k.a. Tacho, took the reins, overseeing the construction of the hydropower plant and reservoir of Lake Apanás in Jinotega; the improved port facilities at Corinto; the highway from San Benito to El Rama, which helped unite the

AUGUSTO CÉSAR SANDINO (1893-1934)

The term Sandinista is easily associated with Nicaragua, but less well known is the story of the man, who, through his fight against imperialism, became a legend in Nicaragua and the world, and is recognized today by just the merest rendering of his famous broad-brimmed hat.

Augusto C. Sandino was born in Niquinohomo (Nahuatl for "valley of warriors"), the bastard son of a wealthy, landed judge and one of his servant women. But while the judge lived well in town, Sandino's family was so poor they often resorted to stealing crops to eat. Sandino grew disgusted at Nicaraguan society, which engendered such inequity, and questioned both civil society and the Catholic church, which he believed was guilty of propping up the aristocracy. At the age of 17, Sandino witnessed the U.S. Marines's invasion of Nicaragua to prop up Adolfo Díaz's failing Conservative presidency. When they crushed a rebellion led by General Benjamin Zeledón, their parading of Zeledón's dead body through the streets of Masaya affected Sandino deeply. Nine years later, Sandino fled to Mexico, where he was inspired by Tampico laborers struggling to unionize in spite of resistance from the U.S.-owned oil companies. Sandino returned to Nicaragua with a new sense of purpose and a strong self-identity shaped by anarchy, socialism, and armed conflict.

He became a renegade general from the Liberals and set up his camp in the mountains outside San Rafael del Norte, Jinotega, where he became one of the first to practice guerrilla warfare, staging effective hit-and-run raids against U.S. Marine installations in Ocotal and the north. Sandino's men, who grew to number nearly 1,800 by 1933, attacked some mining and lumber companies with enough force to drive them away from the Atlantic coast.

Sandino and his troops were brutal – they sometimes killed prisoners of war or slit the throats of the dead and pulled the tongue out and down through the gash, like a necktie. The U.S. military struggled diligently but fruitlessly for seven years to flush Sandino out of the hills. In the words of one U.S. Army lieutenant, "Sandino poses as the George Washington of Nicaragua but he is only a cut-throat

Atlantic and Pacific coasts; and the nation's first social security system (INSS). In 1963, Tacho lost in popular elections to the Liberal Renée Schick, and died of a heart attack four years later.

The third of the Somozas was the most avaricious and cruel. As "Tachito," a 1964 graduate of the West Point Military Academy, rose to power, the nascent Sandinista (FSLN) movement was gaining attention in the north through attacks and kidnappings; over the next decade, they would goad Tachito into becoming the most bloodthirsty president the nation had ever seen. The earthquake of December 1972 provided Tachito a unique opportunity: Appointing himself head of the Emergency Committee, he did little more to rebuild the country than funnel aid money into his own bank accounts. He was reelected in 1974, but Tachito's increasingly flagrant human rights violations including the assassination of journalist Pedro Joaquín Chamorro, and his increasingly violent responses to FSLN attacks earned him international opprobrium. When the FSLN finally ousted him on July 16, 1979, he fled to Miami, and then to Paraguay, where on September 17, 1980, he was assassinated with an anti-tank rocket.

THE SANDINISTA REVOLUTION (1977-1979)

Guerrilla groups opposed to the Somoza dynasty and inspired by Fidel Castro began training in clandestine camps in the northern mountains of Nicaragua in the early 1950s and coalesced a decade later when Carlos Fonseca Amador, Silvio Mayorga, and Tomás Borge formed the **Frente Sandinista de Liberación Nacional (FSLN).** Carlos Fonseca's ideas, an and a bandit, preying upon foreigners and the law-abiding citizens of his country." But he was slippery: In Sandino's advantage was a profound knowledge of the land, vast popular support, the willingness to live poor, and an uncanny ability to vanish into thin air.

While Sandino's struggle was ostensibly to force the U.S. military and business interests out of Nicaragua, he represented much more than brute nationalism. In the Segovias, where Sandino enjoyed massive popular support, he formed agricultural cooperatives of landless peasants, imposing taxes on wealthy ranchers and businessmen to support them. He also fought in support of the exploited timber, banana plantation, and mine workers.

During the Great Depression, the Marines eventually left Nicaragua, and the new president of Nicaragua, Anastasio Somoza García, had Sandino assassinated in February 1934. Sandino's body was never found.

Thirty years after Sandino's death, a young idealistic student named Carlos Fonseca Amador resurrected Sandino's image and ideals as the basis of a new political and guerrilla movement, which he called the Frente Sandinista de Liberación Nacional (FSLN) – the Sandinista Front for National Liberation. The FSLN greatly exaggerated Sandino's reputation as a peasant who fought righteously against the imperialistic designs of the United States, because it suited their ideology. Contrary to FSLN doctrine, Sandino was no communist. Rather, Sandino's crusade was often against the bourgeois Nicaraguan Conservatives. His ideology was a mix of his own peculiar leftism with a curious indigenous mysticism; he changed his middle name from Calderón to César in honor of the Roman emperor, claimed he could give orders to his troops using silent mental communication, and predicted Nicaragua would be the site of Armageddon, where "armies of angels would do battle alongside more temporal troops."

Nevertheless, to this day, Sandino remains a hero to Nicaraguans and the world's leftist community. He spearheaded a movement that fought for drastic social and political change and sought to make up for centuries of class discontent that continues even today.

inspired combination of Marxism (which he'd experienced firsthand in a trip to Moscow) and the nationalist, anti-imperialist beliefs of Augusto Sandino formed their ideological framework: Sandinismo.

Early Sandinista insurrections in Río Coco and Bocay (1963) and Pancasán (1967) were easily crushed but legitimized the FSLN. As trade unions, student organizations, and private and religious organizations all threw their weight behind the Sandinista insurgency, Tachito grew more brutal and outraged. In January 1978, Pedro Joaquín Chamorro, editor of *La Prensa* and a relentless critic of Somoza, was gunned down in Managua. His death fooled no one. One month later, the largely indigenous population of the Masaya neighborhood of Monimbó protested for five days until the National Guard responded by massacring hundreds. By May 1979, the guerrillas were ready for the final insurrection, which would last 52 days.

Combat erupted simultaneously around Chinandega, León, and Chichigalpa in the Pacific, and in the mining triangle in the northeast. At the same time, Sandinista troops began pressing north from the border with Costa Rica. They entered León, capturing the city after a two-day battle. The rest of the nation began a massive general labor strike. On June 8, 1979, Sandinista soldiers and supporters began marching from Carazo, just south of Managua, into the capital itself. The National Guard responded by shelling Managua. Most of the fighting in Managua took place in the lower-middle-class neighborhoods of Bello Horizonte and El Dorado, where extensive networks of concrete drainage ditches made easy battle trenches. The people tore up the concrete *adoquines* (paving stones) of the streets and erected barricades with them. The world watched, appalled, as Somoza's aircraft indiscriminately strafed the capital.

The FSLN captured Matagalpa on July 2, 1979, and the strategic town of Sébaco the day after. The Estelí military barracks—the last and most important one after Managua—fell on July 16. Finally, with complete control of the north, FSLN forces surrounded the capital. Trapped by the Sandinistas and abandoned by the United States, Somoza fled Nicaragua in the predawn hours of July 17.

THE FSLN GOVERNMENT (1979-1991)

The exuberance of military victory quickly faded as the new leaders struggled to convert revolutionary fervor into support for the new nation they wanted to build. They were starting from scratch: Somoza had run Nicaragua as his own personal farm, and overthrowing him had implied dismantling the national economy. The sweeping economic, political, and social reforms of the Sandinista revolution therefore made Nicaragua a real-time social experiment, and the entire world looked on with anticipation and anxiety.

The new Nicaraguan government was a battleground of competing interests exacerbated by the dire need to reactivate the economy. The "Group of Nine" fatigue-clad FSLN *comandantes* elbowed a supporting conservative alliance aside and revealed their legendary **Plan 80,** which revealed the FSLN as Marxist-Leninist and their planned economy as a delicate balance between private ownership ceding to increasing state control. Appalled, betrayed, and frequently victimized as "supporters of the dictator," the upper class abandoned ship and fled to Miami, where they stayed for a decade. Their personal boycott of the Revolution hastened its demise.

Land reform proceeded immediately. The Sandinistas confiscated two million acres of Somoza's holdings and distributed it to the poor for farming. Though this was true social revolution, the environmental impact of previously unexploited and delicate hillsides being cleared and planted was massive deforestation and erosion. Worse, the Sandinista elite kept most profitable lands for themselves, a hypocrisy that did not go unnoticed.

A massive and world-acclaimed literacy campaign saw thousands of volunteers—typically zealous university students—teaching reading, writing, and basic math skills to the illiterate majority. The literacy rate soared to nearly 90 percent, but the Cuban-inspired mix of education and revolutionary propaganda meant many *campesinos'* first reading lessons taught revolutionary dogma, and the math exercises frequently involved counting items like rifles and tanks. Nonetheless, the literacy campaign encouraged young idealists to explore and take pride in their own country and culture, and has reinforced Nicaragua's nationalism and self-identity to the present.

THE CONTRA WAR (1980-1991)

In their zeal to "defend the revolution at all costs," Sandinista leaders ran into opposition from all sides—from the business community (headed by the business organization COSEP and future president Enrique Bolaños); from Somoza's former cronies who missed their days of wealth and privilege and were enraged by the policy of confiscation; from the former members of the National Guard, many of whom regrouped outside of Nicaragua and became the nucleus of the military *contra-revolucionarios* (Contras); and lastly, from the United States government under President Reagan, which remained deeply distrustful of the Sandinistan Communist tendencies.

The Sandinistas openly collaborated with Cuba and the Soviet Union and supported El Salvador's FMLN, a similar revolutionary group, three policies that led the United States to impose an economic embargo in 1985. Many moderate Nicaraguans supported the U.S. government intervention. They had supported overthrowing the dictator, not the establishment of a repressive Marxist-Leninist economy. Furthermore, land confiscation didn't end with Somoza's land; the Sandinistas confiscated the land of any Nicaraguan that opposed them. To moderate Nicaraguans, the FSLN had simply imposed themselves as a new elite.

Negligent Sandinista economic mismanagement and the embargo hastened economic collapse. By 1985, export earnings were half the pre-revolution figures, and much of the confiscated agricultural land remained unproductive in cooperatives. The business class recoiled in fear of further expropriation, and skilled laborers fled the country in search of profitable employment elsewhere. In order to combat the Contras, the Sandinistas increased military spending and sent much of the country's productive labor force into battle. Austerity measures didn't earn the Sandinista government many friends either, as previously common goods, like toothpaste and rice, were parsimoniously rationed and shoddy Eastern-bloc goods replaced imports of better quality. Finally, to counter the increasingly violent Contra attacks in Matagalpa, Jinotega, and much of the east, the Sandinistas instituted a much despised obligatory draft, forcing Nicaraguans to defend—with their sons' lives—a revolution in which they were rapidly losing faith. *Servicio militar patriotico* (patriotic military service), or SMP, was parodied by young men as *Seremos muertos pronto* (soon we will be dead).

Regardless, in 1984 the Sandinistas easily won an election international observers declared fair and transparent while the economy spiralled and the military conflict grew bloodier. Washington continued to fund the Contras, and Cuba and the Soviet Union continued to fund the Sandinistas, in a proxy war that made Nicaragua a geopolitical pawn.

At the close of the 1980s, both the Contras and the Sandinista government were physically and economically exhausted. The collapse of the Soviet Union left the Sandinistas without a sponsor, while the Contras had little real hope of a military victory. The Iran-Contra scandal in the United States exposed the illegal mechanisms President Reagan's team were employing to fund their Contra "Freedom Fighters" and torpedoed the Contras' funding source. The moment was propitious for Costa Rican president Oscar Arías to propose a peace initiative. In 1987, five Central American presidents attended talks at Esquipulas, Guatemala, and emerged with a radical peace accord. The Sandinistas organized elections in 1990 to show the world that their government was committed to democratic principles and to give Nicaraguans the chance to reaffirm their support for the FSLN. To their surprise, the Nicaraguan people overwhelmingly voted them out of office. The revolution had ended.

If Nicaragua was going to revert to capitalism, the Sandinista elite wanted to ensure they got their share, so on their way out the door, the Sandinistas signed over hundreds of millions of dollars of state property to themselves in a hypocritical disgrace now known as the Piñata. FSLN party heads privatized many state companies under anonymous cooperatives and passed a series of decrees ensuring they would retain some power—and the new bourgeoisie of former bourgeoisie-haters was born.

THE NEW DEMOCRACY (1991-2006)

Violeta Barrios de Chamorro, widow of the slain journalist Pedro Joaquín Chamorro, became president with a coalition of Sandinista opposition groups called the Unión Nacional Opositora (UNO). Her charisma and leadership led the nation through a period of reconciliation and rebuilding. She reestablished diplomatic and economic ties with the rest of the world, ended the draft, reestablished the army and the police under civil control, and disarmed the Contras. To help them reassimilate into the agrarian workforce, they were offered 1,600 square kilometers of land, including much of the Río San Juan area and some parts of Jinotega and Matagalpa. Failure to live up to some of these land promises set the stage for further unrest in the 21st century. The international donor community pardoned much of Nicaragua's debt, but did little else to help: Once the proxy war ended, it seemed as though the world had lost interest in Nicaragua.

The elections of 1996, run without the

massive international funding that characterized previous elections, were rife with abnormalities, near-riots, and chronic disorder: Polling places opened hours late, bags of discarded ballots were found afterward in the houses of officials, and the communication network failed. Not surprisingly, in the aftermath, all sides had reason to accuse the others of vote-rigging and fraud. Even so, Nicaraguans turned out in record numbers and elected Managua's slippery mayor, Arnoldo Alemán.

Arnoldo Alemán was a political conservative and hard-core capitalist lawyer with a sworn aversion to all things Sandinista and a professed admiration for the Somozas. Alemán oversaw the continued growth of the economy, boosted the development of *zonas francas* (free trade zones) and the construction

OF BEANS AND BULLETS: WHO WERE THE CONTRAS?

The Contras remain one of the most powerful, divisive, and enigmatic elements of Nicaragua's recent history. They owe their name to the Sandinista leaders who christened them *contra-revolucionarios*. The Contras preferred to call themselves La Resistencia, and others called them "freedom fighters," "bandits," "heroes," and "outlaws."

Not long after the Sandinistas took power in 1979 and long before the Contra movement even had a name, discontent was already swelling among some groups of *campesinos*, who sensed that the Sandinista revolution had gone wrong: Small farmers were being forced to join collectives or were jailed; political meetings were frequent; government propaganda smacked of atheism (or dubious support for the Catholic church); the government was full of Cuban advisors; price controls were making it hard to turn a profit in agriculture; and a lot of people were incarcerated, including many indigenous Miskito people, who had never wanted much more than to be left alone. The revolution was supposed to have made the lives of the poor farmers easier, not harder.

As the first *campesinos* picked up arms and slipped across the northern border into Honduras, they encountered another group eager to see the Sandinistas return to where they had come from: former members of Somoza's National Guard, professional military personnel who longed for their former positions of power and prestige and thirsted for one more battle.

Though they received some early training and organizational help from Argentine military advisers, the Contras weren't an organized force per se until late in the game. Even then, they were composed of numerous factions rife with internal divisions, petty grudges, and ambition among and within their units. Many were simple farm boys looking for fame and fortune at the end of a rifle; others were would-be warlords who used the armed maneuvers to settle old civil disputes or have some vengeance on former drinking buddies. The Contras survived on limited supplies, donations from sympathizers in Miami, and whatever they could take at gunpoint.

The only thing that united the various Contra groups was the feeling that the Sandinista revolution had been a step in the wrong direction. That group included U.S. President Ronald Reagan, who in March 1986, said, "I guess in a way they are counterrevolutionary, and God bless them for being that way. And I guess that makes them Contras, and so it makes me a Contra, too." At various points in the 1980s, the U.S. government played a critical part in the financing and arming of the Contras, in violation of its own laws and without the knowledge of the public.

Based out of camps along the Honduran border, the Fuerza Democrática Nicaragüense (FDN) staged raids in Jinotega, Matagalpa, and Chinandega, and was led primarily by ex-National Guard officers and groups of farmers who called themselves Milicia Popular Anti-Somoza (MILPA, a play on the Spanish word for corn patch). Fighting a completely separate battle along the Río San Juan from camps of *maquiladoras* (export clothing assembly plants). Politics returned to the back room, where endless scandals of kickbacks, insider deals, and frenzied pocket-filling embarrassed and infuriated the nation. His personal fortune soared from $20,000 when he took office as mayor of Managua, to $250 million, when he was voted out in 2001. But as he came under increased political and popular pressure for corruption, he and Ortega (accused of allegedly molesting his stepdaughter Zoilamerica Narvaez) engineered the infamous **El Pacto.** The agreement provided them both diplomatic immunity and a lifetime seat in the Assembly, and divided up the government's most important roles between the FSLN and PLC, including the Supreme Court and the Consejo Supremo Electoral (which

---

over the Costa Rican border was the Alianza Revolucionaria Democrática (ARDE), led by the infamous Edén Pastora, a.k.a. Comandante Cero (Zero), former Sandinista militant turned Contra. ARDE was a military disaster from the start, so thoroughly riddled with Sandinista spies it never had any hope of victory. Pastora was a would-be *caudillo* who hated organization, refused to delegate authority, and kept his own men divided to prevent any claims to his throne. His macho posturing and reputation for womanizing made him an easy target for sexy female Sandinista spies, a half dozen of whom coaxed him to pillow-talk away just about every military secret he had. Pastora's own men feared he was really a Sandinista sympathizer sent to lead them into military devastation.

Though the Sandinista military committed its share of mistakes and atrocities, the Contras' propensity for brutality and terror is well documented and undeniable. Militarily, they were best at short, sharp raids and random ambushes of military and civilian vehicles. Complicated operations that required timing or planning nearly always went awry, and communication and coordination problems plagued them throughout the war. What they were best at was seeding terror in the hillsides. Their tactics were barbaric: Reagan's "Freedom Fighters" regularly disemboweled victims, chopped their limbs off, and tore bones out of bodies which they shook at the victims' family members. Columns of hungry Contra troops didn't think twice about taking at gunpoint anything they needed from local *campesinos*, from cat-

tle to liquor to boots. On the way, many young women and girls were taken away to be raped and killed, sometimes by decapitation. Young boys and men were routinely castrated and mutilated before being killed.

The Contras commonly targeted suspected Sandinista sympathizers, including government workers in nonmilitary organizations. They brutalized and killed mayors, doctors, nurses, judges, schoolteachers, clergy, policemen, even the staff of utility offices and wealthy townspeople suspected of supporting the new government. Often, those victims who escaped death at the hands of the Contras were forced into the mountains at gunpoint to become soldiers. Intent on derailing the Sandinista economy by preventing the harvest, Contras frequently burned the installations of agricultural cooperatives and massacred anyone who stayed to defend them.

The Contras never had the satisfaction of a military victory. Rather, when the Sandinistas lost public elections and handed power over to the Chamorro government, the incentive to be a Contra vanished. Though some Contras rejected the peace accords and slipped back into the mountains to continue fighting, most disarmed and went back to farming their beans and corn. In the end, though foreign powers had helped the Nicaraguans to nearly destroy themselves over ideology and geopolitics, the Contras who returned to the land knew the struggle to defeat the Sandinista government was simple – the right to a piece of land, to be left alone to work it, and to sell their crops at a fair price.

runs elections). Other political parties were excluded from the power sharing arrangement. Together, Nicaragua's top two *caudillos* (political strongmen) had eviscerated Nicaraguan democracy and divided the spoils.

Enrique Geyer Bolaños, Arnoldo Alemán's nondescript vice-president and former head of COSEP (the Nicaraguan private industry association) won the 2001 election for the PLC party on an anticorruption platform that resonated with Nicaraguans appalled with Alemán's avarice and duplicity. Upon entering office, Bolaños moved quickly to bring indictments against high-ranking PLC officials, including Alemán himself. Alemán, under other conditions, might have been able to muster the support to resist the charges, but, as his allies slipped away, he was found guilty of corruption and money laundering, and sentenced in December 2003 to 20 years in prison. This was the first time in recent Latin American history that a overtly corrupt leader had been convicted and punished. But Alemán continued to wield considerable political influence even from house arrest, and the majority of the PLC turned against Bolaños in retribution for biting the hand that fed him. Congress, evenly divided between PLC and FSLN members, mostly opposed Bolaños's legislation, and the PLC mounted a vindictive effort to convict him of corruption himself. Ironically, Enrique Bolaños had better political support from the outside world than he did from his own political party, and relinquished his mandate in 2006 having accomplished very little of value despite the best of intentions.

THE RETURN OF ORTEGA (2006-PRESENT)

The Pact strengthened Ortega's hand, and through the Sandinistas in the National Assembly he methodically weakened and divided the political opposition. Mayoral elections in 2004 went overwhelmingly to the Sandinista party, while Bolaños's new coalition, APRE, suffered significant defeats in most departments. Alemán, under house arrest, could do little to counter him, and in late 2004 Ortega's and Alemán's people again conspired to change the criteria under which one could become president: the threshold for victory was lowered from 45 percent to 35 percent and the mandatory margin over the second candidate was set at 5 percent, both criteria skillfully tailored to Ortega's proven electoral capacity. The FSLN party was by then largely only Daniel supporters or "Danielistas," the old guard of the Revolution having been blocked in an FSLN primary, while breakaway Sandinistas' new party, the Movimiento Renovador Sandinista (MRS) lost its chance when its popular candidate, Herty Lewites, was felled by a mysterious heart attack while campaigning. Ortega, ever the opportunist, embraced the Catholic church by supporting a total abortion ban, assured the private sector and Brettons Woods institutions that he had no intention of returning to a policy of land confiscation, and that he would support free enterprise and a capitalist economy. He married his longtime partner Rosario Murillo and "atoned for the sins committed during the FSLN in the 1980s." Says Álvaro Vargas Llosa, "What this farcical saga tells us is that Daniel Ortega was much more interested in being president than in being principled." And in November 2006, Nicaraguans turned out in record numbers to vote and were stunned to discover Daniel Ortega had won the presidency with only 38 percent of the vote.

Ortega kept his promise to respect private enterprise, but he worked vigorously to ensure his return to power would be permanent. But despite rhetoric about the continuation of the 1979 Revolution, there was nothing revolutionary about Ortega's mandate. His administration relentlessly pursued political foes and solidified FSLN control of the courts, the National Assembly, and attempted the same with the police and military to lesser effect. State agents ransacked the offices of a leading investigative journalist, Carlos Fernando Chamorro (son of the former president and slain newspaper man) and a women's NGO, and sent agents to confiscate the computers of 15 other organizations including Oxfam, under

President Ortega's ubiquitous billboards equate the people's mission with God's, a new twist for the FSLN, the Sandinista party.

suspicion of money laundering and "subversion," a provocative accusation of supporting opposition political parties. At least 10 journalists have been beaten and opposition radio stations have had their equipment destroyed. Masked gangs attacked both major newspapers in November 2009, launching mortars and rockets at the building. Meanwhile, youth spray-painted "Viva Daniel" from one end of Managua to the other.

Under the new administration, Sandinista "supporters" were required to register with their local Consejo Popular Ciudadano (Community Citizen Committee, CPC) and receive a membership card. Non-cardholders found life close to impossible, as suddenly doors were closed to them. Cardholders were permitted to skip certain college exams, non-cardholders could not; cardholders got chosen for scholarships, non-cardholders did not; cardholders got discounted food at the markets, non-cardholders did not. Government workers have also been subjected to intimidating and illegal workplace recruitment campaigns by the Sandinista party, facing the threat of dismissal if they refuse to accept the party card. Once signed up, one of

their new political obligations is to turn up at party rallies, and stand at key intersections in the capital waving party flags in their spare time.

Within the same strategy, the CPCs aligned themselves with criminal gangs and disaffected youth to ensure opposition protestors were unable to assemble in public places. With thinly veiled threats of "the Sandinistas control the streets," popular protests were quickly put down over 30 times in 2008 alone by stone-throwing Sandinista "supporters"—little more than paid mobs—and dissent of any form was stifled. An opposition march organized by civil society groups brought more than 50,000 people on to the streets to protest at the 2008 electoral fraud and Ortega's reelection plans. Thanks to a massive police turnout—70 percent of the 10,000-strong national police force—the march was protected from threatened attacks by Sandinista thugs.

Ortega strengthened diplomatic ties with Libya's Mohammar Qhadaffi, Iran's Mahmoud Ahmadinejad, Venezuela's Hugo Chávez, and of course Cuba's Fidel Castro. Nicaragua was the only nation to recognize the two republics

Russia liberated from Georgia (South Ossetia and Abkhazia), and the abortion ban claimed its first female victims, starting with an 18-year-old who was denied the right to terminate a pregnancy that had developed life-threatening medical complications. Both she and the five-month-old fetus perished.

In 2008, municipal elections for regional officials were overtly sabotaged to engineer a victory for the Danielistas. It drew the immediate ire of the international community, who withdrew financial support for development projects. Between the United States, which suspended its Millennium Challenge program, and the member states of the European Union, over $300 million in funding were suspended. Ortega responded by threatening to send a trillion dollar bill to the European Union to compensate for the ravages of colonialism, and Hugo Chávez offered to substitute the $300 million, which he never did. But Ortega's obstinate march toward dictatorship continued. He was, however, unable to gather the votes for the National Assembly to abolish term limits, something his Honduran and Bolivian colleagues were doing. So the Supreme Court justices loyal to Daniel met over a weekend in August 2009 and ruled that term limits were a violation of Daniel Ortega's constitutional rights. Despite blustering by the opposition members of the National Assembly, Ortega insisted, "this decision is stone; it cannot be altered." An increasingly skeptical populace is gauging whether they are ready to accept Ortega as their newest leader-for-life.

William Easterly quotes, "It took the Sandinistas twelve years to make a saint of Somoza; it took Violeta only five years to make saints of the Sandinistas; Alemán needed only two years to make a saint of Violeta." But Ortega made Alemán look good almost as soon as he took power. Sadly, Ortega's violent and self-serving government has put the final nail in the coffin of the Revolution's reputation, as Ortega has become a dictator just as bad as the one he overthrew. Meanwhile, in the mountains north of Jinotega, a group of disaffected miltants calling itself the Fuerza Democratica Nicaragüense (FDN) emerged in late 2009. "We oppose the second dictatorship of Daniel Ortega," they announced, and angry, disaffected Nicaraguans are gradually joining and supporting them. To date, no military action has been attributed to them, but analysts speculate it will just be a matter of time. Sound familiar?

Government and Politics

With the exception of perhaps Violeta Chamorro and Enrique Bolaños it seems Nicaraguan politicians' sole purpose for governing is to gerrymander the system sufficiently to ensure their indefinite power and/or enrichment. But it's more complicated than just that: talk to any Nicaraguan and you will find Nicaraguan politics are infinitely subtle and the battlefield is constantly being redrawn.

ORGANIZATION

The Republic of Nicaragua is a constitutional democracy; Nicaragua gained its independence from Spain in 1821. The two autonomous regions of the Atlantic coast are governed somewhat separately, and choose their leaders through elections independently of the national government.

Branches of Government

Nicaragua's government is divided into four branches. The executive branch consists of the president and vice president. The judicial branch includes the Supreme Court, subordinate appeals courts, district courts, and local courts, plus separate labor and administrative tribunals. The Supreme Court oversees the entire judicial system and consists of 12 justices elected by the National Assembly for seven-year terms. Though the judicial system is relatively ineffective and plagued by party interests and manipulation by the wealthy elite, it does have some points in its favor, including an approach that attempts to reduce crowding in jails by having the aggressor and the aggrieved meet to strike a deal. For minor offenses, this is effective. There is no capital punishment in Nicaragua, the maximum sentence being 30 years (though the abominable conditions of Nicaraguan prisons makes one wonder if the sentence isn't equally harsh).

The legislative branch consists of the Asamblea Nacional (National Assembly), a chamber in which 90 *diputados* (deputies) representing Nicaragua's different geographical regions vote on policy. The *diputados* are elected from party lists provided by the major political parties, though defeated presidential candidates that earn a minimum requirement of votes automatically become lifetime members, and by law, former presidents are also guaranteed a seat.

The fourth branch of Nicaraguan government is unique to Nicaragua: The Consejo Supremo Nacional runs the elections and oversees the campaign period. Politicized since the Pact of 2000, the body is rampantly abused to further the interests of Arnoldo Alemán and Daniel Ortega.

Prior to his election in 2006, Ortega attempted repeatedly to implement a parliamentary system that would weaken the executive and permit a sort of power sharing favorable to the Sandinistas, without success. Upon regaining the presidency, he immediately instituted direct or participatory governance through Chávez-esque **Consejos Populares Ciudadanos (CPCs)**. Though they ostensibly reach down to permit the poor a more direct engagement with the government, in practice they undermine the other layers of government and facilitate rabble-rousing by Nicaragua's populist and billigerent president.

Elections

The president and *diputados* are elected every five years. The president could not run for consecutive terms until 2009, when Ortega had a

THE PACT

Seldom have two bitter enemies been such good friends. In January 2000, outgoing president Arnoldo Alemán was struggling to find a way to avoid charges of embezzling over $100 million during his presidency, and sideliner Daniel Ortega was looking for a way to avoid facing charges of sexual abuse of his stepdaughter Zoilamerica Narvaez, the gentlemen's (may we use that word?) agreement now known as El Pacto suited them both politically.

The Pact is essentially a power-sharing agreement between the two men's respective political parties. It granted political impunity to ex-presidents (which, when later revoked, landed Alemán in jail), and guaranteed seats on the Assembly to outgoing presidents. It also ensured all government bodies were enlarged and filled with an equal number of PLC and FSLN party representatives.

To ensure no additional parties arise to challenge either party's power, the Pact enacted more stringent requirements for the formation of new parties as well as the requirements for individual candidates for mayor, which worked marvellously to its intended effect, the political abandonment of potential political menace Pedro Solorzano.

The Pact has single-handedly eviscerated the democratic apparatus of post-revolutionary Nicaragua and ensured the ongoing political shenanigans of both Ortega and Alemán are not only tolerated, but lead inevitably to their personal political benefit. As such it is universally criticized as the single most important factor in Nicaragua's future political and economic development. And an entire generation of Nicaraguans suddenly looks back on the Somoza years with a bit of nostalgia, wondering in a sense of horror if things were actually better back then.

Supreme Court justice overrule that decision (to the dismay of many). The Consejo Supremo Electoral (Supreme Electoral Council, or CSE)

consists of seven magistrates elected by the National Assembly for five-year terms. The CSE has the responsibility of organizing, running, and declaring the winners of elections, referendums, and plebiscites. However, electoral reforms put in place in 2000 allowed the FSLN and the PLC the new ability to name political appointees to the Council, politicizing the CSE to the extreme. The international community decried the fact that the entire process of recognizing new political parties, declaring candidates, and managing the mechanics of holding elections could be so easily subverted to ensure the two strongest parties—the PLC and the FSLN—divide the spoils of government between themselves. These "reforms" have led to a perceived reduction in the transparency of the Nicaraguan government as a whole.

Note another trend as well: Nearly every Nicaraguan presidential candidate (with the exception of Doña Violeta), has been, at one time or another, jailed by a previous administration. Tachito jailed Ortega, and Ortega in turn jailed at one point or another both Arnoldo Alemán and Enrique Bolaños.

THE CONSTITUTION

The present constitution, written in 1987 by the FSLN administration, was amended in 1995 to balance the distribution of power more evenly between the legislative and executive branches. The National Assembly's ability to veto was bolstered and the president's ability to veto reduced. It was revised in 2000 to increase the power of the Supreme Court and the comptroller-general's office, and in 2008 to do away with mandated term limits.

Civil Liberties

Prior to Ortega's return in 2006, Nicaraguans enjoyed far greater freedoms than most other Latin American nations, including unparalleled freedom of speech, freedom of religion, freedom of movement, and the right to assembly and to form unions. In practice, these freedoms have slipped dramatically under the new Ortega administration. While officially, there is no government censorship of journalists, in practice, journalists and photographers report unsubtle harrassment, interference, and threats of violence, and Ortega has not hesitated to send the police through offices of newspapers and NGOs that don't fully toe the party line. The Nicaraguan constitution prohibits discrimination by birth, nationality, political belief, race, gender, language, religion, opinion, national origin, or economic or social condition. And Nicaraguans are permitted to form labor unions. Nearly half of the workforce, including much of the agricultural labor, is unionized.

POLITICAL PARTIES

You'd think the political party in Nicaragua is more for organizational convenience than for conviction of principles. Nicaraguan politicians change from one political party to another as necessary to suit their own ambitions while smaller parties coalesce into alliances that later fracture into new arrangements. Infighting and division have been an integral part of the Nicaraguan political scene since the 1800s' Liberal-Conservative split. No other major political party came onto the scene until the FSLN took power in the 1980s. By 1990, no fewer than 20 political parties had risen in opposition to the FSLN; Doña Violeta's UNO coalition was formed from 14 of them. In the 1996 election, 35 different parties participated either on their own or as one of five coalitions. In 2000, new legislation made more stringent the requirements for a political party to participate in elections. While the exclusionary tactics diminished the previous election's free-for-all, skeptics believe the purpose of the law was to deny newcomers a piece of the pie.

Four parties participated in the presidential election of 2001: the FSLN; the PLC; the Partido Conservador Nicaragüense (PCN), the moderate-right representatives of the Conservative party; and the PLC-dominated

Alianza Liberal (Liberal Alliance) under Enrique Bolaños, who ultimately won the election. Five competed in the 2006 election: the FSLN; the PLC; and three new ones—a liberal alliance by the name of ALN-PC, a Sandinista splinter party called the MRS (Movimiento Renovador Sandinista) headed by Managua's well-loved mayor Herte Lewites, and the tiny AC party (Alternativa para Cambio) under ex-Contra rebel Eden Pastora.

The Economy

Two successive governments have had to jump-start the Nicaraguan economy from a standstill: the Sandinistas, who picked up the shattered remains upon ousting Tachito, and Doña Violeta, who had to recover from the war and a decade of socialism. Her administration made dramatic progress, reducing the foreign debt by more than half, slashing inflation from 13,500 percent to 12 percent, and privatizing several hundred state-run businesses. The new economy began to expand in 1994 and grew at 4 percent until 2006, weathering several major catastrophes, including Hurricane Mitch in 1998.

Nevertheless, Nicaragua remains the second poorest nation in the Western hemisphere with a per capital gross domestic product of $780 and its external debt ratio—nearly twice the gross national product. Unemployment is pervasive: More than half of the adult urban population scrapes by in the informal sector (selling water at the roadside, for example), and population growth is probably going to keep it that way. High demand for jobs means employers can essentially ignore the minimum-wage requirement, especially in the countryside, where agricultural laborers typically earn as little as $1 a day, insufficient for survival even by Nicaraguan standards. Nearly 600,000 people face severe malnutrition.

Nicaragua's economy is based almost entirely on agricultural export of primary material, plus recently, tourism and several nontraditional exports like sesame, onions, melons, and fruit. Export earnings are $700 million and rising: Agricultural programs in 2000 and 2001 that helped increase Nicaragua's ability to export beef and milk give hope that exports will rise in the latter part of the decade. Traditional export products include coffee, beef, and sugar, followed by bananas, shellfish (especially lobster tails and shrimp), and tobacco.

The upward trajectory of Nicaragua's economy has slowed radically under President Ortega, and rolling blackouts left much of Nicaragua without energy in 2006 and 2007. This was the combined result of Hugo Chávez's failure to deliver the cheap petroleum he'd promised and ostracism by foreign energy

© JOSHUA BERMAN

Many Nicaraguans rely on subsistence farming and fishing for their livelihood.

suppliers. Ortega's long-term economic plans remain muddled.

DEBT, THE HIPC, AND FOREIGN AID

For years, Nicaragua has been one of the most highly indebted nations of the world. When Somoza fled the country, he took the capital reserves of the banks with him, leaving behind $1.6 billion of debt. The Sandinistas, through a combination of gross economic mismanagement, extensive borrowing (primarily from Eastern bloc nations), the U.S. economic embargo, and high defense expenditures augmented the national debt by a factor of 10, nearly half of which was in arrears. By 1994, Nicaragua had the highest ratio of debt to GDP in the world, a challenge every successive administration has had to deal with. Germany, Russia, and Mexico were the first nations to forgive Nicaraguan debt entirely.

Propitious to Nicaragua's future economic growth was its inclusion in the Highly Indebted Poor Countries (HIPC) debt relief initiative in 2000. Inclusion in the initiative means Nicaragua will be exonerated from the majority of its international debt upon compliance with an International Monetary Fund (IMF) and World Bank program, but that program mandates several austerity measures, debt restructuring, and the opening of its economy to foreign markets. More hotly contested is the mandated privatization of public utilities, including the telephone system (privatized in 2002) and municipal water distribution. City water systems have not yet been privatized and the issue is extremely controversial with those who consider water a human right rather than a commodity. Central to the HIPC initiative is Nicaragua's continued effort toward macroeconomic adjustment and structural and social policy reforms, particularly basic health and education.

AGRICULTURE

Nicaragua is, above all, an agricultural nation—a third of its gross domestic product is agriculture-based, and agriculture represents the fastest growing economic sector, at 8 percent growth per year. However, much of the new land put into agricultural production is opened at the expense of the forests, the indiscriminate harvesting of which has a negative overall effect on the environment and water supply. Agriculture employs 45 percent of the workforce. Outside of the small, upscale producers who export to international markets, the majority of Nicaraguan agriculture is for domestic consumption, and much of that is subsistence farming. Drought years often require importing of basic grains.

Subsistence farmers typically grow yellow corn and red beans. The choice of red beans over black beans and yellow corn over white corn is cultural and presents additional challenges to farmers, as red beans are more susceptible to drought (and less nutritious) than black or soybeans.

The Sébaco Valley is an agriculturally productive area and the primary source of wet rice for local consumption; it's also widely planted with onions. Extensive irrigation of rice plantations caused the water table in the Sébaco Valley to drop more than three meters in the 1990s. Jinotega's cool climate is a major source of fruit and vegetable production, including cabbage, peppers, onions, melons, watermelons, squash, and tomatoes.

THE COFFEE ECONOMY

There's no underestimating the importance of coffee to the Nicaraguan economy. Coffee is produced on more than 100,000 hectares of Nicaraguan land, contributes an average of $140 million per year to the economy, includes more than 30,000 farms, and employs more than 200,000 people, about 10–20 percent of the agricultural workforce. Nicaragua exports its beans primarily to North America, Europe, and Japan—to the tune of 1 million 100-pound burlap sacks every year. These beans are roasted and ground (usually abroad) to produce 11 billion pounds of java.

Because most Nicaragua growers produce full-bodied arabica beans under the shade of diverse trees at altitudes of 900 meters and higher, the quality of its crop is recognized the world over. The June 2004 issue of *Smithsonian* magazine reported Nicaragua as "the 'hot origin' for gourmet coffee, with its beans winning taste awards and its decent wages for many small farmers a hopeful beacon for a global coffee market under siege." It also declared Nicaragua a country where "the goals of a better cup of joe, social justice and a healthier environment are nowhere more tightly entwined." This is important as Nicaragua struggles to emerge from the worst crash in the global coffee economy in a century.

The Coffee Crisis

Producing and selling Nicaraguan coffee, challenging even in good times, was dealt a staggering blow in 1999, when low-quality Vietnamese and Brazilian robusta beans drove world prices to their lowest rates in 30 years (discounting for inflation, they were the lowest prices in a century). This was compounded by corporate consolidation in the trading and roasting industries, which dealt coffee farmers a blow while well-off overseas consumers were spared the extra costs. With market prices well below the costs of production, the effect on rural Nicaraguan coffee workers has been devastating.

Conditions bottomed out when hacienda owners could no longer afford to even feed their workers, let alone pay them wages, and thousands of families (called *plantónes*) migrated to the cities, marched and camped along the highways, and demanded assistance from the government, including land, food, education, and temporary work. With the help of the cooperatives and some of the hacienda owners, the farmworkers union finally negotiated most of their demands and now more than 2,000

CAFTA: BOON OR BUGBEAR?

CAFTA, the Central American Free Trade Agreement, was ratified in 2005 and resembles the similar North American Free Trade Agreement. While the agreement generated much debate and more than a few anxious farmers, CAFTA's immediate economic provisions appear amenable to Nicaragua. The United States agreed to import a greater quantity of Nicaraguan goods – notably beef and sugar – while permitting Nicaragua to protect domestic farmers from most American foodstuffs. Quotas were raised for most Nicaraguan exports and they are scheduled to increase further over time, giving Nicaraguan farmers a better opportunity to export their crops. But Nicaragua's biggest win was for the textile industry, where Nicaragua negotiated the right to import cloth from Asia, assemble clothing, and sell it duty-free in the United States.

But you've got to give to receive, and not surprisingly, CAFTA comes with a sting. The United States earned the right to export yellow corn for chicken feed, as well as powdered milk. While Nicaraguan farmers produce white (not yellow) corn, they and the cattle ranchers are understandably anxious about the effect corn and milk imports will have on their livelihood.

Opponents of CAFTA bring up other concerns as well. For one, CAFTA promotes the Washington consensus export-economy model, where Nicaragua exports cash crops and imports basic foodstuffs. With little leverage in the marketplace, that increases Nicaragua's vulnerability to prices. The textile provisions will certainly promote job creation, but because the Nicaraguan government has taken few steps to protect its workers, women working in the Free trade zones are subject to abuse and are often not permitted to freely form unions. Finally, studies of CAFTA's predecessor, NAFTA, have failed to show a notable improvement in the lives of the Mexicans it claims to affect. Whether CAFTA will be any more beneficial to the Nicaraguans will largely depend on whether the big shots in Managua are willing to protect their people, and history has shown they are not.

families are getting the title to their own land. The next step will be to see, if the crisis continues, whether they will be able to keep their small allotments in the face of neo-liberal national governmental policies.

The Future of Coffee

Discerning North American and European java swillers have created an enormous demand for a superior cup of coffee—and they are willing to pay extra for it, as we all well know. If the Nicaraguan coffee industry is to continue to gain ground, it must maintain its reputation for quality coffee. This requires a government-level effort to address environmental issues, like soil fertility and water contamination, the modernization of processing methods, and the resolution of severe microcredit and marketing issues. The industry will also need to pay higher prices for top-quality coffee, and even Fair Trade and organic coffee price premiums have failed to keep up with the costs of sustainable production. Addressing the coffee crisis may provide the framework for dealing with the social ills inherent in modern coffee production, such as the feudal system of ownership and labor that still exists at many of the larger hacienda-style plantations; on these farms, seasonal pickers and their families are paid the barest survival wages and are sucked into a never-ending debt cycle that keeps them desperate and working.

The future of sustainable coffee production, many agree, is in family-run cooperatives in which small-scale farmers, rather than a single, rich hacienda owner, possess the power to control their product. At present, nearly 20 percent of Nicaraguan coffee is grown by 8,000 small-scale *campesino* producers working as members of nine cooperatives in the country's northlands (that's an increase of 10 percent and 2,000 farms since our last edition). As much as 80 percent of their coffee can be marketed as specialty coffee for the specialty, Fair Trade, and organic markets, making these growers less vulnerable to the extreme price oscillations of conventional coffee.

Nicaragua has a number of other advantages over other similarly struggling coffee-producing nations in the region. First of all, nearly 95 percent of Nicaraguan coffee is grown under a forest canopy that provides shade for coffee bushes and, at the same time, habitat for migratory birds. This can earn a grower a "Bird Friendly" sticker, which, like organic certification (not using chemicals and properly disposing of waste products), gains a significantly higher market price.

Coffee families and their communities also benefit enormously from the Fair Trade certification program (www.transfairusa.org), in which participating companies must comply with strict economic, social, and environmental criteria, guaranteeing producers a fair price. The small-scale farmers who represent most of the certified-organic producers and those linked to Fair Trade markets recently organized to represent their interests at the national and international level by forming an association of small-scale coffee farming co-ops called **Cafenica.**

Finally, a number of coffee growers, especially those who own their own land, have diversified their income with various noncoffee crops and activities, including several awesome ecotourism projects.

INDUSTRY

Industrial production in Nicaragua reached its zenith in 1978 under Anastasio Somoza, who encouraged industrial expansion in Managua at the expense of the environment, especially Lake Xolotlán. Investment policies of the time exonerated industries from the need to worry about environmental protection. Industry—even agro-industry—has been underdeveloped in the years following the revolution. There is a small amount of production for domestic and regional markets, including cement processing, petroleum refining, and some production of plastic goods. Another aspect of Nicaragua's export industry is the steadily increasing number of *zonas francas* (free trade zones) near Managua, Sébaco, Masaya, and Granada, where tens of thousands of Nicaraguans are employed in foreign-owned sweatshops.

FREE TRADE AND THE *MAQUILAS*

Free trade zones *(zonas francas)* – areas that assemble manufactured goods (usually clothing) for duty-free export – have multiplied like rabbits since the Alemán administration and currently employ somewhere between 50,000 and 70,000 Nicaraguan workers, mostly women. Free trade zones don't generate any tax revenue for the government but provide jobs for a nation that desperately needs them. That desperation has not been overlooked by those who do business there.

Apparel magazine reports that Nicaragua's "disciplined and low-cost work force" make it the newest regional competitor in the free-trade factory frenzy, as evidenced by the Korean, Taiwanese, and North American garment companies raising scores of assembly warehouses in Tipitapa, Sébaco, Ciudad Sandino, and Masaya (the largest free trade zone, Las Mercedes, abuts the airport in Managua and is clearly visible from your plane). These firms scour the globe for the absolute cheapest production sites, and Nicaragua is a prime option. At last count, there were 60 such assembly plants in the aforementioned areas, producing goods for well-known brands like Target, J.C. Penney, Talbots, Polo Ralph Lauren, Levi Strauss & Co., Gap, Wal-Mart, Kohl's, Kmart, and Mervyns.

Proponents of this industry argue that in a nation with nearly 70 percent unemployment, *maquila* jobs are better than nothing, regardless of the pay or conditions. But labor activists, human rights monitors, and other critics counter that the mere creation of jobs is unjustifiable if it comes at the cost of conditions that deprive workers of dignity, respect, and basic human rights, like the right to assemble or organize. Someone is making lots of money in these free trade zones (exports grew from $2.9 million in 1992 to $400 million in 2003 at a rate only surpassed by Costa Rica) but it's not the workers: They are paid in continuously-devaluing *córdobas* at a fixed rate that makes their pay worth less every month, halving their monthly earnings over the aforementioned period of export growth.

Critics of free trade zones call it a global "race to the bottom," in which international companies flock to the nations where they can both pay the least and encourage governments like Nicaragua's to overlook fundamental labor rights, i.e. paying a living wage and paying it on time, compensating for overtime, and allowing the workers to form unions. Every one of these abuses has occurred in the *zonas francas;* some have been addressed, many have been ignored, and, on more than one occasion, the company has closed its doors and relocated to other nations even more desperate for foreign investment.

Nicaragua's sweatshops pay by the piece, not by the hour, and enforce minimum-piece counts before a worker earns her first *córdoba.* A favorite subterfuge is to raise the minimum whenever it seems the workers are attaining it. *Maquila* workers thus work long (usually 10-hour) shifts and endure frequent verbal, physical, and sexual abuse from factory supervisors who, among other things, strip-search them on the way out (to "prevent theft") and monitor bathroom breaks. Workplace injuries are ignored, and attempts to form unions are met with mass firings, trumped-up criminal charges, and use of riot police. The Nicaraguan government has made no effort to protect workers and does not intervene in these cases, fearing mass unemployment would be worse than mistreated workers. Indeed, the Nicaraguan workforce was abused long before the days of foreign investment.

The alternative? One idea is the **Fair Trade Zone**, like that formed by a group of unemployed women in Ciudad Sandino called the **Nueva Vida Womens Sewing Cooperative** (tel. 505/269-7073, jhc@jhc-cdca.org, www.fairtradezone.jhc-cdca.org). As owners of their factory, workers at Nueva Vida decide what hours they work, what salaries they are paid, what their labor policies are, and how they share their business's profits amongst themselves. Contact them directly to place an order for your company or organization, or support them by shopping at Michigan-based **Maggie's Functional Organics** (U.S. tel. 800/609-8593, www.maggiesorganics.com). To learn more about the labor rights movement, check in with Campaign for Labor Rights (www.campaignforlaborrights.org) or Global Exchange (www.globalexchange.org).

TOURISM

The so-called "industry without smokestacks" is widely hoped to be a panacea to Nicaragua's economic ills. The governmnet agency in charge of tourism development and marketing is El Instituto Nicaragüense de Turismo, better known as **INTUR** (www.intur.gob.ni). At present, tourism represents the third largest source of foreign exchange. Public Law 306 provides a 10-year tax break to newly constructed tourist facilities that meet certain criteria. More beneficial still are travelers like you, who spend a little money and hopefully take home a good impression of Nicaragua. Since the mid-1990s, investment in tourism has skyrocketed, notably in Managua, Granada, and San Juan del Sur. The total number of visitors to Nicaragua has increased from under 600,000 visitors in 2001 to more than 800,000 in 2005, the majority arriving from Central and South America. Most foreign visitors come from North America and Europe. In 2007, nearly half a million people arrived by international flight to Nicaragua.

Ecotourism

The word ecotourism was created in the 1980s with the best of intentions. The idea is to prevent tourism from spoiling the environment, or to use it to provide an alternative to spoiling the environment. The success of the concept and its marketing value led to a worldwide boom in the usage of that prefix that we know so well, even when its actual practice has sometimes fallen short of original intentions. Indeed, the warm and fuzzy "eco" has been used, abused, prostituted, and bastardized all over the world, and Nicaragua is no exception. Alternative tourism goes by many other names as well: "sustainable," "responsible," "ethical," "rural," or "fair trade" tourism, to name a few.

The concept of protected areas and national parks is relatively new in Nicaragua and is, in some places, viewed with skepticism—especially by poor *campesinos* who live near (or sometimes within) these areas and have always used the forests to supplement their paltry incomes. They need wood for fuel, land for farmland, and game for protein. MARENA, the government ministry charged with protecting Nicaragua's vast system of parks and refuges, has scant resources to prevent such activities. If money comes from nature-loving visitors, an alternative use for the forest has been created. Foreigners come to see the local waterfall or coffee cooperative and need to eat breakfast, hire a guide, rent a horse, and witness how people in this particular corner of the continent live. We've pointed out community-sponsored tourism efforts wherever we found them, namely in Granada, Isla de Ometepe, Matagalpa, and the Miraflor region of Estelí. Here, existing cooperatives have arranged homestay opportunities that involve volunteer work, Spanish language class, alternative agriculture, and trips to local sites.

The People

POPULATION

Nicaragua's population is fast approaching six million, about a full third of whom live in Managua. Nicaragua is both the least populous Central American nation and the fastest growing, at just over 3 percent annually. At this rate, the country's strained resources will have to support between 9 and 12 million people by the year 2030. In addition, well over a million Nicaraguans live outside of the country, particularly in Costa Rica (679,000) and the United States (500,000), not to mention thousands more living in Mexico and other Central American nations.

ETHNIC GROUPS

While Nicaraguans can trace their ancestry back to many sources, most of the population is a blend of Spanish, Native American, and sometimes other European stock. Indigenous blood runs most strongly in the northeast, where the Spanish had less influence, and on

WOLVES, DOGS, AND THE BEST PIECE OF CHICKEN: POPULAR NICARAGUAN SAYINGS

Nicaraguans in general, and *campesinos* in particular, love to speak using *refranes* (sayings or refrains). They're an easy way to make a point, and both the way they are phrased and the points they make say much about the country folks' way of thinking. If you learn a refrain or two and throw one out once in a while in casual conversation, you will be sure to earn broad smiles.

Hay más tiempo que vida. – There is more time than life. (There's no need to rush things.)

Él que a buen árbol se arrima, buena sombra le cobija. – He who gets close to a good tree will be covered by good shade. (He who seeks protection will find it.)

Perro que ladra no muerde. – Dogs who bark don't bite.

No hay peor sordo que él que no quiere escuchar. – There's no deaf person worse than he who doesn't want to hear.

A cada chancho le llega su sábado. – Every pig gets his Saturday. (Everyone eventually gets what he deserves.)

Indio comido, puesto al camino. – An Indian who has eaten, gets up immediately from the table. (A way of pointing out someone ready to leave as soon as he/she gets what he/she wants.)

Quien da pan a un perro ajeno, pierde el pan y pierde el perro. – If you give bread to someone else's dog, you'll lose the bread and lose the dog.

Él que madruga come pechuga, él que tarda, come albarda. – He who gets up early eats the best piece of chicken, he who gets up late eats the saddle.

Él que no llora no mama. – He who does not cry does not suckle. (If you don't complain, you'll never get any attention.)

Él que anda con lobos, aullar aprende. – He who walks with wolves, learns to howl. (A warning about the company you keep.)

Barriga llena, corazón contento. – Full belly, happy heart. (Lean back and use this one after a big meal.)

Él que tiene más galillo, traga más pinol. – He who has a bigger throat, drinks more *pinol*. (Being aggressive will get you farther.)

---

the mid-Atlantic coast, where English and African influences were dominant.

In the Pacific region, the indigenous population thinned from 800,000 when the Spanish arrived to less than 60,000 after a couple centuries of conquistador policy (i.e., war, slavery, genocide, and diseases). The native peoples of the northeast, including Matagalpa and Jinotega, were less affected, and thus retain larger indigenous populations today.

Mestizos

The term mestizo refers to any mixture of Spanish and indigenous blood and describes the majority of Nicaraguan citizens, whose Spanish colonial ancestors began intermingling with the locals about as soon as they got off the boat. A second wave of *mestizaje* (mixing) occurred from the 1860s through the 1890s, during the wave of rubber and banana production along the Atlantic coast, and again in the 1950s as Pacific farmers moved eastward in search of new agricultural lands at the expense of the Sumu-Ulúa and Miskito peoples. Note: Mestizo Nicaraguans sometimes use the term "indio" as a derogatory label for anyone with Native American features (high cheekbones, straight black hair, short eyelashes, and dark brown skin).

Creoles

After decimating the indigenous peoples of the New World, the Spanish realized they lacked laborers; so they imported African slaves to their colonies in the Americas. Beginning in 1562, English slave traders, and later Dutch,

Spanish, and others, supplied the colonies with human cargo. Along the Atlantic coast of Nicaragua, African slaves intermingled with Miskitos, giving birth to the Zambo (or Sambo) people. They also bred with the Spanish and English, forming the Creoles, primarily found today in Bluefields and San Juan del Norte. Creoles speak a form of English that still bears traces of 19th-century Queen's English, as well as Caribbean and Spanish traits. Their culture includes distinct African elements, including the belief in a form of African witchcraft called *obeah* or *sontín,* the latter a corruption of the English "something," or "something special."

Miskitos

Modern-day Miskitos are really a mixture of several races, and include traces of English and African blood. The Native American Bawihka people, whose territory extended from the Río Coco (Wangki) at Cabo Gracias a Dios south to Prinzapolka, mixed with the African-slave refugees of a Portuguese ship that wrecked on the Miskito Cays in 1642. They later mixed with the English during their long occupation of the Atlantic coast. Over the centuries, the word "Miskito" has been written many other ways, including "Mosquito," "Mosca," "Mískitu," and others. The name derives not from the insect but from the Spanish word *mosquete* (musket), a firearm the British provided the locals to ensure a tactical advantage over their neighbors.

The Miskitos' warlike nature and superior firepower helped them subdue twenty other Native American tribes along the Atlantic coast of Central America. They were valuable allies to the English, who used them in raids against inland Spanish settlements, and crowned their "kings" in an Anglican church in Belize City. The Miskitos also absorbed the Prinsu tribe (located along the Bambana and Prinzapolka Rivers) and the Kukra tribe.

Today the Miskitos inhabit much of the Atlantic coast of Nicaragua, from Bluefields northward and all along the Río Coco, which they consider their spiritual home. There are additional Miskito settlements on both Corn Islands, but their two principal centers are Bilwi (Puerto Cabezas) and Waspám. Their language, Miskito, is the old indigenous Tawira language enriched with English and African vocabulary.

The Kukra

The Kukra people were assimilated by the Miskitos over the last two centuries and no longer exist as a tribe. Of unknown but reportedly cannibalistic Caribbean origin, they once inhabited Bluefields, the Corn Islands, and the area around Pearl Lagoon. Today, the only trace of them is the name of the small Pearl Lagoon community of Kukra Hill.

The Garífuna

The Garífuna, as a distinct culture, are relative newcomers to the world. Their history began on the Lesser Antillean island of San Vicente (Saint Vincent), which in the 1700s had become a refuge for escaped slaves from the sugar plantations of the Caribbean, including Jamaica. These displaced Africans were accepted by the native Carib (Arawak) islanders, with whom they freely intermingled. As the French and English settled the island, the Garífunas (as they had become known), established a worldwide reputation as expert canoe navigators and fierce warriors, resisting the newcomers. The English finally got the upper hand in the conflict after tricking and killing the Garífuna leader, and in 1797, they forcefully evacuated the Garífunas from San Vicente to the Honduran Bay Island of Roatán. From there, many of the Garífunas migrated to the mainland communities of Trujillo, Honduras and Dangriga, Belize. Today, they exist up and down most of the Central American Caribbean coast, with a small but distinct presence in Nicaragua, primarily around Pearl Lagoon. Orinoco (originally Urunugu) is the largest settlement of Garífunas in Nicaragua, established in 1912 by the Garífuna John Sambola. The communities of San Vicente and Justo Point are both Garífuna as well. During the 1980s, the Contra war forced many Garífunas out of

CORN CULTURE

The planting cycle of *maíz* (corn) has governed the life of Nicaraguans and their Mesoamerican descendants ever since the first yellow kernels were laid in the dark volcanic soil. *Maíz* is as central to the Nicaraguan diet as white rice is to the people of Southeast Asia. Beans are just as critical a staple (and a nutritionally critical complement), but in Nicaragua, corn is prepared with more variety, taste, and frequency.

Corn is prepared and consumed in more than a hundred different ways: hot, cold, cooked, ground, and liquefied, in both food and in beverages. Tortillas are, of course, flat cakes of corn dough softened with water and cooked on a slightly rounded clay pan known as a *comal*. The only place you'll find a flour tortilla is in a Mexican restaurant in Managua; Nica corn tortillas are thick, heavy, and (hopefully) hot off the woodstove and slightly toasted. When the same dough is fortified with sugar and lard, then rolled into small lumps and boiled while wrapped in yellow corn husks, the result is a *tamal*, steaming heavy bowls of which market women balance on their heads and loudly vend in the streets. *Nacatamales*, a Nicaraguan classic, are similar but with meat – often spiced pork – in the middle. *Atol* is corn pudding, and *güiríla* is a sweet tortilla of young corn, always served with a hunk of *cuajada* (salty white cheese).

Elote is corn on the cob, especially tasty when roasted directly over open coals until the kernels are dry, hot, and a little chewy. When harvested young, the ears of corn are called *chilotes* and are served in soup or with fresh cream. Corn is also oven-baked into hard, molasses-sweetened cookie rings called *rosquillas*, flat cookies called *ojaldras*, and many other shapes. The same dough is also combined with cheese, lard, and spices to produce dozens more items, including *perrerreques*, *cosas de horno*, and *gofios*.

What do you wash it down with? More corn, of course. *Pinol*, drunk so frequently in Nicaragua the Nicaraguans proudly call themselves *pinoleros*, is toasted and ground corn meal mixed with water. *Pinolillo* is *pinol* mixed with cacao, pepper, and cloves; *tiste* is similar. *Pozol* is a ground cornmeal drink prepared from a variety of corn with a pinkish hue. The ultrasweet, pink baggies of *chicha* are made from slightly fermented cornmeal (especially strong batches are called *chicha brava*). Then, of course, there is crystal clear, Nicaraguan corn tequila, or *la cususa*.

Corn: It's what's for breakfast, lunch, and dinner.

---

their communities and into Bluefields, Puerto Limón (Costa Rica), and Honduras.

The Mayangna

"Sumu," is a derogatory word the Miskito used for all other peoples of Ulúa descent (it means stupid; conversely, the Mayangna name for the Miskito was *wayas*, which means "stinky"). The Mayangna, as they prefer to be called, are a combination of several Ulúa tribes, including the Twahka, Panamka, and Ulwa, who once settled the Kurinwas, Siquia, Mico, Rama, and Grande Rivers of the Atlantic coast. Mayangna tradition has it that in the 9th and 10th centuries they were the inhabitants of a territory that extended from the Atlantic coast and Río Coco to the Pacific, but they were forced off the Atlantic coastal lands by the more aggressive and warring Miskito and out of the Pacific by the Nahuatls, Maribios, and Chorotegas. The Mayangna are now centered around the mining triangle and the massive forest reserve of Bosawás.

The Rama

The Rama are the least numerous indigenous people in Nicaragua, numbering only several hundred. Their language is distinct from Miskito and Mayangna and is closely related to the ancient tribal languages of Native American tribes of Panamá and Colombia. Today, only several dozen people can still speak Rama and anthropologists are scrambling to document what they can of the language before it disappears entirely. The Rama people inhabit the pleasant bay island of Rama Cay in the Bay of Bluefields, where they fish and collect oysters. They also grow grains and traditional crops on small plots of land on the mainland of Bluefields Bay and along the Kukra River. The Rama people are reserved and keep mostly to their traditional ways, even using traditional tools and implements. They are excellent navigators and fishers.

Culture, Conduct, and Customs

Nicaraguans are generally open, talkative, and hospitable. In most areas of the country, Nicaraguans are accustomed to seeing foreigners, but they are still curious—and not very discreet about it. Expect blunt questions right off the bat about your age, marital status, and your opinions about Nicaragua. The reaction is nearly always one of curiosity, hospitality, and friendliness.

Despite their directness, Nicaraguans are prone to circuitous, indirect behavior associated with the cultural concept of "saving face." When asked something they don't know, people often invent an answer so that neither party is embarrassed (this is especially true about directions and distances; as Allan Weisbecker observed, "no one, *no one,* south of the Mexican border has any idea how long it takes to go from anywhere to anywhere else"). Business contracts are rife with implied obligations neither party wants to discuss openly, even simple payment details and the work to be done.

Many Nicaraguan city dwellers are, in fact, recently immigrated *campesinos,* and they often bring their country ways—and livestock—with them to the city.

Anti-Americanism, in our experience, is rare, Nicaraguans being particularly adept at distinguishing between a nation's people and its government's policy. In addition, because most Nicaraguan families adore cable TV and have at least one relative sending money back from Miami, Houston, or Los Angeles, many are quite fond of the United States and maintain the dream of traveling there one day. The word "gringo" is used more often as a descriptive, casual term for anyone who comes from

north of the Mexican border. In rare cases, it is meant as an insult (in which case, it will likely be preceeded by *"pinche"*). Likewise for *chele, chela,* and their diminutives, *chelito* and *chelita,* all of which simply mean pale or light-skinned, and are in no way disrespectful. In fact, many cries of, *"¡Oye, chele!"* ("Hey, whitey!") are used as much for light-skinned Nicaraguans as for foreigners.

FAMILY

The Nicaraguan family is the most basic and strongest support structure of society, and, like in most developing world nations, it is usually large—rural women have an average of 4–6 children, and families of a dozen or more aren't uncommon. Urban couples, particularly in Managua, typically have no more than three or four children. In addition, extended families—cousins, in-laws, aunts, and uncles—are all kept in close contact and relied upon during hard times (which, for many, is their whole lives). Families live close together, often in small quarters, and the North American and European concepts of independence and solitude are not well understood.

Nicaraguans' traditional dependence on large family structures mandates that they take care of stragglers. If, for example, you were stranded in a strange country town in the pouring rain, it would not be strange or uncommon for someone to invite you into their home for coffee—or a bed.

CLOTHING AND NEATNESS

Nicaraguans place a great deal of importance on cleanliness. Even the poorest *campesino* with

OLD WIVES' TALES: NICARAGUAN *CREENCIAS*

Like any society with a tradition of rural folk culture, Nicaraguans have hundreds of unique beliefs, or *creencias*, which explain mysteries, offer advice, and dictate practices that prevent or cure common health ailments. In general, most behaviors are associated with causing harm to oneself, and Nicaraguan mothers can be heard admonishing their children, *"¡Te va a hacer daño!"* ("It will cause you harm!").

Nicaraguans are sensitive to subtle differences in temperature, and many of the *creencias* involve avoiding hot things when you are cold, or vice versa. Conventional wisdom dictates that intense bodily harm can come from drinking a cold beverage after eating something hot, bathing in the evening after a hot day in the sun (or bathing with a fever), and ironing with wet hair. If you come in from the fields on a hot day and you're sweaty, drinking a cold glass of fruit juice or water can make you sick, especially your kidneys. Better is a cup of hot coffee. If you want to walk outside at night after drinking coffee, however, you should protect yourself by draping a cloth over the top of your head, being careful to cover the ears. Dietary rules tie into the same theme and other worries as well: no fish, eggs, or beans while menstruating, no citrus when sick, and no fish soup when *agitado* (worked up or sweaty).

The belief in the *mal de ojo* (evil eye) is not unique to Nicaragua, although the local version states that a drunkard who looks directly into an infant's eye can kill the child or make it evil. A person well versed in the art of applying the evil eye can cause birth defects in newborn babies, stroke, paralysis among the living, and other woes like the loss of a job or bad luck. You'll frequently see children wearing a red bracelet with two small gray beads – this is to protect the child from *mal de ojo*. Similarly, if a sweaty man looks at a baby, the only cure is to wrap the baby up in the man's sweaty clothes. To guard against the risk, many babies are kept well covered when out of the house. Allowing dew to fall on a baby's brow will stunt its growth (look for women holding umbrellas over their children on a clear night), and letting a baby look in a mirror will cause his or her eyes to cross permanently.

If you have trouble with bats, you can keep them away by hanging a red cloth from the rafters. To keep flies off your food, suspend a bag of water over the table. To avoid family fights, don't cook with a knife in the pan.

Some Nica *creencias* coincide with North American and European practices even if the reasoning is different. For example, Nicaraguans recommend you don't walk around barefoot, but not because you run the risk of contracting ringworm; rather, walking barefoot, they claim, is an unhealthy temperature combination (hot feet on cold floor). Foreigners tempted to make fun of the "crazy" Nicaraguan beliefs will do well to remember our own societies' *creencias*. Whether scientifically grounded or not, Nicaraguan beliefs are popular because they have been passed from generation to generation, and should be given proper regard.

the threadbare and patched clothing takes great care to tuck his shirt in and keep his clothes clean and wrinkle-free. Managuans are just as conscientious about looking good and smelling clean. Nicaraguans only wear shorts for playing sports or lounging around the house. Nicaraguan women dress the spectrum from long, conservative dresses to bright, tight, and revealing outfits.

Unshaven *internacionalistas* wearing stained shorts, ripped T-shirts, and natty dreads stand out like sore, malodorous thumbs, even without their trademark bulky backpacks. If you plan on being taken seriously in any kind of day-to-day business activities, a little effort into your wardrobe and hygiene will go a long way…and will help do away with the question, "Is it true that people in your country don't bathe because it's too cold?" If, however, you prefer to remain true to your filth, seek out the bohemian population of tattooed Managuans who take well to carefully unkempt foreigners with Che T-shirts and creative facial hair.

CONCEPT OF TIME

Hay más tiempo que vida. (There is more time than life.) So why hurry? The day-to-day approach to living life in Nicaragua may come from the necessity of survival, or it may just be an effect of the hot sun. Probably both. Nicaraguan life, in general, goes according to La Hora Nica (Nica Time), which means a meeting scheduled in Managua for 2:30 P.M. might not start until 3 P.M., or an hour later in the countryside. Foreign travelers accustomed to La Hora Gringa, in which everything starts and stops exactly when planned, will spend their days in Nicaragua endlessly frustrated (and consistently early for meetings). Appointments and meetings are loose, and excuses are easy to come by and universally accepted. Gradually, as you experience Nicaragua, this concept of time will win you over; just be careful when you go home.

ALCOHOL
Rum

It goes largely undisputed that Nicaragua makes the best rum in all of Central America. Flor de Caña is the highest caliber, of which the caramel-colored, 7-year Gran Reserva is only surpassed by the 12-year Centenario (which is twice as expensive). Flor de Caña produces a half-dozen varieties of rum, which increase in price and quality as they age. A *media* (half-liter) of seven-year, bucket of ice, bottle of Coke, and plate of limes (called a *servicio completo*) will set you back only $5 or so. Rum on the rocks with a squirt of Coca-Cola and a spurt of lime is called a Nica Libre. A national competition in search of Nicaragua's new "official drink" awarded the prize to the creator of the **Macuá,** a pediatrician from Granada. The drink is a refreshing combination of one part guava juice, one part white rum, a half part lemon juice, and some sugar and ice, and was chosen not only for its suitability to Nicaragua's agriculture but its suitability for the tropical climate. We have never

seen the drink in the wild, but it's worth asking for.

Reach for a clear plastic bottle of Caballito or Ron Plata, and take a giant step down in price, quality, and class. Enormously popular in the *campo*, "Rrrrron Plata!" is the proud sponsor of most baseball games—and not a few bar brawls. Bottles are $1 or less.

But wait—you can get drunk for even less! Most street corners and town parks are the backdrop for many a grimacing shot of Tayacán, or its homemade, corn-mash equivalent, often served in clear plastic baggies. West Virginians call this stuff "that good 'ole mountain dew"; Nicaraguans call it *la cususa, el guaro,* or *la lija,* brought down from the hills by the moonshine man on his mule. *La cususa* is gasoline-clear, potent in smell (including when you sweat it out the next day), and will bore a hole through your liver quicker than a 9-millimeter. It's sold by the gallon for about $4, often in a stained, sloshing, plastic container that used to contain some automobile product, and then resold in baggie-size portions that look like they should have a goldfish swimming in them.

Beer

The national beers—Victoria and Toña—are both light-tasting pilsners and, well, you can't really say anything bad about an ice-cold beer in the tropics. Expect to pay anywhere from $0.80 to $2 a beer, depending on your environs. Recent additions to the beer selection are Premium, Bufalo, and Brahva, largely indistinguishable, and the Victoria Frost, an ice-filtered beverage with slightly higher alcohol content. Brahva is the only alcoholic beverage whose production or distribution isn't controlled by the Pellas family, which produces every other beverage mentioned in this book. Together, Victoria, Toña, and Flor de Caña are known affectionately as "Vickie, Toni, and Flo."

Alcoholism

Alcohol abuse is rampant in Nicaragua and increasingly acknowledged as a problem. Most towns have an Alcoholics Anonymous chapter,

Toña is one of Nicaragua's national beers.

and many churches forbid their members to drink. Nevertheless, most otherwise religious holidays (including Sundays)—in addition to all nonreligious events—serve as excuses to get falling-down drunk. Just about all men drink and are firm believers in the expression *"una es ninguna"* ("one is none"). Their benders often start before breakfast and end when the liquor does. In small towns, women are socially discouraged from drinking, though they sometimes do so in the privacy of their own homes or with close friends. Bigger towns and cities, of course, are more modern in this regard.

Should you decide to partake in this part of the culture and find yourself drunk *(borracho, bolo, picado, hasta el culo),* be sure you have a decent understanding of your environment and feel good about your company. Remember that most travelers' disaster stories begin with "Man, I was so wasted…" Always take it slow when drinking in a new place, and remember that your hydration level has an enormous impact on how drunk you get.

And oh, by the way, rum does *not* make you a better dancer, but it may improve your Spanish.

RELIGION

Officially, the Republic of Nicaragua endorses no religion. In practice, the overwhelming majority of Nicaraguans call themselves Catholic, with over a hundred evangelical Protestant sects comprising about 9–15 percent and increasing annually. Beginning in the early 1970s and continuing through the revolution, Nicaragua created its own version of liberation theology, a school of Christianity and bourgeois thought that equated Jesus's teachings with Marxism. The degree to which biblical parables were equated to the Marxist struggle varied, and the most radical versions placed Sandino as Jesus or Moses, Somoza as the Pharaoh, and the Nicaraguan masses as the Israelites searching for their promised land through revolutionary struggle.

A tiny percentage of Nicaraguans are descendents of one of the several Jewish families that found refuge here during World War II. Some of them still identify themselves as Jewish, but there is no real practicing community. The only synagogue was dismantled and sold in 1980. A Torah did not return to Nicaragua until 2008. Most Nicaraguans, especially in

At the Purísima procession in Granada, expect fireworks, parties, and midnight mass.

© JOSHUA BERMAN

the countryside, have little concept of Judaism as a modern religion, relating the word *judío* only to the ancient race of *hebreos* they read about in the Old Testament. In 2008, the construction of a mosque in Managua raised eyebrows in the diplomatic community, who feared increasing Iranian influence. It was instead the work of the growing Lebanese community, present in Nicaragua for a century but only now numerous enough to consider building their own place of worship.

LANGUAGE

Spanish is, according to the Nicaraguan constitution, the official language of the republic, though indigenous languages are respected and even used officially in certain areas of the Atlantic coast. Ninety-six percent of Nicaraguans speak Spanish as their first language, 3 percent speak indigenous languages (Miskito, Mayangna, and Rama), and 1 percent speak languages of African origin (Criollo and Garífuna). To hear pure

Miskito, travel north from Bluefields or visit Puerto Cabezas or any village along the Río Coco; in some of these villages, Spanish is completely unknown.

Nicaraguan Spanish is probably unlike any Spanish you've ever come across. The chameleon-like ability of the Spanish language to adapt to new areas of the world is strong in Nicaragua, where it is spoken rapidly and liquidly, the words flowing smoothly together and eating each other's tails. Central Americans enjoy making fun of how their Latin neighbors talk, and the Honduran nickname for Nicaraguans, *mucos* (bulls whose horns have been chopped off), is a reference to the Nicaraguans' habit of chopping the "s" off the ends of spoken words. Backcountry *campesino* Nicaraguan Spanish is inevitably less intelligible to the untrained ear than its urban counterpart, but it is also distinctly more melodic, with a cadence and rhythm distinct to the countryside and celebrated in many of Carlos Mejía Godoy's songs.

A FEW *NICARAGUANISMOS*

The textbook Spanish you learned back home will be understood without trouble, but Nicaraguans take pride in the fact that their version of the old-country Castilian is decidedly unique. When you try to look up some of the new words you're hearing and realize they're not in the dictionary, you'll see what we mean.

Blame it on *campesino* creativity and the Nicas' propensity for inventing words they need; blame the centuries of educational starvation, during which language evolved on its own; blame the linguistic mishmash of pre-Columbian Central America and the words left behind. Or just get out your pencil and paper and try to write down some of the unique vocabulary and phrases you hear, because you won't hear it anywhere else. Nicaraguan Spanish uses some old, proper Spanish no longer used in the Old World, and has assimilated pre-Columbian words from Nahuatl and Chorotega tongues as well (especially local plant and animal names). Still other words are pure onomatopoeia. Those interested in pursuing the topic should seek out Joaquim Rabella and Chantal Pallais's *Vocabulario Popular Nicaragüense*, available in some bookstores in Managua. Here's an incomplete sampling (with the Castilian in parentheses when possible).

arrecho: extremely angry *(enfurecido)*
bochinche: a fistfight among several people
boludo: lazy, unmotivated *(haragán)*
bullaranga: loud noises, ruckus *(tumulto, alboroto)*
curutaca: diarrhea *(diarrea)*
cususa: country moonshine *(aguardiente)*

chapa: earring *(arete)*
chigüin: little kid *(bebé)*
chinela: sandal *(sandalia)*
chingaste: the granular residue of a drink like coffee *(poso, resíduo)*
chunche: any small, nameless object *(cosita)*
chusmón: mediocre
guaro: general term for booze or alcoholic beverages
hamaquear: to rock something rhythmically *(mecer rítmicamente)*
moclín: perverted old man
ñaña: excrement *(excremento)*
panzona: big bellied, implies pregnant *(embarazada)*
pinche: cheap *(tacaño)*
pipilacha: small airplane *(avioneta)*
salvaje: awesome; literally, "savage;" fun response to *"¿Como estás?"*
timba: big belly *(barriga)*

EXCLAMATIONS

¡Chocho!: Holy cow! Dude!
¡A la puchica!: Wow!
¿Ideay? (eedee-EYE?): What was that all about? What do you mean?
Va pué: OK then; see you; I agree; or whatever (short for *va pués*)
Dalepué: OK, I agree, let's do that.
¡Qué barbaridad!: What a barbarity! How rude! What a shame!
¡Sí hombre!: Yeah man!
hijueputa: extremely common, from the vulgarity *hijo de puta* (son of a whore), pronounced hway-POO-tah and used liberally.
Tranquilo como Camilo: Chillin' like Dylan; fun response to *"¿Como estás?"*

And then, of course, there are the vulgarities. Ernest Hemingway wrote, "There is no language so filthy as Spanish. There are words for all the vile words in English and there are other words and expressions that are used only in countries where blasphemy keeps pace with the austerity of religion."

In Nicaragua, even a simple fruit or vegetable name can cause a room to break out in wild laughter if said in the right tone and context (and if accompanied by the appropriate hand gesture). After you've learned a few dirty words, be careful—the degree to which most *vulgaridades* are considered offensive varies depending on the gender of your company, their age, your relationship with them, and a variety of other factors. Cussing can be a fun, complex, and subtle game if you have the patience to learn—*y los huevos*....

Body Language

Limber up your wrist and stretch out those lips. You'll need 'em both if you want to communicate like a true native. Watch people interact on the buses, in the markets, and on the streets, and see if you can spot any of the following gestures in action—then try some out yourself.

Probably the single most practical gesture is a rapid side to side wagging of the index finger. It means "no," and increases in strength as you increase the intensity of the wagging and the amount of hand and arm you use in the motion. In some cases, a verbal "no" in the absence of the **Finger Wag** is disregarded as not serious enough. Use this one liberally with pushy vendors, beggars, and would-be Romeos.

To pull off the **Nicaraguan Wrist Snap,** simply join the tips of your thumb and middle finger and let your index finger dangle loosely. Then with a series of rapid wrist flicks, repeatedly let your index finger slap against the middle one, exactly as you would do with a round tin of tobacco dip. The resulting snapping noise serves to either emphasize whatever it is you're saying, refer to how hard you've been working, or, when combined with a nod and a smile, infer something like, "Damn, that's good!"

You can ask, "What?" (or "What do you want?") with a quick **Cheek Scrunch,** occasionally performed with a subtle upward chin tilt. Use the **Lip Point** rather than your finger to indicate something by puckering up as if for a kiss and aiming where you want. Or, if you are listening to a friend's dumb story, point to the speaker with your lips while looking at everyone else to imply, "This guy's crazy or drunk."

The gesture North Americans would normally use to shoo something away—the outstretched, waving, down-turned hand—means just the opposite in Nicaragua, where the **Downward Wave** (occasionally combined with the whole arm for emphasis) means "Come here." This one is a favorite with drunks in the park who love to talk at foreigners for as long as they are tolerated. The North American "come here," i.e., the upturned and beckoning index finger, is a vulgar, possibly offensive gesture. Speaking of vulgar, a closed fist atop a rigid forearm indicates the male sex organ, and an upturned, slightly cupped hand with the fingertips pressed together into a point is its female counterpart. Here's one more for the road: Make a fist, lock your elbow into the side of your body, and move your hand up and down; combined with a dramatic grimace, the **Plunger Pump** tells the whole world you have diarrhea.

ETIQUETTE AND TERMS OF ADDRESS

Latin America is not homogenous across state borders when it comes to addressing each other: While Costa Ricans tend to gravitate toward the formal *usted* form of address among themselves, Nicaraguans prefer the friendly *vos* (second person) form with each other, although *tú* is widely understood. For travelers, it's best to use *usted* until you've really gotten to know someone (or mastered the tricky *vos* form), particularly after a night out or a long drinking session (you'll be surprised how quickly alcohol lubricates friendships at this latitude).

The term *don* for men and *doña* for women is a colonial term of respect usually related to aristocracy or landownership, but in Nicaragua it's far more commonly used than elsewhere in Latin America, and indicates a higher level of respect or affection, particularly for the elderly, the important, or the wealthy. Practitioners of certain careers sometimes drop their names entirely and go by their profession. That is, it's not uncommon to be presented to someone everyone calls simply *"la doctora," "el ingeniero,"* or *"la abogada."* Just go with it and smile.

a typical Nicaraguan meal: *tostones, gallo pinto, cuajada,* and *frijoles*

It's customary to kiss women on the cheek when greeting, but women will provide the signal whether that's appropriate or not by turning their cheek toward you. Men will offer you their hands for a stiff handshake. When someone new enters the room, rise from your seat to greet them, and when you're ready to end a conversation or leave the room, a friendly *"con permiso"* will pave the way to the door.

TABLE MANNERS

Dig in! Grab that fried chicken between two hands and gnaw at it, shovel down *vigorón* from its banana-leaf wrapper as best as you can without letting all the shaved cabbage and *chile* spill down your shirt. Chase it with long swigs of a cold drink. Nicaraguans enjoy good food and good times, and if you're too dainty, the signal is all too clear you're not pleased with the meal. There are limits, of course, so keep an eye on your dining companions for what's appropriate and what's not, but while you're picking away at your fried cheese and sweet plantains, the guy next to you has finished his meal, pulled his shirt up with one hand and is happily rubbing his belly with the other. Don't be afraid to enjoy what's on your plate. If you'd like to get a laugh out of your Nicaraguan hosts or waiters, after you've finished your plate, tell them, *"Barriga llena, corazón contenta"* ("Belly full, happy heart").

PAINTED ROOSTER:
A GUIDE TO NICARAGUAN DINING

Desayuno	Breakfast
Huevos	Eggs
Enteros, revueltos, volteados	Hardboiled, scrambled, over-easy

Almuerzo y Cena	Lunch and Dinner
Carne/res	Beef
Desmenuzada	Shredded and stewed
A la plancha	Served on a hot plate
Churrasco	Grilled steak
Filete jalapeño	Steak in a creamy pepper sauce
Puerco/cerdo	Pork
Chuleta	Pork chop
Pollo	Chicken
Empanizado	Breaded
Frito	Fried
Al vino	Wine sauce
Rostizado	Rotisserie
Valenciano	A chicken and rice dish
Mariscos	Seafood
Pescado entero	The whole fish
Langosta al ajillo	Lobster in garlic sauce
Camarones al vapor	Steamed shrimp
Sopa de conchas	Conch soup
Huevos de Paslama	Endangered turtle eggs

Platos Tradicionales	Traditional Dishes
Baho	Plantain and beef stew
Nacatamales	Meat-filled corn tamal, wrapped and boiled in banana leaves
Indio viejo	Beef, veggie, and cornmeal mush
Caballo bayo	A sampler's plate of traditional dishes
Gallo pinto	Red beans and rice, generously doused in oil and salt
Cuajada	White, farmer's cheese
Leche agria	A sour cream-yogurt combo
Vigorón	Pork rinds with yucca and coleslaw, served on a banana leaf

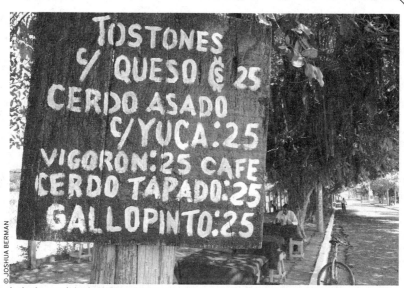

© JOSHUA BERMAN

today's special: plantains, cheese, roast pork, boiled yucca, and *gallo pinto*

Bocadillas	**Appetizers**
Tostones plantain chips	Thick, fried, green
Tajadas	Crunchy, thin strips of green plantain
Maduro	Ripe, sweet plantains fried in their own sugar
Ensalada	Shredded cabbage, tomatoes, and a toasted white corn

Bebidas y (Re)Frescos	**Drinks and Fruit Juices**
Tiste	Toasted cooked corn with cacao, pepper, and cloves

Pinol	Toasted, milled corn
Pinolillo	Pinol with pepper, cloves, and cacao
Horchata	Toasted and milled rice with spices
Chicha	Rough-milled corn with vanilla and banana flavors, sometimes fermented

Postres	**Desserts**
Flan	Flan
Sorbete	Sherbet
Helado	Ice cream

The Arts

Nicaraguans are by nature a creative people, and the many countries and cultures that have taken part in their country's history have each left an unmistakable mark on dance, sculpture, painting, writing, and music. There are many opportunities to experience traditional dance and song, but equally vibrant are the artisans, writers, and performers who are creating in the present, helping to form an artistic environment that's very much Nicaragua's own.

LITERATURE

"Nicaragua," wrote the poet Pablo Neruda, "where the highest song of the tongue is raised." José Miguel Oviedo called the writing of Nicaragua, "the richest and most tragic national literary tradition on the continent." Most start the story of Nicaraguan literature with the groundbreaking words of Rubén Darío. It continues with the vanguardists of the 1950s and 1960s, the subsequent generation of revolutionary poets and novelists, and the current wave of soul-searchers.

Though poverty has placed books out of the economic reach of most Nicaraguans, the Casa de los Tres Mundos art gallery in Managua doubles as ground zero for the Society of Nicaraguan Writers, and is a good place to start if you have questions about readings, book releases, or other events. There are a few bookstores in Managua that carry Nicaraguan and Latin American selections, as well as Spanish translations of foreign works; Estelí and León also boast interesting bookstores to explore.

Poet and author Gioconda Belli was called one of the 100 most important poets of the 20th century. Her work deals with the themes of feminism, mystical realism, and history, all mixed with a breath of sensuality. Her books *Wiwilí, Sofía de los Presagios,* and *El País Bajo Mi Piel* (The Country Under My Skin) are widely acclaimed.

The writing of Ricardo Pasos Marciacq reflects not only his appreciation for the long and tumultuous history of Nicaragua but for the richness of its society. His books *Maria Manuela Piel de Luna* and *El Burdel de las Pedrarias* are modern classics; the former evokes the years when British-armed Miskitos were wreaking havoc on the Spanish settlements of the Pacific.

Rubén Darío is loved throughout the world of Latin American literature and is considered the father of modernism in Spanish literature. A few of the many other books by Nicaraguan writers worth reading if you have the time and the facility of the language include *El Nicaragüense* by Pablo Antonio Cuadra, *Nicaragua, Teatro de lo Grandioso* by Carlos A. Bravo, and *El Estrecho Dudoso* by Ernesto Cardenal.

DANCE AND THEATER

Nicaragua's traditional folk dances are often mixed with a form of theater, like a play in a parade. There are several dance institutions in Managua that teach folk classics alongside modern dance and ballet, and sponsor frequent performances. The presence of dance schools outside the capital is on the rise, which means fortunate travelers have a good chance of seeing a presentation outside of Managua, especially in Masaya, Diriamba, Matagalpa, León, and Granada. "El Güegüense," for example, is a 19th-century dance of costumed dancers in wooden masks that satirically represents the impression Nicaragua's indigenous people first had of the Spanish and their horses. This dance and others are often featured at *fiestas patronales* (patron saint celebrations), notably in the Masaya and Carazo regions. "El Viejo y La Vieja" ("The Old Man and Woman") pokes ribald fun at old age and sexuality. One dancer, dressed up as an old gentleman with cane and top hat, and the other, dressed up as a buxom old woman, perform a dance that usually involves the old man trying to dance with young female members of the audience while his wife chases him, beating him with her cane. "Aquella Indita" is a celebration of

THE POET IS THE HIGH PRIEST

In *Risking a Somersault in the Air,* Margaret Randall wrote, "Throughout Nicaraguan culture, the poet is the high priest. The prophet. The maker of visions. The singer of songs. The one who knows and can say it for others the way others feel it but cannot say it for themselves." Salman Rushdie was equally impressed when, during his tour of Nicaragua and the Sandinista government in the mid-1980s, he found himself surrounded by young warrior-poets at all levels of society.

Indeed, an inordinate number of the revolution's leaders were published writers – including Minister of the Interior and Head of State Security Tomás Borge, and President Daniel Ortega, both of whom published poems from Somoza's prisons in the 1970s (Somoza's forces found and destroyed the only manuscript of the book Ortega wrote during the same time period). Ortega once told Rushdie, "In Nicaragua, everybody is considered to be a poet until he proves to the contrary."

Literature (and painting, pottery, theater, music, and crafts) was strongly supported by the Sandinista government, whose Ministry of Culture, Father Ernesto Cardenal, stayed busy instituting poetry workshops and publishing magazines and books. Cardenal's poetry is internationally acclaimed and widely translated. Another revolutionary, Gioconda Belli, whose work evokes the sensuality of her country's land and people, was named one of the 100 most important poets of the 20th century. But Nicaraguan poetry, no matter how entwined with the revolution, goes way back, before the life of Sandino.

Invariably, one must turn to Nicaragua's literary giant, Rubén Darío, who 100 years ago set the stage for his nation's love affair with poetry by producing a style unprecedented in Spanish literature. Darío is called the father of the modernist movement in Spanish poetry, a literary style that shed long, grammatically intricate Spanish phrases for simplicity and directness. His experimentation with verse and rhythm made him one of the most acclaimed Latin American writers of all time. Darío's legacy stands firm, and stories about his drinking bouts and international exploits still abound. Poet, journalist, diplomat, and favorite son of Nicaragua, Rubén Darío has become the icon for all that is artistic or cultural in Nicaragua. Today, his portrait graces the front of the 100 *córdoba* bill, his name is on most of the nation's libraries and bookstores, and his sculpted likeness presides throughout the land. His legacy is incredible, and Randall asks if today's poets owe everything to him or to the fact that they, like their hero, glean their inspiration "from that violent expanse of volcanic strength called Nicaragua."

A hundred years later, the Sandinistas pointed to Darío's anti-imperialist references, including a passage written at the time of the Spanish-American War in which he denounces the North Americans as "buffaloes with silver teeth."

The muse still reigns in today's generation. *Rubén's Orphans* is an anthology of contemporary Nicaraguan poets, with English translations by Marco Morelli, published in 2001 by Painted Rooster Press. Also, seek out Steven F. White's book, *Poets of Nicaragua, a Bilingual Anthology,* which covers the poets following Darío up to the revolution (1983, Unicorn Press).

---

the Nicaraguan woman and her reputation for being graceful and hardworking. "El Solar de Monimbó" ("Monimbó's Backyard") is a traditional dance from the indigenous neighborhood of Masaya, which captures the spirit of community and celebration.

Besides the traditional folk pieces, Nicaraguans love to dance. Period. And there is no occasion (except maybe a funeral) at which it is inappropriate to pump up the music and take to your feet. The ultrasuave, loose-hipped movements associated with merengue, salsa, *cumbia,* and reggae are most commonly seen at discos, street parties, or in living rooms around the nation. The Palo de Mayo is a popular, modern Caribbean dance form featuring flamboyant costumes, vibrating chests, and not-so-subtle sexual simulations. When you see mothers rocking their babies to loud Latin rhythms, and two-year-old girls receiving hip-gyrating lessons, you'll understand why Nicaraguans are able to move so much more fluidly on the dance floor than you are.

VISUAL ARTS

There are a number of Nicaraguan sculptors and painters whose work is displayed at galleries in Managua, Granada, León, and other places. Though the primitivist painters of Solentiname have gotten the lion's share of the press, there is much more in Nicaragua to be seen. In Managua, there are frequent expos of art, often accompanied by buffets or musical performances.

MUSIC

Music, in an infinite variety of forms, is esssential to Nicaraguan society. Expect to find loud, blaring radios in most restaurants, bars, vehicles, and homes. It may seem strange at first to find yourself listening to fast, pulsing merengue beats at six in the morning on a rural chicken bus (or in your hotel lobby at midnight for that matter) when the only people listening are sitting calmly in their seats or rocking chairs. Realize, however, that this behavior is seen as a way to inject *alegría* (happiness) into the environment, or alternately, to get rid of the sadness that some Nicaraguans associate with silence.

Radio mixes are eclectic, featuring the latest Dominican merengues, Mexican and Miami pop, cheesy *romanticas,* plus a bizarre U.S. mélange of Backstreet Boys ("Los Back," for those in the know), Air Supply, and Guns N' Roses. Another wildly popular genre is the *ranchera,* which comes in the form of either polka beats or slow, drippy, lost-love, mariachi tearjerkers, performed by one of a handful of super-celebrity Mexican crooners. Old, rootsy, U.S. country music is extremely popular on the Atlantic coast, and in northern Nicaragua, Kenny Rogers (pronounced "Royers") is recognized as the undisputed king of "La Musica Country."

Did someone request a *ranchera* song?

© JOSHUA BERMAN

Managua is host to a small, exciting scene of young local bands and solo musicians, most of whom are direct descendants—children, nephews, cousins—of the generation of musicians that brought Nicaraguan folk music to the world. Their acts range from quiet acoustic solo sets to the head-banging throaty screams of a couple of angry, politically minded metal bands. You can hear a lot of them at **El Caramanchel.**

Live music is also found at most *fiestas patronales,* performed by one of several Nicaraguan commercial party bands whose sets imitate the radio mixes of the day. Among the most popular bands is Los Mokuanes (named after the enchanted mountain and its resident witch in La Trinidad, Estelí), who have been around in one form or another for more than three decades. During the war, they were conscripted by the government to don fatigues and perform at army bases throughout the country. Other favorite bands are Macolla and, representing the Palo de Mayo side of things, Sir Anthony and his Dimensión Costeño.

NICARAGUAN BASEBALL FEVER

A hundred years of North American and Cuban influence has engendered a nation of baseball fanatics unrivalled in Latin America. Soccer (*fútbol*) has a few fans in Nicaragua – especially in the Carazo region – but it's *el béisbol* that gets most Nicas' blood boiling.

Throughout Nicaragua, very few pueblos lack a ball field of some sort, even if the kids put together games with homemade bats and balls of wound twine and tape. The casual traveler is more often than not welcome to join. A plethora of municipal leagues, town leagues, little leagues, competitions between universities, and even between government ministries, make up the bulk of the national sport. Nicaragua's pro league seems to be constantly in flux, often to due to funding problems. At last check, only four teams were competing in the top division – Managua (El Boer), Masaya (San Fernando), the León Lions, and Chinandega Tigers. These teams play with professional ringers from the U.S. who come to Nicaragua to stay in shape during their off-season. The other division consists of ballclubs from Estelí, Granada (Los Tiburones, or the Sharks), Matagalpa, and Rivas. **The Federación Nicaragüense de Beisból Asociado** (tel. 505/222-2021) has an office in the national stadium in Managua.

There are several concurrent seasons, with the pros playing November–February, and the minors starting around January. Playoff games and a seven-game championship series are played in the spring. The games are serious – as are the fans – but the series' charm is its humility: Unlike elsewhere, baseball is a sport and a pastime, not a mega-marketed seven-figure-salary circus. Not that Nicaraguan players don't dream of one day making it big in "The Show" like their colleagues, Vicente Padilla and Marvin Bernard. Padilla is a star pitcher who, at the age of 26, signed a $2.6-million contract with the Philadelphia Phillies in 2004. Bernard took $4.2 million from the San Francisco Giants in 2003. Like all Nicas who make it to the big leagues, their every move is followed passionately in the Nicaraguan sports pages.

Going back a few years, one of Nicaragua's most admired national heroes is **Dennis "El Presidente" Martínez,** the kid from Granada who left home in 1976 to make it to the big leagues, where he pitched more winning games than any other Latino. In 1991, he pitched the 13th perfect game in major league history against the first-place Dodgers. Nicaraguans followed every detail of his career with avid determination, as he pitched for the Baltimore Orioles (1976-1986), Montreal Expos (1986-1993), Cleveland Indians (1994-1996), Seattle Mariners (1997), and finally the Atlanta Braves (1998). Martínez was a breath of fresh air and a source of much-needed relief throughout the 1980s, when his pitching and hitting stats were the only good news associated with this war-torn nation; talking baseball was a popular respite from the tragedy and destruction. Martínez retired in 1998 and today, his name graces the stadium in Managua, as well as several charitable foundations, like the **Dennis Martínez Foundation** (www.dennismartinezfoundation.org).

Also respected is Puerto Rican-born Pittsburgh Pirate, **Roberto Clemente.** Clemente was so moved by the distress in Nicaragua's capital after the 1972 earthquake that he rounded up a planeload of clothes, blankets, and food, and flew to Managua to personally distribute it. He never arrived. Immediately after taking off from San Juan, Puerto Rico, his DL-7 plane faltered and plunged into the Caribbean. Investigators suggested the unrestrained cargo shifted during flight and threw the plane off balance; five additional people perished trying to rescue him.

ESSENTIALS

Getting There and Away

BY AIR

American Airlines has daily flights via Miami, Continental Airlines via Houston, and Delta Airlines via Atlanta. The Salvadoran airline TACA also has daily flights from Miami with a brief stopover in San Salvador; this is typically a less expensive flight, but the cheapest possible flight is from Fort Lauderdale, Florida, on Spirit Airlines (you are permitted far less luggage on Spirit).

Nicaragua's annoying old $30 cash-only exit fee has been eliminated, and the Augusto C. Sandino is a surprisingly decent airport after major reconstruction that lasted four years. From the airport you can arrange rental cars, stop by the INTUR desk for hotel recommendations, and even buy or rent a cell phone. Skycaps will help you with your luggage for about $2; don't use the services of anyone not sporting a skycap uniform.

BY LAND

The three northern border posts are (from west to east): Guasale, Chinandega; El Espino, Somoto; and Las Manos, Somoto. Travelers who entered the region via Guatemala, Honduras, or El Salvador can enter Nicaragua without getting additional visas thanks to Nicaragua's participation in the CA-4 Border Control Agreement of 2006. Under the

© JOSHUA BERMAN

agreement, your initial entry visa is valid for the whole region for up to 90 days and can be extended once with little hassle.

On the southern border, Peñas Blancas is the principal corridor on the Pan-American Highway leading to Costa Rica, and no such agreement exists, so you'll need a stamp if arriving from Costa Rica. You can also enter Nicaragua in the south from Los Chiles, Costa Rica, a trip that involves a lovely boat ride to San Carlos at the head of the Río San Juan.

We provide detailed border-crossing instructions in the corresponding regional chapters of this book. Note that every overland crossing involves two steps: exiting the first country and entering the second. If you forget to get the second stamp in your passport you will regret it.

Driving Across the Border

If you are driving your own vehicle, the process to enter Nicaragua is lengthier, but usually not difficult. You must present the vehicle's title, as well as your own driver's license and passport. You will be given a temporary (30-day) permit to drive in Nicaragua, which will cost $10—should you lose the permit, you will be fined $100. Alamo Rent a Car shares cars among Costa Rica and Nicaragua, permitting you to pick up in one country and drop off in another.

By International Bus

A half-dozen long-haul bus companies run between Managua and other Central American capitals, and most are based out of Barrio Martha Quezada in Managua. They each offer competing schedules and prices. Several have affiliate offices in other Nicaraguan cities, like Rivas and León. From Managua to San José, Costa Rica takes about 10 hours and costs $23 each way. To Tegucigalpa, Honduras, is a bit longer and more expensive (up to 12 hours, depending on the line at immigration, and up to $41 each way). Many departures are before dawn, leaving Managua at 3:30–6 A.M., so plan accordingly.

TicaBus (two blocks east of the Antiguo Cine Dorado, tel. 505/2222-6094 or 505/2222-3031, ticabus@ticabus.com, www. ticabus.com) is the oldest and best-established Central American international bus company, with three daily departures to San José, as well as service to the rest of Central America with connections all the way to Mexico. The other companies with stations in Managua (all within a few blocks of each other) are **King Quality** (tel. 505/2222-3065), **Del Sol Bus** (tel. 505/2222-7785), **Central Line** (tel. 505/2254-5431), and **Transnica** (tel. 505/2277-2104).

Getting Around

BY AIR

La Costeña (tel. 505/2263-2142, 505/2263-2143, or 505/2263-2144, reservacion@lacostena.com.ni, www.lacostena.com.ni) is Nicaragua's sole domestic airline, whose humble fleet of seven small craft fly between Managua and the Atlantic coast, Mining Triangle, Puerto Cabezas, Waspám, Bluefields, Corn Island, and San Carlos. Seats are limited on the 12-passenger twin-prop Cessna Grand Caravans (they have one 40-passenger Short 360 aircraft as well), and cost about $80 one-way, $120–160 round-trip. It is almost imperative that you reserve your flight before arriving in Nicaragua; this has been difficult in the past, but La Costeña's new online booking system will help matters.

BY BUS

Nicaragua intercity bus system is made up primarily of retired American yellow school buses, each one lovingly customized with stickers and plastic streamers. Modern, air conditioned coaches are increasingly joining the line-up for popular express routes. Bus coverage is excellent though the ride is bumpy and often slow. Each major population center has one or two bus hubs, with regular and express service to

© JOSHUA BERMAN

Nicaragua's sole domestic air carrier, La Costeña, has a small fleet of planes to get you to remote corners of the country.

nearby cities and to Managua, plus rural routes to the surrounding communities. If you've got the time in your travels, riding the Nicaraguan bus network will provide endless memories and probably make you a couple of friends, as there's little else to do on the ride but chat.

Local buses are called *ordinarios* or *ruteados* and they stop for anyone standing by the roadside and flapping their hand. *Expresos* are more expensive and make fewer stops; they are also often better quality vehicles as well, and are well worth the extra 25 percent you will pay for a ticket. In addition, expresos usually work on a reserved/numbered seat basis. Before you settle into town it's worth spending a couple more minutes at the bus station to make your ownward reservations, if possible.

To points west and south from Managua, there is an especially large number of express microbuses (minivans or *interlocales*) that leave every 20 minutes—or whenever they fill up.

On the *ruteados,* you'll board the bus, find a seat, and then wait for the *ayudante* (driver's helper) to come around and collect your *pasaje* (fare). Ask a fellow traveler how much the ride should cost just to be sure, though our experience is that the *ayudantes* are typically honest. The *ayudante* will write the amount owed to you on your ticket if he doesn't have exact change, returning later in the trip to pay you. Most buses have overhead racks inside where you can stow your bags. Less desirable, but common, is for the *ayudante* to insist you put your backpack on the roof or in some cargo space in the back of the bus. It is safer to keep your stuff on your lap or at least within sight, if possible, but we've never had a problem stowing bags out of sight.

We strongly advise against using the Managua bus system unless you are with a Nicaraguan; the routes are long and confusing and the money you save—a couple of dollars, usually—is not worth the dramatically increased risk of robbery. Even Nicaraguans lose their belongings at knifepoint on these crowded, dilapidated buses. In other Nicaraguan cities *urbanos* are usually much safer and have shorter routes.

TAXIS

The old Russian Ladas that plied the city streets in the 1980s and '90s are fast giving way to newer Japanese and Korean imports. Taxis are a great way to get around and are well worth the extra money if you want to save time; in Managua, they're essential for security reasons.

In every city except Managua, urban taxis operate on a fixed zone rate, usually under $1 within the central city area. In the capital, however, it's a different story, and you are expected to bargain out a rate before sitting down. In all cases, avoid taxis where the driver is traveling with a friend, and pay attention to where you're going.

SHUTTLE SERVICES

This is a relatively new option in Nicaragua, a direct response to travelers in Granada and León who would rather not negotiate taxi fees or muck around with the chicken buses. You'll board a new minivan filled with other tourists willing to spend $15–20 to be whisked between the pueblos, beach towns, and ferry docks. Most offer airport service as well.

Start with **Nica Express** (tel. 505/2552-8461, info@nica-adventures.com, www.nica-adventures.com); they maintain a set schedule of departures throughout the country. **Paxeos** (tel. 505/2552-8291 or 505/8465-1090, www.paxeos.com) is another reliable shuttle service, based in Granada, specializing in personal airport pickups at any time of night (and they have an online booking service). **Adelante Express** (tel. 505/8850-6070, www.adelanteexpress.com) is based in San Juan del Sur and also offers full service shuttles and transport; 24-hour advance reservation required.

You can also check tour operators, especially **Vapues Tours** and **Tierra Tours,** who offer shuttles and airport transfers.

RENTING A CAR AND DRIVING
Renting a Car

While it seems convenient to zip out of the airport in a rented car, the hassle of driving and the risk of making sure the car doesn't get stolen or damaged are not to be underestimated. If you are traveling with a lot of luggage, children, or surfboards, it's a no-brainer, but be aware that if you have just a little bit more time, you can get around extremely easily in taxis, shuttles, and public buses.

That said, all the major car rental agencies have set up shop at the Managua airport, and you can also arrange a car through most hotels costing $50 or higher. Be sure to reserve in advance: **Alamo Rent A Car** (tel. 505/2233-3718, www.alamonicaragua.com), **Avis** (www.avis.com.ni), **Budget** (tel. 505/2255-9000, U.S. tel. 305/433-7708, www.budget.com.ni), **Hertz** (tel. 505/2233-1237, www.hertz.com.ni), **National** (tel. 505/2270-8492 or 505/2233-3718, www.nationalnicaragua.com), **Thrifty** (tel. 505/2233-2192, www.thrifty.com.ni); several other chains are listed at www.nicaraguarentalcars.com. In addition to the airport, Thrifty has an office at Plaza España, and National has an office adjacent to the Hotel Hilton Princess and in the Hotel Colonial Granada.

Plan on spending about $30 per day, $175 a week during the high season for the smallest four-seater "econobox," or $75 a day, $450 a week for a pickup truck, plus insurance costs and gasoline, which is well over $4 per gallon.

Vehicular Safety

The most dangerous thing you will do in Nicaragua, without a doubt, is travel on its highways. Outside the cities, roads are poorly lit, narrow, lacking shoulders, and are often full of axle-breaking potholes, unannounced speed bumps, fallen rocks, and countless other obstacles. Even in Managua, you can expect to find ox carts and abandoned vehicles in the lanes, and hungry dogs and grazing horses wandering the streets. Because there are no shoulders for taxis to use when boarding passengers, they stop in the right lane and let traffic swerve around them. There are also macho, testosterone-crazed bus drivers trying to pass everything they can on blind, uphill curves. The fact that beer and rum are sold at most gas stations should give you an idea of how many drivers are intoxicated, especially late at night.

When possible, avoid traveling during peak rush hours in the cities, and after dark anywhere. New highway projects since 2000 have improved the roads in many parts of the country, but many drivers take advantage of the improved straightaways to speed like bats out of hell. Take time before entering a city to plan your route, as you will not have the luxury of reading the map while you navigate traffic. That goes double for Managua, where choosing the wrong lane can be disastrous!

Traffic Accidents and Getting Pulled Over

So how's that Spanish coming along, amigo? Nicaragua's police force is poorly paid and not adverse to a little pocket money (if you catch our drift). Foreign drivers without diplomatic plates are frequent targets for document checks, but if you commit a *mala maniobra* (moving

violation, literally "bad move") in their presence, you'd better have your papers ready. (Here's a really bad move: calling your interlocutor *"compañero"* is likely to double the bribe.) Crooked cops will demand to confiscate your license and threaten to hold it hostage until you come in the following week to pay the fine—unless, of course, you'd rather take care of the issue right then, hint hint, wink wink.

If you are involved in a vehicular accident, *do not* move your vehicle from the scene of the crime until authorized by a police officer, even if it is blocking traffic. Lacking high-tech crime-scene equipment, Nicaraguan police will try to understand how the accident occurred based on what they see at the site. Drivers who move their vehicle at the scene of the accident (thus altering the crime scene) are legally liable for the incident. Any driver in Nicaragua that causes injuries to another person will be taken into immediate custody, regardless of insurance and circumstances, and remain there until the courts reach a decision—sometimes weeks later—or until the injured party signs a waiver releasing the driver of liability. To avoid

© JOSHUA BERMAN

There are many hazards on the Nicaraguan highways.

a lengthy court proceeding and horrifying jail stay, it may be worth your while to plead guilty and pay a fine (which historically does not exceed $1,000, even in the case of a death). But call your embassy and get a lawyer immediately, nevertheless; this is what they do best.

MOTORCYCLES AND BICYCLES

If you intend to ride a motorcycle or bicycle in Nicaragua, be sure to bring a helmet, an item largely ignored by Nicaraguans, many of whom manage to fit a family of four on one bike. Good quality helmets are not easy to purchase in Nicaragua. If biking, keep your eyes on the road; the entrances to Matagalpa and Granada have unmarked speed bumps which serve as invisible bike-launchers-of-death.

Biking Central America is a breathtaking experience (not just because of the heat!) but puts you at risk in a couple of new ways. We have met dozens of thru-bikers, who report that Nicaragua is no better nor worse than the rest of Central America. Small shoulders at roadside are par for the course, as is the occasional

bottle-throwing idiot careening by in a fast car. Travelers have reported some harassment and even robbery of bikers in the stretch between San Juan del Sur and the Costa Rican border.

BOATS

In several regions of Nicaragua—notably Solentiname, Río San Juan, Río Coco, and the entire Atlantic coast—a boat will be your only means of transportation. Here, rising gasoline prices determine the fare, which will be more expensive than you expect. Locals get around in public water taxis called *colectivos* that help cut costs. Any water-bordering community will likely have small boats the owners use for fishing or transport. Ask for a *canoa, panga,* or *botecita,* and see what shows up. Dugout canoes are common throughout the country, and you can ask to rent one along the Río San Juan and other areas. For recreation, there are a handful of sailboats that can take you out in San Juan del Sur, and some boat-based tour companies out of Granada and León. **Ibis Exchange** (www.ibis-kayaking.com) offers paddle trips in the Estero Padre Ramos in expedition ocean kayaks.

© RANDALL WOOD

getting around the land of lakes and volcanoes

Visas and Officialdom

PASSPORT AND VISA REQUIREMENTS

Every traveler to Nicaragua must have a passport valid for at least six months following the date of entry. A visa is required only for citizens of the following countries: Afghanistan, Albania, Bosnia-Herzegovina, Colombia, Cuba, Haiti, India, Iran, Iraq, Jordan, Lebanon, Libya, Nepal, Pakistan, People's Republic of China, People's Republic of Korea, Somalia, Sri Lanka, Vietnam, and Yugoslavia. Everyone else is automatically given a tourist visa at the airport or land border, good for three months, in the form of a $5 tourist card. Don't lose the card! You'll need to return it when you leave the country. Technically, you must have an onward/return ticket, and evidence of sufficient funds; in practice, this is never checked.

Renewing a visa has gotten easier in the new tourist-friendly Nicaragua. In Managua at the Metrocentro shopping mall, there's an Immigration branch office (no phone, open 10 A.M.–6 P.M. Mon.–Fri., 10 A.M.–1 P.M. Sat. and Sun.) that will process your request for an extension. You'll pay $0.25 for the form, and must present photocopies of your passport's information page as well as the page with your visa. A 30-day tourist visa extension is $10, and if you've overstayed your current visa you will pay an additional $1 for each day over the limit. Many travelers in San Juan del Sur prefer to just take a bus over the Costa Rican border, and return the same day on a fresh, new tourist visa. Furthermore, Nicaragua entered into the CA-4 Border Control Agreement permitting travelers to travel among Nicaragua, Guatemala, Honduras, and El Salvador without getting additional visas: Your initial entry visa is valid for the whole region for up to 90 days and can be extended once with little hassle.

Anything more serious than a basic tourist visa extension requires a trip to the main **Office of Immigration** (Dirección General de Migración y Extranjería, 1.5 blocks north of the *semáforos* Tenderí, tel. 505/2244-0741, 505/2244-1320, or 505/2244-3960, open 8:30 A.M.–noon and 2–4:30 P.M. Mon.–Fri.); show up at least four days before it expires with your passport, current visa, and $25.

CUSTOMS

Tourists are invariably ignored by customs officials, who have their eyes peeled for wealthy Nicas returning from shopping binges in Miami. Should they go through your luggage, you can expect to be taxed for carrying items you obviously don't intend to use yourself, including electronics, jewelry, and perfume. To save trouble for yourself, avoid carrying more of anything valuable (such as a laptop) than a traveler would typically need. Surfers, that goes for your boards, too: If it looks like you're importing sales stock, you will be stopped and hassled.

FOREIGN EMBASSIES AND CONSULATES IN NICARAGUA

All diplomatic missions in Nicaragua are located in Managua, mostly along Carretera Masaya and Carretera Sur. The city of Chinandega hosts consulates from El Salvador, Honduras, and Costa Rica, and the city of Rivas has a consulate from Costa Rica.

United States and Canada

Americans living or traveling in Nicaragua can register with the **U.S. Embassy** in Nicaragua (Kilometer 5.5, Carretera Sur, Managua, tel. 505/2252-7100, nicaragua.usembassy.gov) at the main international travel page of the U.S. State Department (www.travel.state.gov). Registering is not a legal requirement but is encouraged by the embassy so that they can send you updated travel and security advisories regarding Nicaragua. These advisories—and the warden messages on the embassy website—are invariably on the conservative side, as far as risk assessment. Other contacts: Information Resource Center (tel. 505/2252-7237) or American Citizens Services (ACS.Managua@state.gov).

NICARAGUAN CONSULATES AND EMBASSIES

Nicaragua does not maintain a consulate in Canada. For additional consulates in Europe and Latin America, visit www.intur.gob.ni.

IN THE UNITED STATES

Washington, DC (Embassy and Consulate)
1627 New Hampshire Ave. NW
Washington, DC 20009
U.S. tel. 202/939-6531 or 202/939-6532
fax 202/939-6574

Houston, TX
8989 Westheimer Rd., Suite 103
Houston, TX 77063
U.S. tel. 713/789-2762 or 276/789-2781

Los Angeles, CA
3550 Wilshire Blvd., Ste. 200
Los Angeles, CA 90010
U.S. tel. 213/252-1171 or 213/252-1174
fax 213/252-1177

Miami, FL
8532 SW 8th St., Suite 270
Miami, FL 33144
U.S. tel. 305/265-1415
fax 305/265-1780

New York, NY
820 2nd Ave., 8th Floor, Suite 802
New York, NY 10017
U.S. tel. 212/986-6562
fax 212/983-2646

San Francisco, CA
870 Market, Suite 1050
San Francisco, CA 94102
U.S. tel. 415/765-6821, 415/765-6823, or 415/765-6825
fax 415/765-6826

IN CENTRAL AMERICA

Costa Rica
Avenida Central No. 2440,
Barrio La California
San José, Costa Rica
tel. 506/222-2373
fax 506/221-5481

El Salvador
71 Avenida Norte y Primera Calle
Poniente No. 164
Colonia Escalon, San Salvador
tel. 503/298-6549
fax 506/223-7201

Guatemala
10 Avenida, 14-72, Zona 10
Guatemala
tel. 502/268-0785
fax 502/337-4264

Honduras
Colonia Tepeyac, Bloque M-1, No. 1130
Tegucigalpa, Honduras
tel. 504/232-7224
fax 504/239-5225

Panamá
Intersección de Avenida Federico Boyd y Calle 50
Apartado 772, Zona 1
Corregimiento Bella Vista
Ciudad de Panamá, Panamá
tel. 507/223-0981
fax 507/211-2080

GUIDE TO NICARAGUA'S FIESTAS

Each community's annual *fiestas patronales* revolve around the local saint's birthday, but the actual party may extend days or even weeks before and after. This guide should help you catch (or avoid) *fiestas patronales* as you travel; the events are associated with special masses, processions, alcohol, dancing, carnivals, show horses, contests, and more alcohol.

Year-round weekly events include the following: Thursdays in Masaya are Jueves de Verbena, Fridays in Granada are Noches de Serenata, and Sundays in León are Tertulias Leónesas. Semana Santa (Easter Week) is a particularly big deal – everyone parties like rock stars at the beach and prices skyrocket across the board.

JANUARY

1: New Year's Day
18: Fiestas Patronales, El Sauce
Third Sunday: Señor de Esquipulas, El Sauce (León)
Third weekend: Viva León Festival, León
Third weekend: San Sebastián, Acoyapa (Chontales), Diriamba, Carazo (San Sebastián)
Last weekend: La Virgen de Candelaria, La Trinidad (Estelí)

FEBRUARY

Second weekend: Music and Youth Festival, Managua

MARCH

Third weekend: Folklore, Gastronomy, and Handicraft Festival, Granada

APRIL

Semana Santa
First week: Religious Ash Paintings in León
19-21: Fiestas Patronales, San Jorge (Rivas)

MAY

1: Labor Day
1: Fiestas Patronales, Jinotega
15: San Isidro Labrador, Condega (Estelí)
30: Mother's Day
Third weekend: Palo de Mayo Festival, Bluefields

JUNE

16: Virgen del Carmen, San Juan del Sur (Rivas)
24: St. John the Baptist, San Juan de Oriente (Carazo), San Juan del Sur (Rivas), San Juan de Jinotega (Jinotega)
29: St. Peter the Apostle, Diriá (Masaya)
Last Friday: El Repliegue Sandinista (Managua)

The **Canadian Embassy** in Managua is actually an outpost of their main embassy in San José, Costa Rica. The address in the Bolonia neighborhood is on Calle El Nogal, one block east from the Casa Nazareth (tel. 505/2268-0433 or 505/2268-3323, fax 505/2268-0437, mngua@international.gc.ca). For emergencies involving Canadian citizens, call the emergency consular service in Ottawa collect at 613/996-6885.

Central America

Costa Rica: half a block east of Estatua Montoya along Calle 27 de Mayo, tel. 505/2268-7460. There is also a consulate in Rivas and Chinandega.

Cuba: Carretera Masaya from the third entrance to Las Colinas, two blocks east, 75 meters to the south, tel. 505/2276-2285.

El Salvador: Las Colinas, Ave. El Campo Pasaje Los Cerros no. 142, tel. 505/2276-0160.

Guatemala: Carretera Masaya Km 11, tel. 505/2279-9834.

Honduras: Carretera Masaya Km 12, 100 meters toward Cainsa, tel. 505/2279-8231.

Panamá: third entrance to Las Colinas, then

JULY
Second Saturday: Carnaval, Somoto
15-25: Fiestas Patronales, Somoto
19: National Liberation Day
25: Santiago, Boaco, Jinotepe (Carazo)
26: St. Ana, Nandaime (Granada), Chinandega, Ometepe

AUGUST
1-10: Santo Domingo (Noches Agostinas), Managua
10: St. Lorenzo, Somotillo (Chinandega)
14: Gritería Chiquita, León
15: The Assumption, Granada
14-15: Fiestas Patronales, Ocotal
15: The Assumption and Fiesta del Hijo Ausente, Juigalpa
Third weekend: Mariachis and Mazurcas Festival, Estelí

SEPTEMBER
10: San Nicolás de Tolentino, La Paz Centro (León)
14: The Battle of San Jacinto
15: Independence Day
14 and 15: Fishing Fair, San Carlos (Río San Juan)
15: Patron Saint Festival of Villa Nueva, Chinandega
20: San Jerónimo, Masaya
24: La Merced, León, and Matagalpa

Fourth weekend: Polkas, Mazurcas, and Jamaquellos, Matagalpa; Festival of Corn, Jalapa

OCTOBER
12: San Diego (Estelí)
Second weekend: Norteño Music Festival in Jinotega
24: San Rafael Arcángel, Pueblo Nuevo
Penultimate Sunday: Fiesta de los Agüisotes, Masaya
Last Sunday: Toro Venado, Masaya

NOVEMBER
2: All Souls' Day
3-5: Equestrian Rally in Ometepe
4: San Carlos Borromeo, San Carlos (Río San Juan)
12-18: San Diego de Alcalá, Altagracia (Ometepe)
Fourth Sunday: Folkloric Festival, Masaya

DECEMBER
First Sunday: Procesión de San Jerónimo, Masaya
6: Lavado de La Plata, Virgen del Trono, El Viejo (Chinandega)
7: Purísimas (Immaculate Conception Celebrations) in Managua, Granada, Masaya, and León

two blocks east and 75 meters south, tel. 505/2276-0212.

Europe and Asia

Austria: from the Rotonda El Güegüense, one block north, tel. 505/2266-0171 or 505/2268-3756.

Belgium: Consulado de Bélica, Reparto El Carmen across from the Esso station, Calle 27 de Mayo, tel. 505/2228-2068.

Denmark: Plaza España one block west, two blocks north, half a block west, tel. 505/2268-0253.

Finland: Bolonia, one block north, 1.5 blocks

west of the Hospital Militar, tel. 505/2266-3415.

France: Reparto El Carmen, 1.5 blocks west of the church, tel. 505/2222-6210.

Germany: 1.5 blocks north of the Rotonda El Güegüense, tel. 505/2266-3917.

Great Britain: Los Robles, from the old Sandy's on Carretera Masaya, one block south, a half-block west, tel. 505/2278-0014 or 2278-0887.

Italy: one block north and half a block west of the Rotonda El Güegüense, tel. 505/2266-6486.

The Netherlands (Holland): Bolonia canal

U.S. SISTER CITIES WITH NICARAGUA

Some of the following pairings were formed during the 1980s to express solidarity with the Nicaraguan people. They have continued to exist as small-scale development organizations that often organize brigades to their sister towns. For more on sister cities or to find ideas of how you can become involved in your local program, contact your city council, or go to www.sister-cities.org.

Amherst, MA	La Paz Centro	Montclair, NJ	Pearl Lagoon
Ann Arbor, MI	Juigalpa	Moscow, ID	Villa Carlos Fonseca
Bainbridge Island, WA	Ometepe	Newark, DE	San Francisco Libre
Baltimore, MD	San Juan de Limay	New Haven, CT	León
Beckley, WV	Mina El Limon	Newton, MA	San Juan del Sur
Bend, OR	Condega	New York, NY	Tipitapa
Bennington, VT	Somotillo	North Plainfield, NJ	Masaya
Berkeley, CA	León	Norwalk, CT	Nagarote
Bloomington, IN	Posoltega	Pittsburgh, PA	San Isidro
Boulder, CO	Jalapa	Pittsfield, MA	Malpaisillo
Brookline, MA	Quezalguaque	Platteville, WI	Mateare
Burlington, VT	Puerto Cabezas	Portland, OR	Corinto
Concord, MA	San Marcos (RAAN)	Racine, WI	Bluefields
Fresno, CA	Telpaneca	Richland Center, WI	Santa Teresa
Gainesville, FL	Matagalpa	Rochester, NY	El Sauce
Gettysburg, PA	León	Sacramento, CA	San Juan de Oriente
Hartford, CT	Ocotal	Santa Cruz, CA	Jinotepe
Holyoke, CO	Las Mangas	South Haven, MI	Quilalí
Hudson Valley, NY	Larreynaga	Stevens Point, WI	Estelí
Lansing, SC	Tipitapa	Tampa, FL	Granada
Madison, WI	Managua	Tucson, AZ	Santo Domingo
Merced, CA	Somoto	Waukesha, WI	Granada
Milwaukee, WI	Ticuantepe	Yellow Springs, OH	Jicaro

2, half a block north, one block west, tel. 505/2266-4392.

Norway: one block west of Plaza España, tel. 505/2266-4199.

Russia: Las Colinas, Calle Vista Alegre No. 214, tel. 505/2276-0131.

Spain: Las Colinas, Avenida Central No. 13, tel. 505/2276-0968.

Sweden: one block west, two blocks north, and half a block west of the Rotonda Plaza España, tel. 505/2266-8097.

Switzerland: Consulado de Suiza, one block west of the Las Palmas Clinic, tel. 505/2266-5719.

China: Planes de Altamira, from the Copa of-fice 200 meters south across from the tennis courts, tel. 505/2267-4024.

Japan: Bolonia, from the Rotonda El Güegüense one block west, one block north, tel. 505/2266-1773.

OFFICIAL HOLIDAYS

Expect all public offices to be closed on the following days. Also remember that Nicaraguan holidays are subject to decree, shutting the banks down without warning to suit some politician's inclination.

• January 1: New Year's Day

• Late March/early April: Semana Santa, including Holy Thursday, Good Friday, and Easter

- May 1: Labor Day
- May 30: Mother's Day
- July 19: National Liberation Day
- August 1: Fiesta Day
- September 14: Battle of San Jacinto
- September 15: Independence Day
- November 2: Día de los Muertes (All Souls' Day)
- December 8: La Purísima (Immaculate Conception)
- December 25: Christmas Day

Other Holidays and Fiestas

Like the rest of Latin America, every single town and city has its own patron saint whom the residents honor each year with a prolonged party that lasts 1–3 weeks. These **fiestas patronales** combine holy religious fervor with the consumption of alcohol in biblical proportions. Most celebrations include Virgin and Saint parades, special masses, fireworks, cockfighting, rodeos, concerts, gambling, dances, and show-horse parades (hípicos). Many towns have additional celebrations of specific events in their history.

Semana Santa (or Holy Week) is the biggest celebration of the year, occurring during the week leading up to Easter Sunday. The weeklong vacation sends most city folk to the beach for sun and debauchery (and usually a couple of drownings, too) while shops close their doors and everyone takes a breather. In popular beach areas like San Juan del Sur, expect hiked prices and few vacancies. In other areas, you may also encounter altered bus schedules and other travel annoyances.

Tips for Travelers

WHAT TO TAKE

Everything you bring to Nicaragua should be sturdy and ideally water-resistant, especially if you intend to visit the Atlantic coast or Río San Juan, where you'll inevitably find yourself in a boat. Also be prepared for rain during any part of the wet season. Choose a small, strong bag not so large you'll be uncomfortable carrying it for long distances or riding with it on your lap in the bus—and secure its zippers with small padlocks. If you're planning to stay in a midrange or upscale hotel for the duration of your trip, your bag is of less concern, but be sure to take a small daypack or shoulder bag for your daily walkabouts.

Clothing

Pick clothes that are light and breathable in the heat, and if your plans include Matagalpa, Jinotega, or Estelí, you may appreciate something a bit warmer, like a flannel shirt. For sun protection, don't forget a shade hat that covers the back of your neck.

No matter what your style, it is very important to look clean. Having a neat personal appearance is important to all Latin Americans, and you'll find being well groomed will open a lot more doors. In the countryside, Nicaraguan men typically don't wear shorts, unless they are at the beach or at home. Jeans travel well, but you will probably find them hot in places like León and Chinandega; khakis are lighter and dry faster.

Roads are rough, even in cities, so good walking shoes will ease your trip considerably; lightweight hiking boots or just sturdy sneakers are sufficient. You'll be hard-pressed to find shoes larger than a men's 10.5 (European 42) for sale in Nicaragua. Take a pair of shower sandals with you, or better yet, buy a pair of rubber *chinelas* anywhere in Nicaragua for about $1.

Miscellany

Bring a small **first-aid kit,** plastic bags and Ziplocs for protections from both rain and boat travel, and a cheap set of **ear plugs** for the occasional early-morning rooster or *chichera* band.

A lightweight, breathable **raincoat** and/or small **umbrella** are a good idea. A small **flashlight or headlamp** is indispensable for walking at night on uneven streets and for those late-night potty runs in your *hospedaje,*

and an **alarm clock** will facilitate catching early-morning buses. If you wear glasses, bring along a little repair kit. Bring a pocket **Spanish dictionary** and **phrasebook.** Photos of home and your family are a great way to connect with your Nica hosts and friends. A simple **compass** is helpful for finding your way around, as directions in this book typically refer to compass directions (finding the hotel three blocks north of the park is a lot easier if you know which direction north is).

Paperwork

Make a photocopy of the pages in your passport that have your photo and information. When you get the passport stamped in the airport, it's a good idea to make a photocopy of that page as well after you get situated in your first hotel, and store the copies somewhere other than with your passport. This will facilitate things greatly if your passport ever gets lost or stolen. Also consider taking a copy of your health and medical evacuation insurance policy.

TRAVEL WITH CHILDREN

Nicaraguans love children and dote on them. We have both traveled with babies and small children in Nicaragua with relative ease. You may find that traveling with children opens doors and forms new connections. That said, your children will have to endure the same lack of creature comforts, change in diet, and long bumpy bus rides you do. Disposable diapers are expensive but readily available in supermarkets, as are powdered milk/formula, pacifiers *(pacificadores* or *chupetas),* and bottles *(pachas).* Ask your doctor and consult the CDC about malaria prophylaxis for your child.

Perhaps the most important thing to pack is strong sun protection for delicate skin and disinfectant hand soap or foam. Travel with a stroller is half useful and half annoying, as Nicaragua's sandy and cobbled streets frequently require bigger-wheeled strollers that are thus harder to pack and carry around. Make sure your rental car company can provide a car seat for you, or you will be required to bring

---

SINFUL SOUVENIRS: RUM AND CIGARS

Looking for a gift that keeps on giving? Nicaragua offers a selection of ephemeral pleasures, including fine cigars and rum.

Nicaragua's hand-rolled cigars start with Cuban seed and the good earth around Estelí. Find them for sale in the Huembes market in Managua, El Mercado Viejo in Masaya, or the cigar shops around Granada's central plaza (or at the source at cigar factories in Estelí). Gringos: Just because you can buy Cuban Cohibas in Nicaragua (which may or may not be genuine), U.S. customs may still enforce their anti-Cuban embargo – whether your cigars are real or counterfeit! Remove the labels to be sure.

The cheapest place to pick up souvenir bottles of **Flor de Caña,** widely accepted as one of the smoothest rums in all Latin America, is in a supermarket or corner *pulpería;* hotel gift shops and airport kiosks often charge double what you should be paying. Nicaragua customs limits you to six liter-sized bottles of rum at the airport and if you're catching a connecting flight in the U.S., you'll have to transfer your liquids to your checked luggage, so plan ahead and make sure you have space to do so.

© CHRIS SICILIANO

Traveling with children, you get to see Nicaragua through their eyes: Joshua's daughter, Shanti, gets her first view of Ometepe.

one (we highly recommend it, considering the danger of Nicaraguan road travel).

WOMEN TRAVELERS

In Nicaragua, as in all of Latin America, women are both adored and harassed to their wits' end by "gentlemen" hoping for attention. Catcalls and whistles are rife, often accompanied with an *"Adios, amorrrr,"* or a sleazy, *"Tss-tss!"* More often than not, the perpetrators are harmless, immature young men with struggling moustaches. It will either comfort or disgust you to know that Nicaraguan women are forced to endure the same treatment every day and you should note how they react—most ignore the comments and blown kisses entirely, and some are flattered and smile confidently as they walk by. Angrily losing your cool is ill-advised, as it will only feed the fire. Be prepared for this part of the culture, and decide ahead of time how you plan to react.

Physical harassment, assault, and rape are less common in Nicaragua than elsewhere in Central America, but they have all happened, especially when alcohol is involved.

Take the same precautions you would anywhere else to avoid dangerous situations. For more, download a copy of "Her Own Way: Advice for the Woman Traveller" at the Canadian Consular Affairs website (www.voyage.gc.ca); also find good advice and tips at www.journeywoman.com.

Feminine Products

Tampons can be difficult to find, as almost all Nicaraguan women use pads *(toallas sanitarias)* due to custom and as social stigma, as tampons are often associated with sexually uninhibited women. Try the bigger supermarkets if you're in a pinch; most pharmacies and *pulperías* carry pads, usually called "Kotex," regardless of the actual brand name.

GAY AND LESBIAN TRAVELERS

As of March 2008, consensual gay sex is no longer a criminal act in Nicaragua, though the Catholic church still forbids it and homophobia is rampant throughout Latin America. Even so, Nica society is generally tolerant of homosexuality. The gay or lesbian traveler should feel neither threatened nor endangered in Nicaragua provided they maintain a modicum of discretion and choose their situations wisely. Managua and Granada have a few openly gay clubs and gay-friendly hotels. Elsewhere same-sex couples may find local gay communities that will help orient them to tolerant clubs and bars.

TRAVELERS WITH DISABILITIES

Travelers with disabilities should contact **AccessibleNicaragua** (accessiblenicaragua@gmail.com, www.accessiblenicaragua.com) before coming. Founder Craig Grimes, a disabled traveler himself, is somewhat of the authority on the matter. Wheelchair-bound travelers to Nicaragua have reported the two most important things to consider bringing are toilet seat extenders and suction cups, and point out Nicaraguans will quite helpfully offer to help you up and down curbs as necessary.

Nicaragua's *descapacitados* (disabled) get around with much difficulty because of ruined sidewalks, dirt roads, aggressive crowds, and open manholes. While Nicaraguans agree people with disabilities have equal rights, no attempt is made to accommodate them, and the foreign traveler with limited mobility will certainly struggle, but will no doubt find ways to get by. The Los Pipitos organization, based in Managua with 24 chapters around the country, is devoted to providing support, materials, and physical therapy to Nicaraguan children with disabilities and their families. Los Pipitos is always looking for volunteers and support. The Managua office is located half a block east of the Bolonia Agfa (tel. 505/2266-8033).

WORKING

In light of Nicaragua's exceeding poverty and sky-high unemployment rate, you'll have a tough time finding paying work. Immigration laws force you to prove your job couldn't have otherwise gone to a Nicaraguan. Still, there are plenty of foreigners who've pulled it off. They work for international corporations with services and products in Nicaragua, they start businesses of their own, and they work for international NGOs like CARE, Save the Children, ADRA, Project Concern International, and Catholic Relief Services. If you are a licensed English teacher you might also try the universities in Managua, though your salary will be the same as a Nicaraguan's (i.e., you'll be able to sustain yourself from day to day but you'll wish you had a cousin in Miami sending you checks). Universidad Centroamericana (UCA), Universidad Nacional Autónoma (UNAN), and Universidad Americana (UAM) all have English departments that may be looking for staff. For more ideas, check out the book, *Work Abroad,* edited by Clay Hubbs, available at www.transitionsabroad.com.

VOLUNTEERING

Nicaragua's poverty and history of social experimentation have always attracted altruistic groups and individual volunteers. Shortly after 1979, hordes of *"Sandalistas"* poured in from around the world to participate in the Sandinista revolution. They picked coffee, taught in schools, wrote poetry and editorials of solidarity, put themselves in the line of fire, and protested in front of the U.S. Embassy. Today, *internacionalistas* come as part of service brigades, government programs, religous missions, academic trips, or independently. Organizations (both faith-based and secular) work throughout the country to assist with construction, education, translation, agriculture, and general solidarity.

Check www.volunteerabroad.com for the most updated listing of available assignments, or inquire about opportunities with the following organizations:

Habitat for Humanity (www.habitat.org) is active building homes throughout Nicaragua. **American Jewish World Service** (www.ajws.com) runs the Jewish Volunteer Corps, providing support for professionals looking to volunteer in Nicaragua and other countries—to practice the Hebrew commandment "to heal the world." And if your social circle wants to participate in a Nicaraguan work trip, **Bridges**

to Community (U.S. tel. 914/923-2200, www. bridgestocommunity.org) will help plan a trip, find a project, and facilitate logistics to connect you with small Nicaraguan communities where your communication, construction, and environmental skills will be put to good use.

Seeds of Learning (www.seedsoflearning. org) is a group based in El Salvador, Ciudad Dario, Nicaragua and northern California; they accept groups of 13 or more to volunteer with a community, help construct a school, and share in Nicaraguan culture; your fee covers living expenses and building materials.

The **Integral Program Educating with Love and Tenderness** (PIEAT, tel. 505/8638-4080, eddycard@yahoo.com or dyoung_pieat@ yahoo.com) is associated with the Americas Association for the Care of Children and is based in Jalapa, Nicaragua. PIEAT is a volunteer association which brings education to primary caregivers (parents, teachers, nurses, therapists) about health, hygiene, education, child development, alternatives to domestic violence, along with 44 other themes. The association hosts delegations or individual travelers in Nicaragua and offers service-learning and Spanish langauge opportunities.

STUDY ABROAD

There are a few possibilities for spending a summer, semester, or extended internship in Nicaragua. Programs range from biological fieldwork at remote research stations to language training and social justice programs. You'll find additional listings at **www. studyabroad.com.**

School for International Training has been running a semester program in Managua for years, entitled "Revolution, Transformation, and Civil Society" (U.S. tel. 888/272-7881, www.sit.edu).

World Leadership School (www.worldleadershipschool.org), based in Denver, Colorado, has extensive experience with international travel, leadership training, and managing student groups overseas and sometimes offers trips for teens in Nicaragua. On La Isla de Ometepe, near the village of San Ramón **Estación**

Biológica de Ometepe (www.lasuerte.org) is a biological field station frequented by student groups and researchers from all over the world. At the **Mariposa Eco-Hotel and Spanish School** (www.spanishschoolnica. com), the owner Paulette Goudge, PhD, offers a three-month course in the "Politics of Development."

SPANISH LANGUAGE SCHOOLS IN NICARAGUA

Nicaragua has a growing network of independent Spanish schools, and an increasing number of visitors to the country choose to combine their travels with a few days, weeks, or even months of language study. With new "schools" (from teenagers in a living room to full-fledged language institutes) popping up all the time, it is increasingly difficult to keep track of them all; we've listed below the schools that stand out for their reputation and experience. Most schools follow the same basic structure, mixing language instruction with cultural immersion: 2–4 hours of class in the morning, community service activities or field trips in the afternoon, and optional homestays with Nicaraguan families.

To a certain extent, choosing a school is as much a question of your geographical preference as anything else, since there are quality schools across the country. If possible, it's a good idea to come down and personally look into a few options before making a long-term commitment. Get a feel for the teachers (ask about their experience and credentials), the professionalism of the business, and the lesson plan. Do not trust everything you see on the websites.

Also, please note that keeping up with prices is difficult in the competitive world of Spanish schools, so always confirm prices. In general, expect to pay around $150–300 per week, depending on the quality of services offered. This usually includes room, board, instruction, and sometimes tours. Schools in the northern regions are generally cheaper. You can create your own language tour by studying at several schools, using your class schedule and

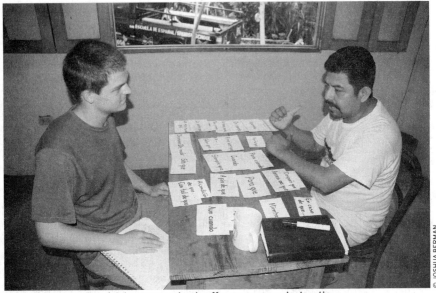

Most Nicaraguan Spanish language schools offer one-on-one instruction.

family homestays as a way to travel throughout Nicaragua.

Once in the classroom, remember that gaining a language takes time—you must learn one word at a time until they start flowing together in sentences and you stop translating everything in your head. Be patient, do your homework, and be ready to laugh at yourself (along with everyone else) as you make mistakes. *¡Suerte!*

Managua

Viva Spanish School (tel. 505/8877-7179 or 505/2270-2339, vivaspanish@btinternet.com, www.vivaspanishschool.com) offers intensive classes to students of all ages and bcakgrounds, catering mainly to NGO members, embassy employees, and missionary workers. The school is located in the heart of Managua, just a couple of blocks from Plaza Metrocentro. Class costs are $90 semi-intensive (10 hrs/week) and $175 intensive program (20 hrs/week). Homestays and other lodging options available. Advanced and specialized classes available as well as online classes and home-office classes.

Granada

Granada's status as ground zero for the Nicaragua tourism scene (from backpackers to upscale) makes it a natural choice for many students who love the city's aesthetic as much as its bar scene. **Casa Xalteva** (across from the church by the same name, tel. 505/2552-2436, www.casaxalteva.com) offers a similar package, $150 per week, with a stress on volunteer activities; it's highly recommended by former students, has a quiet location, and is part of a small group home for boys, which is supported by your tuition.

Roger Ramirez's **One-on-One Spanish Tutoring Academy** (on the Calle Calzada, four blocks west of the central park, tel. 505/2552-6771, oneononetutoring.granada@yahoo.com, www.1on1tutoring.net) offers 20 hours of instruction per week ($110, or hourly for $6), which includes various instructors and five afternoon activities (city tour, salsa lesson, field trips, etc.), plus an end-of-week dinner celebration. Homestays are an additional $85 paid directly to the family.

You'll also find Spanish classes in the patio of **Maverick Reading & Smoothie Lounge,** and in the beautiful **Palacio de Cultura** (tel. 505/2552-7114), in a grand building on the west side of Granada's main plaza.

Los Pueblos Blancos and Carazo

Tucked into the forest off the road to the village of San Juan de la Concepción (also known as La Concha, 12 kilometers west of Ticuantepe, under an hour from Managua), **Mariposa Eco-Hotel and Spanish School** (tel. 505/2418-4638, www.spanishschoolnica.com) offers language classes in an isolated-feeling setting which is only an hour from Managua or Granada; there are views of Volcán Masaya, riding horses, hiking trails, and a library. We've received rave reviews of Mariposa's all-inclusive Spanish school packages ($300/week).

Just outside Jinotepe, **Futuro Mejor** (tel. 505/8871-4705, info@futuromejor.org, www. futuromejor.org) offers room and board, 20 hours of Spanish instruction for $200 a week, and an English-teaching exchange where you can volunteer in associated communities. It's part of a larger project led by a Danish traveler Brian Wolter, who is helping to start a soccer academy.

Laguna de Apoyo

If you prefer to avoid the bustle and nightlife of the city, **Proyecto Ecologico Spanish School and Hostel** (tel. 505/8882-3992, econic@guegue.com, www.gaianicaragua.org) is the only Spanish school in Nicaragua in a purely natural setting—the lakeside lodge is in the crater of an ancient volcano. The spot is incredible, only an hour from Managua, less to Granada, yet still tucked away in its own green world. Lodging and food are excellent (homestays are possible too), and the organization is not-for-profit. One week costs $190 and includes classes, activities, and room and board in their lodge.

San Juan del Sur and Isla de Ometepe

One of the best deals in the country is **Doña Rosa Silva's Spanish School** (located 30 meters west of the Mercado Municipal, tel. 505/8682-2938 or 505/8958-5262, spanish_silva@yahoo.com, www.spanishsilva.com), offering four hours of daily instruction ($100 a week for just lessons, $200 includes homestay and meals). Classes are small (or private, costs a bit more), mix conversation with grammar, and include readings by Nicaragua's best authors and poets. Rosa also has a school on La Isla de Ometepe (in the center of Altagracia, 50 meters east of the mayor's office).

Latin American Spanish School (tel. 505/8820-2252, info@nicaspanish.org, www. nicaspanish.org) is a good option, run by a half dozen entrepreneurial and professional Nicaraguan Spanish instructors with significant experience teaching foreigners. They offer a basic 20-hour instruction and activity package for $120, plus $90 a week for lodging with private bath and three meals a day, plus homestay and volunteer activities.

Across from the BDF bank, in the Lago Azul restaurant (right on the beach!), the **San Juan del Sur Spanish School** (tel. 505/8372-4666, sjdsspanish@yahoo.com, www.sjdsspanish.com) has all-inclusive packages for $200 per week; the teachers are experienced and very friendly. Homestays include private bathroom. They also have opened a sister school in Ometepe.

León

Vapues Tours (tel. 505/2606-2276, www. vapues.com) recently began offering an intensive, full-immersion Spanish course: $195 for 20 hours of one-on-one class (over five days), includes room and board. There are new schools all the time in León. Check the **Casa de Cultura** class schedule, or the bulletin board at the **Vía Vía Hospedaje** for private tutors and lessons.

La Isla Foundation (from Movistar, half a block south, tel. 505/2311-3101, laislafoundation@gmail.com, www.laislafoundation.org)

is a nonprofit organization which offers both English classes to local residents and Spanish immersion courses to international travelers and students in León. Beginner, intermediate, and advanced classes plus opportunities for tours and work exchanges.

Estelí

You'll find a cool climate and a number of natural excursions available at these schools in Estelí, all of which have been around since the early 1990s. **Spanish School Horizonte Nica** (located two blocks east and half a block north of INISER, tel. 505/2713-4117, horizont@ibw. com.ni, www.escuelahorizonte.edu.ni) has one of the longest track records in town and proffers the lofty vision of "promoting peace and social justice for those living in poverty, those struggling against class, race, and gender prejudices, and those fighting for political freedom." It donates part of your $220 weekly fee to local organizations and has an afternoon activity program that includes visits to local cooperatives and community-development programs. Price includes 20 hours of intensive study, afternoon activities, and homestay; service projects sometimes available.

Centro Cultural Juventus (from the southwest corner of the central plaza, two blocks west, tel. 505/2713-3756, walter_delgado_2007@yahoo.com, www.vianica.com/juventus) is a super-*tranquilo* little compound with dorm facilities, nicer rooms, a shared kitchen, and a breezy café with cappuccino and fruit shakes. Various language professors are on hand to tailor your Spanish curriculum; $100 for 20 hours, lodging $35 per week in the dorm or $60 a night for lovely, modern private rooms.

Spanish School Güegüense (six blocks east of the Autolote car lot, , tel. 505/2713-7580) offers afternoon activities, including trips to Jinotega, Quilalí, San Juan del Río Coco, and local Estelí attractions. Class and homestay cost $150 per week.

Matagalpa

This is a remarkable, off-the-beaten-path city in which to spend a few weeks, attending **Spanish School Matagalpa** (tel. 505/2772-0108 or 505/8647-4680, escuela@matagalpa. info, www.matagalpatours.com). As a part of Matagalpa Tours, you'll have immediate access to a range of day trips and backcountry hiking expeditions in the surrounding mountains. The school is conveniently located next door to one of the country's most *suave* cafés, El Artesano.

Health and Safety

BEFORE YOU GO
Resources

Dirk G. Schroeder's *Staying Healthy in Asia, Africa, and Latin America* is an excellent and concise guide to preventative medicine in the Developing World and is small enough to fit in your pocket. Consult the "Mexico and Central America" page of the U.S. Centers for Disease Control (CDC) website for up-to-date health recommendations and advice (www.cdc.gov) or call their International Travelers Hotline (U.S. tel. 404/332-4559 or 877/394-8747). You can also contact the Nicaraguan embassy in your country.

Vaccinations

Required: A certificate of vaccination against yellow fever is required for all travelers over one year of age and arriving from affected areas.
Recommended: Before traveling to Nicaragua, be sure your tetanus, diphtheria, measles, mumps, rubella, and polio vaccines are up-to-date. Protection against hepatitis A and typhoid fever is also recommended for all travelers.

MEDICAL ATTENTION

Medical care is in short supply outside of Managua, and even in the capital city, doctors in public hospitals are underpaid (earning about $200 a month) and brutally overworked. Though there are many qualified medical professionals in Nicaragua who studied abroad in Mexico, Cuba, or the United States, there are also many practicing doctors and medical staff who have less-than-adequate credentials. Use your best judgment. Private hospitals and clinics typically expect immediate payment for services rendered, but their rates are ridiculously cheaper than they are back home. Larger facilities accept credit cards and everyone else demands cash.

Government-run health clinics, called **Centros de Salud,** exist in most towns throughout the country, usually near the central plaza. They are free—even to you—but poorly supplied and inadequately staffed.

We've pointed out the main hospital or private clinic in most regional chapters, but we should also mention here that the most modern hospital in the country is **Hospital Vivian Pellas,** a $23-million private institution seven kilometers south of Managua on the Carretera Masaya. For **dental emergencies,** or even just a check-up, seek out the bilingual services of Dr. Esteban Bendaña McEwan (300 meters south of the ENITEL Villa Fontana, tel. 505/2270-5021 or 505/8850-8981, estebanbm@hotmail.com); Dr. Bendaña is accustomed to dealing with foreign patients and his prices are reasonable.

Natural Medicine

Many *campesinos* have excellent practical knowledge of herbal remedies that involve teas, tree barks, herbs, and fruits. The first medicines came from the earth, and the Nicaraguans haven't lost that connection. Try crushed and boiled papaya seeds, oil of *apazote* (a small shrub whose seed is crushed for medicinal use), or coconut water to fend off intestinal parasites, *manzanilla* (chamomile) for stress or menstrual discomfort, or *tamarindo* or papaya for constipation. A popular cold remedy involves hot tea mixed with two squeezed limes, *miel de jicote* (honey from the *jicote* bee), and a large shot of cheap rum, drunk right before you go to bed so you sweat out the fever as you sleep.

Medications and Prescriptions

Many modern medicines, produced in Mexico or El Salvador, are sold in Nicaragua. Because of a struggling economy and plenty of competition, some pharmacies may sell you medicine without a prescription. For simple travelers' ailments, like stomach upsets, diarrhea, or analgesics, it's worth going to the local pharmacy and asking what they recommend. Even relatively strong medications like codeine can be purchased over the counter (in fizzy tablet form).

Birth Control: Condoms are cheap and easy to find. Any corner pharmacy will have them, even in small towns of just a few thousand people; a three-pack of prophylactics costs less than $2. Female travelers taking contraceptives should know the chemical name for what they use. *Pastillas anticonceptivas* (birth control pills) are easily obtained without prescription in pharmacies in Managua and in larger cities like León, Granada, and Estelí. Other forms of birth control and sexual protection devices, such as IUDs and diaphragms, are neither used nor sold.

STAYING HEALTHY

Ultimately, your health is dependent on the choices you make, and chief among these is what you put in your mouth. One longtime resident says staying healthy in the tropics is more than just possible—it is an "art form." As you master the art, expect your digestive system to take some time getting accustomed to the new food and microorganisms in the Nicaraguan diet. During this time (and after), use common sense: wash or sanitize your hands often. Eat food that is well cooked and still hot when served. Avoid dairy products if you're not sure whether they are pasteurized. Be wary of uncooked foods, including ceviche and salads. Use the finger wag to turn down food from street vendors and be aware that pork carries the extra danger of trichinosis, not to mention a diet of garbage (and worse) on which most country pigs are raised.

Also, be aware of flies as transmitters of food-borne illness. Prevent flies from landing on your food, glass, or table setting. You'll notice Nicaraguans are meticulous about this, and you should be too. If you have to leave the table, cover your food with a napkin or have someone else wave their hand over it slowly. You can fold your drinking straw over and put the mouth end into the neck of the bottle to prevent flies from landing on it, and put napkins on top of the bottle neck and your glass, too. Have the waiter clear the table when you've finished with a dish—and beware the waiter who, in response to your complaints about the flies, comes back and douses you and your dinner in an aerosol cloud of Baygon pesticide.

Sun Exposure

Nicaragua is located a scant 12 degrees of latitude north of the equator, so the sun's rays strike the Earth's surface at a more direct angle than in northern countries. The result is that

When traveling off the beaten track, be prepared for a bucket bath: Randy's daughter, Valentina, cools off in Managua.

© RANDALL WOOD

you will burn faster and sweat up to twice as much as you are used to. Did we mention that you should drink lots of water?

Ideally, do like the majority of the locals do, and stay out of the sun between 10 A.M. and 2 P.M. It's a great time to take a nap anyway. Use sunscreen of at least SPF 30, and wear a hat and pants. Should you overdo it in the sun, make sure to drink lots of fluids—that means water, not beer. Treat sunburns with aloe gel, or better yet—find a fresh *sábila* (aloe) plant to break open and rub over your skin.

Drinking the Water

While most Nicaraguan municipal water systems are well treated and safe (sometimes overcholorinated), there is not much reason to take the chance, especially when purified, bottled water is widely available. But rather than contribute to the growing solid waste problem in Nicaragua, why not bring a single reusable plastic water bottle and refill it in your hotel lobby's five-gallon purified water dispensers? If you are diligent about refilling, it is entirely possible to spend a week or more in Nicaragua drinking purified water without using a single plastic throwaway bottle.

If you'll be spending time in rural Nicaragua, consider a small water filter or, alternately, use six drops of iodine (or three of bleach) in a liter of water; this will kill every organism that needs to be killed, good if you're in a pinch, but not something you'll find yourself practicing on a daily basis. Bringing water to a boil is also an effective means of purification.

Standard precautions include avoiding ice cubes unless you're confident they were made with boiled or purified water (which they are in many restaurants). Canned and bottled drinks without ice, including beer, are safe, but should never be used as a substitute for water when trying to stay hydrated.

Oral Rehydration Salts

Probably the single most effective item you can carry in your medical kit are the packets of powdered salt and sugar known in Spanish as *suero orál*. One packet of *suero* mixed with a

GETTING IN HOT WATER

In the cooler parts of the country, namely Matagalpa and Jinotega, some hotels and *hospedajes* offer hot water by means of electric water-heating canisters attached to the end of the shower head. Cold water passing through the coils is warmed before falling through the spout. The seemingly obvious drawback to the system is the presence of electric wires in and around a wet (i.e., conductive) environment. While not necessarily the electric death traps they appear to be, they should be approached with caution. Before you step into the shower, check for frayed or exposed wires (or the burned carcasses of former hotel occupants on the shower floor). Set the control knob to II and, very carefully, turn the water on. Once you're wet and water is flowing through the apparatus, it's in your best interest not to mess with the heater again.

To save you many cold showers trying to figure out how the darned thing works, we'll let you in on the secret: If the water pressure is too low, the heater isn't triggered on, and the water will not be heated, but if the water pressure is too high, it will be forced through the nozzle before it's had sufficient contact with the coils, and the water will not be heated. Open the faucet to a moderate setting, and rub-a-dub-dub, you're taking a hot shower. When you've finished, turn the water off first and dry off, then turn the little knob back to Off.

often the difference between being just a little sick and feeling really, really awful (we know at least one expat who swears by the stuff for hangovers, too).

Sport drinks like Gatorade are super-concentrated *suero* mixtures and should be diluted at a ratio of three to one with water to make the most of the active ingredients. If you don't, you'll urinate out the majority of the electrolytes. Gatorade is common in most gas stations and supermarkets but *suero* packets are more widely available and much cheaper, available at any drugstore or health clinic for about $0.50 a packet. It can be improvised even more cheaply, according to the following recipe: Mix one-half teaspoon of salt, one-half teaspoon baking soda, and four tablespoons of sugar in one quart of boiled or carbonated water. Drink a full glass of the stuff after each time you use the bathroom. Add a few drops of lemon to make it more palatable.

DISEASE AND COMMON AILMENTS
Diarrhea and Dysentery

Everyone's body reacts differently to the changes in diet, schedule, and stress that go along with traveling, and many visitors to Nicaragua stay entirely regular throughout their trip. Some don't. Diarrhea is one symptom of amoebic (parasitic) and bacillic (bacterial) dysentery, both caused by some form of fecal-oral contamination. Often accompanied by nausea, vomiting, and a mild fever, dysentery is easily confused with other diseases, so don't try to self-diagnose. *Examenes de heces* (stool-sample examinations) can be performed at most clinics and hospitals and are your first step to getting better (cost is $2–8). Bacillic dysentery is treatable with antibiotics; amoebic is treated with one of a variety of drugs that kill off all the flora in your intestinal tract. Of these, Flagyl is the best known, but other non–FDA approved treatments like Tinedazol are commonly available, cheap, and effective. Do not drink alcohol with these drugs, but do eat something like yogurt or acidophilus pills to refoliate your tummy.

liter of water, drunk in small sips, is the best immediate treatment for all of the following: diarrhea, sun exposure, fever, infection, or hangovers. Rehydration salts are essential to your recovery as they replace the salts and minerals your body loses from sweating, vomiting, or urinating, thus aiding your body's most basic cellular transfer functions. Whether or not you like the taste (odds are you won't), consuming enough *suero* and water is very

Generally, simple cases of diarrhea in the absence of other symptoms are nothing more serious than "traveler's diarrhea." If you do get a case of Diriangén's Revenge, your best bet is to let it pass naturally. Diarrhea is your body's way of flushing out the bad stuff, so constipating medicines like Imodium-AD are not recommended, as they keep the bacteria (or whatever is causing your intestinal distress) within your system. Save the Imodium (or any other liquid glue) for emergency situations like long bus rides or a date with Miss Nicaragua. Most importantly, drink water! Not replacing the fluids and electrolytes you are losing will make you feel much worse than you need to. If the diarrhea persists for more than 48 hours, is bloody, or is accompanied by a fever, see a health professional immediately.

Malaria

Risk of malaria is higher in rural areas, especially those alongside rivers or marshes, but malaria-infected mosquitoes breed anywhere stagnant pools of water (of any size, even in an empty bottle cap) are found, including urban settings. At times, western Nicaragua is declared malaria-free, at other times, the U.S. CDC recommends weekly prophylaxis of chloroquine, specifically Aralen-brand pills (500 mg for adults). Begin taking the pills two weeks before you arrive and continue taking them four weeks after leaving the country. A small percentage of people have negative reactions to chloroquine, including nightmares, rashes, or hair loss. Alternative treatments are available, but the best method of all is to not get bitten.

The malaria bacterium (there are four different kinds) settle in your liver and begin replicating; the bacteria invades your red blood cells and causes them to burst, producing the telltale symptoms of fever followed by chills, fever, and even nausea and vomiting on a 24 hours good/24 hours bad cycle. If you observe this pattern, seek medical attention immediately, as failure to treat malaria promptly is the primary cause for the disease becoming dangerous. They'll most likely take a blood test and if it tests positive, prescribe you a huge dose of chloroquine. Allow time to recover your strength.

Dengue Fever

Dengue ("bone-breaking") fever is the only thing we can think of that's worse than malaria. You know have it if you truly believe you will die, and you feel relief that death will make the pain stop. You probably are *not* going to die of course (unless you contract the

---

¿DONDE ESTÁ EL BAÑO? A GUIDE TO NICARAGUA'S TOILETS

Nicaragua boasts an enormous diversity of bathrooms, from various forms of the common *inodoro* (modern toilet, a.k.a. *el trono*) to the full range of dark, infested *letrinas* (outhouses). Despite so many options, many regions of Nicaragua suffer a shortage of actual toilet seats, so having to squat over a bare bowl is common. Because water supplies are sometimes sporadic, even in cities, you may occasionally be forced to take a bucket bath and or employ a manual toilet flush. Mastering this move is important. Use the plastic bucket that should be sitting beside the toilet and dump the water into the bowl, all at once, forcefully and from high up to ensure maximum turd swirlage.

In most mid-range and expensive hotels, you can probably safely flush your toilet paper, but the norm in Nicaragua is still to put used toilet paper in the waste basket next to the toilet, *not* in the bowl, so as not to clog up the weak plumbing. Sure, it's gross, but you'll get used to it. It's never a bad idea to travel with a roll or two of store-bought toilet paper (*papel higiénico*) protected in a plastic bag and easily accessible. Otherwise, try the following phrase with your host: *"Señor, fijase que no hay papel en el baño."*

LAND MINES IN NICARAGUA

Nicaragua has the ignominious honor of having had more land mines – more than 135,000 in place and another 136,000 stockpiled in the wilds of the northeast – than any other country in the Western Hemisphere. This is one of the most brutal and pernicious legacies of the conflicts of the 1980s, and the focus of a major de-mining cleanup effort by the Nicaraguan Army and the Organization of American States (OAS). In fact, no other country in the world is making a greater effort than Nicaragua to clear the land of mines.

The de-mining process, though ongoing, can largely be considered a success: Since the beginning of operations, 75 percent of installed antipersonnel mines have been located and destroyed, and more than 3.8 million square meters of minefield have returned to productive use. The de-mining effort takes place in six-month modules that concentrate on known trouble spots, during which specially trained troops and dogs trained to sniff out explosives comb the territory. After every square meter has been checked for explosives, the region is certified mine-free. The weapons, when uncovered in the field, are detonated on-site. Stockpiles are transferred to and destroyed at one of two special detonating zones: the Escuela de Sargentos Andres Castro outside Managua and the ENABI army base a few kilometers south of Condega, Estelí.

There are currently four areas where OAS troops are actively searching for and destroying land mines: outside of Matagalpa and Jinotega, outside of Murra (Nueva Segovia), and the lands around Jalapa (Nueva Segovia). Both Sandinista and Contra troops mined Nueva Segovia heavily during their repeated confrontations, and, in 1998, flooding and mudslides caused by Hurricane Mitch washed many known minefields downstream, burying other sites under a layer of earth.

Since 2002, OAS troops have been combing the Honduran border from Las Sabanas (Madriz, just south of Somoto) through Jalapa to Wamblán, Jinotega, a distance of nearly 150 kilometers. The department of Chinandega and the border with Costa Rica were declared free of mines in late 2001, and the Río San Juan in 2002.

Antipersonnel explosives have crippled nearly a thousand Nicaraguans and injured countless more (to this day, about 20 people per year). More frequent still are losses of cattle, which go unreported but are the subject of many a *campesino* story. For this reason, an intensive education campaign aimed at the *campesinos* in the affected areas employs comic books with a story line discussing the danger of land mines and what to do if you suspect you've found one.

What does the presence of land mines mean to the traveler? That you should ask a lot of questions if you leave the beaten trail, particularly in the north: Nueva Segovia, Jinotega, Matagalpa, and Jalapa, as well as eastern parts of Boaco. Loose mines don't lie scattered randomly in the hillsides; they were placed at strategic locations, like radio towers, bridges, air strips, and known Contra border crossings. The locals are your best sources of information. They'll be able to tell you if there were battles or heavy Contra presence in the area, if there are known minefields, and if the OAS teams have already passed through. In towns like El Cuá and Bocay, you'll find parcels of land in chest-high weeds even though the land on both sides is intensely farmed. Ask around, and look for the yellow Area Minada signs, then move on.

Numerous international organizations work both to clear minefields around the world, such as the UN-sponsored Adopt-a-Minefield program (www.landmines.org), and to ban the devices (www.icbl.org).

rare hemorrhagic strain of dengue), but you're going to suffer royally. The symptoms may include any or all of the following: sudden high fever, severe headache (think of nails in the back of your eyes), muscle and back pain, nausea or vomiting, and a full-bodied skin rash, which may appear 3–4 days after the onset of the fever. Although the initial pain and fever may only last a few days, you may be out of commission for up to several weeks, possibly bedridden, depressed, and too weak to move. There is no vaccine, but dengue's effects can be successfully minimized with plenty of rest, Tylenol (for the fever and aches), and as much water and *suero* as you can manage. Dengue itself is undetectable in a blood test, but a low platelet *(plaquetas)* count indicates its presence. If you believe you have dengue, you should get a blood test as soon as possible to make sure it's not the rare hemorrhagic variety, which can be fatal if untreated.

HIV and AIDS

Although to date Nicaragua has been spared a major HIV outbreak, health professionals estimate that geography, cultural, political, and social factors mean an outbreak isn't far off. Currently, there are about 1,500 HIV-positive cases registered with MINSA (the Government Health Ministry), but one World Bank official estimated actual cases at 8,000. Exacerbating the spread of AIDS (SIDA in Spanish) is the promiscuous behavior of many married males, an active sex-worker trade, poor use of condoms, and growing drug trouble. AIDS is most prevalent in urban populations, mainly Managua and Chinandega, and is primarily transmitted sexually, rather than through needles or contaminated blood.

We don't recommend you have a blood transfusion, obviously, but furthermore, travelers should avoid sexual contact with persons whose HIV status is unknown. If you intend to be sexually active, use a fresh latex condom for every sexual act and every orifice. Condoms are inexpensive and readily available in just about any local pharmacy; in Spanish, a condom is called *condón* or *preservativo*.

Other Diseases

Cholera is present in Nicaragua, with occasional outbreaks, especially in rural areas with contaminated water supplies. Vaccines are not required because they offer incomplete protection. You are better off watching what you put in your mouth. In case you contract cholera (the symptoms are profuse diarrhea the color of rice water accompanied by sharp intestinal cramps, vomiting, and body weakness), see a doctor immediately and drink your *suero:* Cholera kills by dehydrating you.

Leptospirosis is caused by a bacteria found in water contaminated with the urine of infected animals, especially rodents. Symptoms include high fever and headache, chills, muscle aches, vomiting, and possibly jaundice. Humans become infected through contact with infected food, water, or soil. It is not known to spread from person to person and can be treated with antibiotics in its early stages.

Hepatitis B also lurks in Nicaragua. Avoid contact with bodily fluids or bodily waste. Get vaccinated if you anticipate close contact with the local population or plan to reside in Nicaragua for an extended period of time.

Most towns in Nicaragua, even rural ones, conduct a yearly **rabies**-vaccination campaign for dogs, but you should still be careful. Get a rabies vaccination if you intend to spend a long time in Nicaragua. Should you be bitten, immediately cleanse the wound with lots of soap, and get prompt medical attention.

Tuberculosis is spread by sneezing or coughing, and the infected person may not know he or she is a carrier. If you are planning to spend more than four weeks in Nicaragua (or plan on spending time in a Nicaraguan jail), consider having a tuberculin skin test performed before and after visiting. Tuberculosis is a serious and possibly fatal disease but can be treated with several medications.

BITES AND STINGS
Mosquitoes

Mosquitoes (Nicas refer to them as *zancudos*) are most active during the rainy season (June–November) and in areas near stagnant water, like marshes, puddles, or rice fields. They are much more common in the lower, flatter regions of Nicaragua than they are in mountains, though even in the highlands and major urban areas, old tires, cans, and roadside puddles can provide the habitat necessary to produce swarms of them. The mosquito that carries malaria bites during the night and evening hours, and the dengue fever carrier is active during the day, from dawn to dusk. They are both relatively simple to combat, and ensuring you don't get bitten is the best prophylaxis for preventing disease.

First and foremost, limit the amount of skin you expose: long sleeves, pants, and socks will do more to prevent bites than the strongest chemical repellent. Choose lodging accommodations with good screens and if this is not possible, use a fan to blow airborne insects away from your body as you sleep. Avoid being outside or unprotected in the hour before sunset, when mosquito activity is heaviest, and use a *mosquitero* (mosquito net) tucked underneath your mattress when you sleep. Hanging-type mosquito nets are available in Nicaragua, or you can purchase *tela de mosquitero* anywhere they sell fabric and have a mosquito net made by a seamstress. Also, many *pulperías* sell *espirales* (mosquito coils), which burn slowly, releasing a mosquito-repelling smoke; they're cheap and convenient, but full of chemicals, so don't breathe in too much smoke.

Spiders, Scorpions, and Snakes

Arachnophobes, beware! The spiders of Nicaragua are dark, hairy, and occasionally capable of devouring small birds. Of note is the *pica-caballo*, a kind of tarantula whose name (meaning horse-biter) refers to the alleged power of its flesh-rotting venom to destroy a horse's hoof. Don't worry, though; spiders do not aggressively seek out people, and do way more good than harm by eating things like Chagas bugs. If you'd rather the spiders didn't share your personal space, shake out your bedclothes before going to sleep and check your shoes before putting your feet in them.

Scorpions (*alacránes*) are common in

Nicaragua, especially in dark corners, beaches, and piles of wood. Nicaraguan scorpions look nasty—black and big—but their sting is no more harmful than that of a bee and is described by some as what a cigarette burn feels like. Your lips and tongue may feel a little numb, but the venom is nothing compared to their smaller, translucent cousins in Mexico. For people who are prone to anaphylactic shock, it can be a more serious or life-threatening experience. Be aware, in Nicaragua the Spanish word *escorpión* usually refers not to scorpions but to the harmless little geckos (also called *perros zompopos*) that scurry around walls eating small insects. And in spite of what your *campesino* friends might insist, those little geckos are neither malevolent nor deadly and would never, as you will often hear, intentionally try to kill you by urinating on you.

There are 15 species of poisonous snakes in Nicaragua, but your chance of seeing one is extremely rare, unless you're going deep into the bush. In that case, walk softly and carry a big machete. Keep an eye out for 1 of 11 pit viper species (family *Viperidae*), especially the infamous fer-de-lance *(Bothrops asper),* or *Barba amarilla;* the most aggressive and dangerous snake in Central America, the fer-de-lance is mostly confined to the humid central highlands and the Caribbean coast. Less common pit vipers, but occasionally seen in western parts of the country, are the Ponzigua *(Porthidium ophryomegas);* the Central American rattlesnake *(Crotalus durissus),* known in Spanish as *cascabel;* and a relative of the copperhead, the Cantil, or Castellana, *(Agkistrodon bilineatus).* In addition, there are four rarely seen species of the *Elapidae* family (three coral snakes and the pelagic sea snake). Remember, there are many coral mimics out there with various versions of the famous colored markings; the true coral (only one species of which is found on the west side of the country) has ring markings in only this order: red, yellow, black, yellow.

Chagas' Disease

The Chagas bug *(Trypanosoma cruzi)* is a large, recognizable insect, also called the kissing bug, assassin bug, and cone-nose. In Spanish it's known as *chinche,* but this word is also used for many other types of beetlelike creatures. The Chagas bug bites its victim (usually on the face, close to the lips), sucks its fill of blood, and, for the coup de grâce, defecates on the newly created wound. Chagas bugs are present in Nicaragua, found mostly in poor *campesino* structures of crumbling adobe. Besides the downright insult of being bitten, sucked, and pooped on, the Chagas bug's biggest menace is the disease it carries of the same name, which manifests itself in 2 percent of its victims. The first symptoms include swollen glands and a fever that appear 1–2 weeks after the bite. The disease then goes into a 5- to 30-year remission phase. If and when it reappears, Chagas' disease causes the lining of the heart to swell, sometimes resulting in death. There is no cure.

CRIME

Believe it or not, Nicaragua was considered one of the safer countries in all of Latin America for a few years, though tourism-related crime like petty theft and scam artists (and the occasional robbery and assault) sometimes occur, usually at night and involving alcohol. There have also been some problems with carjackings by criminals posing as police. For the moment, Nicaragua has *mostly* escaped the gang violence that has plagued the cities of Guatemala, El Salvador, and Honduras.

The single biggest area of concern when it comes to security in Nicaragua is the country's place in the Colombia–U.S. drug route. Smugglers, mafiosos, dealers, and crackheads are found along the Atlantic coast, where rising drug-related crimes threaten the very fabric of some communities. The Corn Islands have experienced several rapes, including violent ones, and San Juan del Sur experienced a wave of violence in 2008 that was excessive by any standards, including a kidnapping. The Tipitapa–Masaya highway, formerly a convenient shortcut for going from the airport to Granada while avoiding Managua, is increasingly dangerous at night as it is the scene of

fake "police inspections" that end up with foreign tourists being forced to go from ATM to ATM, withdrawing cash.

Before traveling, check official reports, including the U.S. State Department's warnings at www.travel.state.gov and the travel forums at www.gotonicaragua.com. Managua is clearly the city with the most crime, but bigger cities, like Estelí and Chinandega have neighborhoods you should skip as well (ask at your hotel to get the most updated local info). Avoid traveling alone, especially in remote areas including beaches, at night or while intoxicated, and pay the extra dollar or two for a cab. No one should take a cab when the driver has a friend riding up front—complain loudly if he tries—and pay attention to your surroundings and where you are going. You are most at risk of pick-pocketing (or hat/watch/bag snatching) in crowds and on public transport: avoid urban buses in Managua. Keep a low profile and leave your flashy jewelry, watches, and expensive sunglasses at home. Keep your cash divided up and hidden in a money belt, sock, or your undergarments (take a cue from the many Nica women pulling soggy *córdoba* bills out of their cleavage).

If you are the victim of a crime, report it immediately to the local police department (dial 118), at a minimum because your insurance company back home will require an official police report before reimbursing you. Nicaraguan police have good intentions but few resources, lacking even gasoline for the few patrol cars or motorcycles they have—don't be surprised if you are asked to help fill up a vehicle with gas. This is annoying but not uncommon, and chipping in for $20 of gas will help them get the job done, which they often do! While police corruption does exist—Nicaraguan police earn a pitiful $55–60 per month—the Nicaraguan police force is notably more honest and helpful than in some Central American nations, and has gotten more professional during the Ortega administration.

Illegal Drugs

Nicaragua is part of the underground highway

that transports cocaine and heroin from South America to North America and, as such, is under a lot of pressure from the United States to crack down on drug traffickers passing through in vehicles or in boats off the Atlantic coast. Drug-related crime is rapidly increasing on the Atlantic coast, particularly in Bluefields and Puerto Cabezas. All travelers in Nicaragua are subject to local drug-possession and use laws, which include stiff fines and prison sentences of up to 30 years.

Marijuana thrives in Nicaragua's climate and conditions. It is known locally as *la mota, el monte,* or, in one remote Matagalpa valley, *pim-pirim-pím.* It is officially prohibited despite popular usage, and the current laws allow harsh penalties for possession of even tiny quantities of *cannabis sativa,* for both nationals and tourists alike. Canine and bag searches at airports, docks along the Atlantic coast, and at the Honduran and Costa Rican border crossings are the norm, not the exception.

As a foreign, hip-looking tourist, you may be offered pot at some point during your trip, especially on the Atlantic coast and in San Juan del Sur. The proposal may be a harmless invitation to get high on the beach, or it may be from a hustler or stool pigeon who is about to rip you off and/or get you arrested. Use the same common sense you would anywhere in the world.

Prostitution

The world's oldest profession nearly tripled in practicioners from 2000–2005, especially in Managua, Granada, Corinto, and border/trucking towns like Somotillo. Since then, flagrant prostitution at roadside has been curbed, forcing the trade underground again. Though illegal, *puterías* (whorehouses), thinly disguised as "beauty salons" or "massage parlors," operate with virtual impunity, and every strip club in Managua has a bank of rooms behind the stage, some with an actual cashier stationed at the door. Then there are the commercial sex workers on Carretera Masaya, and the nation's numerous auto-

hotels, which rent rooms by the hour. The situation is nowhere near as developed as the sex tourism industries of places like Thailand and Costa Rica, but it is undeniable that foreigners have contributed in no small way to Nicaragua's sex economy. Travelers considering indulging should think seriously about the social impacts that result from perpetuating this institution, and should start by reading the section on AIDS in this chapter.

BEGGING

It is generally assumed that foreigners with the leisure time to travel to Nicaragua have lots and lots of money, no matter the actual size of your bank account or how much you scraped and saved for your trip. Expect poor children and adults to occasionally ask you for spare change wherever you travel, usually by either a single outstretched index finger or a cupped, empty hand, both accompanied with an insistent, *"Chele, deme un peso"* ("Whitey, give me a coin," though in Granada, this has evolved into *"deme un dolar"*). It's low-key, nothing like the aggressive beggars in India, so don't be worried or afraid. Another poignant sight, encountered at sidewalk restaurants and market eateries, are wide-eyed, hungry children watching as eagerly as the skeletal dogs standing behind them as you finish your meal. Your leftovers will not go to waste here as they would at home—a small concession. In many cities, including Granada, many children and adolescents asking for money are *huele-pegas* (glue sniffers) and your money will only go to buy them more of H. B. Fuller's finest. *Huele-pegas* are identified by glazed eyes, unkempt appearances, and sometimes a jar of glue tucked under a dirty shirt. Do not give them money, but feel free to give them some time, attention, and maybe a little food. In general, giving money to beggars, especially in tourist centers, is a bad idea which perpetuates dependency, bad habits, and children skipping school (sometimes at their parents' request) to ply tourists for coins and dollars. There are many other ways to direct your good intentions.

Information and Services

MONEY
Currency

Since 1912, Nicaragua's currency has been the *córdoba*, named after Francisco Hernández de Córdoba, the Spanish founder of the colony of Nicaragua. It is divided into 100 *centavos* or 10 *reales*. In common usage, the *córdoba* is also referred to as a *peso*. The U.S. dollar is also an official currency in Nicaragua and the only foreign currency you can hope to exchange (although many communities along the Río San Juan also use Costa Rican *colones*).

Under the Sandinistas, inflation ran to 30,000 percent. These days the córdoba is better managed and essentially stable, but to offset inflation, it is being steadily devalued at the rate of approximately US$0.37 every six months. You can do the arithmetic yourself before arriving in Nicaragua (the exchange rate is currently hovering around 20 *córdobas* to 1 dollar, making for simple calculations), or find the actual rates at the Central Bank of Nicaragua's website, www.bcn.gob.ni.

In 2003, a new C$500 bill was introduced, and in 2007 the ratty old paper bills were phased out in lieu of crisp, newly designed currency that feels a bit like there's some plastic wrap mixed in with the paper. Be careful about confusing the C$20 and C$200 bills.

U.S. Dollars and ATMs

Since this book was first published in 2002, two things have made money management a lot easier: widespread use of U.S. dollars, and dramatically increased prevalance of ATMs. Travelers should bring U.S. dollars, preferably, or euros otherwise, as hardly any other currencies can be exchanged in Nicaragua, including those of the neighboring countries (exchange

© JOSHUA BERMAN

It is usually okay to use the licensed money changers you'll find on the street corners, often in front of banks.

your Costa Rican or Honduran currency on the border before entering). Make sure your greenbacks are good quality, as ripped, tattered bills may be refused.

While it's easier to change money and travel using *córdobas,* virtually any merchant will take dollars these days, and give you the bank rate (which means you too need to know what the bank rate is, just to be sure) as change; they usually have trouble breaking anything bigger than a twenty-dollar bill. ATMs, known in Spanish as *cajeros automáticos,* litter all major cities and bigger gas stations; you won't find them outside of the cities though, so plan accordingly. They dispense both *córdoba* (unfortunately, often in the larger, C$500 denominations) and U.S. dollars, and take cards from the Cirrus and Star networks, plus most Visa and Mastercards. Of course you will pay a bank fee for each withdrawal, but it's worth it. You cannot rely on just one card, as some establishments will accept Visa but not MasterCard, or the opposite. And make sure you have photocopied front and back of your cards and stashed the page somewhere safe, in case they are stolen; likewise, inform your credit card companies you will be traveling in Nicaragua so they don't balk and block your card, thinking the sudden spate of charges in Nicaragua indicate theft.

Travelers Checks

Travelers checks are nearly impossible to change in banks, and at exceedingly bad rates. Travelers checks for currencies other than U.S. dollars will not be cashed. You will need to show your passport to cash travelers checks, and be sure that your signature matches your previous one or you'll convert your precious dollars into a worthless piece of paper. Some banks actually demand to see your original receipts (the ones you are supposed to keep physically separate from the checks!). If you truly get stuck, every Nicaraguan city has a branch of Western Union, permitting family back home can wire you money, for a steep fee (up to 25 percent).

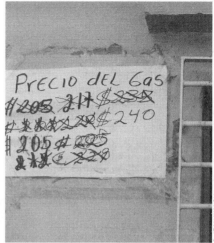

© JEAN WALSH

The cost of living is always on the rise.

Bank Hours

Unless noted otherwise in this book, all bank hours are 8:30 A.M.–4 P.M. Monday–Friday and 8:30–noon Saturday. Nicaraguans receive their pay on the 15th and 30th or 31st of every month (*días de pago* are the best nights to go out dancing in Managua and beyond). Should you need to go to a bank on those days, you can expect the lines to be extra long. Bide your time by watching businesspeople carry away large sums of cash in brown paper lunch bags.

Costs and Your Travel Budget

Nicaragua remains a budget travel destination, with generally cheaper prices across the board than nearby Costa Rica and Belize. You can comfortably exist in Nicaragua on $50 per day, or half of that by eating the way the locals do and forgoing the jalapeño steak and beer. Budget travelers interested in stretching their money to the maximum should eat at *fritangas* and market stalls, take the slow bus, and stay at the simplest *hospedajes*. In Granada, León, and Managua, you can now choose to pay $50–150 for a room, so budget accordingly if you prefer extra comforts (like air-conditioning, security, and cleanliness).

Sales Tax

Nicaragua's sales tax (IGV or Impuesto General de Valor) is a whopping 15 percent—the highest in Central America. You'll find it automatically applied to the bill at nicer restaurants, fancy hotels, and upscale shops in major cities: check on your receipt, where it should be clearly indicated. Elsewhere, sales tax is casually dismissed. Should you decide to splurge on a fancy dinner (places where you'd expect to spend more than $6–10 a meal), expect to pay 25 percent of your bill for tax and tip. Prices in this book usually do not include the IGV. If a hotel does not charge you this tax, they (and you) are breaking the law.

Tipping

In better restaurants, a 10–15 percent *propina* (tip) will be graciously added on to your bill, even if the food was undercooked, the beer flat, and the service atrocious. You are under no obligation to pay it if it is unmerited. You might want to give a little something after getting your hair cut: 10 percent is appropriate. Skycaps at the International Airport in Managua will jostle to carry your luggage out to a waiting taxi for about $2. Taxi drivers and bartenders are rarely tipped and don't expect to be unless they are exceptionally friendly or go out of their way for you. If you accept the offer of children trying to carry your bags, find you a hotel, or anything else, you have entered into an unspoken agreement to give them a few *córdobas:* (5–20 *córdobas* or $1 or less).

Bargaining

Looking for a good deal is a sport in Nicaragua—half social, half business, and is expected with most outdoor market vendors and taxi drivers. But be warned: Bargaining in Nicaragua is *al suave!* Aggressive, prolonged haggling is not cool, won't affect the price, and may leave ill feelings. To start off the process, after you are given the initial price, act surprised and use one of the following phrases: *"¿Cuánto es lo menos?"* ("What is your lowest price?") or *"¿Nada menos?"* ("Nothing less?").

Remember these guidelines when bargaining:

- Bargaining is social and friendly, or at least courteous. Keep your temper under wraps and always smile.

- Go back and forth a maximum of two or three times, and then either agree or walk away. Remember that some Nicaraguans, to save face, may lose a profit.

- Once you make a deal, it's done. If you think you've been ripped off, remember the $2 you got overcharged is still less than you'd pay for a double-tall mocha latte back home. Keep it in perspective and be a good sport.

- When bargaining with taxi drivers in Managua, bargain hard, but agree on a price *before* you enter the cab—once the vehicle is moving, your leverage has vanished in a puff of acrid, black exhaust.

MAPS

The longtime champion map of Nicaragua is published by **International Travel Map** (ITM, www.itmb.com), scaled at 1:750,000, colored to show relief, and with good road and river detail. They also offer an excellent Central America regional map. It's found in many bookstores and travel shops, but not in Nicaragua.

A new favorite is produced by German cartographers **Mapas NaTurismo** (salsa_klaus@yahoo.de, www.mapas-naturismo.com). Their gorgeous 1:500,000 country map is water resistant and features detailed tourist attractions and natural reserves better than any other; it also has a few handy inserts, including Isla de Ometepe at 1:200,000; samples available on their site and they are currently producing city maps of Masaya and Granada, and a regional map of Managua to Rivas. They go for about $7 at www.omnimap.com or www.gotrekkers.com.

The **Nelles Central America** map (1:1,750,000) offers a quality overview of the region (plus more detail on Costa Rica) and is good if you are traveling the whole area

BUYING REAL ESTATE IN NICARAGUA: CAVEAT EMPTOR

For better or worse, Nicaragua is the latest tropical country chosen by international speculators with hopes of carefree retirement and lucrative appreciation on their new plot of Central American soil. A steady stream of aging baby boomers, aspiring financial managers, and alcoholic ne'er-do-wells on the run from ex-spouses and the tax man continue to find their way to southwestern Nicaragua. Healthy foreign investment? Or the new face of Yankee imperialism? You decide.

Potential real estate moguls typically wind up in Granada (and its nearby *isletas*), Rivas, and San Juan del Sur, all of which buzz with both independent and corporate real estate agents of mostly U.S. and Canadian origin. Before signing that check, however, take a breath, open your eyes, and ask a lot of questions. Start by visiting your embassy. The U.S. Embassy (www.usembassy.state.gov) has made land reform a priority for its relations with the Nicaraguan government; experienced buyers also seek out Pro-Nicaragua (www. pronicaragua.org), an "Investment Promotion Agency" that can help with information and contacts. We also recommend the companion volume to this book, by the same authors: *Moon Living Abroad in Nicaragua.*

Good deals are still found, but not without some risk. Much of the valued property that is up for grabs has two distinct and viable chains of title ownership: one that dates back to the Somoza period, and one that dates to the Sandinista government's failed agrarian reforms in which they confiscated land,

Robin Hood-style, and redistributed it to the masses. Some of this land is still owned by cooperatives and *campesino* families, and some was given to powerful supporters (and leaders) of the Sandinistas. In the aftermath of the revolution, many of these seizures have been contested, many still stand, and very frequently two or three people present legitimate claims to the same lot. Make sure you – and your lawyer – know the history of the property back to 1978, and consider buying title insurance. More than one new land owner has been surprised to have a stranger confront him with an obviously falsified property title. The Nicaraguan court system may or may not back you up. In the case of contested property, your policy may cover fraud and forgery.

Don't completely entrust the job to others – do your own research on the region, the lot, community relations, year-round road conditions, etc. Was an environmental-impact statement done, as is required by law? If so, what did it conclude? Does your new piece of paradise have a freshwater supply? Lastly, watch out for the word "beachfront". Under Nicaraguan law, land 30-80 meters from the high tide line (depending on who you ask) cannot be bought or sold, but only leased from either the national government or the local municipality as a "concession." Newly elected municipal governments (i.e., small-town mayors with grudges) often change policies on concessions, frustrating many a would-be gringo beach bum.

and don't intend to venture too far off the beaten track.

INETER, the Nicaraguan Institute of Territorial Studies, produces the only complete series of 1:50,000 maps (or topo quads) of Nicaragua, now available online at www. ineter.gob.ni. Produced in the 1960s and photo-revised in the 1980s with Soviet help, these are the most detailed topographical maps

of Nicaragua that exist. They can be purchased from the INETER office in Managua (and occasionally at regional offices) for $3 each. The Managua office is located across from Policlinica Oriental and Immigration (tel. 505/2249-2768, open 8 A.M.–4:30 P.M. Mon.–Fri.).

Tactical Pilotage Charts (TPC K-25B and TPC K-25C) cover northern and southern

TOUR OPERATORS

Nicaragua's range of independent tour companies offer a variety of trips, from afternoon city tours to week-long expeditions to the farthest reaches of the country, the logistics of which would be nearly impossible for the solo traveler. You can pay for exclusive personal guides and drivers, or visit Nicaragua as part of a group. Doing so decreases your independence, but provides added security and freedom from making plans. In general, all-inclusive nine-day tours cost $1,000-2,000, but each company varies. Following are the most reliable outfitters we've found.

TOUR OPERATORS

Tours Nicaragua (tel. 505/2265-3095, info@toursnicaragua.com, www.ToursNicaragua.com) offers private, fully guided trips using the best hotels in each locale. Their expert guides include working biologists, national museum archaeologists, historians, etc. Customize your own learning trip by asking to meet with current political figures, artists, or ex-combatants from both sides of the Contra war, for example.

Nicaragua Adventures (tel. 505/2552-8461, info@nica-adventures.com, www.nica-adventures.com) is a full-service, very professional Granada-based outfit with a wide range of services including tailor-made package tours and private transportation (car and drivers, rentals, etc.). They can also help book your La Costeña flight within the country.

Explore Nicaragua Tours (U.S. tel. 800/800-1132, www.explorenicaragua.com) has 15 years of experience leading both individual and group tours in Nicaragua and staying at top properties; included in your price is a personal cell phone and bottled water.

Solentiname Tours (tel. 505/8421-5689 or 505/2270-9981, info@solentinametours.com, www.solentinametours.com) has offices in Managua and San Carlos, and specializes in bird-watching, nature tours, and the Río San Juan region.

Vapues Tours (tel. 505/2315-4999, info@vapues.com, www.vapues.com) has offices around the country and offers a huge range of reasonably priced trips, plus shuttle services between cities. They have some unique community tourism connections and lots of experience with groups and packages.

Tierra Tours (tel. 505/2311-0599, tierratour@gmail.com, http://tierratour.com) has offices in Granada and León, and has a long menu of volcano or history tours, countrywide all-inclusive packages, international bus tickets, and domestic flight booking.

ALTERNATIVE TOUR OPERATORS AND CAMPING TRIPS

Be sure to read regional chapters for information on local, specialist tour guides, and unique

---

Nicaragua, respectively, with some coverage of Costa Rica, Panamá, and Honduras at 1:500,000 scale. Designed for pilots, these maps have good representation of topography and are useful if you do any adventuring in the eastern parts of the country (far easier than carrying a stack of topo maps). Many smaller towns are shown, but only major roads.

TOURISM INFORMATION

Begin with our website **www.GoToNicaragua.com,** where you can ask the authors of *Moon*

Nicaragua—and your fellow travelers—about specific concerns regarding Nicaragua travel.

The **Instituto Nicaragüense de Turismo** (INTUR, one block west and one north of the Crowne Plaza Hotel, tel. 505/2222-3333, www.intur.gob.ni, open 8:30 A.M.–2 P.M. Mon.–Fri.) has a sometimes-useful kiosk in the airport arrival area (just before you claim your baggage). The regional offices can give you a list of the year's upcoming festivals, a fistful of brochures, and can sometimes help arrange tours with local operators. Also visit their tourist-directd site www.visitanicaragua.com.

trip offerings (León is particularly rich in this department). There are also a few small companies operating across the country:

¡Un Buen Viaje! (U.S. tel. 612/386-0839, info@ToursToNicaragua.com, www.ToursToNicaragua.com) is a unique grassroots tour company started by former Peace Corps volunteer Jessica Schugel. "You'll meet people who live, work, and play in the places we visit. We'll visit their homes and communities. You'll learn about Nicaragua from the inside out, through the voices of its people, its complex history, and rich culture."

Nicadventure (tel. 505/2532-2344, info@nicadventure.net, www.nicadventure.net) is a Nicaraguan-run tour company based about 1 hour from Managua in Jinotepe, Carazo. They specialize in adventure (volcanos, jungles, etc.), custom trips, or packages focusing on history, geography, culture, heritage, and food.

Eco Camp Expeditions (tel. 505/8400-0455 or 505/2311-2219, geraldpavn@gmail.com, www.ecocampexpeditions.blogspot.com) is a locally owned and operated agency that specializes in overnight camping trips. We like to take people to unique, hidden locations that most others tend to miss. They offer multiday expeditions to volcanos, beaches, lagoons, and organic farms. Prices are very reasonable ($35-80 per day; guide, food, camping gear and transportation included).

Roadmonkey Adventure Philanthropy (www.roadmonkey.net) expeditions combine physically challenging adventures with sustainable, custom-designed volunteer projects that team members finish on site, working with Nicaraguan communities in need.

Wildland Adventures (tel. 800/345-4453, www.wildland.com) has a number of both family-oriented and experiential trip offerings, with many knowledgeable Nica guides on their staff.

REALITY TOURS AND LEARNING DELEGATIONS

Global Exchange (www.globalexchange.org) offers a Reality Tours in Nicaragua. These educational trips explore various social justice issues, including the fair-trade coffee economy, monitoring elections, and learning about labor rights in free trade zones.

Witness for Peace (www.witnessforpeace.org) is a grassroots organization "committed to nonviolence and led by faith and conscience." Based in Managua, Witness for Peace has maintained a permanent presence in this Central American country since 1983; they offer a huge range of delegations "combine international travel and education with the struggle for peace, economic justice, and sustainable development."

Other online resources include www.vianica.com and www.nicaragualiving.info. *Anda Ya!* (www.andayanicaragua.com) is a free Spanish language booklet packed with helpful contacts and listings in Granada, San Juan del Sur, León, Managua and Estelí. An ever-shifting group of free glossy English-language magazines, like *Between the Waves* are found at the airport, bookstores, and hotels. Other tourist-targeted, real estate–funded glossy publications are always on hand in hotel lobbies across the country.

FILM AND PHOTOGRAPHY
Film Processing and Supplies

Really? You still use film? Don't worry, quality film and basic camera supplies are available in Nicaragua, and there are modern camera shops in most cities. Film processing is considerably more expensive (up to $20 a roll with no doubles) and often lower quality than back home. The biggest company is Kodak Express with a presence in nearly every major city. Black-and-white film and slide film are rarely available and processed at great expense.

For digital, always come equipped with a

large memory card or your own laptop to store and edit your photos; otherwise, find a reliable cybercafe, where most provide the service of burning your shots onto a CD at minimal cost. For extra safety, burn two copies of the disk and mail one to yourself, in case your camera and/or bag are stolen.

Photo Etiquette

Cameras are by no means foreign objects in Nicaragua, but in many towns and neighborhoods, they are owned only by a few local entrepreneurs who take pictures at weddings, baptisms, graduations, etc. and then sell the print to the subject. Because of this, some rural Nicaraguans may expect that the photo you are taking is for them, and that you will either charge them for the photo or that you are going to send them a free copy. In general, people love getting their pictures taken, but often insist on dressing up, stiffening their bodies, and wiping all traces of emotion from their faces. The only way to avoid this (apart from making monkey noises to get them to laugh) is to take candid, unsolicited photos, something adults may perceive as bizarre and possibly rude. A solution is to ask first, concede to a few serious poses, and then snap away later when they are more unsuspecting but accustomed to your happy trigger finger. If you promise to send someone a copy, take down their address and actually do it.

COMMUNICATIONS AND MEDIA
Mail

The national postal system is called **Correos de Nicaragua,** and is surprisingly effective and reliable. Every city has at least one post office, often near the central plaza and adjacent to the telephone service (but not always). Legal-size letters and postcards cost about $0.70 to the United States, and a little more to Europe. Post offices in many cities have a gorgeous selection of stamps. *Correos* are open standard business hours (with some variations), almost always close during lunch, and are open until noon on Saturday.

To receive packages, have the sender use a padded envelope instead of a box, even if the shipment must be split into several pieces; keep the package as unassuming as possible, and try writing Dios Te Ama (God Loves You) on the envelope for a little help from above. In general, mail service to Nicaragua is reliable, even to remote areas. Boxes, on the other hand, of whatever size, are routed through the *aduana* (customs). This means traipsing to their office at the airport in Managua and enduring a horrific and uncaring bureaucracy intent on *not* giving you your goods. Most major international courier services have offices all over Nicaragua, including DHL and Federal Express, but they too are subject to the *aduana.*

Telephone and Fax

The national phone company **ENITEL** (Empresa Nicaragüense de Telecomunicaciones, tel. 505/2278-3131, fax 505/2278-4012, www. enitel.com.ni) was privatized in 2003 and is modernizing quickly under private ownership. Note that it is sometimes called TELCOR, its old name. A 24-hour ENITEL customer service operator is available by dialing 121. Every major city has an ENITEL office, as do many small towns, and elsewhere you'll find families offering their phones for pay instead. But these offices are quickly becoming obsolete in the age of cell phones, which have permeated into the poorest villages in just a year or two. You can also purchase phone cards that work in ENITEL and Publitel pay phones, located in any town bigger than Estelí. Most ENITEL offices have fax machines. A two-page international fax may cost you $4–5; a local fax will cost about $1. Also check in copy shops, Internet providers, and post offices. Many local cybercafes offer VOIP calls as well; of note is the **Llamadas Heladas** chain, present in at least 29 locations.

In 2009, Nicaragua switched from a 7-digit to an 8-digit phone number system. All land lines earned an additional "2" at the beginning, and all cell phones took on an additional "8." If you see a number with only seven digits, follow this formula.

Cell Phones

Nicaragua's two networks are Claro and Movistar (formerly Bell South). Claro has better coverage nationwide (even in Waspám!) but calls are more expensive; Movistar works best in city centers but drops out while you're on the road, but has more attractive pricing. Calls between networks are a bit more expensive than calls within networks, hardly enough to worry about, but enough for many Nicas to carry two cell phones.

Getting your own cell phone for travel is easy and inexpensive. Rent a cell phone from a booth in the airport in the luggage pick-up area (open during daylight business hours only), but it may make more sense to purchase a nearly-disposable cell phone *(chiclero)*, available in Claro and Movistar outlets and at most gas stations for less than $20.

You can also put a local SIM card in your own dual-band cell phone (Nicaragua operates on the 800 and 900 Mhz frequencies); it's easy to get a chip for either of Nicaragua's two competing cell phone networks.

As you travel, you'll notice there are little booths all over the nation that offer *"recarga"* of minutes, and many other stores can recharge your phone as well. Just give them your money and your cell number and they'll dial it in; you'll get an SMS within 60 seconds confirming the added time. C$250 is probably enough for a week's worth of travel, depending on how long you chat or how often you phone home.

Important Numbers

- Information: 113
- To place a collect-call within Nicaragua: 110
- International operator: 116
- Police: 118
- Firefighters: 115 and 120
- Red Cross: 128

International Calls

Cybercafes throughout the nation offer Internet calling, and **Llamadas Heladas** specializes in VOIP-based, cheap international calls. Connection quality can be dodgy, but with rates as low as $6 per hour to call the United States, Canada, or Europe, this is a great way to quickly get in touch back home. Of course you can also call home on skype. com or other broadband services, especially if you have a laptop, since many hotels now offer Wi-Fi in your room.

INTERNET AND COMPUTERS

Internet cafés exist throughout the nation, and even in smaller towns you'll find several *cybers* (pronounced SEE-bear), run off a wimpy ADSL connection and a pirated copy of Windows XP (the authors have yet to find a computer whose keyboard is configured properly in any of these village *cybers*). Prices start at about $1 per hour and go as high as $15 an hour in some hotel business centers. Furthermore, free Wi-Fi connections are spreading like the plague across Nicaraguan

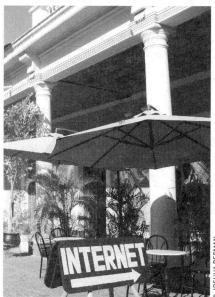

Internet access is easily found in Nicaragua, especially in Granada.

© JOSHUA BERMAN

restaurants, hotels, and cafés. Note that these free networks are often riddled with security threats, so use them to check your email, not your bank account.

If you are staying a significant time in Nicaragua and need a connection in your home or business, visit a Claro or Movistar kiosk to inquire about cell phone dongles that let you access the Internet the way you'd make a cell phone call, with the same coverage. For landlines, IBW Communications (from Hospital Monte España, one block north, one block east, tel. 505/2278-6328, www.ibw.com.ni) offers dial-up access starting at about $10 per month.

Apple and Macintosh
Most of Nicaragua runs on Windows XP, but if you have a Mac you can get repair services at **Mac Center** (located near the UCA, from the Metrocentro rotunda, 2 blocks west, 1.5 south, tel. 505/2270-5918, raguilar@mac.com). They are a certified dealer and service provider, with all kinds of Apple-related services, repairs, and products; also free Nica coffee and Wi-Fi.

PRINT MEDIA
Newspapers
Street vendors are out before 6 A.M. every day hawking the various daily papers, but you can often pick one up in most corner stores. *La Prensa* (www.laprensa.com.ni) was so aggressively anti-Somoza in the 1970s the dictator allegedly had the editor, Pedro Joaquín Chamorro, assassinated. Not long after the revolution, *La Prensa* turned anti-Sandinista and remains anti-Danielista to this day. In the days before an election, *La Prensa* typically runs a regular series of "flashback" articles recalling the atrocities of the Contra war in the 1980s and dredging up every unresolved Sandinista scandal available. *El Nuevo Diario* (www.elnuevodiario.com.ni) offers competing coverage of local news and events, sometimes with a *New York Post*–ish tabloidy spin.

International papers and magazines are sold in Managua at the Casa de Café, a kiosk on the first floor of the Plaza Metrocentro, and in the lobbies of the major hotels.

Print Magazines
Created in 1981 to spread the news about the revolution to the English-speaking world, **Envío** (www.envio.org.ni) remains an interesting print and online magazine, providing "information and analysis of Nicaragua from Nicaragua." **HECHO** (www.hechomagazine. com) is a gorgeously designed, thoughtful Managua-based magazine, created in 2009 to celebrate Nicaraguan culture and art; HECHO is a great resource for live music and event information.

WEIGHTS AND MEASURES
Time
Nicaragua is in standard time zone GMT-6, i.e., six hours earlier than London. Daylight saving time is not observed. During standard time, when it's 8 P.M. in New York it's 7 P.M. in Managua, and during daylight savings time, when it's 8 P.M. in New York it's 6 P.M. in Nicaragua. But no matter what your watch says, you're always on Nica time—i.e. everything starts a little late and meeting times are considered approximate.

Electricity
Nicaragua uses the same electrical standards as the United States and Canada: 110V, 60 Hz. The shape of the electrical socket is the same as well. Laptop users should bring a portable surge protector with them, as the electrical current in Nicaragua is highly variable, and spikes, brownouts, and outages are commonplace.

Measurements
Distances are almost exclusively in kilometers, although for smaller lengths, you'll occasionally hear feet, inches, yards, and the colonial Spanish *vara* (about a meter). The most commonly used land-area term is the *manzana*, another old measure, equal to 1.74 acres. Weights and volumes are a mix of metric and nonmetric: Buy your gasoline in gallons, your chicken in pounds, and so on.

RESOURCES

Glossary

alcaldía mayor's office
arroyo stream or gully
artesanía crafts
ayudante "helper" – the guy on the bus who collects your fee after you find a seat
barrio neighborhood
beneficio coffee mill
bombero firefighter
bravo rough, strong, wild
cabo cape
cafetín light-food eatery
calle street
cama matrimonial "marriage bed" – motels and hotels use this term to refer to a double, queen, or king-size bed; a bed meant for two people.
camión truck
campesino country folk
campo countryside
carretera highway, road
cayo cay
centro de salud public MINSA-run health clinic; there is one in most towns
centro recreativo public recreation center
cerro hill or mountain
cerveza, cervecita beer
chele, chela gringo, whitey
chinelas rubber flip-flops
ciudad city
colectivo a shared taxi or passenger boat
colonia neighborhood
comedor cheap lunch counter
comida corriente plate of the day
complejo complex (of buildings)
cooperativa cooperative
cordillera mountain range

córdoba Nicaraguan currency
corriente standard, base
coyote illegal-immigrant smuggler; or profit-cutting middleman
cuajada white, homemade, salty cheese
departamentos subsection of Nicaragua, akin to states or counties
empalme intersection of two roads
entrada entrance
estero estuary or marsh
expreso express bus
farmacia pharmacy, drugstore
fiestas patronales Saint's Day parties held annually in every town and city
fresco natural fruit drink
fritanga street-side barbecue and fry-fest
gallo pinto national mix of rice 'n beans
gancho gap in a fence
gaseosa carbonated beverage
gringo North American, or any foreigner
guaro booze
guitarra guitar
guitarrón mariachi bass guitar
hospedaje hostel, budget hotel
iglesia church
isla island
laguna lake
lancha small passenger boat
lanchero lancha driver
malecón waterfront
manzana besides an apple, this is also a measure of land equal to 100 square varas, or 1.74 acres
mar sea or ocean
mariachi Mexican country/polka music
mercado market

mesa/meseta geographical plateau
mosquitero mosquito net
muelle dock, wharf
museo museum
ordinario local bus (also *ruteado*)
panga small passenger boat
panguero *panga* driver
pinche stingy, cheap
playa beach
pueblo small town or village
pulpería corner store
puro cigar
quintal 100-pound sack
rancheras Mexican drinking songs
rancho thatch-roofed restaurant or hut
rato a short period of time
reserva reserve or preserve
río river
sala living room
salida exit, road out of town
salon large living room, gallery
salto waterfall
sierra mountain range
suave soft, easy, quiet
tope a dead-end, or T intersection
tranquilo mellow
urbano public urban bus
vara colonial unit of distance equal to roughly one meter
volcán volcano

ABBREVIATIONS

ENEL Empresa Nicaragüense de Electricidad (electric company)
ENITEL Empresa Nicaragüense de Telecomunicaciónes (telephone company)
FSLN Frente Sandinista de Liberación Nacional (Sandinista party)
IFA (EEH-fa) East German troop transport, used commonly in Nicaraguan public transportation system; it probably stands for something in German, but in Nicaragua, it means *imposible frenar a tiempo* (impossible to brake on time).
INETER Instituto Nicaragüense de Estudios Territoriales (government geography/geology institute)
MARENA Ministerio del Ambiente y los Recursos Naturales (Ministry of Natural Resources and the Environment), administers Nicaragua's protected areas
MYA Million Years Ago
NGO Nongovernmental Organization
PCV Peace Corps Volunteer
PLC Partido Liberal Constitucionalista, the conservative anti-Sandinista party
SINAP Sistema Nacional de Areas Protegidas (National System of Protected Areas)
UCA Universidad de Centroamerica
UN United Nations
UNAN Universidad Nacional Autónoma de Nicaragua
USAID United States Agency for International Development, channels congressionally approved foreign aid

Spanish Phrasebook

PRONUNCIATION GUIDE

Spanish pronunciation is much more regular than that of English, but there are still occasional variations.

Consonants

c as "c" in "cat," before "a," "o," or "u"; like "s" before "e" or "i"
d as "d" in "dog," except between vowels, then like "th" in "that"
g before "e" or "i," like the "ch" in Scottish "loch"; elsewhere like "g" in "get"
h always silent
j like the English "h" in "hotel," but stronger
ll like the "y" in "yellow"
ñ like the "ni" in "onion"
r always pronounced as strong "r"
rr trilled "r"
v similar to the "b" in "boy" (not as English "v")

y similar to English, but with a slight "j" sound. When standing alone, it's pronounced like the "e" in "me."

z like "s" in "same"

b, f, k, l, m, n, p, q, s, t, w, x   as in English

Vowels

a as in "father," but shorter
e as in "hen"
i as in "machine"
o as in "phone"
u usually as in "rule"; when it follows a "q," the "u" is silent; when it follows an "h" or "g," it's pronounced like "w," except when it comes between "g" and "e" or "i," when it's also silent (unless it has an umlaut, when it is again pronounced as English "w")

Stress

Native English speakers frequently make errors of pronunciation by ignoring stress. All Spanish vowels – a, e, i, o, and u – carry accents that determine which syllable of a word gets emphasis. Often, stress seems unnatural to nonnative speakers – the surname Chávez, for instance, is stressed on the first syllable – but failure to observe this rule may mean that native speakers may not understand you.

USEFUL WORDS AND PHRASES

Nicaraguans and other Spanish-speaking people consider formalities important. Whenever approaching anyone for information or some other reason, do not forget the appropriate salutation – good morning, good evening, etc. Standing alone, the greeting *hola* (hello) can sound brusque.

Hello. *Hola.*
Good morning. *Buenos días.*
Good afternoon. *Buenas tardes.*
Good evening. *Buenas noches.*
How are you? *¿Cómo está?*
Fine. *Muy bien.*
And you? *¿Y usted?*
Awesome! *De acachimba!*
So-so. *Más o menos.*
Thank you. *Gracias.*

Thank you very much. *Muchas gracias.*
You're very kind. *Muy amable.*
You're welcome. *De nada* ("It's nothing").
yes *sí*
no *no*
I don't know. *No sé.*
It's fine; okay *Está bien.*
Good; okay *Bueno.*
please *por favor*
Pleased to meet you. *Mucho gusto.*
Excuse me (physical) *Perdóneme.*
Excuse me (speech) *Discúlpeme.*
I'm sorry. *Lo siento.*
Goodbye. *Adiós.*
See you later. *Hasta luego* ("Until later").
more *más*
less *menos*
better *mejor*
much, a lot *mucho*
a shot of strong liquor *un cachimvaso*
very drunk *hasta el culo*
a little *un poco*
large *grande*
small *pequeño, chico*
quick, fast *rápido*
slowly *despacio*
bad *malo*
difficult *difícil*
easy *fácil*
He/She/It is gone; as in "She left" or "he's gone." *Ya se fue.*
I don't speak Spanish well. *No hablo bien el español.*
I don't understand. *No entiendo ni papas.*
How do you say. . . in Spanish? *¿Cómo se dice. . . en español?*
Do you understand English? *¿Entiende el inglés?*
Is English spoken here? (Does anyone here speak English?) *¿Se habla inglés aquí?*

TERMS OF ADDRESS

When in doubt, use the formal *usted* (you) as a form of address. If you wish to dispense with formality and feel that the desire is mutual, you can say, *"Me puedes tutear"* ("You can call me 'tu'").

I *yo*
you (formal) *usted*
you (familiar) *vos*
you (familiar) *tú*
he/him *él*
she/her *ella*
we/us *nosotros*
you (plural) *ustedes*
they/them (all males or mixed gender) *ellos*
they/them (all females) *ellas*
Mr., sir *Señor or Don*
Mrs., madam *Señora or Doña*
Miss, young lady *Señorita*
wife *esposa*
husband *marido or esposo*
friend *amigo* (male), *amiga* (female)
sweetheart *novio* (male), *novia* (female)
son, daughter *hijo, hija*
brother, sister *hermano, hermana*
father, mother *padre, madre*
grandfather, grandmother *abuelo, abuela*

GETTING AROUND
Where is . . .? *¿Dónde está. . . ?*
How far is it to . . .? *¿A cuanto está . . . ?*
from. . . to . . . *de. . . a . . .*
highway *la carretera*
road *el camino*
street *la calle*
block *la cuadra*
kilometer *kilómetro*
north *norte*
south *sur*
west *oeste; poniente*
east *este; oriente*
straight ahead *al derecho; adelante*
to the right *a la derecha*
to the left *a la izquierda*

ACCOMMODATIONS
Is there a room? *¿Hay cuarto?*
May I (we) see it? *¿Puedo (podemos) verlo?*
What is the rate? *¿Cuál es el precio?*
Is that your best rate? *¿Es su mejor precio?*
Is there something cheaper? *¿Hay algo más económico?*

single room *un sencillo*
double room *un doble*
room for a couple *matrimonial*
key *llave*
with private bath *con baño*
with shared bath *con baño general; con baño compartido*
hot water *agua caliente*
cold water *agua fría*
shower *ducha*
electric shower *ducha eléctrica*
towel *toalla*
soap *jabón*
toilet paper *papel higiénico*
air-conditioning *aire acondicionado*
fan *abanico; ventilador*
blanket *frazada; manta*
sheets *sábanas*

PUBLIC TRANSPORT
bus stop *la parada*
bus terminal *terminal de buses*
airport *el aeropuerto*
launch *lancha; tiburonera*
dock *muelle*
I want a ticket to . . . *Quiero un pasaje a . . .*
I want to get off at . . . *Quiero bajar en . . .*
Here, please. *Aquí, por favor.*
Where is this bus going? *¿Adónde va este autobús?*
round-trip *ida y vuelta*
What do I owe? *¿Cuánto le debo?*

FOOD
menu *la carta, el menú*
glass *taza*
fork *tenedor*
knife *cuchillo*
spoon *cuchara*
napkin *servilleta*
soft drink *agua fresca*
coffee *café*
cream *crema*
tea *té*
sugar *azúcar*
drinking water *agua pura, agua potable*
bottled carbonated water *agua mineral con gas*

bottled uncarbonated water *agua sin gas*
beer *cerveza*
wine *vino*
milk *leche*
juice *jugo*
eggs *huevos*
bread *pan*
watermelon *sandía*
banana *banano*
plantain *plátano*
apple *manzana*
orange *naranja*
meat (without) *carne (sin)*
beef *carne de res*
chicken *pollo; gallina*
fish *pescado*
shellfish *mariscos*
shrimp *camarones*
fried *frito*
roasted *asado*
barbecued *a la parrilla*
breakfast *desayuno*
lunch *almuerzo*
dinner (often eaten in late afternoon) *comida*
dinner, or a late-night snack *cena*
the check, or bill *la cuenta*

MAKING PURCHASES
I need . . . *Necesito. . .*
I want . . . *Deseo. . .* or *Quiero. . .*
I would like. . .(more polite) *Quisiera . . .*
How much does it cost? *¿Cuánto cuesta?*
What's the exchange rate? *¿Cuál es el tipo de cambio?*
May I see . . . ? *¿Puedo ver . . . ?*
This one *ésta/ésto*
expensive *caro*
cheap *barato*
cheaper *más barato*
too much *demasiado*

HEALTH
Help me please. *Ayúdeme por favor.*
I am ill. *Estoy enfermo.*
pain *dolor*
fever *fiebre*

stomachache *dolor de estómago*
vomiting *vomitar*
diarrhea *diarrea* or *curutaca*
drugstore *farmacia*
medicine *medicina*
pill, tablet *pastilla*
birth-control pills *pastillas anticonceptivas*
condom *condón; preservativo*

NUMBERS
0 *cero*
1 *uno* (masculine)
1 *una* (feminine)
2 *dos*
3 *tres*
4 *cuatro*
5 *cinco*
6 *seis*
7 *siete*
8 *ocho*
9 *nueve*
10 *diez*
11 *once*
12 *doce*
13 *trece*
14 *catorce*
15 *quince*
16 *dieciseis*
17 *diecisiete*
18 *dieciocho*
19 *diecinueve*
20 *veinte*
21 *veintiuno*
30 *treinta*
40 *cuarenta*
50 *cincuenta*
60 *sesenta*
70 *setenta*
80 *ochenta*
90 *noventa*
100 *cien*
101 *ciento y uno*
200 *doscientos*
1,000 *mil*
10,000 *diez mil*
1,000,000 *un millón*

TIME

While Nicaraguans mostly use the 12-hour clock, in some instances, usually associated with plane or bus schedules, they may use the 24-hour military clock. Under the 24-hour clock, for example, *las nueve de la noche* (9 P.M.) would be *las 21 horas* (2100 hours).

What time is it? *¿Qué hora es?*
It's one o'clock *Es la una.*
It's two o'clock *Son las dos.*
At two o'clock *A las dos.*
It's ten to three *Son las tres menos diez.*
It's ten past three *Son las tres y diez.*
It's three fifteen *Son las tres y cuarto.*
It's two forty-five *Son las tres menos cuarto.*
It's two thirty *Son las dos y media.*
It's six A.M. *Son las seis de la mañana.*
It's six P.M. *Son las seis de la tarde.*
It's ten P.M. *Son las diez de la noche.*

today *hoy*
tomorrow *mañana*
morning *la mañana*
tomorrow morning *mañana por la mañana*
yesterday *ayer*
week *la semana*
month *mes*
year *año*
last night *anoche*
the next day *el día siguiente*

DAYS OF THE WEEK

Sunday *domingo*
Monday *lunes*
Tuesday *martes*
Wednesday *miércoles*
Thursday *jueves*
Friday *viernes*
Saturday *sábado*

Suggested Reading and Viewing

SUGGESTED READING

A prodigious amount of literature emerged from the Sandinista years, when Nicaragua was the setting of the hemisphere's most celebrated—and criticized—socialist experiment of the century. You'll find more titles on Nicaragua in the used-book section than you will on the new releases shelf. Following is an extremely eclectic (and incomplete) list of your options.

Fiction

Sirias, Silvio. *Bernardo and the Virgin.* Chicago: Northwestern University Press, 2005. *Bernardo*'s real-life texture and ingenious use of voices and characters portrays a thick slice of Nicaragua's past and present while recounting the true story of the Virgin Mary's appearances to a *campesino* in Cuapa.

Sirias, Silvio. *Meet Me Under the Ceiba.* Houston, TX: Arte Publico Press, 2009. Sirias's second novel is also set in small-town Nicaragua and continues the vibrant cultural portrait he began in *Bernardo*. It is based on a 1998 hate-crime murder in La Curva and addresses many issues, including homophobia and gay rights in Latin America. The narrator explains the story's importance: "Adela Rugama's murder is a chilling story. It's a sobering portrait of human frailty, of what can happen when we allow our weaknesses, our emotional flaws, to take control of our actions."

Nonfiction and Memoir

Babb, Florence. *After Revolution: Mapping Gender and Cultural Politics in Neoliberal Nicaragua.* Austin, Texas: University of Texas Press, 2001. Professor of Anthropology and Women's Studies at the University of Iowa, Babb has also published scores of academic papers on Nicaragua, mainly on issues of gender and sexuality.

Barrios de Chamorro, Violeta. *Dreams of the Heart*. New York: Simon & Schuster, 1996. A very human history of Nicaragua from the Somoza years through Doña Violeta's electoral triumph in 1990 (she served as Nicaragua's president in the early 1990s).

Belli, Gioconda. *The Country Under My Skin: A Memoir of Love and War*. New York: Anchor Books, 2003. This is a phenomenal book that provides a close-up look at various stages of *la lucha* (the struggle), written by one of the country's premier living poets. Stephen Kinzer writes, "Belli's memoir shows us a side of the Sandinista revolution we have not seen. It also introduces us to an astute veteran of two eternal wars, one between the sexes and one that pits the world's poor against its rich."

Cabezas, Omar. *Fire from the Mountain (La Montaña es Algo Más que una Grán Estapa Verde)*. Phoenix, AZ: Crown, 1985. A ribald, vernacular account of what it's like to be a guerrilla soldier in the mountains of Nicaragua; one of the few books about the early stages of the revolution.

Cardenal, Ernesto; Walsh, Donald D. (translator). *The Gospel in Solentiname*. Maryknoll, NY: Orbis Books, 1979. Transcripts of the masses given by Cardenal on Solentiname that helped spawn the *Misa Campesina* and liberation theology movements.

Chomsky, Noam. *Turning the Tide: U.S. Intervention in Central America and the Struggle for Peace*. Cambridge, MA: South End Press, 1985. Succinctly and powerfully shows how U.S. Central American policies implement broader U.S. economic, military, and social aims, with Nicaragua and El Salvador as examples.

Dando-Collins, Stephen. *Tycoon's War: How Cornelius Vanderbilt Invaded a Country to Overthrow America's Most Famous Military Adventurer*. Philadelphia: Da Capo Press, 2008. This account of one of Nicaragua's most fascinating historical periods (the mid-19th century) is painstakingly researched and told in an exciting narrative. Dando-Collins weaves the stories of Vanderbilt and William Walker with a striking degree of detail. The *Wall Street Journal* said this book "reads . . . [like a] screenplay treatment for a hell of a movie."

Davis, Peter. *Where is Nicaragua?* New York: Simon & Schuster, 1987. Davis breaks down the revolution and Contra war, and ties them into the country's greater history; he articulates the complexity of the situation in a graspable manner.

Dickey, Christopher. *With the Contras*. New York: Simon & Schuster, 1985. Dickey was the *Washington Post* correspondent in Honduras and gives an exciting account of his experience with the secret Contra army.

Kinzer, Stephen. *Blood of Brothers: Life and War in Nicaragua*. New York: G. P. Putnam's Sons, 1991. Kinzer, the *New York Times* Managua bureau chief during the war, sensed that Nicaragua was "a country with more to tell the world than it had been able to articulate, a country with a message both political and spiritual."

Lancaster, Roger N. *Life Is Hard: Machismo, Danger, and the Intimacy of Power in Nicaragua*. Berkeley: University of California Press, 1992. Lancaster is an anthropologist and this is an ethnography studying not current events, but their effect on the Nicaraguan individual and family. It is intimate and offers details about Nicaraguan life that one can only get living with the people in their very homes. Lancaster pays attention to issues often passed over, like homosexuality, domestic violence, broken families, and the roots of machismo.

Marriot, Edward. *Savage Shore: Life and Death with Nicaragua's Last Shark Hunters*. New York: Owl Books, 2001. A curious and descriptive journey up the Río San Juan and beyond.

Pastor, Robert. *Not Condemned To Repetition: The United States and Nicaragua.* Boulder, CO: Westview Press, 2002. Robert Pastor was a U.S. policymaker in the period leading up to and following the Sandinista revolution of 1979. A decade later, he organized the International Mission led by Jimmy Carter that mediated the first free election in Nicaragua's history. This updated edition covers the events of the democratic transition of the 1990s and extracts lessons to be learned from the past.

Randall, Margaret. *Sandino's Daughters: Testimonies of Nicaraguan Women in Struggle.* Point Roberts, WA: New Star Books, 1981. Explores the role of feminism in the Sandinista revolution, via a series of interviews with participants.

Rushdie, Salman. *The Jaguar Smile.* New York: Viking, 1987. Representing the pro-Sandinista Nicaragua Solidarity Campaign in London, Rushdie takes readers on a poetic, passionate jaunt through Nicaragua as part of a government cultural campaign; he offers a careful (if short) examination of their policies.

Squier, Ephraim George. *Nicaragua: Its People, Scenery, Monuments, and the Proposed Interoceanic Canal.* New York: D. Appleton, 1852. Squier remains one of Nicaragua's most prolific writers; this massive, multivolume tome is available for hundreds of dollars in rare bookstores. The discussion is divided into five parts in which he describes geography and topography; the events during the author's residence, including accounts of his explorations; observations on the proposed canal; notes on the indigenous of the country, including information regarding geographical distribution, languages, institutions, religions, and customs; and the political history of the country since its independence from Spain.

Volz, Eric. *Gringo Nightmare: A Young American Framed for Murder in Nicaragua.* New York, NY: St. Martin's Press, 2010. It is definitely every traveler's worst nightmare to end up in a filthy Third World prison, but Volz's case goes way beyond his cramped cell, and it is also much greater than the volatile social conditions in San Juan del Sur that helped lead to his arrest. This is a harrowing tale by any account, and proof that Nicaragua is *not* "the next Costa Rica." Not by a long shot. One reviewer remarked, "This story should be issued with every passport" (Bill Kurtis, A&E).

Zimmerman, Matilde. *Sandinista: Carlos Fonseca and the Nicaraguan Revolution.* Durham, NC: Duke University Press, 2001. This is the first English-language biography of the legendary leader of the FSLN and arguably the most important and influential figure of the post-1959 revolutionary generation in Latin America.

Photography

Belli, Alejandro et al. *The Nicaraguans.* Managua, 2006. One of the best photography book about Nicaragua. Period. Go to www.thenicaraguans.com to learn more about this stunning collection of images celebrating the people of the country. In the foreword, Sergio Ramírez Mercado writes, "these photographs, taken by Nicaraguans observing other Nicaraguans who are simply getting through the day, reveal the multi-faceted face of peace, which today also embodies our identity."

Gentile, William Frank. *Nicaragua: Photographs by William Frank Gentile* New York: W. W. Norton & Company, 1989. These are some of the deepest, most powerful photos you'll ever see, with fantastic juxtapositions of Contra and FSLN soldiers.

Kunzle, David. *The Murals of Revolutionary Nicaragua 1979–1992.* Berkeley: University of California Press, 1995. Many murals were strictly political, but most intertwined the revolutionary process with cultural, historical, and literary themes. All are celebrated in Kunzle's book; 83-page introduction and 100 color plates.

Meiselas, Susan. *Nicaragua* New York: Aperture, 2008. Originally published in 1981 to document both the carnage and hope of the year leading up to the Revolution, this book includes some of the most iconic images of the period. This new edition comes with a DVD called "Pictures from a Revolution," in which the photographer returns to the scenes and subjects of her famous photographs.

Poetry, Language, and Literature
Morelli, Marco, ed. *Rubén's Orphans.* New Hyde Park, NY: Painted Rooster Press, 2001. An anthology of contemporary Nicaraguan poets, with English translations.

Rabella, Joaquim and Pallais, C. *Vocabulario Popular Nicaragüense.* This big, red linguistic bible is a wonderful, dictionary celebrating Nicaraguan Spanish, complete with regional usages, sayings, and a plethora of profanities; available (hopefully) in the UCA bookstores in Managua.

Randall, Margaret. *Risking a Somersault in the Air: Conversations with Nicaraguan Writers.* San Francisco: Solidarity Publications, 1984. Just as much about literature as it is about the revolution, this is a fascinating series of interviews with Nicaraguan authors and poets, most of whom were part of the FSLN revolution and government.

White, Steven, trans. *Poets of Nicaragua: A Bilingual Anthology 1918–1970.* London: Unicorn Press, 1983.

Miscellaneous
Hulme, Krekel, and O'Reilly. *Not Just Another Nicaragua Travel Guide.* Redwood, CA: Mango Publications, 1990. An ebullient and fascinating guidebook for traveling Sandinista Nicaragua in the 1980s. Get it if you can find it; only 1,000 copies were printed.

SUGGESTED VIEWING
Carla's Song, a 1996 drama by Ken Loach, stars Robert Carlyle and Oyanka Cabezas. Set in 1987, Scottish bus driver George Lennox meets Carla, a Nicaraguan exile living a precarious, profoundly sad life in Glasgow. George takes her back to her village in northern Nicaragua to find out what has happened to her family, boyfriend, and country. Notable for its real and gritty location shots, in both Scotland and Nicaragua, *Carla's Song* is enjoyable and touching and, notes its writer, Paul Laverty, "is just one of thousands of statistics, hopefully reminding the viewer that everyone in this war had a story." *Carla's Song* was awarded a gold medal at the Italian Film Festival in Venice.

The World Stopped Watching, a 2003 Canadian film by Peter Raymont and Harold Crooks, was shot in 56 mm. Nicaragua dropped from the spotlight after the end of the Contra war. This documentary, shot in late 2002 and early 2003, picks up the pieces of what happened next. Essentially, this is a sequel to *The World is Watching,* a critically acclaimed documentary from the 1980s, involving many of the same characters.

Walker, a bold 1987 anachronistic biography of the infamous soldier-of-fortune from Tennessee, starring Ed Harris. Filmmaker Alex Cox (of *Sid & Nancy* fame), wanted to show that "nothing had changed in the 140-odd years between William Walker's genocidal campaign and that of Oliver North and his goons." One reviewer wrote, "What is so amazing about *Walker* is that it got made at all. It's a film condemning capitalism funded by a capitalist studio. Since it was filmed on location, its production money went straight into a country that the United States was currently at war with." Critics mostly panned the film as "sophomoric black comedy," but confirmed Nicaphiles will surely get a kick out of the familiar scenery.

Internet Resources

THE AUTHORS' SITES
www.GoToNicaragua.com
This is our home base, where you can chat with fellow Nicaphile travelers and expats, ask us travel questions, post travelogues, read the latest Nicaragua headlines, and check for updates to this edition. See you there.

www.therandymon.com
Randy Wood's personal site.

www.joshuaberman.net
Joshua Berman's personal site and blog.

NICARAGUA PORTALS
www.ibw.com.ni
IBW Internet Gateway is a Spanish language portal that is a good introduction to the nation's print and visual media, plus links to Nicaraguan government and NGO websites.

www.lanic.utexas.edu/la/ca/ nicaragua
The Latin American Network Information Center boasts a ton of Nica-sites, including many academic links.

www.nicanet.org
For more than 25 years, The Nicaragua Network, a coalition of U.S.-based nonprofits (many of them regional sister city organizations), has been committed to social and economic justice for the people of Nicaragua.

OFFICIAL
www.nicaragua.usembassy.gov
he U.S. embassy page in Nicaragua.

www.travel.state.gov/travel
U.S. State Department fact sheet for travelers in Nicaragua, including security overview.

www.voyage.gc.ca
Ditto, from the Canadians. The Canadian government has never really been politically involved in Nicaragua, so its travel warnings provide a good reality check for what you read at the U.S. State Department's site.

TRAVELING AND TOURISM
www.intur.gob.ni
www.visitanicaragua.com
Nicaraguan government tourism agency.

www.nicaragua-guide.com
This thorough, diverse traveler portal is run by expats living in Granada who wanted "to show the positive side of Nicaragua and…community life here."

www.marena.gob.ni
For more information on visiting specific parks and reserves, this is the Nicaraguan Natural Resources Ministry.

www.vianica.com
Vianica is an independent, well-designed, informative overview of travel destinations throughout Nicaragua and can help you plan your trip. They even maintain updated Nicaragua bus schedules!

www.xolo.com.ni
Xolo is a Nica-run portal focusing on music, books, and theater, plus links to many of the hotels and restaurants mentioned here.

www.hechomagazine.com
Culture and arts magazine in Managua with current event listings.

www.nicaliving.com
A vibrant online community of opinionated expats and travelers.

Index

List of Maps

www.moon.com

DESTINATIONS | ACTIVITIES | BLOGS | MAPS | BOOKS

MOON.COM is ready to help plan your next trip! Filled with fresh trip ideas and strategies, author interviews, informative travel blogs, a detailed map library, and descriptions of all the Moon guidebooks, Moon.com is all you need to get out and explore the world—or even places in your own backyard. While at Moon.com, sign up for our monthly e-newsletter for updates on new releases, travel tips, and expert advice from our on-the-go Moon authors. As always, when you travel with Moon, expect an experience that is uncommon and truly unique.

MOON IS ON FACEBOOK—BECOME A FAN!
JOIN THE MOON PHOTO GROUP ON FLICKR

MAP SYMBOLS

▦ Expressway		**C** Highlight		✗ Airfield		⚲ Golf Course	
Primary Road		○ City/Town		✈ Airport		**P** Parking Area	
Secondary Road		◉ State Capital		▲ Mountain		⬟ Archaeological Site	
Unpaved Road		⊛ National Capital		✛ Unique Natural Feature		▪ Church	
Trail		★ Point of Interest				⛽ Gas Station	
Ferry		• Accommodation		☂ Waterfall		Glacier	
Railroad		▼ Restaurant/Bar		▲ Park		Mangrove	
Pedestrian Walkway		▪ Other Location		⬛ Trailhead		Reef	
Stairs		⋀ Campground		⛷ Skiing Area		Swamp	

CONVERSION TABLES

°C = (°F - 32) / 1.8
°F = (°C x 1.8) + 32
1 inch = 2.54 centimeters (cm)
1 foot = 0.304 meters (m)
1 yard = 0.914 meters
1 mile = 1.6093 kilometers (km)
1 km = 0.6214 miles
1 fathom = 1.8288 m
1 chain = 20.1168 m
1 furlong = 201.168 m
1 acre = 0.4047 hectares
1 sq km = 100 hectares
1 sq mile = 2.59 square km
1 ounce = 28.35 grams
1 pound = 0.4536 kilograms
1 short ton = 0.90718 metric ton
1 short ton = 2,000 pounds
1 long ton = 1.016 metric tons
1 long ton = 2,240 pounds
1 metric ton = 1,000 kilograms
1 quart = 0.94635 liters
1 US gallon = 3.7854 liters
1 Imperial gallon = 4.5459 liters
1 nautical mile = 1.852 km

°FAHRENHEIT / °CELSIUS thermometer:
230 / 110
220
210 / 100 WATER BOILS
200
190 / 90
180 / 80
170
160 / 70
150
140 / 60
130
120 / 50
110
100 / 40
90 / 30
80
70 / 20
60
50 / 10
40
30 / 0 WATER FREEZES
20
10 / -10
0
-10 / -20
-20 / -30
-30
-40 / -40

Clock face showing 24-hour and 12-hour markings.

Ruler: INCH scale 0 to 4; CM scale 0 to 10.

MOON NICARAGUA
Avalon Travel
a member of the Perseus Books Group
1700 Fourth Street
Berkeley, CA 94710, USA
www.moon.com

Editor: Shaharazade Husain
Series Manager: Kathryn Ettinger
Copy Editor: Emily Lunceford
Graphics and Production Coordinator:
  Lucie Ericksen
Cover Designer: Lucie Ericksen
Map Editor: Mike Morgenfeld
Cartographers: Kat Bennett, Chris Henrick
Indexer: Jean Mooney

ISBN: 978-1-59880-594-9
ISSN: 1539-1019

Printing History
1st Edition – 2003
4th Edition – October 2010

5 4 3 2 1

Some photos and illustrations are used by permission and are the property of the original copyright owners.

Front cover photo: Volcán Concepción and La Isla de Ometepe © Nik Wheeler/Corbis
Title page photo: Chicken bus to nowhere, rural Nicaragua © Joshua Berman
Other front matter photos: pages 5–7, 10–11, 14–16, 18–23: © Joshua Berman; pages 4, 8 bottom, 13: © Randall Wood; pages 12, 17: © Jean Walsh; page 8 top: © Robert Lerich/123RF; page 15: © Holgs/Dreamstime.com; page 24: © David Webster Smith

Printed in Canada by Friesens

KEEPING CURRENT

If you have a favorite gem you'd like to see included in the next edition, or see anything that needs updating, clarification, or correction, please drop us a line. Send your comments via email to feedback@moon.com, or use the address above.

ABOUT THE AUTHORS

Randall Wood

Born on the sandy shore of New York's Atlantic coast, Randall Wood spent his childhood on various small sailboats, developing a mariner's curiosity for what lies over the horizon. His first opportunity to find out was at age 11, when his family drove from New York to California in a '68 Volkswagen bus. He's been exploring ever since, venturing from the salmon boats of Ketchikan to the Bolivian Andes; from the Seychelle Islands to the volcanoes of Java.

Randall first ventured to Nicaragua in 1998, and remained there for the next five years, working as an agronomist and engineer. When Hurricane Mitch swept away the only bridge that led to his mountain village, he found himself marooned for several days; his Nica friends still laugh that he was the first one to cross the storm-swollen river because he was the best swimmer and, at 6'2", tall enough to touch the bottom. He stayed in the country to help manage the Hurricane Mitch reconstruction program. He fell in love with and married Nicaraguan Ericka Briceño, with whom he now has two children.

Randall has a masters degree in international relations and development economics, and spends his free time playing the 12-string folk guitar, swimming and surfing, dancing salsa and merengue, backpacking, making maps, and fiddling around with Linux-based computers. He is an insufferable gearhead whose challenge to find the perfect backpack, and its contents, continues unabated. His work has appeared in the *BC Journal of International Affairs, Between the Waves* magazine, *SAIS Review, Wooden Boat* magazine, and *National Geographic Explorer.*

Randall and his family divide their time between Nicaragua and Benin, West Africa, where Randall is deputy resident country director for a major development program. You can see more of his work on his website, www.therandymon.com.

Joshua Berman

Joshua Berman was born in Clarksburg, West Virginia, in the Year of the Ox. When he was 12, his family moved to Long Island, where, in his high school valedictorian speech, he implored his classmates to "get out" – out of their town, out of New York, and out of the country, if they could. He has since tried to follow his own advice as often as possible.

After earning a degree in environmental studies from Brown University in 1995, Joshua worked as a fisheries biologist with the U.S. Forest Service, a firefighter with the National Park Service, and an instructor for Outward Bound. In 1998, the U.S. Peace Corps shipped him to Nicaragua, where he worked with the Ministry of Education and Hurricane Mitch relief efforts. There he teamed up with his future co-author, Randall Wood, to co-edit the quarterly Peace Corps magazine, ¡Va Pué!

Joshua has led trips for the American Jewish World Service (AJWS) in nearly every Central American nation, as well as in Mexico and Israel. In 2005 and 2006, Joshua and his new bride, Sutay, a registered nurse (and fellow Returned Peace Corps Volunteer), visited 16 countries in 16 months on an extended, round-the-world honeymoon; they spent half of their time abroad completing assignments for the AJWS Volunteer Corps.

Joshua is currently a freelance writer, editor, Spanish teacher, and father. He and his family divide their time between Central America and the Rocky Mountains. In addition to Moon Nicaragua, Joshua and Randall Wood are co-authors of Moon Living Abroad in Nicaragua; Joshua is also the author of Moon Belize, which won a Lowell Thomas Travel Journalism award in the Guidebook category. His articles have appeared in National Geographic Traveler, Yoga Journal, Outside, The Boston Globe, Denver Post, Sunset, 5280, Worldview, and Transitions Abroad. Joshua's blog, "The Tranquilo Traveler," is a celebration of slow travel, voluntourism, and all things Belize and Nicaragua. Visit it at www.joshuaberman.net.

Moon Handbooks give you the tools to make your own choices, with

- Can't-miss sights, activities, restaurants, and accommodations, marked with 🌙

- Suggestions on how to plan a trip that's perfect for you, including:

    The 21-Day Best of Nicaragua
    Hiking the Ring of Fire
    The Great Green North
    Down the Río San Juan
    Celebrations and Fiestas

- 41 detailed and easy-to-use maps

- The firsthand experience and unique perspective of authors Randall Wood and Joshua Berman

"America's finest travel guidebook series . . . extensively researched, engagingly written, intelligently indexed, and packed with helpful maps and sidebars."

—*MONEY* MAGAZINE

ALSO AVAILABLE

LIVING ABROAD IN
NICARAGUA

MOON HANDBOOKS
COSTA RICA

Raincoast/PGC
CDN $24.50

WWW.MOON.COM

FOURTH EDITION
AVALON TRAVEL
A Member of the Perseus Books Group
Distributed by Publishers Group West

PRINTED ON RECYCLED PAPER

ISBN: 978-1-59880-594-9   US $19.95

TRAVEL

51995

9 781598 805949